Hidden Riches

Hidden Riches

A Sourcebook for the Comparative Study
of the Hebrew Bible and Ancient Near East

Christopher B. Hays

WESTMINSTER
JOHN KNOX PRESS
LOUISVILLE · KENTUCKY

Book design by Sharon Adams
Cover design by Dilu Nicholas
Cover illustration: 1846 Antique Map of Turkey in Asia. Iraq/Image ID 1212192 © Steven Wright/
shutterstock.com. A lion of the Ishtar Gate of Babylon in the Pergamon Museum in Berlin, © Robert Jakatics/
shutterstock.com.

Library of Congress Cataloging-in-Publication Data

Hays, Christopher B., 1973–
  Hidden riches : a sourcebook for the comparative study of the Hebrew Bible and ancient Near East / Christopher B. Hays.
      pages cm
  Includes indexes.
  ISBN 978-0-664-23701-1 (paperback)
  1. Middle Eastern literature—Relation to the Old Testament. 2. Bible. Old Testament—Comparative studies. 3. Bible. Old Testament—Criticism, interpretation, etc. 4. Bible. Old Testament—Extra-canonical parallels. I. Title.
  BS1184.H39 2014
  221.6'7—dc23
                                                                                    2014012702

Most Westminster John Knox Press books are available at special quantity discounts when purchased in bulk by corporations, organizations, and special-interest groups. For more information, please e-mail SpecialSales@wjkbooks.com.

I will give you the treasures of darkness
and riches hidden in secret places.
                                    —Isaiah 45:3

What has been is what will be,
and what has been done is what will be done;
there is nothing new under the sun.
Is there a thing of which it is said, "See, this is new"?
It has already been, in the ages before us.
                                    —Ecclesiastes 1:9–10

I am about to do a new thing;
now it springs forth, do you not perceive it?
                                    —Isaiah 43:19

Contents

Permissions and Credits

Miriam Lichtheim, *Ancient Egyptian Literature, Volume I: The Old and Middle Kingdoms*. (Oakland: University of California Press, 1973). Republished with permission of University of California Press; permission conveyed through Copyright Clearance Center, Inc.

Miriam Lichtheim, *Ancient Egyptian Literature, Volume II: The New Kingdom*. (Oakland: University of California Press, 1976). Republished with permission of University of California Press; permission conveyed through Copyright Clearance Center, Inc.

J. M. Lindenberger, trans. "Ahiqar: A New Translation and Introduction," *Old Testament Pseudepigrapha* vol. 2, ed. James H. Charlesworth. (New Haven: Yale University Press, 1985). Reprinted with permission.

Tremper Longman, *Fictional Akkadian Biography: A Generic and Comparative Approach* (Winona Lake: Eisenbrauns, 1991), used by permission of Eisenbrauns.

Piotr Michalowski, *The Lamentation over the Destruction of Sumer and Ur* (Winona Lake: Eisenbrauns, 1989), used by permission of Eisenbrauns.

Allan Millard, *The Eponyms of the Assyrian Empire, 910–612 BC*. State Archives of Assyria Studies, 2. (Helsinki: Neo-Assyrian Text Corpus Project, 1994) is reprinted by permission of The Neo-Assyrian Text Corpus Project.

Martti Nissinin, *Prophets and Prophecy in the Ancient Near East* (Atlanta: Society of Biblical Literature, 2003). Used by permission.

Simo Parpola and Kazuko Watanabe, *Neo-Assyrian Treaties and Loyalty Oaths*. State Archives of Assyria, 2. (Helsinki: University of Helsinki Press, 1988). Reprinted by permission of The Neo-Assyrian Text Corpus Project.

Simo Parpola, *Assyrian Prophecies*. State Archives of Assyria, 9. (Helsinki: University of Helsinki Press, 1997). Reprinted by permission of The Neo-Assyrian Text Corpus Project.

Martha Roth, *Law Collections from Mesopotamia and Asia Minor, Second Edition* (Atlanta: Society of Biblical Literature, 1997). Used by permission.

William K. Simpson, ed., "Instruction of Amenemope" in *The Literature of Ancient Egypt* (New Haven: Yale University Press, 1973). Reprinted with permission.

Ithmar Singer, "Mursili's 'First' Plague Prayer to the Assembly of Gods and Goddesses (CTH 378.1)," *Hittite Prayers* (Atlanta: Society of Biblical Literature, 2002). Used by permission.

Mark Smith, trans., and Simon B. Parker, ed., *Ugaritic Narrative Poetry*, (Atlanta: Society of Biblical Literature, 1997). Used by permission.

Figures

Map by Ben Pease. Coastlines mapped using IndieMapper. Shaded relief adapted from imagery by Natural Earth.

Figure 1. Seals from the Vassal Treaties of Esarhaddon: Courtesy of Simo Parpola

Figure 2. Statue of Gudea Seated: © Science and Society (superstock.com; #1895-10612)

Figure 3. Lachish: © DeAgostini (superstock.com; #1788-15602)

Figure 4. Karatepe Gate and Inscription: Courtesy of Tayfun Bilgin

Figure 5. Stela of Neferabu: Courtesy of Allison Taylor; © Westminster John Knox Press

Figure 6. Taanach Cult Stand: Courtesy of Nancy Lapp

Figure 7. Stela with Akhenaten, Nefertiti, and Children: © tkachuk (shutterstock.com; #24893296)

Figure 8. Udjahorresne: © Scala/Art Resource, NY (artres.com; #ART456441)

Acknowledgments

The seed for this book was planted when I was a master's student at Princeton Theological Seminary and took J. J. M. Roberts's doctoral seminar on ancient Near Eastern religion. The seminar centered on direct engagement with primary texts. Encountering the world of the ancient Near East at length, and reading its texts side by side with comparable biblical texts, made the Bible come alive for me in a new way, and I have read it differently ever since. It was an experience like scales falling from my eyes, and for that reason this book is dedicated to Professor Roberts.

A project this ambitious in its scope does not come to press without the support of many people and institutions, and it is a pleasure to thank them here. The Louisville Institute's Sabbatical Grant for Researchers allowed me to spend the 2010–11 academic year drafting much of the book. The same grant encouraged me to use my drafts in the classroom, and the feedback from numerous students here at Fuller Theological Seminary has been invaluable in shaping the chapters.

I am very grateful to a number of individuals who contributed translations of primary texts. These include Billie Jean Collins's translations of the Hittite Ritual of Ashella in chapter 8 (which will appear in her forthcoming SBLWAW volume on Hittite rituals) and Julye Bidmead's translations of the Babylonian *akitu* text in the same chapter. Alan Lenzi's translation of *Ludlul bēl nēmeqi* in chapter 21 reflects some refinements of his work with Amar Annus in SAACT 7. Jim Eisenbraun was also extremely kind in giving me advance access to W. G. Lambert's posthumously published *Babylonian Creation Myths*. Simo Parpola generously gave me the right to reproduce translations in the State Archives of Assyria series, and Leigh Anderson and the Society of Biblical Literature made translations from their Writings from the Ancient World series affordable to use. Finally, Tayfun Bilgun kindly gave the right to use photos of the Karatepe Gate in chapter 19.

Many friends in the field have read drafts and offered their input along the way; ideally the book reflects some of the collective wisdom of this great cloud of witnesses. I am particularly grateful to Patrick D. Miller, who read and commented on the entire manuscript. Feedback on specific chapters came from Brent Strawn, Matthew Suriano,

Sara Koenig, Alan Lenzi, Ingrid Lilly, Meira Kensky, Cameron Richardson Howard, Kelly Murphy, James Butler, John Goldingay, Yael Avrahami, and Emily Cole. Many of these friends (and others) have used drafts in their classes and have sent feedback that has helped to refine the final versions.

I am grateful to my students Jason A. Riley, Denise Flanders, Zachary Schoening, Daniel Freemyer, Evan Bassett, and Leland Merritt for their assistance with indexing and proofreading the manuscript, and to Andrew Giorgetti for his research assistance.

Finally, I have been blessed to work with the editors at Westminster John Knox Press, starting with Jon Berquist, who saw the potential in the project at the very beginning. Marianne Blickenstaff and Bridgett Green have shepherded the project, and David Dobson has given it his gracious oversight.

Tantur Ecumenical Institute, Jerusalem
Simchat Torah 2013

Abbreviations

AB	Anchor Bible
ABD	*Anchor Bible Dictionary*. Edited by D. N. Freedman. 6 vols. New York, 1992
AEL	*Ancient Egyptian Literature*. M. Lichtheim. 3 vols. Berkeley, 1973–80
ANE	Ancient Near East(ern)
ANET	*Ancient Near Eastern Texts Relating to the Old Testament*. Edited by J. B. Pritchard. 3rd ed. Princeton, 1969
AOAT	Alter Orient und Altes Testament
ARM	Archives royales de Mari
c.	century
CANE	*Civilizations of the Ancient Near East*. Edited by J. Sasson. 4 vols. New York, 1995
CBQ	*Catholic Biblical Quarterly*
COS	*The Context of Scripture*. Edited by W. W. Hallo. 3 vols. Leiden, 1997–
CTH	*Catalogue des textes hittites*. Emmanuel Laroche. Paris, 1971
FAT	Forschungen zum Alten Testament
JANES	*Journal of the Ancient Near Eastern Society*
JAOS	*Journal of the American Oriental Society*
JBL	*Journal of Biblical Literature*

JNES	*Journal of Near Eastern Studies*
JSOTSup	Journal for the Study of the Old Testament: Supplement Series
KTU²	*Die Keilalphabetischen Texte aus Ugarit*. Edited by M. Dietrich, O. Loretz, and J. Sanmartín. 2d enlarged ed. of *KTU: The Cuneiform Alphabetic Texts from Ugarit, Ras Ibn Hani, and Other Places*. Münster, 1995.
obv.	obverse (front) of a tablet
OT	Old Testament
OtSt	Oudtestamentische Studiën
r.	reigned
rev.	reverse (back) of a tablet
SAA	State Archives of Assyria
SAACT	State Archives of Assyria Cuneiform Texts
SBLABS	Society of Biblical Literature Archaeology and Biblical Studies
SBLSymS	Society of Biblical Literature Symposium Series
SBLWAW	Society of Biblical Literature Writings from the Ancient World
SBT	Studies in Biblical Theology
VT	*Vetus Testamentum*
VTSup	Vetus Testamentum Supplements

Time Lines of Ancient Periods

Egyptian Periods

Early Dynastic	3000–2686
Old Kingdom	2686–2160
First Intermediate Period	2160–2055
Middle Kingdom	2055–1650
Second Intermediate Period	1650–1550
New Kingdom	1550–1069
Third Intermediate Period	1069–715
Late Period	715–332

Mesopotamian Periods

Akkad Dynasty	2334–2154
Third Dynasty of Ur	2112–2004
First Dynasty of Babylon	1894–1595
Kassite Dynasty of Babylon	1374-1155
Neo-Assyrian Empire	1114–612
Neo-Babylonian Empire	626–539
Persian Empire	559–330

Hittite Periods

Old Kingdom	1650–1500
Middle Kingdom	1500–1420
Empire	1420–1200

Archaeological Periods of the Levant

Early Bronze I	3300–3050
Early Bronze II–III	3050–2300
Early Bronze IV/Middle Bronze I	2300–2000
Middle Bronze IIA	2000–1800/1750
Middle Bronze IIB–C	1800/1750–1550
Late Bronze I	1550–1400
Late Bronze IIA–B	1400–1200

Iron IA	1200–1150
Iron IB	1150–1000
Iron IIA	1000–925
Iron IIB	925–720
Iron IIC	720–586
Iron III	586–536
Persian Period	536–330

Periods and Dates in Israelite and Judean History

United Monarchy	ca. 1000–922
Division of Israel from Judah	922
Divided Monarchy	922–722
Fall of Samaria	721
Judean Monarchy	721–586
Fall of Jerusalem	586
Babylonian Exile	586–536
Persian Rule of Yehud	536–330
Completion of Second Jerusalem Temple	515
Death of Alexander the Great	323

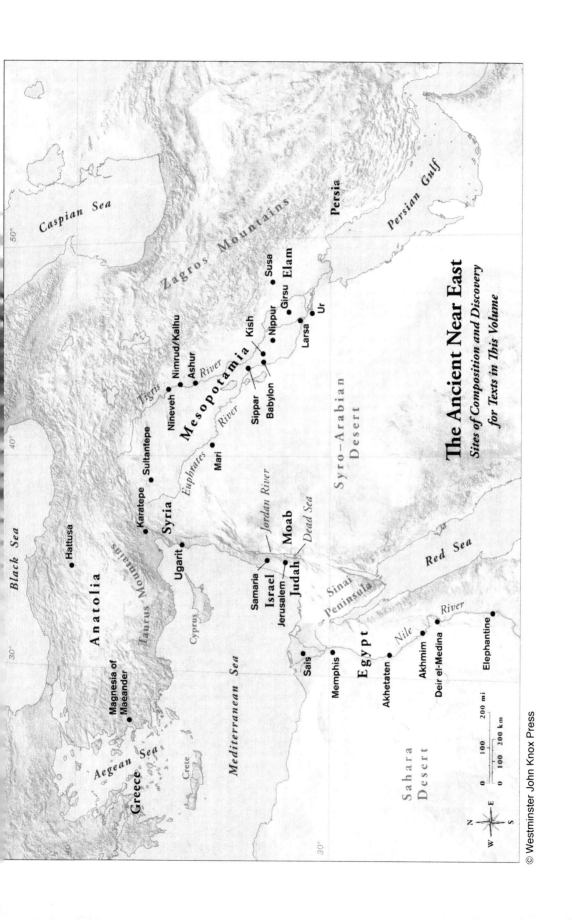

The Ancient Near East
Sites of Composition and Discovery
for Texts in This Volume

© Westminster John Knox Press

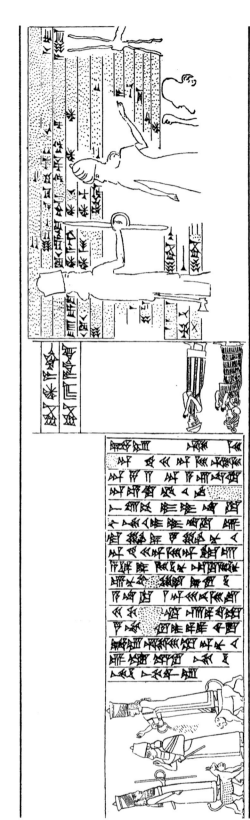

Figure 1. Seals from the Vassal Treaties of Esarhaddon

Image source: Simo Parpola and Kazuko Watanabe, *Neo-Assyrian Treaties and Loyalty Oaths* (State Archives of Assyria 2; Helsinki: Helsinki University, 1988), xxxvi. In the tablet attesting the Vassal Treaty of Esarhaddon, there are three seals between this introductory text and the rest of the document. They are described by Parpola and Watanabe. "The middle seal, with the short legend 'Of the God Aššur and the City Hall,' dates from the time of the Old Assyrian city-state. The impression on the left, from a Neo-Assyrian seal, shows the king of Assyria standing between the gods Aššur and Mullissu, and has the following legend: 'The Seal of Destinies, with which Aššur, king of the gods, seals the destinies of the Igigi and Anunnaki of heaven and earth, and of mankind. What he seals with it, he does not alter. He who should alter (it), may Aššur, king of the gods, and Mullissu, together with their children kill him with their mighty weapons. I am Sennacherib, king of Assyria, a prince who fears you. Whoever erases my name and discards this Seal of Destinies of yours, erase his name and seed from the land!' The impression on the right, showing the king kneeling between the gods Aššur and Ninurta, is from a Middle-Assyrian seal; both gods are mentioned in the largely illegible legend." See chapter 9 for further discussion.

Figure 2. Statue of Gudea Seated
Image source: SuperStock (http://www.superstock.com; #1895-10612)
Present location: Louvre Museum, Paris (AO 2)
This diorite statue of Gudea ("Statue B") holding plans for a temple was found in Tello, Iraq
(ancient Girsu), in excavations by E. de Sarzec in 1880. It dates to ca. 2100 BCE and shows
the prince of Lagash in a pious pose, though he has lost his head sometime in the intervening
millennia. See chapter 11 for further discussion.

Figure 3. Lachish
Image source: SuperStock (http://www.superstock.com; #1788-15602)
Present location: British Museum (ME 124906)
This stone-carved relief from the South-West Palace of Sennacherib in Nineveh depicts the exile of men and women after the siege and capture of the city of Lachish in 701 BCE. At the left and center of the frame are men and boys with emaciated oxen pulling carts. In front of them, women and girls carry provisions. See chapter 13 for further discussion.

Figure 4. Karatepe Gate and Inscription
Image source: Tayfun Bilgin, Bora Bilgin, Ertugrul Anil (http://www.hittitemonuments.com/karatepe/)
Present location: Karatepe, southern Turkey (*in situ*)
A gate of the citadel, made of imported basalt, is flanked by guardian lions carved in high relief, while inscriptions in Phoenician and Luwian run down the length of the walls that form an enclosure. See chapter 19 for further discussion.

Figure 5. Stela of Neferabu
Image source: Sketch by Allison Taylor. Copyright © Westminster John Knox Press.
Present location: British Museum (EA589)
Votive Stela of Neferabu with Hymn to Ptah from Deir el-Medina, Egypt, is a round-topped limestone stela. Ptah is seated in the top left, wearing his characteristic skullcap. Neferabu is kneeling in the bottom right in a pose of adoration. See chapter 22 for further discussion.

Figure 6. Taanach Cult Stand
Image source: Nancy Lapp, Bible Lands Museum, Pittsburgh Theological Seminary
Present location: Israel Museum, Jerusalem
Size: 53.7cm H x 24.5cm W x 22cm D.
This fired-clay stand from the late tenth century BCE was discovered in excavations at the former site of Taanach, near Megiddo. See chapter 23 for further discussion.

Figure 7. Stela with Akhenaten, Nefertiti, and Children
Image source: Shutterstock (http://www.shutterstock.com; #24893296)
Present location: Staatliche Museen zu Berlin, Ägyptisches Museum
This limestone stele, probably used as a home shrine, portrays a rare scene of an Egyptian royal family relaxing together: the pharaoh Akhenaten, Nefertiti, and children. Note the similarity of the male and female body forms and the way the children are portrayed as miniature adults. Some of the rays of the sun disk are represented with ankhs at their tips, symbolizing the life-giving power of the sun. The stele was found in the ruins of Akhenaten's capital city of Akhetaten, present-day Tell el-Amarna, and it dates to Dynasty 18, ca. 1340 BCE. See chapter 23 for further discussion.

Figure 8. Udjahorresne

Image source: Art Resource (www.artres.com; #ART456441)

Present location: Gregoriano Egizio, Vatican City, Rome, Italy (cat. nr. 22690)

This statue of the Egyptian high official Udjahorresne holding a naos (or shrine) is carved in dark green basalt and bears an autobiographical inscription. The statue dates to about ca. 520 BCE, when Egypt was under Persian rule, and was found in the subject's tomb in Sais, Egypt. See chapter 27 for further discussion.

PART I

Prolegomena

1

Introduction

The Hebrew Bible (commonly called the Old Testament) is a compendium of ancient Near Eastern texts. It's a mundane observation, but its vast consequences are not always recognized or honored.

The goal of reading the Bible in its context is simply to gain cultural literacy, a basic prerequisite for any interpreter who aspires to any authority. The prominent biblical scholar H. H. Rowley criticized interpreters who could not read Hebrew: "One who made it his life's work to interpret French literature, but who could only read it in an English translation, would not be taken seriously; yet it is remarkable how many ministers of religion week by week expound a literature that they are unable to read save in translation!"[1]

Much the same could be said of one who made it his life's work to interpret *Les Miserables*, but had never read any other French literature. That person might consider *Les Miserables* the greatest French novel, but how could he argue for that, without at least reading other French novels carefully? How would one appreciate Victor Hugo's interpretation of his times while knowing nothing about them apart from the novel itself? Indeed, without studying the history of the period, how would one grasp that *Les Miserables* is an interpretation at all, rather than a window through which one can view reality? In the same way, to appreciate the worldviews, messages, and artistic qualities of the Bible, one also has to understand its historical and literary context.

Nevertheless, nearly every reader today comes to the Bible without the cultural literacy to make sense of it as its first hearers could. That competence is scarcely taught today, as both ancient history and languages are marginalized in Western education.

There is no shame in being shaped by the cultural assumptions and reading strategies of our communities. That is inevitable for everyone. But at worst, we lay those assumptions and strategies over the biblical text so that they obscure it. We may well want to keep the perspectives that we had before; there is much of value in them, but if we do not

---

1. H. H. Rowley, *Expository Times* 74 (1963): 383.

lay them aside and enter into the thought-world (the "discursive universe") of ancient texts, we can never even see them for what they are. As I tell my students: There is a whole world back there in history. Real people, just like us, told these stories, prayed these prayers, and wrote these histories. Ancient Near Eastern studies is one of our poor, faltering attempts to encounter those people and do justice to their writings.

What does it mean to give proper attention to the ancient Near Eastern nature of the Hebrew Scriptures? Minimally, it means reading other ancient Near Eastern texts. The Scriptures are exceedingly "respiratory": they breathe in the culture of their times, and breathe it back out in a different form. To the reader who learns to breathe the same air—the one who becomes familiar with the context—it is increasingly hard to believe that he or she once read the Bible without it. Reading the Hebrew Scriptures in context is intoxicating, like breathing pure oxygen: everything is clearer and sharper, and the energy is immeasurably higher.

WHY COMPARE?

Some readers, accustomed to assertions of the Bible's uniqueness, may ask why one should compare it at all. Is the Bible unique? And if so, what would that mean for comparative study?

The Bible itself can be understood to argue both for and against its own literary originality. Ecclesiastes 1:9–10 says that "there is nothing new under the sun," while Isaiah 43:19 says that God does new things, and various psalms invite the hearer to "sing a new song." The best solutions combine these two viewpoints, as when Julia Kristeva describes texts as fabrics woven out of citations of other texts:[2] in this metaphor, the author begins with materials already at hand but has the potential to create something not previously known to the reader.

Comparison of multiple texts is not an alternative to immersion in a single text; it can never replace careful reading of individual texts, because careful reading is a precondition of comparison. But when one has read multiple texts, then comparison is inevitable.[3] We compare cultural products all the time in an offhand way: *I enjoy U2's earlier albums more than the later stuff; she's so into indie movies, and she makes fun of Hollywood blockbusters*, and so on. Because of this inevitability, the only alternatives to thoughtful comparison are thoughtless comparison and ignorance of the things that are potentially comparable.

One simple answer to the question, *why compare?* is that comparison brings things into focus. Humans form their self-identities by comparison every day: Am I tall? Am I well spoken? Am I talented at math? Categories such as "tall," "well spoken," and "talented" turn out to be relative, and people discern their identities and purposes in life on the basis

---

2. Julia Kristeva, *Semeiotiké: Recherches pour une sémanalyse* (Paris: Éditions du Seuil, 1969), 144.

3. On the psychological underpinnings of comparison, see Meir Malul, *The Comparative Method in Ancient Near Eastern and Biblical Legal Studies* (AOAT 227; Neukirchen-Vluyn: Neukirchener, 1990), 1–2.

of such comparisons. In a first-grade classroom, I'm tall. In an NBA locker room, I would be short. Context matters.

Literary and theological features come into focus through comparison as well. An example may be found in the comparison of biblical and ancient Near Eastern flood stories (see chap. 4): the biblical flood story in Genesis 6–9 concludes with a heavy emphasis on covenant, a theme not found in the otherwise similar Mesopotamian stories. This tells us something distinctive about the religious milieu of each text. If one wants to know what is distinctive about the Bible, one needs something to compare it to. Needless to say, it is not only the distinctive that is valuable. For example, the Bible's calls to protect the widow and the orphan turn out to have numerous precise cognates in ancient Near Eastern literature (see, for example, chaps. 7 and 11), but they are no less laudable because they are not unique.

Even complex concepts like justice, goodness, and beauty turn out to be relative, and our comprehension and appreciation of them are dependent on comparison. There is the famous comment by Winston Churchill: "Many forms of government have been tried and will be tried in this world of sin and woe. No one pretends that democracy is perfect or all-wise. Indeed, it has been said that democracy is the worst form of government except all those other forms that have been tried."[4] In other words, democracy looks bad until you compare it to something else. Readers' experience of comparison between the Hebrew Bible and other ancient Near Eastern texts will vary, but many will gain a greater appreciation for the biblical texts that they have always known, just as Churchill appreciated his own democracy more when he compared it with other forms of governments throughout history.

THE AIMS OF THIS VOLUME

The reader who perceives the basic value of the comparative project next faces the overwhelming flood of information that is potentially relevant. Ancient Near Eastern texts are usually encountered by introductory students in one of two ways: in snippet form in textbooks introducing the biblical texts (a few of Hammurabi's laws here, a fragment of the Assyrian version of Sennacherib's siege there) or in a compendium of ancient Near Eastern texts. It is the latter sort of book that this volume aspires to improve on.

This volume is both less and more than some comparable books. It gives up something in the scope of texts sampled: even the slimmest student collections of ancient Near Eastern texts comprise samples of about one hundred texts. But they also contain almost no discussion of what these texts are, where they came from, and so forth. In teaching ancient texts, I have found that giving students substantial context for the texts in advance made class discussion vastly richer and better. I went looking for a book that assembled the background data relevant to comparison of specific biblical and ancient Near Eastern texts—much of which is still found in widely scattered sources that are expensive and difficult to find—and at a level that an undergraduate or master's student could understand

4. Speech in the House of Commons, November 11, 1947, *The Official Report*, House of Commons, 5th ser., vol. 444, cols. 206–7.

and digest. Failing to find it, I wrote introductions myself. Eventually, I decided to expand and publish my materials.

The overarching goal of this book is simply to make intelligent comparison between biblical and ancient Near Eastern texts possible. To that end, its first goal is to anticipate questions that will occur to an inquisitive reader:

> Where did these texts come from?
> When were they written, and by whom?
> What were they written on?

Second, this book tries to give a wider view of the texts; sometimes this means discussion of the genre or the literary corpus into which a text fits. When a text must be excerpted, it means giving the reader a sense of the larger composition from which the excerpt was drawn.

Third, this book offers starting points for analysis and comparison. For readers without a strong background in literary study, who might be distracted by superficial difficulties in the texts, this is intended to get them started and take them part of the way, so that they can begin to see the payoffs of the method.

Fourth and finally, the book tries to open up avenues for motivated readers to explore further. The reflection questions typically point beyond the material that is presented; they are not aimed primarily at assessing reading comprehension but at sparking discussion and debate. This book doesn't just leave room for disagreement, it expects it. There are many contested issues and judgment calls in comparative studies, and wherever possible I have indicated that there is room for debate.

For all that this book sets out to do, it is certainly only a beginning. It needs a skilled teacher and thoughtful investment on the part of students. The things that are most desirable in a reader are these:

1. *Cultural and historical knowledge.* This book will complement, but not replace, a course or other textbook that gives students a broader sense of the history of the ancient Near East and the interactions between ancient Israel and its neighbors. For example, the book may allude to the impact of Mesopotamian culture on Judeans during the Babylonian exile, but it does not discuss the events of the period in detail.
2. *Skill in literary interpretation.* Reading well, like any skill, requires practice and training. Strong readers will be better prepared for comparative study of the Bible than those who are less attentive to nuance.
3. *Familiarity with ancient languages.* Of course many readers of this book will not know Hebrew, Aramaic, or the other languages of the Ancient Near East, but for higher-level work, such knowledge is greatly valuable. The method depends more upon close analysis of primary texts in their original languages than can be conveyed in an introductory book, though some linguistic features are briefly noted.

INTRODUCTORY CRITICAL ISSUES

Another piece of the background for the comparative method is the scholarly study of the Bible itself. The results of that study are presupposed throughout this book.

First of all, we are dependent on the study of the development of Hebrew language. Except for a few small pieces in Aramaic, the religious texts of ancient Israel and Judah were written entirely in Hebrew. Since there is no evidence that Hebrew texts were written until the tenth century BCE, no biblical text in this volume has a proposed date before then. It is possible that some biblical texts (primarily archaic poems such as Exod. 15, which are not part of this book) could have been transmitted orally or otherwise existed in a form of the language that preceded the Hebrew that we now read, but that theory is not demonstrable.

Second, this book is conversant with dominant critical theories of biblical composition and redaction, although prior knowledge of these is not presupposed. Chapters 4 and 17 each bring comparative data to bear on questions of composition and redaction in specific instances, in an attempt to suggest how comparison with demonstrable processes of ancient writing, copying, and editing might affect common scholarly theories. Throughout the book, texts are assigned dates conventional to critical treatments, but except for chapter 4 the emphasis is not on internal divisions. For our purposes, what is important is to recognize that the Hebrew Bible was formed of sometimes disparate parts through a lengthy process of scribal transmission and compilation; it is less important for the introductory student to master all the details of that process.[5]

Finally, the discussion sections address the connections between the biblical authors and the ancient Near Eastern cultures that produced the extrabiblical texts. There are numerous sorts of relationships among texts:

> In some cases (such as the comparison of Lamentations with Sumerian city laments in chap. 25) the two texts are separated by thousands of years and many miles, so that one can rule out direct contact and reckon instead with a lengthy preservation of literary and theological traditions.
>
> In other cases (such as the comparison of Moabite and biblical historiography in chap. 10) one is dealing with concurrent cultural developments in similar societies.
>
> In still other cases (as in Deuteronomy's summons to faithfulness to Yhwh alone in chap. 9) one is probably dealing with the biblical author's reaction against similar and competing claims by an imperial power.
>
> As a final example, one may in rare cases see biblical authors more or less borrowing from texts and adapting them to their own purposes. (The similarities between Prov. 22:17–24:22 and an Egyptian wisdom text in chap. 20 may be one such example.)

There is an effort throughout the book to consider texts within the real life of the ancient Near Eastern world, taking seriously questions such as, How did scribes actually work? How did cultural contacts between nations happen? How would cultural influence have taken place between peoples who spoke and wrote different languages? The intention is to respect the complex web of interconnections between ancient Israel and Judah and the other cultures that surrounded and preceded them.

---

5. As Otto Eissfeldt urged, "The important point is not this or that individual dissection of the material, but the total outlook" (*The Old Testament: An Introduction* [trans. Peter Ackroyd; New York: Harper & Row, 1956], 241).

THE DESIGN OF THE CHAPTERS

Since the primary goal is to introduce the student of the Hebrew Bible to the value of the comparative method, diverse case studies have been selected from all parts of the Bible, reflecting the fact that there is no book or passage to which ancient Near Eastern data is irrelevant.

In many cases, merely selecting texts for comparison was daunting. Sometimes, as with prayer texts (chap. 22), the assortment of possibilities was very large (in both the biblical and ANE spheres), and so a selection of short, representative texts had to be chosen. In some cases where hard choices had to be made, I have cited snippets of other texts in the discussions to fill out the picture.

Texts are presented in as complete a form as possible, because it is important to be aware of "the broader contexts of the comparable items so that one avoids excerption that would skew the comparison."[6] The selection of too-narrow excerpts has, in my view, marred certain previous sourcebooks of ancient Near Eastern texts. At times it has been impossible to avoid using excerpts (for example, one cannot present the whole Epic of Gilgamesh in comparing flood narratives, and it would not add a great deal to do so), but I have identified those places and tried to give a sense of what is missing.

Date, Provenance, and Physical Form

No text exists in a disembodied, ahistorical form. Every text comes from somewhere; every text is written in a certain language at a certain time, by certain people, to a certain audience. Time, place, and language all shed light on how a text functions, and students new to the study of the ancient Near East need guidance to see the significance of it all. Language determines who can read it; time and place shed light on the culture and the people that produced it.

In light of the clear significance of a text's historical and cultural backgrounds, its literary context, and its physical form for interpretation, it is surprising how difficult it can be to glean these basic facts from many anthologies of ancient Near Eastern texts.[7] I was generally compelled to assemble them from first editions of the texts in question.

Often there is a significant gap between the historical situation in which a text is thought to have been produced and the period from which copies actually survive. This is the case with nearly every biblical text in this volume, as well as many of the extrabiblical texts, and the effects on interpretation are discussed on a case-by-case basis.

Each extrabiblical text's physical form is specified, and dimensions are supplied where possible. The physical form of a text sheds light on how it was intended to function. A text written on a monument (chap. 10), public wall (chap. 19), or statue (chaps. 11, 27) has at least the potential to function very differently from a text on a tablet or scroll stored in an

6. Brent A. Strawn, "Comparative Approaches: History, Theory, and the Image of God," in *Method Matters: Essays on the Interpretation of the Hebrew Bible in Honor of David L. Petersen* (ed. J. M. LeMon and K. H. Richards; Atlanta: SBL, 2009), 131.

7. See similar remarks by Barbara N. Porter, *Images, Power, and Politics: Figurative Aspects of Esar-haddon's Babylonian Policy* (Philadelphia: American Philosophical Society, 1993), 181.

archive. For example, if a text was inscribed on a large public monument, then even those who could not read it (and most people were illiterate through most of ANE history) may have had some idea of what it said on the basis of public readings or word of mouth.

In some cases, images of the artifacts are supplied to give the reader an idea of how a text appeared. Many ancient Near Eastern texts were accompanied by images, although iconography is still too little studied in this volume.

Primary Texts

Primary texts are placed before discussion and explanation in this volume. This is intended to encourage readers to encounter them first without too many preconceived notions. Although I hope the discussions and the context they supply will be valuable, there is no substitute for careful reading of primary texts. "Lay readers" may well come up with interesting questions based on their reading that they might have overlooked if they had begun thinking they knew what to expect. Of course, the choice of what to read first lies with the reader. Students have sometimes commented that they wanted to have the discussions to understand what was going on and thought they should have been placed first. Ideally, students would read the primary text twice: once with fresh eyes, and again after being introduced to some of the critical issues.

Many students will be surprised to encounter ancient Near Eastern texts that are not complete—that are only partly preserved—but this is the normal state of affairs. (Such gaps in the text are rare in the Bible, but they do occur, as in 1 Sam. 13:1, where there are blanks in the Hebrew text, as reflected in the NRSV translation: "Saul was . . . years old when he began to reign; and he reigned . . . and two years over Israel.") Many of the ancient Near Eastern texts are translated from clay tablets, which can degrade and break over time; or from scrolls, which are even more subject to decay and damage. I have made every effort to select texts that are coherent, but where there are breaks, these are marked by ellipses within square brackets: [. . .].

In many cases, it is possible to restore the text that should have appeared in a break, because there are other copies of a text or parallel passages within a text. Such restorations are indicated within square brackets. Where words are supplied for the sake of clarity that are not in the original text, these are indicated in parentheses.

Another help supplied in this volume is footnotes on ancient Near Eastern phenomena that often go unexplained in other compendia. These notes—on the proper names of people, deities, places, and also on obscure technical terms—have been placed on the page where they are needed rather than tucked away in a glossary. The goal always is maximum readability and comprehension.

In the body text of the translations, words transliterated from ancient languages, especially personal names and place names, are not rendered with a strict, academic system. Instead they are rendered approximately, with the goal of allowing students who do not know the languages to pronounce them as easily as possible. Diacritic marks (e.g., š, ḥ) are normally omitted, as are indications of vowel length (e.g., ā, â, ă). However, in certain footnotes intended for instructors and others with advanced knowledge, technical transliterations are supplied, to facilitate locating them in reference works.

Most of the biblical texts are not reproduced in this volume, which is intended to allow readers to choose their own translation. All biblical verse numbers correspond to those of most English translations, which sometimes differ from Hebrew verse numbers. Readers of translations that follow the Hebrew versification, such as the JPS Tanakh and *Jerusalem Bible*, will hopefully be able to surmount this small inconvenience.

Suggestions for Comparison

Particularly with lengthy pairs (or groups) of texts, it has seemed useful to offer specific suggestions for comparison as a guide for the reader. The purpose of these suggestions is usually fleshed out in the discussion section. Even where offered, such suggestions are by no means exhaustive; there are many other points at which one can see common cultural "fabric" in the texts, and occasionally these are indicated in a footnote.

Students have commented that they would find it useful to have the text of the suggested comparisons placed side by side. I can think of only two ways to accomplish that within the book: to reproduce sometimes large passages twice in the chapter (which length constraints would not allow), or to dismember the original texts in order to set the relevant passages side by side in the original presentation, which would do violence to the literary integrity of the texts. One way to address this issue through pedagogy is to assign one or more students per class session to make a handout that sorts the texts in order to make side-by-side comparisons.

Discussions and Reflection Questions

Many of the discussion points offered in this volume have arisen out of my own teaching. They are intended to start conversations based on good information that drive toward significant issues. Furthermore:

- They are *methodologically diverse*, because different comparisons press toward different questions and approaches.
- They are *not exhaustive*, because they are meant to open up teaching and learning opportunities rather than close them off.
- They are *not entirely conclusive*, because there is usually room for debate around key issues.

Ideally, the diversity and openness of the discussion sections will encourage students to think creatively about ancient texts and their interpretation. Interpretation of texts is not a simple process of reading them, placing them in their contexts, and turning a crank. Authors and audiences each bring their own ideas to any act of communication, and so texts continue to produce new and surprising interpretations.

Further Reading

The goal of the brief bibliographies at the end of each chapter is to offer next steps for the student who wants (or needs) to research a topic further and the instructor who wants to explore secondary literature more deeply in preparation.

The reading lists favor sources that are accessible and up-to-date. They are emphatically not intended to cite all of the most important original research in the history of a given topic, which is often in other languages that few students can read or in specialized sources that relatively few libraries hold. The researcher who wants a thorough bibliography or history of scholarship on a topic can usually find those things in the sources cited.

THEOLOGY, IDEOLOGY, AND TERMINOLOGY

I have just noted that this book does not intend to settle most critical issues; that is true of theological issues as well—although it will almost inevitably raise them. The discussions rarely allude to present-day theology or religion, but some of the reflection questions do invite students to think about the theological claims of texts and the comparative task's impact on their own beliefs.

In part, this reticence is a necessary limitation of the book's scope. More importantly, I hope it will allow the book to be useful in a wide array of teaching settings, including pluralistic ones. When it comes to theology, I have taken the view that each professor is the best judge of what is appropriate in his or her own context; this book is intended to help anyone who is interested in the data that inform biblical interpretation.

A field with the rich history and present controversies of biblical and ancient Near Eastern studies will inevitably generate competing terminology. Any writer must choose certain terms, often among imperfect alternatives.

First, when the term "Bible" is used in this book, it generally means the "Hebrew Bible" (not all of which is in Hebrew), a term invented by scholars. In Jewish circles, this may also be called the Tanakh (an abbreviation for the tripartite divisions: Torah [Pentateuch], Nebi'im [Prophets], and Kethuvim [Writings]). In Christian circles, it is known as the Old Testament (or occasionally as the First Testament), which presupposes a New Testament. To me, it is the Old Testament, yet I have attempted to write for all.

The divine name raises a different set of issues. For some Jews, the name of the god of Israel is too holy to be spoken. Thus already in antiquity, they substituted the Hebrew word *adonay*, "lord," for the divine name. The use of the Greek word for "lord," *kyrios*, in the Septuagint translation of the Hebrew Bible reflects the same preference, and most modern English translations reflect that translation as well. This book, however, prefers to convey the fact that *the divine name is a name*, not a title. In deference to those who prefer not to pronounce it, however, and because its correct pronunciation is genuinely in doubt, the name is presented without vowels: Yhwh.

Terms for the land of the Bible are often freighted with ideological meaning. In particular, the decision to designate it as "Israel" or "Palestine" often suggests a stance on the present-day political conflict between Israelis and Palestinians. "Levant" is frequently used as an alternative. However, it is taken from the French term *soleil levant*, "rising sun," and indicates the land to the east of Europe, Rome, and Greece. Thus it is too broad for some purposes. In general, this book seeks to use the most precise political terminology possible: "proto-Israel(ite)" for the period before the institution of the monarchy, "Israel(ite)," for the period of the united monarchy and for the northern kingdom thereafter, and "Judah/Judean" for the southern kingdom. The whole region may be referred to as "Palestine," including Aram, Ammon, Edom, Moab, and the Philistine and Phoenician coastal states. "Palestine" is somewhat anachronistic when applied to the ancient Near East—it is a Latinized form of "Philistine"—but it is not intended to carry political weight for the present day.

In no case does this book amend quotations from other authors to conform to its style.

GENERAL BIBLIOGRAPHY

This section offers background reading on various essential topics. It would also serve as a list of texts worth having close at hand as one undertakes comparative study of the Hebrew Bible—just as someone learning to cook would want to buy certain staple ingredients that go into many different recipes. Emphasis has been placed on works that are recent, affordable, and in English.

History and Religion of Ancient Israel

Albertz, Rainer. *A History of Israelite Religion in the Old Testament Period.* Translated by J. Bowden. 2 vols. Louisville, KY: Westminster John Knox Press, 1994.
Miller, J. Maxwell, and John H. Hayes. *A History of Ancient Israel and Judah.* 2nd ed. Louisville, KY: Westminster John Knox Press, 2006.
Miller, Patrick D. *The Religion of Ancient Israel.* Louisville, KY: Westminster John Knox Press, 2000.
Smith, Mark S. *The Early History of God: Yahweh and the Other Deities in Ancient Israel.* 2nd ed. Biblical Resource Series. Grand Rapids: Eerdmans, 2002.

Maps and Atlases

Curtis, Adrian, ed. *Oxford Bible Atlas.* 4th ed. Oxford: Oxford University Press, 2007.
Rainey, A. F., and R. S. Notley. *The Sacred Bridge: Carta's Atlas of the Biblical World.* Jerusalem: Carta, 2006.
Roaf, Michael. *Cultural Atlas of Mesopotamia and the Ancient Near East.* New York: Facts on File, 1990.

Resources for Primary Texts in Translation

General

Hallo, W. W., ed. *The Context of Scripture.* 3 vols. New York: Brill, 1997.
Pritchard, James B., ed. *Ancient Near Eastern Texts Relating to the Old Testament.* Princeton, NJ: Princeton University Press, 1969.
Sparks, Kenton L. *Ancient Texts for the Study of the Hebrew Bible: A Guide to the Background Literature.* Peabody, MA: Hendrickson, 2005.
Volumes in the Writings from the Ancient World (SBLWAW) series by the Society of Biblical Literature (see a list at http://www.sbl-site.org/publications/Books_WAW.aspx).

Mesopotamian

Dalley, Stephanie, ed. *Myths from Mesopotamia.* Rev. ed. New York: Oxford University Press, 2000.
Foster, Benjamin R. *Before the Muses: An Anthology of Akkadian Literature.* 3rd ed. Bethesda, MD: CDL Press, 2005.

George, Andrew. *The Epic of Gilgamesh*. Reprint, London: Penguin, 2003.

Egyptian

Lichtheim, Miriam. *Ancient Egyptian Literature*. 3 vols. Berkeley: University of California Press, 1973–[80].
Simpson, W. K., ed. *The Literature of Ancient Egypt: An Anthology of Stories, Instructions, and Poetry* 3rd ed. New Haven, CT: Yale University Press, 2003.

Ugaritic

Pardee, Dennis. *Ritual and Cult at Ugarit*. SBLWAW 10. Atlanta: SBL, 2002.
Parker, Simon B., ed. *Ugaritic Narrative Poetry*. SBLWAW 9. Atlanta: Scholars Press, 1997.

Introductions to ANE History, Culture, and Religion

General

Kuhrt, Amélie. *The Ancient Near East*. Vol. 2, *From c. 1200 B.C. to c. 330 B.C.* Routledge History of the Ancient World. London: Routledge, 1995.
Mieroop, Marc van de. *A History of the Ancient Near East*. 2nd ed. Malden, MA: Blackwell, 2007.
Sasson, Jack, ed. *Civilizations of the Ancient Near East*. Peabody, MA: Hendrickson, 2006.
Snell, Daniel C., ed. *Religions of the Ancient Near East*. New York: Cambridge University Press, 2011.

Mesopotamia

Black, Jeremy, and Anthony Green. *Gods, Demons, and Symbols of Ancient Mesopotamia*. Austin: University of Texas Press, 1992.
Schneider, Tammi J. *An Introduction to Ancient Mesopotamian Religion*. Grand Rapids: Eerdmans, 2011.

Egypt

Assmann, Jan. *The Search for God in Ancient Egypt*. Ithaca, NY: Cornell University Press, 2001.
Dunand, Francoise, and Christiane Zivie-Coche. *Gods and Men in Egypt: 3000 BCE to 395 CE*. Translated by David Lorton. Ithaca, NY: Cornell University Press, 2005.
Hornung, Erik. *Conceptions of God in Ancient Egypt: The One and the Many*. Translated by J. Baines. Ithaca, NY: Cornell University Press, 1982.
Shaw, Ian, ed. *The Oxford History of Ancient Egypt*. Oxford: Oxford University Press, 2000.

Ugarit

Olmo Lete, Gregorio del. *Canaanite Religion according to the Liturgical Texts of Ugarit*, Second English Edition, thoroughly Revised and Enlarged. Translated by W. G. E. Watson. AOAT 408. Münster: Ugarit-Verlag, 2014.
Wyatt, Nicolas. "The Religion of Ugarit: An Overview." In *Handbook of Ugaritic Studies*. Edited by Wilfred G. E. Watson and Nicolas Wyatt. Handbuch der Orientalistik 39. Boston: Brill, 1999.

Hatti

Bryce, Trevor. *The Kingdom of the Hittites*. Oxford: Clarendon Press, 1998.
Collins, Billie Jean. *The Hittites and Their World*. SBLABS 7. Atlanta: SBL, 2007.

Persia

Boyce, Mary, et al. *A History of Zoroastrianism*. Vol. 1, *The Early Period*. New York: Brill, 1996.
Briant, Pierre. *From Cyrus to Alexander: A History of the Persian Empire*. Winona Lake, IN: Eisenbrauns, 2002.

2

History and Methods of Comparative Study

With enough creativity, practically anything can be compared to anything else. In Shakespeare's Sonnet 18, one lover says to another, "Shall I compare thee to a summer's day?"—and the poem delights and surprises because the comparison was not obvious or common. Language and thought are flexible, so that comparison is finally limited only by the decisions of the interpreter. Nevertheless, everyone plays by some set of rules, even if they go unstated—and they often do. Raising our methods to consciousness warrants the effort it requires because, as with any undertaking, some rules are more helpful than others.

One danger, in any study of method, is that it may become overly prescriptive and detailed. Given the vast variety of ancient Near Eastern literature, including biblical literature, it seems far more useful to describe the history of the conversation, touching on a few general principles along the way.

There has been a long scholarly debate about the proper parameters and methods for the comparative study of the Hebrew Bible. The history of comparativism is a story of heroic efforts by excellent scholars, even if it inevitably reflects the trial and error that any pursuit of knowledge entails. One could say that we are standing on the shoulders of those giants, but that would presume that we have arrived at a higher place, which remains to be seen. If we have, it is mostly because the available data have continued to increase in quantity and accessibility. It is an exciting time in biblical and ancient Near Eastern studies as more pieces of the puzzle emerge every year.

PREMODERN CONCEPTIONS OF THE ANCIENT NEAR EAST

It is difficult today to imagine the lack of good sources related to the ancient Near East only two hundred years ago. The classical histories were generally the best sources apart from the Bible, and their interpretation was plagued with innumerable problems.[1] Many Greeks and Romans had a fascination with the Orient, but few had firsthand knowledge (let alone access to primary sources), and so they transmitted unreliable accounts. Their purposes were didactic, and they reveled in telling stories about legendary figures such as Ninus and Semiramis (the former a made-up founder of Nineveh, the latter loosely based on the ninth-century Babylonian queen Shammuramat). Some works that were based on actual travels, such as the *Periegesis* and *Genealogiai* of Hecataeus of Miletus, have been lost.

Most of ancient Near Eastern history was simply overlooked in classical sources, and the descriptions of periods and people that were written were rife with errors and distortions. A few examples will suffice: In his *Persica*, Hellanicus of Lesbos (5th c. BCE) collapsed Esarhaddon and Ashurbanipal into a single king, whom he called Sardanapalus. Herodotus (5th c. BCE) not only garbled events—placing the building of the pyramids after the New Kingdom, for example—he also viewed the Near East as a rival because of the wars between the Greeks and Persians, and so was prone to portray it negatively. Ctesias (5th c. BCE), who was a physician at the Persian court, appears to have transmitted in his *Persica* a version of ancient Near Eastern history so colored by pro-Persian biases as to be largely unrecognizable. Xenophon (4th c. BCE) traveled right past the ruins of Assyrian Nimrud and Nineveh without recognizing them, because he thought he was in the territory of ancient Media.[2] Berossus and Manetho (both 3rd c. BCE) were native to the regions whose history they were writing about—Mesopotamia and Egypt, respectively—and so in some ways surpassed other ancients in accuracy; but they also periodized history to such a degree that they distorted many details. Josephus (1st c. CE) had an apologetic bent in asserting the primacy of Judaism; his *Antiquities of the Jews* largely follows the contours of the biblical narratives, but he was prone to insert curious details, for example, to emphasize the tyranny of the Mesopotamians. Josephus, quoting Berossus, mislocated the hanging gardens in Babylon (rather than Nineveh, where they actually were), an error that was canonized as one of the seven wonders of the ancient world.[3] Lucian (2nd c. CE), in his description of Levantine religion in *On the Syrian Goddess*, seems to have been so intent on entertaining that he made up details; he describes, for example, an 1,800-foot-tall statue of a phallus standing in the forecourt of a temple.

---

1. See further László Kákosy, "Egypt in Ancient Greek and Roman Thought," and Amelie Kuhrt, "Mesopotamia in Ancient Greek and Roman Thought," in *CANE* 1:3–14, 55–65, respectively.

2. Mark W. Chavalas, "Assyriology and Biblical Studies: A Century and a Half of Tension," in *Mesopotamia and the Bible: Comparative Explorations* (ed. M. W. Chavalas and K. L. Younger Jr.; Sheffield: Sheffield Academic, 2002), 23.

3. See Stephanie Dalley, *The Mystery of the Hanging Garden of Babylon: An Elusive World Wonder Traced* (Oxford: Oxford University Press, 2013).

Under these conditions, it is no pious exaggeration to say that the Bible was in many cases the best historical source available for the ancient Near East. Of course, the Bible has its own complexities and ideologies that can mislead modern historians; the primary goal of its authors was not to portray ancient Near Eastern history and culture accurately. But the biblical authors often accurately distinguished Assyria from Babylon, or Egypt from Kush; and they recorded events that were otherwise unknown until the decipherment of other ancient Near Eastern languages.

DISCOVERY AND DECIPHERMENT
OF ANCIENT NEAR EASTERN TEXTS

Eventually it became possible to encounter ancient Near Eastern cultures through their own words. The first ancient Near Eastern language to be deciphered was Egyptian. Hieroglyphic inscriptions had been reported in the West since classical antiquity, and they were already being studied in Europe in the sixteenth century, but without much success. In the 1650s, however, the polymath German Jesuit Athanasius Kircher recognized that hieroglyphic Egyptian was a precursor to Coptic, a later form of Egyptian written with Greek letters and additional signs. Just a few years later, Jean-Jacques Barthélemy suggested that the cartouches in hieroglyphic inscriptions encapsulated proper names.

The beginnings of ancient Eastern studies are tied up with the history of European colonialism in the Middle East; the earliest "Orientalists" were in the service of the Western powers exploring the East. For example, the real breakthrough in the decipherment of hieroglyphic writing came in 1799, when French soldiers serving in Napoleon's campaign to Egypt found the Rosetta Stone. Named for the nearby Egyptian port city of Rosetta (called Rashid in Arabic), the stone bore a trilingual Ptolemaic-period inscription written in hieroglyphs, demotic, and Greek. It was taken to Cairo, where it was kept by the French for eighteen months until they surrendered to the British, who took the Rosetta stone as a spoil of war. (It is on display in the British Museum to this day.)

By the time the British captured the Rosetta Stone, it had already been copied and disseminated to some extent. Still, it took decades for its hieroglyphs to be deciphered. Since Greek was already understood, translators began by recognizing that the names within the cartouches could be matched up with the names in the Greek text, and then worked backward to decipher the hieroglyphs. The greatest advances were made by Jean-François Champollion, an assistant professor of history at Grenoble and a linguistic savant, who systematized the understanding that hieroglyphs could represent not only whole words but also letters and syllables. (Some groundwork had been laid for him by other scholars who gained insight from other bilingual Egyptian inscriptions, and by comparison with the Chinese writing system.) In 1824, Champollion published his study of the language and writing system, *Précis du système hiéroglyphique*. Although many details have been refined (and some are still debated), this gave the modern study of Egyptian a solid foundation.

Even before most other ancient Near Eastern languages were deciphered and the texts understood, the artifacts that were being recovered from the East in the early years of the nineteenth century began to make a strong impression on European intellectuals. Painters portrayed Napoleon on horseback at the Giza pyramids, and great poets tried their hand at capturing antiquity. One famous example is Byron's "The Destruction of Sennacherib" (1815), with its famous opening lines describing the attack on Jerusalem by the Assyrian emperor in 701 BCE:

> The Assyrian came down like the wolf on the fold,
> And his cohorts were gleaming in purple and gold;
> And the sheen of their spears was like stars on the sea,
> When the blue wave rolls nightly on deep Galilee.

Of course, the poem is based entirely on the account of the siege from the Bible (see chap. 13), and Byron betrays his ignorance of Mesopotamian religion by referring to the Assyrians as Baal worshipers in the closing lines. But we see here already the way that the East was inspiring the imagination of the West.

Still more revealing about Europeans' view of the Near East was Percy Bysshe Shelley's "Ozymandias," published in 1818:

> I met a traveller from an antique land
> Who said: Two vast and trunkless legs of stone
> Stand in the desert. Near them, on the sand,
> Half sunk, a shattered visage lies, whose frown,
> And wrinkled lip, and sneer of cold command,
> Tell that its sculptor well those passions read
> Which yet survive, stamped on these lifeless things,
> The hand that mocked them and the heart that fed:
> And on the pedestal these words appear:
> "My name is Ozymandias, king of kings:
> Look on my works, ye Mighty, and despair!"
> Nothing beside remains. Round the decay
> Of that colossal wreck, boundless and bare
> The lone and level sands stretch far away.

Here, even the king's name is refracted through Western eyes: "Ozymandias" is a hellenized version of Usermaatre-setepenre, a throne name of Ramesses II as given by Diodorus Siculus.[4] The poem is an imagined scene of archaeological discovery, and its art lies in the way it reimagines the king's boast as a failure, an embodiment of the saying "Pride goes before the fall" (cf. Prov. 16:18). Ozymandias thought his mighty works would cause despair in those who seek to surpass them, but now that they are fallen, they instead invite despairing reflection on the transience of human achievement. At the same time, the contemporary reader might have been expected to derive some satisfaction from Ozymandius's failure. The Bible repeatedly says that the ancient empires that had oppressed and conquered God's people—including Egypt, Assyria, Babylon, and Greece—would

---

4. Diodorus Siculus reported an inscription on a statue base as reading: "I am Ozymandias, king of kings. If anyone would know how great I am and where I lie, let him surpass one of my works" (*Bib. Hist.* 1.47.4).

themselves stand under divine judgment, and so its readers were prone to view the ruins of those once-powerful civilizations as a tangible vindication. (Of course, at a deeper level, Shelley's poem could be read as a warning to the powers of his own times that they too would fall into dust.)

Many people of faith were quick to embrace the barely known ancient Near East. William W. Hallo recounts stories of a "little old seventeenth-century lady who used to say to her pastor that she 'had found great support in that blessed word 'Mesopotamia,'" and of the eighteenth-century evangelist George Whitefield, who "could reduce grown men to tears by the mere pronunciation of the word 'Mesopotamia.'" Hallo goes on to note that "the word lost some of its magic . . . with the successful decipherment of the cuneiform scripts. . . . Now fantastic and baseless speculations about the Mesopotamian past gradually gave way to more sober assessments."[5]

The discovery of ancient Near Eastern texts and the decipherment of their languages indeed changed the conversation considerably and shed great light. In the nineteenth century, a wide array of cuneiform languages came to light. Cuneiform script is named for the wedge shapes that form its characters (*cuneī* is Latin for "wedges"). Although its forms varied depending on the time and place, the same basic writing system was used for many ancient Near Eastern languages (including Sumerian, Akkadian, Hittite, Persian) over more than 2,000 years. In the 1760s, Carsten Niebuhr traveled in the East and brought back to Europe accurate squeezes[6] of Persian inscriptions from Persepolis, which he published in the 1770s. Success was not immediate, but by the 1840s, Old Persian had also been deciphered. Some progress was also made on languages such as Elamite and Urartian.

The decipherment of Akkadian was perhaps the most important linguistic breakthrough. Invented in Mesopotamia, it became the common language of trade and diplomacy throughout much of the Near East, especially during the Late Bronze Age (ca. 1550–1200 BCE). The earliest Western discovery of Akkadian inscriptions was by Europeans traveling in the region during the seventeenth century, but decipherment did not began in earnest until the 1840s, when Assyrian monuments and inscriptions were brought back to England by A. H. Layard, both physically and in pictures.

Layard began working in 1845 at a site he thought was Nineveh; instead, he had uncovered Kalhu, Ashurnasirpal II's capital city. The French consul in Mosul, Paul-Émile Botta, had actually begun working in 1842 at the site that turned out to be Nineveh. After failing to meet with immediate success there, he eventually excavated significant artifacts from the palace of Sargon II at Khorsabad, but the French were less successful at both publicizing and transporting their finds. Steven W. Holloway has described the British and European public as "mad to see the monuments" from ancient Mesopotamia when the first major exhibition was mounted at the British Museum in 1847. "For a year," he writes, "the public had pored over sketches from . . . Layard's Mesopotamian excavations in the *Illustrated London News*."[7]

---

5. W. W. Hallo, "Biblical History in Its Near Eastern Setting: The Contextual Approach," 1.

6. A squeeze is an impression of an inscribed surface, usually made with wet paper.

7. Steven W. Holloway, "Mad to See the Monuments," *Bible Review* 17 (December 2001): 39; John Malcolm Russell, *From Nineveh to New York: The Strange Story of the Assyrian Reliefs in the*

In the atmosphere of public fervor, the most important work on the decipherment of Akkadian was done between 1848 and 1853. It has become increasingly clear in recent decades that the most important early decipherer was Edward Hincks, an Irish clergyman. A recent study of the correspondence and publications of the period suggests that it was he who first realized that Akkadian was basically written in a syllabic (nonalphabetic) system, determined that Akkadian incorporated another non-Semitic language (Sumerian), and made the greatest strides in identifying what specific signs signified.

In the past, Henry C. Rawlinson was often credited with the decipherment of Akkadian, and the reasons are fairly easy to see: he was a prominent public figure throughout his life, serving in the military and in Parliament; he was elected a Fellow of the Royal Society; and his brother, George, was an Oxford professor who wrote an account of Henry's life that completely omitted Hincks's role in the decipherment. However, a survey of Rawlinson's correspondence shows he was well behind Hincks and even explicitly and wrongly disagreed with him on a number of points. Rawlinson did eventually produce a number of significant editions of cuneiform texts in Persian, Akkadian, and so forth, and these established his fame. But it is probably correct to call this the story of "the genius Hincks and the hard-working Rawlinson."[8]

The Akkadian language and its writing system seemed so complex and difficult that the decipherers' proposed solutions sparked incredulity. Instead of letters, cuneiform signs represent syllables, and because of the variety of possible syllables there are hundreds of these phonetic signs. Furthermore, a single sign usually has multiple values depending on its context. Finally, the signs can also represent whole words in another language (Sumerian), interspersed with syllabic signs. As W. H. Fox Talbot wrote,

> Many persons have hitherto refused to believe in the truth of the system by which Dr. Hincks and Sir H. Rawlinson have interpreted the Assyrian writings, because it contains many things entirely contrary to their preconceived opinions. For example, each cuneiform group represents a syllable, but not always the same syllable; sometimes one and sometimes another. To which it is replied that such a license would open the door to all manner of uncertainty; that the ancient Assyrians themselves, the natives of the country, could never have read such a kind of writing, and that, therefore, the system cannot be true, and the interpretations based upon it must be fallacious.[9]

Therefore, a major way station toward the decipherment of Akkadian was a famous contest held by the British Royal Asiatic Society in 1857. Talbot, Rawlinson, Hincks, and Julius Oppert were given copies of an unpublished cuneiform inscription of the Assyrian king Tiglath-pileser I, and they sent their independent translations to the Royal Asiatic Society to be compared. In the end, they were deemed close enough to confirm that the language was understood.

Metropolitan Museum and the Hidden Masterpiece at Canford School (New Haven, CT: Yale University Press, 1997).

8. Kevin J. Cathcart, "The Earliest Contributions to the Decipherment of Sumerian and Akkadian," *Cuneiform Digital Library Journal* (2011): 9. Accessed at http://www.cdli.ucla.edu/pubs/cdlj/2011/cdlj2011_001.html.

9. W. H. Fox Talbot, "Comparative Translations," *Journal of the Royal Asiatic Society* 18 (1861): 150.

The decipherment of the Hittite language was similarly controversial. As the primary language of one of the great powers of the Late Bronze Age, in which many significant treaties and prayers were written, Hittite was a significant missing piece in understanding the wider ancient Near East. It was first encountered in just two tablets in the large archive of the Amarna letters in Egypt. J. A. Knudtzon identified it in 1902 as an Indo-European language, but the claim was heavily criticized. Just over a decade later, on the basis of a much larger archive found at Boğazköy in present-day Turkey, Bedřich Hrozný was able to decipher Hittite cuneiform, and he confirmed Knudtzon's hypothesis.

There was one final major chapter in the unveiling of ancient Near Eastern cultures: the discovery of Ugarit, which began in 1928 when a Syrian farmer struck a stone with his plow near the Mediterranean coast. He had run into an ancient tomb. Eventually, the French authorities who then governed that part of Syria sent archaeologists and antiquities experts to explore. On the site, called Minet el-Beida ("White Harbor"), and the nearby ruin mound at Ras Shamra ("Fennel Head," named after the plants that grew on it), they discovered the capital of a wealthy city-state from the Late Bronze Age.

Less than a week after the archaeologists began working on the tell,[10] they made the first of the finds that secured the site's fame: cuneiform tablets—and not of a syllabic variety like Akkadian, but rather a previously unknown alphabetic type of cuneiform. An entirely new language had come to light, part of the same West Semitic family as Hebrew and Aramaic, but used hundreds of years earlier. The excavations eventually revealed that Ugarit had been destroyed at the beginning of the twelfth century BCE, and that the tablets mostly dated from the century leading up to its demise. Charles Virolleaud led the way in the decipherment and had already published his findings by late 1929. Further progress came from Hans Bauer of Germany and Édouard Dhorme of France, who had been military cryptoanalysts (on opposing sides) during World War I. The language was effectively deciphered by 1930, and with the publication of Virolleaud's sign list in 1932, it was in the public domain.

The impact of the Ugaritic texts went far beyond their linguistic significance; they also shed light on the Syro-Palestinian religions in which Baal, El, and Asherah were worshiped. These deities were frequently condemned (or their characteristics imputed to Yhwh; see chap. 19) by the biblical authors. In the Ugaritic texts, readers had the clearest picture to date of how those deities looked from a sympathetic, internal perspective. Furthermore, many stylistic aspects of Ugaritic poetry proved comparable to biblical poetry. For all these reasons, the discovery of Ugarit forged a stronger link between the Bible and its ancient Near Eastern context, and strengthened scholars' ability to compare and contrast the two.

By the early twentieth century, historians and biblical scholars had benefited from an unprecedented revolution in their knowledge of the past. Much refinement and further exploration remained, but in the space of two centuries, dozens of centuries of ancient Near Eastern history had become available for study in a way that had been impossible for millennia. We are still sorting through the implications of all this new information, and many texts still await translation and publication.

---

10. "Tell" is the Arabic word for a ruin mound, and it has become a technical term in archaeology.

EARLY COMPARATIVE SCHOLARSHIP

Although the discovery and decipherment of so many ancient Near Eastern languages meant a vast new trove of information for scholars of the Bible and religion, it also brought a whole new set of debates and controversies.

George Smith: Promise Unfulfilled

It did not take long for the British advances in Assyriology to yield dividends. In 1872, George Smith, an assistant at the British Museum, discovered on a tablet from Nineveh an Akkadian version of the flood story that resembled the biblical story in Genesis 6–9 (see chap. 4). The tablet that Smith found was broken, but he presented it in a paper to the Society of Biblical Archaeology in December of the same year. The paper created such great interest that a London newspaper, the *Daily Telegraph*, offered a thousand pounds to send Smith back to Kuyunjik (the site of ancient Nineveh) to try to locate the rest of the account. Despite being a novice in archaeology, Smith had great luck. Within days, he found tablets that completed the text, a copy of what is now recognized as Tablet XI of the Gilgamesh Epic (chap. 4). Again pressed by public excitement, Smith quickly published the epic, along with other Akkadian texts, in *The Chaldean Account of Genesis* (1876).[11] Tragically, Smith was less fortunate in his health than he was in his discoveries. When he returned again to Kuyunjik in 1876, he contracted dysentery, and he died the same year. Assyriology thus lost "one of its most valued students."[12]

Smith's writings reveal that he was not only a gifted decipherer, but also a judicious scholar. He recognized that "furious strife has existed for many years" about the meaning and date of the Genesis narratives.[13] Smith was not a biblical scholar or theologian; insofar as he commented on religion, he perceived a "total difference between the religious ideas" of Mesopotamia and Israel,[14] but he was not prone to make rash statements or to disparage one culture at the other's expense. He was circumspect about the question of the relationship between the flood stories, laying out many of the same details that are still widely accepted today. Even so, Smith assumed that some more complete Mesopotamian "version of Genesis" was still out there, which could fill in some of the blanks that have confounded biblical interpreters. For example, he writes, "The brief narration given in the Pentateuch omits a number of incidents and explanations—for instance, as to the origin of evil, the fall of the angels, the wickedness of the serpent, etc. Such points as these are included in the Cuneiform narrative."[15] This comment represents one of the

---

11. George Smith, *The Chaldean Account of Genesis: Containing the Description of the Creation, the Fall of Man, the Deluge, the Tower of Babel, the Times of the Patriarchs, and Nimrod: Babylonian Fables, and Legends of the Gods: From the Cuneiform Inscriptions* (London: Sampson Low, Marston, Searle, and Rivington, 1876).

12. A. H. Sayce, preface to Smith's posthumously published *History of Sennacherib* (London: Williams and Norgate, 1878), iii.

13. Smith, *Chaldean Account of Genesis*, 13.

14. Ibid., 285.

15. Ibid., 14.

major early stances regarding ancient Near Eastern texts: that they primarily clarified the Bible and brought it into better focus. Smith elsewhere suggests that they might be used to clarify "many of the obscure points in the mythology of Greece and Rome" as well.[16] Although he did not live to pursue much detailed comparative work, he seems to have believed in an essential unity underlying all ancient mythologies.

Max Müller: A Linguistic Model

One of the towering figures in the early modern comparative study of religions, Max Müller, popularized a similar view. He famously applied Goethe's paradox—"He who knows one, knows none"—to religion.[17] That is, the person who knows only one religion does not even really know that one. This claim did not only mean that comparative study of religion can spare people from countless errors and mistaken ideas; Müller's vision for his studies went well beyond that. He was searching for a fundamental common ground among all religions, or as he put it, "something that makes the world akin."[18] If one added up all the religious knowledge in the world, somewhere in the common ground among them one could find "the inward nature" of religion. This is noble in its unifying hopes and characteristic of the boundless optimism of Western thinkers around the turn of the twentieth century. But Müller's project was based on the model of comparative linguistics, and just as languages remain divided into distinct families, so too religions have not proved susceptible to universal comparison.

William Robertson Smith: An Anthropological Approach

The anthropological approach of William Robertson Smith (1846–1894) compared ancient Israel to nineteenth-century pastoralist Bedouin tribes in the Middle East. In his view, life for such tribes had changed so little since ancient times that their beliefs and practices could shed light on ancient Semitic cultures. This led him to conclude that Israelite religion had developed in stages, such as fetishism, that are scarcely alluded to in the Bible. Although his work led to his dismissal from the chair of Old Testament at Free Church College in Aberdeen, it also proved highly influential. In the preface to his *Lectures on the Religion of the Semites* (1894), he made an essentially exegetical case for the comparative study of the Bible, in that "the doctrines and ordinances of the Old Testament cannot be thoroughly comprehended until they are put into comparison with the religions of the nations akin to the Israelites."[19] In his view, that was because

---

16. Smith, *Assyrian Discoveries: An Account of Explorations and Discoveries on the Site of Nineveh, During 1873 to 1874* (New York: Scribner, Armstrong and Co., 1875), 451.

17. Goethe originally said this of languages. Max Müller, *Introduction to the Science of Religion: Four Lectures Delivered at the Royal Institution in February and May, 1870* (1872; new ed., London: Longmans, Green, 1893), 11–16.

18. Ibid., 15.

19. William Robertson Smith, *Lectures on the Religion of the Semites* (London: Adam and Charles Black, 1894), vi.

the positive Semitic religions had to establish themselves on ground already occupied by these older beliefs and usages; they had to displace what they could not assimilate, and whether they rejected or absorbed the elements of the older religion, they had at every point to reckon with them. . . . No positive religion that has moved men has been able to start with a *tabula rasa*, and express itself as if religion were beginning for the first time; in form, if not in substance, the new system must be in contact all along the line with the older ideas and practices which it finds in possession. A new scheme of faith can find a hearing only by appealing to religious instincts and susceptibilities that already exist in its audience, and it cannot reach these without taking account of the traditional forms in which all religious feeling is embodied, and without speaking a language which men accustomed to these old forms can understand.[20]

Robertson Smith went on to compare the Hebrew Bible's rhetorical use of precursor religions to the New Testament's use of biblical concepts such as priesthood and blood sacrifice even as it transformed them. He also shared in Müller's universal and humanistic apologetic for the work, however: he looked forward to a future in which the "crudities recorded alike in sacred and profane literature shall have been purged away in a nobler humanity."[21]

James G. Frazer: Comparison on a Grand Scale

Perhaps most famous among those who followed in Robertson Smith's path was James G. Frazer (1854–1941), whose work was both anthropological, in that it gathered up traditions from living human cultures, and universalizing, in that it spanned the globe. Frazer's most famous work is *The Golden Bough*, but it was in his *Folk-lore in the Old Testament: Studies in Comparative Religion, Legend and Law* (1918) that he discussed the Bible most extensively. He described the comparative method as "the instrument for the detection of savagery under civilization . . . Applied to the human mind, [it] enables us to trace man's intellectual and moral evolution, just as, applied to the human body, it enables us to trace his physical evolution from lower forms of animal life."[22] This comment shows how great was the impact of Charles Darwin's *The Origin of Species* (1859) on various fields, and indeed when Frazer came to compare creation accounts, he opined that "roughly speaking, these two theories [creation and evolution] still divide the civilized world between them."[23]

Frazer wrote with regret that "the scope of my work has obliged me to dwell chiefly on the lower side of ancient Hebrew life revealed in the Old Testament, on the traces of savagery and superstition which are to be found in its pages." He believed it was possible, however, to separate the chaff from the wheat, "that higher side of the Hebrew genius which has manifested itself in a spiritual religion and a pure morality, and of which the Old Testament is the imperishable monument." As is typical of evolutionary schemes that

20. Ibid., 2.
21. Ibid., xii.
22. James G. Frazer, *Folk-lore in the Old Testament: Studies in Comparative Religion, Legend and Law* (London: Macmillan: 1918), viii.
23. Ibid., 44.

were propounded in the enthusiasm of the early twentieth century, however, there is a discernible bias toward the modern and the Western:

> The revelation of the baser elements which underlay the civilization of ancient Israel, as they underlie the civilization of modern Europe, serves . . . as a foil to enhance by contrast the glory of a people which, from such dark depths of ignorance and cruelty, could rise to such bright heights of wisdom and virtue, as sunbeams appear to shine with a greater effulgence of beauty when they break through the murky clouds of a winter evening than when they flood the earth from the serene splendour of a summer noon.[24]

In actuality, Frazer's writings do not often indulge in broad analysis of the material. For example, his discussion of flood stories spans more than 250 pages and every populated continent, but his interest in the end was far more in their origins and diffusion than on the moral or religious value of the various versions. Nor did he show much interest in how comparative data affected biblical interpretation. Instead, he offered vast storehouses of cultural (especially literary) material from all over the world, gathered and sorted but not assessed. (*The Golden Bough* appeared in 1890 as a two-volume work, but grew to twelve volumes by 1915!) Unfortunately these materials are generally presented in paraphrase, and so one may reasonably worry about the reliability of the far-flung and diverse sources of the reports. Frazer was not trained as an anthropologist, but held a post in classics at Cambridge.

Assertions of Biblical Superiority

Other early readers of ancient Near Eastern texts were not so reserved in their analyses. Rawlinson, who had played a role in deciphering Akkadian and built his fame on the ancient Near Eastern findings, opened his *Outline of Assyrian History* with this bold assertion: "Every new fact which is brought to light from the study of the Cuneiform inscriptions tends to confirm the scriptural account of [Mesopotamia]."[25] And Archibald H. Sayce (1845–1933), an Oxford professor and Anglican clergyman, published a number of books and articles asserting the compatibility of ancient Near Eastern data with the biblical texts, with titles such as *Fresh Light from the Ancient Monuments: A Sketch of the Most Striking Confirmations of the Bible* (1888).[26]

Early interpreters also tended to assess the religious value of ancient Near Eastern texts as being far below that of biblical literature. For example, Sayce wrote in 1903,

> Between Judaism and the coarsely polytheistic religion of Babylonia, as also between Christianity and the old Egyptian faith,—in spite of its high morality and spiritual insight,—there lies an impassable gulf. . . . It is like that "something,"

---

24. Ibid., x–xi.

25. H. C. Rawlinson, *Outline of Assyrian History as Collected from the Inscriptions Discovered by Austin H. Layard, Esq., in the Ruins of Nineveh* (Journal of the Royal Asiatic Society; London: John W. Parker and Son, 1852), 3.

26. London: Religious Tract Society, 1888.

hard to define, yet impossible to deny, which separates man from the ape, even though on the physiological side the ape may be the ancestor of the man.[27]

John Arendzen's entry on "Babylonia" in the *Catholic Encyclopedia* (1907) was similarly disparaging: "Babylonian . . . songs to the gods . . . are indeed often either weird incantations or dreary litanies; and when after perusal of a good number of them one turns to the Hebrew Psalter, no fair-minded person will deny the almost immeasurable superiority of the latter."[28] In general, it was typical for interpreters to emphasize the differences between the Old Testament and other ancient religious texts. Another scholar wrote in 1912 in a church-sponsored publication,

> The special religious value of the Old Testament literature does not lie in what is common to it and Babylon, but in the elements in which they differ. The points of contact must not blind the eye to the points of contrast. These points of contrast are in the spirit and atmosphere pervading the Hebrew Scriptures, which are quite distinct, not simply from Babylonian, but from all other literatures. . . . In many cases is agreement in form, but how far superior the spirit and substance of the Hebrew![29]

Early comparisons tended to assert the superiority of the "Hebraic religious spirit" and the biblical literature.

Friedrich Delitzsch: Babel and Bibel

A forceful countertestimony soon entered the conversation. From 1902 to 1904, the eminent German Assyriologist Friedrich Delitzsch gave a series of lectures titled "Babel und Bibel" ("Babel and Bible"), in which he bluntly asserted both the priority and the superiority of Babylonian religion over that of the Hebrew Bible. He was not, of course, the first to make such statements, but they created a larger impact than ever. This was partly because of his own stature—he had recently been appointed professor in Berlin and would put German Assyriology on its path toward dominance—and it was partly the magnitude of the lectures, which were delivered to the German Oriental Society and an audience full of dignitaries. Even Kaiser Wilhelm II, the German emperor, was in attendance. The opportunity to address such an audience attests to the immense public interest that discoveries of ancient Near Eastern artifacts and texts continued to generate in Europe.[30]

27. Archibald Henry Sayce, *The Religions of Ancient Egypt and Babylonia* (The Gifford Lectures on the Ancient Egyptian and Babylonian Conception of the Divine; Edinburgh: T & T Clark, 1903), vi.

28. John Arendzen, "Babylonia," in *The Catholic Encyclopedia*, vol. 2 (New York: Robert Appleton Co., 1907). Accessed at http://www.catholic.org/encyclopedia/view.php?id=1363.

29. Frederick Carl Eiselen, *The Christian View of the Old Testament* (New York: The Methodist Book Concern, 1912), 220–22.

30. Simo Parpola reports that the lectures were the subject of more than 1,650 newspaper and journal articles in Germany alone. See Parpola, "Back to Delitzsch and Jeremias: The Relevance of the Pan-Babylonian School to the Melammu Project," in A. Panaino and A. Piras, eds., *Schools of Oriental Studies and the Development of Modern Historiography* (Melammu Symposia 4; Milano: Mimesis, 2004), 237–47.

Delitzsch began his lectures on uncontroversial ground, noting that "from now till all futurity the names of Babel and Bible will remain inseparably linked together."[31] He pointed out that Mesopotamian (and Egyptian) religious traditions had their roots in periods much earlier than that during which the Hebrew Bible was composed: "Now that the pyramids have opened their depths and the Assyrian palaces their portals, the people of Israel, with its literature, appears as the youngest member only of a venerable and hoary group of nations."[32] Historical priority often carries with it a presumption of originality, and thus superiority, but in this first lecture Delitzsch expressed admiration for Israelite monotheism and for "those titanic minds, the prophets, [who] discovered in Yahweh the god of the universe, and pleaded for a quickening of the inner spirit of religion."[33]

Something had changed significantly in Delitzsch's thinking by the second lecture, given in 1903. This time, he said that it can only be "ignorance, indifference or blindness" to call the prophets agents of revelation, because they are religiously and ethically deficient. "The more deeply I dive into the spirit of the prophetic writings of the Old Testament," he said, "the more I shrink from Yahweh."[34] He claimed in passing that biblical authors probably had Babylonian texts in front of them and copied from them, and he eventually moved to a broader comparison of Israelite ethics versus those of the Mesopotamians:

> It seems to me a particularly unwise proceeding on the part of certain hotspurs to portray the ethical level of Israel, even that of the pre-exilic period, as elevated far above that of the Babylonians. It is undeniable that the warfare of the Assyrio-Babylonians was cruel and sometimes barbarous. But so was the conquest of Canaan by the Hebrew tribes accompanied by a torrent of innocent blood.[35]

It becomes clear in this lecture that Delitzsch was pursuing not only historical comparison but also a program of religious progressivism. He viewed the Hebrew Bible "as a unique monument of a great religio-historical process which continues even into our own times,"[36] but warned in the next breath, "let us not blindly cling to antiquated and scientifically discredited dogmas from the vain fear that our faith in God and our true religious life might suffer harm."[37]

Although these statements may not seem shocking by present-day standards, the scandal in 1903 was very great. Delitzsch was not only a leading professor speaking in a distinguished public forum, but also son of the eminent Old Testament scholar and (rather conservative) Lutheran churchman Franz Delitzsch. Yet the younger Delitzsch seemed to many people to be denigrating the Bible in both theological and humanistic terms. He was criticized as irresponsible in a statement by the emperor himself, and his third

---

31. Friedrich Delitzsch, *Babel and Bible: Three Lectures on the Significance of Assyriological Research for Religion* (Chicago: Open Court, 1906), 2.
32. Ibid., 3.
33. Ibid., 59, 66.
34. Ibid., 70.
35. Ibid., 106.
36. Ibid., 113.
37. Ibid., 114.

series of lectures in 1904 was relegated to smaller and less central venues. In these, his anti-Semitic tendencies seem to have hardened; he spoke, for example, of a "history of civilization which is constantly fettered by Semitic prejudices."[38]

Despite their flaws, Delitzsch's lectures merit significant attention because they raise a number of key issues in comparative studies: First, does historical priority matter to one's assessment of the value of religious ideas? That is, does the relative "youth" of Israel's religion indicate that it is derivative and less valuable? And second, apart from historical priority, can one compare the quality and importance of different ancient religions? Finally, even if it were possible, is it the proper role of comparative study to make such value judgments?

Alfred Jeremias: Revising Pan-Babylonism

A less polemical approach to Pan-Babylonism can be found in Alfred Jeremias's early comparative handbook *The Old Testament in Light of the Ancient Near East* (1904). Although Jeremias was a (German) Lutheran clergyman, he saw religions as fundamentally unified—not only ancient Israelite religion and other ancient Near Eastern religions, but Christianity as well. Within the first hundred pages of the aforementioned volume, he suggested Babylonian cognates for the Trinity and the dual nature of Christ. It was not, according to him, a question of literary dependence between the Bible and Mesopotamian texts, but rather a shared "conception of the world lying at their root." He conceived of this shared conception in terms of historical influence, however, so that a biblical author's "mind unconsciously but of necessity moved in the cycle of thought of . . . his surrounding world."[39] The historical rootedness of cultural influence would become a major component of the comparative method.

At its peak, Pan-Babylonism grew beyond a mere argument for the priority of Mesopotamian culture over Hebrew culture. In Jeremias's magnum opus, *Handbook of Ancient Near Eastern Spiritual Culture* (1913), he argued for the derivative nature of ancient Near Eastern religions generally, including Egypt's. The Pan-Babylonian school produced reams of work in the early years of the twentieth century, but World War I interrupted their productivity. After the war, with the leading proponents aging and their ideas unpopular, Pan-Babylonism sputtered.

Benno Landsberger: Conceptual Autonomy

After the war, Benno Landsberger, the most eminent Assyriologist of his era, advocated the view that Assyriology needed to be an essentially independent field rather than a comparative one. In a 1926 article, he argued that the field needed its own conceptual autonomy (*Eigenbegrifflichkeit*). For him "the most important key to understanding" a culture was to

---

38. Ibid., 172–73. This trend in Delitzsch's thinking culminated in his book *Die Grosse Täuschung* (*The Great Deception*).

39. Alfred Jeremias, *The Old Testament in the Light of the Ancient East: Manual of Biblical Archaeology* (New York: Putnam, 1911), 195–96.

understand it in its own right, rather than in comparison to something else.[40] This might seem to be a retreat from the ambitions advocated by the likes of Müller and Robertson Smith, but Landsberger viewed it as ambitious enough to describe a single ancient culture. From his perspective, practitioners of Assyriology had been overwhelmed both by the enormous amount of textual data and by widespread interest, which together had "hardly ever allowed Assyriology leisure to reflect upon itself and to reach an awareness of where it was heading."[41] Although he did not make this explicit, his argument was for a kind of détente in the struggle between theologians and Assyriologists over which culture or religion was superior. Although the division of the fields that Landsberger sought to create has been transgressed regularly ever since, he (along with his students) did help to create the independent field of Assyriology that is often practiced independently of biblical studies.

The case for conceptual autonomy was so effectively prosecuted that Simo Parpola recently lamented that although comparative work on specific issues goes on, since Landsberger there has been no "systematic, well-documented attempt to reconstruct the Mesopotamian world-view and correlate it with other comparable systems in the ancient world."[42] Parpola has consciously tried to resurrect the methods of the Pan-Babylonian school, for example, by comparing aspects of Assyrian religion to Judaism, Christianity, and Kabbalah.[43]

Landsberger's warning was in many ways wise, however. It is hard to appreciate a Mesopotamian text on its own merits when it comes under the heading "The Babylonian Genesis" or "The Babylonian Job." And in many of these cases, the form and function of these Mesopotamian texts were quite different from the biblical texts to which they were being compared. Interpreters of those texts often gave little reflection to the different time periods and processes of formation that each text went through. Usually this process of comparing apples to oranges resulted in the exaltation of the biblical texts at the expense of the other, as when Morris Jastrow stated that "Job is of an infinitely higher order" than the much earlier Babylonian text *Ludlul bēl nēmeqi*.[44] It may be fine to conclude that Job is artistically superior, but *infinitely*? What standard is being applied in such a case?

These questions continued to be hotly debated throughout the early twentieth century. At the same time, the barriers to (at least moderately) informed participation in the conversation continued to drop, in that ancient Near Eastern texts were becoming increasingly accessible in translation. German scholars led the way in this undertaking, and some of the most successful early compendia of ancient Near Eastern texts in English were translations of German originals.[45] Eventually, however, George Barton's *Archaeology and the Bible* became a touchstone for readers of English. It sought to provide a kind of all-purpose handbook to ancient Near Eastern history, culture, and literature, including

40. Landsberger, "Die Eigenbegrifflichkeit der Babylonischen Welt," *Islamica* 2 (1926): 355–72. Translated as *The Conceptual Autonomy of the Babylonian World* (trans. T. Jacobsen et al.; Malibu: Undena, 1967). Cited here, 6.

41. Landsberger, *Conceptual Autonomy*, 5.

42. Parpola, "Back to Delitzsch and Jeremias," 240.

43. Simo Parpola, *Assyrian Prophecies* (SAA 9; Helsinki: Helsinki University, 1997), xiii–xliv.

44. Morris Jastrow, "A Babylonian Parallel to the Story of Job," *JBL* 25 (1906): 189. See further in chap. 21.

45. Good summaries of early comparative compendia can be found in Pritchard, *ANET*, xix–xx; and Hallo, "Ancient Near Eastern Texts and Their Relevance for Biblical Exegesis," passim.

translations of numerous primary texts, and its popularity is reflected by the fact that it went through seven editions between 1916 and 1937.

New Assertions of the Bible's Uniqueness

Some scholars were eager to embrace the independence of Israelite culture and religion from those of its neighbors, because this allowed them to assert the unique purity of "biblical religion." This was true in both Jewish and Christian circles.

Yehezkel Kaufmann published his massive history of the religion of Israel from 1937 to 1956, and in it he posits that although the ancient Israelites lived right next to polytheistic cultures, they were unaware of the real nature of those neighboring religions. He repeatedly characterizes the biblical authors as "naïve." For example, the prophets' mockery of idol worship as mere fetishism (e.g., Isa. 44:19: "Shall I fall down before a block of wood?") shows that it was not practiced or understood in Israel.[46] Even the structure of his book, with its identification of a "First Idolatrous Period" and a "Second Idolatrous Period," seems intended to suggest that religious purity was the norm except for a couple of brief periods. The methodological reasons for his conclusions are clear, since he criticizes the "deeply ingrained habit" of scholars of religion to found their interpretations on the "testimony of obscure passages, on ingenious combinations of isolated 'hints' and 'clues' scattered here and here."[47] By contrast, Kaufmann (who attended a yeshiva before earning his doctorate in philosophy) thought one should follow what he saw as the broad theohistorical claim of the text, that Israel's religion was fundamentally different from those of other nations.

Similarly, G. Ernest Wright argued in *The Old Testament Against Its Environment* (1950) that far from reflecting polytheism or other common traits of ancient Near Eastern religion, the Hebrew Bible was primarily a long diatribe against the religious practices of neighboring nations.[48] Wright perceived "elements of Israel's faith which distinguish it sharply from the religions of its environment." Indeed, the world of the Hebrew Bible was "a totally different religious atmosphere" —not because of different intellectual development but because of Israel's foundational experience of revelation at Sinai. For Wright, Israel continued to be formed by its ongoing encounter with a God who is radically Other.

Both Kaufmann and Wright were attempting to reckon with a significant feature of Israelite religion: the claim that its own texts make to distinctiveness (and even uniqueness). This claim itself was not unique in the ancient Near East, but the repetitiveness and forcefulness with which it was made are distinctive.[49] Still, neither Kaufmann nor Wright

---

46. Kaufmann's work is available in a heavily abridged form in *The Religion of Israel, from Its Beginnings to the Babylonian Exile* (trans. M. Greenberg; Chicago: University of Chicago Press, 1960). Cited here, 7–20.

47. Ibid., 3.

48. This argument has been made again, and even more sharply, by John D. Currid, *Against the Gods: The Polemical Theology of the Old Testament* (Wheaton, IL: Crossway, 2013).

49. For a more careful discussion of this claim, see Peter Machinist, "The Question of Distinctiveness in Ancient Israel: An Essay," in *Ah, Assyria . . . Studies in Assyrian History and Ancient Near Eastern Historiography Presented to Hayim Tadmor* (ed. M. Cogan and I. Eph'al; Scripta Hierosoly-

reckons carefully enough with the textual and archaeological data, which complicate the picture of Israel as a nation set apart and devoid of foreign elements.

Morton Smith: A "Common Theology"

Alongside these voices arguing for Israel's uniqueness in the middle of the twentieth century were others who continued the older comparative-religions project of finding similarities. One example is Morton Smith's "The Common Theology of the Ancient Near East" (1952), which asserted, "The striking thing about the theological material of the great majority of these ancient Near Eastern texts is that, despite superficial differences, it shows *one overall pattern.*"[50] He did not stop there, but added that this pattern also applies to "most periods and countries where polytheism has been the religion of civilized peoples," and is therefore probably rooted in "social, psychological and rhetorical patterns," rather than in cultural influence in history.[51] Smith did not deny that different religions have distinctive points; for example, he thought that Israelite religion was distinguished by the notion of Yhwh's jealousy and by its neglect of the underworld and the dead.

Later in his career, and less cautiously, Smith mocked the "pseudorthodoxy" of those biblical scholars who "attempt to separate the OT from the near eastern culture of its time and to prove that it teaches a 'higher truth.'"[52] His opening salvo against this group was confrontational:

> I do not know any competent OT critic now living who would not have been excommunicated 250 years ago by any of the major Christian or Jewish groups. Nobody I know accepts the OT chronology, or thinks the nature miracles really happened, or even attributes the whole of the Pentateuch to the direct authorship of Moses; and *a fortiori*, nobody has that notion of the world and of how it works which is pre-supposed throughout the OT and taught in many passages. Nobody, so far as I know, believes in the existence of Yahweh as the OT describes him—a North-Arabian mountain god who traveled in thunderstorms and liked the smell of burning fat. But everywhere there are persistent efforts to square the facts of the OT as far as possible with the traditional teachings of the institutions, and even more, to make them serviceable for homiletic presentation.[53]

It may not be such a damning rebuke of modern biblical theology that it would have shocked religious institutions around 1700. And many of Smith's generalizations here are vast oversimplifications; the views of biblical scholars are not so monolithic. Yet this diatribe usefully calls attention to the effect of differing outlooks, presuppositions, and social locations on interpretation. Generalizing about the situation in the mid-twentieth

---

mitana 33; Jerusalem: Magnes Press, 1991), 196–212. Reprinted in *Essential Papers on Israel and the Ancient Near East* (ed. F. E. Greenspahn; New York: New York University Press, 1991), 420–42.

50. Morton Smith, "The Common Theology of the Ancient Near East," *JBL* 71 (1952): 137 (emphasis added).

51. Ibid., 146.

52. Morton Smith, "The Present State of Old Testament Studies," *JBL* 88 (1969): 32.

53. Ibid., 21.

century, Smith contrasted the tendency of comparative-religions scholars to find similarity with the tendency of theologians to find difference.

Summary: Parallelomania vs. Parallel-onoia

The field of comparative studies has often alternated between those extremes (similar vs. different)—between "parallelomania" (which Samuel Sandmel diagnosed as a "disease" in a presidential address delivered at the 1961 meeting of the Society of Biblical Literature[54]) and "parallel-onoia," which Howard Eilberg-Schwartz more recently warned against.[55] A cyclical pattern in comparative approaches can be discerned: new data would spark a burst of hypercomparativism (as with the Pan-Babylonism that Delitzsch espoused, or the Pan-Ugaritism that reared its head later); the excitement of the new data would be so great that everything would be thought to be explicable by it; then the field would regret its excesses, and begin to reassess the work that had been done.

THE PAST 50 YEARS: NEW TOOLS AND NEW DIRECTIONS

The last half century or so has seen a gradual maturing of comparative study. It has helped to have increasingly useful tools for students. In 1950, James B. Pritchard published *Ancient Near Eastern Texts Relating to the Old Testament*, which was not only "the largest collection of translations of texts relating to the Old Testament yet made,"[56] but was also blessed by authoritative and often artful translators. Unlike some comparable volumes before and since, *ANET* offered little commentary on the texts, an omission that probably helped the volume to last as fads and fashions in comparative studies came and went. *ANET* was soon joined by *The Ancient Near East in Pictures Relating to the Old Testament* (1954), which opened up art-historical (iconographic) interpretation of the Old Testament in its ancient Near Eastern context to new audiences. Both volumes were great successes and were updated a final time in 1969. *ANET* stood as the primary English-language compendium of ancient Near Eastern texts for half a century, and it is still useful, though *The Context of Scripture* (3 vols.; 1997–2002), edited by William W. Hallo and K. Lawson Younger, has now superseded it in many ways. The maturity of these works is marked by the fact that recent German compendia such as *Texte aus der Umwelt des Alten Testaments* (1983–97) have not been translated into English.

Shemaryahu Talmon: A New Focus on Method

The last fifty years have also seen moderation with respect to method. Shemaryahu Talmon articulated a pragmatic approach that both summarized some of the best practices

---

54. Samuel Sandmel, "Parallelomania," *JBL* 81 (1962): 1–13.
55. Howard Eilberg-Schwartz, "Beyond Parallel-onoia," in *The Savage in Judaism: An Anthropology of Israelite Religion and Ancient Judaism* (Bloomington: Indiana University Press, 1990), 87–102.
56. James Pritchard, ed., *Ancient Near Eastern Texts Relating to the Old Testament* (Princeton, NJ: Princeton University Press, 1950), xv.

up to that point and laid out guidelines for the future. Talmon criticized ahistorical "comparison on the grand scale" based on "diverse cultural contexts," which in his view "produces staggering and indeed nonsensical results." He pointed out that "seemingly identical phenomena which may occur in different cultures are often quite differently weighted."[57] Instead, Talmon argued that the most effective and convincing comparisons involved texts with certain similarities: (1) chronological proximity, (2) geographic proximity, and (3) cultural affinity. (This last qualification was not well defined by Talmon, but may be marked at least in part by similarity of language, which allows easier transmission of cultural ideas.) In sum, Talmon emphasized "the analysis of cultures *lying within a given historic stream.*"[58]

Somewhat more controversially, Talmon also explicitly reaffirmed Landsberger's *Eigenbegrifflichkeit*, the emphasis on the study of cultures in themselves. This was based on Talmon's perception of Israel's distinctiveness. He wrote that an "insistence on the particularity of the Hebrew culture and its dissimilarity from neighbouring cultures should serve students of the Old Testament as a guideline in their comparative studies."[59] This sounds perilously close to returning to the naiveté of Kaufmann or Wright, but in practice what Talmon meant to emphasize was simply that comparison reveals difference as well as similarity: "Comparativists generally, and in the field of biblical studies especially, would do well to pay heed to differences between cultures and not only to likenesses. Adequate attention must be given to the interpretation of the dissimilarities from other cultures of the ancient Near East which made biblical civilization the peculiar and particular phenomenon it was."[60]

A different but related misconception arises from the project of finding similarities, or "parallel-hunting," namely the idea that, generally, similarities between texts mean that one author borrowed directly from another. Students are at risk of inferring this even from good comparative work such as John Walton's *Ancient Israelite Literature in Its Cultural Context*, which repeatedly discusses "cases of alleged borrowing," as if literary influence were a criminal charge from which the Bible needed to be exonerated.[61]

In fact, it is very rare that one can confidently assert cross-cultural literary borrowing in the ancient Near East (for discussion and one possible instance, see chap. 20). When one speaks of (for example) Mesopotamian influence on the Bible, that does not mean that there was some original literary genius in Mesopotamia who dwarfed the biblical authors in creativity. After all, later Mesopotamian authors also owed much to earlier Mesopotamian authors. Instead, it means that both the Mesopotamian and biblical authors were part of ancient Near Eastern streams of tradition in which authors tended to conserve

---

57. Talmon, "The 'Comparative Method' in Biblical Interpretation—Principles and Problems," in Greenspahn, *Essential Papers on Israel and the Ancient Near East*, 384–85.

58. Ibid., 386, emphasis in original. The italicized phrase is adopted from the anthropologist Melville J. Herskovits.

59. Ibid., 389.

60. Ibid., 414–15.

61. By contrast, Walton himself would later write, "Borrowing is not the issue, so methodology does not have to address that. Likewise this need not concern whose ideas are derivative. There is simply common ground across the cognitive environment of the cultures of the ancient world." John H. Walton, *Ancient Near Eastern Thought and the Old Testament: Introducing the Conceptual World of the Hebrew Bible* (Grand Rapids: Baker, 2006), 21.

previous literary artifacts while also reshaping them and recombining them in new ways. Although one may not find the exact route of a cultural artifact's historical transmission,[62] it is worth the effort to identify the pathways and processes.

A certain modesty with respect to claims about the originality or dependence of literary works is not only a feature of the discussion of ancient Near Eastern literature; it is very much an emphasis of recent literary theory in general. "In literature there is no creation *ex nihilo*," says Alastair Fowler.[63] Delbert Hillers agrees: "'Books are made out of other books,' and . . . biblical books are no exception."[64] The point is taken, yet somehow this does not abolish the potential for newness in a text or the creativity of its author.[65] To be sure, the materials, the words, are always in some sense "recycled"—the literary critic Marjorie Perloff has sought to honor the effective reuse of cultural materials by dubbing it "unoriginal genius"[66]—but there is excitement and enjoyment in recognizing the things that have been done with those existing materials.

William W. Hallo: The Contrastive Approach

One of the most important twentieth-century voices in the conversation about comparative method was the aforementioned William W. Hallo, the great Assyriologist who taught for many years at Yale. The same year that Talmon's essay appeared, Hallo wrote an essay calling for a "contrastive approach" to comparison.[67] Two decades later, he would coedit (with K. Lawson Younger) the magisterial compendium of ancient Near Eastern texts *The Context of Scripture*. In the introduction, he restated his approach: "Given the frequently very different settings of biblical and ancient Near Eastern texts . . . it is useful to recognize such contrasts as well as comparisons or, if one prefers, to operate with negative as well as positive comparison."[68] In short, difference is not something that only theologians are likely to discover. The eminent comparative-religions scholar Jonathan Z. Smith has written that "as practiced by scholarship, comparison has been chiefly an affair of the recollection of similarity. . . . The issue of difference has been all but forgotten."[69] Clearly,

---

62. William W. Hallo, "Compare and Contrast: The Contextual Approach to Biblical Literature," in *The Bible in the Light of Cuneiform Literature: Scripture in Context III* (ed. William W. Hallo et al.; Ancient Near Eastern Texts and Studies 8; Lewiston, NY: Edwin Mellen, 1990), 6.

63. *Kinds of Literature*, 156.

64. Hillers, *Lamentations* (2nd ed.; AB 7A; New York: Doubleday, 1992), 33.

65. The claim of the Bible's uniqueness is often bound up with claims about its status as revelation; that is to say, if the Bible is divinely revealed, then it is not comparable to products of human literary invention. That assumption is problematic, at least from the standpoint of classical Christian (in this case, Chalcedonian) theology: If human flesh was good enough for God's self-revelation in Christ, why should human literary texts not also have been good enough?

66. Marjorie Perloff, *Unoriginal Genius: Poetry by Other Means in the New Century* (Chicago: University of Chicago Press, 2010).

67. W. W. Hallo, "New Moons and Sabbaths: A Case-Study in the Contrastive Approach," in Greenspahn, *Essential Papers on Israel and the Ancient Near East*, 420–42.

68. Hallo, "Ancient Near Eastern Texts and Their Relevance for Biblical Exegesis," *COS* 1.xxv.

69. Jonathan Z. Smith, "In Comparison a Magic Dwells," in *Imagining Religion: From Babylon to Jonestown* (Chicago Studies in the History of Judaism; Chicago and London: University of Chicago Press, 1982), 25–26.

Smith is not advocating the sort of difference-finding that has too often been hastily practiced in a naive, apologetic mode; rather, like everyone else in the conversation, he is looking for a way to address both similarity and difference accurately and responsibly.

In assessing similarity and difference, the mind-set of the interpreter is important; as Hallo says elsewhere, the goal "is not to find the key to every biblical phenomenon in some ancient Near Eastern precedent, but rather to silhouette the biblical text against its wider literary and cultural environment."[70] His choice of the term "silhouette" is significant, in that it emphasizes *perception*. Interpretation is not simply a decision after the fact about what to emphasize. Instead, our knowledge (or lack thereof) often *determines what we are able to perceive*. Education in ANE studies thus provides a bulwark against the tyranny of idiosyncratic perceptions; it forms or socializes those who undertake it within a certain way of thinking.

WAYS FORWARD FROM HERE

In the case of comparative ancient Near Eastern studies, one of the goals of this socialization is a deep immersion in the cultures of those times and places. Most scholars view this as a desirable thing. Following in the path of Landsberger, we aspire to get inside the heads of ancient authors; and how could that be wrong? Some comparativists, however, have argued that strict adherence to historical-cultural horizons can be overly dogmatic and limiting. One of those who have recently suggested new directions is Brent A. Strawn. Beginning from J. Z. Smith's dissatisfaction with the historical constraints of the method as it has often been practiced, and on Earl Miner's work on "comparative poetics," Strawn suggests a more creative and playful approach to comparison: "Ideally, the best comparisons are intercultural, which means they include historically unrelated and/or noncontiguous cultural and/or linguistic traditions."[71]

There is no doubt that far-ranging comparisons can be useful; an excellent example is Strawn's own "Imprecatory Psalms: Ancient and Modern," which compares the "cursing psalms" to protest music from our own times, including "gangsta rap."[72] While Strawn is perfectly capable of interpreting the psalms in light of their own cultural context, something different is achieved by interpreting them in ours. By means of such comparisons, the psalms may come alive in a new way for readers who would otherwise be unable to understand them.

---

70. Hallo, "Compare and Contrast," 3.

71. Brent A. Strawn, "Comparative Approaches: History, Theory, and the Image of God," in *Method Matters: Essays on the Interpretation of the Hebrew Bible in Honor of David L. Petersen* (ed. J. M. LeMon and K. H. Richards; Atlanta: SBL, 2009), 129.

72. Brent A. Strawn, "Sanctified and Commercially Successful Curses: On Gangsta Rap and the Canonization of the Imprecatory Psalms," *Theology Today* 69 (2013): 403–17; idem, "Imprecatory Psalms: Ancient and Modern," in *Teaching the Bible: Practical Strategies for Classroom Instruction* (ed. Mark Roncace and Patrick Gray; Atlanta: SBL, 2005), 203–4. Strawn draws inspiration from Carol Antablin Miles, "'Singing the Songs of Zion' and Other Sermons from the Margins of the Canon," *Koinonia* 6 (1994): 151–73.

The methodological question turns into a hermeneutical one, as Strawn is quite aware: "the purpose(s) or end(s) of the comparative endeavor matter."[73] The rhetorical context or moment also seems to matter: one might use a more free comparative method in pedagogy, while adhering to historical constraints in scholarly publication. In this way, the classroom can generate interpretive ideas that can then be investigated and checked. To build on the example just given: One can ask whether present-day protest music really functions as the imprecatory psalms did, since the latter (a) may well have been more the literature of high-level religious officials in their society; and (b) may, in light of the cursing practices of neighboring societies, have had an explicitly supernatural purpose in their composition.

In some hands, setting aside historical context would open the door to bad interpretation, because not every interpreter is an expert. Smith and Strawn are able to do it because of their hard-earned knowledge of their material. Probably every student of the ancient world perceives echoes of it in our world every day, but only by submitting oneself to the work of understanding the cultural matrix of ancient texts will one know how accurate such impressions are.

A final point of method for comparative study is that ideally it should illuminate both (or all) the texts that are compared. Meir Malul has asked why the Bible should always be privileged in the comparison:

> It is not that clear why the division should be such that the Old Testament always occupies one side of the equation, and the rest of the ancient world the other side. Why should the comparative method not be perceived as a research tool for comparing any two or more phenomena from the general cultural milieu of the ancient Near East, including the Old Testament being perceived as another one of the ancient sources left to us by that ancient and prolific civilization of the ancient Near East?[74]

While this book is intentionally bibliocentric, I do hope it is possible for readers to perceive the Bible as one of many ancient Near Eastern sources. Even for those who hold the Bible's uniqueness most dear, it is worth provisionally decentering the Bible in order to grasp the way it takes part in a much larger cultural matrix.

IN LIEU OF A CONCLUSION

Has progress been made through the history of comparative study? If nothing else, the volume and quality of our data continue to increase, if not at the rate they once did. A recent example is the 2014 publication of a remarkable Babylonian tablet that contains more information about the ark than previously published texts had (see chap. 4). New information can open new doors and clarify existing theories.

---

73. Strawn, "Comparative Approaches," 129.
74. Meir Malul, *The Comparative Method in Ancient Near Eastern and Biblical Legal Studies* (AOAT 227; Neukirchen-Vluyn: Neukirchener, 1990), 4–5.

In terms of method, we are often still prone to repeat the errors of our forebears, and so only a chastened awareness of the magnitude and incompleteness of the data can protect us. Of course, the only greater error than the ones the data tempt us toward would be the error of ignoring the data entirely. In 1985, J. J. M. Roberts expressed concern about the "perceptible shift away" from comparative study of the Bible, which "bodes ill" for the interpretive task. And so he issued a summons that needs to be sounded continually:

> Despite the abuses and the need for a more self-critical methodology, the attention to extra-biblical sources has brought new understanding to the biblical text. . . . However, if this light from the East is to continue shining and grow brighter, biblical scholars must continue to be conversant with fields outside their own discipline. To some extent one can and must depend on experts in these related fields, but unless one has some firsthand acquaintance with the texts and physical remains with which these related fields deal, one will hardly be able to choose which expert's judgment to follow. There is no substitute for knowledge of the primary sources.[75]

With ancient Near Eastern data ever more accessible, Roberts's call can be understood as deeply democratic. Comparative study of the Bible is not a task to be carried out by a few experts who can then deliver their results to the world; instead, it is a personal journey that any person ought to take who wishes to read in an informed way. In *Four Quartets*, T. S. Eliot wrote,

> We shall not cease from exploration
> And the end of all our exploring
> Will be to arrive where we started
> And know the place for the first time.

That should be the hope for education: that it transforms our understanding of our own heritage and history. In this case, those who begin the comparative journey knowing only the biblical texts may in the end return to the biblical texts, knowing them for the first time.

FURTHER READING

Chavalas, Mark W. "The Comparative Use of Ancient Near Eastern Texts in the Study of the Hebrew Bible." *Religion Compass* 5 (2011): 150–65.

Cross, Frank Moore. "Alphabets and Pots: Reflections on Typological Method in the Dating of Artifacts." Pages 233–46 in *From Epic to Canon: History and Literature in Ancient Israel*. Baltimore: Johns Hopkins University Press, 1998.

Eilberg-Schwartz, Howard. "Beyond Parallel-onoia." Pages 87–102 in *The Savage in Judaism: An Anthropology of Israelite Religion and Ancient Judaism*. Bloomington: Indiana University Press, 1990.

---

75. J. J. M. Roberts, "The Ancient Near Eastern Environment," in *The Hebrew Bible and Its Modern Interpreters* (Minneapolis: Fortress; Atlanta: Scholars Press, 1985), 96.

Finkelstein, Jacob J. "Bible and Babel: A Comparative Study of the Hebrew and Babylonian Religious Spirit." Pages 355–80 in *Essential Papers on Israel and the Ancient Near East*. Edited by F. E. Greenspahn. New York: New York University Press, 1991.

Hallo, William W. "Compare and Contrast: The Contextual Approach to Biblical Literature." In *The Bible in the Light of Cuneiform Literature: Scripture in Context III*. Edited by William W. Hallo et al. Ancient Near Eastern Texts and Studies 8. Lewiston, NY: Edwin Mellen, 1990.

———. "New Moons and Sabbaths: A Case-Study in the Contrastive Approach." Pages 420–42 in *Essential Papers on Israel and the Ancient Near East*. Edited by F. E. Greenspahn. New York: New York University Press, 1991.

Hays, Christopher B. "Echoes of the Ancient Near East? Intertextuality and the Comparative Study of the Old Testament." Pages 20–43 in *The Word Leaps the Gap: Essays on Scripture and Theology in Honor of Richard B. Hays*. Edited by J. Ross Wagner, C. Kavin Rowe, and A. Katherine Grieb. Winona Lake, IN: Eerdmans, 2009.

Landsberger, Benno. "Die Eigenbegrifflichkeit der Babylonischen Welt." *Islamica* 2 (1926): 355–72. Translated by T. Jacobsen et al. as *The Conceptual Autonomy of the Babylonian World* (Malibu, CA: Undena, 1967).

Machinist, Peter. "The Question of Distinctiveness in Ancient Israel: An Essay." Pages 196–212 in *Ah, Assyria . . . Studies in Assyrian History and Ancient Near Eastern Historiography Presented to Hayim Tadmor*. Edited by M. Cogan and I. Eph'al. Scripta Hierosolymitana 33. Jerusalem: Magnes Press, 1991. Reprinted in *Essential Papers on Israel and the Ancient Near East* (ed. F. E. Greenspahn; New York: New York University Press, 1991), 420–42.

Malul, Meir. *The Comparative Method in Ancient Near Eastern and Biblical Legal Studies*. AOAT 227. Neukirchen-Vluyn: Neukirchener, 1990.

Saggs, H. W. F. *The Encounter with the Divine in Mesopotamia and Israel*. London: Athlone Press, 1978. Pages 1–29.

Sandmel, Samuel. "Parallelomania." *JBL* 81 (1962): 1–13.

Smith, Jonathan Z. "*Adde Parvum Parvo Magnus Acervus Erit*." *History of Religions* 11 (1971): 67–90.

———. "In Comparison a Magic Dwells." Pages 19–35 in *Imagining Religion: From Babylon to Jonestown*. Chicago: University of Chicago Press, 1982.

Smith, Morton. "The Common Theology of the Ancient Near East." *JBL* 71 (1952): 135–47.

Strawn, Brent A. "Comparative Approaches: History, Theory, and the Image of God." Pages 117–42 in *Method Matters: Essays on the Interpretation of the Hebrew Bible in Honor of David L. Petersen*. Edited by J. M. LeMon and K. H. Richards. Atlanta: SBL, 2009.

Talmon, Shemaryahu. "The 'Comparative' Method in Biblical Interpretation: Principles and Problems." Pages 320–56 in *Congress Volume: Gottingen, 1977*. VTSup 29. Leiden: Brill, 1978.

PART II

Pentateuch

3

Creation Accounts

Enuma Elish, *the Memphite Theology, and Genesis 1–2*

GENESIS 1–2

When: Sixth century BCE (?)
Where: Jerusalem
Language: Hebrew

ENUMA ELISH ("WHEN ABOVE . . .")

What: Copies survive in 181 clay cuneiform tablets and fragments from various cities
   in Assyria and Babylon, attesting to a seven-tablet composition
When: Ca. 1100 BCE (?)
Where: Babylon
Language: Akkadian
Translation: W. G. Lambert[1]

Tablet I

When the heavens above did not exist,
   And earth beneath had not come into being—
There was Apsu, the first in order, their begetter,
   And demiurge Tiamat, who gave birth to them all;
5   They had mingled their waters together
   Before meadow-land had coalesced and reed-bed was to be found—
When not one of the gods had been formed
   Or had come into being, when no destinies had been decreed,

---

1. W. G. Lambert, *Babylonian Creation Myths* (Mesopotamian Civilizations 16; Winona Lake, IN: Eisenbrauns, 2013), 45–133.

The gods were created within them;
10   Laḫmu and Laḫamu were formed and came into being.
While they grew and increased in stature
         Anshar and Kishar, who excelled them, were created.
They prolonged their days, they multiplied their years.
         Anu, their son, could rival his fathers.
15   Anu, the son, equalled Anshar,
         And Anu begat Nudimmud, his own equal.
Nudimmud was the champion among his fathers;
         Profoundly discerning, wise, of robust strength;
Very much stronger than his father's begetter, Anshar
20   He had no rival among the gods, his brothers,
The divine brothers came together,
         Their clamour got loud, throwing Tiamat into a turmoil.
They jarred the nerves of Tiamat,
         And by their dancing they spread alarm in Anduruna.
25   Apsu did not diminish their clamour,
         And Tiamat was silent when confronted with them.
Their conduct was displeasing to her,
         Yet though their behaviour was not good, she wished to spare them.

Apsu and Mummu plot the destruction of the gods

Thereupon Apsu, the begetter of the great gods,
30   Called Mummu, his vizier, and addressed him,
"Vizier Mummu, who gratifies my pleasure,
         Come, let us go to Tiamat!"
They went and sat, facing Tiamat,
         As they conferred about the gods, their sons.
35   Apsu opened his mouth
         And addressed Tiamat . . .
"Their behaviour has become displeasing to me
         And I cannot rest in the day-time or sleep at night.
I will destroy and break up their way of life
40   That silence may reign and we may sleep."
When Tiamat heard this
         She raged and cried out to her spouse,
She cried in distress, fuming within herself,
         She grieved over the (plotted) evil,
45   "How can we destroy what we have given birth to?
         Though their behaviour causes distress, let us tighten discipline graciously."
Mummu spoke up with counsel for Apsu—
         (As from) a rebellious vizier was the counsel of his Mummu—
"Destroy, my father, that lawless way of life,
50   That you may rest in the day-time and sleep by night!"

Apsu was pleased with him, his face beamed
  Because he had plotted evil against the gods, his sons.
Mummu put his arms around Apsu's neck,
  He sat on his knees kissing him.

Ea kills Apsu and captures Mummu

55 What they plotted in their gathering
    Was reported to the gods, their sons.
  The gods heard it and were frantic.
    They were overcome with silence and sat quietly.
  The one who excels in knowledge, the skilled and learned,
60   Ea, who knows everything, perceived their tricks.
  He fashioned it and made it to be all-embracing,
    He executed it skillfully as supreme—his pure incantation.
  He recited it and set it on the waters,
    He poured sleep upon him as he was slumbering deeply.
65 He put Apsu to slumber as he poured out sleep,
    And Mummu, the counsellor, was breathless with agitation.
  He split (Apsu's) sinews, ripped off his crown,
    Carried away his aura and put it on himself.
  He bound Apsu and killed him;
70   Mummu he confined and handled roughly.

Ea builds a house on Apsu's remains

  He set his dwelling upon Apsu,
    And laid hold on Mummu, keeping the nose-rope in his hand.
  After Ea had bound and slain his enemies,
    Had achieved victory over his foes,
75 He rested quietly in his chamber,
    He called it Apsu, whose shrines he appointed.
  Then he founded his living-quarters within it,
    And Ea and Damkina, his wife, sat in splendour.

The birth of Marduk

  In the chamber of the destinies, the room of the archetypes,
80   The wisest of the wise, the sage of the gods, Bēl was conceived.
  In Apsu was Marduk born,
    In pure Apsu was Marduk born.
  Ea his father begat him,
    Damkina his mother bore him.
85 He sucked the breasts of goddesses,
    A nurse reared him and filled him with terror.
  His figure was well developed, the glance of his eyes was dazzling,
    His growth was manly, he was mighty from the beginning.

Anu, his father's begetter, saw him,
90   He exulted and smiled; his heart filled with joy.
Anu rendered him perfect: his divinity was remarkable,
       And he became very lofty, excelling them in his attributes.
His members were incomprehensibly wonderful,
       Incapable of being grasped with the mind, hard even to look on.
95   Four were his eyes, four his ears,
       Flame shot forth as he moved his lips.
His four ears grew large,
       And his eyes likewise took in everything.
His figure was lofty and superior in comparison with the gods,
100   His limbs were surpassing, his nature was superior:
'Mari-utu, Mari-utu,
       The Son, the Sun-god, the Sun-god of the gods.'
He was clothed with the aura of the Ten Gods, so exalted was his strength,
       The Fifty Dreads were loaded upon him.
105   Anu formed and gave birth to the four winds,
       He delivered them to him, "My son, let them whirl!"
He formed dust and set a hurricane to drive it,
       He made a wave to bring consternation on Tiamat.

Tiamat is moved to action

Tiamat was confounded; day and night she was frantic.
110   The gods took no rest, they . . . .
In their minds they plotted evil,
       And addressed their mother Tiamat,
"When Apsu, your spouse, was killed,
       You did not go at his side, but sat quietly.
115   The four dreadful winds have been fashioned
       To throw you into confusion, and we cannot sleep.
You gave no thought to Apsu, your spouse,
       Nor to Mummu, who is a prisoner. Now you sit alone.
Henceforth you will be in frantic consternation!
120   And as for us, who cannot rest, you do not love us!
Consider our burden, our eyes are hollow.
       Break the immovable yoke that we may sleep.
Make battle, avenge them!
       [. .] . . . . reduce to nothingness!"
125   Tiamat heard, the speech pleased her,
       She said, "Let us do now all you have advised."
The gods assembled within her.
       They conceived [evil] against the gods their begetters.
They . . . . . and took the side of Tiamat,
130   Fiercely plotting, unresting by night and day,

Lusting for battle, raging, storming,
> They set up a host to bring about conflict.

Mother Hubur, who forms everything,
> Supplied irresistible weapons, and gave birth to giant serpents.

135 They had sharp teeth, they were merciless . . . .
> With poison instead of blood she filled their bodies.

She clothed the fearful monsters with dread,
> She loaded them with an aura and made them godlike.

(She said,) "Let their onlooker feebly perish,

140 May they constantly leap forward and never retire."

She created the Hydra, the Dragon, the Hairy Hero,
> The Great Demon, the Savage Dog, and the Scorpion-man,

Fierce demons, the Fish-man, and the Bull-man,
> Carriers of merciless weapons, fearless in the face of battle.

145 Her commands were tremendous, not to be resisted.
> Altogether she made eleven of that kind.

Tiamat elevates Qingu

Among the gods, her sons, whom she constituted her host,
> She exalted Qingu, and magnified him among them.

The leadership of the army, the direction of the host,

150 The bearing of weapons, campaigning, the mobilization of conflict,

The chief executive power of battle, supreme command,
> She entrusted to him and set him on a throne,

"I have cast the spell for you and exalted you in the host of the gods.
> I have delivered to you the rule of all the gods.

155 You are indeed exalted, my spouse, you are renowned,
> Let your commands prevail over all the Anunnaki."

She gave him the Tablet of Destinies and fastened it to his breast,
> (Saying) "Your order may not be changed; let the utterance of your mouth
> be firm."

After Qingu was elevated and had acquired the power of Anuship,

160 He decreed the destinies for the gods, her sons:

"May the utterance of your mouths subdue the fire-god,
> May your poison by its accumulation put down aggression."

Tablet II

Tiamat gathered together her creation
> And organized battle against the gods, her offspring.

Henceforth Tiamat plotted evil because of Apsu.
> It became known to Ea that she had arranged the conflict.

5 Ea heard this matter,
> He lapsed into silence in his chamber and sat motionless.

After he had reflected and his anger had subsided
    He directed his steps to Anshar his father.
He entered the presence of the father of his begetter, Anshar,
10   And related to him all of Tiamat's plotting.
"My father, Tiamat our mother has conceived a hatred for us,
    She has established a host in her savage fury.
All the gods have turned to her,
    Even those you[2] begat also take her side. . . .

[Ea repeats the report of Tiamat's preparations from the previous tablet.]

Anshar heard; the matter was profoundly disturbing.
50   He cried "Woe!" and bit his lip.
His heart was in fury, his mind could not be calmed.
    Over Ea his son his cry was faltering.
"My son, you who provoked the war,
    Take responsibility for whatever you alone have done!
55 You set out and killed Apsu,
    And as for Tiamat, whom you made furious, where is her equal?"

[Anshar tries to send Ea to deal with Tiamat, but he returns from a scouting expedition saying that she is "too much" for him. Ea implores Anshar to send someone else, since "though a woman's strength is very great, it is not equal to a man's." Anshar next sends Anu, and the same thing happens.]

Anshar and Ea send Marduk against Tiamat

Anshar lapsed into silence, staring at the ground,
120   Nodding to Ea, shaking his head.
The Igigi and all the Anunnaki had assembled,
    They sat in tight-lipped silence
No god would go to face . . [. .]
    Would go out against Tiamat . . . . [. .]
125 Yet the lord Anshar, the father of the great gods,
    Was angry in his heart, not summoning any one.
A mighty son, the avenger of [his] father,
    He who hastens to war, the warrior Marduk,
Ea summoned (him) to his private chamber
130   To explain to him his plans.
"Marduk, give counsel, listen to your father.
    You are my son, who gives me pleasure,
Go reverently, before Anshar,
    Speak, take your stand, appease him with your glance."
135 Bēl rejoiced at his father's words,

2. Plural.

He drew near and stood in the presence of Anshar.
Anshar saw him, his heart filled with satisfaction,
  He kissed his lips and removed his fear.
"My father, do not hold your peace, but speak forth,
140 I will go and fulfil your desires!
Anshar, do not hold your peace, but speak forth,
  I will go and fulfil your desires!
Which man has drawn up his battle array against you?
  And will Tiamat, who is a woman, attack you with (her) weapons?
145 ["My father], begetter, rejoice and be glad,
  Soon you will tread on the neck of Tiamat!
Anshar, begetter, rejoice and be glad,
  Soon you will tread on the neck of Tiamat!"
"Go, my son, conversant with all knowledge,
150 Appease Tiamat with your pure spell,
Ride the storms, proceed without delay,
  And with an appearance which cannot be repelled turn her back."
Bēl rejoiced at his father's words,
  With glad heart he addressed his father,
155 "Lord of the gods, Destiny of the great gods,
  If I should become your avenger,
If I should bind Tiamat and preserve you,
  Convene an assembly, and proclaim for me an exalted destiny.
Sit, all of you, in Upshu'ukkinakku with gladness.
160 And let me, with my utterance, decree destinies instead of you.
Whatever I instigate must not be changed.
  Nor may my command be nullified or altered."

Tablet III

Anshar opened his mouth
  And addressed Kaka, his vizier,
"Vizier Kaka, who gratifies my pleasure,
  I will send you to Laḫmu and Laḫamu.
5 You are skilled in making inquiry, learned in address.
  Have the gods, my fathers, brought to my presence.
Let all the gods be brought,
  Let them confer as they sit at table.
Let them eat grain, let them drink ale,
10 Let them decree the destiny for Marduk their avenger."
[*Anshar repeats the story for Kaka to report.*]
  Kaka went. He directed his steps
    To Laḫmu and Laḫamu, the gods his fathers.

He prostrated himself, he kissed the ground before them,
70   He got up, saying to them as he stood,
"Anshar, your son, has sent me,
And I am to explain his plans. . . ."

[*Kaka repeats the story.*]

125   When Laḫḫa and Laḫamu heard, they cried aloud.
All the Igigi moaned in distress,
"What has gone wrong that she took this decision about us?
We did not know what Tiamat was doing."

The pre-battle feast of the gods

All the great gods who decree destinies
130   Gathered as they went,
They entered the presence of Anshar and became filled with [joy],
They kissed one another as they [. . .] in the assembly.
They conferred as they [sat] at table,
They ate grain, they drank ale.
135   They strained the sweet liquor through their straws,
As they drank beer and felt good,
They became quite carefree, their mood was merry,
And they decreed the fate for Marduk, their avenger.

Tablet IV

The gods delegate their power to Marduk and decree his destiny

They set a lordly dais for him
And he took his seat before his fathers to receive kingship.
(They said,) "You are the most honoured among the great gods,
Your destiny is unequalled, your command is like Anu's.
5   Marduk, you are the most honoured among the great gods,
Your destiny is unequalled, your command is like Anu's.
Henceforth your order will not be annulled,
It is in your power to exalt and abase.
Your utterance is sure, your command cannot be rebelled against,
10   None of the gods will transgress the line you draw.
Shrines for all the gods need provisioning,
That you may be established where their sanctuaries are.
You are Marduk, our avenger,
We have given you kingship over the sum of the whole universe.
15   Take your seat in the assembly, let your word be exalted,
Let your weapons not miss the mark, but may they slay your enemies.
Bēl, spare him who trusts in you,
But destroy the god who set his mind on evil."

They set a constellation in the middle
20   And addressed Marduk, their son,
"Your destiny, Bēl, is superior to that of all the gods,
    Command and bring about annihilation and re-creation.
Let the constellation disappear at your utterance,
    With a second command let the constellation reappear."
25   He gave the command and the constellation disappeared,
    With a second command the constellation came into being again.
When the gods, his fathers, saw (the effect of) his utterance,
    They rejoiced and offered congratulation: "Marduk is the king!"
They added to him a mace, a throne, and a rod,
30   They gave him an irresistible weapon that overwhelms the foe.
(They said,) "Go, cut Tiamat's throat,
    And let the winds bear up her blood to give the news."
The gods, his fathers, decreed the destiny of Bēl,
    And set him on the road, the way of prosperity and success.
35   He fashioned a bow and made it his weapon,
    He set an arrow in place, put the bow string on.
He took up his club and held it in his right hand,
    His bow and quiver he hung at his side.
He placed lightning before him,
40   And filled his body with tongues of flame.
He made a net to enmesh the entrails of Tiamat,
    And stationed the four winds that no part of her escape.
The South Wind, the North Wind, the East Wind, the West Wind,
    He put beside his net, winds given by his father, Anu.
45   He fashioned the Evil Wind, the Dust Storm, Tempest,
    The Four-fold Wind, the Seven-fold Wind, the Chaos-spreading Wind, the
    . . . Wind.
He sent out the seven winds that he had fashioned,
    And they took their stand behind him to harass Tiamat's entrails.

Marduk goes to battle

Bēl took up the Storm-flood, his great weapon,
50   He rode the fearful chariot of the irresistible storm.
Four steeds he yoked to it and harnessed them to it,
    The Destroyer, The Merciless, The Trampler, The Fleet.
Their lips were parted, their teeth bore venom,
    They were strangers to weariness, trained to sweep forward.
55   At his right hand he stationed raging battle and strife,
    On the left, conflict that overwhelms a united battle array.
He was clad in a tunic, a fearful coat of mail,
    And on his head he wore an aura of terror.
Bēl proceeded and set out on his way,

60   He set his face toward the raging Tiamat.

In his lips he held a spell,

He grasped a plant to counter poison in his hand,

Thereupon they milled around him, the gods milled around him,

The gods, his fathers, milled around him, the gods milled around him.

65   Bēl drew near, surveying the maw of Tiamat,

He observed the tricks of Qingu, her spouse.

As he looked, he lost his nerve,

His determination went and he faltered.

His divine aides, who were marching at his side,

70   Saw the warrior, the foremost, and their vision became dim.

Tiamat cast her spell without turning her neck,

In her lips she held untruth and lies,

[*Broken lines*]

75   Bēl [lifted up] the Storm-flood, his great weapon,

And with these words threw it at the raging Tiamat,

"Why are you aggressive and arrogant,

And strive to provoke battle?

The younger generation have shouted, outraging their elders,

80   But you, their mother, hold pity in contempt.

Qingu you have named to be your spouse,

And you have improperly appointed him to the rank of Anuship.

Against Anshar, king of the gods, you have stirred up trouble,

And against the gods, my fathers, your trouble is established.

85   Deploy your troops, gird on your weapons,

You and I will take our stand and do battle."

The defeat of Tiamat and her allies

When Tiamat heard this

She went insane and lost her reason.

Tiamat cried aloud and fiercely,

90   All her lower members trembled beneath her.

She was reciting an incantation, kept reciting her spell,

While the (battle-)gods were sharpening their weapons of war.

Tiamat and Marduk, the sage of the gods, came together,

Joining in strife, drawing near to battle.

95   Bēl spread out his net and enmeshed her;

He let loose the Evil Wind, the rear guard, in her face.

Tiamat opened her mouth to swallow it,

She let the Evil Wind in so that she could not close her lips.

The fierce winds weighed down her belly,

100   Her inwards were distended and she opened her mouth wide.

He let fly an arrow and pierced her belly,

He tore open her entrails and slit her inwards,
    He bound her and extinguished her life,
    He threw down her corpse and stood on it.
105   After he had killed Tiamat, the leader,
    Her assembly dispersed, her host scattered.
Her divine aides, who went beside her,
    In trembling and fear beat a retreat.
    [. . .] to save their lives,
110   But they were completely surrounded, unable to escape.
He bound them and broke their weapons,
    And they lay enmeshed, sitting in a snare,
Hiding in corners, filled with grief,
    Bearing his punishment, held in a prison.
115   The eleven creatures who were laden with fearfulness,
    The throng of devils who went as grooms at her right hand,
He put ropes upon them and bound their arms,
    Together with their warfare he trampled them beneath him.
Now Qingu, who had risen to power among them,
120   He bound and reckoned with the Dead Gods.
He took from him the Tablet of Destinies, which was not properly his,
    Sealed it with a seal and fastened it to his own breast.
After the warrior Marduk had bound and slain his enemies,
    Had [. . .] the arrogant enemy [. . .],
125   Had established victory for Anshar over all his foes,
    Had fulfilled the desire of Nudimmud,
He strengthened his hold on the Bound Gods,
    And returned to Tiamat, whom he had bound.

Marduk creates from Tiamat's carcass

Bēl placed his feet on the lower parts of Tiamat
130   And with his merciless club smashed her skull.
He severed her arteries
    And let the North Wind bear up (her blood) to give the news.
His fathers saw it and were glad and exulted;
    They brought gifts and presents to him.
135   Bēl rested, surveying the corpse,
    In order to divide the lump by a clever scheme.
He split her into two like a dried fish:
    One half of her he set up and stretched out as the heavens.
He stretched the skin and appointed a watch
140   With the instruction not to let her waters escape.
He crossed over the heavens, surveyed the celestial parts,
    And adjusted them to match the Apsu, Nudimmud's abode.
Bēl measured the shape of the Apsu

And set up Ešarra, a replica of Ešgalla.
145   In Ešgalla, Ešarra which he had built, and the heavens,
       He settled in their shrines Anu, Enlil, and Ea.

Tablet V

He fashioned heavenly stations for the great gods,
       And set up constellations, the patterns of the stars.
He appointed the year, marked off divisions,
       And set up three stars each for the twelve months.
5   After he had organized the year,
       He established the heavenly station of Nēberu to fix the stars' intervals.
That none should transgress or be slothful
       He fixed the heavenly stations of Enlil and Ea with it.
Gates he opened on both sides,
10   And put strong bolts at the left and the right.
He placed the heights (of heaven) in her (Tiamat's) belly,
       He created Nannar, entrusting to him the night.
He appointed him as the jewel of the night to fix the days,
       And month by month without ceasing he elevated him with a crown,
15   (Saying,) "Shine over the land at the beginning of the month,
       Resplendent with horns to fix the calling of days.
On the seventh day the crown will be half size,
       On the fifteenth day, halfway through each month, stand in opposition.
When Šamaš [sees] you on the horizon,
20   Diminish in all the proper stages and shine backwards.

[*Intervening broken lines describe Marduk's formation of the heavenly bodies.*]

The foam which Tiamat [. . .]
       Marduk fashioned [. . .]
He gathered it together and made it into clouds.
50   The raging of the winds, violent rainstorms,
The billowing of mist—the accumulation of her spittle—
       He appointed for himself and took them in his hand.
He put her head in position and poured out . . [. .] .
       He opened the abyss and it was sated with water.
55   From her two eyes he let the Euphrates and Tigris flow,
       He blocked her nostrils, but left . .
He heaped up the distant [mountains] on her breasts,
       He bored wells to channel the springs.
He twisted her tail and wove it into the Durmaḫu,
60   [. . .] . . the Apsu beneath his feet.
[He set up] her crotch—it wedged up the heavens—
       [(Thus) the half of her] he stretched out and made it firm as the earth.

[After] he had finished his work inside Tiamat,
    [He spread] his net and let it right out.
65   He surveyed the heavens and the earth . . [.] .
    [. .] their bonds . . . .
After he had formulated his regulations and composed [his] decrees,
    He attached guide-ropes and put them in Ea's hands.
[The Tablet] of Destinies which Qingu had taken and carried,
70   He took charge of it as a trophy (?) and presented it to Anu.
[The .] . of battle, which he had tied on or had put on his head,
    [.] . he brought before his fathers.
[Now] the eleven creatures to which Tiamat had given birth and . . . ,
    He broke their weapons and bound them (the creatures) to his feet.
75   He made images of them and stationed them at the [Gate] of the Apsu,
    To be a sign never to be forgotten.

The gods rejoice and bless Marduk

[The gods] saw it and were jubilantly happy,
    (That is,) Laḥmu, Laḥamu and all his fathers.
Anshar [embraced] him and published abroad his title, "Victorious King."
80   Anu, Enlil and Ea gave him gifts.
Mother Damkina, who bore him, hailed him,
    With a clean festal robe she made his face shine.
To Usmû, who held her present to give the news,
    [He entrusted] the vizierate of the Apsu and the care of the holy places.
85   The Igigi assembled and all did obeisance to him,
    Every one of the Anunnaki was kissing his feet.
They all [gathered] to show their submission,
    [. . .] they stood, they bowed down, "Behold the king!"
His fathers [. . .] and took their fill of his beauty,
90   Bēl listened to their utterance, being girded with the dust of battle.
[. . .]
    Anointing his body with . [. . .] cedar perfume.
He clothed himself in [his] lordly robe,
    With a crown of terror as a royal aura.

[Broken lines]

Opened their mouths and [addressed] the Igigi gods,
"Previously Marduk was our beloved son,
110   Now he is your king, heed his command!"
Next, they all spoke up together,
    "His name is Lugaldimmerankia, trust in him!"
When they had given kingship to Marduk,
    They addressed to him a benediction for prosperity and success,
115   "Henceforth you are the caretaker of our shrine,

Whatever you command, we will do!"
Marduk opened his mouth to speak
    And addressed the gods his fathers,
"Above the Apsu, the emerald (?) abode,
120   Opposite Ešarra, which I built for you,
Beneath the celestial parts, whose floor I made firm,
    I will build a house to be my luxurious abode.
Within it I will establish its shrine,
    I will found my chamber and establish my kingship.
125   When you come up from the Apsu to make a decision,
    This will be your resting place before the assembly.
When you descend from heaven to make a decision,
    This will be your resting place before the assembly.
I shall call its name 'Babylon,' "The Homes of the Great Gods,"
130   Within it we will hold a festival, that will be the evening festival,
[The gods], his fathers, [heard] this speech of his,

[*Broken lines*]

(They said:) In Babylon, as you have named it,
    Put our [resting place] forever.

[*About 20 broken lines*]

Tablet VI

Marduk creates humankind from the blood of Qingu

When Marduk heard the gods' speech
    He conceived a desire to accomplish clever things.
He opened his mouth addressing Ea,
    He counsels that which he had pondered in his heart,
5   "I will bring together blood and form bone,
    I will bring into being Lullû,[3] whose name shall be 'man,'
I will create Lullû–man
    On whom the toil of the gods will be laid that they may rest.
I will skillfully alter the organization of the gods:
10   Though they are honoured as one, they shall be divided into two."
Ea answered, as he addressed a word to him,
    Expressing his comments on the resting of the gods,
"Let one brother of theirs be given up.
    Let him perish that people may be fashioned.
15   Let the great gods assemble
    And let the guilty one be given up that they may be confirmed."
Marduk assembled the great gods,

---

3. A Sumerian loan word into Akkadian, meaning "(primeval) man."

Using gracious direction as he gave his order,
As he spoke the gods heeded him:
20   The king addressed a word to the Anunnaki,
"Your former oath was true indeed,
      (Now also) tell me the solemn truth:
Who is the one who instigated warfare,
      Who made Tiamat rebel, and set battle in motion?
25   Let him who instigated warfare be given up
      That I may lay his punishment on him; but you sit and rest."
The Igigi, the great gods, answered him,
      That is, Lugaldimmerankia, the counsellor of the gods, their lord,
"Qingu is the one who instigated warfare,
30   Who made Tiamat rebel and set battle in motion."
They bound him, holding him before Ea,
      They inflicted the penalty on him and severed his blood-vessels.
From his blood he (Ea) created mankind,
      On whom he imposed the service of the gods, and set the gods free.
35   After the wise Ea had created mankind
      And had imposed the service of the gods upon them—
That task is beyond comprehension
      For Nudimmud performed the creation with the skills of Marduk—
King Marduk divided the gods,
40   All the Anunnaki into upper and lower groups.
He assigned 300 in the heavens to guard the decrees of Anu,
      And appointed them as a guard.
Next he arranged the organization of the netherworld.
      In heaven and netherworld he stationed 600 gods.

Marduk has the gods build Babylon and its temples

45   After he had arranged all the decrees,
      And had distributed incomes among the Anunnaki of heaven and netherworld,
The Anunnaki opened their mouths
      And addressed their lord Marduk,
"Now, lord, seeing you have established our freedom
50   What favour can we do for you?
Let us make a shrine of great renown:
      Your chamber will be our resting place wherein we may repose.
Let us erect a shrine to house a pedestal
      Wherein we may repose when we finish (the work)."
55   When Marduk heard this,
      He beamed as brightly as the light of day,
"Build Babylon, the task you have sought.
      Let bricks for it be moulded, and raise the shrine!"
The Anunnaki wielded the pick.

60   For one year they made the needed bricks.
When the second year arrived,
        They raised the peak of Esagil, a replica of the Apsu.
They built the lofty temple tower of the Apsu
        And for Anu, Enlil, Ea and him they established it as a dwelling.
65   He sat in splendour before them,
        Surveying its horns, which were level with the base of Ešarra.
After they had completed the work on Esagil
        All the Anunnaki constructed their own shrines.
        {300 Igigi of heaven and 600 of the Apsu, all of them, had assembled.}
70   Bēl seated the gods, his fathers, at the banquet
In the lofty shrine which they had built for his dwelling,
        (Saying,) "This is Babylon, your fixed dwelling,
Take your pleasure here! Sit down in joy!"
        The great gods sat down,
75   Beer-mugs were set out and they sat at the banquet.
        After they had enjoyed themselves inside
They held a service in awesome Esagil.
        The regulations and all the rules were confirmed:
All the gods divided the stations of heaven and netherworld.
80   The college of the Fifty great gods took their seats,
The Seven gods of destinies were appointed to give decisions.
        Bēl received his weapon, the bow, and laid it before them:
His divine fathers saw the net which he had made.
        His fathers saw how skillfully wrought was the structure of the bow
85   As they praised what he had made.
        Anu lifted it up in the divine assembly,
He kissed the bow, saying, "It is my daughter!"
        Thus he called the names of the bow:
"Long Stick" was the first; the second was, "May it hit the mark."
90   With the third name, "Bow Star," he made it to shine in the sky,
He fixed its heavenly position along with its divine brothers.
        After Anu had decreed the destiny of the bow,
He set down a royal throne, a lofty one even for a god,
        Anu set it there in the assembly of the gods.
95   The great gods assembled,
        They exalted the destiny of Marduk and did obeisance.
They invoked a curse on themselves
        And took an oath with water and oil, and put their hands on their throats.
They granted him the right to exercise kingship over the gods,
100   They confirmed him as lord of the gods of heaven and netherworld.
Anshar gave him his exalted name, Asalluḫi:
        "At the mention of his name, let us show submission!
When he speaks, let the gods heed him,

Let his command be superior in upper and lower regions.
105 May the son, our avenger, be exalted,
Let his lordship be superior and himself without rival.
Let him shepherd the black-heads, his creatures,
Let them tell of his character to future days without forgetting.
Let him establish lavish food offerings for his fathers,
110 Let him provide for their maintenance and be caretaker of their sanctuaries,
Let him burn incense to rejoice their sanctums.
Let him do on earth the same as he has done in heaven:
Let him appoint the black-heads to worship him.
The subject humans should take note and call on their gods,
115 Since he commands they should heed their goddesses,
Let food offerings be brought [for] (?) their gods and goddesses,
May they (?) not be forgotten, may they remember their gods,
May they . . . their . . , may they . . their shrines.
Though the black-heads worship someone, some other god,
120 He is the god of each and every one of us!
Come, let us call the fifty names
Of him whose character is resplendent, whose achievement is the same."
(1) Marduk as he was named by his father Anu from his birth,
Who supplies pasturage and watering, making the stables flourish.
125 Who bound the boastful with his weapon, the storm flood,
And saved the gods, his fathers, from distress.
He is the son, the sun-god of the gods, he is dazzling,
Let them ever walk in his bright light.
On the peoples that he created, the living beings,
He imposed the service of the gods and they took rest.
Creation and annihilation, forgiveness and exacting the penalty
Occur at his command, so let them fix their eyes on him.
(2) Marukka: he is the god who created them,
Who put the Anunnaki at ease, the Igigi at rest.
135 (3) Marutukku: he is the support of land, city, and its peoples,
Henceforth let the peoples ever heed him.
(4) Meršakušu: fierce yet deliberating, angry yet relenting,
His mind is wide, his heart is all-embracing.
(5) Lugaldimmerankia is the name by which we all called him,
140 Whose command we have exalted above that of the gods his fathers.
He is the lord of all the gods of heaven and netherworld,
The king at whose injunctions the gods in upper and lower regions shudder.
(6) Narilugaldimmerankia is the name we gave him, the mentor of every god,
Who established our dwellings in heaven and netherworld in time of trouble,
145 Who distributed the heavenly stations between Igigi and Anunnaki,
Let the gods tremble at his name and quake on their seats.
(7) Asalluḫi is the name by which his father Anu called him,

He is the light of the gods, a mighty hero,
Who, as his name says, is a protecting angel for god and land,
150   Who by a terrible combat saved our dwelling in time of trouble.
(8) Asalluḫi-Namtilla they called him secondly, the life-giving god,
    Who, in accordance with the form (of) his (name), restored all the ruined gods,
The lord, who brought to life the dead gods by his pure incantation,
    Let us praise him as the destroyer of the crooked enemies.
155   (9) Asalluḫi-Namru, as his name is called thirdly,
    The pure god, who cleanses our character.
Anshar, Laḫmu, and Laḫamu (each) called him by three of his names,
    Then they addressed the gods, their sons,
"We have each called him by three of his names,
160   Now you call his names, like us."
The gods rejoiced as they heard their speech,
    In Upšuukkinaki they held a conference,
"Of the warrior son, our avenger,
    Of the provisioner, let us extol the name."
165   They sat down in their assembly, summoning the destinies,
    And with all due rites they called his name:

Tablet VII

[The first 134 lines of Tablet VII continue with the ascription of names to Marduk, including names 10–49.]

135   Since he created the heavens and fashioned the earth,
    Enlil, the father, called him by his own name, (50) 'Lord of the Lands'.
Ea heard the names which all the Igigi called
    And his spirit became radiant.
"Why! He whose name was extolled by his fathers
140   Let him, like me, be called (51) 'Ea'.
Let him control the sum of all my rites,
    Let him administer all my decrees."
With the word "Fifty" the great gods
    Called his fifty names and assigned him an outstanding position.
145   They should be remembered; a leading figure should expound them,
    The wise and learned should confer about them,
A father should repeat them and teach them to his son,
    One should explain them to shepherd and herdsman.
If one is not negligent to Marduk, the Enlil of the gods,
150   May one's land flourish, and oneself prosper,
(For) his word is reliable, his command unchanged,
    No god can alter the utterance of his mouth.
When he looks in fury, he does not relent,

When his anger is ablaze, no god can face him.
155   His mind is deep, his spirit is all-embracing,
        Before whom sin and transgression are sought out.
    Instruction which a leading figure repeated before him (Marduk):
        He wrote it down and stored it so that generations to come might hear it
        [. . .] Marduk, who created the Igigi gods,
160   Though they diminish . . . let them call on his name.
        . . . . the song of Marduk,
        Who defeated Tiamat and took kingship.

THE MEMPHITE THEOLOGY

What: Text on slab of black granite, 66 cm × 137 cm
When: Late eighth century BCE (but see below)
Where: Memphis
Language: Hieroglyphic Egyptian
Translation: Miriam Lichtheim, *AEL* 1.51–57.

The living Horus: Who prospers the Two Lands; the Two Ladies: Who prospers the Two Lands; the Golden Horus: Who prospers the Two Lands; the King of Upper and Lower Egypt: Neferkare; the Son of Re: Sha[baka], beloved of Ptah-South-of-his-Wall, who lives like Re forever.

This writing was copied out anew by his majesty in the House of his father Ptah-South-of-his-Wall, for his majesty found it to be a work of the ancestors which was worm-eaten, so that it could not be understood from beginning to end. His majesty copied it anew so that it became better than it had been before, in order that his name might endure and his monument last in the House of his father Ptah-South-of-his-Wall throughout eternity, as a work done by the Son of Re [Shabaka] for his father Ptah-Tatenen, so that he might live forever.

[A lengthy section describing the unification of the lands under Horus, and identifying Horus with Ptah, is omitted here.]

    The gods who came into being in Ptah:
        Ptah-on-the-great-throne [. . .]
        Ptah-Nun,[4] the father who [made] Atum.
        Ptah-Naunet,[5] the mother who bore Atum.
        Ptah-the-Great is heart and tongue of the Nine [Gods].[6]
        [Ptah . . .] who bore the gods.
        [Ptah . . .] who bore the gods.

4. Nun was the deified primeval waters of life, also called "father of the gods." He is here identified with Ptah.
    5. Naunet is the feminine counterpart or aspect of Nun.
    6. The primary deities of the Heliopolitan pantheon.

[Ptah . . .]
[Ptah . . .] Nefertem[7] at the nose of Re every day.

There took shape in the heart, there took shape on the tongue the form of Atum. For the very great one is Ptah, who gave [life] to all the gods and their *ka*s[8] through this heart and through this tongue, in which Horus[9] had taken shape as Ptah, in which Thoth had taken shape as Ptah.[10]

Thus heart and tongue rule over all the limbs in accordance with the teaching that it (the heart, *or:* he, Ptah) is in every body and it (the tongue, *or:* he, Ptah) is in every mouth of all gods, all men, all cattle, all creeping things, whatever lives, thinking whatever it (*or:* he) wishes and commanding whatever it (*or:* he) wishes.

His (Ptah's) Ennead[11] is before him as teeth and lips. They are the semen and the hands of Atum. For the Ennead of Atum came into being through his semen and his fingers. But the Ennead is the teeth and lips in this mouth which pronounced the name of every thing, from which Shu and Tefnut[12] came forth, and which gave birth to the Ennead.

Sight, hearing, breathing—they report to the heart, and it makes every understanding come forth. As to the tongue, it repeats what the heart has devised. Thus all the gods were born and his Ennead was completed. For every word of the god came about through what the heart devised and the tongue commanded.

Thus all the faculties were made and all the qualities determined, they that make all foods and all provisions, through this word. [Thus justice is done] to him who does what is loved, [and punishment] to him who does what is hated. Thus life is given to the peaceful, death is given to the criminal. Thus all labor, all crafts are made, the action of the hands, the motion of the legs, the movements of all the limbs, according to this command which is devised by the heart and comes forth on the tongue and creates the performance of every thing.

Thus it is said of Ptah: "He who made all and created the gods." And he is Tatenen,[13] who gave birth to the gods, and from whom every thing came forth, foods, provisions, divine offerings, all good things. Thus it is recognized and understood that he is the mightiest of the gods. Thus Ptah was satisfied after he had made all things and all divine words.

> He gave birth to the gods,
> He made the towns,

7. A youthful god associated with the lotus flower.
8. The *ka* is an aspect of the Egyptian soul.
9. A god associated with the sky and kingship, Horus was the son of Osiris. He is also identified with Ptah in this text.
10. *Alternative rendering:* "Heart took shape in the form of Atum, Tongue took shape in the form of Atum. It is Ptah, the very great, who has given [life] to all the gods and their *ka*s *through this heart and through this tongue, from which Horus had come forth as Ptah, from which Thoth had come forth as Ptah.*"
11. From the Greek *ennea,* "nine," this term refers to the group of nine gods (see above).
12. Shu and Tefnut were the first pair of deities born from Nun.
13. Ptah is here identified with Tatenen, the deified primeval mound from which life sprang, often associated with the fertile silt of Nile inundation.

He established the nomes,
He placed the gods in their shrines,
He settled their offerings,
He established their shrines,
He made their bodies according to their wishes.
Thus the gods entered into their bodies,
Of every wood, every stone, every clay,
Every thing that grows upon him[14]
In which they came to be.

Thus were gathered to him all the gods and their *ka*s, content, united with the Lord of the Two Lands.[15]

The Great Throne that gives joy to the heart of the gods in the House of Ptah[16] is the granary of Ta-tenen, the mistress of all life, through which the sustenance of the Two Lands is provided.

[*The text closes with a brief version of the myth of Osiris, who is then incorporated into the Memphite theology.*]

DISCUSSION

What better way could there be to compare cultures and religions than by analyzing their creation accounts? This is where it all begins: the origins of life, the universe, and everything. These stories are indeed foundational for some aspects of their religions, but the relationship between the biblical creation accounts and those of other ancient Near Eastern cultures is a complex and difficult topic, compared to some others. Indeed, the texts presented in this chapter are likely to look completely different from each other at first glance. However, close attention also yields striking points of similarity.

It is best to set aside certain preconceived notions at the outset. For example, many readers may expect that each civilization had one creation story—a *single* account of origins. Popular titles of translations probably contribute to this misconception; for example, some studies call *Enuma Elish* "*The* Babylonian Epic of Creation." It proves untrue, however. Instead, wherever we have large bodies of preserved literature from the ancient Near East, we also find multiple accounts of origins. The best examples are Egypt and Mesopotamia. Each had various creation stories, each of which might have its home in a certain city or temple and might have been more or less influential in a given era.

The diversity within any individual civilization invites study of the internal conversation among texts in a single cultural stream, but the focus here is on comparison *between* cultures. The stories presented here are distinct, but they allow one to ask and answer a common set of questions: Who is the Creator, and what is the Creator like? Who, if anyone, was with the Creator in the beginning? What is the purpose of creation, particularly

14. I.e., Ptah-Tatenen, the mound.
15. The Two Lands are Upper and Lower Egypt. An earlier portion of the text describes their unification.
16. The temple of Ptah at Memphis.

the creation of humankind? And in the end, one must ask the question that has the most diverse answers: What *is* this story, and why was it told?

Babylon: *Enuma Elish*

In the case of Mesopotamia, W. G. Lambert notes that "other than *Enūma Eliš* there is no systematic treatment of cosmology in Sumero-Babylonian literature. . . . But this does not mean that *Enūma Eliš* presents all that is known of Babylonian cosmology. On the contrary, the Epic uses only a selection of the wealth of available material."[17] Seventeen other brief (and sometimes fragmentary) "creation tales" are collected in his *Babylonian Creation Myths*, and there are still more passing references to creation in other genres. Mesopotamians did not tell only one story about creation.

Enuma Elish is not systematic in the sense that Lambert's comment might lead some readers (especially those in the Christian tradition) to anticipate. Indeed, there was no "systematic theology" in the ancient Near East in the sense of a rationalized system of religion. There were many ways for ancient Near Eastern authors to express theological ideas, from hymns to prayers to prophetic pronouncements to ritual prescriptions (all discussed elsewhere in this book), but philosophical argumentation in the manner of later Western thinkers was not operative. In the texts in this chapter, theology was expressed through stories. When stories focus on the gods, they can be classified as *myths*. The term "myth" has long carried the connotation of "fiction," but it derives from the Greek *mythos*, a term that originally meant simply "story," without reference to historical truth.

Enuma Elish is a remarkable work of storytelling and theology. The story begins with a *theogony*—a story about the origins of the gods themselves. (The best-known theogony is probably that of the Greek author Hesiod.) In *Enuma Elish*, the stuff of the universe itself preexists most of the gods; they are formed by the intermingling of Apsu, the primordial watery chaos who begets them, and Tiamat, the monstrous mother goddess who bears them. In time, the clamor of the younger deities begins to antagonize Tiamat and Apsu, and although Tiamat wants to spare them, Apsu plots their demise. The younger gods hear of this, and send Ea as their champion to kill Apsu and confine his vizier, Mummu. He fashions Apsu's remains into his homeland, dwelling, and shrines, and there he begets his son: Marduk (aka Bel).

Tiamat, however, is enraged at the death of Apsu, and prepares for battle against the younger gods, elevating the terrifying Qingu as her general. Seeing her fearsome preparations for battle, all of the younger gods return dismayed from their scouting missions. Finally, however, Marduk is called forward to go against Tiamat and Qingu. He joyfully accepts the nomination, after which the gods outfit him and delegate their powers to him. He goes to battle claiming the righteousness of his cause, and he slays the raging Tiamat. As his father, Ea, did with Apsu, Marduk creates from the carcass of Tiamat. He splits it, and with part of it he makes the heavens and shrines for the gods, and with other parts he forms the earth—its weather, bodies of water, and geographical features.

---

17. Lambert, *Babylonian Creation Myths*, 169.

The gods celebrate Marduk's victory and hail him as their new king. In his first act as king, Marduk cleverly decides to create humankind in order to bear the burden of the gods' labor. Qingu is sacrificed, and from his lifeblood Ea creates humankind. But unlike other myths in which the creation of humankind plays a large role (e.g., Atrahasis), in *Enuma Elish* it is presented in a brief digression. Much more emphasis is placed on Marduk's establishment of Babylon as his holy city, and its temples as the locations at which humankind are to present offerings to the gods.

Enuma Elish closes with a lengthy section in which the gods continue to celebrate Marduk by ascribing to him fifty names in addition to his own. The names are in many cases those of other gods, culminating with his father Ea's giving him his own name; in effect, the text asserts that a wide array of divine names finally point to Marduk. This is a very strong theological claim; although it falls short of monotheism, since other gods continue to be recognized, it has been called "summodeism," in which "the deities are regarded as aspects or functions of a chief god, with political power often key to its expression"[18] (for further discussion, see chap. 23). The same tendency can be seen even more explicitly in various Late Babylonian texts.[19]

How was this text, with its surprising theological claims, used in Babylon? There are many clues in *Enuma Elish* to its social and historical contexts. In its announcement of Babylon's founding, the text says, "within it we will hold a festival" (V:130), and indeed *Enuma Elish* features prominently in the Babylonian *akitu* festival (see chap. 8). The *akitu* festival as a whole seems to have revolved around vanquishing chaos and restoring order at the beginning of each new year,[20] so the story of Ea and Marduk's defeat of the chaos monsters and subsequent establishment of the heavens and earth would have been one of its central myths.

Because Marduk was the city god of Babylon, the claims about his exaltation also have specific political meaning in history: it was an assertion of Babylon's preeminence as well. Marduk had not always been king of the gods; in fact, "the god, his city Babylon, and its cult were utterly unimportant in Sumerian times."[21] It was only with Hammurabi's reign in Babylon (1792–1750 BCE) that Marduk joined the ranks of major deities. And it appears that it was not until Nebuchadnezzar I (r. 1125–1104) reclaimed Marduk's cult statue from captivity with the Hittites that the god was celebrated through the composition of *Enuma Elish*. Even after rhetoric pointing to Marduk's sole supremacy became common in the first millennium, competition among the gods (and their worshipers) continued; Nabu and Sîn in particular continued to inspire similar claims to lordship. In sum, the exaltation of Marduk took place after a period in which his worship had been adversely affected, and it continued to be in dispute within Mesopotamia.

If the creation account in Genesis 1 dates to the period around the Babylonian exile (see below), then the circumstances of its composition were somewhat similar: the Jerusalem

---

18. Mark S. Smith, *God in Translation: Deities in Cross-Cultural Discourse in the Biblical World* (Forschungen zum Alten Testament 57; Tübingen: Mohr Siebeck, 2008), 169.

19. Lambert, *Babylonian Creation Myths*, 265.

20. Benjamin D. Sommer, "The Babylonian Akitu Festival: Rectifying the King or Renewing the Cosmos?" *JANES* 27 (2000): 81–95.

21. Lambert, *Babylonian Creation Myths*, 248.

temple had been destroyed and its vessels stolen (2 Kgs. 25), and theology and worship continued to be disputed in the exilic and postexilic periods.[22] Worshipers of both Marduk and Yhwh had to assert their theological visions anew.

There are also striking differences between the social and historical backgrounds of *Enuma Elish* and Genesis 1, however. For one example, the texts' views of cities is very different: In *Enuma Elish*, Babylon is one of Marduk's most important creations, dominating large sections of the narrative, and it is the place where he rules in joy (VI.45–73). By contrast, cities are not mentioned at all in Genesis 1–2; the images of human authority focus exclusively on the pastoring of the natural world. This might be taken for an oversight or simply an effort at historical verisimilitude (there could not have been cities when there were only two humans!), but the rest of Genesis 1–11 strongly suggests it is an intentional omission. In Genesis 4:17, the founder of the first city is the disgraced Cain, and the Tower of Babel story strongly associates city-building with sin and hubris (Gen. 11:4–8).[23]

Egypt: The Memphite Theology

Like *Enuma Elish*, the Egyptian Memphite Theology was linked to a specific locale—in this case the city of Memphis, just south of the Nile Delta. The only surviving copy of the text was made under the Twenty-fifth Egyptian dynasty, during the reign of the pharaoh Shabaka; it is found on a large slab of granite sometimes called the "Shabaka Stone." Unfortunately, the slab was later reused as a millstone, which damaged some of the hieroglyphs, accounting for the gaps in the text above. The text opens with Shabaka's claim that he found it in the temple of Ptah on a worm-eaten scroll (compare 2 Kgs. 22) and had it copied. The date of the text's composition is not settled; if it was not composed in the time of the existing copy (the 8th century), then it may have been composed during the Nineteenth Dynasty (13th century).

Thus, like *Enuma Elish*, the Memphite Theology was composed at a relatively late date, in an environment where other myths had long been known. The oldest Egyptian creation accounts come from Heliopolis and Hermopolis. They are attested not as whole stories, but piecemeal within larger compositions—mostly funerary texts such as the Pyramid Texts (Old Kingdom) and the Coffin Texts (Middle Kingdom). The Hermopolitan and Heliopolitan myths describe, in different ways, the emergence of the gods out of primeval waters. (In that respect, they bear a basic similarity to *Enuma Elish*.) Since the yearly inundation brought fertility and life to the land of Egypt, it is natural that water would have seemed the wellspring of all life to the Egyptians. At Heliopolis, the primeval waters were called Nun, and the creator sun-god Re-Atum emerged from the waters and created the rest of the Ennead, the nine original gods.[24] Because, for the Egyptians, creation was

---

22. The date of the Priestly author's work is increasingly disputed, with some placing it in the preexilic period. Here as elsewhere, an exilic or postexilic date seems to make sense, but the comparisons are illuminating regardless of the period.

23. The Mesopotamian rulers who had been dominating the Judeans were also negatively associated with city-building (Isa. 14:21).

24. An extended citation may help to elucidate the underlying logic of the myth: "Before the creation, the Monad existed as a single, undifferentiated seed of potentiality, floating inert in the

naturally thought of in relation to procreation, Atum's act of creation was often portrayed as an act of self-insemination, in which the deity swallowed his own semen. The imagery of Atum's semen is partially adapted for Ptah in the Memphite Theology (e.g., "[Ptah's] Ennead is . . . the semen and the hands of Atum"). In Mesopotamia, similar imagery was attested in Sumerian texts,[25] but was not adopted by the authors of *Enuma Elish.*

As an example of the way in which Egyptian creation myths were most commonly expressed, a spell of the pharaoh Pepi I from the Pyramid Texts claims that he was born from Atum "when the sky had not yet come into being, when the earth had not yet come into being, when people had not yet come into being, when the gods had not yet been born, when death had not yet come into being" (Pyramid Texts, 1466). Since the pharaoh expected to be a god in his afterlife, this was no great theological stretch. But there is no further narrative; this is all that is reported about creation in this context. Other spells contain other fragmentary references to creation myths.

The different Egyptian creation traditions centered on different deities. The Heliopolitan tradition (from the city of Heliopolis) focused on the sun-god; the Hermopolitan tradition (from the city of Hermopolis) came to emphasize Thoth. Other cities also had myths that viewed their primary deities as creator: Min in Coptos, Khnum in Elephantine, Amun in Thebes. And when Akhenaten brought about the religious revolution of the Amarna period, he portrayed Aten as sole creator (see chap. 23).

The Memphite tradition, however, revolved around Ptah. Ptah was a major deity, particularly during the New Kingdom and thereafter. He was foremost a craftsman god (he was later identified with Hephaestus by the Greeks), which makes the association with creation natural. He was also associated with scribes through Imhotep, the Egyptian wise man who was accorded divine status and eventually described as Ptah's son. Ptah's most important shrine was in Memphis, but he had temples at all of the major Egyptian religious centers. (For another text about Ptah, see chap. 22.)

As with the other creation accounts in the chapter, the Memphite Theology can be better understood in its political context: Shabaka's Twenty-fifth Dynasty was from Nubia (Kush) in the far south—a major break from earlier dynasties that had been based farther north. Therefore the new dynasts invested heavily in archaism and tradition in order to assert themselves as the rightful heirs of Egypt's ancient royal traditions. However, they also needed to reshape and relocate Egyptian religion away from the earlier narratives to stake their own place in it. The Memphite Theology thus begins from the same place as

Primeval Waters. Creation is the process through which the One became the Many—through which the Monad developed into the Ennead, sum of all the diverse forces and elements that constitute the biosphere. The Egyptians described the process in generational terms, reflecting both the proximate and the material causality of the creation. The world developed from the Monad as a plant develops from a seed. Each of its numberless constituent parts derives both its substance and its energy from the one original source. The process is developmental, not historical. In creation the Monad is not disintegrated but realized." James P. Allen, *Genesis in Egypt: The Philosophy of Ancient Egyptian Creation Accounts* (New Haven, CT: Yale University Press, 1988), 57–58.

25. In stories from the city of Eridu, the deity Enki is said to create by ejaculating and filling the river Tigris with water, and other similarly sexualized water imagery. Richard J. Clifford, *Creation Accounts in the Ancient Near East and in the Bible* (Catholic Biblical Quarterly Monograph Series 26; Washington, DC: Catholic Biblical Association of America, 1994), 32–49.

the Heliopolitan narrative (and to a certain extent depends upon it) but then takes it into a new direction. The text's claim to antiquity is generally thought to be a false appeal to the authority of tradition.

In the Memphite Theology, Ptah's primacy and centrality are even more strongly expressed than Marduk's in *Enuma Elish:* Ptah is the ruler of the gods ("on his throne"), and he is identified with the Nun and as the source of (the one "who bore") all the gods. He is the "heart and tongue of the Nine [Gods]" of the Ennead; presumably this means that their thoughts and words emanate from him. His mastery extends also to earthly things, to "every body and . . . every mouth of all gods, all men, all cattle, all creeping things, whatever lives, thinking whatever he wishes and commanding whatever he wishes." Some interpreters perceive here a kind of *panentheism:* the idea that the god is in everything and everyone.

The most striking facet of the Memphite Theology in comparison with the biblical text is that Ptah, like Yhwh, is said to create by means of the spoken word: "according to this command which is devised by the heart and comes forth on the tongue and creates the performance of every thing." Egyptian creation accounts (like many other aspects of Egyptian religion) are founded on dualities: male-female, earth-sky, water-dry land, and so forth. Another duality might be perceived in the distinction between Ptah's conceptualization of all things in his mind (or "heart"), and their subsequent creation—i.e., between concept and reality. Something similar may be alluded to in the biblical affirmations that "God saw that it was good" (Gen. 1:4, 10, 12, 18, 21, 25, 31)—presumably the creation is being judged good in light of the divine purposes.

The Egyptian text is distinguished by its repeated emphasis on the mouth of Ptah—specifically the teeth, lips, and tongue—whereas the biblical authors avoid anthropomorphisms. Still, the emphasis on creation through the word of a god has inspired comparisons not only with Genesis 1, but even with the "Logos theology" of the prologue to the Gospel of John in the New Testament: "In the beginning was the Word, and the Word was with God, and the Word was God. He was in the beginning with God. All things came into being through him, and without him not one thing came into being" (John 1:1–3).[26]

Finally, the Memphite Theology also shares with the biblical creation account the idea that the creator took satisfaction in the creation. At the end of his creating, "Ptah was satisfied after he had made all things and all divine words." Similarly, Genesis 2:2–3 reads, "God saw everything that he had made, and indeed, it was very good. . . . he rested on the seventh day from all the work that he had done." One key difference here is the link between God's rest and Sabbath rest in Genesis (made explicit in Exod. 20:8–11), which is not found in any other ancient Near Eastern creation text.

In light of these similarities between the biblical and Memphite creation accounts, it may be significant that Ptah was widely known in the southern Levant, near ancient Israel and Judah.[27] Egypt ruled most of Palestine throughout much of the Late Bronze Age (ca.

26. Allen, *Genesis in Egypt,* 46. See also Col. 1:15–18.

27. Othmar Keel, "Reflections of Ptah and Memphite Theology from the Soil of Palestine: Iconographic and Epigraphic Evidence," in *Text, Artifact, and Image: Revealing Ancient Israelite Religion* (ed. Gary M. Beckman and Theodore J. Lewis; Brown Judaic Studies 346; Providence, RI: Brown University, 2006), 239–72.

1550–1200 BCE). Even when Egypt's direct power over Palestine waned in the Iron Age I (ca. 1200–1000) and Israel appeared, there continued to be extensive contact between the neighboring regions because of trade and diplomacy. It is quite possible that the biblical authors had direct knowledge of the creation myths about Ptah.

Genesis 1–2 and the Backgrounds of the Bible

Not only were there ancient creation myths in neighboring regions, ancient Israel emerged in a region that had its own creation accounts already. Myths of divine combat with watery monsters had a long history in the Levant, and these were linked to the divine imposition of order in much the same way as Marduk's victory over Tiamat was. In the Late Bronze Age, before Israel existed, authors at Ugarit composed myths in which their national god, Baal, slayed river and sea. It is no surprise that there were conflicting views about creation and other theological matters within the lands of Israel and Judah; stories about religious conflicts and diversity are told in the biblical histories and the prophetic books.

In fact, the Bible itself preserves multiple creation accounts. The differences between the terminology and theology in Genesis 1:1–2:4a and in Genesis 2:4b–25 are the first of many clues that multiple authors were involved in writing and editing the Pentateuch into the forms that we have today.[28]

The first biblical creation account (Gen. 1:1–2:4a) describes how God spoke the universe into being, with humankind created *last*, as the crowning act. It avoids using the divine name Yhwh, presumably because it has not yet been revealed to Moses (Exod. 3). It also culminates in the phrase "these are the generations"; that is a formula found throughout the Pentateuch, usually to establish human lineages. The concern for ordering and lineage has been thought to be characteristic of the Priestly author, or P source, working in the exilic or postexilic period. There are also indications that this author was reacting in some way to Babylonian claims about creation that would have been encountered by Judeans most directly during the Babylonian exile (587–536 BCE).

This story is followed immediately by another (Gen. 2:4b–25), which uses the name "Yhwh" for God. Therefore, it has been dubbed the "Yahwistic" source, or J source.[29] It describes how God formed man from the dust, like a potter forming clay—and did so *first*, before creating all other life. Its embodied portrayal of God as one who forms as if with hands (and later walks around in Eden; Gen. 3:8) has been thought to be more characteristic of early theology, and so J is usually thought to derive from the tenth or ninth century BCE.

In both stories, God delegates the caretaking of the earth to humankind, but in other ways they differ in emphasis. The first is focused on the divine role in ordering the cosmos:

---

28. A somewhat more extensive discussion of the "sources" of the Pentateuch may be found in chap. 4, but in reality the reader must have other resources for more thorough discussions of the theory. If such a discussion is not readily at hand in an introductory textbook, the reader may consult, for example, Joel Baden's *The Composition of the Pentateuch: Renewing the Documentary Hypothesis* (New Haven, CT: Yale University Press, 2012).

29. J is short for the German term *Jahwist*.

light and darkness; earth and sky; dry land and sea. The second emphasizes that Yhwh is the creator and caretaker of living things in all their diversity.

Nor are these two the only stories about creation in the Bible. In Proverbs 8, for example, one reads that personified Wisdom also played a role in creation, which is not mentioned in the other accounts. She says, "Yhwh created me, the beginning of his work,[30] the first of his acts of long ago. Ages ago I was set up, at the first, before the beginning of the earth . . . then I was beside him, like a master worker" (vv. 22–23, 30). She says that she came before the depths, the dust, the heavens, and the establishment of the boundaries of the waters; all of these figure prominently in the Genesis accounts, which creates a dialogue among these texts. Proverbs 8 can be seen as a kind of innerbiblical midrash, a retelling and reinterpretation of the story. By calling Wisdom "the beginning of [God's] work," the author inserts her into Genesis 1:1, so that one can read, "With the beginning (one), God created," that is, "With Wisdom at his side, God created. . . ." One can discuss whether Proverbs 8's insertion is compatible with Genesis 1:1 when the latter is read on its own, but in any case the author of Proverbs 8 seemingly set out to transform and redefine the reader's view of creation.

It is clear that biblical authors also knew stories in which Yhwh created the heavens and earth by means of a primordial conflict, just as in *Enuma Elish*. For example, Psalm 74:13–17:[31]

> You shook the sea by your might;
>> you broke the heads of the dragons in the waters.
> You crushed the heads of Leviathan;
>> you gave him as food for the creatures of the wilderness.
> You cut openings for springs and torrents;
>> you dried up ever-flowing streams.
> Yours is the day, yours also the night;
>> you established the luminaries and the sun.
> You have fixed all the bounds of the earth;
>> you made summer and winter.

This account of slaying the watery chaos (here embodied by the sea monster Leviathan) followed by ordering the natural universe could not be much closer to *Enuma Elish*.

On the surface, there is a stark distinction between the Genesis 1–2 creation stories, which are abstract, and the violence of Psalm 74 and the Babylonian myth. However, it has sometimes been suggested that Yhwh's acts of separating (light from darkness, sky from sea, day from night) are comparable to Marduk's splitting of Tiamat's corpse. But whereas *Enuma Elish* uses very physical verbs for Marduk (IV.102–31: tore open, slit, bound, threw down, smashed, severed), the Hebrew term for dividing in Genesis 1 is abstract; it is never used of physical cutting.[32] Notably, nonviolent references to divine

---

30. Some translations read, "*at* the beginning of his work." That translation is defensible, but there is no preposition in the Hebrew.

31. See also Ps. 89:10–11; Isa. 51:9–10; Job 9:13; 26:12–13. For a more extensive inventory of references to creation in the Bible in general, see Clifford, *Creation Accounts*, 137–97.

32. In Egyptian cosmological traditions other than the Memphite one, there are references to the primordial division of the gods Nut (sky) and Geb (earth). Like *Enuma Elish*, this image

dividing at creation are also present in the Mesopotamian tradition, such as when Enlil hastens to separate heaven from earth in lines 4–5 of a text called "Praise of the Pickaxe."[33]

The use of wind in each story sets up a similar comparison and contrast. It has been suggested that the wind on the water in Genesis 1:2 is comparable to the wind that Marduk casts into the face of Tiamat to distend her innards and prepare her for slaughter. But again, what is striking is not the similarity, but the difference: Marduk's fierce battle has been transposed into Yhwh's lordly fiat.

Comparing and Contrasting

Given that these texts form a kind of conversation around certain issues and images, how should a reader think about the relationship between them? Palestine has sometimes been called "The Sacred Bridge." This narrow, fertile strip was flanked by ocean to the west and desert to the east, and it stood between the major political powers of its day, so it became a crossing point for trade, travel, and cultures. This is apparent in the material remains that are discovered archaeologically, and in the texts as well.

Is Genesis 1 a direct response to "pagan" ideas about creation such as the myths presented above? It is a common conclusion that Genesis at least responds to Babylonian theology. Although it makes good sense to assume that the Priestly creation account was a Judean effort of theological self-definition in the context of the Babylonian exile, it is unlikely that a Yhwh-worshiper in Babylon had the luxury of sitting down with a copy of *Enuma Elish* (if he could even read it). Rather, it is likely that theological ideas were aired in less formal ways, so that the Priestly creation account as we know it was not a point-by-point rejoinder to a specific text, but rather a polemic response to the cultural pressure of the author's imperial surroundings. That is to say, it is not a commentary on a specific composition.

Again, it is not only the biblical authors who simultaneously incorporated and reacted to elements of earlier texts. The examples of ways in which the ancient Near Eastern texts in this chapter also shared elements of their cultural precursors could be expanded significantly. For example, *Enuma Elish* "borrowed" especially from the Anzu myth, in which the youthful god Ninurta is summoned by the other gods to battle against the supernatural bird Anzu, and after his victory is acclaimed with many names. The fact that *Enuma Elish* borrows is marked by the somewhat random occurrences of the Tablet of Destinies (I:157; IV:121). It appears out of the blue in *Enuma Elish*, whereas in the Anzu myth, Anzu's theft of the tablet is a major plot element.[34] Ancient authors did not view their reliance on earlier traditions as any sort of scandal; much of their creativity was in their interactions with earlier texts.

Ideally, reading these texts alongside each other allows us to perceive the uniqueness of each one. In the case of the biblical account, certain things stand out.

---

embraces the physicality of creation, but without the violence. There is a common motif in Egyptian art of Shu (the god of air) holding up Nut as Geb reclines below.

33. Clifford, *Creation Accounts*, 31.
34. Ibid., 84–85.

First, both *Enuma Elish* and the Memphite Theology are focused on a certain locale, even as they ascribe universal dominion to their creator God: Marduk rules from his house in Babylon and Ptah from his house in Memphis. This is not to say that those deities' spheres of influence were limited to their primary host cities, since they were both worshiped elsewhere, but these literary works each portray the deity as ruling from a definite central location. By contrast, in Genesis 1, the vision for God's habitation seems less geographically limited. Unlike the others, Genesis 1 does not mention any place; there is no reference to Israel or Jerusalem (or Eden).

The lack of localization and temple accords well with the roughly contemporaneous claims of Isaiah: "Thus says Yhwh: Heaven is my throne and the earth is my footstool; what is the house that you would build for me, and what is my resting place?" (Isa. 66:1). The idea was that God's reign is too expansive to be contained in a house or a city. Indeed, the idea that God dwelled in a house seems to have sat uneasily with certain Yahwistic theologians in general (in 2 Sam. 7:5–7, Yhwh rejects David's plan to build a temple). It is true that if Genesis 1 was composed by an exilic or postexilic Priestly author, then there was no temple for Yhwh in Jerusalem, because it had been destroyed by the Babylonians in 586. With the benefit of hindsight, one can see that the biblical authors' prodigious leap to universal monotheism was a response to the vast claims of imperial powers that they faced, but it was in no way a common or obvious leap when they took it. Genesis 1's gracious and peaceful vision for all the earth would have been a remarkable response to its authors' historical suffering.

Second: The question of *creatio ex nihilo* ("creation out of nothing") is a complicated one. The intention of Genesis 1:1–2 is disputed. Essentially: Is the "formless void" in 1:2 the stuff out of which God creates, or does God create the formless stuff before working with it? Because of complexities within the Hebrew of the verse, the question cannot be answered on the basis of close reading; it is also possible to translate, "In the beginning of God creating of the heavens and the earth . . ." It depends, finally, on the interpreter's sense of the whole.[35] At a minimum, one can contrast Genesis 1 with *Enuma Elish* in that the former contains no theogony, no story about the creation or birth of the creator. Marduk comes on to the scene in the midst of the story; he has a genealogy; there was a time when he was not. By contrast, the reader of Genesis never learns of any precursor to the God of Israel.[36]

Insofar as the Memphite Theology identifies Ptah with the primordial elements of being (Nun and Atum), the Memphis theologians may have envisioned something like *creatio ex nihilo* as well. They offer no theogony of Ptah. One difference is that Ptah therefore creates from his own being, like a seed giving birth to a plant. As noted above, this lends an element of panentheism that differs from the biblical account. God does not inhabit all things in Genesis 1. Then again, the idea that "Ptah is in every living thing"

---

35. Alexander Heidel, *The Babylonian Genesis: The Story of Creation* (Chicago: University of Chicago Press, 1951), 76–82, makes a strong case in favor of *creatio ex nihilo*, but the matter is by no means settled.

36. One can again hear resonances with the absolutist theology of Second Isaiah: "Before me no god was formed, nor shall there be any after me" (Isa. 43:10); "Who has performed and done this, calling the generations from the beginning? I, Yhwh, am first, and will be with the last" (41:4).

God has no physical home (

God is not a created being

might find an echo in Genesis's creation of humankind in the image of God (Gen. 1:26–27) or its image of God breathing life into humankind (2:7)—but in either biblical passage this divine gift is given only to humankind; its scope is much more circumscribed, and the hymnody of ancient Israel did not fail to note that remarkable confession (Ps. 8:4–5). As for the rest of creation, although God formed it and called it good, there is no indication that it is part of God's being.[37]

This special connection in Genesis between God and humanity means that in both accounts there is the assumption that humankind is to function as a kind of surrogate for God within the created world, ruling and taking care of it (1:28; 2:15). Humans are even to imitate God in resting on the seventh day (2:3). In *Enuma Elish*, humankind is created to serve the gods—which pertains at least to temple service, but perhaps also alludes to other Mesopotamian myths such as Atrahasis (see chap. 4) in which humans are created to do work so that gods don't have to. (The same idea may lie in the background of the Genesis stories, but their sense of honoring and empowering humans—for example, in the emphasis on "dominion" or Adam's authority to give names—is not present in the Mesopotamian myths.) The only human being who serves as the gods' representative on earth in Mesopotamian theology is the king.[38] In the Memphite Theology, the close relationship between the creator and the creation means that all labor is somehow the work of Ptah; he "creates the performance of every thing." Since the creation essentially has no independent being, it is not clear what that means for the freedom of will for created beings. Doesn't the created order sometimes function poorly or break down? Some have even perceived in the Memphite Theology a "doctrine of predestination," but this is perhaps an overreading.[39] The text does not seem interested in answering that question.

The division between creator and creation in Genesis 1 is particularly pointed in the case of the heavenly bodies. It is remarkable that the author did not use the very common Hebrew terms for sun (*shemesh*) or moon (*yare'ach*), but rather the unusual circumlocutions "the greater light to rule the day and the lesser light to rule the night" (Gen. 1:16). This may be because the Hebrew terms had close cognates in Semitic languages that were the names of the sun-god and moon-god—that is, to avoid giving the impression that divinities other than Yhwh ruled the day and night. This amounts to a demythologization of heavenly bodies and natural elements. Even the monsters of watery chaos—the *tehom*/Tiamat and the *tannin* (the word for "sea monsters" in Gen. 1:21, which is elsewhere a proper name)—are more than defeated; they are domesticated, no threat at all before their maker (much like Leviathan in Job 41). In *Enuma Elish* and the Memphite Theology, creators are glorified by being identified with other familiar deities. In Genesis 1,

---

37. This is another case in which a later text makes only selective use of earlier texts, and there are other Egyptian traditions that are even more similar to Gen. 1–2. For example, the Teaching for Merikare, a Tenth Dynasty text, says that humans "are [Re-Atum's] images who came forth from his body" (line 137), and that the creator god "created the winds so that their nostrils might live." Similarly, in a fourteenth-century Egyptian hymn, the deity Aten is called "giver of breath." (This hymn is presented in chap. 23; see lines 50–57.)

38. For example, Marduk delegates rule to Hammurabi in the prologue to his law code (chap. 7).

39. See, for example, George Hart, *Egyptian Myths* (Austin: University of Texas Press, 1990), 19.

Yhwh is glorified by the denial of other deities. In the text's ancient Near Eastern context, the refusal to acknowledge other gods creates a loud silence.

REFLECTION QUESTIONS

1. What are some similarities and differences among Apsu in *Enuma Elish*, Nun in the Memphite Theology, and the "deep" in Genesis 1?

2. How would you compare and contrast the portrayals of the creator deities in each text?

3. One scholar has written that "Genesis is about the Creation, while *Enuma Elish* is about the creator."[40] What are some reasons to agree or disagree with this statement?

4. There is a long-running debate in the interpretation of Genesis 1:1–2 about whether the verse indicates creation out of nothing (*creatio ex nihilo*) or out of preexisting matter. Engaging that problem requires reading the text in its original language, but *what is at stake* in the question? Why does it matter?

5. How close do you think the Memphite Theology's doctrine of creation by the word of Ptah is to the creation account in Genesis 1, or the Logos theology of John 1?

6. What problems and issues do you think the authors of each text were trying to address?

7. What is the relationship between science and the texts presented in this chapter?

8. What inferences might you draw from these texts about the religions in which they were composed?

9. S. R. Driver wrote in 1907 that "we have in the first chapter of Genesis the Hebrew version of an originally Babylonian legend."[41] What do you find in this statement to agree or disagree with?

FURTHER READING

Allen, James P. *Genesis in Egypt: The Philosophy of Ancient Egyptian Creation Accounts*. New Haven, CT: Yale University Press, 1988.

Batto, Bernard F. *In the Beginning: Essays on Creation Motifs in the Bible and the Ancient Near East*. Winona Lake, IN: Eisenbrauns, 2013.

Clifford, Richard J. *Creation Accounts in the Ancient Near East and in the Bible*. Catholic Biblical Quarterly Monograph Series 26. Washington, DC: Catholic Biblical Association of America, 1994.

Gunkel, Hermann. "The Influence of Babylonian Mythology upon the Biblical Creation Story." Pages 25–52 in *Creation in the Old Testament*. Edited by B. W. Anderson. Philadelphia: Fortress Press, 1984.

Heidel, Alexander. *The Babylonian Genesis: The Story of Creation*. Chicago: University of Chicago Press, 1951.

Hendel, Ronald. "Genesis 1–11 and Its Mesopotamian Problem." Pages 23–36 in *Cultural Borrowings and Ethnic Appropriations in Antiquity*. Edited by Erich S. Gruen. Oriens et Occidens.

40. Victor Hurowitz, "The Genesis of Genesis: Is the Creation Story Babylonian?" *Bible Review* 21 (2005): 43.

41. S. R. Driver, *The Book of Genesis with Introduction and Notes*, 6th ed. (London: Methuen & Co., 1907), 31.

Studien zu antiken Kulturkontakten und ihrem Nachleben 8. Stuttgart: Franz Steiner Verlag, 2005.

Hess, Richard S., and David Toshio Tsumura, ed. *"I Studied Inscriptions from before the Flood"*: *Ancient Near Eastern, Literary, and Linguistic Approaches to Genesis 1–11.* Sources for Biblical and Theological Study 4. Winona Lake, IN: Eisenbrauns, 1994.

Hoffmeier, James K. "Some Thoughts on Genesis 1 and 2 and Egyptian Cosmology." *JANES* 15 (1983): 39–49.

Lambert, W. G. *Babylonian Creation Myths.* Mesopotamian Civilizations 16. Winona Lake, IN: Eisenbrauns, 2013.

———. "A New Look at the Babylonian Background of Genesis." Pages 96–113 in *"I Studied Inscriptions from before the Flood": Ancient Near Eastern, Literary, and Linguistic Approaches to Genesis 1–11.* Edited by Richard S. Hess and David Toshio Tsumura. Sources for Biblical and Theological Study 4. Winona Lake, IN: Eisenbrauns, 1994.

Sommer, Benjamin D. "The Babylonian Akitu Festival: Rectifying the King or Renewing the Cosmos?" *JANES* 27 (2000): 81–95.

Tobin, Vincent Arieh. "Myths." Pages 464–72 in *Oxford Encyclopedia of Ancient Egypt.* Edited by Donald B. Redford. New York: Oxford University Press, 2001.

4

Flood Stories

Gilgamesh XI and Genesis 6–9

EPIC OF GILGAMESH XI

What: Fifteen cuneiform tablets, mostly fragmentary, reflecting eight different copies
of the story[1]
When: ca. thirteenth–twelfth century BCE (but see discussion)
Where: The most complete copies of Tablet XI have been found in Nineveh, but
other copies exist from Ashur, Nimrud, and Babylon
Language: Akkadian
Translation: Andrew George, *The Epic of Gilgamesh* (Penguin, 2003)

[*The Epic of Gilgamesh is about a mighty king of Uruk who compiles great achievements, but then
suffers a crisis when his friend and fellow warrior, Enkidu, dies. He journeys to find Uta-napishti,
the hero of the primordial flood, whom the gods granted "eternal life," to see if he will disclose its
secret.*]

"[My friend, whom I loved so dear,]
   [who with me went through] every danger,
[my friend Enkidu, whom I loved so dear,]
   [who with me] went through every danger:
[the doom of mortals overtook him.]
X.235 "[Six days] I wept for him [and seven nights:]
   [I did not surrender his body for] burial
[until a maggot dropped from] his [nostril.]
   [Then I was afraid that I too would die,]
[I grew] fearful of death, [and so wander the] wild.
X.240 "What became of [my friend was too much] to [bear,]
   so on a far road [I wander the] wild;

---

1. This only includes copies of Tablet XI's flood story in the Standard Babylonian language. See
below on the wider distribution of the Gilgamesh Epic as a whole and of flood stories in general.

what became of my friend Enkidu [was too much to bear,]
    so on a far path [I wander the wild.]
"How can I keep silent? How can I stay quiet?
X.245   My friend, whom I loved, has turned to clay,
my friend Enkidu, [whom I loved, has turned to clay.]
    [Shall] I not be like him and also lie down,
never to rise again, through all [eternity?]"
Said Gilgamesh to him, to Uta-napishti:
X.250   "I thought, 'I will find Uta-napishti the Distant, of whom men tell,'
and I wandered journeying through every land.
    Many times I passed through terrible mountains,
many times I crossed and recrossed all the oceans.
"Of slumber sweet my face had too little,
X.255   I scourged myself by going sleepless.
I have filled my sinews with sorrow,
    and what have I achieved by my toil?"

[*Gilgamesh continues his story and Uta-napishti responds, somewhat scornfully, that Gilgamesh is foolish to exhaust himself in this quest, because no one can know about his own death. Gilgamesh, who seems to have thought that he would earn immortality by fighting and defeating some super-human figure, responds:*]

Said Gilgamesh to him, to Uta-napishti the Distant:
    "I look at you, Uta-napishti:
your form is no different, you are just like me,
    you are not any different, you are just like me.
XI.5   I was fully intent on making you fight,
    but now in your presence my hand is stayed.
How was it you stood with the gods in assembly?
    How did you find the life eternal?"
Said Uta-napishti to him, to Gilgamesh:
    "Let me disclose, O Gilgamesh, a matter most secret,
XI.10   to you I will tell a mystery of gods.
The town of Shuruppak, a city well known to you,
    which stands on the banks of the river Euphrates:
this city was old—the gods once were in it—
    when the great gods decided to send down the Deluge.
XI.15   Their father Anu[2] swore on oath,
    and their counselor, the hero Enlil,[3]

---

2. Anu was the father of the gods, and the primary figure in Mesopotamian creation accounts. He was viewed as a chief deity throughout Mesopotamian history, but he was also a distant and somewhat mysterious figure.
    3. Son of Anu, Enlil had a royal aspect like Anu, and was also associated with storms.

their chamberlain, the god Ninurta,[4]
    and their sheriff, the god Ennugi.[5]
"Princely Ea[6] swore with them also,

XI.20   repeating their words to a fence made of reed:
'O fence of reed! O wall of brick!
    Hear this, O fence! Pay heed, O wall!
O man of Shuruppak, son of Ubar-Tutu,[7]
    demolish the house, and build a boat!

XI.25 Abandon wealth, and seek survival!
    Spurn property, save life!
Take on board the boat all living things' seed!
"'The boat you will build,
    her dimensions all shall be equal:

XI.30 her length and breadth shall be the same,
    cover her with a roof, like the Ocean Below.'
"I understood, and spoke to Ea, my master:
    'I obey, O master, what thus you told me.
I understood, and I shall do it,

XI.35   but how do I answer my city, the crowd and the elders?'
"Ea opened his mouth to speak,
    saying to me, his servant:
'Also you will say to them this:
    "For sure the god Enlil feels for me hatred.

XI.40 In your city I can live no longer,
    I can tread no more [on] Enlil's ground.
[I must] go to the Ocean Below, to live with Ea, my master,
    and he will send you a rain of plenty:
[an abundance] of birds, a profusion of fishes,

XI.45 [he will provide] a harvest of riches.
In the morning he will send you a shower of bread-cakes,
    and in the evening a torrent of wheat."'

"At the very first glimmer of brightening dawn,
    at the gate of Atra-hasis[8] assembled the land:

---

4. Son of Enlil, Ninurta was a god associated with war and farming.

5. A deity sometimes called "canal inspector of the great gods."

6. God of the *abzu*, what the Mesopotamians believed was a subterranean freshwater ocean, Ea (aka Enki) was also often associated with magic and wisdom.

7. Shuruppak was a Sumerian city in southern Mesopotamia. Ubar-Tutu is recorded in certain king lists as its last king before the flood.

8. A. R. George considers "Atra-hasis" (which means "exceedingly wise") to be an epithet of Uta-napishti. Other scholars, however, think that the occurrences of "Atra-hasis" here and in line 197 indicate that the author of Gilgamesh drew material from a different tradition related to the myth of Atra-hasia (see discussion section).

XI.50   the carpenter carrying [his] hatchet,
        the reed-worker carrying [his] stone,
    [the shipwright bearing his] heavyweight axe.
    The young men were [. . .]
        the old men bearing ropes of palm-fiber;
XI.55   the rich man was carrying the pitch,
        the poor man brought the [. . .] tackle.
    By the fifth day I had set her hull in position,
        one acre was her area, ten rods the height of her sides.
    At ten rods also, the sides of her roof were each the same length.
        I set in place her body, I drew up her design.
XI.60   Six decks I gave her,
        dividing her thus into seven.
    Into nine compartments I divided her interior,
        I struck the bilge plugs into her middle.
XI.65   I saw to the punting-poles and put in the tackle.
    "Three myriad measures of pitch I poured in a furnace,
        three myriad of tar I [. . .] within,
    three myriad of oil fetched the workforce of porters:
        aside from the myriad of oil consumed in libations,
XI.70   there were two myriad of oil stowed away by the boatman.
    For my workmen I butchered oxen,
        and lambs I slaughtered daily.
    Beer and ale, oil and wine
        like water from a river [I gave my] workforce,
XI.75   so they enjoyed a feast like the days of New Year.
    At sun-[me] I set my hand [to] the oiling,
        [before] the sun set the boat was complete.
    [. . .] were very arduous:
        from back to front we moved poles for the slipway,[9]
XI.80   [until] two-thirds of [the boat had entered the water.]
    "[Everything I owned] I loaded aboard:
        all the silver I owned I loaded aboard,
    all the gold I owned I loaded aboard,
        all the living creatures I had I loaded aboard.
XI.85   I sent on board all my kith and kin,
        the beasts of the field, the creatures of the wild, and members of every skill
          and craft.
    "The time which the Sun God appointed—
        'In the morning he will send you a shower of bread-cakes,
    and in the evening a torrent of wheat.
        Go into the boat and seal your hatch!'—

---

9. I.e., they rolled the boat into the water on round poles.

XI.90   that time had now come:
       'In the morning he will send you a shower of bread-cakes,
    and in the evening a torrent of wheat.'
       I examined the look of the weather.
    The weather to look at was full of foreboding,
       I went into the boat and sealed my hatch.
XI.95   To the one who sealed the boat, Puzur-Enlil[10] the shipwright,
       I gave my palace with all its goods.
    "At the very first glimmer of brightening dawn,
       there rose on the horizon a dark cloud of black,
    and bellowing within it was Adad the Storm God.[11]
XI.100   The gods Shullat and Hanish[12] were going before him,
       bearing his throne over mountain and land.
    The god Errakal[13] was uprooting the mooring-poles,
       Ninurta, passing by, made the weirs overflow.
    The Anunnaki gods[14] carried torches of fire,
XI.105   scorching the country with brilliant flashes.
    The stillness of the Storm God passed over the sky,
       and all that was bright then turned into darkness.
    [He] charged the land like a bull [on the rampage,]
       he smashed [it] in pieces [like a vessel of clay.]
    For a day the gale [winds flattened the country,]
XI.110   quickly they blew, and [then came] the [Deluge.]
    Like a battle [the cataclysm] passed over the people.
       One man could not discern another,
    nor could people be recognized amid the destruction.
    Even the gods took fright at the Deluge,
XI.115   they left and went up to the heaven of Anu,
    lying like dogs curled up in the open.
    "The goddess cried out like a woman in childbirth,
       Belet-ili[15] wailed, whose voice is so sweet:
    'The olden times have turned to clay,
XI.120   because I spoke evil in the gods' assembly.
    How could I speak evil in the gods' assembly,
       and declare a war to destroy my people?

10. The name of the builder of Uta-napishti's ark means "Protected by Enlil."

11. Adad was a storm-god who was particularly prominent in Syria and Lebanon, where he was regarded as a supreme power.

12. These minor deities were Adad's attendants.

13. A manifestation of Nergal (god of plague and war) as a god of wanton devastation.

14. A traditional name for one of the two divisions of the Mesopotamian pantheon. In later periods, the Anunnaki were considered gods of the Netherworld.

15. "Lady of the gods"; she helped to create humankind and was worshiped as a goddess of human fertility and childbirth.

'It is I who give birth, these people are mine!
    And now, like fish, they fill the ocean!'
XI.125   The Anunnaki gods were weeping with her,
    wet-faced with sorrow, they were weeping [with her,]
their lips were parched and stricken with fever.
"For six days and [seven] nights,
    there blew the wind, the downpour,
the gale, the Deluge, it flattened the land.
XI.130   But the seventh day when it came,
    the gale relented, the Deluge ended.
The ocean grew calm, that had thrashed like a woman in labour,
    the tempest grew still, the Deluge ended.
I looked at the weather, it was quiet and still,
XI.135   but all the people had turned to clay.
The flood plain was flat like the roof of a house.
    I opened a vent, on my cheeks fell the sunlight.
'Down sat I, I knelt and I wept,
    down my cheeks the tears were coursing.
XI.140   I scanned the horizons, the edge of the ocean,
    in fourteen places there rose an island.
On the mountain of Nimush[16] the boat ran aground,
    Mount Nimush held the boat fast, allowed it no motion.
One day and a second, Mount Nimush held the boat fast, allowed it no motion,
XI.145   a third day and a fourth, Mount Nimush held the boat fast, allowed it no
       motion,
a fifth day and a sixth, Mount Nimush held the boat fast, allowed it no motion.

"The seventh day when it came,
    I brought out a dove, I let it loose:
off went the dove but then it returned,
XI.150   there was no place to land, so back it came to me.
I brought out a swallow, I let it loose:
    off went the swallow but then it returned,
there was no place to land, so back it came to me.
I brought out a raven, I let it loose:
XI.155   off went the raven, it saw the waters receding,
finding food, bowing and bobbing, it did not come back to me.

"I brought out an offering, to the four winds made sacrifice,
    incense I placed on the peak of the mountain.
Seven flasks and seven I set in position,

---

16. A high peak of the Zagros mountains, probably Pir Omar Gudrun near Suleimaniyah in
northern Kurdistan.

XI.160   reed, cedar, and myrtle I piled beneath them.
        The gods did smell the savor,
                the gods did smell the savor sweet,
        the gods gathered like flies around the man making sacrifice.

        "Then at once Belet-ili arrived,
XI.165   she lifted the flies of lapis lazuli that Anu had made for their courtship:
        'O gods, let these great beads in this necklace of mine
                make me remember these days, and never forget them!
        All the gods shall come to the incense,
                but to the incense let Enlil not come,
XI.170 because he lacked counsel and brought on the Deluge,
                and delivered my people into destruction.'

        "Then at once Enlil arrived,
                he saw the boat, he was seized with anger,
        filled with rage at the divine Igigi:[17]
XI.175   '[From] where escaped this living being?
        No man was meant to survive the destruction!'

        "Ninurta opened his mouth to speak,
                saying to the hero Enlil:
        'Who, if not Ea, could cause such a thing?
XI.180   Ea alone knows how all things are done.'

        "Ea opened his mouth to speak,
                saying to the hero Enlil:
        'You, the sage of the gods, the hero,
                how could you lack counsel and bring on the Deluge?
XI.185 On him who transgresses, inflict his crime!
                On him who does wrong, inflict his wrongdoing!
        Slack off, lest it snap! Pull tight, lest it [slacken!]
        Instead of your causing the Deluge,
                a lion could have risen, and diminished the people!
XI.190 Instead of your causing the Deluge,
                a wolf could have risen, and diminished the people!
        Instead of your causing the Deluge,
                a famine could have happened, and slaughtered the land!
        Instead of your causing the Deluge,
XI.195   the Plague God could have risen, and slaughtered the land!

17. A traditional name for one of the two divisions of the Mesopotamian pantheon. In later periods, the term was assigned to the great gods of heaven.

It was not I who disclosed the great gods' secret:
>   Atra-hasis[18] I let see a vision, and thus he learned our secret.
And now, decide what to do with him!'

"Enlil came up inside the boat,
XI.200   he took hold of my hand and brought me on board.
He brought aboard my wife and made her kneel at my side,
>   he touched our foreheads, standing between us to bless us:
'In the past Uta-napishti was a mortal man,
>   but now he and his wife shall become like us gods![19]
XI.205 Uta-napishti shall dwell far away, where the rivers flow forth!'
>   So far away they took me, and settled me where the rivers flow forth.
But you now, who'll convene for you the gods' assembly,
>   so you can find the life you search for?
For six days and seven nights, come, do without slumber!"
XI.210 As soon as Gilgamesh squatted down on his haunches,
>   sleep like a fog already breathed over him.
Said Uta-napishti to her, to his wife:
>   "See the fellow who so desired life!
Sleep like a fog already breathes over him."

[*When Uta-napishti asks Gilgamesh, "Who'll convene for you the gods' assembly, so you can find the life you search for?" (1.207–8) he dashes Gilgamesh's hopes: the events of Uta-napishti's life are unrepeatable. He suggests a couple of other methods for Gilgamesh to achieve eternal life, such as staying awake for a week (overcoming sleep is practice for overcoming death; this is probably meant to be humorous) but these fail as well.*]

GENESIS 6:1–9:17

When: See discussion
Where: Jerusalem
Language: Hebrew
Translation: NRSV, but substituting "Yhwh" for "the LORD"

Note: The text has been formatted to show the sources commonly identified within the text.[20] The roman text represents the Yahwistic (J) source, the *italic text* the Priestly (P) source, and the **boldface text** indicates editorial additions. For explanation of these sources, see discussion.

---

18. See note to line 49, above.
19. Compare Gen. 1:27; 3:5, 22; 11:6.
20. These divisions are from Antony F. Campbell and Mark A. O'Brien, *Sources of the Pentateuch: Texts, Introductions, Annotations* (Minneapolis: Fortress Press, 1993). They closely follow Martin Noth's *A History of Pentateuchal Traditions* (trans. Bernhard W. Anderson; Englewood Cliffs, NJ: Prentice-Hall, 1972), 262.

6:1 When people began to multiply on the face of the ground, and daughters were born to them, ²the sons of God saw that they were fair; and they took wives for themselves of all that they chose. ³Then Yhwh said, "My spirit shall not abide in mortals forever, for they are flesh; their days shall be one hundred twenty years."

⁴The Nephilim were on the earth in those days—and also afterward when the sons of God went in to the daughters of humans, who bore children to them. These were the heroes that were of old, warriors of renown.

⁵Yhwh saw that the wickedness of humankind was great in the earth, and that every inclination of the thoughts of their hearts was only evil continually. ⁶And Yhwh was sorry that he had made humankind on the earth, and it grieved him to his heart. ⁷So Yhwh said, "I will blot out from the earth the human beings I have created—people together with animals and creeping things and birds of the air, for I am sorry that I have made them." ⁸But Noah found favor in Yhwh's sight.

⁹*These are the descendants of Noah. Noah was a righteous man, blameless in his generation; Noah walked with God. ¹⁰And Noah had three sons, Shem, Ham, and Japheth. ¹¹Now the earth was corrupt in God's sight, and the earth was filled with violence. ¹²And God saw that the earth was corrupt; for all flesh had corrupted its ways upon the earth.*

¹³*And God said to Noah, "I have determined to make an end of all flesh, for the earth is filled with violence because of them; now I am going to destroy them along with the earth. ¹⁴Make yourself an ark of cypress wood; make rooms in the ark, and cover it inside and out with pitch. ¹⁵This is how you are to make it: the length of the ark three hundred cubits, its width fifty cubits, and its height thirty cubits. ¹⁶Make a roof for the ark, and finish it to a cubit above; and put the door of the ark in its side; make it with lower, second, and third decks. ¹⁷For my part, I am going to bring a flood of waters on the earth, to destroy from under heaven all flesh in which is the breath of life; everything that is on the earth shall die. ¹⁸But I will establish my covenant with you; and you shall come into the ark, you, your sons, your wife, and your sons' wives with you.*

¹⁹*"And of every living thing, of all flesh, you shall bring two of every kind into the ark, to keep them alive with you; they shall be male and female. ²⁰Of the birds according to their kinds, and of the animals according to their kinds, of every creeping thing of the ground according to its kind, two of every kind shall come in to you, to keep them alive. ²¹Also take with you every kind of food that is eaten, and store it up; and it shall serve as food for you and for them."*

²²*Noah did this; he did all that God commanded him.*

7:1 Then Yhwh said to Noah, "Go into the ark, you and all your household, for I have seen that you alone are righteous before me in this generation. ²Take with you seven pairs of all clean animals, the male and its mate; and a pair of the animals that are not clean, the male and its mate; ³**and seven pairs of the birds of the air also, male and female**, to keep their kind alive on the face of all the earth. ⁴For in seven days I will send rain on the earth for forty days and forty nights; and every living thing that I have made I will blot out from the face of the ground." ⁵And Noah did all that Yhwh had commanded him. ⁶*Noah was six hundred years old when the flood of waters came on the earth.* ⁷And Noah **with his sons and his wife and his sons' wives** went into the ark to escape the waters of the flood. ⁸**Of clean animals, and of animals that are not clean, and of birds, and of everything that creeps on the ground, ⁹two and two, male and female, went into the ark with Noah, as God had commanded Noah.** ¹⁰And after seven days the waters of the flood came on the earth. ¹¹*In the six hundredth year of Noah's life, in the second month, on the seventeenth day of the month, on that day all the fountains of the great deep burst forth, and the windows of the heavens were opened.* ¹²The rain fell on the earth forty days and forty nights. ¹³*On the very same day Noah with his sons, Shem and Ham and Japheth, and Noah's wife and the three wives of his sons entered the ark,* ¹⁴*they and every wild animal of every kind, and all domestic animals of every kind, and every creeping thing that creeps on the earth, and every bird of every kind—every bird, every winged creature.* ¹⁵*They went into the ark with Noah, two and two of all flesh in which there was the breath of life.* ¹⁶*And those that entered, male and female of all flesh, went in as God had commanded him*; and Yhwh shut him in.

¹⁷**The flood continued forty days on the earth**; and the waters increased, and bore up the ark, and it rose high above the earth. ¹⁸*The waters swelled and increased greatly on the earth; and the ark floated on the face of the waters.* ¹⁹*The waters swelled so mightily on the earth that all the high mountains under the whole heaven were covered;* ²⁰*the waters swelled above the mountains, covering them fifteen cubits deep.* ²¹*And all flesh died that moved on the earth, birds, domestic animals, wild animals, all swarming creatures that swarm on the earth, and all human beings;* ²²everything on dry land in whose nostrils was the breath of life died. ²³He blotted out every living thing that was on the face of the ground, human beings and animals and creeping things and birds of the air; **they were blotted out from the earth**. Only Noah was left, and those that were with him in the ark. ²⁴*And the waters swelled on the earth for one hundred fifty days.*

8:1 *But God remembered Noah and all the wild animals and all the domestic animals that were with him in the ark. And God made a wind blow over the earth,* and the waters subsided; ²the fountains of the deep and the windows of the heavens were closed, the rain from the heavens was restrained, ³and the waters gradually receded from the earth.

At the end of one hundred fifty days the waters had abated; ⁴*and in the seventh month, on the seventeenth day of the month, the ark came to rest on the mountains of Ararat.* ⁵*The waters continued to abate until the tenth month; in the tenth month, on the first day of the month, the tops of the mountains appeared.* ⁶At the end of forty days Noah opened the window of the ark that he had made ⁷*and sent out the raven; and it went to and fro until the waters were dried up from the earth.* ⁸Then he sent out the dove from him, to see if the waters had subsided from the face of the ground; ⁹but the dove found no place to set its foot, and it returned to him to the ark, for the waters were still on the face of the whole earth. So he put out his hand and took it and brought it into the ark with him. ¹⁰He waited another seven days, and again he sent out the dove from the ark; ¹¹and the dove came back to him in the evening, and there in its beak was a freshly plucked olive leaf; so Noah knew that the waters had subsided from the earth. ¹²Then he waited another seven days, and sent out the dove; and it did not return to him any more. ¹³*In the six hundred first year, in the first month, the first day of the month, the waters were dried up from the earth*; and Noah removed the covering of the ark, and looked, and saw that the face of the ground was drying.

¹⁴*In the second month, on the twenty-seventh day of the month, the earth was dry.* ¹⁵*Then God said to Noah,* ¹⁶*"Go out of the ark, you and your wife, and your sons and your sons' wives with you.* ¹⁷*Bring out with you every living thing that is with you of all flesh—birds and animals and every creeping thing that creeps on the earth—so that they may abound on the earth, and be fruitful and multiply on the earth."* ¹⁸*So Noah went out with his sons and his wife and his sons' wives.* ¹⁹*And*

every animal, every creeping thing, and every bird, everything that moves on the earth, went out of the ark by families.

[20]Then Noah built an altar to Yhwh, and took of every clean animal and of every clean bird, and offered burnt offerings on the altar. [21]And when Yhwh smelled the pleasing odor, Yhwh said in his heart, "I will never again curse the ground because of humankind, for the inclination of the human heart is evil from youth; nor will I ever again destroy every living creature as I have done. [22]As long as the earth endures, seedtime and harvest, cold and heat, summer and winter, day and night, shall not cease."

9:1 *God blessed Noah and his sons, and said to them, "Be fruitful and multiply, and fill the earth. [2]The fear and dread of you shall rest on every animal of the earth, and on every bird of the air, on everything that creeps on the ground, and on all the fish of the sea; into your hand they are delivered. [3]Every moving thing that lives shall be food for you; and just as I gave you the green plants, I give you everything. [4]Only, you shall not eat flesh with its life, that is, its blood. [5]For your own lifeblood I will surely require a reckoning: from every animal I will require it and from human beings, each one for the blood of another, I will require a reckoning for human life. [6]Whoever sheds the blood of a human, by a human shall that person's blood be shed; for in his own image God made humankind. [7]And you, be fruitful and multiply, abound on the earth and multiply in it." [8]Then God said to Noah and to his sons with him, [9]"As for me, I am establishing my covenant with you and your descendants after you, [10]and with every living creature that is with you, the birds, the domestic animals, and every animal of the earth with you, as many as came out of the ark. [11]I establish my covenant with you, that never again shall all flesh be cut off by the waters of a flood, and never again shall there be a flood to destroy the earth."[21] [12]God said, "This is the sign of the covenant that I make between me and you and every living creature that is with you, for all future generations: [13]I have set my bow in the clouds, and it shall be a sign of the covenant between me and the earth. [14]When I bring clouds over the earth and the bow is seen in the clouds, [15]I will remember my covenant that is between me and you and every living creature of all flesh; and the waters shall never again become a flood to destroy all flesh. [16]When the bow is in the clouds, I will see it and remember the everlasting covenant between God and every living creature of all flesh that is on the earth." [17]God said to Noah, "This is the sign of the covenant that I have established between me and all flesh that is on the earth."*

DISCUSSION

The ancient stories of a great flood provide an excellent case study in comparing the Hebrew Bible to other ancient Near Eastern texts. On the one hand, the stories contain "the most remarkable parallels between the Old Testament and the entire corpus of

---

21. Gary A. Rendsburg, "The Biblical Flood Story in the Light of the Gilgamesh Flood Account," in *Gilgamesh and the World of Assyria: Proceedings of the Conference held at Mandelbaum House, The University of Sydney, 21–23 July 2004* (ed. J. Azize and N. Weeks; Leuven: Peeters, 2007), 120–21, reports on an unpublished Late Babylonian fragment of Atrahasis housed in the Metropolitan Museum of Art, New York, which includes this promise from Ea: "From this day no Deluge shall take place, and the human race [shall] endure for ever!"

cuneiform inscriptions from Mesopotamia";[22] on the other hand, the comparison is not at all simple, and the complexities that arise introduce certain difficulties that are characteristic of the whole enterprise.

The Flood in World Literature and in Archaeology

Before focusing on the questions of these stories' meanings in their contexts, one should note how far back into human history flood stories reach and how widely they are distributed. There are more than 300 known accounts of a great flood, and they come from every continent except Antarctica.[23] However, many of these stories recorded by anthropologists since the nineteenth century did not develop independently, but were the result of missionary influence in the preceding centuries.[24] Still others, especially those from Europe, Asia Minor, Africa, and Asia, may have resulted from cultural diffusion from the ancient Near East—and later from Greece and Rome as those cultures adapted older myths (see below).

Still, not all the versions of the story can be accounted for by means of diffusion, which has left some scholars to see them as indications of an actual global cataclysm, or the "common structure of the human mind" across civilizations.[25] Neither conclusion is likely; the problems with universalizing theories of comparison are addressed in the general introduction to this volume. And the idea of a historical global flood is not only contrary to scientific data, it renders the story internally illogical. A global flood such that "all the high mountains under the whole heaven were covered" (Gen. 7:19) would require water at a depth of almost 30,000 feet. For this amount of rain to fall in forty days and forty nights would require rainfall of about thirty feet per hour.[26] The hardest rainfall ever recorded was one foot in an hour;[27] more to the point, thirty feet per hour would sink any ship. Such a storm is not only impossible, it is unimaginable.

As for modified historical theories that attempt to connect the Mesopotamian or biblical flood stories to more localized flood events, these must be sharply qualified.[28] No flood covered any great percentage of the earth in ancient times, and there is no archaeological indication of mass deaths caused by flooding in early antiquity. Regional flooding afflicted certain coastal settlements in the Neolithic period (ca. 8000–5000 BCE), probably in the area of the

---

22. Alexander Heidel, *The Gilgamesh Epic and Old Testament Parallels* (Chicago: University of Chicago Press, 1949), 224.

23. Brian B. Schmidt, "Flood Narratives of Ancient Western Asia," in *Civilizations of the Ancient Near East*, Volume 4, ed. Jack M. Sasson (New York: Simon & Schuster Macmillan, 1995), 2337.

24. Bernhard Lang, "Non-Semitic Deluge Stories and the Book of Genesis: A Bibliographical and Critical Survey," *Anthropos* 80 (1985): 605–16.

25. Ibid., 614.

26. The highest mountain on earth is Everest, at 29,029 feet. Forty days × 24 hours = 960 hours; 29,029 feet/960 hours = 30.2 feet/hour.

27. According to the World Meteorological Organization (http://wmo.asu.edu/). The greatest rainfall for a single minute was 1.23 inches, which would amount to about six feet in an hour, if it continued at such a furious intensity. The point is that the story requires an intensity of rainfall at least five times harder than has ever been recorded on earth, for forty days straight.

28. Schmidt, "Flood Narratives of Ancient Western Asia," 2338.

Black Sea and possibly on the Levantine coast as well.[29] For some reason these Stone Age settlements were abandoned, and they are now submerged, but the exact causes are still debated. However, connecting the Stone Age flooding with Mesopotamian texts requires an oral tradition spanning almost two thousand years, since writing did not appear until the end of the fourth millennium BCE. In other words, even the Sumerian flood stories would be relatively "late" literary versions of an oral tradition that could have been only a bare mythologoumenon—that is, a mythological fragment susceptible to various interpretations by storytellers.

Finally, a theory of origins in *local* flooding may be entertained. There is mixed evidence of local flooding in Mesopotamia (including at Shuruppak) in the early third millennium BCE.[30] But lest the reader miss the point: These floods do not seem to have devastated life in the sense of killing people and other living things. There was a solution to such local and regional floods: move to a slightly higher elevation!

In sum, as Nahum Sarna has written:

> The widespread popularity of flood stories, their prevalence among such a large variety of peoples living at different times as well as different places, argues against literary interdependence, a common source, or reference to a single historic event. Whatever historical foundations may possibly underlie such traditions, it is clear that popular imagination has been at work magnifying local disastrous floods into catastrophes of universal proportions.[31]

Mesopotamian Flood Stories

Flood stories had a long history in Mesopotamia, even before one was incorporated into the Epic of Gilgamesh. A flood marks a new period of history in the Sumerian King List (2000–1700 BCE), which names eight kings who ruled before "the Flood swept over." This is also implicitly true of the Lagash King List (also from the early second millennium), since it begins its story of the world immediately after the flood. The so-called Eridu Genesis (ca. 1600 BCE) is a Sumerian composition that describes the creation of humanity and the decision of the gods to destroy it. In it, Ziusudra king of Shuruppak is warned by the god Enki about the coming flood. He builds a boat, and a terrible storm floods the country for seven days and seven nights. Afterward, he sacrifices to the gods and is dubbed "the preserver of small animals and the seed of humankind." (It is not clear what the Sumerians thought became of the large animals!)

The Babylonian story of Atrahasis (first half of second millennium) is certainly the most famous Mesopotamian flood story apart from the one in Gilgamesh, and comparing it to the biblical story bears fruit as well.[32] (Its great length and fragmentary condition preclude

29. Sean Kingsley, "From Carmel to Genesis: A Neolithic Flood for the Holy Land?" *Bulletin of the Anglo-Israel Archaeological Society* 26 (2008): 75–93.

30. Schmidt, "Flood Narratives of Ancient Western Asia."

31. Nahum M. Sarna, *Understanding Genesis* (New York: Schocken Books, 1966), 38.

32. The whole shape of the Genesis primeval history has been compared to the Atrahasis Epic (Bernard F. Batto, *In the Beginning: Essays on Creation Motifs in the Bible and the Ancient Near East* [Winona Lake, IN: Eisenbrauns, 2013], 50–69; David M. Carr, *Reading the Fractures of Genesis: Historical and Literary Approaches* [Louisville, KY: Westminster John Knox, 1996], 241–48), and indeed

including it in this volume.) As with Eridu Genesis, it is more than a flood story. It begins with a theogony, a story about the creation of the gods. In this case, one group of gods creates another group of gods to do their work. When the newer gods also tire of the labor, they rebel, and humanity is created to do the work instead. However, the noise from the humans annoys the god Enlil, and so he rouses the gods to destroy humankind. (For more on Enlil as a destroyer of human civilization, see chap. 25.) When plague and drought do not succeed, flood is tried next. As in Eridu Genesis, Enki warns a human (here named Atrahasis) about the flood, and the construction of the ark to preserve life and the postflood sacrifice ensue in a very similar fashion. Therefore even in the fragmentary literary remains that have survived, one can see the emergence of a standard form for the flood story in Mesopotamia.

More remarkable still is that the story of Atrahasis and the flood is still emerging. In 2014, Irving Finkel, an Assyriologist with the British Museum, published a Mesopotamian tablet that supplies previously unknown details about Atrahasis and his boat.[33] Perhaps the most striking new detail in this "Ark Tablet" for readers of the Bible is that Atrahasis is said to have led animals onto the ark "two by two," just as Noah is told to do in Genesis 6:19–20 (and as he does in Gen. 7:9, 15).[34] Another previously unattested detail given is that Atrahasis's ark was round—a coracle, essentially a giant basket sealed with bitumen. This type of boat is still used on rivers in Mesopotamia and elsewhere.

The Mesopotamian flood tradition was incorporated into other later works, such as the Erra Epic, in which the underworld god Erra persuades Marduk to turn over the control of his city, Babylon, and then destroys it (see also chap. 18). The endurance of the flood tradition is reflected in Hellenistic works, especially the third-century History of Babylon (aka *Babyloniaca*) by Berossus, in which the hero of the flood is called (in Greek) Xisuthros. This name is a hellenized version of the Sumerian name Ziusudra, demonstrating what a long memory the ancient Near Eastern scribal tradition had.[35]

THE FLOOD IN THE GILGAMESH EPIC

The list of examples is intended to emphasize that when one speaks of Mesopotamian influence on the Bible, it is not as if the adaption of older stories was something that only biblical authors did; instead it was a pervasive part of scribal culture in the ancient Near

---

both share a broader set of overlapping topics (e.g., the creation of humankind). So although the structure of the Gilgamesh flood account specifically is closer to that of Genesis, broader comparison is warranted here. For example, the ten generations from Adam to Noah (Gen. 5) parallel the number of antediluvian kings in certain Mesopotamian flood stories (the number varies from eight to ten). The way that the biblical flood story overlaps with multiple Mesopotamian texts points to the complexity of the relationships between biblical and Mesopotamian literature. One is dealing with a set of traditions being used and interwoven in different ways, successively throughout ancient Near Eastern history.

33. Irving Finkel, *The Ark before Noah: Decoding the Story of the Flood* (London: Hodder & Stoughton, 2014).

34. This detail depends on the reading of a broken section of the tablet which had not undergone scholarly peer review as of this writing.

35. Schmidt, "Flood Narratives of Ancient Western Asia," 2344–45.

East. This is true not only of the flood stories, but of the Gilgamesh stories as well. The Gilgamesh epic had a complicated history of composition and compilation. The earliest stories about Gilgamesh were written in the third millennium BCE in Sumerian; five such stories have survived, each as an individual composition. In the Old Babylonian period, those stories were combined to form a lengthier epic, and the whole in turn was propagated more widely than any other ancient story—copies or fragments have been discovered from the Bronze Age in Syria, Anatolia, and Palestine (at Megiddo). Scribes used it as a practice text to learn to copy, and it was translated into foreign languages such as Hittite and Hurrian.

Despite all the copies of Gilgamesh that have been found from the Bronze Age, it is not clear that the flood story was part of it at that stage, since none of the (fragmentary) Gilgamesh tablets in Old Babylonian or Middle Babylonian contain it. It is likely, therefore, that the flood story was incorporated into it during the Kassite period (13th–12th centuries BCE). A legendary scribe named Sîn-leqi-unninni was later credited as the ultimate author of the Standard Babylonian version of the epic. That version took the somewhat variable Middle Babylonian versions of the epic, and, with great literary genius, transformed them into a "canonical" form—that is, one that became fairly standard and was copied extensively. In the process, the author likely added a new prologue and the flood account, and adjusted other details as well.[36]

The evident evolution of the Gilgamesh Epic formed the basis for a significant defense of the Documentary Hypothesis of the formation of the Pentateuch. Jeffrey Tigay showed that "many of the phenomena presumed to have taken place in the development of biblical literature demonstrably occurred in the development of *Gilgamesh*." Although not all of these phenomena identified by Tigay can be demonstrated here, they warrant enumerating at some length:

> . . . the origin of the epic in unconnected tales about the hero, their collection and transmission into an integrated series of episodes illustrating themes that the author sought to highlight, and the enhancement of the series by the addition of further material originally unrelated to the hero. In the course of this development, one can see the early malleability of the materials, permitting easy integration, reinterpretation, and revision of the elements, and the increasing reluctance of later editors to tamper with their sources when adding their own contributions, so that the latest additions to the epic are less well integrated.[37]

In sum, Gilgamesh provides a good example of the way that other ancient literature helps bring into focus not only the meaning of biblical texts, but also how they were composed.

Like the authors of the Pentateuch, the author of Gilgamesh used source material. Parts of the Gilgamesh flood story are borrowed almost directly from Atrahasis; most strikingly, the hero of the flood in Gilgamesh, who is named Uta-napishti, is called

---

36. A. R. George, *The Babylonian Gilgamesh Epic: Introduction, Critical Edition, and Cuneiform Texts* (Oxford: Oxford University Press, 2003), 1–33.

37. Jeffrey H. Tigay, introduction to *Empirical Models for Biblical Criticism* (Philadelphia: University of Pennsylvania Press, 1985), 21.

Atrahasis in XI.49 and 197! Another marker of the flood story as an insertion is that it calls Uta-napishti's wife his "woman" (*sinnishtu* in Akkadian) whereas the rest of the epic calls her his "spouse" (*marhitu*). Similar distinctions are used by biblical scholars to identify sources in the Bible (see below).

Despite the literary relationship between the flood stories in Gilgamesh and Atrahasis, the story functions entirely differently in each case. In Atrahasis (and in Eridu Genesis), the flood story is about a struggle between gods and humans in which a single figure helps to preserve life on earth through wisdom and heroism. In Gilgamesh, such cosmic concerns are not in view. As noted above, in the introduction to the text, the latter parts of the epic revolve around Gilgamesh's quest for "eternal life" after the death of his friend. There is also a profoundly existential angle as Gilgamesh comes to terms with mortality and his failures to overcome it, but the universal themes are grounded in individual experience. In Gilgamesh XI, the flood story is merely Uta-napishti's recounting of how he personally won eternal life. The details of the flood are rendered incidental, and the whole story is probably repeated only due to its entertainment value and cultural popularity.

The Biblical Flood Story and Its Sources

The complexity of the flood story in Genesis is comparable to that of Gilgamesh. The story may seem unified on a cursory reading, but it is usually recognized to be a composite of more than one source. In the Genesis 6:1–9:17 passage presented above, "sources" within the text are indicated with different typefaces, and a few words of explanation will help to explain their significance.

The dominant theory about the formation of the book of Genesis is that its earliest literary layer is a version of Israel's epic traditions compiled by an author called the Yahwist (abbreviated J[38]), because he used the name "Yhwh" for God (the divine name Yhwh is often translated "the LORD" in ancient and modern translations; it appears repeatedly in the J passages). There is also thought to be a separate version of the epic tradition by an author called the Elohist (E) because he used the Hebrew term "Elohim," meaning "God," instead of the divine name. However, E is the least well preserved Pentateuchal source, and there is no E version of the flood. So, in the case of the flood story, the J source is the earliest version, and it was later augmented. The additions to the J story are attributed to a Priestly writer (P), who was careful not to use the name Yhwh because in the overall shape of the Pentateuchal story that he was revising, the divine name was not revealed until Exodus 3. Therefore, P used "God" instead of "Yhwh" for texts that he composed, but he was conservative enough as a copyist not to remove the divine name from the Yahwist's earlier stories.

There are other reasons to conclude that two different versions of the flood story are combined in Genesis. There are numerous "doublets" in the story, in which a single thing is narrated twice; for example, why is the reason for the flood given twice in slightly different terms (6:6–7 [J]; 6:11–12 [P])? (Other examples are noted in the chart below.) There are also disagreements between the sources; for example, in the P story, Noah is

---

38. "J" reflects the German spelling (*Jahwist*) used by the earliest proponents of the theory.

told to put "two of every kind" on the ark (6:20), whereas in J, it is seven pairs of the ritually clean animals and one pair of the unclean (7:2).[39] Furthermore, in J the flood is said to last 40 days (7:4, 12; 8:6), whereas P suggests that the flood lasts 150 days (7:24; 8:3).

There have been consistent efforts over time to harmonize the two stories,[40] but the best and most straightforward way to explain the whole set of data is to say that two stories have been combined. Thus in both Mesopotamia and Judah, the flood stories had deeper roots in the culture but were incorporated into their present narrative contexts at a relatively later date.

A final question is how the Priestly author worked: The sources as they are presented above presume that there was once a complete Yahwistic story of the flood and a complete Priestly story of the flood, and that these two were harmonized by a redactor (or editor, whose work is hypothetically indicated in boldface). There are other ways to conceive of the story's formation, but an intelligent analysis of the options depends on an awareness of the form of a typical flood story. The key elements of that form as it appears in Genesis and Gilgamesh are presented here.[41]

Elements of the Flood Stories Compared

	Genesis	*Gilgamesh*
Reason for the flood	6:5; 6:11–13 (J/P)	—[42]
Divine decision to destroy	6:6–7, 13 (J/P)	XI.14–19
Reason for hero's salvation	6:8–9 (J/P)	(XI.23)[43]
Warning to flood hero	6:13 (P)	XI.20–23
Command to build ark	6:14–21 (P)	XI.24–31
Hero's obedience	6:22; 7:5 (P/J)	XI.32–85
Command to enter	6:18 (?); 7:1–3 (P[?]/J)	XI.87–89
Entry into the ark	7:7–16 (P/J)	XI.81–84
Closing door	7:16 (J)	XI.94
Description of flood	7:17–24 (P/J)	XI.97–128

39. The J source has its own internal logic here: At the end of J's story, Noah sacrifices some of "every clean animal" (Gen. 8:20)—had he only brought two of each, he would have thereby made extinct the very animals he had just saved!

40. In particular, Wenham's explanation of the chronology of the flood may reveal that the Priestly tradent (the one helping to pass along the tradition) imposed a coherent timeline, and that the conflict between the 40 days and the 150 days is more apparent than real (Gordon J. Wenham, "The Coherence of the Flood Narrative," *Vetus Testamentum* 28 [1978]: 342–45). However, Wenham is still working with a two-source model.

41. The chart comparing elements of the flood stories is indebted to various previous studies, notably Heidel, Sarna, Wenham, and Rendsburg.

42. Much later, in XI.183–86, Ea scolds Enlil: "You, the sage of the gods, the hero, / how could you lack counsel and bring on the Deluge? / On him who transgresses, inflict his crime! / On him who does wrong, inflict his wrongdoing!" In other words, the flood was unjustified in Ea's view. The reason for the flood seems to be immaterial in Gilgamesh.

43. Implicitly, Uta-napishti is chosen for salvation because he is a worshiper of Ea and the king of his people. In Eridu Genesis, however, Ziusudra is explicitly portrayed as being righteous before the gods, like Noah.

Destruction of life	7:21–23 (P/J)	XI.135
End of rain	8:2 (J)	XI.130–34
Waters begin to recede	8:1, 3 (J/P)	XI.140–41
Ark grounding on mountain	8:4 (P)	XI.142–46
Hero opens window	8:6 (J)	XI.137
Birds' reconnaissance	8:6–12 (J/P)	XI.147–56
Exit from the ark	8:15–19 (P)	XI.157
Sacrifice	8:20 (J)	XI.157–60
Divine smelling of sacrifice	8:21–22 (J)	XI.161–63
Divine promise to humanity	8:21–22; 9:12–17 (J/P)	XI.163–67
Conflict among the gods	—	XI.168–98
Blessing on flood hero	9:1–3, 7 (P)	XI.199–206
Covenant	9:8–11 (P)	—

There is no overlooking the striking and numerous similarities of detail and structure between the two texts. The two clearly have the same overall structure, and the differences can be explained by reference to the unique purposes of each (see below). The chart shows that it is only when the passages attributed to J and P are *combined* that the fit is as close as it is. This is why scholars generally now conclude that there was only "one epic source [of the flood story, i.e., J] which has been reworked by a later priestly editor."[44] This is more economical than assuming that two complete earlier versions existed and were combined, and that for some reason the redactor who combined them sometimes preserved doublets and sometimes cut out whole sections of each story. In sum, the Yahwistic story, which is usually assumed to have been written down in the tenth or ninth century, would have been reworked by a Priestly tradent,[45] probably in the postexilic period.

If a Priestly tradent was working under greater Mesopotamian influence than the earlier Yahwistic author, it is not surprising that the Priestly portion of the story has two of each animal entering the ark—which correlates with the number used for Atrahasis in the newly published Ark Tablet—rather than the seven pairs that the Yahwist names.

It is usually thought that the Priestly author worked after the Babylonian exile, and it makes particular sense in this case since Judeans in exile would have been exposed to Babylonian culture at the imperial court.[46] In much the same way that the Standard Babylonian story of the flood superseded earlier versions and became canonical after it was reworked by Sîn-leqi-unninni, the earlier Israelite flood story seems to have been

---

44. Wenham, "Coherence," 348. This would fit well with F. M. Cross's portrayal of P as a tradent instead of a distinct narrative source: "The Flood has been completely rewritten by P. . . . The interweaving of the sources is not the work of a redactor juxtaposing blocks of material, but that of a tradent reworking and supplementing a traditional story" (Cross, *Canaanite Myth and Hebrew Epic: Essays in the History of the Religion of Israel* [Cambridge, MA: Harvard University Press, 1973], 303). Notably, this requires a reevaluation of the boldface passages attributed to a third-party redactor.

45. A tradent is one who plays a role in passing along a tradition.

46. Second Kgs. 25:27–30 tells that Jehoiachin, former king of Judah, "dined regularly in the king's presence" and was given "a regular allowance"—a story that is supported by Babylonian records.

reworked by the Priestly tradent and became canonical. (Of course, the preservation of the Yahwist's account of the flood suggests that the earlier version already had a certain significance, as did the Middle Babylonian versions of Gilgamesh.)

Since the Gilgamesh Epic preceded the biblical flood story by centuries, it is clear that the former can only have influenced the latter, if there was literary influence at all. Probably there was. The influence of the Mesopotamian story on the biblical one can be seen from the fact that flooding was part of natural conditions in Mesopotamia and not in Israel/Judah, and also the fact that the only place named in the biblical story is Ararat (Gen. 8:4), probably equivalent with the region of Urartu in Asia Minor, which was on the western periphery of the Mesopotamian empires.

In describing this influence, a sensitive and precise literary interpreter must use words carefully. It was not that the Priestly author "borrowed" or "copied" the story from the Babylonian version, because the two end up having very different emphases, but rather the later biblical author was probably impressed by the Babylonian tradition and took it to be the authoritative shape of the story. He adopted that shape, but transposed it, adapting it to his own purposes.

Some contrasts between the stories are apparent from the chart above. In the first place, Genesis is essentially monotheistic.[47] In the biblical story, Yhwh is both the one who destroys and the one who saves, whereas in Gilgamesh and other Mesopotamian versions, there is strife among the multiple gods. This creates greater complexity in the portrayal of Yhwh. It also means that unlike Enlil, Yhwh is portrayed as one whose purposes are not thwarted.

Another major difference concerns the reasons for the flood. The biblical flood is repeatedly attributed to moral wrongdoing, although the language ("evil," "corruption") is mostly vague. The references to violence in Genesis 6:11–13 point in one direction, while the unions between "sons of God" and "daughters of humans" in Genesis 6:1–4 might lead one to think of sexual transgression. (Not coincidentally, these are assigned to separate sources.) In Gilgamesh, no motivation is given for the flood, because the point of the story is to close off from Gilgamesh the possibility of receiving Uta-napishti's gift. In Atrahasis and other versions, the reason given is excessive noise by the humans. Elsewhere in the story, "noise" indicates complaining about excessive work, and it could also refer to the general growth and striving of human civilization (cf. Gen. 11), but it is not a moral reason. Indeed, it is often argued that part of the point of the Mesopotamian stories is to portray of humanity as subject to the whims of sometimes destructive and inscrutable gods.

Related to this last point, the Bible also describes Noah's righteousness as the reason for his salvation. The Gilgamesh Epic gives no explicit reason for Uta-napishti to be saved, although one could infer from Ea's scolding of Enlil that Uta-napishti was guilty of nothing.

---

47. Other divine beings are mentioned in Genesis (e.g., 6:1–4, and perhaps the plural pronouns for YHWH in Gen. 11), but none are on the level of God. For a more complete discussion of monotheism, see chap. 21.

In general, the Gilgamesh Epic seems more interested in its human characters, whereas the biblical flood story seems more interested in the character of God. Gilgamesh is the complex main character of the Babylonian story and the gods are mostly functionaries to advance the plot, while in the primeval stories in Genesis, God is the complex main character, and the human characters of the Noah story look flat by comparison.

Another difference is that although both stories end with a blessing on the hero, only the Bible frames the salvation in covenantal terms. This fits with the periodization of the biblical history according to covenants (primarily with Noah, Abraham, and David). And at the beginning of this new covenantal period, the biblical account focuses much more on the "new creation" aspects of the banishment of the flood: a division is reestablished between the water and land, life flourishes again, Noah is told to "be fruitful and multiply" just as Adam was (Gen. 1:28; 9:1). This theme is absent in Gilgamesh, where the flood is taken out of its setting in primordial history. Whether this would be true of other versions of the flood told in the Neo-Babylonian period is difficult to tell, since the surviving copies are incomplete.

In conclusion, literary context matters. The reader should note that neither the Gilgamesh flood story nor its counterpart from the book of Genesis is a self-contained whole. Each of them is only a single episode within a larger story. Partly for that reason, the flood functions somewhat differently in each context, despite the similarities of form and content. Gilgamesh goes on to attempt to overcome death in other ways, by trying to stay awake for a week or retrieve an underwater plant that is supposed to grant immortality, but these methods fail. The epic closes with a translation of an ancient Sumerian poem in which Gilgamesh asks his friend Huwawa about the afterlife: one of the primary messages of Gilgamesh is that the real hope for eternal happiness is not in immortality, which is impossible, but in ongoing mortuary care by one's offspring. The final tablet closes with positive descriptions of the afterlife of men with many sons: the man with seven sons "sits on a throne among the junior deities" (XII.116). The biblical call to "be fruitful and multiply" (Gen. 9:1, 7) might be an echo of the importance of procreation, but by contrast, the Genesis flood story closes with covenantal promises: humankind is called to renounce improper bloodshed (9:5–6), and God in turn renounces the extreme measure of destroying the earth by flood (9:9–16). In the larger narrative structure of the book of Genesis and the Bible, the flood appears to be only one of the early attempts by God to deal with human wrongdoing (see also the banishment of Cain in Gen. 4, and the scattering of the builders from Babel in Gen. 11).

REFLECTION QUESTIONS

1. Beyond the similarities and differences noted above, are there details in either story that stand out as distinguishing its style from the other story?
2. What reasons would the biblical authors have had for incorporating a preexisting type of flood story into their own national religious traditions?
3. Are there past events in your own life or the history of your country that you would claim as part of your own story although you cannot verify them?

4. What is the theological effect of transposing the story from polytheism to monotheism in this case?

5. Which makes for more compelling literature: a pantheon of gods, some of whom could be dangerous while others were helpful, or a single god who exhibited both wrath and mercy? Why?

6. Are the source divisions of the flood narrative convincing and apparent when they are pointed out? Why or why not?

7. What are some of the ways in which these two structurally similar flood accounts are made to mean different things in their different literary contexts?

8. Why do you think the authors of Gilgamesh and the Pentateuch incorporated older stories into their compositions? Can you think of modern examples of incorporating old stories into new ones?

FURTHER READING

George, Andrew. *The Babylonian Gilgamesh Epic: Introduction, Critical Edition, and Cuneiform Texts.* Oxford: Oxford University Press, 2003.

———. *The Epic of Gilgamesh: The Babylonian Epic Poem and Other Texts in Akkadian and Sumerian.* London: Penguin, 2000.[48]

Heidel, Alexander. *The Gilgamesh Epic and Old Testament Parallels.* Chicago: University of Chicago Press, 1949.

Lambert, W. G., and A. R. Millard. *Atra-Hasis: The Babylonian Story of the Flood.* Oxford: Oxford University Press, 1969.

Lang, Bernhard. "Non-Semitic Deluge Stories and the Book of Genesis: A Bibliographical and Critical Survey." *Anthropos* 80 (1985): 605–16.

Moran, William L. *The Most Magic Word: Essays on Babylonian and Biblical Literature.* Edited by Ronald S. Hendel. Washington, DC: Catholic Biblical Association of America, 2002. (Esp. 33–86.)

Noort, Ed. "The Stories of the Great Flood: Notes on Gen 6:5–9:17 in Its Context of the Ancient Near East." Pages 1–38 in *Interpretations of the Flood.* Edited by Florentino García Martínez and Gerard P. Luttikhuizen. Leiden: Brill, 1999.

Rendsburg, Gary A. "The Biblical Flood Story in the Light of the Gilgamesh Flood Account." Pages 115–27 in *Gilgamesh and the World of Assyria: Proceedings of the Conference Held at Mandelbaum House, The University of Sydney, 21–23 July 2004.* Edited by J. Azize and N. Weeks. Leuven: Peeters, 2007.

Sarna, Nahum M. *Understanding Genesis.* New York: Schocken Books, 1966. (Esp. 37–62.)

Tigay, Jeffrey H., ed. *Empirical Models for Biblical Criticism.* Philadelphia: University of Pennsylvania Press, 1985.

Wenham, Gordon J. "The Coherence of the Flood Narrative." *VT* 28 (1978): 336–48.

48. The Oxford edition will be preferred by technically inclined scholars, but the Penguin volume offers enough introduction and commentary for generalists and most students.

Court Stories

Ahiqar and Joseph

GENESIS 39 AND 41

When: See below
Where: Jerusalem
Language: Hebrew

AHIQAR

What: Papyrus fragments
When: Late fifth century BCE
Where: Elephantine, Egypt (but probably composed in Syria)
Language: Aramaic
Translation: J. M. Lindenberger[1]

§A1 (1–4) [These are the wor]ds of one Ahiqar, a wise and skillful scribe, which he taught his son. N[ow he did not have offspring of his own, but] he said, "I shall nevertheless have a son!" Prior to this, Ahiqar had [become a gre]at man; he had [become counselor of all Assyria and ke]eper of the seal of Sennacherib, king of Assy[ria. He used to say, "I] may not have any sons, but Sennacherib, king of Assyria, relies [on my counsel] and advice."

§A2 (5–10) A[t that time Senna]cherib, k[ing of Assyria, died, and] his son Esarhaddon [arose] and became king in Assyria in pla[ce of his fa]ther [Sennacherib]. T[hen I said (to myself), "I am] growing old." [So I] se[nt] for [my] nep[hew, so that he might succeed me at] my death [and become scribe and keeper of the se]al for [King] Es[arhaddon just as I was for Sennacherib, king] of Assyria. Then I [adopted Nadin, my] ne[phew, as my son.

---

1. "Ahiqar: A New Translation and Introduction," in *Old Testament Pseudepigrapha* (ed. J. H. Charlesworth; 2 vols.; New York: Doubleday, 1985), 2:479–507.

I reared him and trained him] and taught him wisdom. And I was generous to him and i[nstalled him in the] palace [ga]te with [me before the king in the midst of] his courtiers.

§A3 (11–13) I brought him before Esarhaddon, king of Assyria. And the k[ing questioned him] concerning wisdom, [and he told him every]thing he asked. Then Esarhaddon, king of Assyria, gave him his approval and said [to me], "May your life [be prolonged], O wise [s]cribe, counselor of all Assyria, who raised up his [neph]ew to be his son, since [he had] no son of his own." [When the king of Assy]ria [said this], I, Ahiqar, bowed low in obeisance to Esarh[addon, king of] Assyria.

§A4 (14–22) [Some time later, when I, A]hiqar, saw that Esarhaddon, king of Assyria, was favorably disposed, I addressed [the king and said], "I [served] your father, King [Sennach]erib, [wh]o ruled [before you] [. . . . .] [Now] I am growing old. I can no longer perform my duties in the palace gate [or continue my service to you.] But my son Nadin has grown up. Let him succeed me as scribe [and counselor of all Assyria], and let him be [kee]per of the seal for you! For [I have taught him] my wisdom and co[unsel." Esarhaddon, ki]ng of Assyria, replied to me, "Very well, [your son] shall [be scribe and counselor and keeper of the seal for me] in your place. He shall do your work [for me." Now when I, Ahiqar, heard him prom]ise [this], I went back home [and went into retirement there.]

§A5 (23–31) [And as for this son of mine, whom] I [had reared] and installed in the palace gate [before Esarhaddon, king of Assyria, in the midst of hi]s [courtiers], I thought, "He will promo[te my] welfare, [just as I did his." (But) then my nep]hew, whom I reared, devised [a wicked] plot against [me and thought to himself], "[This is what] I can s[ay (to the king): 'This old Ahiqar, who was keeper of the seal] for your father, King Sennache[ri]b, [is subverting the land against you, for] he is a wise [counselor and scribe], on whose counsel and ad[vice all Assyria used to rely.' Then], when [Esarhaddon] hears [my report], he will be greatly enraged, [and will order Ahiqar killed." So] when this false son of mine had devised [this lie against me, . . .] [. . . . .]

§A6 (32–39) [Then Es]arhaddon, king of Assyria, [flew into a rage], and said, ["Bring me Nabusumiskun, on]e of my father 's officers, who [was] on his staff." [(Then) the king said (to Nabusumiskun)], "Seek [Ahiqar] out, (and) wherever you find (him), [kill him!] Otherwise that old [Ah]iqa[r]—wise scribe [and counselor of all Assy]ria that he was—is liable to subvert the land against us." When [the king of A]ssyria [had said this], he appointed two other men with him to observe how [(the execution) should be carried out]. (Then) officer [Nab]usumiskun rode [away] on a swif[t h]orse, accompanied by [those men].

§A7 (40–45) After three d[a]ys had gone by, [he and the o]ther [men] accompanying him c[aught sight of me] as I was walking along among the vineyards. [As soon as] officer [Nab]usumiskun saw me, he tore his cloak and lamented: ["Is it you], O wise scribe and master of good counsel, who [used to be a righteous] man, [and o]n whose counsel and advice all Assyria used to rely? [Your son whom you rear]ed, whom you installed in the palace gate, has denounced you. He has ruined you, and turn[ed on you wickedly."]

§A8 (46–54) [Sudde]nly I, Ahiqar, was afraid, and I answered [officer] Nabusum[iskun, "Indeed], I am the same Ahiqar who once long ago rescued you from an undeserved death, [when] King Esarhaddon's father [Sennacherib] was so angry with you [that he sought to kill you.] I took you [direc]tly to my own house and provided for you there, as a man would care for his own brother. I concealed you from him, saying, 'I have killed him,' until an oppor[tune ti]me. Then, after a long time, I presented you to King Sennacherib and cleared you of the charges against you in his presence, so that he did you no ha[rm]. Indeed, King Sennacherib was grateful to me for having kept you alive rather than killing you. Now it is your turn to treat me as I treated you. Do not kill me, (but) take me to your house un[til] the times change. King Esarhaddon is known to be a merciful man. He will eventually think of me and wish for my counsel. Th[en] you can [br]ing me to him, and he will let me live."

§A9 (55–69) Then officer Nabusumiskun [re]plied to me, "Have no fear, my [lor]d Ahiqar, father of all Assyria, on whose counsel King Sennacherib and [all] the Assyrian Army [used to rely]!" At once officer Nabusumiskun said to his companions, those two men who were accompanying him, ["List]en! Co[me near] to me and I will tell you [my] plan, and a [very] good plan it is." Th[en] those two [men] replied to hi[m, "You t]ell us, officer Nabusumiskun, what [yo]u th[ink, and we will obey] you." Then [of]ficer [Nabu-sumiskun] said [in reply] to them, "Listen to me: This [Ahi]qar was a great man. He was [King] Esarhaddon's [keeper of the se]al, and all the [Assyr]ian army used to rely on his counsel and advice. Far be it from us to kill him! [There is a] eunuch-[slave] of mine. Let him be killed between [the]se two mountains in place of this Ahiqar. Whe[n it is reported], the king will [se]nd other [m]en [af]ter us to see the body of this Ahiqar. Then [they will see the body] of [th]is eunuch-slave of mine (and that will be the end of the matter) until eventually [King] Esarhaddon [thinks of Ahiqar and wishes for his counsel, and grieves] over him. (Then) [King] Esarhaddo[n]'s thoughts [will turn to me, and he will say to his officers and courtiers], 'I would give you riches as num[erous as grains of sand, if only you could find Ahiqar.'" Now this plan] seemed good to his t[wo] companions. [They replied to officer Nabusumiskun], "Do as you suggest. [Let us not kill him, but you give us] that eunuch-[slave] in place of [this] Ahiqar. [He shall be killed between these two mountains."]

§A10 (70–78) At that time word spread through the la[nd of Assyria that Ahiqar,] King [Esarhaddon's scribe,] had been put to death. Then [officer] Nabus[umiskun took me to his house and hid me. Indeed,] he provided for me there as [a man would care for his own brother. And he said to me . . . . "Bread and water] will be provided to my lord. I[f . . . ."] He gave me] plenty of food and abun[dant] supplies. [Then officer Nabusumiskun] went to Ki[ng] Esarhaddon [and said, "I have done as you commanded me.] I went and found [that] Ahiqar [and put him to death." Now when King Esarhaddon heard this,] he questioned the t[wo] men [whom he had appointed along with Nabusumiskun. And they said, "It happened just as] he said." T[he]n, while [King] Esarha[ddon . . . .]

[[*The rest of the story is lost in the Aramaic version, although a section of proverbs survives. The ending supplied here is from the Syriac version, which is significantly later, and significantly longer.*]]

What: Syriac version of Ahiqar
When: Twelfth–seventeenth century CE, but probably based on an earlier translation
Language: Syriac
Translation: Adapted from F. C. Conybeare et al.[2]

---

2. F. C. Conybeare, J. R. Harris, and A. S. Lewis, *The Story of Ahikar: From the Aramaic, Syriac, Arabic, Armenian, Ethiopic, Old Turkish, Greek and Slavonic Versions* (Cambridge: Cambridge University Press, 1913).

§S1 Now when Pharaoh, king of Egypt, heard that I, Ahiqar, had been slain, he was overjoyed, and he wrote a letter to Sennacherib, saying: "Pharaoh, king of Egypt, to Sennacherib, king of Assyria and Nineveh, greetings. I am planning to build a castle between heaven and earth, so seek out and send me from your kingdom a man who is a skilled architect, that he may give me reply concerning all that I shall ask him. And when you send me such a man, I will collect and send you the revenue of Egypt for three years: but if you do not send me a man who can answer everything that I ask him, then you will collect and send me the tribute of Assyria and Nineveh for three years, by these ambassadors that come to you."

§S2 And when this letter was read before the king, he cried out to all the nobles and landowners of his kingdom, and said unto them: "Which of you will go to Egypt to answer for the king everything that he may ask? And who will build him the castle that he plans, and bring back the three years' tribute of Egypt and return?"

§S3 And when the nobles heard this, they answered the king: "My lord the king, you know that not only in the years of your reign, but also in the years of your father Sahardum,[3] Ahiqar the Secretary was in the habit of resolving questions like these. But now look: his son Nadan is also instructed in his father's book-lore and wisdom." And when my son Nadan heard these things, he cried out before the king and said: "The gods themselves cannot do things like these; let alone men."

§S4 And when the king heard these words, he was greatly disturbed, and he descended from his throne and sat on the ground, and said: "Alas for you, Ahiqar the wise, that I destroyed you on account of a boy's words! Who will return you to me for such a time as this? I would give him your weight in gold."

§S5 And when Nabusemakh [=Nabusumiskun][4] . . . heard these words, he fell down before the king and said to him: "He who has despised the commandment of his lord, is guilty of death; and I, my lord, have despised the command of your kingship. Therefore, order them to crucify me—for Ahiqar, whom you commanded me to kill, is still alive."

§S6 And when the king heard these words, he answered and said, "Speak on, speak on, Nabusemakh, speak on, you good and clever man, unskilled in evil. If it is indeed as you say, and you show me Ahiqar alive, then I will give you presents of silver, a hundred talents in weight, and of purple, fifty talents in value."

§S7 And Nabusemakh answered and said, "Swear to me, my lord the king, that, if you do not find other sins of mine, this sin shall not be remembered against me." And the king gave him his right hand on this matter. And promptly the king mounted his chariot, and hurried to me, and opened [my prison] over me, and I ascended and came and fell before the king; the hair of my head had grown down on my shoulders, and my beard reached my chest; and my body was foul with the dust, and my nails were grown long like those of eagles.

---

3. Note that in the Syriac version, the order of the reigns of Esarhaddon (=Sahardum) and Sennacherib has been switched (cf. §A2).

4. Nabusumiskun is instead called Nabusemakh in the Syriac version.

§S7 And when the king saw me, he wept and was ashamed to talk with me, and in great grief he said to me, "It was not I who sinned against you, Ahiqar; but your son whom you raised, he sinned against you." Then I answered and said to him, "Because I have seen your face, my lord, no evil is in my mind." And the king said to me, "Go to your house, Ahiqar, and shave off your hair, and wash your body, and recover your strength for forty days; and after that come to me."

§S8 Therefore I went to my house, and I was in my house about thirty days. When I had recovered, I came to the king, and he said to me: "Have you seen, Ahiqar, what a letter Pharaoh, king of Egypt, has written me?" And I answered, "My lord the king, let there be no trouble to you over this affair. I will go to Egypt and build the king a castle: and I will answer anything he asks me: and I will bring back with me the three years' tribute of Egypt." And when the king heard these things he was overjoyed, and he gave me gifts. And as for Nabusemakh he set him at the head of all.

§S9 After this I wrote a letter to Eshfagni, my wife, as follows: "When this letter reaches you, command my huntsmen to catch me two young eagles, and command the workers in flax to make me ropes of hemp; the length of each one of them shall be a thousand ells,[5] and their thickness that of one's little finger. And bid the carpenters to make me cages for the young eagles: and deliver over Ubael and Tabshelim, the two boys, who do not yet know how to talk, and let them teach them to say on this wise: 'Give the builders mud, mortar, tiles, bricks, for they are idle.'" And Eshfagni my wife did all that I commissioned her.

§S10 Then I said to the king: "Order, my lord, that I should go to Egypt." And when the king ordered me to go, I took me a force of soldiers and went. And when we came to the first resting place, I let out the young eagles and bound the ropes to their feet and made the boys ride on them; and they took them and went up to a great height, and the boys cried out as they had been taught, "Supply mud, mortar, tiles, and bricks to the builders who are idle!" Then I pulled them in again. And when we came to Egypt, I went to the king's gate, and his nobles told the king, "There is come the man whom the king of Assyria has sent." And the king commanded and gave me a place to reside in.

§S11 On the following day I came in before him and worshiped him and inquired after his health. And the king answered me, "What is your name?" And I said to him, "My name is Abikam: one of the contemptible ants of the kingdom."[6] And the king answered and said to me, "Am I thus despised of your lord, that he has sent me a despised ant of his kingdom? Go, Abikam, to your lodging, and come to me early in the morning."

§S12 Then the king commanded his nobles, "Tomorrow clothe yourselves in red," and the king dressed himself in fine linen, and sat on his throne. And he commanded and I came in to his presence, and he said to me, "What am I like, Abikam and what are my nobles like?' And I answered and said to him, "My lord the king, you are like Bel, and your nobles are like his priests." And again he said to me, "Go to your lodging, and come to me tomorrow.'

5. An ell is about half a meter; its precise value varied.
6. Ahiqar does not reveal his real name.

§S13 And the king commanded his nobles, "Tomorrow clothe yourselves in robes of white linen," and the king himself put on white and sat on his throne. And he commanded and I came into his presence, and he said to me, "What am I like, Abikam, and what are my nobles like?" And I said to him, "My lord the king, you are like the sun, and your nobles his rays." And again he said to me, "Get you to your lodging, and come to me tomorrow."

§S14 And again the king commanded his nobles, "Tomorrow clothe yourselves in black," and the king put on crimson. And he commanded, and I came into his presence, and he said to me, "What am I like, Abikam; and what are my nobles like?" And I said to him, "My lord the king, you are like the moon, and your nobles the stars." And again he said to me, "Go to your house: and come to me tomorrow."

§S15 And the king commanded his nobles, "Tomorrow dress in diverse and varied colors, and let the doors of the palace be covered with red hangings." And the king himself was robed in fine needlework. And he commanded and I came into his presence; and he said to me, "What am I like, Abikam? And my nobles, what are they like?" And I said to him, "My lord the king, you are like the month Nisan, and your nobles its flowers."

§S16 Then the king said to me, "The first time you compared me to Bel, and my nobles to his priests. The second time you compared me to the sun, and my nobles to its rays. The third time you compared me to the moon, and my nobles to the stars. And the fourth time you likened me to Nisan, and my nobles to the flowers thereof. And now tell me, Abikam, to what is your lord like?" And I answered and said to him, "Be it far from me, my lord the king, that I should make mention of my lord Sennacherib,[7] while you are seated. My lord Sennacherib is like [the God of Heaven] and his nobles to the lightning in the clouds: for when he wills, he fashions the rain and the dew [and] the hail; and if he thunders, he restrains the sun from rising, and its rays from being seen; and he will restrain Bel from coming in and from going forth in the street, and his nobles from being seen; and he will hinder the moon from rising and the stars from appearing."

§S17 And when the king heard these things he was exceedingly angry, and said to me, "By the life of your lord, I adjure you tell me: What is your name?" And I answered and said to him, "I am Ahiqar the Secretary and Great Seal of Sennacherib king of Assyria and Nineveh." And the king said to me, "Did I not hear that your lord had killed you?" And I said to him, "I am still alive, my lord the king: and God saved me from something which my hands did not." And the king said to me, "Go, Ahiqar, to your house, and come to me tomorrow, and tell me a word which I never heard nor anyone of my nobles; and which was never heard in the city of my kingdom."

§S18 Then I sat down and thought, and wrote a letter as follows: "From Pharaoh, king of Egypt, to Sennacherib, king of Assyria and Nineveh, greetings. Kings have need of kings and brethren of brethren; and at this time my gifts have become scant, because silver is scarce in my treasury: command, therefore, to send me from your treasury 900 talents[8] of silver, and in a little while I will return them to their place."

---

7. See n. 3 on Sahardum/Esarhaddon.
8. A talent is roughly sixty-seven pounds.

§S19 I folded this letter and held it in my hands, and the king commanded and I came into his presence, and I said to him, "Perhaps in this letter there is a word that was never heard by you." And when I read it before the king and before his nobles, they cried out, as they were ordered by the king to do, and said, "This has been heard by all of us, and it is so." Whereupon I said to them, "Behold, [in that case] there is a debt of 900 talents from Egypt to Assyria." And when the king heard this, he marveled.

§S20 Then he said to me, "I am planning to build a castle between earth and heaven. Its height from the earth shall be one thousand fathoms." Then I brought out the young eagles and bound the ropes to their feet, and set the boys on their backs; and they were saying, "Provide mud, mortar; [foreman, mix] tiles and bricks for the builders, because they are idle." And when the king saw it, he was confounded. Then I, Ahiqar, took a switch and beat the king's nobles, till they all took to flight. Then the king was indignant with me, and said to me, "You are quite mad, Ahiqar: who is able to carry up anything to these boys?" And I said to him, "Concerning the affairs of Sennacherib my lord, say nothing; for if he had been at hand, he would have built a couple of castles in one day." And the king said to me, "Forget about the castle, Ahiqar, and go to your lodging; and in the morning come to me."

§S21 And when it was morning, I came into his presence, and he said to me, "Explain to me, Ahiqar, the following matter. The horse of your lord neighs in Assyria, and our mares hear his voice here, and their foals miscarry." Then I went forth from the king's presence, and commanded my servants to catch me a cat, and I whipped it in the streets of the city; and when the Egyptians saw it, they went and told the king that Ahiqar had lifted himself up against our people and makes mock of us. "For he has caught a cat and whips it in the streets of our city." And the king sent for me and called me; and I came into his presence. And he said to me, "In what way art you insulting us?" and I answered and said to him, "This cat has seriously damaged me in no slight matter; for a cock had been entrusted to me by my lord, whose voice was extremely beautiful, and by the time that he crowed I understood that my lord wished for me, and I went to the gate of my lord. And last night this cat went to Assyria and tore off the head of this cock of mine and returned." And the king answered and said to me, "As far as I can see, Ahiqar, since you have grown old you have become stark mad. For it is 360 parasangs from here to Assyria; and how can you say that in a single night this cat went and cut off the head of the cock and came back?" Then I said to him, "And if it is 360 parasangs from Egypt to Assyria, how do your mares in this place hear the voice of the horse of my lord, and their foals miscarry?"

§S22 And when the king heard this, he was sore vexed, and he said to me, "Ahiqar, expound to me this riddle: A pillar has on its head twelve cedars; in every cedar there are thirty wheels, and in every wheel two cables, one white and one black." And I answered and said to him, "My lord the king, the ox-herds in our country understand this riddle that you tell. The pillar of which you spoke to me is the year: the twelve cedars are the twelve months of the year; The thirty wheels are the thirty days of the month; the two cables, one white and one black, are the day and the night."

§S23 Again he said to me, "Twine me five cables from the sand of the river." And I said to him, "My lord the king, bid them bring me from your treasury one rope of sand, and I will make one to match it." Then he said to me, "Unless you do this, I will not give you the Egyptian tribute." Thereupon I sat down and calculated in my heart how I should do it. And I went out from the king's palace and bored five holes in the eastern wall of the palace. And when the sun entered the holes I scattered sand in them, and the sun's path began to appear as if [the sand] were twined in the holes. Then I said to the king; "My lord, bid them take up these, and I will weave you others in their stead." And when the king and his nobles saw it, they were amazed.

§S24 And again the king commanded to bring me an upper millstone that was broken: and he said to me, "Ahiqar, sew up for us this broken millstone." Then I went and brought a nether millstone, and cast it down before the king and said to him, "My lord the king, since I am a stranger here, and have not the tools of my craft with me, bid the cobblers cut me strips from this lower millstone which is the fellow of the upper millstone; and I will immediately sew it together."

§S25 And when the king heard it, he laughed and said, "The day in which Ahiqar was born shall be blessed before the god of Egypt; and since I have seen you alive, I will make it a great day and a feast." Then he gave me the revenue of Egypt for three years, and straightway I returned and came to my lord the king Sennacherib: and he came forth to meet me and received me. And he made it a great day and set me at the head of his household; and he said to me, "Ask whatever you desire, Ahiqar; and I worshiped the king and said, "Whatever you wish to give me, give it to Nabusemakh . . . because he gave me my life; and for myself, my lord, bid them give me my son Nadan, that I may teach him a further lesson. For he has forgotten my former teaching." And the king commanded and gave me my son Nadan; and the king said to me, "Go your way, Ahiqar, and work your will on your son Nadan; for no man shall rescue his body from your hands."

§S26 Thereupon I took Nadan my son, and brought him to my house; and I bound him with iron chains whose weight was twenty talents, and I fastened the chains in rings, and I fastened collars on his neck; and I struck him one thousand blows on the shoulders and a thousand and one on his loins; and I put him in the porch of the door of my palace, and gave him bread by weight and water by measure. And I delivered him to my boy Nabuel to guard, and told my boy, "Write down in a tablet whatever I say to my son Nadan, when I go in or come out." And I answered and said to my son Nadan as follows:

§S27 My son, he who does not hear with his ears, they make him hear with the nape of his neck.

[[*Other proverbs follow in the Syriac version. In the Syriac and Armenian versions, the proverbs are split into two sections, one when the boy is first instructed, and another at the end. In the Aramaic version, the sayings seem not to have been integrated with the narrative, but rather transmitted separately.*]]

SUGGESTIONS FOR COMPARISON

§A5	Gen. 39:11–18
§A6	Gen. 39:19–20
§A8–9	Gen. 39:21–23
§S11	Gen. 41:14–15

§S12–24   Gen. 41:1–7, 17–24
§S12–24   Gen. 41:25–36
§S25   Gen. 41:39–45

DISCUSSION

In ancient Near Eastern history, writing was practiced most intensively at royal courts. Kings and their officials kept records, wrote letters, issued propaganda, and documented events. Royal courts were also, of course, the site of intrigues, so it is not surprising that court stories are widely attested. The ones presented here might be viewed as a subset of a broader genre that also includes Daniel 1–6 and Esther.

The story of Ahiqar invites close comparison with the Joseph stories. Ahiqar was clearly one of the most popular and widely circulated tales in antiquity, and it survives in multiple versions: in Aramaic, Syriac, Greek, Ethiopic, and Armenian. The earliest of these is the Aramaic version that is presented above; because it is incomplete, an ending to the narrative is supplied from the later Syriac version. This of course risks creating a literary hodgepodge, but the two halves are intelligible as a whole.

Ahiqar is the story of a high official and leading counselor at the Assyrian court of Sennacherib. When the latter dies and is succeeded by Esarhaddon, Ahiqar decides that it is time to train a successor and retire. Since he has no children, he selects his nephew Nadin and tries to educate him. When Ahiqar steps down, however, Nadin betrays him to Esarhaddon by telling the king that Ahiqar is subverting him. Esarhaddon becomes enraged and orders Ahiqar to be killed. Fortunately for Ahiqar, Esarhaddon assigns the task to one of his father's officers, Nabusumiskun, who knows Ahiqar and indeed owes the wise man his life. So Nabusumiskun instead hides Ahiqar (though he kills another man in his place!). This is where the Aramaic version breaks off.

Significantly, Ahiqar's troubles begin *after* Esarhaddon succeeds Sennacherib. Presumably Sennacherib would not have believed that his trusted adviser would betray him, whereas the newly enthroned Esarhaddon might.[9] Transitions of power were always dangerous times for ancient Near Eastern empires—uprisings around the empire were common at such junctures—so paranoia on the part of a new king would have been understandable. But this detail also evokes the story of the Israelites' sufferings in Egypt, which began when "a new king arose . . . *who did not know Joseph*" (Exod. 1:8; emphasis added).

If the end of the story is faithfully supplied by the Syriac version,[10] the Egyptian pharaoh sees an opportunity to take from Esarhaddon now that his wisest counselor is out

---

9. Historically, Esarhaddon's brothers killed their father, Sennacherib, and he had to fight them for the throne. This experience surely helped inspire him to draft and propagate his well-known loyalty oath (see chap. 9) in an attempt to ensure that his son's succession would go more smoothly. It is by no means clear that a knowledge of these events inspired the Ahiqar story, but it is possible.

10. The fact that the motif of one king riddling another extends back more than a thousand years, into Sumerian literature, may argue for the antiquity of the shape of this story. For the earliest example of the form, see "Enmerkar and the Lord of Aratta," in H. L. J. Vanstiphout, *Epics of Sumerian Kings: The Matter of Aratta* (Atlanta: Society of Biblical Literature, 2003), 49–96.

of the picture, and he asks for an architect who can build him "a castle between heaven and earth." The Assyrian king is distressed, so Nabusumiskun produces Ahiqar from his hiding place. The king sends Ahiqar to the pharaoh, and Ahiqar calls himself Abikam so as not to be recognized. He solves riddles posed to him by the pharaoh, and stumps him when he cannot get supplies into the sky to build the castle he requested. He thereby wins (on the king of Assyria's behalf) the bet that the pharaoh had proposed. Finally, Ahiqar returns home, where he imprisons and beats his treacherous nephew, and the text closes with wisdom sayings by which the wise man tries a second time to educate the nephew.

Ahiqar is alluded to in the intertestamental book of Tobit, which is part of Catholic and Orthodox Bibles.[11] There, he is presented as Tobit's nephew (1:21–22) and supporter (2:10). The author of Tobit also knows the traditions of Ahiqar's service to Sennacherib and Esarhaddon (whom he gets in the right order) and of his betrayal by his adopted son, who is called Nadab (14:10; cf. 11:18) instead of Nadin. Therefore, prior to the discovery of the Aramaic text, it was assumed that Ahiqar was originally a Jewish story, like the biblical court tales.

However, the Aramaic version makes it clear that the tale predates its adoption into Jewish tradition. In particular, the proverbs make reference to "the gods," and to specific foreign deities. For example, Ahiqar proverb 12 reads, "There are two things that are good, and a third that is pleasing to Shamash." (Compare Prov. 6:16: "There are six things that Yhwh hates, seven that are an abomination to him.") Or again in Ahiqar proverb 13: "Wisdom is of the gods . . . she has been exalted by Shamayn." The combination of the Mesopotamian Shamash and the Levantine (Baal) Shamayn suggests a kind of syncretism that would have been at home in the western part of the Mesopotamian empires of the first millennium.

The narrative portions of Ahiqar may also be grounded in the Neo-Assyrian period. It has been proposed that the tale of Ahiqar was based in some way on a real court adviser from the time of Esarhaddon. A tablet from Uruk (copied much later, in 165 BCE) lists kings and their advisers, and mentions that a man named Aba-enlil-dari served Esarhaddon,[12] further noting that the Arameans called him "Aḥûqari." Given its late date, this record could have been influenced by the tales, but the Mesopotamian scribal tradition was highly conservative, and so it is also possible that an Ahuqar or Ahiqar indeed served Esarhaddon. (Lindenberger suggests that Ahiqar himself collected the proverbs, but that is even more speculative.) A further supporting detail is that one of the sons of the Babylonian king Marduk-apla-iddina II was named Nabu-shuma-ishkun, and was taken captive by Sennacherib; this figure has been understood to be the Nabusumiskun who is one of Sennacherib's officers in the tale.[13]

---

11. There are also similarities between the proverbs of Ahiqar and certain biblical proverbs, and even certain New Testament teachings (see Lindenberger, "Ahiqar"; and James C. VanderKam, "Ahikar/Ahiqar [Person]," *ABD* 1:114).

12. The Akkadian term used is *umm(i)ānu,* which means "scholar, scribal expert."

13. For citations and discussion, see James C. VanderKam, "Ahikar/Ahiqar (Person)," *ABD* 1:114. For discussion of recent and even more ambitious attempts to locate Ahiqar in Assyrian history, see Tawny L. Holm, "Memories of Sennacherib in Aramaic Tradition," in Isaac Kalimi and

Related to the story's possible Assyrian roots, it has been argued that it was composed in Akkadian and later translated to Aramaic. However, closer study of the language suggests that it was instead composed in Aramaic in the late seventh or early sixth century, with the proverbs perhaps having preexisted the narrative, since they are of a slightly older linguistic type. Aramaic was already the administrative language of the western part of the Assyrian Empire at that time.

These complex cultural backgrounds not only shed light on the story, they are its raison d'être. Both stories reflect the struggle of nonnative peoples to prove themselves trustworthy to an imperial ruler. Consider: Ahiqar, like Joseph, Daniel, and Esther, seems to have been a foreigner who was elevated. The fact that he "*became* counselor of all Assyria" and had no family might suggest that he too was specially favored, rather than born to the courtier class. The name Ahiqar is also not Akkadian, but rather West Semitic (i.e., Aramaic; it would mean "My brother is honored/precious"). To a contemporary audience, Ahiqar's name likely cast him as a Westerner, as surely as the name José would lead a hearer today to interpret a character as Hispanic.

The sequence of Joseph stories in Genesis 37–50 has long been recognized as a distinctive component within Genesis and the Pentateuch. These stories are connected by numerous themes and motifs, and unlike some of the terse stories elsewhere in Genesis, they are intricately crafted, with a long and complex plot and depth of characterization. For these reasons, the Joseph cycle is usually deemed a different genre: a novella—a short novel. (Other biblical novellas include the books of Ruth, Jonah, and Esther.)

Joseph's story has numerous ups and downs. The reader meets him in Genesis 37 as a seventeen-year-old who angers his brothers by flaunting their father's favoritism toward him. They throw him in a pit, and from there he is taken and sold into slavery in Egypt. In Genesis 39, he rises to a position of some authority as a servant of an Egyptian captain, Potiphar. But when Potiphar's wife tries to seduce him and fails, she accuses him of attempting to rape her. He is thrown into captivity, but there (in Gen. 40) he distinguishes himself as an accurate interpreter of dreams. One of the prisoners whose dreams Joseph rightly interpreted eventually returns to service in Pharaoh's court, and he mentions Joseph to the ruler when he has dreams that his experts cannot interpret. Giving glory to God, Joseph interprets the dreams as referring to coming years of abundance and famine, which allows the Egyptians to prepare and flourish. In this unlikely manner, Joseph secures a status as a vizier and near equal to pharaoh, and is able to provide for his own family when they come to Egypt out of starvation and desperation.

The similarities between the stories of Ahiqar and Joseph are thus striking:

1. A foreigner is incorporated into an imperial court.
2. He shows himself to be wise.
3. The wise man is falsely charged with treachery and imprisoned.
4. A crisis arises that can only be solved with extraordinary wisdom or insight.
5. A friendly courtier who is in the wise man's debt delivers him.

Seth Richardson, eds., *Sennacherib at the Gates of Jerusalem: Story, History and Historiography* (Culture and History of the Ancient Near East 71; Leiden: Brill, 2014), 303–6.

6. The wise man is able to solve the crisis.
7. The wise man is rewarded.

Many of these elements are also found, in various forms, in other court stories, such as Daniel and Esther.

The most striking differences between the Ahiqar and Joseph stories are found not in the sections presented above but in the sections that frame the Joseph stories within the larger novella: Genesis 37 and 42–50 have no parallel in the Ahiqar story. That probably is because the novella is made up of smaller parts. The term "novella" emphasizes that the composition is written and crafted, but it is widely recognized that the Joseph novella incorporates stories within it that have an oral character.

Smaller stories within the Joseph cycle can be analyzed individually. For example, the scene in Genesis 41 in which the pharaoh questions Joseph (like the scene in which the pharaoh questions Ahiqar) has a recognizable folkloric structure. Folklorists collected thousands of folktales and cataloged them according to elements of content (motifs) and the structure of their content elements.[14] This resulted in a large number of folktale types—one of which (no. 922) contains the following elements:

1. A person of lower status is called before a person of higher status.
2. A person of higher status expounds the problem.
3. A person of lower status is able to answer.
4. A person of lower status is rewarded.

Clearly, that form fits both Ahiqar and Genesis 41 rather well.[15] Both stories also include elements akin to orally transmitted stories, such as repetition (e.g., pharaoh's outfits in the Ahiqar story and pharaoh's dreams in Gen. 41). This sort of patterning reflects the stories' long process of shaping, which likely included oral transmission.[16]

How far back does the Joseph story go? Some scholars have argued that it finds a literary and historical home where the narrative is set, in second-millennium BCE Egypt, since it shows cultural awareness of certain aspects of Egyptian culture, and since stories of courtiers were also being composed there at that time.[17] These claims for a very early date merit discussion.

---

14. See also A. Aarne and S. Thompson, *The Types of the Folktale* (Folklore Fellows Communications 184; 2nd ed.; Helsinki: Suomalainen tiedeakatemia, 1964).

15. Susan Niditch and Robert Doran, "The Success Story of the Wise Courtier: A Formal Approach," *JBL* 96 (1977): 179–93.

16. One cannot be sure, since "the presence of formulaic language and conventional literary structures in ancient Semitic literatures . . . does not in and of itself bespeak a background in oral performance. Features of originally orally composed texts are incorporated into written literature as well." See Edward L. Greenstein, "Some Developments in the Study of Language and Some Implications for Interpreting Ancient Texts and Cultures," in *Semitic Linguistics: The State of the Art at the Turn of the 21st Century* (ed. S. Izre'el; Israel Oriental Studies 20; Winona Lake, IN: Eisenbrauns, 2002), 462.

17. E.g., K. A. Kitchen, *On the Reliability of the Old Testament* (Grand Rapids: Eerdmans, 2003), 343–72.

There is no extrabiblical attestation at all for Joseph, but the idea of a Semite in a pharaoh's court during the Late Bronze Age is hardly far-fetched. The Egyptians interacted
extensively with the Levant in that period; primarily, they ruled Palestine as imperial governors. One of the Egyptians' methods of rule during the Late Bronze Age was to bring
the princes of Levantine states to the pharaonic court to become familiar with Egyptian
customs and court etiquette. This could be effective in creating sympathy and loyalty, as
reflected in certain Amarna letters. In one, a Levantine nobleman named Yaḫtiru writes,

> A brick may shift from beneath its neighbor, but I shall never shift from beneath
> the feet of the king, my lord. . . . When I was young, he took me to Egypt. I served
> the king, my lord, and I stood in the city gate of the king, my lord. . . . [Now]
> wherever the archers of the king, my lord, go, I go with them. (El Amarna Letter
> No. 296)

This is not the place to survey what is known about the ethnogenesis of ancient Israel (i.e.,
its emergence as a people), but it is certainly conceivable that some of the later Israelites
could trace their roots not only to Semitic slaves, but to Semitic courtiers in Egypt.

The Amarna letters, written in the late thirteenth century BCE between Egyptian
pharaohs and their client-rulers in Palestine, show that one of the challenges Palestine
faced was tribal bands of Semites called ḫapiru (or ḫabiru), who were considered lawless,
low-class outsiders. There have been attempts over the years to relate these outsiders to
the nascent Israelites—that is, the Hebrews.[18] These attempts are not without problems,
but if the association is correct, it is interesting that Pharaoh's wife repeatedly calls Joseph
a "Hebrew" in an apparently derogatory manner when she accuses Joseph of assaulting
her (Gen. 39:14, 17). Perhaps the author intended to have her issue a reminder of Joseph's
humble roots.

It is also true that certain aspects of the stories reflect contact with Egyptian culture—
for example, Joseph's Egyptian wife Asenath (Gen. 41:45) is named for the Egyptian
goddess Neith, and the forty-day period of Jacob's embalming in Genesis 50:3 accurately
reflects an Egyptian ideal burial. However, such knowledge of Egyptian culture could
have been absorbed by Hebrew authors well into the first millennium BCE; that influence
does not require an early date. Indeed, as noted in the general introduction, Hebrew did
not emerge until the first millennium, so the Joseph story could not have been written in
anything like its current form until then.

It is sometimes claimed that the Joseph story is akin to Egyptian court tales of the second millennium, but comparison of the latter with the Joseph and Ahiqar stories shows
that they are not of the same type at all. The only one that really bears comparison is the
story of Sinuhe, from Dynasty 12, in the nineteenth century BCE.[19] In the story, Sinuhe
fears that he, like Ahiqar and Joseph, is out of favor with the royal (in this case, Egyptian)
court. After the death of a king, he hears talk of sedition against the heir, and he fears that
he will be accused of treason. In a moment of panic, he flees; only at the end of his life is

---

18. For discussion, see N. P. Lemche, "ḫabiru/ḫapiru," *ABD* 3:6–10.
19. For the text of the Sinuhe story, see W. K. Simpson, ed., *The Literature of Ancient Egypt: An
Anthology of Stories, Instructions, and Poetry* (3rd ed.; New Haven, CT: Yale University Press, 2003),
54–66.

he invited back and restored to honor. Sinuhe was once thought to be a copy of an actual Egyptian autobiography; however, no such figure is known historically, and the form and content of the story diverge significantly from real tomb inscriptions.[20] Sinuhe is also of an entirely different nature from the court stories mentioned thus far: Instead of succeeding at the court, Sinuhe flourishes while in exile in Palestine, and his restoration to the Egyptian court does not emphasize his wisdom but rather serves as propaganda for the grace of the king. It is a paean to an Egyptian who wishes to go home to his own land and account of an insider's return rather than an outsider's success.

Furthermore, Sinuhe is a native to the court he flees, whereas Ahiqar, Joseph, Daniel, and Esther are foreigners. Unlike Sinuhe, each is a person initially of low standing who is raised up by royal favor. Sinuhe begins the story as a hereditary nobleman and an official of the royal harem. His is not a rags-to-riches story like that of Joseph, who begins as a slave and ends by being told by Pharaoh, "only with regard to the throne will I be greater than you" (Gen. 41:40)—truly a fantastic claim.

When the Egyptian stories are set aside, all of the court stories that fit the type are set in *Eastern* courts—in Assyria, Babylon, and Persia. It is not surprising, then, that the Joseph cycle reflects the concerns of the exilic or postexilic period, when diaspora Jews found themselves having to survive in various foreign settings, including foreign courts.

Comparative, literary, and linguistic data all supply meaningful information about the context of the composition of the Joseph stories, but the combination of oral and written stages of the story's transmission makes it complex and difficult to describe that composition: Does one mean the date at which the story was first told? Or the date at which an author wrote down the story for the first time? Or the date at which the story reached the form in which we read it? These dates surely differ significantly—and they may span centuries. Source critics generally analyze chapters 39–41 as a combination of J (Yahwist) and E (Elohist) sources (note the use of "Yhwh/LORD" in Gen. 39 versus the use of "God" in Gen. 41; see chap. 4 for a discussion of these sources). This would mean that Genesis 39–41 contains a folklore story about Joseph that may have been transmitted orally, but was later written down in the ninth–eighth century BCE (according to the usual dates assigned to J and E). In a parallel or later process, these stories would have been incorporated into the larger national narrative about the salvation of Jacob's family, which was to become the nation Israel.

The stories of the wise son of Israel at the Egyptian court would have meant different things to different people at different times. Whatever they meant to those who first heard them and wrote them down, they came to encapsulate a wise man's duty to glorify God even at a foreign court and to rescue his people even when he was estranged from them. The formation of the Pentateuch as we have it is usually assigned to the period just after the exile, a time when that message would have had special relevance for diaspora Jews.

Why were these stories relevant in a diaspora context? In their successes, Joseph and Ahiqar both embodied (or enacted) court wisdom. In Genesis 41:33, Joseph says, "Let

20. R. B. Parkinson, *The Tale of Sinuhe and Other Ancient Egyptian Poems, 1940–1640 BC* (Oxford: Clarendon Press, 1997).

Pharaoh select a man who is discerning and wise," and this turns out to be Joseph himself. Joseph's wisdom is manifest in his flourishing under Potiphar and even in jail, and his ability to interpret Pharaoh's dreams is to be understood as another manifestation of it. Ahiqar is introduced as "a wise and skillful scribe," and he becomes a teacher of wisdom to Nadin, albeit a failed one. Indeed, the story is paired with a collection of proverbs. Ahiqar's wisdom is also acted out in his clever responses to the pharaoh. Since each story is set in an exotic, foreign land, the message seems to be that one can survive and flourish even in an unfamiliar place with the help of wisdom.

Here one begins to see how the biblical court stories differ from each other, partly because of their different historical contexts. Daniel 2, for example, has a very different perspective on wisdom. Although Daniel 2 shares both a basic outline and numerous more specific details with Genesis 41, it eschews wisdom's promise of universally applicable knowledge that fosters human flourishing in favor of a more sectarian and inward-looking perspective. Joseph's dream interpretations help the empire to flourish, whereas Daniel repeatedly foretells doom for the foreigners (2:36–45; 4:31; 5:26–31); indeed, the Daniel tales are entirely uninterested in the well-being of the empire. Furthermore, Daniel and his compatriots fiercely maintain their Jewish identity by refusing to accept the court's food and wine (Dan. 1) or bow to the statue that Nebuchadnezzar sets up (Dan. 3). By contrast, when Joseph takes his Egyptian office, he is dressed as an Egyptian (Gen. 41:42), so that when his brothers come to Egypt, they do not even recognize him (42:8); he does not use his native language, speaking through an interpreter instead (42:23); and he is buried in Egypt in the style of an Egyptian courtier (50:26).[21]

Both of these stories were read throughout antiquity, and such conflicting views of empire surely coexisted in postexilic Jewish history. Still, the ideology of the Daniel court tales might be said to be more characteristic of a later period, which is why they are more coherent with the apocalyptic visions of the latter half of the book instead of the wisdom traditions that characterize Joseph and Ahiqar. As John Collins wrote,

> The problems with which the tales deal were not likely to arise in the theocratic administration in Jerusalem. On the other hand, those problems were of daily and vital interest to Jews in the diaspora, and especially to Jews who functioned as courtiers or aspired to be "wise men" after the manner of Chaldean and other Gentile wise men.[22]

If one compares the court wisdom of Proverbs, Joseph, and Daniel, one can see a picture of increasing skepticism about governing power and alienation from it. There is a grimness to the Daniel court tales that is foreign to folk literature.[23] Clearly Jews sensed that the God of Israel was growing more and more distant from the reigning king as the

---

21. Both Daniel and Joseph are renamed (Gen. 41:45; Dan. 1:7), though neither name ever sits easily; Joseph's "Zaphenath-paneah" is never used again, while "Belteshazzar" is hardly ever used without the reminder that he is really Daniel.

22. John J. Collins, "The Court-Tales in Daniel and the Development of Apocalyptic," *JBL* 94 (1975): 220.

23. "The more overtly polemical and ideological the narrative is, the more it is removed from mere folktale" (Niditch and Doran, "Success Story," 181).

joyful return of the Persian period gave way to persecutions under Hellenistic rule. This sociopolitical context is one of a number of reasons that the Daniel court stories are usually assigned to a later period than their Babylonian setting would suggest.

In sum, analysis of the court tales of Joseph and Ahiqar by means of historical and literary methods suggests that both stories have some authentic historical flavor, but that both are heavily shaped to suit the interests and needs of later periods. The question of how it looked to live out divine wisdom in the world continued to be answered in different ways at different times.

REFLECTION QUESTIONS

1. Why would stories of foreigners serving at imperial courts be more at home in later periods of ancient Near Eastern history?
2. What effect does the sages' status as foreigners have on the narrative?
3. Why do you think stories of the betrayal and restoration to honor of courtiers would have been popular? What social purpose would they have served?
4. What is the connection between wisdom and court life?
5. How do you imagine these court stories to have been shared? Were they originally only for people at royal courts? Why or why not?
6. What is the role of God or the gods in each text? How do the texts convey their theological messages?

FURTHER READING

Collins, John J. "The Court-Tales in Daniel and the Development of Apocalyptic." *JBL* 94 (1975): 218–34.

Lindenberger, J. M. "Ahiqar: A New Translation and Introduction." Pages 479–507 in vol. 2 of *Old Testament Pseudepigrapha*. Edited by James H. Charlesworth. 2 vols. New York: Doubleday, 1985.

Niditch, Susan, and Robert Doran. "The Success Story of the Wise Courtier: A Formal Approach." *JBL* 96 (1977): 179–93.

Parkinson, R. B. *The Tale of Sinuhe and Other Ancient Egyptian Poems, 1940–1640 BC*. Oxford: Clarendon Press, 1997.

Rindge, Matthew S. "Jewish Identity under Foreign Rule: Daniel 2 as a Reconfiguration of Genesis 41." *JBL* 129 (2010): 85–104.

VanderKam, James C. "Ahikar/Ahiqar (Person)." *ABD* 1:114.

Wills, Lawrence M. *The Jewish Novel in the Ancient World*. Myth and Poetics. Ithaca, NY: Cornell University Press, 1995.

6

Birth Accounts

Sargon and Moses (Exodus 1:7–2:10)

EXODUS 1:7–2:10

When: Ninth century BCE (?); see discussion
Where: Jerusalem
Language: Hebrew

THE BIRTH LEGEND OF SARGON

When: Eighth century BCE
Where: Nineveh
Language: Akkadian
Translation: By the author[1]

> I am Sargon,[2] the mighty king, the king of Akkad.
> My mother was high priestess; I did not know my father.
> My father's kin live in the mountains;
> My city is Azupiranu, which is on the banks of the Euphrates.[3]
> 5   My mother conceived and bore me in secrecy.
> She placed me in a vessel of reeds and sealed its hatch with pitch.
> She gave me over to the river, but it did not overwhelm (me).
> The river carried me away; it brought me to Aqqi, the water bearer.
> Aqqi the water bearer dipped his bucket and lifted *me* up!
> 10   Aqqi the water bearer raised me—as his adopted son.
> Aqqi the water bearer set me to his gardening work.

---

1. Akkadian text: Jerrold S. Cooper and Wolfgang Heimpel, "The Sumerian Sargon Legend," *JAOS* 103 (1983): 67–82.
2. Sargon's name in Akkadian (*Sharru-kin*) means "legitimate king."
3. The location of Azupiranu is unknown; it is unattested outside this text.

While I was gardening, Ishtar took a liking to me,
so that I ruled fifty-five years as king.

I became lord over the black-headed people[4] and governed them.
15   I [cut through] mighty mountains with copper picks;
Over and over again, I ascended the mountain heights;
Over and over again, I traversed the foothills.
Three times I circumnavigated the sea.[5]
I conquered Dilmun [. . .]
20   I went up to great Der [and . . .]
I destroyed [Ka]zallu [. . .]

Whatever king may arise after me,
[Let him rule fifty-five years as king.]
Let him become lord over the black-headed people [and govern them.]
25   Let him cut through mighty [moun]tains with cop[per picks;]
Let him ascend the mountain heights over and over again;
[Let him traverse the foothills over and over again;]
Let him circumnavigate the [sea] three times.
[Let him conquer Dilmun.]
30   Let him go up to great Der
[. . .] from my city Agade . . .

DISCUSSION

Authors have always been prone to turn history into legend, and not only in ancient times. The making of legends has persevered into modern times, from George Washington and the cherry tree to Davy Crockett and the Alamo. Indeed, all of us are surrounded by legends and myths, so that it would appear to be a tendency of the human mind and memory.

Legends have tended to spring up around powerful people. The birth legend of Sargon purports to recount the birth, childhood, and reign of Sargon of Akkad, one of the great kings in Mesopotamian history. Sargon was a real historical figure; he reigned ca. 2340–2284 BCE. Beginning from the city of Akkad, he founded one of the first empires of the ancient Near East, campaigning eastward into Iran, and westward to Mari, Ebla, and perhaps even as far as northern Palestine. This empire helped to establish Akkadian

---

4. This term originated as a designation for the Sumerians in southern Mesopotamia, but by the Neo-Assyrian period it probably referred to all Mesopotamians.

5. This line is partly broken and more woodenly could be translated, "I encircled the land of Tiamat." Since Tiamat is the divine personification of the sea in Mesopotamian mythology, it is possible that this is a reference to a military siege of the "Sealand" region of southern Mesopotamia. But since the context describes feats of exploration, and since Dilmun is usually identified as an island or a distant seacoast, the translation above seems preferable.

(which takes its name from the city of Akkad) as the language of diplomacy and trade in the Near East.

After the discovery of the Sargon text, it was suggested that it might be a copy of an authentic text of the Sargonic period, perhaps copied from a statue. However, no copy of it from anywhere close to the period of Sargon himself has survived, and so it is now accepted that it must be a far later composition. The most natural assumption about its authorship is that it came from the court of Sargon II, a Neo-Assyrian king (722–705) who adopted Sargon's name and thus had a stake in propagating legends about him.

There is an entire genre of Mesopotamian literature called pseudo-autobiography (or fictional autobiography). The form is based on inscriptions by Mesopotamian kings that included three parts: an opening self-introduction, a first-person narrative of the king's accomplishments, and an epilogue with a blessing for those who preserve his words, or a curse for anyone who would efface them. When that inscription form was adapted to pseudepigraphical use, it tended to be poetic and didactic, and to have a message for future kings (i.e., primarily the king who actually had the text written).[6]

Some of the narrative about Sargon's reign is stereotypical for Mesopotamian royal inscriptions—many Neo-Assyrian kings made similar boasts about ascending mountains and conquering distant lands. The fictional nature of the text is clear, since "the historical Sargon could not very well have asserted 'I ruled 55 years as king.'"[7] That would be a bit like the claim (which is at least as early as Philo[8]) that Moses wrote about his own death and burial in Deuteronomy 34:5–7.

The description of Sargon's mother as a high priestess (enētu in Akkadian) has generated a large amount of scholarly conversation: What is the significance of this detail? Such priestesses—one of whom likely would have been associated with temples in many major cities—are thought to have been sworn to chastity except for participation in the ritual of "sacred marriage," in which she might portray a goddess, having intercourse with a king portraying the god. But if Sargon's father were a king, why would a legend glorifying him not say so? Some have concluded that the father must have been someone inappropriate, which would explain why the priestess mother hid her pregnancy and birth and sent Sargon away in secrecy. From another perspective, the mystery surrounding Sargon's paternity leaves open the interpretation that he was fathered by a god. This was a claim that other Mesopotamian kings, such as Eanatum of Lagash, had made before Sargon's time. And indeed, Sargon's successor Naram-Sin explicitly claimed to be divine, calling himself "The God of Agade."

Whatever message about the father the text intended to convey, it seems that the pregnancy would have been deemed socially inappropriate; this would explain why Sargon's mother hid the pregnancy and sent him away. There is a comparison to be made between Sargon and Moses already, in that Moses too is descended from a priestly family, the Levites (Exod. 2:1).

---

6. The genre of didactic instructions in the name of deceased kings was also very active in ancient Egypt, but the comparisons do not concern us here.

7. Tremper Longman, *Fictional Akkadian Autobiography: A Generic and Comparative Study* (Winona Lake, IN: Eisenbrauns, 1991), 56.

8. *De vita Mosis* 2.291.

It is the distinctive opening of Sargon's narrative, however, that is the primary reason this text has fascinated biblical scholars and students. Like Moses, Sargon is placed by his mother in a basket of reeds sealed with pitch, and put on a river. However, the similarity of the act of placing the child on a river may mask different motivations. In the case of Moses, it is an act of desperation; in the case of Sargon, the motive is less clear. Mesopotamian laws attest a practice known as the River Ordeal in which someone whose innocence is in question was cast into a river so that the river-god could determine his fate; the one who survived the ordeal was deemed innocent. Sargon's ordeal is not the same, of course, but a similar abandonment to fate might have been intended for a child whose parentage was seemingly unusual.

Sargon is drawn out by a water bearer called Aqqi. That name can be understood as a verb meaning "I poured," essentially identifying him by his profession—like a baker named Baker or a fisherman named Fisher. Moses' name was similarly given a folk etymology that connected it with being drawn from water: The Hebrew verb *mashah* means "to draw water," and sounds very much like the Hebrew form of Moses' name, *Mosheh*; thus Exodus 2:10 recounts that pharaoh's daughter "named him Moses, 'because,' she said, 'I drew him out of the water.'" Typically, however, scholars identify the real etymology of Moses' name as an Egyptian one, arguing that "Moses" is derived from the common element in names such as Thutmosis ("Thoth created him") or Ramesses ("Ra created him").

It is remarkable how few names are used in either story: Sargon's mother and father are unnamed, as are Moses' father, mother, and sister, and the pharaoh and his daughter. This would seem to support the idea that we are dealing with fables here: the characters are flat stereotypes and agents, rather than being fleshed out.

Aqqi first lifts Sargon out of the water, and then raises him up, putting him to work in his garden. This is by no means a typical upbringing for an Assyrian king. The bestowal of favor by Ishtar (line 12) is a more typical qualification to rule; Ishtar was frequently invoked by Assyrian rulers for blessings and support (see chap. 13).

The closing blessing wishes the future king long rule and success just as Sargon himself had experienced. If Sargon II had this text composed, then he would have been claiming this blessing for himself as the namesake and spiritual heir of Sargon the Great. This would be similar to the situation with another pseudo-autobiographical text from Mesopotamia, the Cuthean Legend, which was written in the persona of Naram-Sin of Akkad (23rd c. BCE) but most likely composed in the time of Naram-Sin of Eshnunna, in the late nineteenth century BCE.[9]

The Sargon text breaks off at the end, so it is difficult to determine whether something else might have followed.[10] One copy of the birth legend has further text on the reverse side of the tablet, but the text is broken and bears no obvious relationship to the Sargon

---

9. Longman, *Fictional Akkadian Autobiography*, 115.

10. Brian Lewis concluded that the structure of the Sargon text was closest to the prologue for a law code, but no such materials have been found as part of any copy of the text. (Brian Lewis, *The Sargon Legend: A Study of the Akkadian Text and the Tale of the Hero Who Was Exposed at Birth* [Cambridge, MA: American Schools of Oriental Research, 1980]).

story, so two different texts may simply have been copied onto opposite sides of one tablet.[11]

The comparison between the Sargon and Moses texts cannot proceed along generic lines. The story from Exodus has none of the features of Mesopotamian autobiographical inscriptions; most basically, it is not even narrated in the first person, but rather the third. Instead, it is the underlying narrative structure—a child is abandoned, saved, and rises to leadership—that is similar. The Moses story unfolds at much greater length, but his leadership of the Hebrews is already foreshadowed immediately after his naming by the account of his killing an abusive Egyptian in 2:11–12.

There are many stories, from the ancient Near East and elsewhere, of an exposed child who is saved and rises to prominence. In the Bible alone, one can point to Genesis 21 (Ishmael), Ezekiel 16 (a personified Jerusalem), and, in a more attenuated form, Genesis 37 and 39 (Joseph). Elsewhere in the ancient Near East, in addition to the Sargon legend, there are fainter echoes from Egypt and Hatti.[12] Scholars have tried to boil such stories down to an archetype to determine the Hebrew author's unique contributions, but this sort of analysis is probably a mistake. There is no archetypal version, only the actual variety found within literary history. Individual stories are best compared to each other, not to an ideal form.

In the case of the Sargon and Moses stories, notable differences emerge:[13]

- Moses is abandoned not for some individual reason (such scandal or economic hardship) but because of a wider threat: genocide.
- Moses is kept by his mother for three months, perhaps to emphasize his parents' reluctance to give him up.
- The sister who watches over Moses is a unique agent, presumably also intended to emphasize the family's concern.
- Moses begins life as a slave, is found and raised by a princess, and then returns to his common roots; Sargon is born to a high priestess, saved by a workman, and then elevated again by a goddess. The patterns of their ascents and descents are thus mirror images of each other.
- Moses' mother maintains contact with him when she is hired by Pharaoh's daughter to be his nursemaid.

This last element is frequently thought to be direct reflection of Mesopotamian legal texts referring to wet-nurse arrangements,[14] but such arrangements were familiar to elites in Egypt as well. A more likely indication that the basic story was at home in a Mesopotamian rather than an Egyptian sphere is that the Egyptians were specifically known for eschewing child exposure.[15]

---

11. Longman, *Fictional Akkadian Autobiography*, 58–59.

12. For a brief discussion, see John D. Currid, *Against the Gods: The Polemical Theology of the Old Testament* (Wheaton, IL: Crossway, 2013), 79–84.

13. Lewis, *The Sargon Legend*, 264.

14. Brevard S. Childs, "The Birth of Moses," *JBL* 84 (1965): 111–12. Such an arrangement was called a *tarbitum* in Akkadian (lit., "enlarging" or "growing").

15. This assumes that it is valid to extrapolate backward from Greek authors such as Diodorus Siculus (1.80.3) and Strabo (17.824).

As the above differences indicate, one distinctive aspect of the Hebrew adaptation of this type-story is its ethnocentrism: it emphasizes the care and humanity of the Hebrew slaves in the face of the evil and inhumanity of the Egyptians. And since Pharaoh's daughter adopts the child her father is trying to kill, and then pays his own mother to raise him, a contrast also is drawn between the foolishness of the Egyptians and the wiliness of the Hebrews. Such ethnic jabs are not a concern of the Sargon text.

Many aspects of these texts point to their literary shaping as legends or fables; but contrary to the connotations that those terms may carry, recognizing the literary features does not necessarily imply a judgment about their historical content. In the case of Sargon, it is quite certain that he was a real king; he is attested in king lists and chronicles. But the line between legend and history turns out to be murkier than some would expect. For example, the early sections of the Sumerian King List, which include legendary figures such as Gilgamesh, were once thought to be literary fictions. Later, however, Sumerologists discovered historical inscriptions from one of those early kings, Enishibbaragesi, so it is now recognized that there is some historical value to the list. Legends may contain history that has become encrusted over time; one has to appraise each case critically.

For that reason, it is difficult to draw firm conclusions about the Moses story. There is no reason that there should not have been a figure such as Moses in the Late Bronze Age, given the general conditions of frequent interchange between Egypt and the Levant, including the holding of Semitic slaves by Egyptians. But absolutely nothing outside the biblical text supports the story, and the biblical story cannot have been written down in anything close to its present form until the emergence of the Hebrew language in the first millennium, so one is looking at a gap of hundreds of years between the (possible) event and the story. The most common scholarly assessment of Moses' birth story is that it is quite old for Hebrew literature. It is part of the J (or Yahwistic) source of the Pentateuch—an author working in the tenth or ninth century BCE who gathered some of Israel's traditions and crafted them into the narrative framework of what is now the Pentateuch. But if so, it probably already then was a traditional tale that was incorporated into that Yahwistic composition.[16]

When the reader is faced with the fact that biblical stories and ancient fables share certain characteristics and features, temptations crowd in: some try to ignore the commonalities in an attempt to affirm the uniqueness and historical truth of the Bible; others reject the idea that the Bible contains any historical data at all in their single-minded focus on its literary formation. A moderate position is both more accurate and more difficult to stake out.

REFLECTION QUESTIONS

1. What are some similarities between the two stories?
2. What are some differences, in either content or form?

16. Childs, "Birth of Moses," 122.

3. One theory about the "Birth of Sargon" text is that Sargon II sought to legitimate his rule by association with his ancient namesake. If one reasoned strictly by analogy, how would this apply to the case of Moses? How is Moses analogous to Sargon of Akkad? Who would be analogous to Sargon II in the case of the Hebrew text?

4. Do you think the argument from analogy suggested in the previous question generates a convincing argument? Why or why not?

5. Tremper Longman classifies the Sargon text as "fictional autobiography." What does "fictional" mean in that case?

6. Should the Moses account be classified as fictional autobiography?

FURTHER READING

Childs, Brevard S. "The Birth of Moses." *JBL* 84 (1965): 109–22.

Lewis, Brian. *The Sargon Legend: A Study of the Akkadian Text and the Tale of the Hero Who Was Exposed at Birth*. Cambridge, MA: American Schools of Oriental Research, 1980.

Longman, Tremper. *Fictional Akkadian Autobiography: A Generic and Comparative Study*. Winona Lake, IN: Eisenbrauns, 1991.

Westenholz, Joan Goodnick. *Legends of the Kings of Akkade*. Winona Lake, IN: Eisenbrauns, 1996. (Esp. 36–49.)

Law Collections

The Laws of Hammurabi and the Covenant Code (Exodus 20–23)

EXODUS 20:1–23:33

When: Tenth–eighth century BCE
Where: Jerusalem
Language: Hebrew

THE LAWS OF HAMMURABI

What: Cuneiform text on black basalt stela, 2.25 m high × 65 cm wide
When: ca. 1750 BCE
Where: Babylon
Language: Akkadian
Translation: Martha T. Roth[1]

When the august god Anu, king of the Anunnaku deities, and the god Enlil, lord of heaven and earth, who determines the destinies of the land, allotted supreme power over all peoples to the god Marduk, the firstborn son of the god Ea, exalted him among the Igigu deities, named the city of Babylon with its august name and made it supreme within the regions of the world, and established for him within it eternal kingship whose foundations are as fixed as heaven and earth, at that time, the gods Anu and Enlil, for the enhancement of the well-being of the people, named me by my name:

Hammurabi, the pious prince, who venerates the gods, to make justice prevail in the land, to abolish the wicked and the evil, to prevent the strong from oppressing the weak, to rise like the sun-god Shamash over all humankind, to illuminate the land.

---

1. Martha T. Roth, *Law Collections from Mesopotamia and Asia Minor* (2nd ed.; ed. Piotr Michalowski; SBLWAW 6; Atlanta: Society of Biblical Literature, 2003).

I am Hammurabi, the shepherd, selected by the god Enlil, he who heaps high abundance and plenty, who perfects every possible thing for the city Nippur, (the city known as) band-of-heaven-and-earth, the pious provider of the Ekur temple;

the capable king, the restorer of the city Eridu, the purifier of the rites of the Eabzu temple;

the onslaught of the four regions of the world, who magnifies the reputation of the city Babylon, who gladdens the heart of his divine lord Marduk, whose days are devoted to the Esagil temple;

seed of royalty, he whom the god Sîn created, enricher of the city of Ur, humble and talented, who provides abundance for the Egishnugal temple;

discerning king, obedient to the god Shamash, the mighty one, who establishes the foundations of the city of Sippar, who drapes the sacred building of the goddess Aja with greenery, who made famous the temple of Ebabbar which is akin to the abode of heaven;

the warrior, who shows mercy to the city of Larsa, who renews the Ebabbar temple for the god Shamash his ally;

the lord who revitalizes the city of Uruk, who provides abundant waters for its people, who raises high the summit of the Eanna temple, who heaps up bountiful produce for the gods Anu and Ishtar;

the protecting canopy of the land, who gathers together the scattered peoples of the city of Isin, who supplies abundance for the temple of Egalmach;

dragon among kings, beloved brother of the god Zababa, founder of the settlement of Kish, who surrounds the Emeteursag temple with splendor, who arranges the great rites for the goddess Ishtar, who takes charge of the temple of Hursagkalamma;

the enemy-ensnaring throw-net, whose companion, the god Erra, has allowed him to obtain his heart's desire, who enlarges the city of Kutu, who augments everything for the Emeslam temple;

the fierce wild bull who gores the enemy, beloved of the god Tutu, the one who makes the city of Borsippa exult, the pious one who does not fail in his duties to the Ezida temple, <the dwelling of> the god of kings;

the one who is steeped in wisdom, who enlarges the cultivated area of the city of Dilbat, who heaps up the storage bins for the mighty god Urash;

the lord, worthy recipient of the scepter and crown bestowed upon him by the wise goddess Mama, who devised the plans of the city of Kesh, who provides the pure food offerings for the goddess Nintu;

the judicious one, the noble one, who allots pasturage and watering place for the cities of Lagash and Girsu, who provides plentiful food offerings for the Eninnu temple;

who seizes the enemies, beloved of (the goddess Ishtar) the able one, who perfects the oracles of the city of Zabala, who gladdens the heart of the goddess Ishtar;

the pure prince, whose prayers the god Adad acknowledges, appeaser of the heart of the god Adad, the hero in the city of Karkara, who installs the proper appointments throughout the Eudgalgal temple;

the king who gives life to the city of Adab, who organizes the Emah temple;

lord of kings, peerless warrior, who granted life to the city of Mashkanshapir, who gives waters of abundance to the Emeslam temple;

wise one, the organizer, he who has mastered all wisdom, who shelters the people of the city of Malgium in the face of annihilation, who founds their settlements in abundance, who decreed eternal pure food offerings for the gods Enki and Damkina who magnify his kingship;

leader of kings, who subdues the settlements along the Euphrates River by the oracular command of the god Dagan, his creator, who showed mercy to the people of the cities of Mari and Tuttul;

the pious prince, who brightens the countenance of the god Tishpak, who provides pure feasts for the goddess Ninazu, who sustains his people in crisis, who secures their foundations in peace in the midst of the city of Babylon;

shepherd of the people, whose deeds are pleasing to the goddess Ishtar, who establishes Ishtar in the Eulmash temple in the midst of Akkad-the-City;

who proclaims truth, who guides the population properly, who restores its benevolent protective spirit to the city of Ashur;

who quells the rebellious, the king who proclaimed the rites for the goddess Ishtar in the city of Nineveh in the Enmesmes temple;

the pious one, who prays ceaselessly for the great gods, scion of Sumu-la-el, mighty heir of Sinmuballit, eternal seed of royalty, mighty king, solar disk of the city of Babylon, who spreads light over the lands of Sumer and Akkad, king who makes the four regions obedient, favored of the goddess Ishtar, am I.

When the god Marduk commanded me to provide just ways for the people of the land (in order to attain) appropriate behavior, I established truth and justice as the declaration of the land, I enhanced the well-being of the people.

At that time:

Laws

§1   If a man accuses another man and charges him with homicide but cannot bring proof against him, his accuser shall be killed.

§2   If a man charges another man with practicing witchcraft but cannot bring proof against him, he who is charged with witchcraft shall go to the divine River Ordeal,[2] he shall indeed submit to the divine River Ordeal; if the divine River Ordeal should overwhelm him, his accuser shall take full legal possession of his estate; if the divine River Ordeal should clear that man and should he survive, he who made the charge of witchcraft against him shall be killed; he who submitted to the divine River Ordeal shall take full legal possession of his accuser's estate.

---

2. The River Ordeal was a way of settling legal disputes that could be resolved through normal means—it symbolized the decision to "refer the case" to the god of the river. The person who was to undergo the ordeal would be cast into the river and had to travel a certain distance. If he came out safely, he was deemed not guilty. If he sank and was overcome, he was deemed guilty and was sentenced. Black states that drowning was not the intended consequence of the ordeal. See further: Jeremy Black and Anthony Green, *Gods, Demons, and Symbols of Ancient Mesopotamia: An Illustrated Dictionary* (Austin: University of Texas Press, 1992), 155–56.

§3   If a man comes forward to give false testimony in a case but cannot bring evidence for his accusation, if that case involves a capital offense, that man shall be killed.

§4   If he comes forward to give (false) testimony for (a case whose penalty is) grain or silver, he shall be assessed the penalty for that case.

[Laws 5–116 are omitted here to limit the length of the reading. They cover crimes such as theft and kidnapping, and also certain business practices, such as regulation of land tenancy, loans, and business partnerships.]

§117   If an obligation is outstanding against a man and he sells or gives into debt service his wife, his son, or his daughter, they shall perform service in the house of their buyer or of the one who holds them in debt service for three years; their release shall be secured in the fourth year.

§118   If he should give a male or female slave into debt service, the merchant may extend the term (beyond the three years), he may sell him; there are no grounds for a claim.

§119   If an obligation is outstanding against a man and he therefore sells his slave woman who has borne him children, the owner of the slave woman shall weigh and deliver the silver which the merchant weighed and delivered (as the loan) and he shall thereby redeem his slave woman.

§120   If a man stores his grain in another man's house, and a loss occurs in the storage bin or the householder opens the granary and takes the grain or he completely denies receiving the grain that was stored in his house—the owner of the grain shall establish his grain before the god, and the householder shall give to the owner of the grain twofold the grain that he took (in storage).

§121   If a man stores grain in another man's house, he shall give 5 silas[3] of grain per kur[4] of grain as annual rent of the granary.

§122   If a man intends to give silver, gold, or anything else to another man for safekeeping, he shall exhibit before witnesses anything which he intends to give, he shall draw up a written contract, and (in this manner) he shall give goods for safekeeping.

§123   If he gives goods for safekeeping without witnesses or a written contract, and they deny that he gave anything, that case has no basis for a claim.

§124   If a man gives silver, gold, or anything else before witnesses to another man for safekeeping and he denies it, they shall charge and convict that man, and he shall give twofold that which he denied.

§125   If a man gives his property for safekeeping and his property together with the householder's property is lost either by (theft achieved through) a breach or by scaling over a wall, the householder who was careless shall make restitution and shall restore to the owner of the property that which was given to him for safekeeping and which he allowed to be lost; the householder shall continue to search for his own lost property, and he shall take it from the one who stole it from him.

§126   If a man whose property is not lost should declare, "My property is lost," and accuse his city quarter, his city quarter shall establish against him before the god that no property of his is lost, and he shall give to his city quarter twofold whatever he claimed.

3. In the Old Babylonian period, a sila was 0.84 liter.
4. A kur was equivalent to 300 silas. Therefore, a kur would have been 252 liters.

§127 If a man causes a finger to be pointed in accusation against an *ugbabtu*[5] or against a man's wife but cannot bring proof, they shall flog that man before the judges and they shall shave off half of his hair.

§128 If a man marries a wife but does not draw up a formal contract for her, that woman is not a wife.

§129 If a man's wife should be seized lying with another male, they shall bind them and cast them into the water; if the wife's master allows his wife to live, then the king shall allow his subject (i.e., the other male) to live.

§130 If a man pins down another man's virgin wife who is still residing in her father's house, and they seize him lying with her, that man shall be killed; that woman shall be released.

§131 If her husband accuses his own wife (of adultery), although she has not been seized lying with another male, she shall swear (to her innocence by) an oath by the god, and return to her house.

§132 If a man's wife should have a finger pointed against her in accusation involving another male, although she has not been seized lying with another male, she shall submit to the divine River Ordeal for her husband.

§133a If a man should be captured and there are sufficient provisions in his house, his wife [. . . she will not] enter [another's house].

§133b If that woman does not keep herself chaste but enters another's house, they shall charge and convict that woman and cast her into the water.

§134 If a man should be captured and there are not sufficient provisions in his house, his wife may enter another's house; that woman will not be subject to any penalty.

§135 If a man should be captured and there are not sufficient provisions in his house, before his return his wife enters another's house and bears children, and afterwards her husband returns and gets back to his city, that woman shall return to her first husband; the children shall inherit from their father.

§136 If a man deserts his city and flees, and after his departure his wife enters another's house—if that man then should return and seize his wife, because he repudiated his city and fled, the wife of the deserter will not return to her husband.

§137 If a man should decide to divorce a *shugitu*[6] who bore him children, or a *naditu*[7] who provided him with children, they shall return to that woman her dowry and they shall give her one half of (her husband's) field, orchard, and property, and she shall raise her children; after she has raised her children, they shall give her a share comparable in value to that of one heir from whatever properties are given to her sons, and a husband of her choice may marry her.

§138 If a man intends to divorce his first-ranking wife who did not bear him children, he shall give her silver as much as was her bridewealth and restore to her the dowry that she brought from her father's house, and he shall divorce her.

§139 If there is no bridewealth, he shall give her 60 shekels of silver as a divorce settlement.

§140 If he is a commoner, he shall give her 20 shekels of silver.

§141 If the wife of a man who is residing in the man's house should decide to leave, and she appropriates goods, squanders her household possessions, or disparages her husband. they shall charge and convict her; and if her husband should declare his intention to divorce her, then he shall divorce her; neither her travel expenses, nor her divorce settlement, nor anything else shall be given to her. If

---

5. A type of priestess.
6. Refers to a class of women, often as second wives.
7. A childless woman, often one dedicated to a god.

her husband should declare his intention to not divorce her, then her husband may marry another woman and that (first) woman shall reside in her husband's house as a slave woman.

§142 If a woman repudiates her husband, and declares, "You will not have marital relations with me"—her circumstances shall be investigated by the authorities of her city quarter, and if she is circumspect and without fault, but her husband is wayward and disparages her greatly, that woman will not be subject to any penalty; she shall take her dowry and she shall depart for her father's house.

§143 If she is not circumspect but is wayward, squanders her household possessions, and disparages her husband, they shall cast that woman into the water.

§144 If a man marries a *naditu*, and that *naditu* gives a slave woman to her husband, and thus she provides children, but that man then decides to marry a *shugitu*, they will not permit that man to do so, he will not marry the *shugitu*.

§145 If a man marries a *naditu*, and she does not provide him with children, and that man then decides to marry a *shugitu*, that man may marry the *shugitu* and bring her into his house; that *shugitu* should not aspire to equal status with the *naditu*.

§146 If a man marries a *naditu*, and she gives a slave woman to her husband, and she (the slave) then bears children, after which that slave woman aspires to equal status with her mistress—because she bore children, her mistress will not sell her; she shall place upon her the slave-hairlock, and she shall reckon her with the slave women.

§147 If she does not bear children, her mistress shall sell her.

§148 If a man marries a woman, and later *la'bum*-disease[8] seizes her and he decides to marry another woman, he may marry, he will not divorce his wife whom *la'bum* disease seized; she shall reside in quarters he constructs and he shall continue to support her as long as she lives.

§149 If that woman should not agree to reside in her husband's house, he shall restore to her her dowry that she brought from her father's house, and she shall depart.

§150 If a man awards to his wife a field, orchard, house, or movable property, and makes out a sealed document for her, after her husband's death her children will not bring a claim against her; the mother shall give her estate to whichever of her children she loves, but she will not give it to an outsider.

§151 If a woman who is residing in a man's house should have her husband agree by binding contract that no creditor of her husband shall seize her (for his debts)— if that man has a debt incurred before marrying that woman, his creditors will not seize his wife; and if that woman has a debt incurred before entering the man's house, her creditors will not seize her husband.

§152 If a debt should be incurred by them after that woman enters the man's house, both of them shall satisfy the merchant.

§153 If a man's wife has her husband killed on account of (her relationship with) another male, they shall impale that woman.

§154 If a man should carnally know his daughter, they shall banish that man from the city.

§155 If a man selects a bride for his son and his son carnally knows her, after which he himself then lies with her and they seize him in the act, they shall bind that man and cast him into the water.

§156 If a man selects a bride for his son and his son does not yet carnally know her, and he himself then lies with her, he shall weigh and deliver to her 30 shekels of silver; moreover, he shall restore to her whatever she brought from her father's house, and a husband of her choice shall marry her.

---

8. This may refer to a contagious skin disease.

§157   If a man, after his father's death, should lie with his mother, they shall burn them both.

§158   If a man, after his father's death, should be discovered in the lap of his (the father's) principal wife who had borne children, that man shall be disinherited from the paternal estate.

§159   If a man who has the ceremonial marriage prestation[9] brought to the house of his father-in-law, and who gives the bridewealth, should have his attention diverted to another woman and declare to his father-in-law, "I will not marry your daughter," the father of the daughter shall take full legal possession of whatever had been brought to him.

§160   If a man has the ceremonial marriage prestation brought to the house of his father-in-law and gives the bridewealth, and the father of the daughter then declares, "I will not give my daughter to you," he shall return twofold everything that had been brought to him.

§161   If a man has the ceremonial marriage prestation brought to the house of his father-in-law and gives the bridewealth, and then his comrade slanders him (with the result that) his father-in-law declares to the one entitled to the wife, "You will not marry my daughter," he shall return twofold everything that had been brought to him; moreover, his comrade will not marry his (intended) wife.

§162   If a man marries a wife, she bears him children, and that woman then goes to her fate, her father shall have no claim to her dowry; her dowry belongs only to her children.

§163   If a man marries a wife but she does not provide him with children, and that woman goes to her fate—if his father-in-law then returns to him the bridewealth that that man brought to his father-in-law's house, her husband will have no claim to that woman's dowry; her dowry belongs only to her father's house.

§164   If his father-in-law should not return to him the bridewealth, he shall deduct the value of her bridewealth from her dowry and restore (the balance of) her dowry to her father's house.

§165   If a man awards by sealed contract a field, orchard, or house to his favorite heir, when the brothers divide the estate after the father goes to his fate, he (the favorite son) shall take the gift which the father gave to him and apart from that gift they shall equally divide the property of the paternal estate.

§166   If a man provides wives for his eligible sons but does not provide a wife for his youngest son, when the brothers divide the estate after the father goes to his fate, they shall establish the silver value of the bridewealth for their young unmarried brother from the property of the paternal estate, in addition to his inheritance share, and thereby enable him to obtain a wife.

§167   If a man marries a wife and she bears him children, and later that woman goes to her fate, and after her death he marries another woman and she bears children, after which the father then goes to his fate, the children will not divide the estate according to the mothers; they shall take the dowries of their respective mothers and then equally divide the property of the paternal estate.

§168   If a man should decide to disinherit his son and declares to the judges, "I will disinherit my son," the judges shall investigate his case and if the son is not guilty of a grave offense deserving the penalty of disinheritance, the father may not disinherit his son.

---

9. A payment; presumably Roth chooses this uncommon English word to distinguish the Akkadian word used here (*biblum*) from the more common *terḫatum*, which is translated "bridewealth" in this law and elsewhere.

§169   If he should be guilty of a grave offense deserving the penalty of disinheritance by his father, they shall pardon him for his first one; if he should commit a grave offense a second time, the father may disinherit his son.

§170   If a man's first-ranking wife bears him children and his slave woman bears him children, and the father during his lifetime then declares to (or: concerning) the children whom the slave woman bore to him, "My children," and he reckons them with the children of the first-ranking wife—after the father goes to his fate, the children of the first-ranking wife and the children of the slave woman shall equally divide the property of the paternal estate; the preferred heir is a son of the first-ranking wife, he shall select and take a share first.

§171   But if the father during his lifetime should not declare to (or: concerning) the children whom the slave woman bore to him, "My children," after the father goes to his fate, the children of the slave woman will not divide the property of the paternal estate with the children of the first-ranking wife. The release of the slave woman and of her children shall be secured; the children of the first-ranking wife will not make claims of slavery against the children of the slave woman. The first-ranking wife shall take her dowry and the marriage settlement which her husband awarded to her in writing, and she shall continue to reside in her husband's dwelling; as long as she is alive she shall enjoy the use of it, but she may not sell it; her own estate shall belong (as inheritance) only to her own children.

§172   If her husband does not make a marriage settlement in her favor, they shall restore to her in full her dowry, and she shall take a share of the property of her husband's estate comparable in value to that of one heir. If her children pressure her in order to coerce her to depart from the house, the judges shall investigate her case and shall impose a penalty on the children; that woman will not depart from her husband's house. If that woman should decide on her own to depart, she shall leave for her children the marriage settlement which her husband gave to her; she shall take the dowry brought from her father's house and a husband of her choice shall marry her.

§173   If that woman should bear children to her latter husband into whose house she entered, after that woman dies, her former and latter children shall equally divide her dowry.

§174   If she does not bear children to her latter husband, only the children of her first husband shall take her dowry.

§175   If a slave of the palace or a slave of a commoner marries a woman of the *awilu*-class[10] and she then bears children, the owner of the slave will have no claims of slavery against the children of the woman of the *awilu*-class.

§176a   And if either a slave of the palace or a slave of a commoner marries a woman of the *awilu*-class, and when he marries her she enters the house of the slave of the palace or of the slave of the commoner together with the dowry brought from her father's house, and subsequent to the time that they move in together they establish a household and accumulate possessions, after which either the slave of the palace or the slave of the commoner should go to his fate—the woman of the *awilu*-class shall take her dowry; furthermore, they shall divide into two parts everything that her husband and she accumulated subsequent to the time that they moved in together, and the slave's owner shall take half and the woman of the *awilu*-class shall take half for her children.

§176b   If the woman of the *awilu*-class does not have a dowry, they shall divide into two parts everything that her husband and she accumulated subsequent to the

10. The *awilu* class referred to free citizens, or gentlemen and gentlewomen of the society.

time that they moved in together, and the slave's owner shall take half and the woman of the *awilu*-class shall take half for her children.

§177   If a widow whose children are still young should decide to enter another's house, she will not enter without (the prior approval of) the judges. When she enters another's house, the judges shall investigate the estate of her former husband, and they shall entrust the estate of her former husband to her later husband and to that woman, and they shall have them record a tablet (inventorying the estate). They shall safeguard the estate and they shall raise the young children; they will not sell the household goods. Any buyer who buys the household goods of the children of a widow shall forfeit his silver; the property shall revert to its owner.

§178   If there is an *ugbabtu*, a *naditu*, or a *sekretu*[11] whose father awards to her a dowry and records it in a tablet for her, but in the tablet that he records for her he does not grant her written authority to give her estate to whomever she pleases and does not give her full discretion—after the father goes to his fate, her brothers shall take her field and her orchard and they shall give to her food, oil, and clothing allowances in accordance with the value of her inheritance share, and they shall thereby satisfy her. If her brothers should not give to her food, oil, and clothing allowances in accordance with the value of her inheritance share and thus do not satisfy her, she shall give her field and her orchard to any agricultural tenant she pleases, and her agricultural tenant shall support her. As long as she lives, she shall enjoy the use of the field, orchard, and anything else which her father gave to her, but she will not sell it and she will not satisfy another person's obligations with it; her inheritance belongs only to her brothers.

§179   If there is an *ugbabtu*, a *naditu*; or a *sekretu* whose father awards to her a dowry and records it for her in a sealed document, and in the tablet that he records for her he grants her written authority to give her estate to whomever she pleases and gives her full discretion—after the father goes to his fate, she shall give her estate to whomever she pleases; her brothers will not raise a claim against her.

§180   If a father does not award a dowry to his daughter who is a cloistered *naditu* or a *sekretu*, after the father goes to his fate, she shall have a share of the property of the paternal estate comparable in value to that of one heir; as long as she lives she shall enjoy its use; her estate belongs only to her brothers.

§181   If a father dedicates (his daughter) to the deity as a *naditu*, a *qadistu*,[12] or a *kulmashitu*[13] but does not award to her a dowry, after the father goes to his fate she shall take her one-third share from the property of the paternal estate as her inheritance, and as long as she lives she shall enjoy its use; her estate belongs only to her brothers.

§182   If a father does not award a dowry to his daughter who is a *naditu* dedicated to the god Marduk of the city of Babylon or does not record it for her in a sealed document, after the father goes to his fate, she shall take with her brothers her one-third share from the property of the paternal estate as her inheritance, but she will not perform any service obligations; a *naditu* dedicated to the god Marduk shall give her estate as she pleases.

§183   If a father awards a dowry to his daughter who is a *shugitu*, gives her to a husband, and records it for her in a sealed document, after the father goes to his fate, she will not have a share of the property of the paternal estate.

11. A type of cloistered woman, usually of high rank.
12. A type of priestess.
13. A cultic prostitute.

§184 If a man does not award a dowry to his daughter who is a *shugitu*, and does not give her to a husband, after the father goes to his fate, her brothers shall award to her a dowry proportionate to the value of the paternal estate, and they shall give her to a husband.

§185 If a man takes in adoption a young child at birth and then rears him, that rearling will not be reclaimed.

§186 If a man takes in adoption a young child, and when he takes him, he (the child?) is seeking his father and mother, that rearling shall return to his father's house.

§187 A child of (i.e., reared by) a courtier who is a palace attendant or a child of (i.e., reared by) a *sekretu* will not be reclaimed.

§188 If a craftsman takes a young child to rear and then teaches him his craft, he will not be reclaimed.

§189 If he should not teach him his craft, that rearling shall return to his father's house.

§190 If a man should not reckon the young child whom he took and raised in adoption as equal with his children, that rearling shall return to his father's house.

§191 If a man establishes his household (by reckoning as equal with any future children) the young child whom he took and raised in adoption, but afterwards he has children (of his own) and then decides to disinherit the rearling, that young child will not depart empty-handed; the father who raised him shall give him a one-third share of his property as his inheritance and he shall depart; he will not give him any property from field, orchard, or house.

§192 If the child of (i.e., reared by) a courtier or the child of (i.e., reared by) a *sekretu* should say to the father who raised him or to the mother who raised him, "You are not my father," or "You are not my mother," they shall cut out his tongue.

§193 If the child of (i.e., reared by) a courtier or the child of (i.e., reared by) a *sekretu* identifies with his father's house and repudiates the father who raised him or the mother who raised him and departs for his father's house, they shall pluck out his eye.

§194 If a man gives his son to a wet nurse and that child then dies while in the care of the wet nurse, and the wet nurse then contracts for another child without the knowledge of his father and mother, they shall charge and convict her, and, because she contracted for another child without the consent of his father and mother, they shall cut off her breast.

§195 If a child should strike his father, they shall cut off his hand.

§196 If an *awilu* should blind the eye of another *awilu*, they shall blind his eye.

§197 If he should break the bone of another *awilu*, they shall break his bone.

§198 If he should blind the eye of a commoner or break the bone of a commoner, he shall weigh and deliver 60 shekels of silver.

§199 If he should blind the eye of an *awilu*'s slave or break the bone of an *awilu*'s slave, he shall weigh and deliver one-half of his value (in silver).

§200 If an *awilu* should knock out the tooth of another *awilu* of his own rank, they shall knock out his tooth.

§201 If he should knock out the tooth of a commoner, he shall weigh and deliver 20 shekels of silver.

§202 If an *awilu* should strike the cheek of an *awilu* who is of status higher than his own, he shall be flogged in the public assembly with 60 stripes of an ox whip.

§203 If a member of the *awilu*-class should strike the cheek of another member of the *awilu*-class who is his equal, he shall weigh and deliver 60 shekels of silver.

§204 If a commoner should strike the cheek of another commoner, he shall weigh and deliver 10 shekels of silver.

§205 If an *awilu*'s slave should strike the cheek of a member of the *awilu*-class, they shall cut off his ear.

§206   If an *awilu* should strike another *awilu* during a brawl and inflict upon him a wound, that *awilu* shall swear, "I did not strike intentionally," and he shall satisfy the physician (i.e., pay his fees).

§207   If he should die from his beating, he shall also swear ("I did not strike him intentionally"); if he (the victim) is a member of the *awilu*-class, he shall weigh and deliver 30 shekels of silver.

§208   If he (the victim) is a member of the commoner-class, he shall weigh and deliver 20 shekels of silver.

§209   If an *awilu* strikes a woman of the *awilu*-class and thereby causes her to miscarry her fetus, he shall weigh and deliver 10 shekels of silver for her fetus.

§210   If that woman should die, they shall kill his daughter.

§211   If he should cause a woman of the commoner-class to miscarry her fetus by the beating, he shall weigh and deliver 5 shekels of silver.

§212   If that woman should die, he shall weigh and deliver 30 shekels of silver.

§213   If he strikes an *awilu*'s slave woman and thereby causes her to miscarry her fetus, he shall weigh and deliver 2 shekels of silver.

§214   If that slave woman should die, he shall weigh and deliver 20 shekels of silver.

§215   If a physician performs major surgery with a bronze lancet upon an *awilu* and thus heals the *awilu*, or opens an *awilu*'s temple with a bronze lancet and thus heals the *awilu*'s eye, he shall take 10 shekels of silver (as his fee).

§216   If he (the patient) is a member of the commoner-class, he shall take 5 shekels of silver (as his fee).

§217   If he (the patient) is an *awilu*'s slave, the slave's master shall give to the physician 2 shekels of silver.

§218   If a physician performs major surgery with a bronze lancet upon an *awilu* and thus causes the *awilu*'s death, or opens an *awilu*'s temple with a bronze lancet and thus blinds the *awilu*'s eye, they shall cut off his hand.

§219   If a physician performs major surgery with a bronze lancet upon a slave of a commoner and thus causes the slave's death, he shall replace the slave with a slave of comparable value.

§220   If he opens his (the commoner's slave's) temple with a bronze lancet and thus blinds his eye, he shall weigh and deliver silver equal to half his value.

§221   If a physician should set an *awilu*'s broken bone or heal an injured muscle, the patient shall give the physician 5 shekels of silver.

§222   If he (the patient) is a member of the commoner-class, he shall give 3 shekels of silver.

§223   If he (the patient) is an *awilu*'s slave, the slave's master shall give the physician 2 shekels of silver.

§224   If a veterinarian performs major surgery upon an ox or a donkey and thus heals it, the owner of the ox or of the donkey shall give the physician as his fee one sixth (of a shekel, i.e., 30 barleycorns) of silver.

§225   If he performs major surgery upon an ox or a donkey and thus causes its death, he shall give one quarter (?) of its value to the owner of the ox or donkey.

§226   If a barber shaves off the slave-hairlock[14] of a slave not belonging to him without the consent of the slave's owner, they shall cut off that barber's hand.

§227   If a man misinforms a barber so that he then shaves off the slave-hairlock of a slave not belonging to him, they shall kill that man and hang him in his own

---

14. The slave-hairlock (in Akkadian: *abbuttu*) refers to a tuft of hair on a certain part of the head, which only slaves had to wear, as a sign of their low status. When a slave was freed, his or her lock was shaved off.

doorway; the barber shall swear, "I did not knowingly shave it off," and he shall be released.

§228   If a builder constructs a house for a man to his satisfaction, he shall give him 2 shekels of silver for each sar[15] of house as his compensation.

§229   If a builder constructs a house for a man but does not make his work sound, and the house that he constructs collapses and causes the death of the householder, that builder shall be killed.

§230   If it should cause the death of a son of the householder, they shall kill a son of that builder.

§231   If it should cause the death of a slave of the householder, he shall give to the householder a slave of comparable value for the slave.

§232   If it should cause the loss of property, he shall replace anything that is lost; moreover, because he did not make sound the house which he constructed and it collapsed, he shall construct (anew) the house which collapsed at his own expense.

§233   If a builder constructs a house for a man but does not make it conform to specifications so that a wall then buckles, that builder shall make that wall sound using his own silver.

§234   If a boatman caulks a boat of 60-kur capacity for a man, he shall give him 2 shekels of silver as his compensation.

§235   If a boatman caulks a boat for a man but does not satisfactorily complete his work and within that very year the boat founders or reveals a structural defect, the boatman shall dismantle that boat and make it sound at his own expense, and he shall give the sound boat to the owner of the boat.

§236   If a man gives his boat to a boatman for hire, and the boatman is negligent and causes the boat to sink or to become lost, the boatman shall replace the boat for the owner of the boat.

§237   If a man hires a boatman and a boat and loads it with grain, wool, oil, dates, or any other lading, and that boatman is negligent and thereby causes the boat to sink or its cargo to become lost, the boatman shall replace the boat which he sank and any of its cargo which he lost.

§238   If a boatman should cause a man's boat to sink and he raises it, he shall give silver equal to half of its value.

§239   If a man hires a boatman, he shall give him 1,800 silas of grain per year.

§240   If a boat under the command of the master of an upstream-boat collides with a boat under the command of the master of a downstream-boat and thus sinks it, the owner of the sunken boat shall establish before the god the property that is lost from his boat, and the master of the upstream-boat who sinks the boat of the master of the downstream-boat shall replace to him his boat and his lost property.

§241   If a man should distrain[16] an ox, he shall weigh and deliver 20 shekels of silver.

§242/243   If a man rents it for one year, he shall give to its owner 1,200 silas of grain as the hire of an ox for the rear (of the team), and 900 silas of grain as the hire of an ox for the middle (of the team).

§244   If a man rents an ox or a donkey and a lion kills it in the open country, it is the owner's loss.

§245   If a man rents an ox and causes its death either by negligence or by physical abuse, he shall replace the ox with an ox of comparable value for the owner of the ox.

---

15. A surface measure equivalent to twelve square cubits.
16. I.e., take an ox in place of a debt payment.

§246   If a man rents an ox and breaks its leg or cuts its neck tendon, he shall replace the ox with an ox of comparable value for the owner of the ox.

§247   If a man rents an ox and blinds its eye, he shall give silver equal to half of its value to the owner of the ox.

§248   If a man rents an ox and breaks its horn, cuts off its tail, or injures its hoof tendon, he shall give silver equal to one quarter of its value.

§249   If a man rents an ox, and a god strikes it down dead, the man who rented the ox shall swear an oath by the god and he shall be released.

§250   If an ox gores to death a man while it is passing through the streets, that case has no basis for a claim.

§251   If a man's ox is a known gorer, and the authorities of his city quarter notify him that it is a known gorer, but he does not blunt (?) its horns or control his ox, and that ox gores to death a member of the *awilu*-class, he (the owner) shall give 30 shekels of silver.

§252   If it is a man's slave (who is fatally gored), he shall give 20 shekels of silver.

§253   If a man hires another man to care for his field, that is, he entrusts to him the stored grain, hands over to him care of the cattle, and contracts with him for the cultivation of the field—if that man steals the seed or fodder and it is then discovered in his possession, they shall cut off his hand.

§254   If he takes the stored grain and thus weakens the cattle, he shall replace twofold the grain which he received.

§255   If he should hire out the man's cattle, or he steals seed and thus does not produce crops in the field, they shall charge and convict that man, and at the harvest he shall measure and deliver 18,000 silas of grain for every buru[17] of land.

§256   If he is not able to satisfy his obligation, they shall have him dragged around through that field by the cattle.

§257   If a man hires an agricultural laborer, he shall give him 2,400 silas of grain per year.

§258   If a man hires an ox driver, he shall give him 1,800 silas of grain per year.

§259   If a man steals a plow from the common irrigated area, he shall give 5 shekels of silver to the owner of the plow.

§260   If he should steal a clodbreaking plow or a harrow, he shall give 3 shekels of silver.

§261   If a man hires a herdsman to herd the cattle or the sheep and goats, he shall give him 2,400 silas of grain per year.

§262   If a man [gives] an ox or a sheep to a [herdsman . . .]

§263   If he should cause the loss of the ox or sheep which were given to him, he shall replace the ox with an ox of comparable value or the sheep with a sheep of comparable value for its owner.

§264   If a shepherd, to whom cattle or sheep and goats were given for shepherding, is in receipt of his complete hire to his satisfaction, then allows the number of cattle to decrease, or the number of sheep and goats to decrease, or the number of offspring to diminish, he shall give for the (loss of) offspring and by-products in accordance with the terms of his contract.

§265   If a shepherd, to whom cattle or sheep and goats were given for shepherding, acts criminally and alters the brand and sells them, they shall charge and convict him and he shall replace for their owner cattle or sheep and goats tenfold that which he stole.

17. A buru is about nineteen acres.

§266   If, in the enclosure, an epidemic should break out or a lion make a kill, the shepherd shall clear himself before the god, and the owner of the enclosure shall accept responsibility for him for the loss sustained in the enclosure.

§267   If the shepherd is negligent and allows mange (?) to spread in the enclosure, the shepherd shall make restitution—in cattle or in sheep and goats—for the damage caused by the mange (?) which he allowed to spread in the enclosure, and give it to their owner.

§268   If a man rents an ox for threshing, 20 silas of grain is its hire.

§269   If he rents a donkey for threshing, 10 silas of grain is its hire.

§270   If he rents a goat for threshing, 1 sila of grain is its hire.

§271   If a man rents cattle, a wagon, and its driver, he shall give 180 silas of grain per day.

§272   If a man rents only the wagon, he shall give 40 silas of grain per day.

§273   If a man hires a hireling, he shall give 6 barleycorns of silver per day from the beginning of the year until (the end of) the fifth month, and 5 barleycorns of silver per day from the sixth month until the end of the year.

§274   If a man intends to hire a craftsman, he shall give, per [day]: as the hire of a . . . , 5 barleycorns of silver; as the hire of a woven-textile worker, 5 barleycorns of silver; as the hire of a linen-worker (?), [x barleycorns] of silver; as the hire of a stone-cutter, [x barleycorns] of silver; as the hire of a bow-maker, [x barleycorns of] silver; as the hire of a smith, [x barleycorns of] silver; as the hire of a carpenter, 4 (?) barleycorns of silver; as the hire of a leatherworker, [x] barleycorns of silver; as the hire of a reedworker, [x] barleycorns of silver; as the hire of a builder, [x barleycorns of] silver.

§275   If a man rents a [. . . -boat], 3 barleycorns of silver per day is its hire.

§276   If a man rents a boat for traveling upstream, he shall give 2½ barleycorns of silver as its hire per day.

§277   If a man rents a boat of 60-kur capacity, he shall give one sixth (of a shekel, i.e., 30 barleycorns) of silver per day as its hire.

§278   If a man purchases a slave or slave woman and within his one-month period epilepsy then befalls him, he shall return him to his seller and the buyer shall take back the silver that he weighed and delivered.

§279   If a man purchases a slave or slave woman and then claims arise, his seller shall satisfy the claims.

§280   If a man should purchase another man's slave or slave woman in a foreign country, and while he is traveling about within the (i.e., his own) country the owner of the slave or slave woman identifies his slave or slave woman—if they, the slave and slave woman, are natives of the country, their release shall be secured without any payment.

§281   If they are natives of another country, the buyer shall declare before the god the amount of silver that he weighed, and the owner of the slave or slave woman shall give to the merchant the amount of silver that he paid, and thus he shall redeem his slave or slavewoman.

§282   If a slave should declare to his master, "You are not my master," he (the master) shall bring charge and proof against him that he is indeed his slave, and his master shall cut off his ear.

Epilogue

These are the just decisions which Hammurabi, the able king, has established and thereby has directed the land along the course of truth and the correct way of life.

I am Hammurabi, noble king. I have not been careless or negligent toward human-kind, granted to my care by the god Enlil, and with whose shepherding the god Marduk charged me. I have sought for them peaceful places, I removed serious difficulties. I spread light over them. With the mighty weapon which the gods Zababa and Ishtar bestowed upon me, with the wisdom which the god Ea allotted to me, with the ability which the god Marduk gave me, I annihilated enemies everywhere, I put an end to wars, I enhanced the well-being of the land, I made the people of all settlements lie in safe pastures, I did not tolerate anyone intimidating them. The great gods having chosen me, I am indeed the shepherd who brings peace, whose scepter is just. My benevolent shade is spread over my city, I held the people of the lands of Sumer and Akkad safely on my lap. They prospered under my protective spirit, I maintained them in peace, with my skillful wisdom I sheltered them.

In order that the mighty not wrong the weak, to provide just ways for the waif and the widow, I have inscribed my precious pronouncements upon my stela and set it up before the statue of me, the king of justice, in the city of Babylon, the city which the gods Anu and Enlil have elevated, within the Esagil, the temple whose foundations are fixed as are heaven and earth, in order to render the judgments of the land, to give the verdicts of the land, and to provide just ways for the wronged.

I am the king preeminent among kings. My pronouncements are choice, my ability is unrivaled. By the command of the god Shamash, the great judge of heaven and earth, may my justice prevail in the land. By the order of the god Marduk, my lord, may my engraved image not be confronted by someone who would remove it. May my name always be remembered favorably in the Esagil temple which I love.

Let any wronged man who has a lawsuit come before the statue of me, the king of justice, and let him have my inscribed stela read aloud to him, thus may he hear my precious pronouncements and let my stela reveal the lawsuit for him; may he examine his case, may he calm his (troubled) heart, (and may he praise me), saying:

"Hammurabi, the lord, who is like a father and begetter to his people, submitted himself to the command of the god Marduk, his lord, and achieved victory for the god Marduk everywhere. He gladdened the heart of the god Marduk, his lord, and he secured the eternal well-being of the people and provided just ways for the land."

May he say thus, and may he pray for me with his whole heart before the gods Marduk, my lord, and Zarpanitu, my lady. May the protective spirits, the gods who enter the Esagil temple, and the very brickwork of the Esagil temple, make my daily portents auspicious before the gods Marduk, my lord, and Zarpanitu, my lady.

May any king who will appear in the land in the future, at any time, observe the pronouncements of justice that I inscribed upon my stela. May he not alter the judgments that I rendered and the verdicts that I gave, nor remove my engraved image. If that man has discernment, and is capable of providing just ways for his land, may he heed the pronouncements I have inscribed upon my stela, may that stela reveal for him the traditions, the proper conduct, the judgments of the land that I rendered, the verdicts of the land that I gave and may he, too, provide just ways for all humankind in his care. May he render their judgments, may he give their verdicts, may he eradicate the wicked and the evil from his land, may he enhance the well-being of his people.

I am Hammurabi, king of justice, to whom the god Shamash has granted (insight into) the truth. My pronouncements are choice, and my achievements are unrivaled; they are meaningless only to the fool, but to the wise they are praiseworthy. If that man (a future ruler) heeds my pronouncements which I have inscribed upon my stela, and does not reject my judgments, change my pronouncements, or alter my engraved image, then may the god Shamash lengthen his reign, just as (he has done) for me, the king of justice, and so may he shepherd his people with justice.

(But) should that man not heed my pronouncements, which I have inscribed upon my stela, and should he slight my curses and not fear the curses of the gods, and thus overturn the judgments that I rendered, change my pronouncements, alter my engraved image, erase my inscribed name and inscribe his own name (in its place)—or should he, because of fear of these curses, have someone else do so—that man, whether he is a king, a lord, or a governor, or any person at all, may the great god Anu, father of the gods, who has proclaimed my reign, deprive him of the sheen of royalty, smash his scepter, and curse his destiny.

May the god Enlil, the lord, who determines destinies, whose utterance cannot be countermanded, who magnifies my kingship, incite against him even in his own residence disorder that cannot be quelled and a rebellion that will result in his obliteration; may he cast as his fate a reign of groaning, of few days, of years of famine, of darkness without illumination, and of sudden death; may he declare with his venerable speech the obliteration of his city, the dispersion of his people, the supplanting of his dynasty, and the blotting out of his name and his memory from the land.

May the goddess Ninlil, the great mother, whose utterance is honored in the Ekur temple, the mistress who makes my portents auspicious, denounce his case before the god Enlil at the place of litigation and verdict; may she induce the divine king Enlil to pronounce the destruction of his land, the obliteration of his people, and the spilling of his life force like water.

May the god Ea, the great prince, whose destinies take precedence, the sage among the gods, all-knowing, who lengthens the days of my life, deprive him of all understanding and wisdom, and may he lead him into confusion; may he dam up his rivers at the source; may he not allow any life-sustaining grain in his land.

May the god Shamash, the great judge of heaven and earth, who provides just ways for all living creatures, the lord, my trust, overturn his kingship; may he not render his judgments, may he confuse his path and undermine the morale of his army; when divination is performed for him, may he provide an inauspicious omen portending the uprooting of the foundations of his kingship and the obliteration of his land; may the malevolent word of the god Shamash swiftly overtake him, may he uproot him from among the living above and make his ghost thirst for water below in the nether world.

May the god Sîn, my creator, whose oracular decision prevails among the gods, deprive him of the crown and throne of kingship, and impose upon him an onerous punishment, a great penalty for him, which will not depart from his body; may he conclude every day, month, and year of his reign with groaning and mourning; may he unveil before him a contender for the kingship; may he decree for him a life that is no better than death.

May the god Adad, lord of abundance, the canal-inspector of heaven and earth, my helper, deprive him of the benefits of rain from heaven and flood from the springs, and may he obliterate his land through destitution and famine; may he roar fiercely over his city, and may he turn his land into the abandoned hills left by flood.

May the god Zababa, the great warrior, the firstborn son of the Ekur temple, who travels at my right side, smash his weapon upon the field of battle; may he turn day into night for him, and make his enemy triumph over him.

May the goddess Ishtar, mistress of battle and warfare, who bares my weapon, my benevolent protective spirit, who loves my reign, curse his kingship with her angry heart and great fury; may she turn his auspicious omens into calamities; may she smash his weapon on the field of war and battle, plunge him into confusion and rebellion, strike down his warriors, drench the earth with their blood, make a heap of the corpses of his soldiers upon the plain, and may she show his soldiers no mercy; as for him, may she deliver him into the hand of his enemies, and may she lead him bound captive to the land of his enemy.

May the god Nergal, the mighty one among the gods, the irresistible onslaught, who enables me to achieve my triumphs, burn his people with his great overpowering weapon like a raging fire in a reed thicket; may he have him beaten with his mighty weapon, and shatter his limbs like (those of) a clay figure.

May the goddess Nintu, august mistress of the lands, the mother, my creator, deprive him of an heir and give him no offspring; may she not allow a human child to be born among his people.

May the goddess Ninkarrak, daughter of the god Anu, who promotes my cause in the Ekur temple, cause a grievous malady to break out upon his limbs, an evil demonic disease, a serious carbuncle which cannot be soothed, which a physician cannot diagnose, which he cannot ease with bandages, which, like the bite of death, cannot be expunged; may he bewail his lost virility until his life comes to an end.

May the great gods of heaven and earth, all the Anunnaku deities together, the protective spirit of the temple, the very brickwork of the Ebabbar temple, curse that one, his seed, his land, his troops, his people, and his army with a terrible curse.

May the god Enlil, whose command cannot be countermanded, curse him with these curses and may they swiftly overtake him.

SUGGESTIONS FOR COMPARISON

Exod. 20:1–2	LH Prologue[18]
Exod. 21:2–6	LH 117, 175, 282
Exod. 21:7–11	LH 117, 148–49, 154–56, 178
Exod. 21:12–14	LH 207
Exod. 21:15–17	LH 192–93, 195

18. List based on table 1.1 in David P. Wright, *Inventing God's Law: How the Covenant Code of the Bible Used and Revised the Laws of Hammurabi* (New York: Oxford University Press, 2009), 9.

Exod. 21:18–19	LH 206
Exod. 21:20–21	LH 208
Exod. 21:22–23	LH 209–14
Exod. 21:23–25	LH 196–97
Exod. 21:23–27	LH 196–201
Exod. 21:28–32, 35–36	LH 250–52
Exod. 21:33–34	LH 229–30
Exod. 22:1, 4	LH 253–65
Exod. 22:6–8	LH 265–66
Exod. 22:9–12	LH 266–67
Exod. 22:13–14	LH 268–71
Exod. 23:20–33	LH Epilogue

DISCUSSION

The category of "laws" will likely appear familiar to most readers. We live in societies with laws today, even if many of us have only a murky idea about how they are constructed and how they function. (For example, are U.S. readers aware that federal law is codified in the United States Code, which is reissued in a major edition every six years?) The question of how law functioned (and what it was) is even more difficult to answer for ancient societies.

From the broadest perspective, the laws of a society may serve as a window into its values: Where does law come from and whom does it serve? What is forbidden? What is valued? Where do social boundaries lie? What form does punishment take? What are the roles of deities and humans? However, laws (like any texts) rarely correlate precisely to reality. They are ideological productions, used to project and maintain a certain order. If this is true today, it was even more so in the ancient Near East.

The cuneiform legal tradition is very ancient, and collections of laws are attested from an array of places and times. Despite the ample data, significant questions remain about why laws were collected, how the collections functioned, and how to explain the similarities among them. The earliest Mesopotamian cuneiform law collections are the Laws of Ur-Namma (ca. 2100 BCE, from the city of Ur) and the Laws of Lipit-Ishtar (ca. 1930 BCE, from the city of Isin), each of which is written in Sumerian and named for the king who propagated it. In both of those cases, the collection and propagation of laws carried an implicit claim to authority. In the case of the Laws of Ur-Namma, it probably helped Ur-Namma (or his son, Shulgi) symbolically to solidify the independence that the city had won from Uruk. In the case of Lipit-Ishtar, the law collection simply reflected Isin's status as the dominant political power in Lower Mesopotamia at that time.

The cuneiform legal tradition remained active at least into the Neo-Babylonian period, since a collection from about 700 BCE has been found in Sippar. Between these two temporal extremes, there are other examples from Babylonia, such as the Old Babylonian Laws of Eshnunna (1770 BCE) and the Laws of Hammurabi, the largest extant collection. Along with a pair of law collections from the Middle Assyrian period (11th c.

BCE), all of these are written in Akkadian. The collections share numerous similar laws, but none is a mere copy or updating of an earlier collection, nor even an updating of earlier language; instead, each one must in some way have responded to the situation in which it was compiled.

Legal traditions similar to those of Mesopotamia are known from other ancient Near Eastern contexts apart from the Bible. The Hittites collected laws as early as the Old Kingdom period (17th and 16th centuries), and these continued to be copied and sometimes reinterpreted for more than five hundred years. Thus it is clear that there was some dispersion of Mesopotamian legal traditions. However, nothing resembling these extensive law codes has been recovered from Egypt or anywhere in the West Semitic sphere except the Bible.

Ancient Near Eastern laws can be grouped into two types, broadly speaking: casuistic and apodictic. Casuistic laws (or case laws) introduce a situation ("If a man accuses another man . . .") and prescribe a course of action in response. Apodictic laws flatly forbid a certain action (e.g., "You shall not steal"). Readers should note which forms are used in each collection and consider the impact and likely social location of each form.

It has often been supposed that apodictic law, which in the case of the Covenant Code is described as having been spoken by God, must have originated within a religious setting, in which it would have been natural for a deity to speak in absolute terms. By contrast, it might appear that casuistic law was intended for use in courts of law. The epilogue to Hammurabi's Code certainly seems to invite the people to use the stela as a standard of justice: "Let any wronged man who has a lawsuit come before the statue of me, the king of justice, and let him have my inscribed stela read aloud to him, thus may he hear my precious pronouncements and let my stela reveal the lawsuit for him."

However, it appears that these law collections were rarely, if ever, referred to in court settings as laws are today. Hundreds of thousands of ancient Near Eastern legal documents record proceedings of various kinds, and scarcely any allude to anyone referencing a written law code. There is one Old Babylonian letter in which an administrator tells one of his functionaries at another site that the wages for workers there are "recorded on a stela."[19] However, the wages described in the letter are three times what is prescribed for workers in Hammurabi's Law No. 274, which is from roughly the same period. Does the Hammurabi stela set a sort of minimum wage, or does the relationship between such laws and actual practice need to be reconsidered in less pragmatic terms? The promulgation of laws by the king in such a stela might have had mostly a propagandistic or votive purpose; that is to say, the king was seeking to make a statement about his authority before the people, and about his piety, before the gods.

Further data aiding the interpretation of laws of Hammurabi are supplied by the iconography of the stela (see fig. 1). Since only a tiny percentage of people could read cuneiform (even where it was the native writing system), the image would have been the primary way that the stela conveyed its message to nonexperts.[20] The interpretation of

19. Roth, *Law Collections*, 5–6.
20. We do not know how the stela was originally displayed, since it was recovered not in Babylonia but in Susa, where it had been taken as plunder by an Elamite king. The same king effaced some

ancient iconography is now a flourishing field in its own right, and the stela provides a case study in why it is useful and not always straightforward. At the top of the stela is an image of the Mesopotamian sun-god Shamash enthroned at the right, and Hammurabi stands to the left with his hand raised in a posture of worship. Discussions of the stela frequently describe this scene as Shamash delivering the laws to Hammurabi, but that is incorrect. Instead, Shamash is handing Hammurabi a scepter, which symbolizes the authority to govern and to give laws. Shamash did not personify justice in the way that Maat did in Egypt, but in his role as the sun-god he was seen as the one who brought all truth into the light. Therefore, he was the divine judge, and he had the authority to delegate that power to the king.

Turning to biblical law, the so-called Covenant Code in Exodus is typically limited to Exodus 20:23–23:19, but the rest of Exodus 20–23 provides literary context. The framing verses include the Ten Commandments (20:1–17), a theophany on Mount Sinai (20:18–22), and Yhwh's closing promises to the people (23:20–33). The laws of the Covenant Code are frequently considered to be the oldest legal collection in the Bible, with their compilation perhaps dating to the tenth century. This is due to a perceived egalitarian outlook that some scholars have thought reflected a premonarchic society. That is to say, although the Hebrew laws refer to slaves, there are no class distinctions among the free Israelites as there were among the Babylonian citizens in Hammurabi's Code (e.g., *awilu* vs. commoner). The agrarian character of the Covenant Code is also frequently remarked upon; it might reflect a society that had not developed large urban centers or the more complex economy that accompanies them.

There are two other major law collections in the Bible: the Priestly Code (in Lev. 1–26) and the Deuteronomic Code (Deut. 4:44–28:68). These collections do not always agree with one another, so at most one can speak of competing sets of authoritative law, which were propagated at different times and under different circumstances.

Such conflicts are not likely to have caused practical problems. There is little indication in the Bible that written law collections were referred to in legal proceedings. This is despite ample references to legal practices: kings as judges (e.g., 2 Sam. 15:2–6; 1 Kgs. 3:28; 3:9–12), judges appointed by kings (2 Chr. 19:5; Deut. 16:18), and local courts where village elders or town councils presided (e.g., Deut. 21:2–3; 1 Kgs. 21:8–11; Ruth 4:2, 9–11; Deut. 25:7–9). Moses does say in Exod. 18:16 that when a dispute comes to him, "I decide between one person and another, and *I make known to them the statutes and instructions of God*" (emphasis added). Jethro then encourages Moses to teach the statutes and instructions to others so that they can lift the burden of judging from his shoulders (18:20). This is surely an etiological story, an explanation for some version of the Israelite judicial system.

Since no ancient law code comes close to covering every imaginable legal dispute, one possible conclusion is that the laws were at most learned as a way of passing along principles that could be adapted to new situations. Some scholars have gone further, arguing that biblical and ancient Near Eastern law codes were merely esoteric treatises that did

---

of the bottom laws from the stela and inscribed his own name—ironic, given the warning against just that action in the epilogue.

not apply to real life, and that the scribes who compiled them were more interested in theory than practice. Still others have thought that law codes were composed primarily for the moral education of kings and other elites. In weighing these options, Bruce Wells points out that there are instances where biblical and ancient Near Eastern laws closely reflect decisions recorded in actual court proceedings; therefore, he concludes that although the collections did not *prescribe* what kings or judges must do, they did *describe* "legal rules and customs that were traditionally practiced."[21]

It is remarkable how similar certain laws are. For example, the laws pertaining to a goring ox in Laws of Hammurabi 250–52 may be compared with Exodus 21:28–32:

> *LH 250:* If an ox gores to death a man while it is passing through the streets, that case has no basis for a claim.
>
> *LH 251:* If a man's ox is a known gorer, and the authorities of his city quarter notify him that it is a known gorer, but he does not blunt (?) its horns or control his ox, and that ox gores to death a member of the *awilu*-class, he (the owner) shall give 30 shekels of silver.
>
> *LH 252:* If it is a man's slave (who is fatally gored), he shall give 20 shekels of silver.
>
> *Exodus 21:28* When an ox gores a man or a woman to death, the ox shall be stoned, and its flesh shall not be eaten; but the owner of the ox shall not be liable.
>
> *Exodus 21:29* If the ox has been accustomed to gore in the past, and its owner has been warned but has not restrained it, and it kills a man or a woman, the ox shall be stoned, and its owner also shall be put to death.
>
> *Exodus 21:30* If a ransom is imposed on the owner, then the owner shall pay whatever is imposed for the redemption of the victim's life.
>
> *Exodus 21:31* If it gores a boy or a girl, the owner shall be dealt with according to this same rule.
>
> *Exodus 21:32* If the ox gores a male or female slave, the owner shall pay to the slaveowner thirty shekels of silver, and the ox shall be stoned.

In each case, the owner of a goring ox is not liable for the goring, *unless* the owner could have known that it was prone to gore. (Though the biblical law distinctively prescribes the destruction of the ox, which would have been a serious economic loss to the owner.)

If the owner of the ox knew it was prone to gore, in Hammurabi's Law he must compensate the loss with a payment. In Exodus 21:32, the Covenant Code allows the owner of a slave to be compensated in the same way. Because the laws are from different times and places, it would be difficult to compare the value of the payments, though at face value they are similar.

The biblical law implicitly values different citizens' lives differently (as the comment about children in v. 31 shows), and both sets of laws value free citizens differently from slaves. The biblical law is sterner in the case of an ox owner whose negligence leads to the death of a free man. In that case the owner is to suffer the death penalty, and the ox is to be stoned; strikingly, Hammurabi's Law makes no provision for the punishment of either the owner or the ox. Does the biblical law reflect a greater legal pressure to maintain the well-being of its community? Sometimes one reads that biblical law is more

---

21. Bruce Wells, "What Is Biblical Law? A Look at Pentateuchal Rules and Near Eastern Practice," *CBQ* 70 (2008): 229.

stringent because of its religious character. The idea is that because God is the biblical lawgiver, mere lawbreaking becomes sin, and biblical law must be harsher to maintain the holiness and purity of the divine. But since the Mesopotamians saw their gods as the ultimate source of the authority behind the law as well, this assertion can be questioned: Why was Yhwh's holiness more zealously protected in some cases than Shamash's? Or why would Yhwh's holiness have been thought to be threatened more than Shamash's by lawbreaking?

Another set of texts frequently compared are the examples of *lex talionis* (law of retribution) from each collection:

> *LH 196:* If an *awilu* should blind the eye of another *awilu*, they shall blind his eye.
> *LH 197:* If he should break the bone of another *awilu*, they shall break his bone.[22]

> *Exodus 21:23–25* If any harm follows, then you shall give life for life, eye for eye, tooth for tooth, hand for hand, foot for foot, burn for burn, wound for wound, stripe for stripe. [See also Deut. 19:21.]

In our times, this sort of retributive justice has been much criticized (e.g., the common bumper sticker, "An eye for an eye makes the whole world blind"[23]), and these laws have led some moderns to think of ancient Near Eastern cultures as barbaric. However, it is important to note that these laws may often have had the effect of *limiting* disproportionate punishment: If someone were to put out your eye, might you not want to kill that person? But the principle of retributive justice forbids it. Furthermore, the punishments that our cultures prefer were not available in the ancient Near East. In particular, there was no system for long-term incarcerations; no "jail terms" are ever referred to in legal texts.[24] What remained were the punishments that *are* frequently attested in ancient Near Eastern texts: monetary retribution, banishment, disfigurement, and death.

Because of the similarities between the laws (and the underlying concerns) of the Laws of Hammurabi and biblical law, they take part in a broader debate about the way that legal traditions were passed along in the ancient Near East. The issues are much the same whether one is talking about the Covenant Code or the Neo-Babylonian Laws. In the simplest terms, did the authors of a new legal code have some sort of copy of an earlier code to work with, or were the contours of legal tradition simply known to educated people in the ancient world in much the same way as people today recognize the conventions of popular music or fairy tales at an almost subconscious level? Both viewpoints are reflected in the list for further reading.

Another example of the diffusion of cuneiform law traditions comes from closer to the world of ancient Israel: Recently, two fragments of a cuneiform tablet were discovered at Hazor that preserve small portions of a law collection. They date to the Middle Bronze Age, well before the emergence of Israel in the region (i.e., when the city was under

---

22. See also LH 229–32.

23. This quotation is regularly attributed to Gandhi or Martin Luther King Jr.; both made similar comments, but apparently not in this exact phrasing.

24. There were certainly jails, but presumably they could not accommodate large numbers of people.

Canaanite rule and Akkadian was the language used for many official purposes). The text specifies payments to compensate for harm done to a slave, and thus parallels other cuneiform law collections from Mesopotamia and Hatti, but it is not a copy of any existing code. The text is written by an expert scribe, and was found on the acropolis of the city, so its excavators hypothesize that it was a royal law collection promulgated by the king of Hazor.[25]

In a later period, Hazor was an Israelite city,[26] but it remains to be determined how much of the Mesopotamian scribal tradition survived in the Levant when many of the Canaanite cities were destroyed at the end of the Late Bronze Age. This transition brought a great disruption of cultural continuity. West Semitic dialects such as Phoenician, Aramaic, and Hebrew replaced Akkadian as the administrative language of the region. It is possible (although the point is debated) that some scribes continued to be able to read cuneiform, and even more likely that some elites were able to understand spoken Akkadian. Certainly these would have been important skills when the Mesopotamian powers rose to dominate the Levant in the first millennium.

Many of the similarities in the chart above ("Suggestions for Comparison") have long been noted, but their significance is still disputed. Recently, David P. Wright argued that the Covenant Code is "directly, primarily and throughout dependent upon the Laws of Hammurabi."[27] He bases this not only on the comparable content, but also on the similar sequencing of certain laws. The reader should set these laws side by side and consider how likely direct literary dependence is. It is important to note that the eighteenth-century BCE Laws of Hammurabi necessarily predate the Covenant Code by at least four hundred to five hundred years. Even on a strictly literalist reading of the biblical account, in which the law was delivered to Moses himself after the exodus, the promulgation of this law collection could have been no earlier than the thirteenth century. Therefore, if there was literary influence, it can only have been exercised by the Mesopotamian laws on the Israelite laws.

Wright's argument is a minority view. Whereas some of the specific laws are similar, the relationship between other texts that Wright compares is much looser (e.g., Exod. 22:6–8 and LH 265–66, which Wright groups as laws of deposit). Wells points out that the Covenant Code shares similar features with *all* of the extant law collections, both earlier and later. He argues that the larger number of similarities to Hammurabi's is due simply to its larger size. Thus he prefers to speak of legal "meta-traditions" that spanned much of the ancient Near East; for him, the basic similarities between the collections are explained not by biblical authors' copying of earlier texts, but by the fact that all these legal scribes were "immersed in the life of the ancient Near Eastern culture."[28]

Despite the similarities between the law collections, it is important to note the different uses to which the various collections were put, which are reflected less in the laws

---

25. W. Horowitz, T. Oshima, and F. Vukosavovic, "Hazor 18: Fragments of a Cuneiform Law Collection from Hazor," *Israel Exploration Journal* 62 (2012): 174.

26. According to the Bible, Hazor was rebuilt by Solomon (1 Kgs. 9:15) and flourished during the divided monarchy under the Israelite (northern) kings Ahab and Jeroboam II.

27. Wright, *Inventing God's Law*, 3.

28. Bruce Wells, "The Covenant Code and Near Eastern Legal Traditions: A Response to David P. Wright," *Maarav* 13 (2006): 116, 118.

themselves than in their framing. The biblical laws have the character of covenantal stipulations since they are issued by a divine sovereign, along with promises of blessings if they are kept, and the people agree to them (Exod. 24; see also chap. 9 of this volume). The prologue and epilogue of the Hammurabi text, by contrast, are works of royal propaganda, portraying the king as a "pious prince" who executes justice on behalf of the gods. As noted above, law collections were ideological compositions that could serve various purposes. The final literary form of each text is thus independent of and secondary to the legal traditions themselves.

Furthermore, there are arguably underlying theological differences between Mesopotamian and Israelite law. In Mesopotamian thought, there was a notion of justice known as *kittum* (in Akkadian). On the one hand, some texts say that *kittum* was handed down by Shamash, who was the sun god and the god of justice, as well as by other major deities, such as Marduk. On the other hand, *kittum* had an authority separate from the gods and could be conceptualized as a deity itself, a daughter of Shamash (comparable to personified Wisdom in Proverbs, or the Egyptian goddess Maat). In that role, *kittum* could be viewed as supradivine, having an authority equivalent at least to some deities, so that not only humans, but even to some extent the gods, were thought to be subject to it (even if the gods are rarely portrayed as being called to account for themselves). For example, in the wisdom dialogue called "The Babylonian Theodicy" (see chap. 21), a speaker who argues for normative theology accuses that a skeptic has "forsaken what is right [*kitta*[29]] and blasphemes against your god's designs." Depending how the parallelism is interpreted, the god's designs might be seen as equivalent with *kittum*, or the two may express distinct sources of authority against which the other interlocutor is accused of sinning. Since "your god" appears to refer to a personal god, and thus a lesser deity than Shamash, the latter interpretation is reasonably likely.

In Israel and Judah, by contrast, Yhwh was most often portrayed as the supreme agent of justice,[30] and his actions often seem to be independent of the moral standards applied to humans. Then again, in the stories of Job[31] and Abraham (who bargains with God in Gen. 18:23–33), humans do challenge God on the basis of an idea of justice that seems to be separate from him: "Shall not the Judge of all the earth do what is just?" (Gen. 18:25).

REFLECTION QUESTIONS

1. What does the prologue of the Laws of Hammurabi seek to accomplish? How does this compare with the opening of Exodus 20? Are there other biblical texts that could be compared with the Hammurabi prologue?

---

29. *Kitta* is the same word as *kittum* with a different nominal case ending.

30. E.g., "Many seek the favor of a ruler, but it is from Yhwh that one gets justice" (Prov. 29:26); "Yhwh of hosts is exalted by justice" (Isa. 5:16); "Yhwh is a God of justice" (Isa. 30:18).

31. For example, God is viewed separately from justice in Job's cry, "Let me be weighed in a just balance, and let God know my integrity!" (31:6), and the statement that Elihu "was angry at Job because he justified himself rather than God" (32:2).

2. What does the epilogue of the Laws of Hammurabi seek to accomplish? How does this compare with the closing of Exodus 23?

3. Taken holistically, how would you compare or contrast the literary settings of these two law collections?

4. Where does law derive from in the Hammurabi Code, how is it delivered, and how is it supposed to be propagated in the human sphere? Apply the same questions to the law in Exodus.

5. How would you compare Moses' role in Exodus to Hammurabi's in his laws?

6. What principles of organization do you perceive for each collection, and how are transitions between topics or sections executed?

7. Choose at least one of the paired "suggestions for comparison" listed above; read both groups of laws carefully and then describe both how they are similar and how they are different.

8. What aspects of each code indicate that they were or were not useful for practical purposes, as reference works in court settings? If they were not used as reference works for ancient courts, why would rulers have produced them?

9. Do you think it is fair to say that each code expresses a legal (or social) "ethos"—that is, does each one crystallize and reveal something about the society that produced it? Or do these collections seem too haphazard to accomplish anything so coherent?

10. What kind of class distinctions are perceptible in each collection, and what sort of social similarities or differences might they indicate between the cultures that produced them?

11. How do gender roles figure in each collection, and what might this tell us about the cultures that produced them?

12. How does a polytheistic worldview affect the idea of justice compared to a monotheistic worldview?

13. From a theological standpoint, what does it mean for God to "give laws" that in some sense have already been given in a similar form?

FURTHER READING

Greengus, Samuel. "Biblical and ANE Law." *ABD* 4:242–52.

Mendenhall, G. E. "Ancient Oriental and Biblical Law." *Biblical Archaeologist* 17 (1954): 25–46.

Roth, Martha T. *Law Collections from Mesopotamia and Asia Minor*. 2nd ed. Edited by Piotr Michalowski. SBLWAW 6. Atlanta: Society of Biblical Literature, 2003.

Wells, Bruce. "The Covenant Code and Near Eastern Legal Traditions: A Response to David P. Wright." *Maarav* 13 (2006): 85–118.

———. "What Is Biblical Law? A Look at Pentateuchal Rules and Near Eastern Practice." *CBQ* 70 (2008): 223–243.

Wells, Bruce, and F. Rachel Magdalene, eds. *Law from the Tigris to the Tiber: The Writings of Raymond Westbrook*. 2 vols. Winona Lake, IN: Eisenbrauns, 2009.

Wright, David P. *Inventing God's Law: How the Covenant Code of the Bible Used and Revised the Laws of Hammurabi*. New York: Oxford University Press, 2009.

8

Ritual Texts

Purgation Rites from Hatti, Babylon, and Judah

LEVITICUS 16:1–34

When: Unknown (estimates range from the tenth–fifth centuries BCE)
Where: Jerusalem
Language: Hebrew

ASHELLA'S RITUAL AGAINST A PLAGUE IN THE ARMY (CTH 394)

What: Cuneiform text reconstructed from six clay tablets
When: ca. 1300 BCE
Where: Hattusas (near modern Boğazkale, Turkey)
Language: Hittite
Translation: Billie Jean Collins[1]

[The paragraphs in this translation reflect breaks indicated in the text of one of the original tablets.]

§1 According to Ashella, man of Hapalla: If an epidemic occurs in the land or in the army camp, I perform this ritual.

§2 I take these things: When day turns to night, all who are army commanders, every one prepares a ram. Nothing is prescribed as to whether the rams should be white or black. I wind twists of white, red, and green wool and he weaves them into one. I string one pearl (?) and one ring of iron and lead, and I tie them to the necks and horns of the rams. They tether them (the rams) before the tents for the night, and as they do so, they say the following: "Whatever deity is stirring/wandering below, whatever deity has caused this plague, for you I have secured these rams. Be satisfied with (these)!"

---

1. *Hittite Rituals from Arzawa*, SBLWAW, forthcoming.

§3 Then in the morning I drive them to the countryside. With each ram they bring one pitcher of beer, one offering loaf, and one cup of fired clay. Before the king's tent, he seats an ornamented woman. He sets one *huppar*[2] of beer and three offering loaves at the foot of the woman.

§4 Afterwards the camp commanders place their hands on the rams and recite as follows: "The deity who has caused this plague, now the rams are standing here and their liver, heart, and thigh are very succulent. May human flesh be repulsive to him (the deity) once again, and may you (O deity) be satisfied with these rams." The army commanders bow down to the rams and the king bows to the ornamented woman. Afterwards, they take the rams, the woman, the bread, and the beer through the army and drive them to the countryside. They go and abandon them at the enemy border (so that) they do not end up at any place of ours. Thereupon they recite as follows: "Whatever evil was among the men, cattle, sheep, horses, mules, and donkeys of this army, these rams and the woman have just carried it away from the camp. Whoever finds them, may that land receive this evil plague!"

§5 At daybreak on the second day they prepare six rams, six billy goats, twelve jugs, twelve cups, twelve offering loaves, one *huppar* of beer, and three small bronze knives and drive them to still another place in the countryside; and they carry all these things along. When they move to the countryside, they slaughter them on the ground and cook them simply.[3] They spread out foliage and arrange the meat, offering breads, and a small knife as follows. Further, they fill the cups and jugs with beer. In addition, at the same time [they say] the follow[ing: ". . .] promptly for the first time [. . .] we have released. Now [to you, O deity] we have given cooked food, including meat, bread, and beer, and raw food. O Deity, eat and drink like a god. Don't cast it aside!" Then they bow down, and come away. While they are worshipping the deity, no one shall place (any) utensil on the ground. It is not permitted; nor shall one take it up for himself.

§6 When they leave the ritual, they pour salt into the water. He washes their hands with it. Then they ignite a fire in two places and they pass through them. They arrange two goats, one *huppar* of wine, and five offering loaves. The two goats are dedicated to the Protective Deity of the Ritual Paraphernalia. He sets the cooked breast, right shoulder, liver, and heart on (some) foliage. He toasts the Protective Deity of the Ritual Paraphernalia three times and they eat. Then they come away.[4]

§7 At daybreak of the third day, they drive in one billy goat, one ram, and one pig. Afterward they prepare three offering loaves and one *huppar* of beer and then drive them into the steppe to another place. They spread out branches and set down the three offering loaves. The billy goat, the sheep, and the pig they present to that very deity who made this plague in the army (saying): "Let that deity eat. Let that deity drink. And in the land of Hatti and in regard to the army of the land of Hatti let there be peace. Let him (the deity) be turned in favor (to the army)." They eat and drink. Then they come away.[5]

---

2. The volume of a *huppar* is unknown.
3. Or: whole.
4. One copy adds: "Second day finished."
5. One copy adds: "Third day finished."

§8 At daybreak on the fourth day, they drive in one bull, one ewe, and one wether[6]—but (it must be) a ewe to which a ram has not yet gone—ten offering loaves, one *huppar* of beer, one *huppar* of wine. They drive them to yet another place in the countryside and they present the cow (i.e., bull) to the Storm God. But the ewe they present to the Sun God. And they present three sheep to all the gods. Then they spread foliage on the ground. He sets down the cooked breast, the right shoulder, the liver, and the heart. Then he toasts the Sun God of Heaven, the Storm God, and all the gods three times. They eat. Then they come away.

[*Colophon*:] One ritual, according to Ashella. When a plague occurs in the land or in the midst of the army camp.[7]

THE RITUAL OF AMBAZZI (CTH 391)

What: Cuneiform text reconstructed from seven clay tablets
When: ca. 1300 BCE
Where: Hattusas (near modern Boğazkale, Turkey)
Language: Hittite
Translation: David P. Wright[8]

    She wraps a little tin on the bowstring.
35   She puts it on the right hand (and) feet of the offerers.
    Then she takes it away
    and puts it on a mouse (saying): "I have
    taken away from you evil and I have put it on
    the mouse. Let this mouse take it to the high mountains,
40   the deep valleys (and) the distant ways."
    She lets the mouse go (saying): "Alawaimi,
    drive this (mouse) forth, and I will give to you a goat to eat."
    (Offerings to Alawaimi and other gods follow.)

DAY FIVE OF THE BABYLONIAN AKITU FESTIVAL

What: Cuneiform text; twenty-second and twenty-third tablets (reconstructed from multiple fragments) of a lengthy compilation
When: Seleucid period (3rd–2nd c. BCE)
Where: Babylon

6. A wether is a castrated ram.
7. A variant ending reads, "The plague ritual of Ashella, man of Hapalla, finished." Another variant ending reads, "One tablet, complete, containing three rituals. When a plague occurs in the land or in the midst of the army."
8. David P. Wright, *The Disposal of Impurity: Elimination Rites in the Bible and in Hittite and Mesopotamian Literature* (Society of Biblical Literature Dissertation Series 101; Atlanta: Scholars Press, 1986).

Language: Akkadian
Translation: Julye Bidmead[9]

285   On the fifth day of the month of Nisannu at two double hours of the night,
           the high priest
       will rise and wash (himself) with water from the Tigris and Euphrates.
       [He will enter before Bel] he will remove the (linen?) curtain in front of Bel
       (Marduk) and Beltiya (Zarpanitu)[10]
       He will recite the following prayer:

[*Lines 289–333 include prayers to Marduk and Beltiya in Sumerian. One section of the prayer
contains a series of lines ending with "my lord, my lord, be calm."*]

       After he has said the prayer, he will open the gates.
335   The *eribbiti* (temple-entering) priests will enter and
       perform their rites in the usual manner;
       the *kalu*-priests and the singers also.
       When, at the first double hour (two hours after sunrise),
       the offering table of Bel and Beltiya are set,
340   he will request the exorcist and he will purify the temple
       with water from a well of the Tigris, and from a well of the Euphrates
       he will sprinkle the temple. He will beat the copper drum inside the temple.
       He will move a censer and a torch in the temple,
       and in the courtyard. He will not enter the cella[11] of Bel
345   and Beltiya. When the purification of the temple
       is complete, he will enter the Ezida, the cella of Nabu[12]
       and purify the temple with a censer, torch, and water,
       and sprinkle the temple (with) water from a well of the Tigris
       and a well of the Euphrates.
350   He will smear the doors of the cella with cedar resin.
       He will put the silver censer in the middle of the courtyard of the cella and
       mix aromatics and juniper around it.
       He will call a slaughterer who will cut off the head of the sheep, and
       the exorcist will purify[13] the temple with the body of the sheep.
355   He will recite the incantations for exorcising the temple.

---

9. This translation is modified from the one Bidmead offered in *The Akitu Festival: Religious
Continuity and Royal Legitimation in Mesopotamia* (Gorgias Dissertations, Near East Series 2; Pis-
cataway, NJ: Gorgias Press, 2002). It is based on the Akkadian text of François Thureau-Dangin,
Rituels Accadiens (Paris: E. Leroux, 1921), 136–46.

10. Marduk's consort, and the goddess of childbirth. "Bel" and "Beltiya" are more generic titles,
meaning "lord" and "my lady," respectively.

11. A cella is a central sanctuary of a temple.

12. Nabu was the moon-god, and the son of Marduk. Ezida was the name of temples to Nabu in
various places (initially in Borsippa, south of Babylon), but here it seems to refer to a chapel within
Esagila, the temple of Marduk in Babylon.

13. The Akkadian verb used here is *kapāru*, cognate with the Hebrew root that gives us Yom
Kippur, the Day of Atonement.

He will purify the entirety of the cella and remove the censer;
the exorcist will lift up the body of the sheep and
go to the river. He will face the west.
He will throw the body of the sheep in the river.
360   He will go into the open country. The slaughterers with the head will go
          also.
The exorcist and the slaughter will remain in the open country as long as
Nabu is in Babylon; they cannot enter Babylon.
From the fifth day until the twelfth day, they remain in the open country.
The high priest of Etusa[14] will not view the purification of the temple
365   If he does view (it), he is not pure.
After the purification of the temple, when one-and-two-thirds double hours
of daytime passes, the high priest of the Etusa will go out and
call the craftsmen.
They will bring the Golden Heaven[15] from Marduk's treasury
370   and cover the Ezida, the cella of Nabu from its crossbeam (highest point)
to the foundation of the temple.
The high priest of the Etusa and the craftsmen
will recite the following prayer.
"They will purify the temple,
375   Asalluhi, son of Eridu, who dwells in Eudul[16]
(God) Kusu [. . .] Kusu
Ningirim,[17] who hears the prayers
Marduk, who purifies the temple
Kusu,[18] who lays down the decrees
380   Ningirim, who casts the spell
Whatever evil, which is in the temple, get out!
Great demon, may Bel kill you!
May he expel you!"
The craftsmen go out to the gate.

[Lines 385–94 are broken, but they refer to offerings on a golden tray—a meal of roasted meat, twelve loaves of bread, salt, and honey, juniper—placed before a statue of Marduk. The high priest makes a libation of wine and offers a prayer of intercession.]

395   He will recite the prayer:
"Marduk, exalted lord of the gods
who lives in the Esagila,[19] who creates order
[. . .] to the great gods

14. The chapel of Marduk.
15. Perhaps a type of canopy.
16. Asalluhi came to be identified with Enki, the god of the Mesopotamian city of Eridu. Enki and Asalluhi were both associated with magic.
17. A goddess associated with exorcism and magic.
18. A Mesopotamian deity, here associated with the determining of fates.
19. The temple of Marduk in Babylon.

[. . .] who sit in the quay
400   [. . .] your heart, the ones who you take by the hand
in the Esizkur, temple of prayer,
may he raise his head."
After he says the prayer, he will clear the offering trays.
He will call for the craftsmen.
405   He will give offerings to the craftsmen
and to Nabu.
They will take it and go
to the bank of the canal.
When Nabu arrives, they will take the king in the presence of Nabu.
410   They will place an offering table before Nabu.
They lift up the leftovers; as soon as Nabu leaves the ship Iddahedu,[20]
place them on the table.
They place water for the hand washing (before) the king and
they make him enter the Esagila. The craftsmen go out to the gate.
415   When he (the king) arrives before Bel, the high priest will go out of the cella and
remove the scepter, circle, and mace (of the king).
He will lift up the "crown of kingship."
He will enter before Bel and in front of Bel.
He will place them on a chair. He will go out and strike the cheek of the king.
420   He will place [. . .] behind him. He will force him to enter before Bel.
He will pull his ears, (and) force him to bow on the ground.
The king will say once:
"[I did not] sin, lord of the lands; I did not neglect your divinity
[I did not] destroy Babylon, I did not order its downfall
425   . . . Esagila, I did not forget its rituals
[I did not] strike the cheek of the 'protected citizens'
I [did not] humiliate them
I honored Babylon and I did not smash its walls."

[*Broken lines*]

Do not fear;
435   Bel has spoken.
Bel [hears] your prayer.
He caused your lordship to become great.
He exalted your kingship.
On the day of the *eššešu* [festival], do . . . .
440   At the opening of the gate, wash your hands.
[. . .] Day and night

---

20. A cultic boat on which the statue of Nabu was transported.

[. . .] of Babylon, his city [. . .]
[. . .] of Esagila, his temple [. . .]
of the sons of Babylon, his "protected citizens."
445   Bel will bless you [. . .] forever.
He will destroy your enemy, and cause your adversaries to fall!
When he has spoken, the king (will regain) his kingship.
(The high priest) will bring (back) the scepter, circle, and crown and give
them to the king.
He will strike the king's cheek (again). When (he strikes) his cheek,
450   if his tears flow, Bel is friendly.
If his tears do not flow, Bel is angry,
and the enemy will rise and bring his downfall.
When he has done this and it is one-third double hour (sunset),
the high priest will tie together forty uncut reeds of three cubits —
455   unbroken, straight, in a bundle (tied) with date palm.
They will open a pit in the Exalted Courtyard,
[and] he puts it in the pit [with offerings of honey, ghee, fine oil]
[. . .] he places. A white bull [. . .]
the king places fire on a reed in its center
460   the king and the high priest recite the following utterance:
O (Divine) Bull, brilliant light which burns the darkness
O burning of Anu.

DISCUSSION

Ancient rituals are difficult for many modern readers to understand because they combine categories that are usually kept separate in our minds. We may know the saying "cleanliness is next to godliness," but few of us would judge a person or place ungodly simply because they were messy. Then again, moderns do still, in extreme cases, consider a place unclean when a terrible thing has happened there—as when the people of Newtown, Connecticut, voted to demolish Sandy Hook Elementary and build a new school after the mass shooting there in 2012, or when Pennsylvania State University recently tore out the showers where a football coach had molested children. But these and similar cases derive from a gut sense of revulsion; we do not practice regular rituals to purify our spaces from sin. Because of this cultural gap, it is especially advisable in this chapter to read each text more than once.

The cultic laws of the Pentateuch were for a long time disproportionately ignored even by critical scholars. Many of the earliest modern practitioners of biblical criticism (including, most prominently, Julius Wellhausen) were Protestants who found these texts dry and legalistic, reminiscent of Jewish and Catholic ritual practices that they considered unworthy of the supposedly more spiritual faith of the prophets and Jesus. Mary Douglas lamented that the study of religion "has inherited an ancient sectarian quarrel about the value of formal ritual" and that this "narrow preoccupation with belief in the efficacy of rites" has left biblical scholars (among others) with very little to say about such texts.[21] In the last quarter century, however, there has been a renewed interest in the theological and social significance of biblical ritual.

The Hittite rituals of Ashella and Ambazzi (above) are among the many Hittite texts that deal with the removal of evil. As this small sampling suggests, these texts show great diversity and specificity. David P. Wright identified ten "purification motifs" (or steps toward purification) in the Hittite corpus:[22]

1. *Transfer*: An evil is transferred from the subject to another object or living being, to be carried away and disposed of.
2. *Substitution*: Akin to transfer, except with the assumption that evil will fall on the object to which the evil is transferred, rather than simply being carried away.
3. *Concretizing*: The evil is symbolically made concrete in something (such as clothing or thread) that can be removed to enact purification. (The evil may remain abstract or invisible in the previous motifs.)
4. *Disposal*: The disposal of the evil can follow any of the above three motifs.
5. *Detergents*: A variety of substances could be used to purify the subject, including water, wine, clay, flours, salt, blood, and fire.
6. *Entreaty and appeasement*: Deities are summoned to remove the evil(s).
7. *Analogy*: The subject is compared to an object that can be purified in some way.[23]
8. *Annulment*: Ritual action cancels the impurity.
9. *Prevention*: Ritual action stops evil from returning or from taking effect in the first place.
10. *Invigoration*: Ritual action brings health and well-being to the patient.

Not all of these purification motifs were used in a given text; they could be combined in various ways.

The ritual of Ambazzi is the simpler of the two presented in this chapter. It was intended to treat sick individuals, as the wider context reveals. The practitioner places a bowstring wrapped in tin on the hands and feet of the subjects, and then attaches it to a mouse. He clearly states that this is to take the evil away from the subjects and put it on the mouse. The ritual therefore exemplifies the motifs of concretizing and disposal. The text goes on to entreat the deity Alawaimi to help the process by driving the mouse away and offers the appeasement of a sacrifice.

The Ashella ritual is more complex, perhaps because it is intended to treat not just sick individuals, but a whole army or land struck by a plague.[24] It is a multiday affair, and a number of motifs are employed. On day one, the multiple rams and the woman (§§3–4) are the objects to which the evil is transferred. Since these are prepared by the leaders of the military, who place their hands on them, it is clear they are driven out for disposal. Nevertheless, this is not stated, as it was in the Ambazzi ritual. The evil is also concretized

21. Mary Douglas, *Purity and Danger: An Analysis of Concepts of Pollution and Taboo* (London: Routledge & K. Paul, 1966), 18–19.
22. Wright, *Disposal of Impurity*, 31–45; see there for examples. I have renumbered the motifs to group them by type.
23. For example, one text reads, "As water flows down from the roof and does not go back again to the gutter, so may the evil . . . be poured out and not come back again."
24. Note the possible historical connection to the Hittite Plague Prayers; see chap. 24.

in the cords, rings, and beads that are tied to them. It seems in this text that the rams serve a dual purpose: on the one hand, they are supposed to carry away the evil so that it can fall on the ones who find them (transfer and disposal); but on the other hand they are supposed to be "very succulent" food for the angry god(s) to devour instead of human flesh (§4: "May human flesh be repulsive to him"); this would be an instance of substitution. The latter is the only reason that the rams would be sent out with bread and beer: these items complete the gods' meal.

The subsequent days of the ritual are more straightforward, involving mostly sacrifices in the interest of entreaty and appeasement. Day two, however, does include the use of salt water and fire as detergents to purify the ritual paraphernalia and personnel (§6). Also on the second day, the sacrifices are laid out for the deity, and he is invited to eat. But although the rams from the first day were also pictured as food for the gods, they were not killed, but only driven away. It is almost as if, in the face of the intractable plague and the theological uncertainty that it brought, the Hittites were not sure whether the gods preferred their food live or dead, and so decided to cover their bases.

The Babylonian purification ritual presented above was part of an _akitu_ festival. The _akitu_, one of the most important festivals in Mesopotamia, was observed for thousands of years. The _akitu_ is sometimes called a "New Year's Festival," but in fact they frequently marked a new "equinox year." That is, the _akitu_ was celebrated twice a year, in the first and seventh months, marking the fall and spring equinox, respectively. However, there was no single form or schedule for an _akitu_ festival; these things changed over time to suit the context.[25]

The Babylonians often symbolized their deities by means of statues. During the _akitu_ festival, the statues of the gods were taken to an "_akitu_-house," often outside the city, where the deity would remain for a few days, and then reenter the city. While residing at the _akitu_-house, the deity would receive offerings and prayers. The reentry into the city, in a grand procession, then symbolized the deity's resumption of rule in the city, essentially electing anew to be the city's god. (Certain biblical psalms have been taken to reflect an Israelite New Year's festival that celebrated Yhwh's rule, particularly those with the refrain "Yhwh reigns!"; e.g., Pss. 29:10; 93:1; 96:10; 97:1; 99:1.)

Akitu festivals are recorded for many gods in many Mesopotamian cities. The oldest reference, from the third millennium, reflects a celebration of the moon god in Ur. The text presented above is much later, from the Late Babylonian (Seleucid) period. It reflects Marduk's rise to prominence (which took place in the second millennium), but since it also still includes a prominent role for the moon god (Nabu), it is in that sense conservative. It may reflect a syncretistic combination of festivals for Nabu and Marduk.[26]

In the first millennium BCE, the _akitu_ festival in Babylon lasted twelve days. The text above prescribes only the events of the fifth day, and so comprises a relatively small piece of the whole. The day includes a multipart purification rite intended to prepare a sanctuary for the god Nabu in the Esagila temple in Babylon. The high priest who carries it out

25. For a detailed discussion of the various forms, see Mark E. Cohen, _The Cultic Calendars of the Ancient Near East_ (Bethesda, MD: CDL Press, 1993), 400–453. The summary here is deeply indebted to Cohen.
26. Ibid., 440.

is supposed to bathe himself and, after prayer and singing, another priest sprinkles water from the Tigris and Euphrates on the outer temple to purify it. Moving to the cella (or chapel) of Nabu, he purifies it with water and a torch and censer, and smears cedar resin in the temple. These substances could be considered detergents, in Wright's terms.

The sacrificial aspect of the Babylonian ritual involves a single ram, which is decapitated. Another priest is instructed to use its body "to purify the temple." (As noted above, the Akkadian verb used for "purify," *kapāru,* is linguistically related to Hebrew *kippur*—as in Yom Kippur, the Day of Atonement. The verbal root common to both languages means, most basically, "to wipe," but it has taken on larger meanings.[27]) The ram is disposed of— its body in a river, and its head in the wilderness; only afterward can Nabu enter his cella. Although the text does not specify what the ram's sacrifice and disposal mean, in light of the Hittite comparisons they almost certainly were intended to "absorb" the temple's impurity by transfer, and then dispose of it. The concern to keep the pure and impure separate is quite clear; both those who dispose of the ram and the priest who carried out the purification are ordered to go into the wilderness, and not to return until the festival is over. Furthermore, the high priest is ordered not to view the purification ritual lest he be rendered impure.

After Marduk and the king have taken their places, the king is struck by the high priest and pulled to the ground by his ears. This enacts his humbling before the god, and he submits his record of treating Babylon well and denies wrongdoing. The priest strikes the king again, and "if his tears flow," he is regarded with favor by Marduk. Otherwise, the king was supposedly fated to be brought down by his enemies. The scene as a whole may have amounted to a ritual "performance review" of the king, carried out by the god. Later, on day 11, in the most important part of the festival, the king would escort the deity back into the city. This "taking the hand of Bel (Marduk)" was a central act of king-ship in first-millennium Mesopotamia.

The ritual of Leviticus 16 for the Day of Atonement (Yom Kippur) is similarly complex. Aaron bathes and purifies himself, dresses in linen, and sacrifices a bull "as a sin offer-ing for himself . . . and for his house" (v. 6). Two rams are brought as burnt offerings, one by Aaron (v. 3) and the other by the people (v. 5). The people also bring two goats; Aaron then casts lots (a form of dice) to designate one each for Yhwh and Azazel. The act of send-ing the "scapegoat" to Azazel is often considered the central act of the ritual, which makes the uncertainty about who or what Azazel is all the more frustrating. Since (1) the name can be translated (with a small emendation) as "angry god";[28] (2) Azazel is parallel with Yhwh in the syntax; and (3) Azazel came to be a prominent demon in postbiblical Jewish texts, it is likely that one was originally dealing with a divine power who needed to be appeased. The fact that Azazel's character is almost entirely obscured in the present form of the text likely indicates that it did not fit with the theology of the text's later tradents. That is, the scapegoat ritual apparently originated in an early period with a less strict monotheism. After all, "it makes little sense to suppose that a de-personalized demon with

---

27. For a nonritual use of the verb in Hebrew, see Gen. 6:14, where Noah is told to smear the ark with pitch to seal it.

28. For discussion and further references, see Wright, *Disposal of Impurity,* 74; and Bernd Janowski, "Azazel," in *Dictionary of Deities and Demons in the Bible* (2nd ed.; Leiden: Brill, 1999), 128–31.

little functional purpose as a demon was cast in a rite that originated with Priestly legisla-
tors. We would expect that [they] would have constructed the rite without such a figure."[29]

Aaron next burns incense in the Holy of Holies, and sprinkles the bull's blood on and
in front of the throne of Yhwh (the "mercy seat" or *kapporet*). He slaughters the goat designated for Yhwh, sprinkles blood as he did with the bull's, and then rubs both types of
blood on the horns of the altar. Then he lays hands on the second goat, confesses "all the
iniquities of the people of Israel, and all their transgressions, all their sins, putting them
on the head of the goat, and sending it away into the wilderness . . . The goat shall bear on
itself all their iniquities to a barren region" (Lev. 16:21–22). Finally, Aaron bathes again,
clothes himself again, and only then offers up the rams as burnt offerings. The remains of
the bull and goat that were sacrificed are burned outside the camp, and those who dispose
of the remains are also instructed to bathe and wash their clothes.

The biblical ritual can be divided into two main sections: first, the sin offering of the
bull, which atones for Aaron and his kindred and purifies the temple; and second, the
scapegoat ritual, which atones for the transgressions of the people. Presumably the sanctuary is made impure by the sins of the people, so there is no point in purifying it without
also removing the people's transgressions.

Various purifying motifs are in evidence in Leviticus 16: The sacrifices presumably
functioned as entreaty and appeasement, although it is never stated. The blood that is
sprinkled and rubbed must have been envisioned as a detergent. The motif of transfer is
the most explicit: the sins are literally "put on the head of the goat," which then carries
them away into the wilderness (disposal).

The similarities between Leviticus 16's rituals and the other ancient Near Eastern rituals presented here have long been noted and studied. Both Hittite texts remove evil from
people by transferring it to animals and then sending them away, much like the biblical
scapegoat. (However, only the Ashella ritual suggests that the evil is supposed to fall on
someone else.) Also like Leviticus 16, both Hittite texts include sacrifices, although the
meaning may not be the same; in Ashella, the sacrifices seem to function partly as a form
of substitution for the human victims of the devouring plague, and partly as agents of
transfer—it is as if they combine the purposes of both the sacrificed goat and the scapegoat
from Leviticus 16. In Ambazzi, the sacrifice is intended to entreat the god to drive the evil
away. Furthermore, Aaron's sacrifices provide the detergent for the sanctuary, although
they probably also were meant to have the effect of entreating and appeasing Yhwh.

Another significant difference between the Hittite and biblical rituals is the former's
use of a *woman* to substitute for the king; perhaps an animal was taken to be an insufficient
substitute for royalty?[30] In addition, there is no reference in the Hittite texts to human
sins or transgressions, as there is in Leviticus 16; since the idea of transgression *is* present
in the Hittite Plague Prayers (chap. 24), it could be implicit in these rituals. However,
the repeated references to the eating of the sacrifices might indicate instead that the gods
were seen as ravenous devourers whose appetites simply needed to be redirected.

29. Wright, *Disposal of Impurity*, 73–74.
30. Other comparable substitution rituals are known from the ancient Near East. For example, a
substitute king ritual could be carried out when a bad omen fell upon the king. A commoner would
be named king for a day so that he would bear the curse, and then he was killed.

The similarities between Leviticus 16 and the temple-cleansing rites in the *akitu* festival are even more striking. In both texts:

- Purification of holy space is combined with propitiatory offerings.
- The priestly figures bathe beforehand.[31]
- Smoke is used in the sanctuary.
- A slaughtered animal or its blood is used to purify the space.
- The deity is presented with roasted meat after the cleansing.
- The carcasses of the slaughtered animals are disposed of outside the civilized area.
- Those who conduct the temple-purification ritual are made unclean; however, the Babylonian functionaries are temporarily banished, whereas Aaron and the temple functionaries are instructed to bathe.

Finally, it may not be a coincidence that the Day of Atonement was instituted in the seventh month (Tishri), on the tenth day. Although the Babylonian *akitu* presented above is for the first month (Nisan), there was another in the seventh month. Furthermore, the Day of Atonement may have been part of a multiday festival beginning with the blowing of horns on the first of Tishri (Lev. 23:23–25); that would make it very similar in length to the eleven- or twelve-day Babylonian festival.[32]

There are also significant differences between the Babylonian and biblical texts:

- The Babylonian high priest cannot even be present during the cleansing (lines 364–65), while Aaron is active in the biblical ritual.
- There is no royal participation in Leviticus 16. (Of course, there *was* no king in the biblical narrative at this point, but the role of the nation's political leader could have been filled by Moses.)
- The precise cleansing motifs are also different: the Babylonian sanctuary is wiped down with a slaughtered ram so that the impurity is transferred and disposed of; its blood is not a detergent as with the sacrificial blood in Leviticus 16. (Instead, water and fire are used as detergents in the *akitu* text.)
- The animal to which the people's impurity is transferred for disposal in Leviticus 16 is not sacrificed or slaughtered, but rather driven away.

There is also the question of sin and purification. Some scholars have seen atonement for sin as a facet of the Babylonian ritual, while others have not. As with the Hittite texts, understanding the reasons for the cleansing in the Babylonian text requires inference. The prayers that precede the purification include the repeated phrase "my lord, be calm," which may indicate a purpose similar to the common Mesopotamian prayers "for appeasing the heart of an angry god," and some of those prayers do confess transgressions (see chap. 22). Still, there is no explicit reference to wrongdoing during the purification ritual, and other parts of the text portray the purification as an exorcism of demons (esp. lines 381–83: "Whatever evil, which is in the temple, get out! Great demon, may Bel kill you!

31. Some translations also interpret the reference to linen at the beginning of the text as indicating that the Babylonian priest dressed in linen just as Aaron did, but that interpretation is not adopted here.

32. Roy E. Gane, *Cult and Character: Purification Offerings, Day of Atonement, and Theodicy* (Winona Lake, IN: Eisenbrauns, 2005), 370–71.

May he expel you!"). Furthermore, in the latter part of the day 5 rituals, the king *denies* wrongdoing rather than confessing sins as Aaron does in Leviticus 16.

Some of the differences between these texts already point to the more complex history of the rituals in Leviticus 16. Not only are they framed in a narrative context, they also include more explanation about the meaning of various actions (which is not to say they are straightforward). There is an ongoing debate among biblical scholars about the date when the Priestly laws of the Pentateuch took on their present form, and the proposed dates vary by centuries, roughly from the ninth century BCE to the fifth. But whenever they were recorded, they represent a text with a layered history: they preserve ritual activities that were probably carried out long before the texts were written down, but they also include the attempts of later authors to explain what the rituals meant.

Even the later explanations do not make it clear *why* this was supposed to atone for anything; they only say that they *do*: "Thus he shall make atonement for the sanctuary, because of the uncleannesses of the people of Israel, and because of their transgressions, all their sins" (Lev. 16:16). Various theories about the underlying logic of purification offerings and rituals have been advanced. It has been said that the things that make Israelites ritually impure (such as diseases, bodily emissions, and contact with the dead) were linked to death, so that they had to be separated from the pure things of God.[33] So perhaps it is because "the life is in the blood" (Lev. 17:11; cf. Gen. 9:4) that blood drives out the impurity of death?[34] It has been said that the sanctuary must be purified because it "receives the impact of human imperfection among the surrounding Israelites," which is incompatible with the holiness and righteousness of the divine King and Judge.[35] These are useful ideas that identify significant patterns in the data, yet many readers will find them speculative and ultimately unsatisfying.

The long tradition of purification rituals in the ancient Near East gives little reason to doubt their antiquity in Israel. They certainly demonstrate theological presuppositions of an archaic sort. As one scholar commented (and as the comparison here shows), "The Levitical ritual is a sublimated form of what is basically a purely magical procedure."[36] Another indicator that it is an independent composition from most of the Priestly literature is the presence of the demonic Azazel (see above).

Finally, the preservation of supernatural rituals and demonic figures in the Bible may seem to present theological difficulty for modern readers—especially those in faith communities where magic is thought of as a forbidden black art, an attempt to control the supernatural in an impermissible way. (The question of magic is addressed in more detail in chap. 22.) If this is a problem, however, then it must be a problem for much of the cultic law in the Pentateuch, because the meanings of other rituals are typically even less well explained than this one. The mystery of these texts can be tamed by a decision of faith to fit them into a different theological worldview than the one from which they emerged.

---

33. Jacob Milgrom, "Rationale for Cultic Law: The Case of Impurity," *Semeia* 45 (1989): 103-9.
34. One might also look at John 6:53–54 and Rev. 12:11 in this connection.
35. Gane, *Cult and Character*, 379.
36. O. R. Gurney, *Some Aspects of Hittite Religion* (Oxford: Oxford University Press for the British Academy, 1977), 47.

But apart from such an effort, it can hardly be denied that one person's meaningful ritual is another person's magic.

REFLECTION QUESTIONS

1. What is the effect of explaining the meaning of a ritual? What is gained? What is lost?
2. How have the rituals of Leviticus 16 been incorporated into the larger narrative? What portion of the text might predate its incorporation?
3. After surveying the similarities and differences between Leviticus 16 and day 5 of the Babylonian *akitu*, Roy Gane wrote that the latter "should not be regarded as a Babylonian 'Day of Atonement'" (*Cult and Character*, 373). Do you agree or disagree, and why?
4. What are the connections between the temple purification rituals and the scapegoat ritual in Leviticus 16? Do you think these were originally separate rituals that were later combined, or were they composed as a whole?
5. What reasons can you see for "acting out" purification or the removal of evil?
6. How do present-day religions deal with sin and impurity? How do notions such as sacrifice and blood figure into their beliefs and practices?
7. Can you think of practices in modern life beyond the scope of formal religions that could be compared to purgation rituals?

FURTHER READING

Bidmead, Julye. *The Akitu Festival: Religious Continuity and Royal Legitimation in Mesopotamia*. Piscataway, NJ: Gorgias Press, 2002.

Cohen, Mark E. *The Cultic Calendars of the Ancient Near East*. Bethesda, MD: CDL Press, 1993. (Esp. 400–453.)

Collins, Billie Jean. "Hittite Religion and the West." Pages 54–66 in *Pax Hethitica: Studies on the Hittites and Their Neighbours in Honour of Itamar Singer*. Edited by Y. Cohen, A. Gilan, and J. L. Miller. SBT 51. Wiesbaden: Harrassowitz Verlag, 2010.

Douglas, Mary. *Purity and Danger: An Analysis of Concepts of Pollution and Taboo*. London: Routledge & K. Paul, 1966.

Feder, Yitzhaq. *Blood Expiation in Hittite and Biblical Ritual: Origins, Context, and Meaning*. Atlanta: SBL, 2011.

Gane, Roy E. *Cult and Character: Purification Offerings, Day of Atonement, and Theodicy*. Winona Lake, IN: Eisenbrauns, 2005. (Esp. 355–78.)

Gurney, O. R. *Some Aspects of Hittite Religion*. Oxford: Oxford University Press for the British Academy, 1977.

Janowski, Bernd. "Azazel." Pages 128–31 in *Dictionary of Deities and Demons in the Bible*. 2nd ed. Leiden: Brill, 1999.

Lemos, T. M. "The Universal and the Particular: Mary Douglas and the Politics of Impurity." *Journal of Religion* 89 (2009): 236–51.

Milgrom, Jacob. *Leviticus 1–16*. AB 3A. New York: Doubleday, 1991. (Esp. 1109–84.)

———. "Rationale for Cultic Law: The Case of Impurity." *Semeia* 45 (1989): 103–9.

Wright, David P. *The Disposal of Impurity: Elimination Rites in the Bible and in Hittite and Mesopotamian Literature*. Society of Biblical Literature Dissertation Series 101. Atlanta: Scholars Press, 1986.

9

Treaty, Oath, and Covenant

Hittite and Neo-Assyrian Treaties, and Deuteronomy

DEUTERONOMY

When: Probably ca. 622 BCE
Where: Jerusalem
Language: Hebrew

TREATY BETWEEN MURSILI II OF HATTI AND MANAPA-TARHUNTA OF THE LAND OF THE SEHA RIVER

What: "File copy" of cuneiform text on clay tablet (CTH 69)
When: Ca. 1320 BCE
Where: Hattusas (near modern Boğazkale, Turkey)
Language: Hittite
Translation: Gary Beckman[1]

Preamble and Historical Introduction

§1 (A i 1–13) Thus says My Majesty, Mursili,[2] Great King, King [of Hatti, Hero]:

Your father left you, Manapa-Tarhunta [behind . . .], and you were a child. Your brothers [. . .] and Ura-Tarhunta plotted to kill [you], and would [have killed] you, [but] you escaped. [They caused] you [to flee] from [the land of the Seha River], and [you went]

---

1. Gary M. Beckman, *Hittite Diplomatic Texts* (ed. Harry A. Hoffner Jr.; 2nd ed.; SBLWAW 7; Atlanta: Scholars Press, 1999), 82–86.
2. The name is transliterated Muršili, and it is not certain whether this is to be pronounced "Murshili" or "Mursili." (The same question applies to other Hittite proper nouns in this text that contain an *s*.) I follow the more common convention.

over to the people of the city of Karkisa.[3] [They took] your land and the house of your father [away] from you, and took them for themselves. [But I, My Majesty, commended you, Manapa-Tarhunta], to the men of Karkisa. [I repeatedly sent] gifts [to] the men of Karkisa. [My brother also] pleaded [with them on your behalf]. Because of our words the men [of Karkisa] protected you.

§2 (A i 14–18) [But] when Ura-Tarhunta proceeded [to transgress] the oath, [the oath] gods seized him, and the men [of the land of the Seha River] drove him [out]. But [because of our words] the men [of the land of the Seha River] received you (back), and because of [our] words they protected you.

§3 (A i 19–33) But [when] it happened that my brother [Arnuwanda died], and I, My Majesty, [seated myself] on the throne [of my father], then I, My Majesty, came and [backed] you. [I caused] the people of the land of the Seha River [to swear an oath] to you, and because of my [words they protected] you. [They . . .] you wholeheartedly.

[*Four lines too fragmentary for translation.*]

But [when it happened that Uhha-ziti, king of the land of Arzawa,[4] began war against My Majesty], then [you, Manapa-Tarhunta, offended against My Majesty]. You backed [Uhha-ziti, my enemy, and made war] on My Majesty. You did not back [me].

Fugitives

§4 (A i 34–62) [But when I went on campaign] against Uhha-ziti and against [the people of Arzawa], because Uhha-ziti [had transgressed the oath] in regard to me, the oath gods seized [him, and I destroyed him]. And because you [had taken the side of Uhha-ziti], I [would] have destroyed you likewise. [But] you fell [down] at [my feet], and [you dispatched old] men [and old women] to me. [And] your messengers [fell] down at [my] feet. You sent [to me] as follows: "Spare me, my lord. [May my lord not] destroy [me]. Take me as a vassal and [. . .] my person. [I will turn over] from here [all] the civilian captives of the land of Mira, [the civilian captives] of Hatti, [or] the civilian captives of Arzawa— whichever come [over] to me."

Then I, My Majesty, had [compassion] for you, [and] because of that I acceded [to you and made] peace with you. And as I, My Majesty, had compassion for you and made peace with you, now seize and hand [over] to me all civilian captives of the land of Arzawa who come over to you—whoever [flees] before me—and whatever civilian captives of the land of Mira [or of] Hatti come [over] to you . . . You shall not leave a single man behind, nor shall you [allow] anyone out of your land, or allow him to cross into another land. Gather up the civilian captives and turn them [over] to me. If you carry out all these matters, [then] I will take [you] as a vassal. Be my ally. In the future this shall be [your] regulation. [Observe it]. It shall be placed under oath for you.

---

3. Location uncertain, but most likely to be identified with Caria in southwest Anatolia. The Seha River was called the Caicus in classical antiquity, and the Bakırçay today.

4. Like Appawiya, Mira, Kuwaliya, and Hapalla, which are mentioned later, this is a region of western Anatolia. Their precise locations and borders are somewhat uncertain.

§5 (A i 63–67) I have now given you the land of the Seha River and the land of [Appawiya]. This shall be your land—protect [it]! You shall not hereafter desire a Hittite person or a border district of Hatti. [If] you do perversely desire a Hittite person or a border district of Hatti, you will have transgressed the oath.

[*The remainder of column I is badly damaged.*]

Defensive Alliance

§6 (B iii 9–14) And now, if someone somehow [carries out] a revolt against [My Majesty, whether it is] some person or some unit of troops [whoever it is]—and you, Manapa-Tarhunta, somehow [hear about him], become his partisan, and turn away [from My Majesty], that too [shall be placed] under oath.

Relations among Subordinates

§7 (B iii 15–19) Furthermore, [I], My Majesty, [have] now [given] you, [Manapa-Tarhunta], the land of the Seha River and the land of Appawiya. This shall be your land—protect it! [And I have given] the land of Mira and the land of Kuwaliya to Mashuiluwa. [And] I have given the land of Hapalla to Targasnalli. This shall be your territory—protect it!

§8 (B iii 20–23) Now you, Manapa-Tarhunta, shall not take anything away from Mashuiluwa, and Mashuiluwa shall not take [anything] away from you. You, Manapa-Tarhunta, shall not quarrel with Mashuiluwa, and Mashuiluwa [shall not] quarrel with [you].

§9 (B iii 24–27) [Now you shall be] favored [by Mashuiluwa], and Mashuiluwa shall be favored [by you]. If [some] legal dispute comes up, you shall place [it] before My Majesty, and I, [My Majesty], will decide it.

§10 (A iii 19'–29') [Furthermore, you], Manapa-Tarhunta, [shall not approach] Mashuiluwa as an enemy, and you shall not [kill] him. [Mashuiluwa] shall not approach [you] as an enemy, [and] he shall not kill you. But if Mashuiluwa does [quarrel] with you and approaches you as an enemy, and kills you, [then] Mashuiluwa will thereby be My Majesty's enemy. I, My Majesty, will continually make war on [Mashuiluwa]. But if you, Manapa-Tarhunta, quarrel [with Mashuiluwa], and approach Mashuiluwa [as an enemy], and kill him, then you, Manapa-Tarhunta, will be My Majesty's enemy. I will continually make war on you. And this matter too will be placed under oath.

§11 (A iii 30'–36') [A subject] of Mashuiluwa shall not [come] as a fugitive to your land, and a subject [of yours] shall not go as a fugitive [to] Mashuiluwa. You shall be favored by one another (in this regard). And if some person from among the civilian captives which the father of My Majesty carried off to Hatti flees from me, and you, Manapa-Tarhunta, do not give him back, this too will be placed under oath.

§12 (A iii 37'–47') Those subjects of mine who are in flight from me, My Majesty, shall be your enemies, just as they are Mashuiluwa's enemies. You shall continually make war on them, just as Mashuiluwa continually makes war on them. And [as] you,

Manapa-Tarhunta, do not allow them [into your land], Mashuiluwa shall likewise not allow them in. They shall be [your] common enemies. [But if] they make peace, then they shall make peace with you in common. They shall [not be] at peace with anyone of you, while hostile to another. And this matter too will be placed under [oath].

Divine Witnesses

§13 (A iii 48′–B i 27) We have now summoned the Thousand Gods to assembly for this oath. They shall stand, observe, and listen. And they shall be [witnesses].

§14 [The Sun-god of Heaven, the Sun-goddess of Arinna, the Storm-god] of Heaven, the Powerful Storm-god, [. . . , Sheri, Hurri], Mount Nanni, [Mount Hazzi, . . .], the Storm-god of the Market (?), the Storm-god of the Army, [the Storm-god of . . . , the Storm-god of Pittiyarik], the Storm-god of Nerik, the Storm-god of the Ruin Mound, [the Storm-god of . . . , the Storm-god of Aleppo], the Storm-god of Uda, the Storm-god of Kummanni,

§15 [the Storm-god of . . . , the Storm-god of Hisashapa], the Storm-god of Samuha, the Storm-god of Sapinuwa, [the Storm-god of . . . , the Storm-god] of Sahpina, the Storm-god of Hurma, the Storm-god of Sarissa, the Storm-god [of . . .], the Storm-god of Help, the Storm-god of Zippalanda,

§16 the Tutelary Deity, the Tutelary Deity of Hatti, Zithariya, Karzi, Hapantaliya, the Tutelary Deity of Karahna, the Tutelary Deity of the Countryside, the Tutelary Deity of the Hunting Bag, Allatu, Enki, Telipinu, Pirwa, the Moon-god, <Lord> of the Oath, Hebat, Great Queen, [. . .], Ishtar, Ishtar of the Countryside, Ishtar of Nineveh, [Ishtar] of Hattarina, Ninatta, Kulitta, [Ishhara], Queen of the Oath,

§17 [the War-god], the War-god of Hatti, the War-god of Illaya, the War-god of Arziya, Yarri, Zappana, Abara of Samuha, Hantitassu of Hurma, Katahha of Ankuwa, the Queen of Katapa, Ammamma of Tahurpa, Hallara of Dunna, Huwassanna of Hupisna, the mountain-dweller gods, all the mercenary gods of Hatti,

§18 [the male deities] and the female deities of Hatti, the Sun-goddess of the Earth, all the primeval deities—Nara, Namsara, Minki, Ammunki, [Tuhusi], Ammizzadu, Alalu, Kumarbi, Anu, Antu, Enlil, Ninlil,

§19 [the mountains, the rivers], the springs, the great sea, [heaven and earth], the winds, the rivers, and the clouds.

[*A short break intervenes.*]

Curse

§20 (A iv 29′–39′) [And if] you, [Manapa-Tarhunta, together with the people of the land] of the Seha River [and] the land of Appawiya, do [not] observe [these words, and in the future, to the first and second generation, you turn] away, or you alter [these words] of the tablet—whatever [is contained] on this tablet, then these [oath gods] shall eradicate you, together with [your] person, your [wives], your sons, your [grandsons], your household, [your land], your infantry, your horses, [your chariots (?)], and together with your [possessions], from the Dark Earth.

Blessing

§21 (A iv 40′–46′) [But If] you, Manapa-Tarhunta, observe these [words] of the tablet, and in the future you do not [turn] away from the [King] of Hatti, together with [my sons, and from the word of the oath, then] these oath gods shall [benevolently] protect you. And [your sons] shall thrive [in the hand of My Majesty].

Colophon

Text A: Single tablet of the treaty of [Manapa-Tarhunta].

VASSAL TREATY OF ESARHADDON

What: Cuneiform text on multicolumn clay tablet[5]
When: Twelfth day of the month of Iyyar, 672 BCE
Where: Kalhu
Language: Akkadian
Translation: Simo Parpola and Kazuko Watanabe[6]

Seal of the god Ashur, king of the gods, lord of the lands—not to be altered; seal of the great ruler, father of the gods—not to be disputed.[7]

Preamble

§1 The treaty of Esarhaddon, (king of the world), king of Assyria, son of Sennacherib, (likewise king of the world), king of Assyria, with Humbaresh, city-ruler of Nahshimarti[8]

5. Hundreds of fragments found in the temple of Nabu in Kalhu attest to eight versions of this treaty, each with a different ruler of a peripheral polity named as the vassal. See discussion below.

6. Simo Parpola and Kazuko Watanabe, *Neo-Assyrian Treaties and Loyalty Oaths* (SAA 2; Helsinki: Helsinki University, 1988), 28–58.

7. There are three seals between this introductory text and the rest of the document. From Parpola and Watanabe, *Neo-Assyrian Treaties*, xxxvi: "The middle seal, with the short legend 'Of the God Aššur and the City Hall,' dates from the time of the Old Assyrian city-state. The impression on the left, from a Neo-Assyrian seal, shows the king of Assyria standing between the gods Aššur and Mullissu, and has the following legend: 'The Seal of Destinies, with which Aššur, king of the gods, seals the destinies of the Igigi and Anunnaki of heaven and earth, and of mankind. What he seals with it, he does not alter. He who should alter (it), may Aššur, king of the gods, and Mullissu, together with their children kill him with their mighty weapons. I am Sennacherib, king of Assyria, a prince who fears you. Whoever erases my name and discards this Seal of Destinies of yours, erase his name and seed from the land!' The impression on the right, showing the king kneeling between the gods Aššur and Ninurta, is from a Middle-Assyrian seal; both gods are mentioned in the largely illegible legend."

8. Nahshimarti was a Median city-state to the east of Assyria.

(etc.), his sons, his grandsons, with all the Nahshimartians (etc.), the men in his hands young and old, as many as there are from sunrise to sunset, all those over whom Esarhaddon, king of Assyria, exercises kingship and lordship, (with) you, your sons and your grandsons who will be born in days to come after this treaty, (concerning Ashurbanipal, the great crown prince designate, son of Esarhaddon, king of Assyria, on behalf of whom he has concluded this treaty with you,)

Divine Witnesses

§2 (which he) confirmed, made and concluded in the presence of Jupiter,[9] Venus, Saturn, Mercury, Mars, and Sirius; in the presence of Ashur, Anu, Ill[il], Ea, Sin, Shamash, Adad, Marduk, Nabu, Nusku, Urash, Nergal, Mullissu, Sherua, Belet-ili, Ishtar of Nineveh, Ishtar of Arbela, the gods dwelling in heaven and earth, the gods of Assyria, the gods of Sumer and [Akka]d, all the gods of the lands.

Adjuration

§3 Sw[ear ea]ch individually by Ashur, father of the gods, lord of the lands!
(Swear)[10] by Anu, Illil and Ea!
(Swear) by Sin, Shamash, Adad and Marduk!
(Swear) by Nabu, Nusku, Urash and Nergal!
(Swear) by Mullissu, Sherua and Belet-ili!
(Swear) by Ishtar of Nineveh and Ishtar of Arbela!
(Swear) by all the gods of the Inner City!
(Swear) by all the gods of Nineveh!
(Swear) by all the gods of Calah!
(Swear) by all the gods of Arbela!
(Swear) by all the gods of Kilizi!
(Swear) by all the gods of Harran!
(Swear) by all the gods of Babylon, Borsippa and Nippur!
(Swear) by all the gods of Assyria!
(Swear) by all the gods of Sumer and Akkad!
(Swear) by all the gods of the lands; ditto by all the gods of heaven and earth!
(Swear) by all the gods of one's land and one's district!

Ashurbanipal Designated Heir to Throne

§4 (This is) the treaty which Esarhaddon, king of Assyria, has concluded with you, in the presence of the great gods of heaven and earth, on behalf of Ashurbanipal, the great crown

---

9. Both here and in the curse section (§§42–43), these names are translations of Akkadian names for the planets. The Roman mythology is not implied.

10. The text places a mark at the beginning of each phrase here that meant, essentially, "Ditto," i.e., repeat the above.

prince designate, son of Esarhaddon, king of Assyria, your lord, whom he has named and appointed to be crown prince: When Esarhaddon, king of Assyria, passes away, you will seat Ashurbanipal, the great crown prince designate, upon the royal throne, and he will exercise the kingship and lordship of Assyria over you. You shall protect him in country and in town, fall and die for him. You shall speak with him in the truth of your heart, give him sound advice loyally, and smooth his way in every respect. You shall not depose him, nor seat (any)one of his brothers, elder or younger, on the throne of Assyria instead of him. You shall neither change nor alter the word of Esarhaddon, king of Assyria, but serve this very Ashurbanipal, the great crown prince designate, whom Esarhaddon, king of Assyria, your lord, has presented to you, and he shall exercise the kingship and dominion over you.

Obligation to Protect Heir

§5 You shall protect Ashurbanipal, the great crown prince designate, whom Esarhaddon, king of Assyria, has presented and ordered for you, and on behalf of whom he has confirmed and concluded (this) treaty with you; you shall not sin against him, nor bring your hand against him with evil intent, nor revolt or do anything to him which is not good and proper; you shall not oust him from the kingship of Assyria by helping one of his brothers, elder or younger, to seize the throne of Assyria in his stead, nor set any other king or any other lord over yourselves, nor swear an oath to any other king or any other lord.

Obligation to Report Opposition to Succession

§6 If you hear any improper, unsuitable or unseemly word concerning the exercise of kingship which is unseemly and evil against Ashurbanipal, the great crown prince designate, either from the mouth of his brothers, his uncles, his cousins, his family,[11] members of his father's line; or from the mouth of magnates and governors, or from the mouth of the bearded and the eunuchs, or from the mouth of the scholars or from the mouth of any human being at all, you shall not conceal it but come and report it to Ashurbanipal, the great crown prince designate.

Succession at Esarhaddon's Untimely Death

§7 If Esarhaddon, king of Assyria, passes away while his sons are minors, you will help Ashurbanipal, the great crown prince designate, to take the throne of Assyria, and you will help Shamash-shumu-ukin, his equal brother, the crown prince designate of Babylon, to ascend the throne of Babylon. You will reserve for him the kingship over the whole of Sumer, Akkad and Karduniash.[12] He will take with him all the gifts that Esarhaddon, king of Assyria, his father, gave him; do not hold back even one.

---

11. Some versions read "his people" instead of "his family."
12. Although Esarhaddon named Ashurbanipal the heir to the imperial throne, he gave southern Mesopotamia to another son, Shamash-shumu-ukin. This eventually led to a civil war.

Definition of Loyalty

§8 You shall keep absolute honesty with respect to Ashurbanipal, the great crown prince designate whom Esarhaddon, king of Assyria, has presented to you, and (with respect to) his brothers, sons by the same mother as Ashurbanipal, the great crown prince designate, on behalf of whom Esarhaddon, king of Assyria has concluded (this) treaty with you; you shall always serve them in a true and fitting manner, speak with them with heartfelt truth, and protect them in country and in town.

Prohibition of Disloyal Conduct

§9 You shall not sin against Ashurbanipal, the great crown prince designate, whom Esarhaddon, king of Assyria, has ordered for you, nor against his brothers, sons by the same mother as Ashurbanipal, the great crown prince designate, concerning whom he has concluded (this) treaty with you; you shall not bring your hands to (do) evil against them nor make insurrection or do anything which is not good to them.

Obligation to Report Treason

§10 If you hear any evil, improper, ugly word which is not seemly nor good to Ashurbanipal, the great crown prince designate, son of Esarhaddon, king of Assyria, your lord, either from the mouth of his enemy or from the mouth of his ally, or from the mouth of his brothers or from the mouth of his uncles, his cousins, his family, members of his father's line, or from the mouth of your brothers, your sons, your daughters, or from the mouth of a prophet, an ecstatic, an inquirer of oracles, or from the mouth of any human being at all, you shall not conceal it but come and report it to Ashurbanipal, the great crown prince designate, son of Esarhaddon, king of Assyria.

Injunction against Treason

§11 You shall not do (anything) that is evil and improper to Ashurbanipal the great crown prince designate, whom Esarhaddon, king of Assyria, your lord, has ordered for you; you shall not seize him and put him to death, nor hand him over to his enemy, nor oust him from the kingship of Assyria, nor sw[ear an oa]th to any other king or any other lord.

Action against Those Suborning Treason

§12 If anyone should speak to you of rebellion and insurrection (with the purpose) of ki[lling], assassinating, and eliminating Ashurbanipal, the [great crown] prince designate, son of Esarhaddon, king of Assyria, your lord, concerning whom he has concluded (this) treaty with you, or if you should hear it from the mouth of anyone, you shall seize the perpetrators of insurrection, and bring them before Ashurbanipal, the great crown prince designate. If you are able to seize them and put them to death, then you shall destroy their name and their seed from the land. If, however, you are unable to seize them and put them to death, you shall inform Ashurbanipal, the great crown prince designate, and assist him in seizing and putting to death the perpetrators of rebellion.

Action against Traitors

§13 If you should come into contact with perpetrators of insurrection, be they few or many, and hear (anything, be it) favorable or unfavorable, you shall come and report it to Ashurbanipal, the great crown prince designate, son of Esarhaddon, king of Assyria, being totally loyal to him. You shall not take a mutually binding oath with (any)one who installs (statues of) gods in order to conclude a treaty before gods, (be it) by sett[ing] a table, by drinking from a cup, by kindling a fire, by water, by oil, or by holding breasts, but you shall come and report to Ashurbanipal, the great crown prince designate, son of Esarhaddon, king of Assyria, your lord, and shall seize and put to death the perpetrators of insurrection and the traitorous troops, and destroy their name and seed from the land.

Action against Open Rebellion

§14 If an Assyrian or a vassal of Assyria, or a bearded (courtier) or a eunuch, or a citizen of Assyria or a citizen of any other country, or any living being at all besieges Ashurbanipal, the great crown prince designate, in country or in town, and carries out rebellion and insurrection, you shall take your stand with and protect Ashurbanipal, the great crown prince designate, wholeheartedly defeat the men who revolted against him, and rescue Ashurbanipal, the great crown prince designate, and his brothers, sons by the same mother.

Obligation to Escape from Rebels

§15 You shall not make common cause with (any)one who may revolt against Ashurbanipal, the great crown prince designate, son of Esarhaddon, king of Assyria, your lord, concerning whom he has concluded (this) treaty with you, but, should they seize you by force, you shall flee and come to Ashurbanipal, the great crown prince designate.

Rejection of Rebellion

§16 You shall not, whether while on a guard duty [. . . . . .] or on a [day] of rest, while resid[ing] within the land or while entering a tax-collection point, set in your mind an unfavorable thought against Ashurbanipal, the great crown prince designate; you shall not revolt against him, nor make rebellion, nor do anything to him which is not good.

Succession of Ashurbanipal

§17 On the day that Esarhaddon, king of Assyria, your lord passes away, (on that day) Ashurbanipal, the great crown prince desi[gnate], son of Esarhaddon, your lord, shall be your king and your lord; he shall abase the mighty, raise up the lowly, put to death him who is worthy of death, and pardon him who deserves to be pardoned. You shall hearken to whatever he says and do whatever he commands, and you shall not seek any other king or any other lord against him.

Rejection of Palace Revolt against Esarhaddon

§18 If anyone in the Palace makes an insurrection, whether by day or by night, whether on a campaign or within the land against Esarhaddon, king of Assyria, you must not obey him. If a messenger from within the Palace at an unexpected time, whether by day or by night, comes to the prince saying: "Your father has summoned you; let my lord come," you must not listen to him nor let him go away but you must guard him strongly until one of you, who loves his lord and feels concern over the house of his lords, goes to the Palace and ascertains the well-being of the king, his lord. (Only) afterwards you may go to the Palace with the prince, your lord.

Prohibition against Seditious Meetings

§19 You shall not hold an assembly to adjure one another and give the kingship to one of you.

Action against Pretenders to Throne

§20 You shall not help (anyone) from among his brothers, his uncles, his cousins, his family, or members of his father's line, whether those who are in Assyria or those who have fled to another country, or (anyone) in the closer palace groups or in the more remote palace groups or (any) groups great or small, or (any) of the old or young, of the rich or the poor, whether a bearded (courtier) or a eunuch, or (one) of the servants, or (one) of the bought (slaves) or any citizen of Assyria or any foreigner or any human being at all, any one of you, to seize the throne, nor shall you hand over to him the kingship and lordship of Assyria. You shall help Ashurbanipal, the great crown prince designate to seize the throne of Assyria, and he will exercise the kingship and lordship over you.

Allegiance to Ashurbanipal

§21 You shall fall and die for Ashurbanipal, the great crown prince designate, son of Esarhaddon, your lord, and seek to do for him what is good. You shall not do for him what is not good, nor give him an improper counsel or direct him in an unwholesome course, but continually serve him in a true and fitting manner.

Action against Murderer of Ashurbanipal

§22 If Esarhaddon, king of Assyria, passes away while his sons are minors, and if either a bearded (courtier) or a eunuch puts Ashurbanipal, the great crown prince designate, to death, and takes over the kingship of Assyria, you shall not make common cause with him and become his servant but shall break away and be hostile (to him), alienate all lands from him, instigate a rebellion against him, seize him and put him to death, and then help a son of Ashurbanipal, the great crown prince designate, to take the throne of Assyria. You shall wait for a woman pregnant by Esarhaddon, king of Assyria, (or) for the wife of Ashurbanipal, the great crown prince designate (to give birth), and after (a son) is born, bring him up and set him on the throne of Assyria, seize and slay the perpetrators of rebellion, destroy their name and their seed from the land, and by shedding blood for blood, avenge Ashurbanipal, the great crown prince designate.

Prohibition against Killing Ashurbanipal

§23 You shall not give Ashurbanipal, the great crown prince designate, son of Esarhaddon, king of Assyria, your lord, a deadly drug to eat or to drink, nor anoint him with it, nor practice witchcraft against him, nor make gods and goddesses angry with him.

Action in Favor of Ashurbanipal's Brothers

§24 You shall love Ashurbanipal, the great crown prince designate, son of Esarhaddon, king of Assyria, your lord, like yourselves.[13] You shall not slander his brothers, his mother's sons, before Ashurbanipal, the great crown prince designate, nor speak anything evil about them, nor lift your hands against their houses or commit a crime against them, nor take anything away from the gift which their father has given them, or the acquisitions which they themselves have made. The gift of lands, houses, orchards, peoples, implements, horses, mules, donkeys, cattle and flocks which Esarhaddon, king of Assyria, has given to his sons, shall be theirs. You shall speak good of them before Ashurbanipal, the great crown prince designate. They shall stand before him and be united with you.

Perpetuating Allegiance to Ashurbanipal

§25 This treaty which Esarhaddon, king of Assyria, has confirmed and concluded with you on behalf of Ashurbanipal, the great crown prince designate and his brothers, sons by the same mother as Ashurbanipal, the great crown prince designate, by making you take an oath, you shall speak to your sons and grandsons, your seed and your seed's seed which shall be born in the future, and give them orders as follows: "Guard this treaty. Do not sin against your treaty and annihilate yourselves, do not turn your land over to destruction and your people to deportation. May this matter which is acceptable to god and mankind, be acceptable to you too, may it be good to you. May Ashurbanipal, the great crown prince designate, be protected for (his) lordship over the land and the people, (and) may his name later be proclaimed for the kingship. Do not place any other king or any other lord over you."[14]

---

13. Compare Deut. 6:5; Lev. 19:18; Matt. 19:19, etc.
14. Compare Isa. 26:13.

Action against Usurper of Esarhaddon's Throne

§26 If anyone makes rebellion or insurrection against Esarhaddon, king of Assyria, and seats himself on the royal throne, you shall not rejoice over his kingship but shall seize him and put him to death. If you are unable to seize him and put him to death, you shall not submit to his kingship nor swear an oath of servitude to him, but shall revolt against him and unreservedly do battle with him, make other lands inimical to him, take plunder from him, defeat him, destroy his name and his seed from the land, and help Ashurbanipal, the great crown prince designate, to take his father's throne.

Injunction against Fomenting Strife between King and Crown Prince

§27 If (any) one of his brothers, his uncles, his cousins, his family, (any) one of his own dynastic line, or any descendant of former royalty or (any) one of the magnates, governors or eunuchs, (or any) one of the citizens of Assyria, (or) any foreigner, involves you in a plot, saying to you: "Malign Ashurbanipal, the great crown prince designate, in the presence of his father. Speak evil and improper things about him," you shall not make it come to a fight between him and his father by stirring up mutual hatred between them.

Response to Fomentors of Strife

§28 (Instead) say to the envious person who commands you and would make you become accursed: "Where are his brothers or the servants who made themselves accursed to his father by slandering him in the presence of his father? Has not what Ashur, Shamash and [Adad] said about him proved to be true? Did your father [. . .] without (the consent of) Ashur and Shamash? Let your brother be honored, and stay alive."

Injunction against Fomenting Strife between Prince and His Brothers

§29 If someone involves you in a plot, be it one of his brothers, his [unc]les, his relations, a member of his father's line, a bearded (courtier) or a e[unuch], an Assyrian or a foreigner, or any human being at all, saying: "Slander his brothers, sons by his own mother, before him, make it come to a fight between them, and divide his brothers, sons of his own mother, from him," you shall not obey nor speak evil about his brothers in his presence, nor divide him from his brothers; you shall not let those who speak such things go free but shall come and report to Ashurbanipal, the great crown prince designate as follows: "Your father imposed a treaty on us and made us swear an oath concerning it."

Response to Attempts to Foment Strife

§30 You shall not look on [. . . Ashurbanipal], the great crown [prince], his brothers [. . .]. You shall contest them as you would on [your] own [behalf], and rouse [fear] in their heart, saying: "Your father set (this) in a treaty and made [us] swear it."

Injunction against Fomenting Strife after Ashurbanipal's Accession

§31 When Esarhaddon, king of Assyria, your lord, passes away and Ashurbanipal, the great crown prince designate, ascends the royal throne, you shall not say any evil word about his bro[thers, sons of] his own mo[ther], before their brother nor try to make them accursed (saying): "Bring your hand against them for an evil deed." You shall not alienate them from Ashurbanipal, the great crown prince designate, nor shall you say any evil word about them in the presence of their brother. (As for) the positions which Esarhaddon, king of Assyria, their father, assigned them, you shall not speak in the presence of Ashurbanipal, the great crown prince designate, (trying to make him) remove them [from these positions].

Prohibition against Invalidation of Oath

§32 You shall not smear your face, your hands, and your throat with . . . against the gods of the assembly, nor tie it in your *lap*, nor do anything to undo the oath.

Prohibition against Undoing the Oath

§33 You shall not revoke or undo (this) oath . . . [. . .]; you shall neither think of nor perform a ritual to revoke or undo the oath. You and your sons to be born in the future will be bound by this oath concerning Ashurbanipal, the great crown prince designate, son of Esarhaddon, your lord, from this day on until what(ever) comes after this treaty.

Attitude toward Swearing the Oath

§34 While you stand on the place of this oath, you shall not swear the oath with your lips only but shall swear it wholeheartedly;[15] you shall teach it to your sons to be born after this treaty;[16] you shall not feign incurable illness but take part in this treaty of Esarhaddon, king of Assyria, concerning Ashurbanipal, the great crown prince designate. In the future and forever Ashur will be your god, and Ashurbanipal, the great crown prince designate, will be your lord. May your sons and your grandsons fear him.

Obligation to Guard the Treaty Document

§35 Whoever changes, disregards, transgresses or erases the oaths of this tablet or [dis]regards . . . this treaty and transgresses its oath, [may the guardian(s) of] this treaty tablet, [Ashur], king of the gods, and the great gods, my lords, [. . . . . .] the statue of Esarhaddon, king of Assyria, or the statue of Ashurbanipal, the great crown prince designate, or the statue of [his] b[rother . . . . . .] the seal of the [great] ru[ler, father] of the gods, [. . . . . .]. You shall guard [this treaty tablet which] is sealed with the seal of Ashur, king of the gods, and set up in your presence, like your own god.

---

15. Compare Deut. 6:5; 26:16.
16. Compare Deut. 4:10; 6:20; 11:19; 29:15; 32:46; Exod. 12:26.

Injunction against Destroying the Document

§36 If you should remove it, consign it to the fire, throw it into the water, [bury] it in the earth or destroy it by any cunning device, annihilate or deface it—

Standard Curse Section

§37 May Ashur, king of the gods, who decrees [the fates], decree an evil and unpleasant fate for you. May he not gra[nt yo]u long-lasting old age and the attainment of extreme old age.

§38 May Mullissu, his beloved wife, make the utterance of his mouth evil, may she not intercede for you.

§38A May Anu, king of the gods, let disease, exhaustion, malaria, sleeplessness, worries and ill health rain upon all your houses.

§39 May Sin, the brightness of heaven and earth, clothe you with leprosy and forbid your entering into the presence of the gods or king. Roam the desert like the wild ass and the gazelle!

§40 May Shamash, the light of heaven and earth, not judge you justly. May he remove your eyesight. Walk about in darkness!

§41 May Ninurta, the foremost among the gods, fell you with his fierce arrow; may he fill the plain with your blood and feed your flesh to the eagle and the vulture.

§42 May Venus, the brightest of the stars, before your eyes make your wives lie in the lap of your enemy; may your sons not take possession of your house, but a strange enemy divide your goods.

§43 May Jupiter, exalted lord of the gods, not show you the entrance of Bel in Esagil;[17] may he destroy your life.

§44 May Marduk, the eldest son, decree a heavy punishment and an indissoluble curse for your fate.

§45 May Zarpanitu, who grants name and seed, destroy your name and your seed from the land.

§46 May Belet-ili, the lady of creation, cut off birth from your land; may she deprive your nurses of the cries of little children in the streets and squares.

§47 May Adad, the canal inspector of heaven and earth, cut off sea[sonal flooding] from your land and deprive your fields of [grain], may he [submerge] your land with a great flood; may the locust who diminishes the land devour your harvest; may the sound of mill or oven be lacking from your houses, may the grain for grinding disappear from you; instead of grain may your sons and your daughters grind your bones; may not (even) your (first) finger-joint dip in the dough, may the [. . .] of your bowls eat up the dough. May a mother [bar the door] to her daughter. In your hunger eat the flesh of your sons! In want and famine may one man eat the flesh of another; may one man clothe himself in another's skin; may dogs and swine eat your flesh; may your ghost have nobody to take care of the pouring of libations to him.

---

17. The temple of Marduk (=Bel) in Babylon.

§48 May Ishtar, lady of battle and war, smash your bow in the thick of ba[ttle], may she bind your arms, and have you crouch under your enemy.

§49 May Nergal, hero of the gods, extinguish your life with his merciless sword, and send slaughter and pes[til]ence among you.

§50 May Mullissu, who dwells in Nineveh, tie a flaming sword at your side

§51 [May] Ishtar, who dwells in Arbela, [no]t show you mercy and compassion.

§52 May Gula, the great physician, put sickness and weariness [in your hearts] and an unhealing wound in your body. Bathe in [blood and pus] as if in water!

§53 [May] the Pleiades, the [heroic] gods, mas[sacre you with their] fierce [weapons].

§54 [May] Aramish, lord of [. . .] you [. . .].

§54A May [Bethel and Ana]th-Bethel hand you over to the paws of [a man-eating] lion.

§55 May Kubaba, the god[dess of] Carchemish, put a serious venereal disease within you; may your [urine] drip to the ground like raindrops.

§56 May all the grea[t go]ds of heaven and earth who inhabit the universe and are mentioned by name in this tablet, strike you, look at you in anger, uproot you from among the living and curse you grimly with a painful curse. Above, may they take possession of your life; below, in the netherworld, may they make your ghost thirst for water. May shade and daylight always chase you away, and may you not find refuge in a hidden cor[ner]. May food and water abandon you; may want and famine, hunger and plague never be removed from you. Before your very eyes may dogs and swine drag the breasts of your young women and the penises of your young men to and fro in the squares of Ashur; may the earth not receive your corpses but may your burial place be in the belly of a dog or a pig.[18] May your days be dark and your years dim, may darkness which is not to be brightened be declared as your fate. May your life end in exha[ustion and slee]plessness. May an irresistible flood come up from the earth and devastate you; may anything good be forbidden to you, anything ill be your share; may tar and pitch be your food; may urine of an ass be your drink,[19] may naphtha be your ointment, may duckweed be your covering. May demon, devil and evil spirit select your houses.

Vow of Allegiance to Ashurbanipal

§57 May these gods be our witnesses: We will not make rebellion or insurrection against Esarhaddon, king of Assyria, against Ashurbanipal, the great crown prince designate, against his brothers, sons by the same mother as Ashurbanipal, the great crown prince designate, and the rest of the sons of Esarhaddon, king of Assyria, our lord, or make common cause with his enemy. Should we hear of instigation to armed rebellion, agitation or malicious whispers, evil, unseemly things, or treacherous, disloyal talk against Ashurbanipal, the great crown prince designate, and against his brothers by the same mother as Ashurbanipal, the great crown prince designate, we will not conceal it but will report it to Ashurbanipal, the great crown prince designate, our lord. As long as we, our sons (and) our grandsons are alive, Ashurbanipal, the great crown prince designate, shall be our king

---

18. Compare 1 Sam. 17:44–46; 1 Kgs. 14:11; 2 Kgs. 9:10, 36; Jer. 15:3, etc.
19. Compare 2 Kgs. 18:27 (= Isa. 36:12).

and our lord, and we will not set any other king or prince over us, our sons or our grand-sons. May all the gods mentioned by name (in this treaty) hold us, our seed and our seed's seed accountable (for this vow).

Ceremonial Curse Section

§58 If you should sin against this treaty which Esarhaddon, king of Assyria, [your] lord, [has concluded] with you concerning Ashurbanipal, the great crown prince designate, (and concerning) his [brother]s, sons by [the same mother as Ash]urba[nipal], the great crown prince designate, and the re[st] of the offspring of Esar[haddon, king] of Assyria, your lord, May Ashur, father of the gods, st[ri]ke [you] down with [his] fierce weapons.

§59 May Palil, the fore[most] lord, let eagles and vultures [eat your f]lesh.[20]

§60 May Ea, king of the Abyss, lord of the springs, give you deadly water to drink, and fill you with dropsy.

§61 May the great gods of heaven and earth turn water (and) oil [into a curse for] you.

§62 May Girra, who gives food to small and great, burn up your name and your seed.

§63 Ditto, ditto, may all the gods that are [mentioned by name] in th[is] treaty tablet make the ground as narrow as a brick for you. May they make your ground like iron (so that) nothing can sprout from it.

§64 Just as rain does not fall from a brazen heaven, so may rain and dew not come upon your fields and your meadows;[21] instead of dew may burning coals rain on your land.

§65 Just as lead does not stand up before a fire, so may you [not s]tand before yo[ur] enemy (or) take your sons and your daughters in your hands.

§66 Just as a m[ule has n]o offspring, may your name, your seed, and the seed of your sons and your daughters disappear from the land.

§67 Just as a germinal shoot of ma[lt, if it] is soaked with ma[sh . . .], does not sprout (and) a [. . .] does not return [. . .], may your [see]d and the seed of y[our] s[ons] and your daughters disappear [from] the face of the ground.

§68 May Shamash with an iron plough [overtu]rn yo[ur] city and your district.

§69 Just as [thi]s ewe has been cut open and the flesh of [her] young has been placed in her mouth, may they make you eat in your hunger the flesh of your brothers, your sons and your daughters.[22]

§70 Just as young sheep and ewes and male and female spring lambs are slit open and their entrails rolled down over their feet, so may (your entrails and) the entrails of your sons and your daughters roll down over your feet.[23]

§71 [If you] should sin [against] this [trea]ty of Esarhaddon, king of Assyria, [concerning Ashurbanipal, the great crown prince design]ate; just as a sna[ke] and a mongoose do

---

20. Compare Prov. 30:17.

21. Compare Deut. 28:23–24.

22. Presumably this and the next paragraph refer to the ritual slaughtering of animals that took place in the covenant ceremony; compare Gen. 15.

23. Compare Jer. 34:18–20. For more information on oath making in Mesopotamia, see Dominique Charpin, *Reading and Writing in Babylon* (trans. J. M. Todd; Cambridge, MA: Harvard University Press, 2010), 154–68.

not enter the same hole to lie there together but think only of cutting each other's throats, so may you and your women not enter the same room to lie down in the same bed; think only of cutting each other's throats!

§72 Just as bread and wine enter into the intestines, [so] may (the gods) make this oath enter into [your] intestines and into those of [your] so[ns] and your [daught]ers.

§73 [J]ust as you blow water out of a t[ub]e, may they blow out you, your women, your sons and your daughters; may your streams and your springs make their waters flow backwards.

§74 May they make bread to be worth gold in your land.

§75 Just as honey is sweet, so may the blood of your women, your sons and your daughters be sweet in your mouth.

§76 Just as a worm eats [. . .], so may the worm eat, while you are (still) alive, your own flesh and the flesh of your wives, your sons and your daughters.

§77 May all the gods who are called by name in this treaty tablet break your bow[24] and subject you to your enemy; may they turn over the bow in your hands and make your chariots run backwards.

§78 As a stag is pursued and killed, so may your [mortal] enemy pursue and kill you, your brothers and your sons.

§79 As a caterpillar does not see and does not return to its cocoon, so may you not return to your women, your sons, your daughters, and to your houses.

§80 Just as one seizes a bird by a trap,[25] so may they deliver you, your brothers and your sons into the hands of your mortal enemy.

§81 May they make your flesh and the flesh of your women, your brothers, your sons and your daughters as black as [bitu]men, pitch and naphtha.

§82 Just as a . . . beast is caught in a snare, may you, your [women], your brothers, your sons and your daughters be seized by the hand of your enemy.

§83 May your flesh and the flesh of your women, your brothers, your sons and your daughters be wasted like the flesh of a chameleon.

§84 Just as the honeycomb is pierced with holes, so may they pierce your flesh, the flesh of your women, your brothers, your sons and your daughters with holes while you are alive.

§85 May they cause locusts, [. . .], lice, caterpillars and other field pests [to] devour your towns, your land and your district.

§86 May they make you like a fly in the hand of your enemy, and may your enemy squash you.

§87 Just as (this) bug stinks, just so may your breath stink before god and king (and) mankind.

§88 May they strangle you, your women, your sons and your daughters with a cord.

§89 Just as an image of wax is burnt in the fire and one of clay dissolved in water, (so) may your figure be burnt in the fire and sunk in water.

24. Compare Ps. 46:9; Jer. 49:35; Hos. 1:5.
25. Compare Ps. 124:7.

§90 ([If you should sin against] this [treaty] of Esarhaddon, king of Assyria, [and of] his sons and grandsons), (then) just as this chariot is drenched with blood up to its baseboard, so may your chariots be drenched with your own blood in the midst of your enemy.

§91 May all the gods who are called by name in this treaty tablet spin you around like a spindle-whorl,[26] may they make you like a woman before your enemy.[27]

§92 May all the gods who are mentioned by name in this treaty tablet make you, your brothers, your sons, and your daughters go backward like a crab.

§93 May they make evil and wicked things surround you like fire.

§94 Just as oil enters your flesh, so may they cause this oath to enter into your flesh, the flesh of your brothers, your sons and your daughters.

§95 Just as those who cursed sinned against Bel and he cut off their hands and feet and blinded their eyes, so may they annihilate you, and make you sway like reeds in water;[28] may your enemy pull you out like reeds from a bundle.

§96 If you should forsake Esarhaddon, king of Assyria, Ashurbanipal, the great crown prince designate, (his brothers, [sons by the same mother] as Ashurbanipal, the great crown prince designate, and the other sons, the offspring of [Esa]rhaddon, king of Assyria), going to the south or to the north, may iron swords consume him who goes to the south and may iron swords likewise consume him who goes to the north;

§96A May they [slaughter] you, your women, your brothers, your sons, and your daughters like a spring lamb and a kid.

§97 Just as the noise of (these) doves is persistent, so may you, your women, your sons and your daughters have no rest or sleep and may your bones never come together.[29]

§98 Just as the inside of a hole is empty, may your inside be empty.

§99 When your enemy pierces you, may there be no honey, oil, ginger or cedar-resin available to place on your wound.

§100 Just as gall is bitter, so may you, your women, your sons and your daughters be bitter towards each other.

§101 May Shamash clamp a bronze bird trap over you, (your sons and your [daught]ers); may he cast you into a trap from which there is no escape, and never let you out alive.

§102 Just as (this) waterskin is split and its water runs out, so may your waterskin break in a place of severe thirst; die [of th]irst!

§103 Just as (these) shoes are split, so may your [shoes] be torn in a region of brier. [Go around barefooted!]

§104 May Illil, lord of the throne, [overthrow] your throne.

§105 May Nabu, bearer of the tablet of fates of the gods, erase your name, and destroy your seed from the land.

§106 May the door [. . .] before your eyes, may your doors [. . . . . .].

---

26. Compare Isa. 22:18.

27. Compare Isa. 19:16, etc.

28. These images mirror those found on Assyrian reliefs that depict the treatment of defeated peoples.

29. Compare Ezek. 37:7.

Date and Colophon

§107 18th day of Iyyar, eponymy of Nabu-belu-utsur, governor of Dur-Sharrukku. The treaty of Esarhaddon, king of Assyria, conclu[ded] on behalf of Ashurbanipal, the great crown prince designate of Assyria, and Shamash-shumu-ukin, the crown prince designate of Babylon.

SUGGESTIONS FOR COMPARISON

	Hittite	Deuteronomy	Assyrian
1. ID of covenant giver	§1	5:6	§§1, 4
2. Historical prologue	§§1–3	1:1–4:14	—
3. Stipulations	§§4–12	4:44–27:8	§§5–32
4. Divine witnesses	§§13–19	4:26 (31:28)	§§2–3
5. Curses	§20	28:15–68	§§37–56, 58–106
6. Blessings	§21	28:1–14	—
7. Oath taking	—	27:9–26	§57
8. Deposit/recital	—[30]	31:10–13, 24–29[31]	§§34–35

DISCUSSION

The word "covenant" comes from the French *convenir*—etymologically, "to come together," but by the time of the coinage it already meant "to come to an agreement." So a covenant is an agreement. (The Hebrew term is *berit*, the etymology of which has proven more difficult to explain.)[32] One might expect to find texts in ancient Near Eastern religious literature that reflect forms similar to biblical covenants; instead, one finds the closest analogues in pragmatic documents: political treaties.

There is a long history of treaties and loyalty oaths in the ancient Near East; exemplars are found as early as the third millennium BCE,[33] and the endurance of their terminology and practices, even into Greek and Roman times, makes the ancient Near East "the cradle

---

30. Uncharacteristically, not present in this text; see discussion.

31. See also Deut. 10:1–2.

32. Some of the theories relate it to a Hebrew verb for feasting (*bārāh*), an Akkadian word for divining the will of a god (*barû*), or an Akkadian noun meaning "space between" (*birītu*)—note the ritual of passing between parts of sacrificed animals in Gen. 15 and Jer. 34:18–20. This last noun has a homonym meaning "fetter," which might also suggest the bond formed by a covenant. The medieval Jewish interpreter Ibn Janah connected it to the lightly attested verb *bērēʾ*, "to cut, clear." See Hayim Tadmor, "Treaty and Oath in the Ancient Near East: An Historian's Approach," in *Humanizing America's Iconic Book: Society of Biblical Literature Centennial Addresses* (ed. G. M. Tucker and D. A. Knight; Chico, CA: SBL, 1982), 137–38.

33. On extant examples of the treaty form, see Amnon Altman, "How Many Treaty Traditions Existed in the Ancient Near East?" in *Pax Hethitica: Studies on the Hittites and Their Neighbours in Honour of Itamar Singer* (ed. Y. Cohen, A. Gilan, and J. L. Miller; SBT 51; Wiesbaden: Harrassowitz Verlag, 2010), 17–36.

of covenant formalities in the ancient world."[34] One of the most diverse and extensive corpora is the Hittite treaties of the Late Bronze Age. The basic elements of the Hittite treaties are

1. A preamble identifying the covenant giver
2. Historical prologue, as motivation for the vassal's loyalty
3. Stipulations of the treaty
4. A list of divine witnesses
5. Blessings and curses
6. Provision for recital of the covenant and deposit of its tablets[35]

The covenant giver is known as a "suzerain," and so the form is often called the "suzerainty treaty." This is used in cases where the two parties are unequal in power, and the lesser power, or vassal, must submit to the more powerful party's demands. Another type, called a "parity treaty," was made between two equally powerful parties who agreed to certain stipulations. These two types of treaties can also be called "unilateral" and "bilateral," respectively. All of the examples here are of the suzerainty/unilateral type.

The Hittite treaty above pertains to a region of western Anatolia. The Hittite king Mursili II had recently become the first Hittite ruler to conquer areas so far to the west, and so this treaty was not intended merely to ensure the submission of the individual vassal to whom it was addressed (Manapa-Tarhunta), but also to create a new polity in the western part of the empire. That is the significance of sections 7–12, which make up a large part of the treaty. The primary duties stipulated for the vassals were to return fugitives to Hatti, help Hatti in wartime, and maintain peaceful relations among themselves. This last stipulation may seem strange, but Mursili was effectively creating a buffer zone to his west of small, self-governing states submissive to him. If they fought among themselves, that would destabilize and weaken his western border.

Mursili's claim to adjudicate among the lesser rulers within his empire was one of the essential functions of the Bronze Age empires in the Near East. In the earliest "empires," the dominant king was only first among equals; in Hatti this was at one earlier point symbolized by an iron scepter that was wielded by the dominant king.[36] By the Late Bronze Age the power differences were more substantial; note that Mursili does not call Manapa-Tarhunta a king, because he does not view the regional ruler as an equal. In other cases the Hittite emperor is distinguished as a "Great King" among the other Syro-Anatolian kings. Only in a few cases does a Hittite text acknowledge a foreign ruler as an equal. A prominent example is in the treaty of Hattusili III with Ramesses II of Egypt, in which both were called "Great King." Indeed, Ramesses is mentioned first, which may mark a recognition of his superiority.

34. Moshe Weinfeld, "Covenant Terminology in the Ancient Near East and Its Influence on the West," *JAOS* 93 (1973): 190–99.

35. G. E. Mendenhall and Gary A. Herion, "Covenant," *ABD* 1:1179–1202.

36. Iron may seem like an unlikely choice for a royal scepter, but it was effectively a precious metal in the Bronze Age, before the technology necessary for large-scale ironworking became available.

The prologue to the treaty is rhetorically effective in portraying Mursili as having been wronged by Manapa-Tarhunta after supporting him. Mursili claims to have protected Manapa-Tarhunta when he was a boy and his succession was at risk, only to have him refuse to send help with Hatti was attacked. There is no way of verifying most of the facts that Mursili put forward, but if they are correct, then the Hittite king would have been justified in being suspicious and wanting the assurance of a written treaty. As it turned out, Mursili eventually deposed Manapa-Tarhunta for failing to support him, and installed the latter's son on the throne instead.[37]

One must also assume that Mursili was concerned throughout to present himself as justified in the eyes of the divine witnesses invoked at the end. The god lists in Hittite treaties usually include the deities of both parties, although the emphasis is on the Hittite gods and goddesses. Sometimes the vassal's gods are simply grouped as "all the gods of the land of X." The detail of the list of foreign deities may have depended on the power of the nation in question and the perceived prominence of its gods. This divine sanction was crucial: these treaties were "the ideological glue which held the Hittite empire together."[38]

The Hittite god list reflects a fairly normal ancient Near Eastern practice of invoking the same deity in many different manifestations, especially for each of the many places they were known to be worshiped. For example, the text mentions at least twenty-three manifestations of the storm god, some connected to specific places, and others to things like the market or army. In extrabiblical Hebrew inscriptions, one finds similar references to "Yhwh of Teman" and "Yhwh of Samaria." The biblical text as it comes to us perhaps preserves fragmentary memories of similar discrete manifestations—especially "Yhwh of Armies" (aka "Lord of Hosts"), which seems to enshrine Yhwh's military aspect; but also such less prominent epithets as "Yhwh Will Provide" (Gen. 22:14); "Yhwh My Banner" (Exod. 17:15); "Yhwh of Peace" (Judg. 6:24); "Yhwh Is There" (Ezek. 48:35).

The Hittite treaty reproduced here was chosen partly for its brevity; it does not include the provision for recital of the covenant and deposit of its tablets that many of the covenants do. For example, a treaty between Suppiluliuma of Hatti and the Shattiwaza of Mitanni reads, "A duplicate of this tablet is deposited before the Sun-goddess of Arinna, since the Sun-goddess of Arinna governs kingship and queenship. And in the land of Mitanni a duplicate is deposited before the Storm-god. . . . It shall be read repeatedly, for ever and ever, before the Storm-god."[39] The text continues with curses for anyone who changes, hides, or destroys the tablet.

The Assyrian oath comes from about 650 years later than the Hittite treaty. It was a new era, and the Assyrians had built the largest empire that the Near East had seen. The composition's circumstances and motivations are different; it is focused on the succession of Esarhaddon's son: "Ashurbanipal, the great crown prince designate." Ashurbanipal was not yet king, but Esarhaddon wanted to ensure that he would take the throne smoothly when the time came. Thus is it called a "loyalty oath" (in Akkadian, adê). However, a

---

37. Billie Jean Collins, *The Hittites and Their World* (Atlanta: SBL, 2007), 53.
38. Beckman, *Hittite Diplomatic Texts*, 3.
39. Ibid., 46.

reading of the text makes it clear that because it is an oath imposed on a lesser power, it takes the form of a treaty. Essentially, the oath is the primary stipulation of the treaty.

The goal of the treaty oath was to protect Ashurbanipal from threats—both from foreign nations and from within Assyria (from his own brothers, for example). Transfers of leadership in the ancient Near East were typically fraught with uncertainty; they brought dangers for the stability of the ruling structures of an empire. Time and time again, one sees battles for succession within a kingdom, and in larger empires the accession of a new ruler often brought uprisings that tested the central government's ability to enforce its rule. Almost every successive Assyrian ruler had to campaign regularly into the surrounding vassal states to reassert Assyrian domination. But Esarhaddon had a personal and specific motivation for his concerns, since he himself had earlier acceded to the throne amid turmoil. His father, Sennacherib, had nominated him as crown prince in favor of his older brothers. The brothers apparently later murdered Sennacherib while Esarhaddon was on a military campaign, probably thinking to usurp power. Esarhaddon returned quickly to fight the coup and was successful.[40]

Although the background and form of the Assyrian text are somewhat different from the Hittite treaty, there are also similarities. Some of Esarhaddon's stipulations are the same as Mursili's; both require military aid and action against traitors. Another similarity to the Hittite situation is that the Assyrian treaty oath was applied to a number of other smaller nations at the same time. Indeed, eight copies of Esarhaddon's treaty have been recovered, and a different ruler of a peripheral city-state is named on each one. This Assyrian treaty was thus a kind of form letter that could be applied to a number of rulers.

The sheer, overwhelming length of the Assyrian treaty, mostly in its stipulations and curses, is reminiscent of an end-user agreement that one must accept by checking a box before installing computer software: it is so detailed that it might contain anything, and the effect is to give the ones who drafted it carte blanche to require or claim whatever they want. In this sense the emperor asserts his power not only through the content of the treaty but also through overwhelming scribal firepower.

In the form presented here, the oath was adapted to be addressed to foreign vassals, and it was initially dubbed a "vassal treaty." However, it has since been recognized that a similar oath must have been imposed on native Assyrians as well. Ashurbanipal reports a national ceremony in which just such a loyalty oath was sworn by all the people:

> Esarhaddon, king of Assyria, my father and begetter, heeded the command of Assur and Mullissu, the gods in whom he trusted, who told him that I was to exercise the kingship. On the 12th of Iyyar, at the noble command of Ashur, Mullissu, Sin, Shamash, Adad, Bel, Nabu, Ishtar of Nineveh, Ishtar of Arbela, Ninurta, Nergal and Nusku, he convened the people of Assyria, great and small, from coast to coast, made them swear a treaty oath by the gods and established a binding agreement to protect my crown-princeship and future kingship over Assyria.[41]

---

40. These events are referred to very briefly in 2 Kgs. 19:36–37//Isa. 37:37–38, and also in Assyrian texts.

41. Parpola and Watanabe, *Neo-Assyrian Treaties*, xxix.

Both this account and the oath itself reflect that the right to inherit the rule was dependent both on the selection of the previous king (the rule did not automatically pass to the eldest son) and on the approval of the gods of the land.

As with the Hittite texts, the god lists in Neo-Assyrian treaties are extensive. Foreign gods, where they are mentioned at all, are listed after Assyrian gods. Both the lists' secondary placement and brevity reflect their lesser importance. In the Esarhaddon treaties, they are mentioned barely at all and in the manner of a form letter: "(Swear) by all the gods of one's land and one's district!" (§3). As with Mursili's refusal to call Manapa-Tarhunta king, every aspect of these treaties was crafted with an eye to establishing the desired political relationship, meaning primarily the subjugation of the vassal.

The structure of the Iron Age loyalty oaths known from Assyrian sources seems to have been flexible, but usually it included these basic elements:

1. Preamble identifying the Assyrian king and the vassal who is placed under oath
2. Designation of the Assyrian ruler or successor to whom loyalty is due
3. Divine witnesses
4. Stipulations
5. Curses for failing to carry out the stipulations[42]

Rubrics calling for vows to be taken could be inserted in various places; in the treaty presented here, one is placed in the middle of the two curse sections (§57). Similarly, Deuteronomy 27:9–26 portrays a ceremony in which the people are also sworn to an oath, this one to keep YHWH's commandments.[43]

The biblical covenants were from the beginning *adaptations* of the treaty form, rather than examples of it. Their overall form can only be aligned with the sort of political covenants presented here in a loose way. The order and weight of the various elements is simply not the same (see "Suggestions for Comparison"). However, the similarities of the rhetoric are undeniable and striking. The biblical covenants clearly draw many of their ideas from ancient Near Eastern treaties and oaths, and the same elements are all present.

1. *Identification of the covenant giver* (Deut. 5:6): "I am Yhwh, your God. . . ."

2. *Historical prologue*: If one prefers to see the historical prologue as following the identification, as in the Hittite treaties, one can see a historical account in vestigial form in 5:6b: ". . . who brought you out of the land of Egypt, out of the house of slavery." This is the core of Yhwh's historical claim on Israel. However, Moses' entire opening monologue in Deuteronomy (1:1–4:14) amounts to a lengthy recounting of the people's history with Yhwh. A representative passage reads,

> "Yhwh your God, who goes before you, is the one who will fight for you, just as he did for you in Egypt before your very eyes, and in the wilderness, where you saw how Yhwh your God carried you, just as one carries a child, all the way that you traveled until you reached this place. But in spite of this, you have no trust

---

42. This list is based on the one in Mendenhall and Herion, "Covenant," 1182. The outline in Parpola and Watanabe, *Neo-Assyrian Treaties*, xxxv–xlvii, is more detailed, incorporating elements that were not found in most treaties.

43. There are other ceremonies narrated in the Bible at which the covenant is renewed (e.g., Josh. 24; 1 Kgs. 8; Ezra 10//Neh. 8–10).

in Yhwh your God. . . . Yhwh said to me, 'Say to them, "Do not go up and do not fight, for I am not in the midst of you; otherwise you will be defeated by your enemies."' Although I told you, you would not listen. You rebelled against the command of Yhwh and presumptuously went up into the hill country." (Deut. 1:30–32, 42–43)

3. *Stipulations* (4:44–27:8): "This is the law that Moses set before the Israelites. These are the decrees and the statutes and ordinances that Moses spoke to the Israelites when they had come out of Egypt" (4:44–45). Although this long section contains primarily legal injunctions that are meant to be obeyed, it is a diverse body of literature, including hortatory interludes, stories, and so forth.

4. *Divine witnesses* (4:26): "I call heaven and earth to witness against you today that you will soon utterly perish from the land that you are crossing the Jordan to occupy" (see also 31:28). The Hittite treaty similarly calls on heaven and earth (as well as other natural phenomena) as witnesses (§19). And although the Assyrian treaty calls instead on "all the gods of heaven and earth" (§3), in the curse section some of the curses involve natural hardships caused by heaven and earth (e.g., §64).

5. *Blessings* (28:1–14): "All these blessings shall come upon you and overtake you, if you obey Yhwh your God" (Deut. 28:2).

6. *Curses* (28:15–68): "But if you will not obey Yhwh your God by diligently observing all his commandments and decrees, which I am commanding you today, then all these curses shall come upon you and overtake you" (Deut. 28:15).

7. *Oath taking* (27:9–26): "The Levites shall declare in a loud voice to all the Israelites: 'Cursed be anyone who makes an idol. . . .' All the people shall respond, saying, 'Amen!'" (Deut. 27:14–15).

8. *Deposit/recital* (10:1–2; 31:10–13, 24–29):[44]

> Moses commanded them: "Every seventh year . . . you shall read this law before all Israel in their hearing. Assemble the people . . . so that they may hear and . . . so that their children, who have not known it, may hear." (Deut. 31:10–13)

> Moses commanded the Levites who carried the ark of the covenant of Yhwh, saying, "Take this book of the law and put it beside the ark of the covenant of Yhwh your God; let it remain there as a witness against you." (Deut. 31:25–26)

Perhaps the largest single distinguishing aspect of the biblical covenants is that Yhwh takes on the role of the human emperor. Despite the form's "continuity with age-old patterns of thought" the switch to a divine suzerain "represented a complete discontinuity from earlier ways of thinking."[45] The casting of Yhwh as a king whose claims mirror those of foreign kings can actually be widely observed in the Bible, and has been called "replacement theology."[46]

---

44. See also 10:1–2.
45. Mendenhall and Herion, "Covenant," 1183.
46. Another example is found in Isa. 30:27–33, in which Yhwh campaigns from far away, takes captives, and punishes the Assyrian king. These are all claims recognizably adapted from those of Assyrian emperors.

A related point is that Yhwh has a speaking role. Although the Assyrian oaths require loyalty to their national god (see below), Ashur does not speak; Esarhaddon dictates the terms of the oath. The situation is analogous to that of the law codes (see chap. 7), where, for example, Hammurabi pronounces the laws, while Shamash is never said to speak for himself. But in both law and covenant, Yhwh speaks for himself. The fact that the oath is made to God also affects the content of the stipulations. If it is correct to view all the laws of the Deuteronomic Code (4:44–27:8) as the stipulations of the covenant, then they cover many topics that are never broached in ancient Near Eastern treaties. (The combination of the two genres, treaty oath and law, is discussed in chap. 7.) And although theology is always in some sense political, Deuteronomy ignores many of the common stipulations of ancient treaties, such as defensive alliances and the return of fugitives;[47] these are simply not the concern of Yhwh.

Then again, there are interesting potential parallels between the prohibition of speaking treason in Vassal Treaty of Esarhaddon §§10, 12 and the prohibition of false prophetic speech in Deuteronomy 18:20–22. Furthermore, in Deuteronomy 2:5–19 Yhwh acts much like Mursili, commanding peace among the nations when he orders the Israelites not to make war with Edom, Moab, or Ammon. It is interesting to consider the relationship of this passage to those such as Isaiah 19:21–25, which suggests that Yhwh had a relationship to Egypt like the one he had with Judah; or Amos 9:7, in which Yhwh tells Israel: "Are you not like the Ethiopians to me, O people of Israel? says Yhwh. Did I not bring Israel up from the land of Egypt, and the Philistines from Caphtor and the Arameans from Kir?" This might suggest that Yhwh, like ancient emperors, made pacts with various "vassals."

Assyrian treaties shed significant light on one of the most famous aspects of Deuteronomy's rhetoric: its call to "love Yhwh your God with all your heart, and with all your soul, and with all your might" (6:5). Esarhaddon issues a similar call for the vassals to love his heir: "You shall love Ashurbanipal . . . your lord, like yourselves" (§24; cf. Lev. 19:18; Matt. 22:37, etc.). Indeed, the language of "love" was used to express political faithfulness in diplomatic texts and letters reaching back into the Bronze Age; they speak of the brotherly love between allied kings.[48] Not surprisingly, Deuteronomy frames the call to love in an explicitly covenantal framework:

> Yhwh your God is God, the faithful God who maintains covenant loyalty with those who love him and keep his commandments, to a thousand generations, and who repays in their own person those who reject him. He does not delay but repays in their own person those who reject him. (Deut. 7:9–10; cf. 5:9–10; Exod. 20:5–6; 34:6–7)

The prophets adapted the language of love to describe the nation as the bride of Yhwh.[49] The most famous example of portraying the covenant relationship as a marriage is Hosea, who says to the people, "Your love is like a morning cloud, like the dew

---

47. Perhaps Yhwh was seen as capable of reclaiming his own fugitives; see Amos 9:1–4.
48. William L. Moran, "The Ancient Near Eastern Background of the Love of God in Deuteronomy," *CBQ* 25 (1963): 77–87; Tadmor, "Treaty and Oath."
49. See Hos. 6:4–5; 12:6; Jer. 2:2; 33:11; Ezek. 16:8.

that goes away early" (6:4), and also accuses them of making a treaty with Assyria (12:1). Although this imagery may have drawn on long-standing traditions about marriage, it was essentially the prophets' own literary invention; the idea of romantic love is not primary when the term is used in treaty or covenant contexts. Even the New Testament preserves an echo of love as the keeping of covenant stipulations, when Jesus says, "If you love me, you will keep my commandments" (John 14:15).

Estimates differ on whether the overall form of the biblical covenants owes more to the Hittite suzerainty treaties or to the Assyrian ones. One striking point at which the Israelite covenants diverge from the Neo-Assyrian model toward the Hittite one is in their inclusion of a lengthy historical prologue. This, in addition to the emphasis on divine grace, which is analogous to the favor of the Hittite rulers in their treaties, differentiates the portrait of Yhwh from that of the Neo-Assyrian king. Moshe Weinfeld points out that the Neo-Assyrian rulers simply saw themselves differently from previous suzerains: "It seems that the Assyrian emperor who saw himself as king of the universe felt that it would be both unnecessary and humiliating to justify his demand of loyalty by referring to the benevolence of the suzerain to the vassal in the manner of the Hittite kings."[50] In Deuteronomy 5, the historical prologue is greatly condensed: the people are told that Yhwh "brought you out of the land of Egypt, out of the house of slavery." Moses' speech in the previous chapter (Deut. 4:32–38) expands greatly on the reasons that Yhwh is justified and the people owe their faithfulness:

> Has anything so great as this ever happened or has its like ever been heard of? Has any people ever heard the voice of a god speaking out of a fire, as you have heard, and lived? Or has any god ever attempted to go and take a nation for himself from the midst of another nation, by trials, by signs and wonders, by war, by a mighty hand and an outstretched arm, and by terrifying displays of power, as Yhwh your God did for you in Egypt before your very eyes? To you it was shown so that you would acknowledge that Yhwh is God; there is no other besides him. From heaven he made you hear his voice to discipline you. On earth he showed you his great fire, while you heard his words coming out of the fire. And because he loved your ancestors, he chose their descendants after them. He brought you out of Egypt with his own presence, by his great power, driving out before you nations greater and mightier than yourselves, to bring you in, giving you their land for a possession, as it is still today.

Like Mursili, who felt unappreciated and wronged by Manapa-Tarhunta, Yhwh portrays himself as wronged by the people. He brought them out of slavery only to have them complain repeatedly (e.g., Exod. 16; Num. 14; 17) and even prefer to be dead or back in Egypt (Num. 14:3–4). Like the Hittite covenant, the biblical covenant is a chance for a ruled people to reaffirm their commitment to their ruler.

However, Deuteronomy looks more like an Assyrian treaty in some of its specific rhetoric, and especially in its lengthy curse sections (27:15–26; 28:15–68), which are about

---

50. Moshe Weinfeld, "Deuteronomy," *ABD* 2:170.

four times as long as its blessings (28:1–14). There is also at least one section of the curses where the biblical and Assyrian curses mirror each other in structure:[51]

Deuteronomy	VTE	Curse
28:26	§41	corpses as food for animals
28:27	§39a	skin disease
28:28–29	§39b–40	blindness and wandering
28:30a	§42a	fiancée raped by enemy
28:30b–33	§42b	plunder of house and goods

Jeffrey Tigay rightly points out that there are numerous points at which the curses of Deuteronomy are paralleled by curses from many ancient Near Eastern texts, but since these parallels are not verbatim, this similarity was probably not due to literary influence. Instead, there was "a literary tradition of curses, in treaties and various other genres, shared by Israelites, Arameans, and Assyrians . . . Even if some curses were drawn more directly from foreign models, they were freely modified in keeping with Israelite ideas."[52] This may also be true of the whole: Deuteronomy adapts the treaty/oath form in a way different from any other known examples, and it seems possible that it is an Assyrian-period reshaping of materials that are not strictly related to the treaty/oath form and may even have preexisted their incorporation into Deuteronomy.

The issue of when the treaty form came into biblical literature is complicated, since the treaties were used for so long in close proximity to ancient Israel. The treaty form "is by its very nature an international form,"[53] and one can assume that a number of kings of Israel and Judah were sworn to loyalty oaths of roughly the kind presented above. This finds biblical support in the reference to the treaty with Assyria in Hosea 12:1, and Ezekiel reports that Nebuchadnezzar, king of Babylon, "took one of the royal offspring and made a covenant with him, putting him under oath" (17:13). The question is when the adaptation of the form took place, not whether it could have taken place.

More than a few scholars remain of the opinion that the idea of covenant with Yhwh is primordial to the religion and national identity of Israel.[54] That is, they think that when Israel first appeared as a people, they already viewed themselves as in a covenantal relationship with Yhwh. The alternative is to say that covenant is a later invention. Given the number, diversity, and theological weight of the biblical covenants, it seems likely that covenant was a relatively ancient concept for Israel. However, the Sinai covenant tradition in Exodus is more likely to preserve an instance of an early covenant with Yhwh (see chap. 7). Deuteronomy, in anything like the form that we have it, is significantly later.

The Bible reports in 2 Kings 22–23//2 Chronicles 34 that in the eighteenth year of Josiah (622), a "book of the law" was found in the temple and was newly propagated

---

51. This chart is based closely on that of Jeffrey H. Tigay, *Deuteronomy: The Traditional Hebrew Text with the New JPS Translation* (Philadelphia: Jewish Publication Society, 1996), 497.
52. Ibid., 496–97.
53. G. E. Mendenhall, "Covenant Forms in Israelite Tradition," *Biblical Archaeologist* 17 (1954): 54.
54. Mendenhall, "Covenant Forms in Israelite Tradition."

by the king at that time. Most scholars conclude that some form of Deuteronomy was Josiah's law book, because (1) Deuteronomy also refers to itself as a "book of the law" (29:21; 30:10; 31:26), and (2) the reforms that the history reports Josiah carried out match some of the laws of Deuteronomy. The motif of "finding an ancient book" is attested elsewhere in the ancient Near East, and appears to have been a way to increase the authority of a document in more traditional cultures in which antiquity was valued over novelty.

What indications are there that Deuteronomy has roots in the Neo-Assyrian period and not earlier? Unlikely as it may seem at first glance, it may have been precisely the absoluteness of the Neo-Assyrians' demand for loyalty that made this oath apt for adaptation to the Israelite context in Josiah's time. Note the strong language of §§34–35:

> In the future and forever Ashur will be your god, and Ashurbanipal, the great crown prince designate, will be your lord. May your sons and your grandsons fear him. . . . You shall guard [this treaty tablet which] is sealed with the seal of Ashur, king of the gods, and set up in your presence, like your own god.

The Assyrians were not monotheists, and usually they did not concern themselves whether other gods were worshiped in other places. As this text reflects, however, the Assyrians ultimately required loyalty, which implicitly put their demands and those of their national god at the top of the divine pecking order. The vassals who were forced to swear this oath may also have been compelled to display a copy of it in the temple of their own god; these tablets were found in the Nabu temple in Kalhu, and there is archaeological evidence that a copy of Esarhaddon's treaty was displayed in a temple in the Neo-Hittite city at Tell Tayinat while it was under Assyrian rule.[55]

Clearly these two demands for absolute allegiance—to Ashurbanipal and to Yhwh—come into conflict with one another. Did the existence and display of a treaty actively interfere with the religion of a vassal such as Judah? No, but it certainly would have frustrated Judean loyalists and staunch adherents to Yahwism, since vassalhood brought both financial hardship and ideological/theological submission. In this context, it becomes clear that the adaptation of the Assyrian covenant form to Yahwistic use was meant to subvert the claims of the empire. That is, the demand of faithfulness to Yhwh probably necessarily precludes complete faithfulness to a foreign emperor, and to frame that demand in the same literary form that the empire used makes the contrast especially stark. Deuteronomy's use of the treaty/oath form is an example of fighting fire with fire.

It is almost certainly not accidental that Josiah's propagation of the Deuteronomic law book came when it did: By 622 Assyria was a very troubled power, having faced another struggle for succession after Ashurbanipal's death in 627 and insurrections by the Babylonians. Its control over outlying areas such as Palestine was decidedly compromised by this time, and by 612 the Neo-Assyrian Empire had come to a rapid end. Thus in addition to their religious significance, Josiah's reforms had the character

---

55. Jacob Lauinger, "Some Preliminary Thoughts on the Tablet Collection in Building XVI from Tell Tayinat," *Canadian Society for Mesopotamian Studies Journal* 6 (2011): 5–14.

of a national liberation movement. It is important to remember that up to this time, Jerusalem had never been conquered under Davidic rule. Although Judah was a vassal or client state, it had not been turned into a province by the Assyrians. Judean national pride—linked to Yhwh the warrior-king—was still alive in Zion, and it burns hot in Deuteronomy.

REFLECTION QUESTIONS

1. It has been said that whereas the Hittite treaties emphasized the vassal's debt of gratitude to the suzerain, the Assyrian treaties emphasized the self-interested desire to avoid destruction. Do you agree, and if so, what supports that case? Which approach do you think would be more effective?

2. Why do you think Yhwh is cast in the role of the suzerain? What problems does it solve? What problems does it raise?

3. Given that Deuteronomy does not line up precisely with the form of either treaty, what reasons would you give for the differences? These could include theological, ideological, and literary factors.

4. How does an awareness of the ancient backgrounds of the covenant form affect your view of the idea of making a covenant with God?

FURTHER READING

Beckman, Gary M. *Hittite Diplomatic Texts*, ed. Harry A. Hoffner Jr. 2nd ed. SBLWAW 7. Atlanta: Scholars Press, 1999.

McCarthy, D. J. *Treaty and Covenant: A Study in Form in the Ancient Oriental Documents and in the Old Testament*. Rev. ed. Analecta Biblica 21A. Rome: Pontifical Biblical Institute, 1978.

Mendenhall, G. E. "Covenant Forms in Israelite Tradition." *Biblical Archaeologist* 17 (1954): 49–76.

Mendenhall, G. E., and Gary A. Herion. "Covenant." *ABD* 1:1179–1202.

Moran, William L. "The Ancient Near Eastern Background of the Love of God in Deuteronomy." *CBQ* 25 (1963): 77–87.

Parpola, Simo, and Kazuko Watanabe. *Neo-Assyrian Treaties and Loyalty Oaths*. SAA 2. Helsinki: Helsinki University, 1988.

Tadmor, Hayim. "Treaty and Oath in the Ancient Near East: An Historian's Approach." Pages 127–52 in *Humanizing America's Iconic Book: Society of Biblical Literature Centennial Addresses*. Edited by G. M. Tucker and D. A. Knight. Chico, CA: SBL, 1982.

Tigay, Jeffrey H. *Deuteronomy: The Traditional Hebrew Text with the New JPS Translation*. Philadelphia: Jewish Publication Society, 1996.

Weinfeld, Moshe. "Deuteronomy." *ABD* 2:168–83.

PART III

Former Prophets

10

The Divine in History

The Mesha Inscription, Judges 2, and 2 Kings 3

JUDGES 2:7–23

When: See discussion
Where: Jerusalem
Language: Hebrew

2 KINGS 3:1–27

When: See discussion
Where: Jerusalem
Language: Hebrew

THE MESHA INSCRIPTION

What: Inscription on black basalt stela, 1.24 m high × 79 cm wide
When: ca. 835 BCE
Where: Moab (present-day Jordan)
Language: Moabite
Translation: By the author (Moabite text: Shmuel Ahituv, *Echoes from the Past: Hebrew and Cognate Inscriptions from the Biblical Period* [Jerusalem: Carta, 2008], 392).

[1]I am Mesha son of Chemosh-[yat] king of Moab, the Dibonite.[1] [2]My father ruled over Moab thirty years and I ruled [3]after my father; and I built this high place for Chemosh in the citadel, a high place of [4][vic]tory because he made me more victorious than all the kings, and because he caused me to dominate all my enemies.

---

1. Dibon was Mesha's capital city. It is in the same place as modern Dhiban, Jordan, east of the Dead Sea.

Omri [5]was king of Israel, and for many days he subjugated Moab because Chemosh was angry with his land. [6]And his son replaced him and he too said, "I will subjugate Moab." In my days he said that, [7]but I dominated him and his house and Israel was completely destroyed forever. Omri had conquered all the land [8]of Madaba,[2] and he ruled it during his reign and half the reign of his son, forty years; but Chemosh [9]returned it in my day.

So I rebuilt Baal-Meon and I made the reservoir in it and I bu[ilt] [10]Qiryaten. The Gadites had lived in the land of Ataroth from of old and the king of Israel [11]built Ataroth for them. But I fought against the city and I seized it and I slew all the people [so that] [12]the city belonged to Chemosh and Moab. I brought back from there the altar-hearth of its David,[3] and I [13]dragged it before Chemosh in Qiryat. I settled in [Ataroth] men of Sharon and m[en] [14]of Maharoth.[4]

And Chemosh said to me, "Go, seize Nebo against Israel," so I [15]went at night and I fought with it from daybreak until midday. I took [16]it and I slew all of them, seven thousand men and boys and women and girls [17]and "wombs" because I had dedicated it to the ban for Ashtar-Chemosh.[5] I took [the ves]sels [18]of YHWH and I dragged them before Chemosh.

The king of Israel had built [19]Yahaz, and he ruled there while he was fighting with me, but Chemosh drove him out before me. [20]I took from Moab two hundred men, all its commanders, and I brought them to Yahaz and I seized it [21]in order to annex it to Dibon.

It was I[6] who built the citadel, "the wall of the forests,"[7] and the wall of [22]the Ophel.[8] It was I who built its gates, and I who built its towers, and [23]I who built a royal palace and I who made the enclosures for the reser[voir . . .] in the midst [24]of the city. But there was no cistern within the city, in the citadel, so I said to all the people, "Each of you make [for] [25]yourselves a cistern in his house." It was I who cut the shafts for the citadel using prisoners [26]of Israel. It was I who built up Aroer, and I who made the highway in the Arnon.

[27]It was I who built Beth Bamoth because it was a ruin. It was I who built Bezer because it was [28]a heap of stones. [. . .] with the fifty men of Dibon, because all of Dibon was under (my) command. I myself rule[d [29]ov]er [the] hundreds in the towns which I had annexed to the land. And it was I who built [30][Mada]ba and Beth-Diblathaim and Beth-Baal-Meon; I brought [my herdsmen] there [31][to herd] the flocks of the land. And as for Horonaim, the [Ho]use of [Da]vid ruled it [. . .] [32][. . .]. Chemosh [s]aid to me, "Go down, fight against

2. A city in Jordan, about twenty miles southwest of present-day Amman.

3. The singular pronoun ("*its* David) may refer to the city, or to the people as above ("their David").

4. After killing the Gadite inhabitants, Mesha repopulated the city with people from nearby areas.

5. "Ashtar-Chemosh" is a composite name for Chemosh, much like "Yhwh Elohim" for the god of Israel. Much earlier in Levantine history, Ashtar was attested as a minor deity at Ugarit.

6. Mesha's repetitive emphasis on himself as the builder of various features in Yahaz seems to be intended to emphasize his work as distinct from that of the Israelite king referred to above. The insistence is just as repetitive and pleonastic in Moabite as it appears in English.

7. The meaning of this name is unclear, but it may refer to cedar columns. Compare 1 Kgs. 7:2; 10:17; Isa. 22:8.

8. See 2 Chr. 27:3, etc.

Horonaim," so I went down [. . . [33]. . .] Chemosh [ret]urned it in my days. Then I went up from there te[n . . .] [34][. . .] righteousness and [. . .].

DISCUSSION

Moab was one of the small Levantine nations of the Iron Age, alongside Israel and Judah. It was to the east of the Dead Sea. These nations regularly found themselves in competition and conflict. The Bible recounts that the Israelite judges fought against the Moabites, the most famous episode being Ehud's slaying of the Moabite king Eglon, starting a war in which 10,000 Moabites were killed (Judg. 3:12–30). Later, David is supposed to have subjected Moab (2 Sam. 8:2). This early history is not independently verifiable, but after the division of the Israelite kingdom, it is undisputed that Moab was a vassal to the northern Omride dynasty (2 Kgs. 1:1; 3:4–5; Mesha lines 4–6).

The Mesha Stela is useful for comparison with the Bible in multiple ways. It helps historians reconstruct the history of the biblical period, and it offers a comparison to the "Deuteronomistic" theology of history that dominates the historical books of Joshua–2 Kings. The stela is written in Moabite, a Northwest Semitic dialect closely related to classical Hebrew; then as now, anyone who could read one of those languages could read the other reasonably well.

With regard to historical events, the stela and the Bible (2 Kgs. 3:4) agree that Moab was subjugated by Israel, and that Mesha eventually threw off the Israelite yoke. Beyond that, it is clear that both accounts reflect the perspectives from which they were written and the concerns of their authors, and that both are stylized for ideological reasons.

King Omri of Israel (r. 876–69) first appears in the Bible as a military commander of the army under the Israelite king Elah; 1 Kings 16 recounts that Omri rose to the throne by popular will after Elah was killed in a coup, and after a period of schism and divided kingship in the north. Omri became the founder of a powerful dynasty; the "house of Omri" played a leading role in coalitions of Levantine states that fought against the Neo-Assyrians during the ninth century and is mentioned in Assyrian inscriptions.

This mighty king of the northern kingdom may not even have been a native Israelite; his name is probably not a Hebrew one, his lineage is not described in the Bible, and he built a new capital city of Samaria outside the territories of the northern tribes. In other words, he seems to have come from one of the other peoples of ancient Canaan and to have had sympathies for them. Omri's rise to power as a foreigner would not be as surprising as it may at first appear; the incorporation of foreigners into militaries is well known throughout the ancient Near East, including in Israel and Judah (David's soldier Uriah the Hittite may be the most famous example). Shifting ethnicities between dynasties in a single nation was not uncommon either; examples include the Kassite dynasty in Babylon and the Kushite pharaohs in Egypt.

Omri's ethnic origins may help to explain why he is judged so negatively by the Yahwistic authors of the biblical history—1 Kings 16:25 reads, "Omri did what was evil in the sight of Yhwh, and did more evil than all who were before him." Despite being powerful and successful kings, both he and his heirs may well have had proclivities toward "Canaan-ite" religious practices if their heritage was outside Israel.

The Mesha Stela certainly disagrees with the Bible when it says that Israel was "com-pletely destroyed forever" (line 7). It is possible to reconcile the accounts by assuming that the stela telescopes history and conflates a successful Moabite uprising against Israel-ite hegemony (cf. 2 Kgs. 3) with the destruction of the house of Omri by Jehu in 843–842 (2 Kgs. 9), so that Mesha refers to the destruction of the house of Omri, not the northern kingdom as a political entity. In any case, fighting continued between Moab and Israel after Mesha's time. Further losses in the same region are reported to have been inflicted on Israel by Hazael of Damascus during Jehu's reign, as reported in 2 Kings 10:32–33, and probably in the Tel Dan Inscription, an Aramaic text on a stone stela that was prob-ably authorized by Hazael.

The Bible and the Mesha Stela also disagree in that Mesha claims to have thrown off Israelite rule during the reign of Omri's son (Ahab, r. 869–850), while 2 Kings 3 places it in the reign of his grandson (Jehoram, r. 849–843). It would be possible to harmo-nize the sources by assuming that Mesha's reference to "Omri's son" actually referred to his grandson, which would hardly be unusual by ancient Near Eastern standards. One memorable instance of confusion from the same period was when the Assyrians referred to Jehu as part of the "house of Omri," which he had murderously overthrown![9] Such details of the internal politics of foreign nations were simply not of primary concern to many ancient Near Eastern kings and their scribes.

Beyond its significance for historical reconstruction, the Mesha passage is a fascinat-ing and rare example of the way Israel's neighbors in the Iron Age Levant wrote their own histories. The scarcity of such inscriptions is probably related more to the writing technologies of the time than to a scarcity of history writing at the time. Unlike in Meso-potamia, where cuneiform writing on clay tablets persisted and allowed vast numbers of Assyrian and Babylonian texts to survive the millennia and be read today, it appears that Levantine nations most commonly wrote their official records in ink on soft media. Inscriptions on potsherds, clay seals, stone, and even silver attest to a relatively vibrant scribal culture. Unfortunately, the climate was not dry enough to preserve parchment or papyrus scrolls from the preexilic period.

The Mesha Inscription demonstrates striking similarities with Judean historical writ-ings pertaining to the same period. When Mesha overthrows Nebo, he kills all the Isra-elite inhabitants, even using the same verb (ḥrm) that is used in the Bible for the same practice of total annihilation of enemies and their property (Num. 21:2; Deut. 2:34; Judg. 1:17; etc.). Mesha also claims to have established a "high place," or outdoor shrine, for the national god Chemosh; Solomon is also said to have sacrificed at high places prior to the construction of the Jerusalem temple (1 Kgs. 3:2–4), and Jeroboam built high places at Bethel and Dan as the primary shrines of the northern kingdom (1 Kgs. 12:26–33). First Kings 11:7 even says that Solomon built a high place for Chemosh, although some take this to be a claim invented by a later historian to criticize Solomon.

---

9. The reference occurs on the Black Obelisk of Shalmaneser III.

From the standpoint of religion, the Mesha Stela represents the earliest secure reference to Yhwh in history.[10] The account of Mesha taking the vessels of Yhwh from the temple is not recorded in the Bible—probably because it did not involve the Jerusalem temple or any of the most significant cultic sites of the time—but it recalls the similar confiscations by the Philistines (1 Sam. 4–6) and the Babylonians (2 Kgs. 25:14). Plundering of temples was a frequent and widespread occurrence in the ancient Near East.

More broadly, the Mesha Inscription serves as a corrective to the older, facile claim that pagan religions were based on the cyclical processes of nature, while Israelite religion was based on its historical experience. Some theologians have sought to distinguish Israel's God as a *god who acts* in history,[11] but the Mesha Inscription claims that Chemosh acted in history as well. In sum, "the idea of divine acts in history is found in much the same form both in Israel and in the neighboring peoples."[12] Specifically, Mesha says that the national deity had become angry with his people and punished them with military failures (line 3), but that he also fought on behalf of his people when his anger subsided (lines 14, 19).

A similar theological worldview was held by the biblical authors; the pattern of divine anger and mercy is crystallized most concisely in Judges 2, which describes a repeated cycle: Human apostasy > Divine anger and abandonment > Human distress > Divine deliverance. Judges 2 can serve as a kind of condensed summary of the biblical historians' view of the nation's fortunes throughout the Deuteronomistic History, the story of Israel and Judah that spans from Joshua through 2 Kings. The history is named after the book of Deuteronomy, which precedes it directly, and which enunciates the theology that governs the history, as in Deuteronomy 4:37–40:

> Because [Yhwh] loved your ancestors, he chose their descendants after them. He brought you out of Egypt with his own presence, by his great power, driving out before you nations greater and mightier than yourselves, to bring you in, giving you their land for a possession, as it is still today. So acknowledge today and take to heart that Yhwh is God in heaven above and on the earth beneath; there is no other. Keep his statutes and his commandments, which I am commanding you today for your own well-being and that of your descendants after you, so that you may long remain in the land that Yhwh your God is giving you for all time.

Whereas Deuteronomy sets up this relationship between faithful obedience and success, the passage in Judges shows Deuteronomistic thinkers interpreting history, with all its national ups and downs.

Much as the Mesha Stela interprets history theologically from at least half a century later, the Judges passage is also thought to have been written significantly later than the events it summarizes—in this case, perhaps hundreds of years later. To say that it is a late

---

10. An Egyptian topographical list from the New Kingdom names a place called "Yahu" in the southern Levant, which may be named after Yhwh. It is quite likely that certain biblical texts were composed earlier than the Mesha Stela, but copies have not survived.

11. G. Ernest Wright, *God Who Acts: Biblical Theology as Recital* (SBT 8; London: SCM Press, 1952).

12. Bertil Albrektson, *History and the Gods: An Essay on the Idea of Historical Events as Divine Manifestations in the Ancient Near East and in Israel* (Lund: C. W. K. Gleerup, 1967), 115.

interpretation is not to pronounce any judgment about the history of the premonarchic period in Israel, which is a different and more complicated matter; it is only to say that this is how the nation's history looked to those who compiled it (almost certainly with the help of existing sources) in the time of Josiah and again during (or after) the Babylonian exile. Judges offers a reason for Yhwh's anger, whereas the reason for Chemosh's is not identified.

A final theological point demonstrates the extent to which the authors of 2 Kings 3 shared in common theological presuppositions of their times. At the end of the passage, the king of Moab, recognizing that the battle is going against him, sacrifices his son and heir, presumably to Chemosh. Apparently it works, since "great wrath came upon Israel, so they withdrew from him and returned to their own land" (3:27). This is likely to surprise readers who expect theological uniformity in the Bible on at least two counts: first, that child sacrifice seems to work; and second, that "pagans" know how to influence the supernatural, that their gods have power. What one sees here is not a strict monotheism as in, for example, Isaiah 45:21 ("There is no other god besides me"), but rather monolatry: the restriction of worship to one god out of many who may exist (see further discussion in chap. 23). Apparently these theologians took a similar view of child sacrifice: it was forbidden (Lev. 18:21; Deut. 12:31) *despite* its potential efficacy.

There were certainly differences in the theology and historiography of ancient Israel and Judah compared with the surrounding nations, but comparison of the texts should press readers to greater nuance and precision in their assessments of the differences.

REFLECTION QUESTIONS

1. From a literary perspective, what aspects of the biblical account of Mesha's victory from 2 Kings 3 are told in form or style that is similar to the Mesha Stela? What parts seem to be written in a different form or style?

2. Scholars tend to assume that ways of writing history developed similarly in the different Iron Age nations; working from that assumption, how could one account for the differences between the two texts?

3. Based on your answers to the two previous questions, how would you describe the relationship between the account in 2 Kings 3 and "history as it really was"?

4. Is it possible to reconstruct ancient history "as it really was"? Why or why not?

5. Can you think of examples of history writing from our own times or recent times that show a process of remembering and recounting similar to that of 2 Kings 3? Is it possible to write "history as it really was" in modern times?

6. The discussion section notes a basic similarity between the theological perspective of Judges 2 and that of the Mesha Stela. How do their perspectives *differ*? How might the relationship between the date of the events recounted and the date of the account itself affect the way events are remembered and retold?

7. How do the portrayals of Yhwh and Chemosh as characters differ between Judges 2 and the Mesha Stela?

8. What does it mean that Mesha dragged the vessels of Yhwh "before Chemosh"? What do you think is the significance of that act?

9. The stereotypical image of Israel's neighbors is that they were polytheistic; do you see indications of polytheism in the Mesha Stela?

FURTHER READING

Albrektson, Bertil. *History and the Gods: An Essay on the Idea of Historical Events as Divine Manifestations in the Ancient Near East and in Israel.* Lund: C. W. K. Gleerup, 1967.

Dearman, J. Andrew, ed. *Studies in the Mesha Inscription and Moab.* Atlanta: Scholars Press, 1989.

Emerton, John A. "The Kingdoms of Judah and Israel and Ancient Hebrew History Writing." Pages 34–49 in *Biblical Hebrew in Its Northwest Semitic Setting: Typological and Historical Perspectives.* Edited by Steven E. Fassberg and Avi Hurvitz. Winona Lake, IN: Eisenbrauns, 2006.

Lemaire, André. "Hebrew and West Semitic Inscriptions and Pre-Exilic Israel." In *In Search of Pre-Exilic Israel: Proceedings of the Oxford Old Testament Seminar.* Edited by John Day. London: T & T Clark, 2004.

Roberts, J. J. M. "Myth Versus History: Re-Laying the Comparative Foundations." *CBQ* 38 (1976): 1–13.

Saggs, H. W. F. "The Divine in History." In *Essential Papers on Israel and the Ancient Near East.* Edited by Frederick E. Greenspahn. New York: New York University Press, 1991.

Wright, G. Ernest. *God Who Acts: Biblical Theology as Recital.* SBT 8. London: SCM Press, 1952.

11

Temple-Building Accounts

Inscriptions of Gudea and Tiglath-pileser I, and 1 Kings 5–9

1 KINGS 5–9

When: Narrates events of the tenth century (on the date of composition, see below)
Where: Jerusalem
Language: Hebrew

STATUE B OF GUDEA OF LAGASH

What: Cuneiform inscription on dark green diorite statue, 93 cm high × 46.5 cm wide × 61.5 cm in diameter
When: ca. 2100 BCE
Where: Girsu
Language: Sumerian
Translation: Dietz Otto Edzard[1]

(*Column i, lines 1–20*) One liter of beer, one liter of bread, half a liter of flour (used) for spreading, (and) half a liter of emmer groats[2] being the regular offering for the statue of Gudea, ruler of Lagash, who built the House of Ningirsu.[3] (If a future) ruler revokes (and cuts off these offerings) from the House of Ningirsu, (Gudea's) master, (and) who (thereby) curtails the innate rights of Ningirsu, may the offerings (of that ruler) be revoked (and cut off) from the House of Ningirsu, and may his mouth stay shut.

(*ii 1–iii 5*) For Ningirsu, mighty warrior of Enlil, did Gudea, who has a "treasured" name, ruler of Lagash, shepherd chosen in the heart of Ningirsu, whom Nanshe[4] regarded

1. Dietz Otto Edzard, *Gudea and His Dynasty* (Royal Inscriptions of Mesopotamia, Early Periods 3/1; Toronto: University of Toronto Press, 1997), 30–38.
2. Hulled grains of emmer wheat, or farro.
3. Ningirsu was a warrior-god and also associated with the fruitfulness of crops. His name means "Lord of Girsu," after a town in the kingdom of Lagash.
4. Nanshe, Nin-dara, Bau, Gatmudu, Ig-alim, Shul-shaga, and Ningishzida are names of deities.

201

in a friendly manner, to whom Nin-dara gave strength, the one keeping to the word of Bau, child born of Gatumdu, to whom Ig-alim gave prestige and a lofty scepter, whom Shul-shaga richly provided with breath of life, whom Ningishzida, his (personal) god, made stand out gloriously as the legitimate head of the assembly—

(*iii 6–11*) when Ningirsu had directed his meaningful gaze on his city, had chosen Gudea as the legitimate shepherd in the land, and when he had selected him by his hand from among 216,000 persons—

(*iii 12–iv 6*) (For Ningirsu, Gudea then) cleansed the city, and let (purifying) fire go over it.[5] He set up the brick-mould, determined the (first) brick by means of an oracle.[6] Persons ritually unclean, unpleasant to look at (?) [. . .] (and) women doing work he banished from the city; no woman would carry the basket, only the best of the warriors would work for him.

(*iv 7–19*) He built Ningirsu's House on ground that was as clean as Eridu (itself).[7] No one was lashed by the whip or hit by the goad, no mother would beat her child. Governor, inspector, overseer, levy supervisor, (whoever) stood watching the work, supervision was, in their hands, as (soft) as combed wool.[8]

(*v 1–11*) No hoe was used at the city cemetery, no bodies were buried, no cult musician brought his harp (or) let a lamentation sound, and no wailing woman sang a dirge. Within the boundaries of Lagash no one took an accused person to the place of oath-taking, and no debt collector entered anyone's house.

(*v 12–20*) (Gudea) made things function as they should for his lord Ningirsu; he built and restored for him his Eninnu,[9] the White Thunderbird, and within (that complex) he installed for him his beloved grove (?),[10] (in) the scent (of) cedars.

(*v 21–36*) When he was about to build the House of Ningirsu, Ningirsu, his master who loves him, opened for him (all) the roads leading from the Upper to the Lower Sea. From the Amanus, the mountain range of the cedar, he (cut) cedars of sixty and fifty cubits [length] and boxwood of twenty-five cubits length, joined them to form rafts, and (thus) made them come down from their mountain.

. . .

(*v 45–52*) Those cedar (beams) he used to make big doors, and he made carvings of shining flowers (?) on them, and he brought them into the Eninnu (for Ningirsu). (Moreover,) he used (the cedars) as roof beams in the lofty building where cold water is sprinkled for (Ningirsu).

---

5. Gudea burned the land to clear it of vegetation.

6. Laying the first brick was analogous to laying the cornerstone of a modern building and was thus a ceremonial occasion.

7. Eridu was a Mesopotamian city that was the mythical "first city" in mythology; thus in this context it had some of the same connotations as Eden in Jewish and Christian traditions—a place of original, unspoiled purity.

8. I.e., there was no coerced labor on the temple. This might be compared to the reaction against Solomon's forced labor (1 Kgs. 9:15; 12).

9. The name of the temple, meaning "House of the Fifty."

10. Sacred groves were common in ANE temple precincts.

(*v 53–vi 2*) From the city of Ursu and the mountain range of Ibla he (brought) juniper, big firs as well as plane trees, mountain wood, joining them to form rafts, and he used them as roof beams (for Ningirsu) in the Eninnu.

(*vi 3–12*) He brought down big stone slabs from Umanum, the mountain range of Menua, and from Basar, the mountain range of the Martu, and he used them to make steles, setting them up (for Ningirsu) in the courtyard of the Eninnu.

[The intervening lines describe other exotic materials brought from various regions and their uses.]

(*vi 51–56*) He brought down a myriad (?) of talents of bitumen[11] from Madga, the mountain range of the Ordeal river (?), and he (used it for) building the retaining wall of the Eninnu.

(*vi 57–58*) He brought down . . . clay.

(*vi 59–63*) From the mountain range of Barme he loaded innumerable stone slabs on big boats, and he placed them (for Ningirsu) around the foundation walls of the Eninnu.

(*vi 64–76*) He defeated the cities of Ansan and Elam and brought the plunder to Ningirsu in his Eninnu. When he had built the Eninnu for Ningirsu, Gudea, ruler of Lagash, made (the plunder) a donation forever.[12]

(*vi 77–vii 20*) No ruler has ever built a house like this one for Ningirsu; but he (Gudea) indeed built it. He inscribed his name, and made things function as they should. He reacted piously to the word Ningirsu had spoken to him. From the mountain of Magan he brought down diorite, and he fashioned it into a statue of himself. "I built his House for my lord, (so) life is my reward"—(this is how) he named (the statue) for (Ningirsu's) sake, and he brought it to him in (his) House.

(*vii 21–25*) Gudea "gives word" to the statue:[13] "Statue, would you please tell my lord:

(*vii 26–33*) When I built for him the Eninnu, his beloved House, I had debts remitted and 'washed all hands.' For seven days no grain was ground.[14] The slave-woman was allowed to be equal to her mistress, the slave was allowed to walk side by side with his master.

(*vii 34–48*) In my city the one (who appeared ritually) unclean to someone was permitted to sleep (only) outside. I had anything disharmonious turned right back where it belongs. I paid attention to the justice ordained by Nanshe and Ningirsu; I did not expose the orphan to the wealthy person nor did I expose the widow to the influential one. In a house having no male child I let the daughter (of the house) become its heir."[15] He installed the statue (in order) to convey messages.

(*vii 49–55*) For this statue nobody was supposed to use silver or lapis lazuli, neither should copper or tin or bronze be a working (material). It is (exclusively) of diorite; let it stand at the libation place.

---

11. A naturally occurring asphalt.
12. Note the comparison to the captured items "devoted to Yhwh" in Josh. 6:17–24; Deut. 13:17; etc.
13. See discussion of votive statues, below.
14. This is a brief reference to the festival of temple dedication.
15. Cf. Moses' decision concerning the daughters of Zelophehad in Num. 27:1–11.

(*vii 56–viii 38*) Nobody will forcibly damage (the stone). O statue, your eye is that of Ningirsu: He who removes from the Eninnu the statue of Gudea, the ruler of Lagash, who had built Ningirsu's Eninnu;

who effaces the inscription thereon;

who destroys (the statue);

who disregards my judgment after (at the beginning of a prosperous New Year) his god Ningirsu, my master, had (directly) addressed him within the crowd, as my god (addressed me);

who revokes my donation;

who deletes my name from the collection of songs (addressed to) me and then puts there his (own) name;

who abandons the chapels set up in the courtyard of my lord Ningirsu, not considering the fact that since earliest days, since the seed sprouted forth, no one was (ever) supposed to alter the utterance of a ruler of Lagash who, after building the Eninnu for my lord Ningirsu, made things function as they should; no (one was supposed) to disregard his judgment.

(*viii 39–ix 11*) (As for) him who changes the word of Gudea, ruler of Lagash, and disregards his judgment, let An,[16] let Enlil, let Ninhursanga, let Enki of trustworthy utterance, let Suen, whose name nobody can explain, let Ningirsu, lord of the weapon, let Nanshe, lady of the boundary, let Nindara, the master and warrior, let the mother of Lagash, shining Gatumdu, let Bau, the lady, eldest daughter of An, let Inanna, lady of battle, let Utu, lord of the blue (skies), let Hendursanga, the herald of the Land, let Ig-alim, let Shulshaga, let Ninmar, eldest daughter of Nanshe, let Dumuzi-abzu, lady of Kinunir, let my (personal) god Ningishzida reverse the promise that had been made to him; let him be slaughtered like a bull on that day, let him be seized like an aurochs[17] by his fierce horn; let him sit down in the dust instead of on the seat they set up for him;

(*ix 12–22*) If in fact (his) mind is fixed on erasing this inscription, let his (own) name (disappear) from the house of his (personal) god (and) be removed from the tablet; let his (personal) god ignore the "striking" among (his) people;[18] let the rain be kept back in heaven, let water be kept back on earth, let years of shortages arise for him, and let there be a famine during his reign;

(*ix 23–30*) Let that person, like someone who did evil to a righteous one [. . .] and let him not go free; let the Land proclaim the prominence of the broad-breasted one among the gods, the lord Ningirsu.

ANNALS OF TIGLATH-PILESER I

What: Cuneiform text reconstructed from numerous clay prisms and fragments
When: First quarter of eleventh century BCE
Where: Ashur

---

16. All of the names in the paragraph are deities invoked in the curses.
17. A type of large wild cattle, now extinct.
18. Presumably a reference to plague (see chap. 25).

Language: Akkadian
Translation: A. Kirk Grayson[19]

(*Column vii, lines 60–70*) At that time 641 years had passed since the temple of the gods Anu and Adad—the great gods, my lords—had been built by Shamshi-Adad (III), vice-regent of Ashur, son of Ishme-Dagan (II) (who was) also vice-regent of the god Ashur. It had become dilapidated. Ashur-dan (I), king of Assyria, son of Ninurta-apil-Ekur (who was) also king of Assyria, tore down this temple but did not rebuild (it), and so for 60 years its foundation had not been relaid. In my accession year, the gods Anu and Adad—the great gods, my lords, who love my priesthood—commanded me to rebuild their shrine.

(*vii 71–84*) I made bricks. I delineated this area, dug down to the bottom of its foundation pit, (and) laid its foundation upon bedrock. I piled up this entire area with bricks like an oven, making it 50 layers of brick deep. I laid thereon the limestone foundation of the temple of the gods Anu and Adad, the great gods, my lords.

(*vii 85–107*) I rebuilt it from top to bottom and made it bigger than before. I constructed two large ziqqurrats[20] which were appropriate for their great divinity. I planned (and) laboriously rebuilt (and) completed the pure temple, the holy shrine, their joyful abode, their happy dwelling which stands out like the stars of heaven and which represents the choicest skills of the building trade. I decorated its interior like the interior of heaven. I decorated its walls as splendidly as the brilliance of rising stars. I raised its towers and its ziqqurrats to the sky and made fast its parapets with baked brick. I installed inside a conduit[21] (suitable for the conduct) of the rites of their great divinity.

(*vii 107–14*) I brought the gods Anu and Adad, the great gods, my lords, inside (and) set them on their exalted thrones. (Thus) did I please their great divinity.

(*viii 1–4*) The *hamru*-temple[22] of the god Adad, my lord—which Shamshi-Adad (III), vice-regent of Ashur, son of Ishme-Dagan (II) (who was) also vice-regent of the god Ashur, had built—was dilapidated and in ruins.

(*viii 5–10*) I delineated its site (and) rebuilt it from top to bottom with baked brick. I adorned it and made it stronger than before.

(*viii 11–16*) Inside I offered pure sacrifices to the god Adad, my lord. At that time I transported obsidian, *haltu*-stone,[23] and haematite from the mountains of the land of Nairi, which I conquered with the support of the god Ashur, my lord. I deposited (them) in the *hamru*-temple of the god Adad, my lord, forever.

(*viii 17–49*) Because I made plans without ceasing and was not slack in the work (but) quickly completed the pure temple, the exalted shrine, for the abode of the gods Anu and Adad, the great gods, my lords, and (thereby) pleased their great divinity: may the gods

---

19. A. Kirk Grayson, *Assyrian Rulers of Early First Millennium BC I (1114–859 BC)* (Royal Inscriptions of Mesopotamia, Assyrian Periods 2; Toronto: University of Toronto Press, 1991), 28–31.

20. This term, more often anglicized as "ziggurats," refers to temple buildings with a stepped, pyramidal form.

21. Presumably a kind of water pipe. Mesopotamian rituals often involved water (see above, Gudea Statue B v 45–52).

22. In Akkadian, *hamru* means "sacred precinct." Lines vii 1–10 are a digression concerning a separate temple.

23. The identity of this stone is unknown.

Anu and Adad faithfully have mercy upon me, may they love my prayers, may they heed my fervent petitions, may they grant abundant rain and extraordinarily rich years during my reign; may they lead me about safely in battle and strife; may they subdue under me all enemy lands, rebellious mountain regions, and rulers hostile to me; may they pronounce a favorable blessing over me and my priestly progeny; and may they firmly place my priesthood in the presence of the god Ashur and their great divinity forever like a mountain.

I wrote on my monumental and clay inscriptions my heroic victories, my successful battles, (and) the suppression of the enemies (and) foes of the god Ashur which the gods Anu and Adad granted me. I deposited (them) in the temple of the gods Anu and Adad, the great gods, my lords, forever. In addition, I anointed with oil the monumental inscriptions of Shamshi-Adad (III) my forefather, made sacrifices, (and) returned them to their places.

(*viii 50–88*) In the future, in days to come, may a later prince, when the temple of the gods Anu and Adad, the great gods, my lords, and those ziqqurrats become old and dilapidated, restore their weakened (portions). May he anoint with oil my monumental and clay inscriptions, make sacrifices, (and) return (them) to their places. His name let him write with mine. (Then) may the gods Anu and Adad, the great gods, my lords, guide him well in joy and success, as they did me.

He who breaks (or) erases my monumental or clay inscriptions, throws (them) into water, burns (them), covers (them) with earth, secretly stores (them) in a Taboo House where they cannot be seen, (who) erases my inscribed name and writes his (own) name, or (who) conceives of anything injurious and puts it into effect to the disadvantage of my monumental inscriptions:

May the gods Anu and Adad, the great gods, my lords, glare at him angrily and inflict an evil curse upon him. May they overthrow his sovereignty. May they tear out the foundations of his royal throne. May they terminate his noble line. May they smash his weapons, bring about the defeat of his army, and make him sit in bonds before his enemies. May the god Adad strike his land with terrible lightning (and) inflict his land with distress, famine, want, (and) plague. May he command that he not live one day longer. May he destroy his name (and) his seed from the land.

SUGGESTIONS FOR COMPARISON

	Gudea	*Tiglath-pileser*	*1 Kings*[24]
Circumstances / decision to build	ii 1–iii 11	vii 60–70	5:1–5
Preparations	iii 12–iv 19	vii 71–84	5:6–18
Description of the building	v 12–vi 76[25]	vii 85–107	6:1–7:51

24. Some readers may wish to consult the longer list of parallels suggested in Richard E. Averbeck, "Sumer, the Bible, and Comparative Method: Historiography and Temple Building," in *Mesopotamia and the Bible: Comparative Explorations* (ed. Mark W. Chavalas and K. Lawson Younger Jr.; Grand Rapids: Baker, 2002), 119–21; however, that list is focused on the Gudea Cylinders rather than the texts presented here.

25. The account of preparations and description of the building are combined in v 21–vi 76.

Dedication rites	vii 26–33	vii 107–114	8:1–11, 54–66
Prayer of the king	vii 26–48	viii 17–49	8:12–30
Blessings and curses	vii 56–ix 30	viii 50–88	9:3–9

DISCUSSION

Along with military exploits, building campaigns were the primary achievements for which ancient Near Eastern kings took credit in their own inscriptions. Building accounts were popular because they reflected both the flourishing of society and the maintenance of earthly order that the gods delegated to the king. Rather than being objective records of events, these inscriptions represent the stories that kings wanted told about themselves. They are shaped and edited to tell a certain story, and they consistently include the same sorts of claims.[26] These stories about divinely elected temple and city builders can be considered a subset of "the broad category of narratives concerning kings who were selected for specific divine missions."[27] Such stories turn out to have a lot in common.

Sometimes building accounts concerned projects that were for the public good—for example, Tiglath-pileser recounts that he rebuilt palaces and royal residences and repaired weakened fortifications. He also speaks of building up stores of grain and the numbers of livestock.[28] However, a sizable number describe the building of temples, and these are usually much more detailed. These are intended to present the king as pious and thus favored by the gods; as a significant additional benefit, they would have reminded priests of the temples (who made up a majority of the small portion of society that could read and write) who their benefactor was.

It is possible to identify an archetypal form of these temple-building accounts. Despite significant variations among them, the most complete (such as the Tiglath-pileser and biblical stories above) include the following structural elements:

1. Circumstances of the project and the decision to build
2. Preparations, such as drafting workmen and gathering materials
3. Description of the building
4. Dedication rites and festivities
5. Blessing and/or prayer of the king
6. Blessings and curses of future generations[29]

For an analysis of how each text can be divided into sections, see the "Suggestions for Comparison" above.

---

26. As an example of the selective nature of the story that such annals tell, it appears from other data that the Assyrians actually were under serious pressure from the Arameans during Tiglath-pileser's reign (Grayson, *Assyrian Rulers*, 5), but no setbacks are mentioned in the annals.

27. Victor Avigdor Hurowitz, *I Have Built You an Exalted House* (JSOTSup 115; Sheffield: JSOT Press, 1992), 48.

28. Grayson, *Assyrian Rulers*, 26.

29. Hurowitz, *I Have Built You an Exalted House*, 64.

The three building accounts presented in this chapter are all embedded in historical narratives, and in each case the concern to memorialize the king is also clear. These were the most common manifestations of such inscriptions, but they could also be embedded in other genres, such as myths and hymns.[30]

The earliest temple-building inscriptions in Mesopotamia come from the late third millennium and were composed in Sumerian on behalf of Gudea, king of Lagash, who calls himself "the shepherd." The most famous of these are the two cylinders that contain a lengthy (fifty-four-column) account of the building of Eninnu. The inscription presented here was chosen for its brevity (it contains most of the same elements in less than a tenth of the space).[31] However, the text still alludes briefly to each element in the six-part form described above, which supports the idea that the form had cultural significance in its wholeness. To put it another way, the ancients seem to have *expected* at least those six elements to be included in a story about building a temple.

The statue on which the above inscription appears is famous because it shows Gudea holding an architectural plan of the temple laid out on his lap. But the fact that the text is written on a statue also illuminates its function. In the ancient Near East, elites frequently had votive statues of themselves placed in the shrines of their deities. The statues were intended to represent their sponsors in a posture of continuous praise and supplication of the deity, and sometimes a prayer in the form of a letter to the god would be inscribed on smaller statues. The Gudea text presented here is more extensive than most. At one point, it says, "Gudea 'gives word' to the statue:[32] 'Statue, would you please tell my lord: . . .'" This is the king's instruction or recording of his message to Ningirsu. The immediate message (vii 34–48) is that Gudea has carried out a proper festival and has ensured justice in his land; the emphasis on the widow and the orphan will be familiar to readers of the Bible (Exod. 22:22, etc.; cf. chap. 5).

The closing curses of the Gudea text may seem somewhat different from those of a typical building account, since they open with a concern for the statue itself. However, the statue was a part of the temple precinct and intended to immortalize Gudea specifically as the builder of the temple, and the curses extend to the neglect of the temple chapels. Thus they mostly overlap with Tiglath-pileser's curses, which include a nearly identical warning against effacing the king's inscriptions.

The Assyrian temple-building account presented above was extracted from the annals of Tiglath-pileser I (r. 1114–1076). Although kings had recorded their deeds in various forms from the beginning of the written word, annals developed later. In annals, "events are narrated in chronological order with a clear division between the years."[33] They are fuller and more narrative than chronicles (see chap. 12), and these from Tiglath-pileser are the first exemplars that are known to us, so it may be that they developed during his

---

30. Ibid., 59.

31. Some interesting detail is lost in the condensing. For example, in the longer cylinder texts, Gudea repeatedly seeks the counsel and approval of the gods, who reveal to him the plan of the temple in detail. Much of the description of the temple is also omitted from the statue inscription, as is nearly the entire description of the celebratory festival.

32. See discussion of votive statues, below.

33. Grayson, *Assyrian Rulers*, 7.

reign. Annals continued to be written and copied over thousands of years (for an extract about a military campaign against Judah from later Assyrian annals, see chap. 13). They were written on clay and archived, and they were sometimes also inscribed on buildings and monuments.

The temple-building account presented above is only about one and a half columns excerpted from an eight-column annalistic text. After introducing himself and touting his greatness and favor with the gods, Tiglath-pileser spent about five columns—the great majority of the tablet—discussing his military campaigns and victories. Even though the temple-building account is not the bulk of the annals, it might be said that the text builds to it and culminates in it, since it is the last event recounted, and it comprises the longest single section. Tiglath-pileser's temple-building account expresses thanks for the grace of the gods during his reign and seeks to affirm his close relationship with them. These annals glorifying the king seem to have achieved their purpose, since his fame endured for hundreds of years in Assyria. Later kings (Tiglath-pileser II and Tiglath-pileser III) took the same name because they wished to associate themselves with the image of his historic successes.

A few nonbiblical West Semitic texts contain pieces of the building account form. The fullest of these is the Karatepe Gate Inscription of Azatiwada (chap. 19), although it omits any mention of preparations for building. The Baal Myth's account of Baal's palace-building also has certain affinities with these accounts, although in a diffuse form.

The Bible includes a number of building accounts in addition to 1 Kings 5–9. These include Exodus 25–31, 35–40, which is supposed to describe the construction of the tabernacle (the tent sanctuary of Yhwh); 2 Chronicles 2–7, the Chronicler's version of Solomon's temple-building; and Ezekiel 40–48, Ezekiel's vision of a restored temple.

As the discussions of the Sumerian and Neo-Assyrian accounts showed, the meaning and purpose of a text depend heavily on the context for which it was composed and the person who composed it (or had it composed). However, the date and purpose of the account of Solomon's temple-building is strenuously debated among biblical scholars. Was it composed to glorify Solomon in his own time, or by a later author who looked back on the project as exemplary? The uncertainty is rooted in the fact that the account is part of a historical work that took shape over many centuries and exists only in later copies. The books of 1–2 Kings alone cover about 350 years of history and were clearly not completed until at least the period of Babylonian exile in the sixth century BCE. This history is a composite work, made up of many layers and genres from various hands and periods. Furthermore, unlike the other texts in this chapter, no version of the 1 Kings account has been found that dates to anywhere close to the time of the Israelite monarchy. (As with many other biblical books, the oldest surviving copies of the books of Kings are among the Dead Sea Scrolls.)

Under these conditions, one of the potential rewards of comparative work is that literary works have tended to change in regular ways throughout history, much like forms of pottery.[34] Therefore, if one can find the period and cultural environment in which a

---

34. See F. M. Cross, "Alphabets and Pots: Reflections on Typological Method in the Dating of Human Artifacts," *Maarav* 3 (1982): 121–36. Certainly there are cultural differences, and

certain biblical text has its most precise fit, this would allow one to argue for a theory of its composition. Solomon reigned in the tenth century BCE, which establishes the earliest point at which a story about his temple-building could have been written. Between the tenth and sixth centuries, Israel and Judah were under Neo-Assyrian and Neo-Babylonian influence.[35] There were a number of differences between the Babylonian building accounts and the earlier Assyrian ones. The foremost difference was a lack of blessings and curses in Babylonian texts; also, the dedication ceremonies are less common, and briefer where they do appear. The presence of these items in the Assyrian accounts may be related to the Assyrians' heavy emphasis on covenants (chap. 9), in which curses and ceremonies played important roles. The fact that these same elements are found in the biblical text *might* suggest that the structure of the biblical account of Solomon's temple derives from the Neo-Assyrian period, rather than later.

Alternatively, one could support the view that the 1 Kings account took shape in or after the Neo-Babylonian period by noting that the Neo-Babylonian royal inscriptions focus on building projects more than military feats, just as the stories of Solomon do.

Conclusive evidence does not exist for either period—the use of the form clearly spanned many centuries, and there is significant diversity even among the relatively small number of surviving texts. Cultural influence is often not as direct and determinative as the above arguments would assume. Still, the comparative data form a starting point for a reasoned discussion.

Many readers will be more interested in comparing the accounts on the basis of theology or ethics. One striking difference is that in 1 Kings 9, Yhwh himself pronounces the blessings and curses, whereas in the other accounts it is the king who does so. This is analogous to the situation in comparative ancient Near Eastern law (chap. 7), in which biblical laws are framed as the word of God instead of human words. The emphasis of the biblical blessings and curses on fidelity to Yhwh and observation of his statutes and ordinances seems at first glance to further distinguish the 1 Kings building account, since the Mesopotamian curses seem primarily concerned with the preservation of the inscriptions themselves. However, on closer inspection, the Sumerian and Assyrian accounts demonstrate similar concerns. Tiglath-pileser emphasizes his faithfulness to the gods by describing the alacrity with which he undertook the temple-building (viii 17–49), and Gudea explicitly links his invocation of blessings for himself to his attention to law and justice (vii 34–48).

The comparison of these theologies or worldviews points to a complex set of relationships among these texts. Rather than a situation in which the Bible stands alone against its environment, there are similarities and differences between any two of the texts that one considers. Of course, there is the irreducible distinction marked by the identity of the gods to whom each text is devoted, and Solomon's God is further distinguished by his

---

sometimes we find what seems to be a surprising innovation, but often such surprises turn out to be simply pieces of data that have not yet been properly contextualized by the addition of other data.

35. This admittedly overlooks the strong Egyptian influence on the region (there are numerous descriptions of temple-building in Egyptian texts, which cannot be surveyed here) and the later advent of Persian rule in the area. The focus on Mesopotamia reflects the conclusion of comparative study on the topic.

jealousy: as the text stands now, the Bible forbids worshiping any other god along with Yhwh (1 Kgs. 9:6–9), whereas at the end of each of the other accounts, numerous gods are invoked to enforce the blessings and curses. This is one of the primary points at which one can perceive the fundamental difference between biblical monotheism and the other cultures' polytheism.

⌐One can combine the historical and theological perspectives that have just been laid ⌐ out. The blessings and curses that link the biblical account to the Assyrian account *also* contain the clearest statements of exclusive Yahwism. It is possible that the basic structure of the temple-building account is relatively early—there is reason to think that an Israelite king could have written an account of his building—but that some of the fleshed-out narrative and theological elements, such as Solomon's extraordinarily long prayer and Yhwh's blessings and curses, are later additions. If this is the case, then the coincidence of Assyrian influence with a strong Yhwh-alone impulse among biblical authors might point to a composition in the seventh century, particularly under the reign of Josiah. This is when the covenant form of Deuteronomy is commonly thought to have evolved (chap. 9), and the blessings and curses here look strikingly similar. To pick one verse as a case study, the language in 1 Kings 9:6 of "turning aside," "keeping commandments and statutes," and "serving other gods" are all quintessentially characteristic of the Deuteronomistic historians who are thought to have been working in Josiah's time. ⌐

To summarize: If Solomon indeed recorded an account of his building, it was certainly dedicated to Yhwh and portrayed Solomon as a faithful king, just as Gudea and Tiglath-pileser expressed their fidelity to their national gods. However, specific comparison of the royal prayers and the blessings and curses suggests that the ones in 1 Kings are on a different scale and have different concerns than most ancient Near Eastern building texts. It would have more likely been under the pressure of imperial neighbors and the associated socioeconomic duress that a more focused and exclusive form of Yahwism developed. It is that later form of Yahwism that seems to have been responsible for augmenting the story of Solomon with these details.

All of these conclusions about the history of Israelite and Judean religion and the composition of biblical texts are built on much broader critical arguments that cannot be restated here, but taken together they show the potential of comparative and historical approaches to sharpen our picture of biblical authors' theologies in their cultural settings.

REFLECTION QUESTIONS

1. What do you think are the purposes for the building accounts' detailed records of the materials gathered?

2. Where is purity mentioned in each text, and what importance does it have?

3. What is the relationship between temple-building accounts and the histories of the reigns in which they often appeared?

4. What indications do you have in these texts about the relationship between kings and gods in the ancient Near East, and are there differences among the texts?

5. How does the role played by Hiram of Tyre and his artisans in the 1 Kings account affect your interpretation of the relationship between Solomon's temple and its cultural

environment? Why do you suppose the biblical account mentions foreign workmen when the others do not?

6. To what extent do you think these literary works were conditioned by unique aspects of their cultures, and to what extent were they part of a more widespread tradition?

FURTHER READING

Averbeck, Richard E. "Sumer, the Bible, and Comparative Method: Historiography and Temple Building." Pages 88–125 in *Mesopotamia and the Bible: Comparative Explorations*. Edited by Mark W. Chavalas and K. Lawson Younger Jr. Grand Rapids: Baker, 2002.

Edzard, Dietz Otto. *Gudea and His Dynasty*. Royal Inscriptions of Mesopotamia, Early Periods 3/1. Toronto: University of Toronto Press, 1997.

Grayson, A. Kirk. *Assyrian Rulers of Early First Millennium BC I (1114–859 BC)*. Royal Inscriptions of Mesopotamia, Assyrian Periods 2. Toronto: University of Toronto Press, 1991.

Hurowitz, Victor Avigdor. *I Have Built You an Exalted House*. JSOTSup 115. Sheffield: JSOT Press, 1992.

12

Annual Chronicles

*The Neo-Babylonian Chronicle, the Neo-Assyrian Eponym List,
and 2 Kings 18:1–13*

2 KINGS 18:1–13

When: See below
Where: Jerusalem
Language: Hebrew

THE NEO-BABYLONIAN CHRONICLE

What: Cuneiform text reconstructed from diverse clay tablets
When: Sixth–second centuries BCE
Where: Babylonia
Language: Akkadian (Late Babylonian)
Translation: By the author[1]

Chronicle 1 i 19–32

The third year of (Nabu)-mukin-zeri: When Tiglath-pileser (III) went
down to Akkad, he destroyed Bit-Amukkannu and captured (Nabu)-
mukin-zeri. For three years (Nabu)-mukin-zeri had ruled Babylon.
Tiglath-pileser (III) took the throne in Babylon.

The second year, Tiglath-pileser (III) died in the month of Tebet. For
<*eighteen*>[2] years Tiglath-pileser (III) ruled Babylonia[3] and Assyria. For
two of those years he ruled in Babylonia.

---

1. Akkadian text: A. K. Grayson, *Assyrian and Babylonian Chronicles* (Winona Lake, IN: Eisenbrauns, 2000), 72–73, 81–82, 99–100, 102, 109–10.
2. A blank space was left here on the tablet. Presumably the scribe meant to check the number
and fill it in, but never did.
3. In Akkadian, "Akkad," a designation for southern Mesopotamia.

727 BCE   On the twenty-fifth day of the month of Tebet, Shalmaneser (V) took
                 the throne in Assyria and Babylonia. He slaughtered Samaria.
722 BCE   In the fifth year, Shalmaneser died in the month of Tebet. Shalmaneser
                 ruled Babylonia and Assyria for five years. On the twelfth day of Tebet,
                 Sargon took the throne in Assyria. In the month of Nisan, Merodach-
                 baladan took the throne in Babylon.

Chronicle 1 iii 34–38

681 BCE   On the twentieth day of Tebet, Sennacherib king of Assyria—his son
                 killed him in a coup. For [24] years Sennacherib ruled over Assyria. From
                 the twentieth day of Tebet until the second of Adar, the revolt continued
                 in Assyria.
                        On the [. . .]eighth[4] of Adar, his son Esarhaddon took the throne in
                 Assyria.

Chronicle 5 OBV. 1–11

605 BCE   [In the twenty-first year,] the king of Babylon was in his country.
                 Nebuchadnezzar, his eldest son and the crown prince, [called] up the
                 [army of Babylonia], took the lead and marched on Carchemish, which is
                 on the bank of the Euphrates. He crossed the river [to face the Egyptian
                 army] which was camped at Carchemish. [. . .] They fought each other,
                 and the Egyptian army fled before him. He inflicted a bloody defeat on
                 them and completely annihilated them.
                        The remnants of the army of [Egypt, which] had escaped from the
                 defeat, and which the army of Babylonia had not wiped out, the army
                 defeated in the district of Hamath[5] so that [not] a single man [returned]
                 to his country. At that time Nebuchadnezzar conquered all of Hamath.
                        Nabopolassar ruled Babylon for twenty-one years. On the eighth of
                 Ab, he died.
                        In the month of Elul, Nebuchadnezzar returned to Babylon; on the
                 first of Elul, he took the royal throne in Babylon.

rev. 11–13

598/597 BCE   In the seventh year, in the month of Kislev, the king of Babylonia called
                 up his army and campaigned to Hatti.[6] He encamped against the city of
                 Judah,[7] and on the second day of Adar he took the city and captured the

---

4. The date should read either the eighteenth or the twenty-eighth; the text is broken.
5. In Syria.
6. A catchall term used by the Mesopotamians for areas to the west.
7. In Akkadian, *Yaḫudu.*

king. He installed a king of his own choosing there, took heavy tribute, and brought it back to Babylon.

Chronicle 7 iii 12b–18

539 BCE

In the month of Tishri, Cyrus (II) fought with the army of Babylonia at Opis on the [bank of] the Tigris, (and) the people of Babylonia retreated. He took plunder and killed the people. On the fourteenth day, Sippar was taken without a fight. Nabonidus fled. On the sixteenth day, Ugbaru governor of Gutium, and the army of Cyrus entered Babylon without a fight. Later, after Nabonidus had surrendered, he was captured in Babylon.

The Gutian troops surrounded the gates of Esagil, but there was no interruption at Esagil or the (other) temples, and no sacred occasion was missed. On the third day of the month of Arachsamnu, Cyrus entered Babylon. Peace settled over the city when Cyrus proclaimed peace to all of Babylon.

THE NEO-ASSYRIAN EPONYM CHRONICLE

What: Cuneiform text reconstructed from ten copies on clay tablets
When: Sixth century BCE
Where: Nineveh, Ashur, Sultantepe
Language: Akkadian
Translation: A. R. Millard[8]

(805 BCE)	(In the eponymate of) Ashur-taklak, chamberlain, to Arpad.[9]
(804 BCE)	(In the eponymate of) Ilu-issiya, governor of the land,[10] to Hazaz.
(803 BCE)	(In the eponymate of) Nergal-eresh, governor of Rasappa, to Baʿal.
. . .	
(773 BCE)	(In the eponymate of) Mannu-ki-Adad, governor of Raqmat, to Damascus.
. . .	
(765 BCE)	(In the eponymate of) Ninurta-mukinnishi, of Habruri, to Hatarikka; plague.
(764 BCE)	(In the eponymate of) Sidqi-ilu, of Tushhan, in the land.
(763 BCE)	(In the eponymate of) Bur-sagale, of Guzan, revolt in the citadel of Ashur; in the month of Siwan the sun had an eclipse.
. . .	
(755 BCE)	(In the eponymate of) Iqisu, of Shibhinish, to Hatarikka.

---

8. A. R. Millard, *The Eponyms of the Assyrian Empire, 910–612 BC* (State Archives of Assyria Studies 2; Helsinki: Neo-Assyrian Text Corpus Project, 1994), 57–59.
9. I.e., "[The Assyrian army campaigned] to Arpad."
10. I.e. the land of Ashur.

(754 BCE)	(In the eponymate of) Ninurta-shezibanni, of Talmush, to Arpad; return from Ashur.
. . .	
(745 BCE)	(In the eponymate of) Nabu-belu-usur, of Arrapha, on (the) 13th (of) Ayar, Tiglath-pileser (III) took the throne; in Teshrit he went to Mesopotamia.
(744 BCE)	(In the eponymate of) Bel-dan, of Kalah, to Namri. 10 years [Ashur-nerari] king of Assyria
(743 BCE)	(In the eponymate of) Tiglath-pileser, king of Assyria, to Arpad, defeat of Urartu made.
(742 BCE)	(In the eponymate of) Nabu-da"inanni, commander in chief, to Arpad.
(741 BCE)	(In the eponymate of) Bel-Harran-belu-usur, palace herald, to Arpad, within three years taken.
(740 BCE)	(In the eponymate of) Nabu-eteranni, chief butler, to Arpad.
(739 BCE)	(In the eponymate of) Sin-taklak, chamberlain, to Ulluba, citadel captured.
(738 BCE)	(In the eponymate of) Adad-belu-ka"in, governor of the land, Kullani conquered.
(737 BCE)	(In the eponymate of) Bel-emuranni, of Rasappa, to Media.
(736 BCE)	(In the eponymate of) Ninurta-ilaya, of Nisibin, to the foot of Mount Nal.
(735 BCE)	(In the eponymate of) Ashur-shallimani, of Arrapha, to Urartu.
(734 BCE)	(In the eponymate of) Bel-dan, of Kalah, to Philistia.
(733 BCE)	(In the eponymate of) Ashur-da"inanni, of Mazamua, to Damascus.
(732 BCE)	(In the eponymate of) Nabu-belu-usur, of Simme, to Damascus.

DISCUSSION

Various types of chronological records were kept in ancient Mesopotamia. These allowed scribes to keep track of their nations' histories and to reckon historical time frames in general. The Babylonian Chronicle texts presented here are excerpts from a lengthy sequence of tablets that record half a millennium of Babylonian history. The term "chronicle" refers to "a prose narration of events in chronological order normally written in the third person."[11] The chronological nature of the texts is marked by the year numbers at the start of each entry (the year numbers recorded to the left of each entry above are guides provided by modern scholars).

The chronicle is subdivided into the Neo-Babylonian Chronicle (which covers from the eighth century up to the conquest of Babylon by Cyrus of Persia in 539) and the Late Babylonian Chronicle (which runs into the Seleucid period, 312–63 BCE). The texts excerpted above are from the Neo-Babylonian Chronicle.

Although the texts may appear fairly uniform and smooth-flowing as they are presented here, the chronicle is actually assembled from an assortment of tablets written at different times and places, and subsequently found in different cities. None of the

---

11. Grayson, *Assyrian and Babylonian Chronicles*, ix.

surviving Babylonian Chronicle tablets predates the sixth century BCE, and many of the chronicles of the Neo-Babylonian period are known from copies from the Seleucid period. This means that there is a gap between the events and their attestation about as large as that which is usually hypothesized for the biblical histories. It also means that in each case one has to reckon with copying by scribes over centuries—painstaking labor over tiny cuneiform signs that were not easy to master. This brings with it the potential for error, of course, but also for revision. Where the tablets overlap with each other, they sometimes preserve significant variations in their wording, prompting some scholars to conclude that they are each excerpts from more extensive compositions. Nevertheless, they are similar enough to represent a single literary tradition.

The Babylonian Chronicles cover various topics. In the examples presented here, political and military events are the dominant topic, but other events also appear, such as the reference to the maintenance of Babylonian religious festivals under Cyrus II. Other types of chronicles from Babylonia focus on the burial places of kings, the keeping of the Akitu festival, and even the market price of goods such as wool, barley, and dates. It is not always clear why these records were kept and copied hundreds of years after the events and dynasties in question, but it reflects the degree to which the Mesopotamian scribal culture was committed to the recording and systematization of knowledge.

The style of the Neo-Babylonian Chronicle is interesting in its inconsistency: For some events it is laconic and terse, reporting only the barest facts. In places it skips over years at a time. In other instances it goes into more narrative detail. This might have been due to the nature of the events—for example, perhaps the accession of Nebuchadnezzar is recounted at greater length because it was deemed more significant. It is not clear at what point the detail was introduced—that is, whether it reflects the earliest version of such chronicles as quotidian records, or whether such records were supplemented later with details (perhaps drawn from narrative annals from the kings in question; cf. chap. 13) to create the genre we know as chronicles.

The Babylonian Chronicle is provincial in that it is focused entirely on events that affect Babylon, but it is not heavily biased to the extent of altering facts to support its ideology. A. Kirk Grayson, who produced the major edition of the chronicles, notes that they are "quite objective and impartial."[12] Unlike many royal inscriptions from the ancient Near East, it does not try to efface major defeats and setbacks for the Babylonians.

In addition to these Babylonian Chronicles, other sorts of chronological records were kept in ancient Mesopotamia. Among these are *limmu* lists, or eponym lists. *Limmu* was an honorary title given to a high-ranking person, and the year was then named after that person. These lists occur in two forms: one with only a list of officials after which each year is "named," and another that adds a major event for each year. Excerpts from the latter type of list are presented above.

Examples of *limmu* lists go back as far as the early second millennium in Mari, and the title *limmu* appears to go back to the earliest periods of Assyrian history. The eponyms were high officials in the Assyrian Empire. By the Neo-Assyrian period, the title was rotated in a relatively regular way: a new king served as eponym in his second year,

---

12. Ibid., 10.

followed by his commander-in-chief (*turtanu*; cf. 2 Kgs. 18:17), and then usually by the "chief cupbearer" (*rab shaqeh*; cf. 2 Kgs. 18–19), the palace herald, the chamberlain, and then various provincial governors.

If there were duties associated with the title *limmu*, they are not well understood;[13] it has been hypothesized that it brought the bearer responsibility for the maintenance of the cult of Ashur, in addition to honor. Nearly a hundred stone stelae bearing the names of eponyms have been recovered from a single location in the former city of Ashur, and they might have been moved there after they stood in a temple during their eponymate. The practice may also have commemorated them after their deaths.

There is also an Assyrian King List that exists in a handful of copies and that seeks to record the reigns of Assyrian kings to the start of the second millennium. For the pre-Sargonic era, it has a distinct lack of detail, but for later periods it includes the king's name, his father, and the length of his reign. Here is a representative excerpt:

> Ashurnasirpal (II), son of Tukulti-Ninurta, ruled for twenty-five years.
> Shalmaneser (III), son of Ashurnasirpal, ruled for thirty-five years.
> Shamshi-Adad (V), son of Shalmaneser, ruled for thirteen years.
> Adad-nerari (III), son of Shamshi-Adad, ruled for twenty-eight years.
> Shalmaneser (IV), son of Adad-nerari, ruled for ten years.
> Ashur-dan (III), brother of Shalmaneser, ruled for eighteen years.
> Ashur-nerari (V), son of Adad-nerari, ruled for ten years.
> Tiglath-pileser (III), son of Ashur-nerari, ruled for eighteen years.
> Shalmaneser (V), son of Tiglath-pileser, ruled for five years.

Occasionally it will add a few more details, such as "Mutakkil-Nusku, his brother, fought him and took him to Karduniash. Mutakkil-Nusku held the throne briefly, then died," or "Shamshi-Adad (IV), son of Tiglath-pileser, came up from Karduniash. He ousted Eriba-Adad, son of Ashur-bel-kala, seized the throne and ruled for four years." But such additions are exceptions to the rule.

The Mesopotamian texts presented here are only a handful of examples from a large corpus of similar texts, but the long process through which they were compiled and copied may shed light on the composition of the biblical histories as well. Although no chronicles like the Mesopotamian ones here are known in Hebrew or any other Iron Age Semitic language, a king list from Ugarit indicates that regnal records were kept in the West as well.[14] There are also Egyptian King Lists from various periods, so one is looking at a widespread phenomenon.[15]

Could king lists of Judah and Israel have served as the framework for the biblical histories of the monarchies in 1–2 Kings? The year notices that punctuate the biblical history are reminiscent of the Babylonian Chronicle. The portion of 2 Kings 18 presented above

---

13. Part of the problem is discerning the word's etymology; it could indicate "turn (in office)" or "leader of a thousand" (Millard, *Eponyms*, 9).

14. Kenneth A. Kitchen, "The King List of Ugarit," *Ugarit-Forschungen* 9 (1977): 131–42.

15. Donald B. Redford, *Pharaonic King-Lists, Annals, and Day-Books: A Contribution to the Study of the Egyptian Sense of History* (Mississauga, ON: Benben, 1986).

was selected for its density of chronological markers. It cannot be overlooked that there are numerous references in the Bible to textual records that apparently have not survived:

- Numbers 21:14:[16] "It is said in *the Book*[17] *of the Wars of Yhwh*. . . ."
- Joshua 10:13: "And the sun stood still, and the moon stopped, until the nation took vengeance on their enemies. Is this not written in *the Book of Jashar*?"
- 1 Kings 11:41: "Now the rest of the acts of Solomon, all that he did as well as his wisdom, are they not written in *the Book of the Acts of Solomon*?"
- 1 Kings 14:19: "Now the rest of the acts of Jeroboam, how he warred and how he reigned, are written in *the Book of the Annals of the Kings of Israel*."
- 1 Kings 14:29: "Now the rest of the acts of Rehoboam, and all that he did, are they not written in *the Book of the Annals of the Kings of Judah*?"
- Nehemiah 7:5: "And I found *the book of the genealogy* of those who were the first to come back, and I found the following written in it: . . . ."

The impression one might glean from all these references (some of the books are mentioned multiple times) is that the biblical historians sat down with a library of historical records and then wrote their own, choosing freely what to include. Against this imaginative reconstruction, it is often pointed out that there are examples in the ancient world of inventing ancient sources to bolster the authority of political or theological claims.

But if the source material is similar, one must account for the differences in the final form of the history. The biblical histories are far more diverse and novelistic than the Mesopotamian chronicles. They also incorporate ideological biases and an overriding theological viewpoint that are absent from the Mesopotamian texts. To take just one example, the accounts of the reigns of Saul, David, and Solomon have more detail, complexity, and narrative artistry than any other surviving historical text from the ancient Near East. It is for similar reasons that Grayson wrote that "in the books of the Old Testament historiography reaches an unprecedented height. The clarity and beauty of style found in the ancient Hebrew narratives is unique among historical documents from the ancient Near East."[18]

Comparing the biblical histories to chronicles, however, is not comparing apples to apples; the better comparison is to royal inscriptions, which have a more coherent narrative structure (see chaps. 10 and 13). Then again, even if the biblical histories did not approximate their final form until the Persian period, as most biblical scholars would say, they still have no peer in the ancient Near East up to that point. They are sometimes compared instead to the work of the Greek historian Herodotus, who worked at about that time.[19]

Neither proof nor disproof of the existence of chronistic sources lying behind the biblical histories is likely to emerge in our lifetimes, so each reader must reflect on the likelihood of the existence of such sources and on the ways that they have been reshaped. That is not to say it is necessarily a matter of faith. Comparative data can both strengthen

---

16. All quotations in this list are from the NRSV, with italics added.
17. These "books" would have been scrolls; books were invented much later.
18. Grayson, *Assyrian and Babylonian Chronicles*, 1.
19. John Van Seters, *In Search of History: Historiography in the Ancient World and the Origins of Biblical History* (New Haven, CT: Yale University Press, 1983).

and weaken the case; on the one hand, books of annals were normally kept in the ancient Near East; on the other hand, there is no indication that such annals were ever rewritten in such a novelistic form as the biblical histories, so some exceptional process of formation much be envisioned. As William W. Hallo wrote, "In the perennial tug-of-war between credulity and skepsis . . . all of us would no doubt like to stake out a place on the middle-ground of sweet reasonableness."[20]

REFLECTION QUESTIONS

1. What aspects of the biblical text are unlike the Mesopotamian chronicles?

2. If you skim through 1–2 Kings, can you identify portions or layers in it that are unlikely to be attributed to source material in the form of chronicles?

3. On the basis of your reading, how would you assess Grayson's claim that "the clarity and beauty of style found in the ancient Hebrew narratives is unique"?

4. How do you imagine the relationship of ancient historians to their sources? That is, to what extent do you think they felt bound to merely copy existing information, or to what extent do you think they felt free to modify their sources and compose new accounts?

FURTHER READING

Glassner, Jean-Jacques. *Chroniques mésopotamiennes*. Paris: Les belles lettres, 1993.

Grayson, A. K. *Assyrian and Babylonian Chronicles*. Winona Lake, IN: Eisenbrauns, 2000.

Kitchen, Kenneth A. "The King List of Ugarit." *Ugarit-Forschungen* 9 (1977): 131–42.

Millard, A. R. *The Eponyms of the Assyrian Empire, 910–612 BC*. State Archives of Assyria Studies 2. Helsinki: Neo-Assyrian Text Corpus Project, 1994.

Redford, Donald B. *Pharaonic King-Lists, Annals, and Day-Books: A Contribution to the Study of the Egyptian Sense of History*. Mississauga, ON: Benben, 1986.

Van Seters, John. *In Search of History: Historiography in the Ancient World and the Origins of Biblical History*. New Haven, CT: Yale University Press, 1983.

20. W. W. Hallo, "The Limits of Skepticism," *JAOS* 110 (1990): 187.

13

Comparative Historiography

*Assyrian and Biblical Accounts of Sennacherib's Siege of Jerusalem
(2 Kings 18:13–19:37 and 2 Chronicles 32:1–22)*

2 KINGS 18:13–16 (THE A [ANNALISTIC] ACCOUNT)

When: Eighth century BCE (?; see below)
Where: Jerusalem
Language: Hebrew

2 KINGS 18:17–19:9A (THE B¹ ACCOUNT)

When: Seventh–sixth century BCE (see below)
Where: Jerusalem
Language: Hebrew

2 KINGS 19:9B–19:37 (THE B² ACCOUNT)

When: Seventh–sixth century BCE (see below)
Where: Jerusalem
Language: Hebrew

[*The division between the B¹ and B² accounts[1] is based on the theory that there are two different, repeated stories about Sennacherib's envoy to Hezekiah, which were presented back-to-back and joined by an editor. The second story starts halfway through v. 9: "He sent messengers again to Hezekiah. . . ." See further discussion below.*]

---

1. Unlike the A[nnalistic] and C[hronicles] accounts, there is no inherent reason why these are abbreviated B. It is merely fortuitous that A-B-C is their chronological order in both canon and (probably) composition.

2 CHRONICLES 32:1–23 (THE C ACCOUNT)

When: Late fifth century BCE (?)
Where: Jerusalem
Language: Hebrew

SENNACHERIB'S WESTERN CAMPAIGN OF 701

What: Cuneiform text on barrel-shaped clay cylinder, 26.35cm long × 11.11cm in diameter; dozens of copies exist
When: 700 BCE
Where: Nineveh
Language: Akkadian
Translation: Mordechai Cogan, *The Raging Torrent: Historical Inscriptions from Assyria and Babylonia Relating to Ancient Israel* (Jerusalem: Carta, 2008), 111–15.

[The text presented here comprises lines 32–58 of the ninety-five-line inscription]

32–35   In my third campaign, I marched to Hatti.[2] The awesome splendor of my lordship overwhelmed Luli, king of Sidon, and he fled overseas far-off. The terrifying nature of the weapon of (the god) Ashur my lord overwhelmed his strong cities, Greater Sidon, Little Sidon, Bit-zitti, Sariptu, Mahaliba, Ushu, Achzib, Acco, walled cities (provided) with food and water for his garrisons, and they bowed in submission at my feet. I installed Tuba'lu on his royal throne over them and imposed upon him tribute and dues for my lordship (payable) annually without interruption.

36–38   The kings of Amurru,[3] all of them—Minuhimmu of Samsimuruna, Tuba'lu of Sidon, Abdili'ti of Arvad, Urumilki of Byblos, Mitinti of Ashdod, Pudu'ilu of Beth-Ammon, Chemosh-nadbi of Moab, Ayarammu of Edom—brought me sumptuous presents as their abundant audience-gift, fourfold, and kissed my feet.

39–41   As for Sidqa, king of Ashkelon[4] who had not submitted to my yoke[5]—his family gods, he himself, his wife, his sons, his daughters, his brothers, and (all the rest of) his descendants, I deported and brought him to Assyria. I set

---

2. The Assyrians used "Hatti" as a catchall term for areas to the west of them.

3. Another blanket term for western regions. Of course, both "Amurru" and "Hatti" had more specific geographic and ethnic meanings, but the Assyrians were not concerned with such distinctions. The kingdoms listed here span a wide range from the northern Levantine seacoast to the south and east of the Dead Sea.

4. A Philistine port city that had taken part, with Ekron and Judah, in a coup to throw off Assyrian rule.

5. The "yoke of Assyria" signified imperial rule, and more specifically the burden of taxation. (The conquered was like an ox or other draft animal working for the benefit of its master, the imperial king. See also 1 Kgs. 12:4.) Jer. 27–28 reflects that this metaphor continued to be used under Babylonian rule. Jer. 2:20 and 5:5 attest that the yoke, like many other symbols of royal power, became a theological metaphor for service to God as well.

Sharru-lu-dari, son of Rukibti, their former king, over the people of Ash-kelon and imposed upon him payment of tribute (and) presents to my lord-ship; he (now) bears my yoke. In the course of my campaign, I surrounded and conquered Beth-dagon, Joppa, Bene-berak, Azor, cities belonging to Sidqa, who did not submit quickly, and I carried off their spoil.

42–45 The officials, the nobles, and the people of Ekron[6] who had thrown Padi, their king, (who was) under oath and obligation to Assyria, into iron fetters and handed him over in a hostile manner to Hezekiah, the Judean, took fright because of the offense they had committed. The kings of Egypt, (and) the bowmen, chariot corps and cavalry of the king of Cush[7] assembled a countless force and came to their (i.e., the Ekronites) aid. In the plain of Eltekeh, they drew up their ranks against me and sharpened their weapons. Trusting in the god Ashur,[8] my lord, I fought with them and inflicted a defeat upon them. The Egyptian charioteers and princes, together with the charioteers of the Cushites, I personally took alive in the midst of the battle.

46–48 I besieged and conquered Eltekeh and Timnah and carried off their spoil. I advanced to Ekron and slew its officials and nobles who had stirred up rebel-lion and hung their bodies on watchtowers all about the city. The citizens who committed sinful acts, I counted as spoil, and I ordered the release of the rest of them, who had not sinned. I freed Padi, their king, from Jerusa-lem and set him on the throne as king over them and imposed tribute for my lordship over him.

49–52 As for Hezekiah, the Judean,[9] I besieged 46 of his fortified walled cities and surrounding smaller towns, which were without number. Using packed-down ramps and applying battering rams, infantry attacks by mines, breeches, and siege machines,[10] I conquered (them). I took out 200,150 people, young and old, male and female, horses, mules, donkeys, camels, cattle, and sheep, without number, and counted them as spoil. He himself, I locked up within Jerusalem, his royal city, like a bird in a cage.[11] I surrounded him with armed posts, and made it unthinkable[12] for him to exit by the city gate.

6. A Philistine city that was a little over twenty miles west of Jerusalem.

7. Cush, or Nubia, was to the south of Egypt. At this point in history, a Cushite dynasty had conquered the traditionally dominant Delta Egyptian powers. It appears that the Assyrians, like the biblical authors, perceived the Cushites and Egyptians as racially and ethnically distinct even though they were fighting together.

8. The national god of Assyria.

9. Another copy of the text (the Chicago Prism) from nine years later, in 691, adds here: "who had not submitted to my yoke." This is one of a handful of variants among the numerous copies of this text.

10. Alternately: storm ladders.

11. "Like a bird in a cage" is a stereotypical phrase that had been used by past Assyrian kings. It is notable that Sennacherib does not make the same claim to have "besieged and conquered" Jeru-salem as he did with other cities in this campaign.

12. Lit., "taboo."

53-54   His cities which I had despoiled, I cut off from his land and gave them to Mitinti, king of Ashdod, Padi, king of Ekron, and Silli-Bel, king of Gaza, and thus diminished his land. I imposed dues and gifts for my lordship upon him, in addition to the former tribute, their yearly payment.

55-58   He, Hezekiah, was overwhelmed by the awesome splendor of my lordship, and he sent me after my departure to Nineveh, my royal city, his elite troops (and) his best soldiers, which he had brought in as reinforcements to strengthen Jerusalem, his holy city, with 30 talents of gold, 800 talents of silver, choice antimony, large blocks of carnelian, beds (inlaid) with ivory, armchairs (inlaid) with ivory, elephant hides, ivory, ebony-wood, boxwood, multicolored garments, garments of linen, wool (dyed) red-purple and blue-purple, vessels of copper, iron, bronze and tin, iron, chariots, siege shields, lances, armor, daggers for the belt, bows and arrows, countless trappings and implements of war, together with his daughters, his palace women, his male and female singers. He (also) dispatched his messenger to deliver the tribute and to do obeisance.

DISCUSSION

Second Kings 18:13–19:37, its parallel in Isaiah 36–37, and its reshaping in 2 Chronicles 32 all tell the story of the Neo-Assyrian king Sennacherib's invasion of Judah and siege of Jerusalem in 701 BCE. This is a rare case where narrative accounts of the same event are preserved both within the Bible and without. Because the accounts neither completely agree nor completely disagree, they present the historian with a fascinating test case for assessing and weighing historical sources.

The Assyrian text is part of an account of the years just after Sennacherib took the throne in 705. In the ancient Near East, transitions of power, even from father to son, were typically viewed by subject nations as a chance to test the new ruler: perhaps he would not be as strong as the previous king. In this case, it does seem that it took Sennacherib a few years to consolidate his rule at home and in other areas. The text presented above recounts Sennacherib's campaign in 701 to reassert Assyria's claim on the western parts of the empire and on the taxes that they provided. "Tribute" is the name given to the payments that ancient empires required of their vassals. It worked very much like a Mafia protection racket: kings of smaller nations had to pay up or be deposed and killed. As the Assyrian texts says, this tax was payable "annually *without interruption.*"

This text preserves a wide array of possible reactions to Sennacherib's offensive. Eight kings pay up immediately, and the reference to paying "fourfold" may reflect that they paid more than usual as a kind of late penalty. (It had been four years since Sennacherib took the throne, so perhaps it was more like back taxes on the missed years. If so, it would have been a backbreaking sum, since the tribute was heavy even when it was paid regularly.) Another king, Lulli of Sidon, is said to have fled rather than face the choice of impoverishment or death; and Sidqa of Ashkelon is deposed and deported along with his entire family. Both kings are replaced with rulers thought to be properly sympathetic to the Assyrians.

The account reaches its crescendo with the attack on Judah and Hezekiah. The musical metaphor is intentional, because these ancient campaign accounts are artistic works—as opposed to, for example, journalistic reports.[13] Such campaign accounts were shaped according to the literary and ideological preferences of the authors. For example, the order in which each of these sites was visited and conquered is unknown. The foreign nations are grouped not by historical order, but by their reaction; there is a set that submitted and a set that did not. Within those sets, they are grouped geographically. It is probable that Judah was Sennacherib's last stop, since he reports returning home afterward, but it was also the focal point of the campaign. Hezekiah had not only failed to pay taxes; he had also taken an active part in an anti-Assyrian coup in nearby Ekron. The Ekronites deposed their pro-Assyrian king and gave him to Hezekiah for imprisonment.

Sennacherib's campaign against Judah was certainly punitive; he reports conquering forty-six fortified cities, and destruction layers from this time have been discovered by archaeologists in many sites. He also reduced Judah's territory by awarding its western areas to the coastal kingdoms. Sennacherib was so proud of his campaign that he had huge reliefs carved into the walls of his palace in Nineveh that depicted his defeat of the Judean fortress town of Lachish.

Despite these punishments, many have found Sennacherib's treatment of Hezekiah curiously lax: whereas other kings were forced to flee or be deported, Hezekiah, who was seemingly most guilty of all, preserves his rule and his capital city. It has often been noted that Sennacherib claims only to have "shut [Hezekiah] up like a bird in a cage"—not only a modest claim by Assyrian standards, but one that is borrowed from an earlier inscription of Tiglath-pileser III.[14]

According to the Assyrian account, the reasons for the city's salvation are straightforward: Sennacherib besieged the city until Hezekiah capitulated and sent him a heavy tribute. But why only a siege and not destruction? Why no deportation or death for Hezekiah? It is most surprising that Sennacherib would allow a rebel king to remain on the throne, when the whole point of the western campaign was to punish rebellious vassals. Assyrian rule of its provinces and client states was not wholly systematic, but the treatment of vassals and the language of these inscriptions is usually standardized enough that these exceptions have warranted an ongoing debate, on internal grounds alone.

The situation becomes even more complicated when one considers the biblical accounts, because they differ from the Assyrian account. One of the first things that historians ask is which sources are the most reliable. Proximity to the events narrated is usually a factor in that judgment; accounts closer to the events are usually assumed to be less changed by oral transmission or later points of view. In the case of these two texts,

---

13. K. Lawson Younger Jr., *Ancient Conquest Accounts: A Study in Ancient Near Eastern and Biblical History Writing* (JSOTSup 98; Sheffield: JSOT Press, 1990).

14. Hezekiah's survival is reminiscent of another rebel king who was also anomalously left on his throne, Hanunu of Gaza. The Sargonid monarch in that instance, Tiglath-pileser III, installed a gold image of himself in Hanunu's palace, perhaps cast from gold taken from Hanunu himself. It may be the case for both Hezekiah and Hanunu that they were more useful alive than dead.

the existing copies of the Assyrian version are obviously closer to the events in question. Sennacherib considered this an important campaign, and so the text was copied numerous times over the years. The earliest copy was within less than a year of the siege of Jerusalem.

The date of the biblical version is more complicated. The oldest *surviving* copy of the account is from the Dead Sea Scrolls, more than 500 years after the events, but there is no doubt that at least parts of the text are much more ancient. For example, although it cannot be conclusively proven, the Bible may preserve a brief, annalistic report from as close to the events as the Assyrian accounts, consisting of 2 Kings 18:13–16. The stories were compiled within the Deuteronomistic History (Joshua–2 Kings), which continued to be edited and rewritten through the seventh and sixth centuries. The rest of the text presented here, 2 Kings 18:17–19:37, has to be considered part of these later strata, although it may well contain earlier material.

If treated separately, the annalistic account (or "A account") of 2 Kings 18:13–16 would be mostly consistent with Sennacherib's inscription. The Bible recounts that Hezekiah gave the Assyrian king "all the silver that was found in the house of Yhwh and in the treasuries of the king's house," even stripping the gold from the doors of the temple. Strikingly, the biblical and cuneiform texts record similar tribute amounts: 30 talents of gold in both cases, plus either 300 (2 Kings) or 800 (Sennacherib) talents of silver.

The discrepancy in the numbers might simply reflect an effort by the Assyrian scribes to glorify Sennacherib by the amount of spoil he took. (Or an attempt by Judean scribes to minimize the loss.) The way that the Assyrians used numbers in their inscriptions is another example of the literary nature of their historical texts. A number such as the 200,150 beings (human and animal) that he is said to have taken as spoil is almost certainly not accurate; it is far too high.[15] Instead, it fits with a tendency to use "very high-exact numbers," that is, numbers created by adding "a very high 'round' numeral with an 'exact' one on the order of some hundreds and some tens."[16] It has been suggested that the figure was actually 2,150, or the number 200,150 may simply have been invented.

Apart from the numbers, there are other minor discrepancies between the A account and the Assyrian version. For example, Sennacherib seems to say that he received his tribute after a siege, while the Bible is less clear on this point—2 Kings 18:14–16 states that Hezekiah sent word to Sennacherib in advance, to try to avert destruction, and that he paid up without further coercion.

More problematically, the bulk of the biblical version, the "B account" in 2 Kings 18:17–19:37, tells a *very* different story. In these accounts, Assyria initiates contact by sending a diplomatic corps to Jerusalem to issue threats and promises intended to win the city's surrender. This causes dismay in the royal court, but through some combination of

15. For comparison, note that 2 Kgs. 24:14–16 says that Nebuchadnezzar, when he conquered Jerusalem in 586, took about 10,000 people into exile, while Jer. 52:28 says it was only 3,023. After he conquered Samaria in 721, the Assyrian king Sargon II claimed to have taken 27,280 captives, and even that figure has been questioned for being high.

16. Marco De Odorico, *The Use of Numbers and Quantifications in the Assyrian Royal Inscriptions* (Helsinki: Neo-Assyrian Text Corpus Project, 1995), 171.

divine intervention and a threat from an approaching Cushite army, the Assyrians suffer a setback and withdraw. This section also includes two different but similar speeches by the Assyrian representative at the wall of Jerusalem, and thus is customarily divided up into two sources, B[1] (18:17–19:9a) and B[2] (19:9b–37). Although the likelihood that these are transcriptions of actual Assyrian speeches is small, they have been shown to preserve genuine elements of Assyrian rhetoric, and they were surely intended to sound realistic.[17]

The Assyrian account disagrees with the B sources in significant ways: First, it mentions a battle against Cush and Egypt *prior to* the siege of Jerusalem, a battle in which Sennacherib says he "inflicted a defeat upon them." More importantly, it describes the siege as a success. Assyrian inscriptions were prone to do so, regardless of actual events. There are a number of battles against the Babylonians for which the Assyrians simply falsely claimed victory.[18]

A final biblical account is supplied by the author of 2 Chronicles 32, writing in the postexilic period. He retells the story again, this time with a heroic Hezekiah who fearlessly prepares the city and speaks encouragingly to the people, saying (vv. 6–7), "Be strong and of good courage!" (Compare the A account, where Hezekiah grovels, saying, "I have done wrong; withdraw from me; whatever you impose on me I will bear" [2 Kgs. 18:14]; or the B account, in which he tears his clothes and says, "This day is a day of distress, of rebuke, and of disgrace" [19:3].) This C account is very much in keeping with the Chronicler's agenda to justify and glorify Davidic rule in Jerusalem. Ideology is another factor that historians consider in assessing the historical value of texts, and the ideological perspective of this text is very strong.

Despite its extensive reshaping, 2 Chronicles 32 does seem to preserve an accurate memory of Hezekiah's preparations for the siege. It says that he protected the city's water supply and fortified the walls (vv. 2–5), works that are attested elsewhere in the Bible (Isa. 22:10–11) as well as being supported by archaeological findings. A tunnel bringing water into Jerusalem from the Siloam spring and a massive wall expanding the city have both been dated to the eighth century. In sum, although the historians' ideology certainly shapes the retelling, that does not abolish the question: *To what extent was this version based on accurate memory or records?*

How does one finally make sense of a set of texts in which both sides of a military confrontation claim victory, and both versions are equally prone to ideological coloring? In his seminal *History of Israel*, John Bright devoted an entire excursus to it,[19] and ended up

---

17. Thucydides' method was probably not unlike that of the historians who recorded this passage: "it was in all cases difficult to carry [the speeches] word for word in one's memory, so my habit has been to make the speakers say what was in my opinion demanded of them by the various occasions, of course adhering as closely as possible to the general sense of what they really said" (*History of the Peloponnesian War* 1.22). Regarding the Deuteronomistic Historian's intention to write accurate history, see Baruch Halpern, *The First Historians: The Hebrew Bible and History* (San Francisco: Harper & Row, 1988), 1–35.

18. A. K. Grayson, "Problematical Battles in Mesopotamian History," in *Studies in Honor of Benno Landsberger on His Seventy-fifth Birthday, April 21, 1965* (ed. Hans G. Güterbock and Thorkild Jacobsen; Assyriological Studies 16; Chicago: University of Chicago Press, 1965), 337–42.

19. John Bright, *A History of Israel* (4th ed.; Louisville, KY: Westminster John Knox Press, 2000), 298–309.

positing that there had been two separate invasions. He argued that 2 Kings 18:13–16 reflects an Assyrian campaign in 701 in which Hezekiah quickly capitulated and paid tribute, and that 2 Kings 18:17–19:37 tells of a *different* siege which the city resisted and survived, probably in 688. One major problem for historians is that Assyrian annals after 689 have not been discovered. These were among the key factors for Bright:

- Egypt is supposed to have been trusted by Hezekiah (according to the Rabshakeh's speech), but why would he have trusted Egypt when it had already been defeated by Assyria at Eltekeh (cf. ll. 42–45 of Sennacherib's inscription and 2 Kgs. 19:9)?[20]
- Sennacherib looks schizophrenic if he first imposed terms on Judah as if he intended to leave it as a vassal, and then suddenly decided to attack it, as he might do with a state that he intended to eradicate and turn into a province.
- Tirhakah (2 Kgs. 19:9) would not have been on the Egyptian throne by 701, according to the usual dating of Egyptian reigns.
- Since 2 Kings 19:37 refers to Sennacherib's murder (in 681) as if it had happened immediately after the campaign in question, a lot of history is being telescoped somewhere. Why not between 18:16 and 18:17 as well? It is easier to imagine that six or seven years were telescoped than twenty. (The simple answer to Bright is that 18:17 does not begin with a new dating marker as we would expect, but this could be a quirk of editing.)

Bright admits that proof is impossible, but he thinks attempts to harmonize the A and B accounts both into the year 701 create a story that makes no sense. He also resists reconstructions that do not "take the Biblical tradition of Jerusalem's deliverance seriously enough."[21] For example, if Sennacherib besieged Jerusalem and then went away because Hezekiah paid tribute, it is hard to see how a doctrine of the city's inviolability (and the promise to the Davidic king) would have been taken seriously and grown as it did. In this, he has the support of Baruch Halpern, who comments,

> [The biblical historian] portrays the plague in Sennacherib's camp as a miracle, as he or his source (a Hezekian dedication?) must have seen it. That something untoward did befall the beleaguerers—whether at Jerusalem or in the Philistine plain—is to be inferred from the fact that Hezekiah, alone among vassals besieged, forwarded his tribute to Assyria, rather than paying up on the spot.[22]

In general, however, Bright's two-campaign theory has not fared well, as most scholars have come to conclude that there was only one campaign. In so doing, they have removed some of the impediments Bright saw for such a reconstruction.

---

20. Bright was not convinced by attempts to explain that it was only a small Egyptian advance attachment, and that a larger force was coming.

21. Bright, *History of Israel*, 306.

22. Baruch Halpern, *The First Historians: The Hebrew Bible and History* (San Francisco: Harper & Row, 1988), 247.

- Younger points out that because of the literary shaping of the Assyrian account, there is no particular reason to assume that the victory over the Egyptians took place prior to the siege of Jerusalem, even though it precedes it in the inscription.[23]
- As noted, one of Bright's major misgivings about dating the B accounts to 701 is that Tirhaka (Taharqa) could not have been on the throne by 701. But James Hoffmeier and others have proposed that the chronology can be reconciled by means of a coregency, that is, two kings reigning at the same time; coregencies were common in Egypt.[24] Shabako, who ruled from Memphis (in the Delta region), would have appointed his nephew Shabataka to rule Cush from Napata, far to the south. Shabataka, responding to calls for help, would have sent Taharqa north with the army, because it was common for the crown prince to go into battle for a more aged monarch.
- Walter Mayer simply dismisses the biblical data, saying that those who construct the events differently are part of a line influenced by biblical inerrancy and a derision of Assyrian sources.[25] The comment that Hezekiah "sent his tribute behind me" does not suggest flight, but rather success: Mayer reasons that Sennacherib's chariot would naturally have traveled back to Nineveh more quickly than his spoil could.

Again, in the absence of more data (such as the Assyrian annals after 689), it seems that historically inclined biblical scholars are opting for the one-campaign solution. A two-campaign theory certainly has its merits, but it is probably better for the time being to seek to reconcile the narrative oddities without making recourse to events for which there is no clear evidence.

On the question of Jerusalem's salvation, new data may suggest new answers. The reasons given in the biblical text for Jerusalem's survival are Egyptian military aid, sickness among the Assyrian troops,[26] and/or divine intervention. It is possible, however, that a friendly history between Judah and Assyria helped; despite the tense relations between the nations, it may be that Judean princesses were married to the Assyrian kings Tiglath-pileser III and Sargon II. Stephanie Dalley also notes that Judeans seem to have served as bodyguards for Sennacherib, and that Sennacherib also praised Hezekiah as "tough and strong" in an inscription, which was exceptional praise for a rebellious foreign king.[27] Finally, from the perspective of economics, it is possible that Assyria did not deem Judah a highly profitable area to control, and so did not expend the energy to conquer it

23. K. Lawson Younger Jr., "Assyrian Involvement in the Southern Levant at the End of the Eighth Century B.C.E.," in *Jerusalem in Bible and Archaeology: The First Temple Period* (ed. Andrew G. Vaughn and Ann E. Killebrew; SBLSymS 18; Atlanta: Society of Biblical Literature, 2003), 235–63.

24. James K. Hoffmeier, "Egypt's Role in the Events of 701 B.C. in Jerusalem," in Vaughn and Killebrew, *Jerusalem in Bible and Archaeology*, 219–34.

25. Walter Mayer, "Sennacherib's Campaign of 701: The Assyrian View," trans. Julia Assante, in *"Like a Bird in Cage": The Invasion of Sennacherib in 701 BCE* (ed. Lester L. Grabbe; JSOTSup 363; London: Sheffield Academic Press, 2003), 168–200.

26. Donald J. Wiseman suggests that it was a case of bacillary dysentery ("Medicine in the Old Testament World," in *Medicine and the Bible* [ed. Bernard Palmer; Exeter: Paternoster, 1986], 25).

27. Stephanie Dalley, "Recent Evidence from Assyrian Sources for Judaean History from Uzziah to Manasseh," *Journal for the Study of the Old Testament* 28 (2004): 387–401.

completely and turn it into a province.[28] In the end, historical surprises rarely arise from single factors; it seems likely that more than one of these reasons came into play.

What *is* clear is that Judah resumed its vassal status to Assyria after 701. The Assyrians continued their southward expansion, and within thirty years, their empire stretched all the way across Egypt. It is hard to imagine that Assyria could have pressed so far south had it not been in firm control of the Levant. Although the biblical narrative seems to lose interest in Assyrian events after 701, an inscription of Esarhaddon reveals that Manasseh of Judah was among the foreign kings compelled by him to bring building supplies to Nineveh for his palace, and a long reign such as his (ca. 698–644) would not have been possible without the tolerance of the empire.

This is not a conundrum with a clearly correct answer. Despite a rare surplus of data, the reconstruction of the events remains subject to critical judgment. The comparison of these texts requires the reader to wrestle, and to clarify methods and presuppositions.

REFLECTION QUESTIONS

1. Are you able to perceive the reasons that scholars have divided the text in 2 Kings into three "accounts"? What features point to that division? Are there features that suggest otherwise?

2. On what points does Sennacherib's account agree with one or more of the biblical accounts?

3. How is communication between Judah and Assyria established in each biblical account (A, B, and C)?

4. How does the outcome vary among the biblical accounts?

5. How does the portrait of Hezekiah vary among the biblical accounts?

6. To what does Sennacherib attribute the sparing of Jerusalem? What about the biblical accounts?

7. What is the outcome for Assyria and Sennacherib in each account?

8. How do you assess the reasons for the reshaping of the story in 2 Kings and 2 Chronicles?

FURTHER READING

Bright, John. *A History of Israel.* 4th ed. Louisville, KY: Westminster John Knox Press, 2000.
Dalley, Stephanie. "Recent Evidence from Assyrian Sources for Judaean History from Uzziah to Manasseh." *Journal for the Study of the Old Testament* 28 (2004): 387–401.
De Odorico, Marco. *The Use of Numbers and Quantifications in the Assyrian Royal Inscriptions.* Helsinki: Neo-Assyrian Text Corpus Project, 1995.
Evans, Paul S. *The Invasion of Sennacherib in the Book of Kings: A Source-Critical and Rhetorical Study of 2 Kings 18–19.* Leiden: Brill, 2009.

---

28. While Sennacherib's pride in defeating a second-tier city like Lachish reflects Judah's political significance, material remains reveal that it was not as wealthy as coastal trading cities or even as its northern neighbor, Israel.

Frahm, Eckart. "Einleitung in die Sanherib-Inschriften." *Beihefte zur Archiv für Orientforschung* 26 (1997): 51–61.

Gallagher, William R. *Sennacherib's Campaign to Judah: New Studies.* Studies in the History and Culture of the Ancient Near East 18. Leiden: Brill, 1999.

Grayson, A. K. "Problematical Battles in Mesopotamian History." Pages 337–42 in *Studies in Honor of Benno Landsberger on His Seventy-fifth Birthday, April 21, 1965.* Edited by Hans G. Güterbock and Thorkild Jacobsen. Assyriological Studies 16. Chicago: University of Chicago Press, 1965.

Hallo, W. W. "Jerusalem under Hezekiah: An Assyriological Perspective." Pages 35–50 in *Jerusalem: Its Sanctity and Centrality to Judaism, Christianity, and Islam.* Edited by Lee I. Levine. New York: Continuum, 1999.

Halpern, Baruch. *The First Historians: The Hebrew Bible and History.* San Francisco: Harper & Row, 1988.

Hoffmeier, James K. "Egypt's Role in the Events of 701 B.C. in Jerusalem." Pages 219–34 in *Jerusalem in Bible and Archaeology: The First Temple Period.* Edited by Andrew G. Vaughn and Ann E. Killebrew. SBLSymS 18. Atlanta: Society of Biblical Literature, 2003.

Mayer, Walter. "Sennacherib's Campaign of 701: The Assyrian View." Translated by Julia Assante. Pages 168–200 in *"Like a Bird in Cage": The Invasion of Sennacherib in 701 BCE.* Edited by Lester L. Grabbe. JSOTSup 363. London: Sheffield Academic Press, 2003.

Millard, A. R. "Sennacherib's Attack on Hezekiah." *Tyndale Bulletin* 36 (1985): 61–77.

Tadmor, Hayim. "Sennacherib's Campaign to Judah." *Zion* 50 (1985): 65–80.

Younger, K. Lawson, Jr. *Ancient Conquest Accounts: A Study in Ancient Near Eastern and Biblical History Writing.* JSOTSup 98. Sheffield: JSOT Press, 1990.

———. "Assyrian Involvement in the Southern Levant at the End of the Eighth Century B.C.E." Pages 235–63 in *Jerusalem in Bible and Archaeology: The First Temple Period.* Edited by Andrew G. Vaughn and Ann E. Killebrew. SBLSymS 18. Atlanta: Society of Biblical Literature, 2003.

PART IV

Latter Prophets

Introduction to Prophecy
in the Ancient Near East

Prophecy is a form of divination, a way for humans to make known the will of God or the gods. In the ancient world, spoken prophecy coexisted with many other types of divination, and it was not typically the most prominent or revered divinatory art in most times and places. For example, although the court at Mari supported and listened to prophets, their words were often checked by means of extispicy, that is, the examination of animal entrails, especially hepatoscopy, the examination of (usually sheep) livers. It seems that extispicy was considered more reliable than prophecy.

Other forms of divination used in the ancient Near East included astrology (Mesopotamians were famous for their study of the heavenly bodies), oneiromancy (revelation through dreams), augury (interpretation of the flight of birds), lecanomancy (interpretation of the behavior of oil on water), necromancy (divination by summoning the dead), and even the interpretation of the bodies of animals born deformed. The assumption of such forms of divination was that the gods had encoded intelligible messages in the liver, in the sky, and so forth. Thus in one sense this diversity reflects a profound faith: the ancients believed that it was possible for the gods to send messages to humankind in nearly any way imaginable; it only required training and skill to interpret the signs.

Of course, the Israelites and Judeans of the Bible were not ignorant of divinatory practices other than prophecy; in fact, they employed some of them. The most prominent example is the Urim and Thummim, holy dice that were kept in the breastpiece of the high priest (Exod. 28:30) and were used to determine the divine will (1 Sam. 14:41, etc.). Oneiromancy also played a major role: God speaks to Solomon in a dream (1 Kgs. 3:5–15), both Joseph and Daniel were dream interpreters, and "visionary" and "seer" (Heb., ḥōzeh and rō'eh) were common prophetic titles. Deuteronomy 13:1–5 certainly suggests that dream interpretation was not viewed as inherently problematic even in a period of religious reform ("If prophets or those who divine by dreams appear among you and promise you omens or portents, and the omens or the portents declared by them take place . . ."). However, dreams can also mislead and thus are subjects of scorn at times (Jer. 23:28; 29:8). Other forms of divination are attested more sporadically: Gideon lays a fleece on the ground and asks God to use it to send a sign (Judg. 6:36–40); Saul practices necromancy (1 Sam. 28). Of course, necromancy was elsewhere condemned (Deut. 18:10–11), as was astrology (Deut. 4:19), but those very condemnations reflect the temptations that the people faced.

Discussions of divination sometimes distinguish divine messages that are solicited (oracles) from those that are unsolicited (omens). Sometimes this distinction holds; for example, extispicies were usually solicited, since they required the sacrifice of an animal and careful inspection, whereas malformed animal births would have had to be unsolicited. However, both prophecy and dreams can be solicited or not. Dream incubation was common in the ancient world, and kings frequently sought approval from court prophets before going to battle or making other decisions. Therefore the distinction of oracles from omens is not of the first importance in dealing with prophecy.

A more useful distinction is between *inductive* and *noninductive* divination. *Inductive* oracles are based on the observation of concrete phenomena (the form of a liver, the flight of a bird, the behavior of oil on water, etc.) and proceed to interpretation on the basis of accepted canons. Such rules for interpretation were collected into extensive series that attempted to cover as many cases as possible. For example, in a series made up of hundreds of liver omens, one pair instructs the diviner how to interpret abnormalities on a part of the sheep's liver that was called the "Presence." The outcome of the divination depended on where the abnormality occurred: For example, one such text reads, "If on the right side of the Presence a hole lies: The army will be defeated. If a hole lies on the left side of the Presence: The enemy army will be defeated."[1]

Clay models functioned as "maps" of the liver, as resources that others could read and check, and as a means to teach hepatoscopy. A divinatory professional (*barû*, in Akkadian) had to know how to "read" a liver, and where to find the correct entry in the written omen series, but ideally the process was otherwise supposed to be objective; theoretically, any trained interpreter could be expected to arrive at the same interpretation.

By contrast, prophecy is a *noninductive* type of divination. Rather than observing and interpreting, prophets "act as direct mouthpieces of gods."[2] Deuteronomy 18:21–22 acknowledges that there is no systematic way to check the words of a prophet in advance; only time can tell whether a prophet spoke the truth:

> You may say to yourself, "How can we recognize a word that Yhwh has not spoken?" If a prophet speaks in the name of Yhwh but the thing does not take place or prove true, it is a word that Yhwh has not spoken. The prophet has spoken it presumptuously; do not be frightened by it.

Thus the prophet derives authority only from his or her track record.

These sources from various places and times suggest that prophecy had significant cultural currency and diffusion in Mesopotamia. Two major corpora allow one to understand

---

1. For text, see Ulla Koch-Westenholz, *Babylonian Liver Omens: The Chapters* Manzāzu, Padānu, *and* Pān tākalti *of the Babylonian Extispicy Series Mainly from Assurbanipal's Library* (CNI Publications 25; Copenhagen: Museum Tusculanum Press, 2000), 87.

2. Martti Nissinen, *Prophets and Prophecy in the Ancient Near East* (ed. Peter Machinist; SBLWAW 12; Atlanta: Society of Biblical Literature, 2003), 1.

in depth how prophecy functioned in a society: the Mari letters from Bronze Age Syria and the Neo-Assyrian archives of Nineveh. Those two corpora provide the primary comparative materials for the ensuing chapters, and they are discussed further there.

The word "prophet" has a Greek etymology: πρό (forth, before, for) + -φητης (speaker), so that a prophet is "one who speaks forth/proclaims," but the practice of prophecy long predates the Greeks. The references to prophecy in the ancient Near East are widespread, and it coexisted with other forms of divination as a consistent part of Mesopotamian religious culture. The earliest reference to a prophet in the ancient Near East is a passing mention from a king of Ur during the final century of the third millennium BCE. Also from Mesopotamia are references in an Old Babylonian (early second millennium) list of occupations, in a Middle Assyrian (late second millennium) rations list, in a lament from Ugarit (ca. 1200), and in a number of Neo-Babylonian texts from the first millennium.

Prophetic oracles are also attested elsewhere in the ancient Near East. In the West Semitic languages of the first millennium, a few texts mention prophets, but they are all either fragmentary or very brief. The late-ninth-century Amman Citadel inscription records an oracle of the Ammonite god Milcom; in the Zakkur Stela, a king of Hamath avowed, "Baal of the Heavens [spoke] to me through seers and visionaries"; and the early-eighth-century Deir ʿAlla Plaster texts tell a story about Balaam son of Beor, who is known to readers of the Bible from Numbers 22–24. Within ancient Judah, letters from Lachish attest that military officials were paying attention to the impact that prophets' words had on their society (see chap. 15).

Farther to the west (in Hatti) and south (in Egypt), it is not clear that prophecy consistently had the same stature as a means of divination, although it was practiced in both places. In one of the Hittite Plague Prayers (see chap. 24), Mursili II implored the gods to reveal the reason for the devastation: "Let me either see it in a dream, or [let] it [be discovered] by means of an oracle, or let a prophet speak of it."[3] Similar references to oracular consultations occur throughout the Hittite royal prayers, though these generally seem to be of a yes-or-no nature. Whereas inquiries regarding divine anger were probably common, there is no evidence that oracles were consulted to determine policy—for example, to decide whether to go to war. Other means of inquiry seem to have had more currency in the Hittite kingdom, including extispicy, augury, symbol oracles (based on the manipulation of tokens symbolizing entities such as the king, his enemies, and the gods; thus somewhat akin to tarot reading). Billie Jean Collins concludes that although "the Hittite shared an interest in dreams [with the Israelites and Judeans], they did not rely heavily on prophecy as a means of communication with the divine."[4]

In Egypt, there is no evidence of oracular consultations of the gods prior to the New Kingdom; the use of omens from the chief god Amun rose in popularity during the Eighteenth Dynasty (ca. 1550–1295 BCE); by the Twenty-first Dynasty (ca. 1069–945) it had taken on such an importance in so many minor decisions that Erik Hornung characterizes

---

3. From Mursili's second plague prayer (CTH 378.2; see translation by Gary Beckman in *COS* 1.60:159). See also Mursili's fourth plague prayer (CTH 378.4) and Muwatalli's prayer to the storm-god (CTH 382).

4. Billie Jean Collins, *The Hittites and Their World* (SBLABS 7; Atlanta: SBL, 2007), 166–69.

the period as a theocracy.[5] However, the records of oracular consultations are hardly comparable to Semitic prophecies. Sometimes questions were asked in a yes-or-no format, so that the representation of the deity had only to nod to answer yes; backing up from the inquirer meant no. Other times, the movement of a god's statue as it was carried through a sacred precinct was interpreted as having meaning; for example, a person might be selected for a specific post if the god's statue stopped in front of the person. Still other inquiries involved laying two papyri before the deity's statue, one with a statement and one with the opposite statement. The papyrus that the statue selected was deemed true.[6] In exceptional cases, the god might be said to have issued an omen spontaneously, as in the case of Hatshepsut's ascension to the pharaonic throne as a woman.[7] Even the rare cases where Egyptian gods speak in an oracular fashion do not bear comparison with Semitic prophecies; for example, the Apanage Stela of Iuwelot (9th c. BCE) simply puts in Amun-Re's mouth the ratification of the land claims of a high priest; it can be understood as a juridical contract document with a theological introduction.

Over the centuries, the Hebrew prophets have been understood in many ways: as ecstatic proclaimers, as charismatic leaders, as cultic officials, as literary geniuses, as religious innovators, and as spiritual figures with a special affinity for the heart and mind of God. Since one can see at least hints of each of these personae in the ancient Near Eastern prophets, comparison brings the biblical prophets into sharper focus.

GENERAL RESOURCES
ON ANCIENT NEAR EASTERN PROPHECY

Heimpel, Wolfgang. *Letters to the King of Mari: A New Translation, with Historical Introduction, Notes, and Commentary.* Winona Lake, IN: Eisenbrauns, 2003.
Nissinen, Martti. *Prophets and Prophecy in the Ancient Near East.* Edited by Peter Machinist. SBLWAW 12. Atlanta: Society of Biblical Literature, 2003.
Parpola, Simo. *Assyrian Prophecies.* SAA 9. Helsinki: Helsinki University Press, 1997.

5. Erik Hornung, *Conceptions of God in Ancient Egypt: The One and the Many* (trans. J. Baines; Ithaca, NY: Cornell University Press, 1982), 193.
6. Jean-Marie Kruchten, "Oracles," in *Oxford Encyclopedia of Ancient Egypt,* ed. Donald B. Redford (New York: Oxford University Press, 2001), 609–12.
7. Jan Assmann, *The Search for God in Ancient Egypt* (Ithaca, NY: Cornell University Press, 2001), 192–93.

14

Prophetic Symbolic Acts

Royal Archives of Mari 26 206 and Isaiah 20

ISAIAH 20:1–6

When: 711 BCE
Where: Jerusalem
Language: Hebrew

JEREMIAH 27–28

When: 596 BCE
Where: Jerusalem
Language: Hebrew

ROYAL ARCHIVES OF MARI, ARM 26 206 (=A. 3893)

What: Cuneiform letter on clay tablet
When: 1775–1762 BCE
Where: Mari (in present-day Syria)
Language: Akkadian
Translation: Martti Nissinen, *Prophets and Prophecy in the Ancient Near East* (ed. Peter Machinist; SBLWAW 12; Atlanta: Society of Biblical Literature, 2003), 38–39.

Sp[eak] to my [lord]: Thus [Yaqqim-Addu, your] servant:

A prophe[t of Dagan] came to me [and spoke as foll]ows. This is what he said: "V[erily, what] shall I eat that belongs to Z[imri-Lim]? [Give me] one la[mb] and I shall eat it!"

[I gave] him one lamb and he devoured it raw [in fr]ont of the city gate. He assembled the elders in front of the gate of Saggaratum and said: "A devouring will take place! Give orders to the cities to return the taboo material.[1] Whoever commits an act of violence shall be expelled from the city. And for the well-being of your lord Zimri-Lim, clothe me in a garment."

This is what he spoke to me. For the sake of the well-being of [my] lord, I clothed [him] in a garment. Now, [I have recorded] the ora[cle that] he spoke [to me] and sent it [to my lord.] He did not utter his oracle in private, but he delivered his oracle in the assembly of the elders.

DISCUSSION

Because of the derivation of the words "prophet" and "prophecy" from the Greek verb φημί, "to speak," and because of the presuppositions of modern cultures, many people do not realize that the *acting out* of oracles was one of the earliest forms of prophecy. Many stories of such "sign-acts" are preserved in both the Bible and other ancient Near Eastern texts.

A number of sign-acts are reported in letters from Mari, a powerful Syrian city-state in the late third and early second millennium. The Mari letters are the earliest surviving collection of reports of prophetic activities. The Mari prophetic oracles were mostly preserved within letters reporting them to the kings Yasmach-Addu and Zimri-Lim (ca. 1792–1760 BCE). These royal archives survived undisturbed when Mari fell to Hammurabi's Babylon. The existence of a smaller number of contemporary prophetic texts from Eshnunna, which was much farther east and nearer to the Babylonian heartland, suggests that prophecy was already active across the Mesopotamian cultural sphere at that time.

The term translated as "prophet" in the Mari text above is *muḫḫum,* meaning "crazy person"; it is perhaps best understood as "ecstatic (prophet)." This common title for a prophet at Mari reflects the idea that one could attain a better connection to the world of the divine by reaching a state of ecstasy. Mystics from many places and periods have sought similar kinds of ecstasy through such means as fasting, praying, and ingesting mind-altering substances. In the modern world, speaking in tongues is one example of an ecstatic state that some believe reflects a connection to God. There are other titles for prophets at Mari, such as *āpilum,* "answerer," which perhaps reflects a different approach to divine revelation.

No prophetic books or compilations have come to us from Mari—probably none existed, unlike in the Neo-Assyrian period (see chap. 17). Mari prophets' oracles are generally reported in just a few phrases, and usually the prophet's name is not even recorded.

The background of this particular Mari oracle is not entirely clear. The prophet refers to "taboo material" that has, in his view, been misappropriated. The taboo material is property belonging to temples, apparently in various cities. This is not an uncommon complaint from those who spoke for the gods. It seems that there was a tendency to use the wealth of temples to help pay for practical civic expenses in times of crisis. For a

---

1. "Taboo material" (Akkadian *asakku*) refers to property set aside for the deity.

biblical example, see 2 Kings 18:16: "Hezekiah stripped the gold from the doors of the temple of Yhwh, and from the doorposts . . . and gave it to the king of Assyria." Like Hezekiah, Zimri-Lim was in a complicated political situation in which temple goods might well have been forcibly requisitioned. It is possible that the uncommon word translated as "an act of violence" could refer to the same theft of property, but it is usually used of physical assault, and so it is more likely that this is a separate word of divine warning.

The prophet's oracle threatens the peace of Zimri-Lim's reign—the predicted "devouring" could refer to some sort of plague or epidemic, but the word is also used to describe divine attacks. Such attacks commonly took the form of enemy invasions (see chap. 25). It is also clear that the author of the letter took the threats seriously—seriously enough to give the ecstatic prophet the food and clothing that he demanded, and to report the word to the king.

Although the prophecy was reported, one should not assume that such words were treated completely credulously. They were commonly conveyed in letters, and so were other events that were thought to have divinatory significance, such as unusual happenings in the skies and deformed births. In contrast to what the reader may assume based on ancient Israel, in Mari spoken prophecy actually had lower status than other forms of divination, and so an oracle like this one might be checked by royal diviners through extispicy (divination by the examination of the organs of a sacrificed animal). The author of another letter (ARM 26 371) reports an ecstatic prophet's screaming in the city gate, but "no one spoke to him"—one can well imagine that prophet as a street-corner preacher shunned by passersby.

Symbolic acts by prophets might be understood as an attempt to bridge the gap between their spoken oracles and forms of divination that were more authoritative. By contrast with the "scientific" appearance of the heavily codified inductive forms of divination, spoken prophecy would have risked seeming arbitrary. Arguably, the genesis of prophetic symbolic acts was the attempt to make the prophet's own body and behavior a kind of readable text for the viewer, just as a liver or the night sky were readable to experts. The prophet's body became the medium through which the gods sent their messages.

Prophetic symbolic acts could also be seen as magical actions intended to bring about the realities they predict. From a perspective that is basically open to supernatural causation, it can seem a fine line between foretelling and magic. Voodoo-like rituals are well attested in both Mesopotamia and Egypt, in which items symbolizing an enemy or evil force were symbolically burned or broken. Is the Mari prophet's devouring of the lamb simply a prediction, or is it a magical act? What about the case of Ahijah in 1 Kings 11:30–31?

> Ahijah laid hold of the new garment [Jeroboam] was wearing and tore it into twelve pieces. He then said to Jeroboam: Take for yourself ten pieces; for thus says Yhwh, the God of Israel, "See, I am tearing the kingdom from the hand of Solomon, and will give you ten tribes."

The verb for "tearing" is a participle. Although it can have a future interpretation ("I am about to tear"), it can just as well be translated, "I hereby tear. . ."

Whatever the roots of such symbolic acts, they became a significant part of a Hebrew prophet's repertoire. There are many prophetic symbolic acts in the Bible, and thus numerous other biblical passages could have been selected for comparison:

- Jeremiah ruins a loincloth (Jer. 13:1–11), shatters a jug (19:1–15), buys a field when the nation is on the brink of destruction (32:1–15), buries stones in a clay pavement (43:8–13), and throws a scroll in the Euphrates (51:59–64).
- Ezekiel lies on his side for more than a year and eats barley-cakes cooked over human dung (Ezek. 4:1–13), shaves his head and beard (5:1–4), drags baggage around and digs through a wall (12:1–16), and writes on sticks (37:15–28).
- Hosea is told to marry a prostitute (Hos. 1–3).
- Zechariah collects gold and silver and makes a crown (Zech. 6:9–15).

These texts span a long period of time; one is dealing not with isolated incidents, but with a long-standing cultural practice. And this is not surprising, since the tradition of prophetic sign-acts stretched at least as far back as the early second millennium.

The reports of the symbolic acts of prophets in the Bible bring into sharp focus the debate about the relationship between historical prophetic figures and the books that bear their names. The Bible's lengthy prophetic oracles are often thought to be literary works that were heavily edited and augmented over time, but the reports of prophets' actions at least purport to be eyewitness accounts. Although in principle these accounts might be late inventions as much as any other text, their explicit references to personal activity would be the marks of bolder fabrications.

It is also necessary, however, to consider the final form of the texts. The Mari report comes to us in a letter that is terse and somewhat difficult to interpret. It does not contain any explanation, unless perhaps the "devouring" is connected to the comment about violence. Presumably these references would have been more clear to the letter's sender and receiver. Isaiah's sign-act, while also briefly reported, is fully explained. It clearly refers to the political situation of the end of the eighth century BCE, in which Judah was under constant threat from Assyrian expansion and was prone to seek military support from Egypt. Isaiah consistently condemned that tendency to rely on Egypt (see also Isa. 30:1–5; 31:1–3).[2] Although these events in Isaiah 20 are fitted into that larger narrative, the terseness of their presentation allows the reader to imagine that this is a primary record of what happened, much like the Mari text.

Finally, the section from Jeremiah shows two different but related sign-acts: Jeremiah's wearing the yoke, and Hananiah's breaking it. One can imagine what dramatic street theater this would have been; but to look at it a different way, the construction of an extended narrative like this one requires a certain amount of time and distance. In this case, it is unlikely that the story was told in this way until at least the time of Hananiah's death, two months after he broke the yoke and still longer after Jeremiah's original oracles. It is no less likely that this story was added significantly later as a legend linked to the prophet that was thought to illustrate the conflicts of his times. In any case, the

---

2. And indeed, although Egyptians intervened at least once in a while in the affairs of the Levant during Isaiah's time (2 Kgs. 19:6–9), in the big picture they were very little help to Judah against Assyria.

motivations of the author of Jeremiah were very different from those of Yaqqim-Addu of Mari. Yaqqim-Addu was doing his duty to his ruler by briefly reporting a strange, and possibly portentous, happening in his town. By contrast, the final editors of the book of Jeremiah were telling a sweeping theological story about God, a prophet, and the people of Judah. The different literary development and purpose of each story create a very different impression on the reader.

REFLECTION QUESTIONS

1. In a few words, what are the symbolic acts in these texts, and what is the relationship of the acts to the oracles being delivered?

2. Why would diviners do such strange things? Why not just tell people the message?

3. What are some of the indications in the biblical texts that they have been edited into literary compositions, as compared to the letter report from Mari?

4. What does it mean, in religious terms, to collect and save oracles? Does a king collecting them in his archives mean something different from their being written down in a compilation in the prophet's name?

5. What are some other differences in the reporting and presentation of the symbolic act in each case? What does this reflect about the production and purpose of each text?

6. The behavior of each of these prophets was certainly not normal, or else it would not have had the desired impact. What else do these accounts suggest about the relationship of prophets to the cultures in which they lived?

FURTHER READING

Roberts, J. J. M. "The Mari Prophetic Texts in Transliteration and English Translation." Pages 157–253 in *The Bible and the Ancient Near East: Collected Essays*. Winona Lake, IN: Eisenbrauns, 2002.

Viberg, Åke. *Prophets in Action: An Analysis of Prophetic Symbolic Acts in the Old Testament*. Coniectanea biblica: Old Testament Series 55. Stockholm: Almqvist & Wiksell, 2007.

15

Oracles of Well-Being

Oracles to Esarhaddon and Oracles of Isaiah

STATE ARCHIVES OF ASSYRIA 9 1.1, 4, 6

What: Cuneiform text on clay tablet
When: 680–679
Where: Nineveh
Language: Akkadian
Translation: Simo Parpola[1]

[*Presented here are three oracles from a set of six collected on a single tablet. For more about the compilation of Neo-Assyrian prophecies, see chapter 17.*]

1.1   [Esarh]addon, king of the lands, fear [not]!

What wind has risen against you, whose wing I have not broken? Your enemies will roll before your feet like ripe apples.

I am the Great Lady; I am Ishtar of Arbela, who cast your enemies before your feet. What words have I spoken to you that you could not rely upon?

I am Ishtar of Arbela. I will flay your enemies and give them to you. I am Ishtar of Arbela. I will go before you and behind you.

Fear not! You are paralysed, but in the midst of woe I will rise and sit down (beside you).

By the mouth of Issar-la-tashiyat of Arbela.

. . .

1.4   Fear not, Esarhaddon!

I am Bel.[2] (Even as) I speak to you, I watch over the beams of your heart. When your mother gave birth to you, sixty great gods stood with me and protected you. Sin was at your right side, Shamash at your left; sixty great gods were standing around you and girded your loins.

---

1. Simo Parpola, *Assyrian Prophecies* (SAA 9; Helsinki: Helsinki University Press, 1997), 4–8.
2. Marduk.

Do not trust in man. Lift up your eyes, look to me! I am Ishtar of Arbela; I reconciled Ashur with you. When you were small, I took you to me. Do not fear; praise me!

What enemy has attacked you while I remained silent? The future shall be like the past. I am Nabu,[3] lord of the stylus. Praise me!

By the mouth of the woman Baya, 'son'[4] of Arbela.

. . .

1.6   I am Ishtar of [Arbela]. Esarhaddon, king of A[ssyria]! In the Inner City, Nineveh, Calah and Arbela I will give long days and everlasting years to Esarhaddon, my king.

I am your great midwife; I am your excellent wet nurse. For long days and everlasting years I have established your throne under the great heavens. I watch in a golden chamber in the midst of the heavens; I let the lamp of amber shine before Esarhaddon, king of Assyria, and I watch him like the crown of my head.

Have no fear, my king! I have spoken to you, I have not lied to you; I have given you faith, I will not let you come to shame. I will take you safely across the River.

Esarhaddon, rightful heir, son of Mullissu![5] With an angry dagger in my hand I will finish off your enemies.

O Esarhaddon, king of Assyria, cup filled with lye, axe of two shekels!

Esarhaddon! I will give you long days and everlasting years in the Inner City. O Esarhaddon, I will be your good shield in Arbela.

Esarhaddon, ri[ghtful] heir, son of Mul[lissu]! I am mindful of you, I have loved you greatly. I keep you in the great heavens by your curl. I make smoke rise up on your right side, I kindle fire on your left.

[*rest fragmentary*]

ISAIAH 7:3–9; 8:5–15

When: ca. 734 BCE
Where: Jerusalem
Language: Hebrew
Translation: Adapted from CEB (by the author and Patricia K. Tull)

7:3   Yhwh said to Isaiah, "Go out to meet Ahaz, you and your son Shear-jashub, at the end of the channel of the Upper Pool, by the road to the field where laundry is washed, [4]and say to him, 'Be careful and stay calm. Don't fear, and don't lose heart over these two pieces of smoking torches, over the burning anger of Rezin[6] and Aram and the son of Remaliah.[7]

---

3. The Mesopotamian god of wisdom and writing.
4. See discussion.
5. A mother goddess (aka Ninlil) who was regarded in Neo-Assyrian times as the wife of the national god Ashur.
6. An Aramean king who was part of a coalition against Judah.
7. I.e., Pekah, king of Israel. According to Dennis T. Olson, "When [Pekah son of Remaliah] murdered King Pekahiah and usurped the throne [2 Kgs. 15:23–25], he may have taken the closely related name Pekah for himself as a means of identifying himself as a legitimate successor. Isaiah 7

[5]"Aram has planned evil against you with Ephraim and Remaliah's son, saying, [6]"Let's march up against Judah, tear it apart, capture it for ourselves, and install Tabeel's son[8] as its king."

[7]"But Yhwh God says: It won't happen; it won't take place. [8]The chief of Aram is Damascus;[9] the chief of Damascus is Rezin (in sixty-five more years Ephraim will be shattered as a nation); [9]the chief of Ephraim is Samaria; and the chief of Samaria is the son of Remaliah. If you aren't steadfast, you won't stand fast.'"

8:5 Yhwh spoke again to me:

[6]Since this people has rejected the waters of Shiloah that flow gently,[10] and instead rejoices over Rezin and Remaliah's son—[7]therefore, look, Yhwh is raising up against them the powerful floodwaters of the Euphrates, the king of Assyria and all his glory.[11] It will rise up over all its channels, overflowing all its banks, [8]and sweep into Judah, flooding, overflowing, and reaching up to the neck. But God is with us; the span of his wings will cover the width of the land.

> [9]Unite yourselves, peoples,
> and be shattered!
> Listen, all distant places of the earth—
> Prepare to be shattered!
> Prepare to be shattered!
> [10]Create a plan, but be frustrated—
> Speak a word, but it won't stand,
> for God is with us.

[11]Yhwh spoke to me, taking hold of me and warning me not to walk in the way of this people: [12]Don't call conspiracy all that this people calls conspiracy. Don't fear what they fear, and don't be terrified. [13]It is Yhwh of heavenly forces whom you should hold sacred, whom you should fear, and whom you should hold in awe.

> [14]God will become a sanctuary—
> but he will be a stone to trip over
> and a rock to stumble on for the two houses of Israel;
> a trap and a snare for those living in Jerusalem.
> [15]Many of them will stumble and fall,
> and be broken, snared, and captured.

---

provides some evidence that the name Pekah may have been perceived as a usurped and illegitimate name for the new king . . . the prophet simply refers to the king of Israel as 'the son of Remaliah' with no mention of his name. Isaiah may thereby signal a refusal to acknowledge the legitimacy of Pekah's reign by avoiding the name stolen from the previous king Pekahiah" ("Pekah," *ABD* 5:214).

8. Probably a king of Tyre in Phoenicia.

9. I.e., Damascus was the leading Aramean city-state.

10. Shiloah (later Siloam) was at this time a channel to bring water from Jerusalem's Gihon spring into a reservoir.

11. The Assyrian military was often portrayed as rushing floodwaters, both in Assyrian texts and in the Bible.

STATE ARCHIVES OF ASSYRIA 9 2.3

What: Cuneiform text on clay tablet
When: 680–679
Where: Nineveh
Language: Akkadian
Translation: Simo Parpola[12]

1–5	[I am the La]dy of Arbela. [Esarhaddon, king of] Assyria, [fear not!] . . . [I will annihilate] whatever enemies you [have]. As for [you, stay] in your palace; I will [reconcile] Assyria with you. I will protect [you] by day and by dawn and [consolidate] your crown.
6–10	Like a winged bird ov[er its young] I will twitter over you and go in circles around you. Like a beautiful (lion) cub[13] I will run about in your palace and sniff out your enemies.
11–16	I will keep you safe in your palace; I will make you overcome anxiety and trembling. Your son and grandson shall rule as kings before Ninurta. I will abolish the frontiers of all the lands and give them to you.
17–20	Mankind is deceitful; I am one who says and does. I will sniff out, catch and give you the corrupt men.[14]
21–23	As for you, praise me! Gather into your innards these words of mine from Arbela:
24–27	The gods of Esaggil languish in the 'steppe' of mixed evil.[15] Quickly let two burnt offerings be sent out to their presence, and let them go and announce your well-being!
28	From the mouth of La-dagil-ili of Arbela.

ISAIAH 31:1–5, 8–9

When: ca. 701 BCE (but see discussion)
Where: Jerusalem, Judah
Language: Hebrew
Translation: Adapted from CEB (by the author and Patricia K. Tull)

31:1 Doom to those going down to Egypt for help!
They rely on horses,
trust in chariots because they are many,
and riders because they are very strong.

---

12. Parpola, *Assyrian Prophecies*, 15–16.

13. Parpola interprets this as a lion cub; it could be argued, however, that the image of sniffing around a palace sounds more like a young dog, which is an equally possible translation of the Akkadian word (*mūrānu*).

14. Lit., "the noisy daughter," a reference to mythical accounts of humankind's creation.

15. "The 'steppe' of mixed evil" appears to be a reference to exile. Statues of gods were often taken away from a city if it was conquered. For Mesopotamians, the steppes were symbols of wastelands.

But they don't look to the Holy One of Israel;
they don't seek Yhwh.
[2]But God also knows how to bring disaster;
he has not taken back his words.
God will rise up
against the house of evildoers
and against the help of those who do wrong.
[3]Egypt is human and not divine;
their horses are flesh and not spirit.
Yhwh will extend his hand;
the helper will stumble,
those helped will fall,
and they will all die together.
[4]Yhwh has said to me:
When the lion growls,
the young lion, over its prey,
though a band of shepherds is summoned against it,
isn't scared off by their noise
or frightened by their roar.
So Yhwh of heavenly forces will go down
to fight on Mount Zion and on her hill.
[5]Like birds flying aloft,
so Yhwh of heavenly forces will shield Jerusalem:
shielding and saving,
sparing and rescuing.
. . . .
[8]Assyria will fall, but not by a human sword—
a sword not made by humans will devour them.
They will flee before the sword;
their young men will become forced laborers.
[9]In horror they will flee from their stronghold;
their officers will be terrified at the signal,
says Yhwh, whose fire is in Zion
and whose oven is in Jerusalem.

DISCUSSION

From early periods in Mesopotamia, there were prophets at royal courts who were sought out for oracular advice and support of various kinds (see also chapters 15 and 16). Very often, they pronounced their blessings on the king and his plans. Such an oracle is found already in Old Babylonian Eshnunna, where the king Ibalpiel (r. 1779–1765 BCE) is told by a god: "I, Kititum, will strengthen the foundations of your throne; I have established a protective spirit for you. Let your ear be attentive to me!"[16]

Oracles pronouncing divine favor on the king, the country, and their activities have come to be known as *shulmu* oracles, after the Akkadian word that is cognate with the

---

16. Martti Nissinen, *Prophets and Prophecy in the Ancient Near East* (ed. Peter Machinist; SBLWAW 12; Atlanta: Society of Biblical Literature, 2003), 94.

Hebrew *shalom*. *Shalom* is commonly translated "peace," and it became a commonplace greeting. At a deeper level, however, it denoted a more comprehensive state of "well-being" (e.g., Gen. 37:14: "Go now, see about the welfare [*shalom*] of your brothers.") It is that state of well-being that positive oracles often wish for the king and the country, as in the biblical exclamation, "How beautiful upon the mountains are the feet of the messenger who announces *shalom*, who brings good news, who announces salvation (Isa. 52:7//Nah. 1:15)—here the poetic parallelism equates *shalom* with both good news and salvation. It is those same oracles that Jeremiah decried: "From prophet to priest everyone deals falsely. They have treated the wound of my people carelessly, saying, '*Shalom, shalom*,' when there is no *shalom*" (Jer. 8:10–11). Although the nation may not have been at war when Jeremiah issued those words, he means that it was also not in a state of well-being.

The practice of seeking a positive prophetic oracle is reflected clearly in the story of 1 Kings 22, in which Ahab, king of Israel, is trying to convince Jehoshaphat, king of Judah, to ally with him in war:

> The king of Israel gathered the prophets together, about four hundred of them, and said to them, "Shall I go to battle against Ramoth-gilead, or shall I refrain?" They said, "Go up; for Yhwh will give it into the hand of the king." But Jehoshaphat said, "Is there no other prophet of Yhwh here of whom we may inquire?" The king of Israel said to Jehoshaphat, "There is still one other by whom we may inquire of Yhwh, Micaiah son of Imlah; but I hate him, for he never prophesies anything favorable about me, but only disaster." (1 Kgs. 22:6–8)

The author of this story portrays Jehoshaphat as being quite aware that a prophet in the employ of the king has a strong incentive to say what the king wants to hear. Micaiah does indeed prophesy disaster, and the story comes out badly—the kings ignore his warning and Ahab is killed: it suggests that a wise king should seek out and listen to such a minority report.

The largest surviving corpus of oracles of well-being from court prophets comes to us from the courts of the Neo-Assyrian kings Esarhaddon (r. 680–669) and Ashurbanipal (r. 668–627)—nearly thirty oracles have survived on their original tablets. These texts are of particular interest to the study of Hebrew prophecy, since the first Hebrew prophets whose words were collected into biblical books (e.g., Amos, Hosea, Isaiah) were prophesying at the same time that the Neo-Assyrian Empire was making its presence felt in Israel and Judah.

Esarhaddon and Ashurbanipal may have had a special affinity for prophecy; they are the only Assyrian kings who are known to have archived prophecies, and the only ones who mention prophets in their inscriptions. They were also closely linked with Ishtar of Arbela, the patron goddess of nearly all the prophets whose words they recorded.[17] The method of these prophets was based on their ability to become "possessed" by a god (again, usually Ishtar) and speak for her or him. The most common Neo-Assyrian term for a prophet is *ragintu* (in the masculine form, *ragimu*), meaning "one who shouts (or proclaims)."[18]

---

17. Names like "Mulissu" and "Lady of Arbela" are essentially epithets of Ishtar.
18. There is also the term *zabbu/zabbatu* ("frenzied one"), found in administrative lists, and *mahhu* ("crazy person") was sometimes used, as at Mari.

The majority of Neo-Assyrian prophets seem to have been female—eight or nine of the thirteen who are named in preserved oracles were women. This may surprise some readers who are accustomed to encountering mostly male prophets in the Bible,[19] but it makes sense in that they were speaking for and representing Ishtar. It also seems that some kind of gender-bending took place in the cult of Ishtar, with men playing the roles of women to speak for the goddess. There is a reference in one text to Ishtar's "changing men into women," perhaps through castration.[20] The prophecy SAA 9 1.4 is attributed to "the woman Baya, 'son' of Arbela"—Baya seems to be a woman's name. It is possible that this was a man speaking as a woman—notably, that oracle is spoken in the personae of deities both male (Marduk, Nabu) and female (Ishtar).[21]

In the Neo-Assyrian context, prophets seem to have enjoyed a higher status than their Mari counterparts had earlier (see chap. 14). They were supported by the state, and their oracles do not seem to have been vetted by comparison with other forms of divination as a matter of course. Reports of their oracles usually mention the name and gender of the prophet, and the city in which she or he was based. One collection of multiple oracles is even thought to be the work of a single prophet, as in biblical prophetic books (see chap. 17). Thus the prophets seem to have possessed a kind of personal authority.[22]

The length of Neo-Assyrian oracle reports varied quite a bit, from the eleven brief lines of SAA 9 8 (see chap. 16) to the twenty-five longer lines of SAA 9 7. The length of the lines depended on the width of the clay tablet; despite the literary character of many of the prophecies, they were not divided into poetic lines, as many biblical prophetic texts are.

The Neo-Assyrian prophecies that have survived are almost always addressed to the king, and they are almost always oracles of well-being. However, in a few cases there are records of prophecy being used against the king, for example, to support a coup attempt. We must assume that the overwhelmingly positive attitude of the surviving oracles toward the ruler is because most of what has been found is from the royal archives. In other words, it is likely that prophecy was used to support various political perspectives (as in ancient Israel and Judah), but that kings did not generally preserve prophecies against themselves and their empires.

Prophets and their actions are also mentioned in many types of Neo-Assyrian sources besides oracle reports. Unlike the Mari letters, few actually are eyewitness reports, but rather most quote from written sources, which provides glimpses into the way prophets' words were viewed and used by their contemporaries in the Assyrian Empire.[23] Royal inscriptions allude to the "messages of prophets," and scribes cited oracles when it suited

---

19. Note, however, the references to Israelite and Judean prophetesses such as Miriam in Exod. 15:20–21; Deborah in Judg. 4:4–5:31; Huldah in 2 Kgs. 22:14–20; and the unnamed prophetess in Isa. 8:3. There is also a surviving prayer by a Hittite priest that refers to the consultation of a female seer.

20. Parpola, *Assyrian Prophecies*, xxxiv, il.

21. It is also possible that "son" here is simply being used as it is in both Akkadian and Hebrew to mean "a member of a group" (cf. Amos 7:14; 1 Kgs. 20:35).

22. Nissinen, *Prophets and Prophecy*, 100.

23. Cf. Parpola, *Assyrian Prophecies*, 133.

them to make an argument. Prophets were also mentioned in royal correspondence, ritual texts, and administrative texts.

As with most Assyrian prophecies, the historical contexts of the oracles presented above are relatively clear: Although it was compiled later, this collection (SAA 9 1) contains oracles related to the events of 681 BCE, when Esarhaddon fought a civil war against his brothers to take the throne after the death of their father, Sennacherib. Another collection (SAA 9 2) contains oracles of comfort to the new king from about 680–679, as he sought to consolidate his rule after defeating his brothers. References to deceitfulness and corruption indicate that his ascension was controversial and difficult, as do contemporaneous historical inscriptions.

It is important to note that the Isaianic oracles above survive in copies that date, at the earliest, to more than five hundred years after the events they reflect. This is in stark contrast to the Assyrian oracles, the copies of which were made either when they were delivered or at most a few months or years later.

The context of the texts from Isaiah 7–8 is the Syro-Ephraimitic War of 734–732 BCE. As the Assyrians spread their empire westward toward the Mediterranean and into Palestine, smaller Syrian and Palestinian states formed an alliance against Assyria to stop its expansion, as their predecessors had successfully done in the previous century. At that time, there were two nations descended from the kingdoms of David and Solomon: one in the north (Israel) and one in the south (Judah). The northern kingdom had joined the anti-Assyrian alliance, but Judah refused. That refusal not only weakened the alliance, but would have given it a serious liability on its rear periphery. Therefore, the Syrian nations and Israel attacked Judah in an effort to remove this liability and force its participation:

> In the days of Ahaz . . . Aram's King Rezin and Israel's King Pekah (Remaliah's son) came up to attack Jerusalem, but they could not overpower it. When the house of David was told that Aram had become allies with Ephraim [i.e., Israel], their hearts and the hearts of their people shook as the trees of a forest shake when there is a wind. (Isa. 7:1–2)

The fears of Ahaz and the Judean people are easy to understand: They were already in danger from Assyria, and then they also made enemies of their neighboring nations. In the face of all this danger and instability, Isaiah reframes the situation, saying of the Syro-Ephraimite alliance: "Unite yourselves, peoples, and be shattered!" (7:9). This subversion of the expectation that strength would come from unity is a word of comfort to Ahaz as he resists the coalition of nations.

Isaiah goes on to caution Ahaz: "Don't call conspiracy all that this people calls conspiracy. Don't fear what they fear" (8:12)—that is, don't be afraid of Assyria, and don't believe that refusing to join the alliance is treason against your neighbors. Instead, Assyria will save Judah by washing away these other nations like a salvific flood: "Yhwh is raising up against them the powerful floodwaters of the Euphrates: the king of Assyria and all his glory" (8:7). It is impossible to prove that this word was delivered in advance, but it was correct: in 731, Tiglath-pileser III campaigned to Syria-Palestine and crushed the coalition resistance, turning some nations into provinces and installing Hoshea on the throne of Israel (2 Kgs. 16:5–9; 17:1).

The situation behind Isaiah 31, which took place more than thirty years later, was very different: Assyria had conquered Syria and the northern kingdom, while Judah had spared itself and bought its independence for a while by siding with Assyria. But in the intervening years, it too had come under pressure. Like all small nations on the Assyrians' periphery, it had to pay a heavy annual tribute. This worked like a Mafia protection scam. *Pay up or else.* It was also a great burden on a relatively small economy, and so under Hezekiah, the Judeans withheld the tribute and the Assyrian emperor Sennacherib campaigned through Judah, leaving a path of destruction like Sherman's march to the sea in the American Civil War (2 Kgs. 18:13–14; see chap. 13). The oracle in Isaiah 31 reflects that renewed Judean terror, probably prior to the actual Assyrian campaign, in which some of the Jerusalem elites were looking to Egypt for support against the Assyrians. It had been a habit of Palestinian nations, as far back as the Bronze Age, to call on Egypt for help. But Isaiah advised that Egypt was neither able nor willing to stand up to Assyria; this was a consistent theme of his later oracles (e.g., Isa. 19:1–15; 20:1–6; 30:1–7, etc.).

The similarities between the words of Yhwh in Isaiah 31 and those of the Assyrian deities in SAA 9 2 are striking. In both, there is an assertion of divine agency in salvation, violent imagery of the destruction of enemies, and an appeal to past activity on behalf of the ruler or nation. There is even the nearly identical combination of images of the deity as a bird hovering over the city to protect it and as a lion facing the enemy (Isa. 31:4–5; SAA 9 2.3:6–10). This may indicate that the two oracles shared more than simply a common purpose; they may have arisen out of a common rhetorical tradition.

The two sets of texts are also comparable in their implied audience. The Assyrian oracles are all addressed to the king, even if they have broader implications. This is also clearly true of the oracle from Isaiah 7. On the basis of Isaiah 31:6–7, it might seem that Isaiah 31 is addressed to a wider audience—"People of Israel, return to the one whom you have deeply betrayed!" However, the reference in those same verses to idols of silver and gold is highly characteristic of the book's sixth-century additions (e.g., Isa. 40:19–20; 44:9–20, etc.). Furthermore, 31:6–7 are prose rather than poetry like the rest of the passage. Therefore, verses 6–7 are almost certainly a later addition, and so they are omitted above.[24] If one reads the passage without those two verses, as it would have been before, it becomes less clear who is being addressed—the charge of 31:1–2 is still addressed to a plural group, but it could well be the court elites who conducted diplomacy and helped determine military strategy.

One central difference between the oracles is that Isaiah's message was a complex mixture of promise and judgment, even in its original form. Thus there is a difference in tone between the two texts, and this is not to be dismissed (as it often has been) as an effect introduced by editing of the biblical text. Part of this difference is surely linked to the

---

24. It has been theorized that the description of Assyria's destruction by "a sword not made by humans" (31:8) marks this as a late composition from the late seventh century, when the Assyrian Empire was crumbling. However, the tradition of Yhwh as Divine Warrior is very ancient, and certainly the prophet who predicted that Assyria would be punished after it punished Judah (Isa. 10:12) could have spoken these words as well. At a minimum, it is just as likely that it came from shortly after Jerusalem's escape from Sennacherib's siege in 701, assuming that the tradition of the city's divine deliverance developed shortly thereafter (see also Isa. 37:36).

social location of each prophet—the Assyrians were court prophets; they worked for the king. Isaiah, on the other hand, seems to have functioned outside the inner circle of the royal court; that is the most likely reason he had to meet Ahaz (7:3) in such an odd, out-of-the-way location ("by the road to the field where laundry is washed"!). This would also help to explain why Ahaz rejected Isaiah's help (7:12–13), so that the prophet eventually had his words written down and sealed—since the court would not listen to him, he wanted proof of his prescience that could be verified later (8:15–18). Isaiah would have been a controversial and marginal figure through most of his career; his prominence and honored position as a prophet developed later.

This comparison brings to mind the old adage that the winners write the history books. The biblical text contains practically no unqualified oracles of well-being, because the "winners" in the competition among Israelite and Judean prophets were those who predicted that the nation was on the wrong track and would pay for it. There were those like Hananiah who said around 594 BCE: "Thus says Yhwh: . . . I will break the yoke of King Nebuchadnezzar of Babylon from the neck of all the nations within two years" (Jer. 28:11). Needless to say, such triumphalistic prophecies proved to be quite wrong. Thus the prophetic books in the Bible include far more negative prophecies about the nation than those from Assyrian royal archives. The Assyrian prophecies were written at the peak of the empire's power, and they were not weeded out or edited decades later, during or after the cataclysmic events that brought Assyria to its knees in the late seventh century BCE. The Bible, too, preserves some prophecies of salvation, and these stem primarily from events like those of the late eighth century, in which Judah *did* experience salvation.

Since this chapter compares poetic texts, it is worth noting that each of these texts has significant artistic value. Part of the success of Isaiah ben Amoz's prophecies is surely attributable to his giftedness as a wordsmith. The great English poet and critic Matthew Arnold, who translated Isaiah, said he enjoyed him more than Shakespeare and Milton, and compared him to Homer.[25] As for the Assyrian oracles, Parpola has written that their poetic features "elevate [their] diction . . . to a surprisingly high stylistic level, keeping in mind that they were written down from oral performance and apparently not subjected to any substantial editing."[26] It is impossible to recognize and appreciate *all* of the literary features of these texts in translation, but some of their artistry is still accessible to the reader.

---

25. Matthew Arnold, *Isaiah of Jerusalem* (London: Macmillan and Co., 1883), 4.

26. He continues in a more defensive vein: "It is true that the oracles are on the whole relatively short and that their thematic repertory is somewhat limited and formulaic. However, under no circumstances can they be considered products of untrained ecstatics 'prophesying' under the influence of drugs or intoxication. Their literary quality can have been achieved only through conscious striving for literary excellence, and their power of expression reflects the prophets' spiritual assimilation to the Goddess who spoke through their lips" (Parpola, *Assyrian Prophecies*, lxvii). Parpola's point about the literary quality and ambitions of the Neo-Assyrian prophecies is well taken, but these are not mutually exclusive with substance-induced ecstasy. In modern times, poets have written some fine work under the influence of drugs and alcohol.

REFLECTION QUESTIONS

1. What other similarities or differences do you find in the Assyrian and biblical texts besides those outlined in the discussion?
2. What poetic features seem significant in these texts?
3. Which passages of the Assyrian oracles seem like good writing to you? Are there others that do not?
4. Given that the majority of the surviving Neo-Assyrian prophecies were issued by women, and prophetesses are mentioned in the Bible, why are there no biblical prophetic books in women's names?
5. In light of the messages of Isaiah and other biblical prophets in their historical worlds, what does it mean in today's world to speak prophetically?

FURTHER READING

Ellis, Maria de Jong. "Observations on Mesopotamian Oracles and Prophetic Texts: Literary and Historiographic Considerations." *Journal of Cuneiform Studies* 41 (1989): 127–86.
Nissinen, Martti. *Prophets and Prophecy in the Ancient Near East.* Edited by Peter Machinist. SBLWAW 12. Atlanta: Society of Biblical Literature, 2003.
———. *References to Prophecy in Neo-Assyrian Sources.* State Archives of Assyria Studies 7. Helsinki: Neo-Assyrian Text Corpus Project, 1998.
Parpola, Simo. *Assyrian Prophecies.* SAA 9. Helsinki: Helsinki University Press, 1997.

16

Oracles Against the Nations

Oracles to Zimri-Lim, Ashurbanipal, and Zedekiah

JEREMIAH 49:34–39

When: ca. 597 BCE
Where: Jerusalem
Language: Hebrew

ROYAL ARCHIVES OF MARI, ARM 26 207

What: Cuneiform letter on clay tablet from Shibtu, queen of Mari, to Zimri-Lim, king of Mari
When: ca. 1775–1762 BCE
Where: Mari (modern Tell Hariri, Syria)
Language: Akkadian
Translation: After Martti Nissinen[1]

1–2 Speak to my lord: Thus (says) Shibtu, your servant:

3–12 Concerning the campaign my lord is planning, I gave drink to male and female prophets to inquire about signs. The oracle is extremely favorable to my lord. Likewise, I inquired of male and female about Ishme-Dagan.[2] The oracle is unfavorable to him. The report concerning him goes: "He will be placed under the feet of my lord."

13–17 They said: "My lord ha[s raised] a rod![3] Raising the rod against Ishme-Dagan he says: 'I will beat you with the rod! Wrestle as much as you can, I shall win the match!'"

---

1. Martti Nissinen, *Prophets and Prophecy in the Ancient Near East* (ed. Peter Machinist; SBLWAW 12; Atlanta: Society of Biblical Literature, 2003).
2. Ishme-Dagan I, king of Assyria.
3. The Akkadian word (ḫumāšum) that is translated here as "rod" is rare and not clear. The meaning is taken from context (for discussion, see Nissinen, *Prophets and Prophecy*, 41).

18-34   I said: "Will my lord come near to a conflict?" They answered: "There will be no armed conflict! For as soon as his (Zimri-Lim's) allies arrive they will be scattered. The he[ad of Ishme]-Dagan will be cut off and placed under the feet of my lord, saying: 'The army of I[shm]e-Dagan is large, but even if [his] a[rmy is la]rge, his allies have scattered it. My allies are Dagan, Shamash, Itur-Mer, Belet-ekallim and Adad, the Lord of Decisions,[4] who g[o] beside my lord.'"

35-45   Perhaps my lord would s[ay] this: "She has [made them speak] by fraudulent means." But [I did] not make [them] speak anything. They speak voluntarily—they could resi[st] as well! They say: "The allies of Ishme-[Dagan] are prisoners. When they fall into deceit and distress with him, they will not take heed of his [word]. Before my lord's arrival, his army will be dissipated."

STATE ARCHIVES OF ASSYRIA 9 8

What: Cuneiform text on clay tablet (oracle report to Ashurbanipal, king of Assyria)
When: 653 BCE
Where: Nineveh
Language: Akkadian
Translation: Simo Parpola[5]

Words [concerning the Elam]ites:[6]
[God] says as follows: "I have go[ne and I ha]ve come."
He s[ai]d (this) five, six times, and then: "I have come from the [m]ace. I have pulled out the snake[7] which was inside it, I have cut it in pieces, and I have broken the mace."
And (he said): "I will destroy Elam; its army shall be leveled to the ground. In this manner I will finish Elam."

DISCUSSION

Oracles against the nations are prophetic proclamations about or addressed directly to foreign nations. They might be considered the opposite counterparts of the oracles of well-being presented in the previous chapter, which affirm the prophet's own ruler or nation. The recorded examples of oracles against the nations are nearly always negative, condemning the foreign entity. The Mari prophecies are introduced in chapter 14. The

---

4. A list of gods. Dagan, Shamash, and Adad are major gods associated with grain, sun, and storm, respectively; politically, Dagan was closely linked to the ruling families of both Assyria and Mari. Itur-Mer was a protective god local to Mari, while Belet-ekallim ("mistress of the house") was a patron goddess of the Mari royal family.

5. Simo Parpola, *Assyrian Prophecies* (SAA 9; Helsinki: Helsinki University Press, 1997), 40.

6. Elam was a nation to the east of Mesopotamia that regularly came into conflict with Assyria in the eighth and seventh centuries.

7. Parpola notes the "prominence of the snake in Elamite religion and art" (*Assyrian Prophecies*, 40).

letter translated here is one of the longer such reports, and it sheds further light on the way prophecy functioned at this city-state on the western end of the Mesopotamian cultural sphere.

The queen Shibtu reports the oracles, and she addresses the king's potential concerns about the validity of the prophecies; she protests that she did not coerce their words. It is not clear whether Zimri-Lim had specific reason to doubt her, but such details about the circumstances of prophets' utterances are not uncommon in the Mari letters. In any case, Shibtu, as queen, may have been somewhat less constrained in speaking to her husband than were some of the lower-ranking reporters of prophecies.

The military background of this letter is quite clear. Like all of the Mari letters, it was written in a time of decentralized power in ancient Mesopotamia, when relatively small city-states vied for influence. A letter from an official at Mari described the situation:

> There is no king who is strong by himself: 10 or 15 kings follow Hammurabi of Babylon, as many follow Rim-Sin of Larsa, Ibalpiel of Eshnunna and Amutpiel of Qatna, while 20 kings follow Yarim-Lim of Yamhad. (ANET p. 628)

In this context, a king's reign would have been under constant threat, and espionage and divination were among the tools that rulers used to try to get a handle on their situation. It was normal for ancient Near Eastern rulers to check the will of the gods before going out to battle; if Mari is representative, in earlier periods this was more often done by checking physical omens, especially extispicy (reading the entrails of sacrificed animals). In later periods, both in Assyria and Israel/Judah, spoken prophecy came to have greater independent prominence in advising the king. In this early period, Shibtu seems to have been concerned that the type of prophecy she was reporting was inherently suspicious, so she insists, "I did not make them speak anything."

Another facet of Shibtu's role is revealed by her comment about giving the prophets something to drink. It is debated whether the drink should be understood as an intoxicating beverage intended to aid in prophetic ecstasy, or whether it is merely a symbolic act in which the prophet "processes" a drink which is understood to contain a sign, just as (for example) sheep's livers were thought to contain a sign that merely needed to be interpreted. The first theory seems more likely in light of the long history of intoxication as a way to get in touch with the divine.

It is often thought that ancient authors portrayed human wars as battles between the gods of the respective nations (see also chap. 10), but such was not always the case. Mari prophecy also reflects a sort of internecine dispute among followers of the same god, Dagan. Ishme-Dagan's name (which means "Dagan has heard") marks him as a Dagan worshiper, and yet Shibtu's prophets speak in his name as well ("My allies are Dagan, . . ."). Although Dagan may have been thought to have as many local manifestations as he had temples (see the discussion of Baal in chap. 19), it is equally possible to imagine the dispute as focusing on the will of a single god. The question would then have arisen: *Who rightly understands the god's will?* The same sort of intersectarian disagreements have taken place throughout history and continue into our own times.

Despite Shibtu's insistence, history shows that many of the Mari letters are examples of *failed* prophecies. Zimri-Lim never did defeat Ishme-Dagan. There is an even clearer example in the case of some prophecies against Hammurabi of Babylon; they include pronouncements such as, "Hammurabi [. . . is rush]ing to his complete undoing," and "You will capture him and stand over him. His days are running short; he will not live long."[8] In fact, Hammurabi conquered Mari and probably killed Zimri-Lim.

The Assyrian prophecy presented here was preserved as a brief report from very close in time to the events about which the prophet spoke. The fact that it contains no epistolary introduction or scene-setting reflects the fact that it was normal practice to record such prophecies. It is unusual for this corpus that the identity of the prophet was not recorded. The text was also not dated, but it is likely to have been written either in 653, when Assyria went to war with Elam and reduced it to vassalhood, or (less likely) in 647–646, when Elam was turned into an Assyrian province.[9] War oracles focused on specific foreign nations, as this one is, are not common in the surviving corpus. However, this is almost certainly an accident of preservation, since the larger oracle collections contain numerous references to divine violence against enemies.

A prophecy such as this one, which was not collected into a literary compilation, was probably recorded partly to check the veracity of a prophet's predictions. Without the systematization that was possible when reading physical omens,[10] such review was the only way to know who was an effective prophet. (As noted in the introduction to this section, Deut. 18:21–22 reflects the same assumptions about verification in Israel and Judah.) Unlike the Mari oracle above, this Assyrian oracle against Elam proved correct.

Turning to the biblical text, the historical context of the Jeremiah oracle is less clear. Some scholars doubt that a Judahite prophet would have had anything to say about a nation as distant as Elam (which was east of Mesopotamia), preferring to treat the oracle as an addition from the Babylonian exile or even from the later Babylonian Jewish diaspora. However, it makes sense that Jeremiah would prophesy against Babylon's enemies, since he had also predicted that all the nations (including his own Judah) must submit to the Babylonians.[11] Elam does seem to have survived to trouble Babylon, even after being provincialized by the Assyrians—or perhaps it regained its independence after Assyria fell. In any case, there is a report of Elam attacking the Neo-Babylonians in around 596.[12] There is no doubt that the oracles against the nations in Jeremiah as a whole were edited much later than the prophet's time—among other reasons, they appear in a completely different place in the book in the Septuagint than in the Hebrew Bible. However, it is

8. Nissinen, *Prophets and Prophecy*, 45–46.

9. Parpola, *Assyrian Prophecies*, lxx.

10. There were canonical guides to the interpretation of physical omens, so that, for example, a bump on a certain part of a sheep's liver was supposed to mean a certain thing. This brought a level of "objectivity" to divination.

11. E.g., Jer. 27:8–10: "If any nation or kingdom will not serve this king, Nebuchadnezzar of Babylon, and put its neck under the yoke of the king of Babylon, then I will punish that nation with the sword, with famine, and with pestilence, says Yhwh, until I have completed its destruction by his hand. You, therefore, must not listen to your prophets, your diviners, your dreamers, your soothsayers, or your sorcerers, who are saying to you, 'You shall not serve the king of Babylon.' For they are prophesying a lie to you, with the result that you will be removed far from your land."

12. Jack R. Lundbom, *Jeremiah 37–52* (AB 21C; New York: Doubleday, 2004), 359–64.

quite possible that the bulk of this particular oracle originated in the context assigned to it, that is, the beginning of Zedekiah's reign in 597 BCE.

If so, then this context sheds light on the theological force of the oracles as well: "Placed in the historical context of the end of the seventh and the beginning of the sixth century BCE, the oracles against the nations bring [a] breathtaking message": that despite "the maelstrom of the destruction" wrought by Assyria and Babylon, "God determines history" and is sovereign over all the nations.[13]

In the Bible, oracles against the nations are recorded not only in prophetic books, but also in the historical books (e.g., 1 Kgs. 22:6; 2 Kgs. 3:18–19), and even in Psalms (e.g., Pss. 60, 83). Many of the biblical prophetic books contain oracles against foreign nations, and in the Major Prophets, they are gathered into collections of significant size (Isa. 13–23; Jer. 46–51; Ezek. 25–32). The earliest example of oracles against the nations among the writing prophets is probably Amos 1–2; it seems that such early oracles are literary adaptations of original war oracles—Israelite variations on the Assyrian oracle presented above. Indeed, these straightforward condemnations of foreign nations have sometimes been taken as one of the most ancient forms of prophetic speech in the Bible.

John H. Hayes suggested that oracles against the nations could be divided into three types:

1. *Curses* meant to disadvantage the opposition supernaturally
2. *Omens* that predict the outcome of battles
3. *Judgment oracles* that supply a reason for divine wrath upon the enemy

The *curse* type of oracle is referred to (though not exemplified) in the biblical story of Balak and Balaam (Num. 22–24). Balak, the king of Moab, fearing the encroachment of the Israelites on his land, summons the prophet Balaam: "Come now, curse this people for me, since they are stronger than I; perhaps I shall be able to defeat them and drive them from the land; for I know that whomever you bless is blessed, and whomever you curse is cursed" (22:6). Relevant to our purposes here, Balaam is known outside the Bible in the lengthy Deir ʿAlla text written on a plaster wall at a site in the east Jordan Valley and dating to the late eighth century. Although the text is fragmentary, and much of it is hard to understand, it presents Balaam as a "seer of the gods" who delivers an oracle from the god El. The word used for "oracle" is equivalent with the Hebrew term (maśśāʾ) used for oracles against the nations in Isaiah (13:1; 14:28; 15:1; 17:1; 19:1; 21:1, 11, 13; 22:1, 15; 23:1).

A good example of an *omen* oracle comes from 1 Kings 22, where Ahab of Israel says to Jehoshaphat of Judah, "Will you go with me to battle at Ramoth-gilead?" And Jehoshaphat replies, "Inquire first for the word of Yhwh." The story continues: "Then the king of Israel gathered the prophets together, about four hundred of them, and said to them, 'Shall I go to battle against Ramoth-gilead, or shall I refrain?' They said, 'Go up; for Yhwh will give it into the hand of the king'" (1 Kgs. 22:6).

---

13. Eric Peels, "God's Throne in Elam: The Historical Background and Literary Context of Jeremiah 49:34–39," in *Past, Present, Future: The Deuteronomistic History and the Prophets* (ed. J. C. de Moor and Harry F. van Rooy; Leiden: Brill, 2000), 226–27.

Such tales clearly reflect the way that ancient Near Eastern kings sought divinatory confirmation to comfort themselves and justify their campaigns.

A brief example of a *judgment oracle* is given in 1 Kings 20:28, where "a man of God approached and said to the king of Israel, 'Thus says Yhwh: Because the Arameans have said, "Yhwh is a god of the hills but he is not a god of the valleys," therefore I will give all this great multitude into your hand, and you shall know that I am Yhwh.'" As a more elaborate example, one could take Amos 1–2, where numerous nations are judged guilty by Yhwh of various transgressions. Tyre, for example, is accused of forgetting "covenant of kinship" (1:9).

Explicit in Amos 1:9 (and implicit elsewhere) is the idea that the nations should be held accountable for adhering to an unwritten code of international justice. Some have treated these oracles as extensions of treaty-curse language, that is, as proclamations of judgment on those who have broken a treaty.[14] Both in Amos and in the Major Prophets, Yhwh is implicitly portrayed as the imperial ruler (or "suzerain") who enforces justice when faced with the wrongdoing of the foreign nations. Such treaty language in prophetic texts is almost certainly a literary device rather than reflecting an actual historical agreement between all these nations.

There has been some doubt, with all of the forms suggested above, how closely the texts preserved in the biblical prophets match any actual historical prophetic speech. Often the literary forms of recorded oracles do not match up neatly with ancient Near Eastern literary forms. The large collections in the major prophetic books are certainly complex, interwoven literary compositions that would not have been uttered as a whole at any specific historical moment; instead, they would have been gathered from various situations and likely reshaped into their present form. Nevertheless, comparison of their component parts with uncurated ancient Near Eastern oracles from other cultures reveals significant similarities.

Careful judgment is required in making comparisons. For example, the last verse of Jeremiah's Elam oracle ("in the latter days I will restore the fortunes of Elam," 49:39) might look patently like a late addition to soften the blow, since the other war oracles presented here include no such promise of restoration. On the other hand, a concluding promise of restoration is common in the ancient Mesopotamian city laments[15] (chap. 25) and indeed laments such as the Curse of Agade are frequently compared with the oracles against the nations, since they too foretell the destruction of a city-state. The final piece of information is that the Curse of Agade is widely taken to be *vaticinium ex eventu* (prophecy after the fact)—and in this case, probably *long* after the fact. Thus it is more plausible that Jeremiah's word of restoration for Elam was added at a later date.

---

14. Delbert R. Hillers, *Treaty-Curses and the Old Testament Prophets* (Rome: Pontifical Biblical Institute, 1964).

15. Lundbom, *Jeremiah 37-52*, 311.

REFLECTION QUESTIONS

1. What do you think was the purpose of collecting and preserving oracles that were originally intended for a specific historical context, so that they could be read in historical contexts that were essentially unrelated, as was done in both Assyria and Judah?

2. Would you classify Jeremiah's oracle against Elam as a curse, omen, or judgment oracle?

3. Given the way in which oracles against the nations were produced, would you use historical details contained in them (e.g., about a military victory or the destruction of a city) to determine the date of an oracle?

4. What aspects of each oracle appear to reflect specific knowledge of the foreign nations in question, and what aspects seem to be formulaic?

5. Do you think the last verse of the Jeremiah passage (49:39) reflects a prediction made at the same time as the rest, or a later addition intended to soften the judgment or reflect subsequent historical events?

FURTHER READING

Christensen, Duane L. *Prophecy and War in Ancient Israel: Studies in the Oracles Against the Nations in Old Testament Prophecy.* Berkeley, CA: Bibal Press, 1989.

Hayes, John H. "The Usage of Oracles against Foreign Nations in Ancient Israel." *JBL* 87 (1968): 81–92.

Hillers, Delbert R. *Treaty-Curses and the Old Testament Prophets.* Rome: Pontifical Biblical Institute, 1964.

Lundbom, Jack R. *Jeremiah 37–52.* AB 21C. New York: Doubleday, 2004.

Peels, Eric. "God's Throne in Elam: The Historical Background and Literary Context of Jeremiah 49:34–39." Pages 216–29 in *Past, Present, Future: The Deuteronomistic History and the Prophets.* Edited by J. C. de Moor and Harry F. van Rooy. Leiden: Brill, 2000.

Petersen, David L. "The Oracles Against the Nations: A Form-Critical Analysis." Pages 39–61 in *Society of Biblical Literature Seminar Papers, 1975,* vol. 1. Missoula, MT: Society of Biblical Literature, 1975.

Compilation of Prophetic Texts

Oracle Collections of La-dagil-ili of Arbela and Isaiah of Jerusalem

STATE ARCHIVES OF ASSYRIA 9 3

What: Cuneiform text on clay tablet (collection of oracles for Esarhaddon, king of Assyria)
When: 681 BCE, collected 680 BCE or later
Where: Nineveh, Assyria
Language: Neo-Assyrian Akkadian
Translation: Simo Parpola[1]

[*The introductory section is very fragmentary.*]

3.2 First oracle

[List]en, O Assyrians! [The king] has vanquished his enemy. [You]r [king] has put his enemy [under] his foot, [from] sun[se]t [to] sun[ris]e, [from] sun[ris]e [to] sun[se]t!

I will destroy [Meli]d.[2] [I will de]stroy [. . .] I will deliver the Cimmerians[3] into his hands and set the land of Ellipi[4] on fire. Ashur has given the totality of the four regions to him. From sunrise to sunset there is no king equal to him; he shines as brilliantly as the sun. This is the (oracle of) well-being placed before Bel-Tarbaṣi[5] and the gods.

---

1. Simo Parpola, *Assyrian Prophecies* (SAA 9; Helsinki: Helsinki University Press, 1997), 22–27. The subheadings used here are not present in the ancient text and are provided for reference.
2. A city in Asia Minor.
3. A nomadic tribe that had moved south into northern Asia Minor and caused problems for the Assyrians.
4. A region to the southeast of Assyria.
5. Lit., "Lord of the Temple Courtyard" or "Lord of the Animal-Pen."

3.3 Second oracle

Now then, these traitors provoked you, had you banished, and surrounded you; but you opened your mouth (and cried): "Hear me, O Ashur!"[6]

I heard your cry. I issued forth as a fiery glow from the gate of heaven, to hurl down fire and have it devour them. You were standing in their midst, so I removed them from your presence. I drove them up the mountain and rained (hail)stones and fire of heaven upon them. I slaughtered your enemies and filled the river with their blood. Let them see (it) and praise me, (knowing) that I am Ashur, lord of the gods. This is the (oracle of) well-being (placed) before the Image.[7]

This covenant tablet of Ashur enters the king's presence on a cushion. Fragrant oil is sprinkled, sacrifices are made, incense is burnt, and they read it out in the king's presence.

3.4 Covenant meal

The word of Ishtar of Arbela[8] to Esarhaddon, king of Assyria: Come, gods, my fathers and brothers, [enter] the cove[nant . . . . . .]

[She placed] a slice . . . on the [ter]race and gave them water from a cooler to drink. She filled a flagon of one *seah*[9] with water from the cooler and gave it to them with the words:

"In your hearts you say, 'Ishtar is slight,' and you will go to your cities and districts, eat (your) bread and forget this covenant. (But when) you drink from this water, you will remember me and keep this covenant which I have made on behalf of Esarhaddon."

3.5 Word of Ishtar of Arbela

The word of Ishtar of Arbela to Esarhaddon, king of Assyria:

As if I did not do or give you anything! Did I not bend the four doorjambs of Assyria, and did I not give them to you? Did I not vanquish your enemy? Did I not collect your haters and foes [like but]terflies?

[As for yo]u, what have you given to me? [There is no fo]od for my banquet, as if there were no temple; I [am depri]ved of my food, I am d[ep]rived of my cup! I am waiting for them, I have cast my eye upon them.

Verily, establish a one-*seah* bowl of food and a one-*seah* flagon of sweet beer! Let me take and put in my mouth vegetables and soup, let me fill the cup and drink from it, let me restore my charms! . . . Let me lift . . .

I went up [. . .] and arranged [a fea]st [. . .]. [When] I was [there, they said: "We know] that you are Ishtar [of A]rbela." I set out [for As]syria to see yo[ur success], to tread the mountains [with my feet], [and to spea]k about Esarhaddon.

---

6. Ashur was the national deity of Assyria and head of the Mesopotamian pantheon from their perspective.

7. The statue of Ašhur in the sanctuary dedicated to him.

8. An Assyrian city that was the center of Ishtar's cult.

9. A large vessel, capable of containing multiple gallons. The use of such large vessels (see also 3.5) may be in accordance with the perceived large stature of the goddess who is serving the drink and food.

[No]w rejoice, Esarhaddon! [I have be]nt [the four doorjamb]s of Assyria and given them to you; I have vanquished yo[ur enemy. The mood of the people] who stand with you has been turned upside down.

[From thi]s you shall see [that] I am [Ishtar of] Arbela. [As soon as the traitors] have been dragged forth, [the 'ones at the right and] left side' shall be there to bear [the punishment].

(As for) those cou]rtiers and palace [personnel who] rebelled [against] you, [I have sur]rounded them and impaled them by their teeth.

[La-dagil-i]li, a prophet of [Arbela, prophesied (this) when . . . . . .] Ishtar [. . . . . .].

ISAIAH 5:8–25

When: Late eighth century BCE
Where: Jerusalem
Language: Hebrew
Translation: NRSV (adapted)

[8]*Hoy*,[10] you who join house to house,
    who add field to field,
until there is room for no one but you,
    and you are left to live alone in the midst of the land!
[9]Yhwh of hosts has sworn in my hearing:
    Surely many houses shall be desolate,
    large and beautiful houses, without inhabitant.
[10]For ten acres of vineyard shall yield but one bath,[11]
    and a homer[12] of seed shall yield a mere ephah.[13]
[11]*Hoy*, you who rise early in the morning in pursuit of strong drink,
    who linger in the evening to be inflamed by wine,
[12]whose feasts consist of lyre and harp,
    tambourine and flute and wine,
but who do not regard the deeds of Yhwh,
    or see the work of his hands!
[13]Therefore my people go into exile without knowledge;
    their nobles are dying of hunger,
    and their multitude is parched with thirst.
[14]Therefore Sheol[14] has enlarged its appetite
    and opened its mouth beyond measure;
the nobility of Jerusalem and her multitude go down,
    her throng and all who exult in her.
[15]People are bowed down, everyone is brought low,

---

10. An exclamatory particle that was usually used in mourning the dead; thus somewhat akin to "Alas!"
11. A measure of liquid volume equivalent in volume to an ephah, i.e., a few gallons. The point of these lines is that the land will produce a pitifully small yield, even from vast planting.
12. A measure of dry volume equivalent to one donkey-load, about 200 pounds.
13. One-tenth of a homer, or about 20 pounds.
14. The Hebrew term for the underworld, here personified as a greedy eater, as it was at Ugarit.

and the eyes of the haughty are humbled.
[16]But Yhwh of hosts is exalted by justice,
    and the Holy God shows himself holy by righteousness.
[17]Then the lambs shall graze as in their pasture,
    fatlings and kids shall feed among the ruins.
[18]*Hoy*, you who drag iniquity along with cords of falsehood,
    who drag sin along as with cart ropes,
[19]who say, "Let him make haste, let him speed his work that we may see it;
    let the plan of the Holy One of Israel hasten to fulfillment, that we may know it!"
[20]*Hoy*, you who call evil good and good evil,
    who put darkness for light and light for darkness,
    who put bitter for sweet and sweet for bitter!
[21]*Hoy*, you who are wise in your own eyes,
    and shrewd in your own sight!
[22]*Hoy*, you who are heroes in drinking wine
    and valiant at mixing drink,
[23]who acquit the guilty for a bribe,
    and deprive the innocent of their rights!
[24]Therefore, as the tongue of fire devours the stubble,
    and as dry grass sinks down in the flame,
so their root will become rotten,
    and their blossom go up like dust;
for they have rejected the instruction of Yhwh of hosts,
    and have despised the word of the Holy One of Israel.
[25]Therefore the anger of Yhwh was kindled against his people,
    and he stretched out his hand against them and struck them;
the mountains quaked,
    and their corpses were like refuse in the streets.
For all this his anger has not turned away,
    and his hand is stretched out still.

DISCUSSION

How did prophecies become prophetic books? One has to begin with the question of how and why prophecies were written down in the first place. In a world where even a mobile phone can record and transcribe our words, the question may not even occur to readers. One just speaks, and text appears. Or one can often go back to audio and video recordings to check what was said. But of course, none of these were options in the ancient Near Eastern world. Instead, writing itself was high technology, the province of an elite class that knew how to use it or could employ others who did.

The question of how prophetic oracles were compiled is bound up with the history of writing itself. The development of writing in Israelite society—who could write and when?—has recently attracted intense scrutiny by scholars, and it is borne out by references to writing in the biblical prophetic books. The epigraphic evidence from archaeological excavations is subject to interpretation, but at a minimum, it is clear that scribal training and the prevalence of literacy in ancient Palestine increased between the earliest monarchic period in Israel (10th c. BCE) and the end of the First Temple period (586 BCE).

Biblical texts reflect the growth in writing. Early prophetic figures such as Elijah and Elisha are said to have been itinerant wonder-workers who manifested God in their actions more than in their words. Although stories were told about them, there is no indication that they had anything to do with those stories' being written down.

In the eighth century, however, Isaiah refers to "binding up" his words as testimony to his predictions (8:1, 16; 30:8), so that people would know in the future that he was correct (cf. Deut. 18:21–22). This is probably a reference to the binding of a scroll with string and a small piece of clay called a bulla (papal bulls are documents that take their name from a similar type of seal). Since the words were said to be bound up "among his disciples," it is possible that someone in that group had scribal training and recorded his oracles. It is also possible that some of Isaiah's words were written down by scribes associated with the Judean royal court. Many of his prophecies pertained to political and religious affairs of the state, and they might have been recorded even when they were not heeded. At both Mari and Nineveh, the only other places from which extensive prophetic records exist, significant energy went into reporting and recording the words of prophets for the king and other high officials.

Later, in late seventh and early sixth centuries, Jeremiah is said to have had a personal scribe, Baruch, who took dictation from him (Jer. 36:1–4). In this case, the reason given is that Jeremiah is banned from the temple, so he delegates Baruch to read his words for him. This serves also as a model for the way biblical prophecies have functioned ever since: they allow a prophet's words to be heard even when he is not present. When King Jehoiakim burns the scroll, Jeremiah and Baruch re-create a scroll with the same words, and the chapter closes with the interesting aside that "many similar words were added to them" (36:32); this is likely a statement about the growth of prophetic books through later additions by those other than the original prophet. The passive voice obscures the agency, probably on purpose.

These examples from Isaiah and Jeremiah reflect that there is no indication that Isaiah or any of the early prophets were writers (thus the term "writing prophets," which is sometimes used for the prophets who have books in their names, is a misnomer in many cases). Although such prophets were almost certainly educated, there was not necessarily a close connection between education and scribal training in the ancient Near East. Socrates was famously suspicious of writing (see *Phaedrus* 274–75), and it is probably no accident that his condemnation of the new technology took place in the fifth century BCE, since the use of writing expanded greatly in Greece beginning around the start of the sixth century, just as it did in the Levant.[15]

This eventual shift toward writing can be seen in the work of Ezekiel, who was ordered to "take a stick and write" (Ezek. 37:16); presumably that means that he was able to do so. Indeed, in such later texts, the form of divine revelation itself is taken to be written (Ezek. 2:9–3:4; cf. Zech. 5:1–2), which no doubt reflects the increasing prominence of the written word in Judean/Jewish culture. Again, however, in the eighth century there was

---

15. Harvey Yunis, ed., *Written Texts and the Rise of Literate Culture in Ancient Greece* (Cambridge: Cambridge University Press, 2003).

little likelihood that the prophets would have written down their own words;[16] scribal intermediaries were needed.

The next stages of the editing of prophetic books can be better understood in light of recent studies comparing them with the compilation and editing of Neo-Assyrian prophecies.[17] There has been a significant reaction against the heavy emphasis on the role of editors (sometimes called "redactors") in the formation of biblical books in general. A particularly forceful comment comes from John van Seters: "The notion of the ancient editor was created out of an obvious anachronism and then developed in the interest of literary and text-critical theories, with the result that it became devoid of all contact with reality."[18] This is only partially true for the books of Genesis–2 Kings, which were Van Seters's primary focus; but in the case of prophetic books, one has very good empirical models for at least the first stages of their compilation and editing.[19]

In the Assyrian royal courts, prophetic oracles were recorded in daily records on a certain type of clay tablet, and then often later taken up and compiled on a different kind of tablet for special occasions, such as a major military campaign or the succession of a new king. The daily tablets on which reports of individual oracles were first recorded were horizontal and were only occasionally archived; the archival tablets, for long-term preservation, were vertical. Although our records are limited, it is almost certain that there was a loss of content at every step of the way: most oracles were not written down; most written oracle reports were not archived; and most archived oracles were never reedited into a compilation.

In general, compilations could be commissioned on the occasion of major public events, and they were intended to support "the public good," that is, the will of the king and the state. At that point, the prophetic oracles are often uprooted from their original context and put into the service of different causes, as Martti Nissinen has noted: "In this phase, not only editorial selection and stylization of the oracles takes place, but prophecy is reused in a new situation and finally becomes a part of written tradition transcending specific historical situations and retaining its relevance in changing circumstances."[20]

For example, in the Neo-Assyrian royal archives at Nineveh there was a collection pertaining to the succession of Esarhaddon after the death of the father (SAA 9 1, excerpted in chap. 15). It contains oracles pertaining to battles in the civil war that he fought, and to the court intrigue that followed his accession to the throne. But the whole composition

16. Even much later, comments by the apostle Paul make it clear that although he could write, he reserved that effort for a few words in closing (1 Cor. 16:21; Col. 4:18), while leaving the bulk of the writing to a professional: "See what large letters I make when I am writing in my own hand!" (Gal. 6:11).

17. Matthijs J. de Jong, *Isaiah among the Ancient Near Eastern Prophets: A Comparative Study of the Earliest Stages of the Isaiah Tradition and the Neo-Assyrian Prophecies* (VTSup 117; Leiden: Brill, 2007).

18. John Van Seters, *The Edited Bible: The Curious History of the "Editor" in Biblical Criticism* (Winona Lake, IN: Eisenbrauns, 2006), 400.

19. Jeffrey H. Tigay, ed., *Empirical Models for Biblical Criticism* (Philadelphia: University of Pennsylvania Press, 1985).

20. Martti Nissinen, *Prophets and Prophecy in the Ancient Near East* (ed. Peter Machinist; SBLWAW 12; Atlanta: Society of Biblical Literature, 2003), 98.

was compiled after all these events, and its purpose was to affirm in retrospect that Esarhaddon was favored by the gods through the entire process and thus had the divine right to rule Assyria.

Other texts, such as Esarhaddon's royal inscriptions, testify to the role of divination generally (and prophecy specifically) in political events. It could help to legitimate a king's rule and consolidate the loyalty of the people.

> [Year 683] "Even though I was younger than my big brothers, at the behest of [the gods], my father duly elevated me among my brothers and declared, 'This is my successor.' He consulted Shamash and Adad by extispicy, and they answered him with a firm yes: 'He will be your replacement.' Respecting their weighty command, he assembled the people of Assyria young and old, my brothers, and the progeny of my dynastic line, and made them swear by the gods of heaven and earth a solemn oath to protect my succession. . . .
>
> [Year 682] Proper guidance was lavished upon my brothers, but they forsook the gods, trusting in their own haughty deeds, and hammered out evil plans. Godlessly they fabricated malicious rumors and untrue slander against me. . . .
>
> [Year 680] . . . Good portents appeared in heaven and on earth. Messages of ecstatic prophets, the messengers of the gods and the Goddess, constantly and regularly came in and encouraged me." (Esarhaddon's Nineveh A inscription, 673 BCE)[21]

This text and others like it testify to the importance of prophecy as a form of royal propaganda in Assyria.[22] The text is silent on the question of whether Esarhaddon's older brothers also had divinatory support for their claims to succession; if so, it is no accident that the records did not survive, since Esarhaddon would have destroyed them. The reader thus cannot determine whether there were competing "testimonies" or how the Assyrians dealt with such conflicts.

Isaiah 5 contains a series of six oracles with the same form. These all begin with the exclamation *Hoy!* which derived from funerary contexts. This use of *hoy* can be seen in various places, such as the burial of a prophet in 1 Kings 13:30. At his graveside, "they mourned over him, saying, '*Hoy*, my brother!'" Or again, Jeremiah's account of the mourning for Jehoiakim: "They shall not lament for him, saying, *hoy*, my brother!" (Jer. 22:18). In Amos 5:16–20 mourning in the squares and streets ("*Ho! Ho!*") turns into mourning (*Hoy!*) for those who desire the Day of Yhwh. This shift within prophetic proclamations introduces a special use of the exclamation in mock mourning for those on whom God's judgment is about to be carried out. In other words, the prophets mourn (whether sincerely or sardonically) for those who are *about to die*. The eighth-century prophets show clear awareness of the *hoy* cry's origin in death or funerary lament.[23] In Isaiah 5:14, those

---

21. Parpola, *Assyrian Prophecies*, lxxii–lxxiii.

22. Another inscription of Esarhaddon from 679 BCE reports about the year 680: "Messages from ecstatic prophets concerning the establishment of the foundation of my sacerdotal throne until far-off days were constantly and regularly conveyed to me. Good omens kept occurring to me in dreams and oracles concerning the establishment of my seat and the extension of my reign. Seeing these signs of good portent, my heart turned confident and my mood became good" (Parpola, *Assyrian Prophecies*, lxxiv).

23. This sense was lost in the postexilic period, as one can see in, e.g., Zech. 2:10–11.

who are condemned are said to descend to the underworld; and it also linked to mourning in Mic. 2:1–4 ("*Hoy*, you who devise wickedness! . . . On that day they shall take up a taunt song against you, and wail with bitter lamentation").

Just as significant, this series of oracles revolves around the same theme: social justice. The series is appended to an oracle in the form of a song comparing the nation to a vineyard that God has cared for diligently, but that has yielded only bad grapes (Isa. 5:1–7). The song closes with an artful play on two pairs of words that sound similar in Hebrew: "He expected justice [*mishpat*], but saw bloodshed [*mispach*]; righteousness [*tsedaqah*], but heard a cry [*tse'aqah*]!" (Isa. 5:7). The oracles of 5:8–25 then characterize those who have failed to carry out justice in various ways: they have squeezed the less privileged off their land; they have overconsumed; they are scornful, impious, deceitful, and prideful. There are numerous indications that there was a crisis of social inequality in the late eighth century,[24] and similar transgressions are condemned in Amos and Micah.

Is it possible that Isaiah delivered all of chapter 5 at one time, in a lengthy monologue? In theory, yes. There are some fairly lengthy oracle reports from the Neo-Assyrian archives, albeit not as long as Isaiah 5. Most of the prophetic pronouncements from the Assyrian prophets were significantly shorter, however—more on the order of the individual *hoy* oracles. It seems more likely, therefore, that Isaiah delivered these oracles on different occasions, and that they were secondarily compiled for their likeness and appended to the artful song of the vineyard. The repetition of certain themes in different sections (e.g., drunkenness in vv. 11–12 and 22) may be another indication that this was not originally a unified utterance.

A final notable feature of Isaiah 5 that many would see as evidence of literary editing is the closing line of the passage excerpted above, "For all this his anger has not turned away, and his hand is stretched out still" (5:25). This is an Isaianic refrain that is repeated in 9:12, 17, 21; and 10:4. It is of course conceivable that this was just a saying that the prophet happened to repeat a lot, but it is also possible that it was a literary device used by a later compiler to lend a sense of unity to Isaiah's repeated warnings. Phrases like "all this" and "still" might suggest a wider historical vista than the individual oracles to which the refrain is appended.

The Isaianic and Assyrian texts have much in common. Like Isaiah, SAA 9 3 was compiled in the name of a single prophet, La-dagil-ili.[25] One might well ask whether the literary compilation of oracles was really the task of a *ragimu*, a "shouter" such as La-dagil-ili, or whether the literary composition was created by someone else and attributed to him because his name gave it more authority.

Also, in their final forms, both Isaiah 28 and the Assyrian text are *literary works*, rather than simply *oracle reports*. As de Jong said of SAA 9 3,

> The prophetic oracles preserved in this text . . . are reworkings of oracles that previously had been orally delivered and reported, and afterwards were inserted in an elaborate form into a new context. This compiled text shows that prophetic

---

24. Marvin L. Chaney, "Whose Sour Grapes? The Addressees of Isaiah 5:1–7 in the Light of Political Economy," *Semeia* 87 (1999): 105–22; Walter Houston, "Was There a Social Crisis in the Eighth Century?" in *In Search of Pre-Exilic Israel: Proceedings of the Oxford Old Testament Seminar* (ed. John Day; London: T&T Clark, 2004), 130–49.

25. Parpola, *Assyrian Prophecies*, l–li. The beginning of the name is broken and would have to be restored, but the oracles in the text resemble those elsewhere attributed to that prophet.

texts and reused oracles were closely related. On the one hand, prophetic oracles received a second life in a reworked form. On the other hand, texts were produced that were literary in origin, but closely resemble the genre of prophecy.[26]

De Jong is working from a distinction between "prophecy," which is spoken, and "literary compositions," which are written (for example, he considers 9 3.3, above, a literary work and not an oracle, even though it is called an oracle of well-being in the text). This discussion, applied to Isaiah 5, suggests that one should speak of at least three stages of compilation:

1. Spoken oracles
2. Recording of the oracles in literary form
3. Secondary reediting into a more elaborate form

It has sometimes been thought that the oracles were "broken" when they were compiled. In particular, the three oracles in verses 18–19, 20, and 21 do not have any explicit judgment clause (often marked by "Therefore . . .") attached to them. However, this is based on a misunderstanding of the form; as noted above, the cry *hoy* already contains its own judgment of death. The lack of a judgment clause is insufficient grounds to assume incompleteness. Nevertheless, there is no way to know with certainty what might have been removed (or added) by a compiler or an editor.

Since the Assyrian oracles were compiled on the occasion of major events, one might also ask what historical event could have prompted someone to compile the oracles of Isaiah 5. The rest of the chapter suggests that it was a devastating attack by the Assyrian army (v. 26: "a nation far away"). The carnage of this attack (v. 25: "corpses were like refuse in the streets") would have seemed to fulfill Isaiah's dire earlier predictions (v. 9: "many houses shall be desolate"). If the oracles were delivered to Judeans, then the most obvious date during Isaiah's career would be 701, when the Assyrians destroyed dozens of fortified Judean cities and even besieged Jerusalem (see chap. 13). But the dual conditions of social injustice and Assyrian domination persisted over decades in the late eighth century. It is possible that something else prompted the compilation, so specific dates remain hypothetical in this case.

One significant difference between the Isaianic and Assyrian oracles is that the former had to be transmitted for centuries by copying, whereas the Assyrian tablets are from very close in time to their composition. There is no doubt that some changes were introduced in the process; one concrete example is in the spelling of the words: in the time of Isaiah ben Amoz, vowel letters were used very sparsely in Hebrew, whereas the standard Hebrew text of the Bible (the Masoretic Text) uses them more extensively, as later scribes would have done. It may help those who do not read Hebrew to consider the analogous example of the New King James Version's updating of forms from the King James Version in Psalm 23:2:

KJV   He maketh me to lie down in green pastures: he leadeth me beside the still waters.

---

26. De Jong, *Isaiah among the Ancient Near Eastern Prophets*, 411–12.

NKJV   He makes me to lie down in green pastures; He leads me beside the still
           waters.

The forms "maketh" and "leadeth" were normal English in the seventeenth century
when the KJV was composed. To those who revised it, those forms were archaic and
somewhat difficult; to help the modern reader, they have emended them to what are
now standard forms, yet they have preserved the vocabulary and cadences of the earlier
translation. This is the minimum sort of updating that took place in the book as we have it
today. Among the Dead Sea Scrolls is a copy of Isaiah (1QIsaᵃ) that updates the spellings
even more than the Masoretic Text does, so the form of the book that one usually reads
in Hebrew could be considered moderately conservative.

Most scholars assume that the later scribes who copied the book and updated its spellings also took other liberties with these early oracles of Isaiah as they added the later
portions of the book. Although Isaiah's words were first compiled in the eighth century,
the compilation was taken up yet again in the late sixth century as a later prophet (or
prophets) added words of comfort and exhortation meant for those returning from exile
in Babylon—the texts that now make up Isaiah 40–66. In all, the compilation and editing
of the book spanned at least two centuries, and probably closer to three. The effect of
these later stages on Isaiah ben Amoz's words is hotly debated. Some scholars think that
very little of the book can be attributed to him, but this is unduly skeptical. Sometimes
there is textual evidence for additions and changes, when other copies and translations
differ from the standard Hebrew text. However, the variations in Isaiah 5 are fairly minor,
so the text appears to have been copied in a relatively stable form through history.

The idea that Isaiah is a book that took shape over centuries troubles some readers, but
it certainly would not have surprised the ancients that their prophets' words were reread
and reinterpreted in new situations. The growth of the book is a reflection of its original
and ongoing power, as its words inspired new words and became rich symbols. Even
seemingly straightforward geographical designations such as Assyria came to symbolize
foreign powers and regions of later eras (e.g., Zech. 10:10–11, written in a time when
Assyria no longer existed as a nation). Perhaps best known to readers of the Bible is the
encoding of Rome as Babylon by New Testament authors in Revelation 18 and 1 Peter
5:13. These texts carry on a tradition of reinterpretation that began with the compilation
of prophetic books themselves. In much the same way, the words of Isaiah ben Amoz,
spoken in the eighth century, received "second life"—and third, and fourth, and so on.
Indeed, they continue to live in the reading of faith communities today.

REFLECTION QUESTIONS

1. How would you characterize the message and tone of La-dagil-ili compared with those
   of Isaiah?

2. How is the tone of each text related to the social location of each prophet? Specifically,
   what was Isaiah's social relationship to the people to whom he was speaking?

3. What is the latest possible date for the Assyrian compilation of prophecies? What is the latest possible date for the compilation of Isaiah's prophecies? What factors do scholars consider in assigning a date to such compositions?

4. Do the individual *hoy* oracles in Isaiah 5 seem like complete utterances to you? Do you imagine them being delivered separately or together?

5. Are there portions of Isaiah 5 that strike you as likely to have been added by a later author rather than spoken by Isaiah?

6. Does the La-dagil-ili compilation seem more or less unified as a composition than the chapter of Isaiah? Why?

FURTHER READING

Chaney, Marvin L. "Whose Sour Grapes? The Addressees of Isaiah 5:1–7 in the Light of Political Economy." *Semeia* 87 (1999): 105–22.

Houston, Walter. "Was There a Social Crisis in the Eighth Century?" Pages 130–49 in *In Search of Pre-Exilic Israel: Proceedings of the Oxford Old Testament Seminar.* Edited by John Day. London: T&T Clark, 2004.

Jong, Matthijs J. de. *Isaiah among the Ancient Near Eastern Prophets: A Comparative Study of the Earliest Stages of the Isaiah Tradition and the Neo-Assyrian Prophecies.* VTSup 117. Leiden: Brill, 2007.

Tigay, Jeffrey H., ed. *Empirical Models for Biblical Criticism.* Philadelphia: University of Pennsylvania Press, 1985.

Troxel, Ronald L. *Prophetic Literature: From Oracles to Books.* Malden, MA: Wiley-Blackwell, 2012.

Van Seters, John. *The Edited Bible: The Curious History of the "Editor" in Biblical Criticism.* Winona Lake, IN: Eisenbrauns, 2006.

18

Divine Abandonment

The Marduk Prophecy, Esarhaddon's Rebuilding, and Ezekiel

EZEKIEL 8–11; 36:16–38; 43:1–11

When: 592–571 BCE
Where: Jerusalem
Language: Hebrew

THE MARDUK PROPHECY

What: Autobiographical account by the Babylonian god Marduk, reconstructed from
multiple clay tablets[1]
When: ca. 1125 BCE
Where: Nineveh and Ashur (copies of Babylonian originals)
Language: Akkadian
Translation: Adapted from Tremper Longman[2]

§1 O Harharnum, Hayyasum, Anum, Enlil, Nudim[mud], Ea, Muati, Nabium![3] Let the
great gods learn my secrets. After I gird my loins, I will give my speech.

---

§2 I am Marduk the Great Lord. I am always watching; walking watchfully over the
mountains, I watch—a watchman roaming the lands. I am he, who in all the lands—from
sunrise to sunset—am constantly roaming.

---

1. The text translated here is reconstructed from approximately twenty fragmentary tablets;
for precise line numbers related to those tablets, see Tremper Longman III, *Fictional Akkadian
Autobiography: A Generic and Comparative Study* (Winona Lake, IN: Eisenbrauns, 1991), or other
editions. A streamlined system of numbered paragraphs is adopted here for the sake of simplicity.
The horizontal lines accurately reflect scribal dividing lines marked in the ancient tablets. Blank
lines between paragraphs mark transitions between tablets.
2. Ibid., 233–35.
3. This is a list of gods who are invoked.

§3 I gave the command that I go to Hatti. I inquired into Hatti. I set up the throne of my Anu-power[4] in its midst. I dwelt in its midst for 24 years. I established [the tr]ade of the citizens of Babylon [in] its midst. I oversaw its [. . .], its goods, and its valuables [in] Sippar, Nippur [and Babyl]on.

§4 [A king of Babylon] arose and led me [to] Babylon. [. . .] were in order (?). The marketplace of Ba[bylon] was fair. [. . .] the crown of my Anu-power [. . .] and the statue [. . .] water, winds [. . .]. Three days [. . .] the crown of my Anu-power [. . .] and statue [. . .] to my body [did I] I went home. [With reference to Babylon, I said:] "Bring [your tribute, O you] la[nds, to Babylon]."

[*Break*]

§5 [. . .] Ashur was good [. . .]. [Make its temples shine] like a precious stone. Abounding [. . .] I gave [it. Monthly, daily, and ye]arly [I blessed it]. I girded [the loins] of the people of Enlil with it. I gave [it] wings like a bird. I filled all [the lands]. I filled [. . .]. I blessed Ashur. I gave it fates [. . .]. I gave it strong approval [. . .]. I went home. With reference to Babylon I said: "Bring your tribute, O you lands, to Babylon [. . .]."

§6 I am Marduk, the great prince. I am Lord of fate and oracle. Who has undertaken this campaign? As I have gone away, I will come back—I have commanded it. I went to Elam—all the gods went—I commanded it. I myself cut off the food-offering[5] of the temples. Shakkan and Nisaba[6] I caused to go away to heaven.

Siris[7] made the heart of the land sick. The corpses of the people block the gates. Brother consumes brother. Friend strikes his friend with a weapon. Aristocrats stretch out their hands (to beg) to the commoner. The scepter grows short. Evil lies across the land. [. . .] kings diminish the land. Lions block off the way. Dogs go mad and bite people; as many as they bite do not live; they die. I fulfilled my days; I fulfilled my years. Then I carried myself back to my city Babylon and to the Ekursagil.[8] I called all the goddesses together. I commanded: "Bring your tribute, O you lands, to Babylon [. . .]."

§7 A king of Babylon will arise and he will renew the house of announcement, the Ekursagil. He will draw the plans of heaven and earth in the Ekursagil. He will change its height. He will establish tax exemptions for my city Babylon. He will lead me and bring me into my city Babylon and the Ekursagil forever. He will renew the ship Matush.[9] He

---

4. "Anu-power" (Akkadian *anūtu*) refers to the authority and power of the highest god. It is named for the sky-god Anu.

5. Akkadian *nindabû*, often a grain offering.

6. Deities related to herding and the harvest, respectively.

7. A minor goddess of alcoholic beverages.

8. A temple in Babylon.

9. Ships were used in Mesopotamian processions, since the Euphrates River and canals ran through and around Babylon.

will fill its rudder with fine gold. He will [cover] its walls with precious metal.[10] He will let sailors who serve on it embark on it. They will face each other on the right and left. A king who like (?) the star (?) of the Ekursagil [. . .].

§8 [He will bring me in] forever. [He will renew the] ship Madah-hedu. [He will fill] its rudder [with fine gold. He will cover] its walls [with precious metal. He will let] the sailors [who serve on it embark] on it. Nabu, the son [. . .] will go who [. . .] and Ekur[11] [. . .] forever [. . .], This prince [. . .].

§9 Ekur [. . .] river of the god [. . .] pure water [. . .] Ekur [. . .], the hand of Nin[. . .].

§10 He will bring me [in forev]er. [. . .] he will establish [. . .] Ekur [. . .] he will give it to her/him. [This prince] will experience the grace of the gods. [The years/days] of his reign will be long.

§11 He will make [Ekur]-Egishnugal[12] shine [like a pre]cious stone. The [temple] of Ning[al] (and) the [temp]le of Si[n],[13] together with its plu[ndered] silver, goods, and its valuables [. . .] in the gate of the god [. . .].

§12 With Sin [. . .] of Egishnugal [. . .] the land together [. . .]. This prince will be strong and [will have] no rival.
§13 He will take care of the city. He will gather the scattered. He will make the Ekur-Egalmah and (all) the temples shine like a precious stone. Ningal, Gula, Kurnunitum, the city Hariddu—they and their favorite houses will be transformed. That prince will cause the land to eat his splendid produce. His days will be long [. . .] cities [. . .] he will make (all) the temples shine like a precious stone. All of the gods he will transform. He will gather together the scattered land. He will make its foundation firm. The gate of heaven will be opened permanently [. . .].

§14 [. . . she] will fear her [husband]. He will be [compassionate] toward the people. Men will regularly pay their taxes. [That prince] will rule [all] the lands. [And I, the god of] all, [will befriend him]. He will destroy [Elam]; he will destroy [its cities]. [The city and its] swamps he will turn away. [The great king of] Der[14] [. . .]

§15 [. . .] the dead he will make alive [. . .] he will have [. . .] he will permanently establish. Ningirsu will rule. The rivers will carry fish. The fields and plains will be full of yield. The grass of winter (will last) to summer. The grass of summer will last to winter. The harvest of the land will thrive. The marketplace will prosper. He will set evil aright. He

---

10. The identity of this metal (Akkadian *pasallu*) is uncertain.
11. "Ekur" was a general term for a temple in Akkadian. It is used in various ways; the meaning here is not clear.
12. Another temple in Babylon.
13. Sin was the Mesopotamian moon-god.
14. A city on the border between Mesopotamia and Elam.

will clear up the disturbed. He will illumine evil. The clouds will be continually present. Brother will love his brother. A son will fear his father as if he were a god. Mother [. . .] daughter. The bride will marry. She will fear her husband. He will be compassionate toward the people. The man will regularly pay his taxes. That prince will [rule all] the lands.

---

§16 And I, the god of all, will befriend him. He will destroy Elam. He will destroy its cities. The city and its swamps he will turn away. He causes the great king of Der to arise in his doorframe. He will change its deathly silence. His evil [. . .]. His hand he will seize. He will ever cause him to enter Der and the Udgalkalamma.[15]

---

§17 [. . .] of god [. . .] 40 quarts [. . .] one of flour [. . .]; one [. . .]; one quart of honey; one of fine oil; one quart [. . .]; one quart raisins; one quart shale; one quart good [. . .]; one normal sheep; a fattened calf I will burn to the ghost.[16] I will bless him monthly, daily, yearly.

---

§18 O Harharnum, Hayyasum—complete.

---

§19 I, Shulgi. Written according to the writing board. Copy of Babylon. Checked. Palace of Ashurbanipal, king of the universe, king of Assyria.

ESARHADDON'S REBUILDING OF BABYLON

What: Cuneiform text on black stone[17] rectangular-sided monument, 8.5 inches tall
When: ca. 680 BCE[18]
Where: Nineveh (?)
Language: Akkadian
Translation: By the author

I:1–18   Esarhaddon, king of the world, king of Assyria, governor of Babylon, king of Sumer and Akkad, the pious prince, worshiper of Nabu and Marduk: Before my time, in the reign of an earlier king, there were evil forces in Sumer and Akkad. The people who dwelt in Babylon answered each other yes (when they meant) no, speaking lies all the time. They stretched out their hands for the property of Esagila, the temple of the gods, and gave away (its) gold, silver, and gems to Elam as payment.[19]

---

15. The name of a temple.
16. Presumably "the ghost" was identified earlier in a broken portion of the text. Ancient Mesopotamians often invoked the spirits of the dead to bless and help the living.
17. The stone has repeatedly been identified as basalt in the literature. However, Barbara N. Porter, in *Images, Power, and Politics: Figurative Aspects of Esarhaddon's Babylonian Policy* (Philadelphia: American Philosophical Society, 1993), 186, cites Julian E. Reade, a curator at the British Museum, with the opinion that it is more likely black limestone.
18. Porter, *Images, Power and Politics*, 169–76.
19. I.e., in exchange for military aid.

I:19–II:11   Marduk, lord of the gods, was enraged. He set his mind to leveling the land and destroying its people. The Arachtu Canal, [*Col. II*] a river of abundance, of waters mighty like the Flood, was brought up and it poured into the city where he dwelled, and into his sanctuary, and turned it into a ruin. The gods (and) goddesses who dwelled there went up to heaven. The people who lived there, having been dealt captivity and degradation, went into slavery.

II:12–18   He had recorded seventy years as the period of its desolation. But the merciful Marduk—after his heart was calmed—transposed (the number) and ordered its repopulation in the eleventh year.[20]

II:19–III:8   You truly called me, Esarhaddon, from among my older brothers in order that these things might be restored, [*Col. III*] and you set your good, protecting shadow over me. All who hate me, you have flattened like the Flood; all of my enemies, you have defeated. You have caused me to reach my goal. In order to give rest to the heart of your great divinity, to put your mind at ease, you entrusted the shepherding of Assyria to my hands.

III:9–13   At the beginning of my reign, in my first regnal year, when I took my seat upon the royal throne in majesty, favorable signs appeared in the heavens (and) on earth. Concerning the resettlement of the city and the renovation of his sanctuary, he sent his sign.

III:14– IV:2a   I was fearful (and) anxious about undertaking that task. I knelt down before Shamash, Adad, and Marduk, the chief justices of the gods, my lords. By the sacrificial food bowls of the diviners, positive omens were revealed—he caused liver-omens to be written concerning the rebuilding of Babylon (and) the restoration of Esagila. [*Col. IV*] I trusted that these were reliable.

IV:2b–15   I summoned all of my experts and the whole population of Babylonia. I made them wield the hoe and imposed forced labor upon them. I sprinkled its retaining walls with good oil, honey, butter, beer, choice wine, (and) pure mountain beer. I took the construction-basket upon my head and I carried it myself. In a brick mold of ivory, ebony, boxwood and sissoo (?),[21] I had (them) make bricks all year.

IV:16–27   I had Esagila, the temple of the gods, rebuilt from its foundations to its peak—together with its shrines, Babylon the special city, Imgur-Enlil, its wall, Nimitti-Enlil, its outer wall—I made them bigger, higher, and more majestic. I restored the statues of the great gods, and had them reinstalled in their sanctuaries, their eternal dwellings. I reestablished their interrupted offerings.

IV:28–34   I gathered together the sons of Babylon who had been enslaved, who were in captivity and degradation, and I counted them as Babylonians; I reestablished their special status.

---

20. In Akkadian, the number seventy becomes eleven if the order of two cuneiform signs is switched.

21. The type of wood (Akkadian *musukannu*) is uncertain.

DISCUSSION

From very early in Mesopotamian history, deities were connected to specific cities where they were worshiped; for example, in Sumerian times, Enki had his capital in Eridu, Enlil in Nippur, An in Uruk, and Nanna in Ur. Later, Marduk was identified with Babylon and Ashur with Assyria.[22] This did not exclude the worship of other deities in each city, and indeed the aforementioned gods were all conceived of as bringing with them a retinue of family and divine "staff." Still, the welfare of the city was thought to be related to the agency of the chief deity: if the god was active and content, then the city thrived; if the god was inattentive or angry, then the city suffered.

In Israel and Judah as well, one could speak of the high god, Yhwh, being related to a specific city—Jerusalem.[23] The idea that Yhwh took a special interest in his holy city is at the heart of what has been called "Zion theology." See, for example, Isaiah 60:14: "They shall call you the City of Yhwh, the Zion of the Holy One of Israel." Yhwh was supposed to fight on behalf of Zion (Isa. 31:4, etc.) and protect it (Ps. 69:35, etc.).

When the fortunes of a city or nation suffered, ancient theologians often explained that suffering by the assertion that the deity had abandoned his or her people. This often reflected a literal departure, since invading armies in the ancient Near East frequently plundered divine statues (as well as other temple paraphernalia) from a city when it was conquered—a practice that has been dubbed "godnapping." Such statues were occasionally returned to their original homes, either as an act of grace on the part of the conquerors or by force.

Those familiar with the Bible may assume that a people's wrongdoing was always the reason that gods were said to abandon their cities. Sometimes that was the case; in the inscription above, Esarhaddon asserts that Marduk became enraged partly by the Babylonians' habit of lying. However, a wide range of reasons are given for divine abandonment. In Sumerian literature, the gods of Ur are said to have been ordered by higher-ranking gods to stand aside as their city is destroyed (see the "Lamentation over the Destruction of Sumer and Ur," chap. 25). In the Erra Epic, Marduk is portrayed as a tired and senile god who is persuaded to step aside by the violent Erra, god of plague and underworld, who then wreaks havoc on the city. Sounding much like Yhwh in Ezekiel, Marduk says, "I shall rise up from my dwelling, and the control of heaven and earth shall be undone."[24]

The variety of explanations for divine absence is refracted humorously in Elijah's mockery of the prophets of Baal: "Cry aloud! Surely he is a god, so either he is meditating, or he has wandered away, or he is on a journey, or perhaps he is asleep and must be awakened!" (1 Kgs. 18:27). Indeed, there are a number of portrayals of gods abandoning their cities in the Bible, often reflecting incidents of "godnapping," such as Isaiah 46:1–2:

---

22. Jean Bottéro, *Religion in Ancient Mesopotamia* (trans. T. L. Fagan; University of Chicago: 2001), 48–55.

23. The link between Yhwh and Jerusalem did not always exist. The name of the city long predates its capture by David and is often thought to reflect the meaning "City of Shalim," where Shalim was an ancient Semitic astral deity. Furthermore, the ark of the covenant, the symbol of Yhwh's presence, was said to have been brought to Jerusalem only in the time of David (2 Sam. 6).

24. Stephanie Dalley, ed., *Myths from Mesopotamia: Creation, the Flood, Gilgamesh, and Others* (Oxford: Oxford University Press, 1989), 292.

Bel bows down, Nebo stoops,
their idols are on beasts and cattle;
these things you carry are loaded
as burdens on weary beasts.
They stoop, they bow down together;
they cannot save the burden,
but themselves go into captivity.

Similarly, Jeremiah 48:7 says of the Moabites' national god: "Chemosh shall go out into exile, with his priests and his attendants." The same is said of the Ammonites' Milcom in Jeremiah 49:3.

There is ample evidence that these were not simply the caricatures of foreigners, but that people often viewed their own misfortunes in the same way, that is, as resulting from the absence or neglect of their gods. One can see this as an implicit assumption in the Moabite inscription of King Mesha, who says, "Omri was king of Israel, and he oppressed Moab many days because Chemosh was angry with his land" (lines 4–5; see chap. 10)— that is, Chemosh allowed Moab to be subjugated. Still clearer evidence comes from the fear that biblical authors frequently expressed that they might be taunted about the absence of Yhwh (e.g., Ps. 79:10: "Why should the nations say, 'Where is their God?'"; cf. Pss. 42:3, 10; 79:10; 115:2; Mic. 7:10; Joel 2:17). The cries of Lamentations also acutely express God's absence; for example, "Why have you forgotten us completely? Why have you forsaken us these many days?" (Lam. 5:20).

In the case of Babylonian literature, the idea of Marduk departing from Babylon became a recurrent theme. It happens also in the Middle Babylonian text titled "The Seed of Kingship," and was even adopted by scribes (probably native Babylonians) working under Cyrus of Persia after he conquered the city. The Cyrus Cylinder ascribed the Persian conquest of Babylon to mismanagement of Marduk's temples by Nabonidus (the Babylonian king whom Cyrus overthrew), among other things:

An incompetent person was installed to exercise lordship over his country. [. . .] By his own plan, he did away with the worship of Marduk, the king of the gods; he continually did evil against his (Marduk's) city. . . . Upon (hearing) their cries, the lord of the gods became furiously angry [and he left] their borders; and the gods who lived among them forsook their dwellings, angry that he had brought (them) into Babylon.

A similar sort of rhetoric is employed by the Assyrians besieging Jerusalem in 701. The Assyrian spokesman suggests that Hezekiah's moves to centralize the worship of Yhwh in Jerusalem angered the deity, causing him to hand over the city just as Marduk did Babylon: "If you say to me, 'We rely on Yhwh our God,' is it not he whose high places and altars Hezekiah has removed, saying to Judah and to Jerusalem, 'You shall worship before this altar in Jerusalem'?" (2 Kgs. 18:22). In both cases—Sennacherib and Cyrus—it is a remarkably aggressive theological move to put words in the mouth of someone else's god, especially when those words condemn the god's own worshipers.

As the foregoing examples show, the contexts in which divine abandonment was perceived were often related to the military defeat of a city or nation. Such narratives tend to span past and future; that is, they tend to describe and interpret historical events, but also allude to the present situation and even predict future events. This is apparent in the Marduk Prophecy, which describes Babylon's suffering and defeat before proclaiming, "A king of Babylon will arise" to restore the city's fortunes. It is widely accepted that this text was commissioned by Nebuchadnezzar I (r. 1125–1104) to glorify himself. If so, then the text was not a prophecy but a piece of royal propaganda. The practice of foretelling events that have already taken place is called *vaticinium ex eventu* (prophecy after the fact), and it is frequently attested in the ancient Near East. Similarly, descriptions of Esarhaddon's rebuilding of Babylon in the seventh century present him as the savior king who is divinely called from his youth and confirmed by omens (II:19–III:13).

Ezekiel, too, recounts Jerusalem's past failures and its downfall only to point toward a future reconstruction, although in his case the line between *vaticinium ex eventu* and genuine attempts at prophecy is less clear. The vision of Yhwh's departure from the temple is dated in the sixth year of Jehoiachin's exile, which would be 592 BCE (Ezek. 8:1; cf. 1:1–2). This would predate the fall of Jerusalem by about five years; it is not clear whether the slaughter and defilement of the temple in Ezekiel 9 reflects the experience of the Babylonian destruction of 586. It is reminiscent of other accounts of that cataclysmic event, but it does not necessarily point to any knowledge of what happened in 586; in its vagueness, it could describe the destruction of any city. It is clearer still that Ezekiel's descriptions of the new temple were attempts to foretell a reality that had not yet arrived; indeed, Ezekiel's temple was never built in Jerusalem.

One major difference between Ezekiel and the Marduk texts is the reason given for the departure of the deity: In Ezekiel, it is primarily the adoption of religious practices that were considered unorthodox, although there is also reference to "filling the land with violence." The Marduk Prophecy reports no reason, only the decision of the deity to depart. (Admittedly, the text is broken and thus difficult to interpret with certainty.) In the Esarhaddon rebuilding text, Marduk is said to have been angered because the people lied and stole the wealth of his temple Esagila to use for political purposes.

Daniel Block proposes another key difference: he says that the Mesopotamian gods had to depart because they were thought to indwell the statues that were periodically stolen; he sees a contrast with Yhwh's freedom to leave "of his own volition."[25] He contrasts Mesopotamian religions with Yahwism, which he calls "a spiritual religion."[26] However, those assertions cannot rest on the data presented here: In both biblical and Mesopotamian texts, the gods' departure is linked to the destruction of their sanctuaries and the interruption of their offerings—Yhwh's religious paraphernalia was stolen; how could he stay with no one to serve him and no means to do so? Yhwh announces his intention to leave before the city is destroyed, but so does Marduk in the Esarhaddon text, implicitly. All three of these texts are concerned with preserving the idea that the gods are free to come and go.

---

25. Daniel I. Block, "Divine Abandonment: Ezekiel's Adaptation of an Ancient Near Eastern Motif," in *The Book of Ezekiel: Theological and Anthropological Perspectives* (ed. Margaret S. Odell and John T. Strong; SBLSymS 9; Atlanta: SBL, 2000), 37.
26. Ibid., 35.

Even more clearly, the return of the deity in each case is linked to the restoration of their temple. Indeed, historically, the Jerusalem temple was the first priority of the returnees; it was rebuilt by 515, decades before the city walls, which would seem to be of greater practical importance. Among other reasons for the rebuilding, the returnees would have felt that Yhwh could not return to his city without a home. Spiritual or not, Yahwism was at that time very much linked to physical space.

Despite some basic similarities among the texts, Ezekiel does adapt the divine abandonment tradition in some distinctive ways. One example is Ezekiel's emphasis on the presence of God with the exiles: "Though I scattered them among the countries, *yet I have been a sanctuary to them for a little while* in the countries where they have gone" (11:16; emphasis added). The idea that a god of the homeland was present among a defeated and exiled people is not characteristic of Mesopotamian literature. Although Ezekiel was writing from Babylon, and was exposed to Mesopotamian culture, he brought a Judean's sensibilities to the themes and motifs that he adopted, partly because Israelites and Judeans had thought and written about divine abandonment and mobility from long before his time. Given the way Israel presented its own history—wandering in the wilderness, suffering slavery in a foreign land—it is not surprising that older traditions had already prepared the way for a prophetic theology of a traveling God.[27]

Each of the texts in this chapter spans a relatively wide swath of history, unlike earlier prophetic and divinatory statements that might concern only the present situation or the immediate future. In each of them, furthermore, history is broken up into periods of divine presence and absence—perhaps most clearly in the Marduk Prophecy. Because of this breadth and periodization of history, and because of Ezekiel's visionary experiences, it has sometimes been suggested that "their closest analogues are to be found in the apocalyptic literature of the Old Testament and the inter-testamental period."[28] As an example of historical breadth and periodization in apocalyptic, note Daniel 7:17–18: "As for these four great beasts, four kings shall arise out of the earth. But the holy ones of the Most High shall receive the kingdom and possess the kingdom forever—forever and ever." Here, broad expanses of history are succinctly summed up in symbolic imagery.[29] An apocalyptic text such as Daniel 9:2 explicitly reaches back into history to these events of divine abandonment, citing Jeremiah's prophecy of a seventy-year Babylonian subjugation: "I, Daniel, perceived in the books the number of years that, according to the word of Yhwh to the prophet Jeremiah, must be fulfilled for the devastation of Jerusalem, namely, seventy years" (cf. Jer. 25:11–12). It is striking that the term handed down here is identical to the seventy years of prescribed punishment in the Esarhaddon inscription (II:12–18).

Like apocalyptic, the Ezekiel and Marduk texts sought to impose order on history—to explain adverse events while still expressing faith that history was under divine control.

---

27. Daniel Bodi, *The Book of Ezekiel and the Poem of Erra* (Orbis biblicus et orientalis 104; Freiburg, Switzerland: Universitätsverlag, 1991), 320. Cf. John F. Kutsko, *Between Heaven and Earth: Divine Presence and Absence in the Book of Ezekiel* (Winona Lake, IN: Eisenbrauns, 2000), 24.

28. Longman, *Fictional Akkadian Autobiography*, 132; but cf. Paul D. Hanson, *The Dawn of Apocalyptic* (Philadelphia: Fortress Press, 1975), 233–36.

29. Much the same thing happens when Daniel interprets Nebuchadnezzar's dream of the statue as representing kingdoms of decreasing grandeur in Dan. 2.

Arguably, the success or failure of these texts depended on their ability to accurately predict the future (Deut. 18:21–22). In the case of Ezekiel, his predictions of mercy, restoration, and temple rebuilding did come to pass, and the rebuilt temple stood for six centuries. When it, in turn, was destroyed by the Romans in 70 CE, the idea was well established that the God whose temple was in Jerusalem was a universal god, so there was no need for him to depart, but the cataclysm did spark a new wave of diverse explanations by the rabbis, some of them similar to those Ezekiel gave. In the Mishnah, *Avot* 5:8–9 attributed the destruction to idol worship, among other factors (compare also Luke 19:41–48).

REFLECTION QUESTIONS

1. What parts of the Marduk Prophecy represent *vaticinium ex eventu* (prophecy after the fact), and what parts seem to be genuine attempts to foretell the future?

2. What reasons are given for the deity's departure in each text?

3. What are the effects of the deity's departure in each case?

4. When the texts refer to the destruction of a city, who carries it out?

5. Why would a theologian want to say that his or her people have been abandoned by their god?

6. In each text, what brings about the return of the deity?

7. In each text, the gods' return is linked to the restoration of their sacred spaces. How does each text describe the role of the god(s) and humans in restoring proper worship?

FURTHER READING

Block, Daniel I. "Divine Abandonment: Ezekiel's Adaptation of an Ancient Near Eastern Motif." Pages 15–42 in *The Book of Ezekiel: Theological and Anthropological Perspectives.* Edited by Margaret S. Odell and John T. Strong. SBLSymS 9. Atlanta: SBL, 2000.

Bodi, Daniel. *The Book of Ezekiel and the Poem of Erra.* Orbis biblicus et orientalis 104. Freiburg, Switzerland: Universitätsverlag, 1991. (Esp. 35–51.)

Dalley, Stephanie, ed. *Myths from Mesopotamia: Creation, the Flood, Gilgamesh, and Others.* Oxford: Oxford University Press, 1989.

Hanson, Paul D. *The Dawn of Apocalyptic.* Philadelphia: Fortress Press, 1975.

Kutsko, John F. *Between Heaven and Earth: Divine Presence and Absence in the Book of Ezekiel.* Winona Lake, IN: Eisenbrauns, 2000.

Longman, Tremper, III. *Fictional Akkadian Autobiography: A Generic and Comparative Study.* Winona Lake, IN: Eisenbrauns, 1991.

Porter, Barbara N. *Images, Power, and Politics: Figurative Aspects of Esarhaddon's Babylonian Policy.* Philadelphia: American Philosophical Society, 1993.

19

Praise and Polemics for Baal

The Baal Myth, the Karatepe Inscription, Hosea 2, 1 Kings 18, and 2 Kings 23

HOSEA 2:1–17

When: ca. 750–722 BCE
Where: Samaria
Language: Hebrew

[*Note the wordplay in Hos. 2:16: The Hebrew word* baal *as a common noun can also mean "lord" or "owner." Because of the views of marriage prevalent in the ancient Near East, it could also mean "husband" (e.g., Deut. 22:22). The other common Hebrew word for "husband,"* ish, *is used earlier in the verse. It does not have the connotation of ownership; rather, it primarily connotes male gender.*]

1 KINGS 18:17–41

When: Eighth–seventh centuries BCE, likely preserving a preexisting story
Where: Gilead (?)[1]
Language: Hebrew

[*The background of the story is that the northern kingdom of Israel has experienced three years of drought and famine. Yhwh sends the prophet Elijah to Ahab king of Israel, although Ahab has been persecuting Yhwh's prophets.*]

---

1. The history of the stories of Elijah and Elisha prior to their incorporation into the larger historical books is subject to dispute. If it is correct, as has been argued, that there are traces of a northern ("Israelian") dialect in the stories, that lends credence to their antiquity. Elijah is portrayed as coming from Gilead (1 Kgs. 17:1) and was a thorn in the side of the court at Samaria, so if his stories were preserved at all, it would have been by his own followers (these are more clearly attested in the case of Elisha; e.g., 2 Kgs. 2).

2 KINGS 23:4–5

When: Sixth century BCE
Where: Jerusalem
Language: Hebrew

EXCERPT FROM THE BAAL MYTH

What: Alphabetic cuneiform text on clay tablets
When: Fourteenth century BCE
Where: Ugarit
Language: Ugaritic
Translation: By the author; Ugaritic text *KTU²* 1.6 vi.9–35[2]

[*This is a brief excerpt from a lengthy myth: more than 1,800 lines have survived, and that may be less than half the original myth. Baal is portrayed as a warlike junior deity fighting for supremacy among the gods who are subordinate to El. El is portrayed as a king who supervises the gods. Thus, this scene encapsulates a number of aspects of the Ugaritic pantheon: Baal is at war with Mot ("Death"), the god of the underworld. Despite Baal's strength, he does not overcome Mot himself. Rather, it is the word of El, delivered by the sun-goddess Shapshu, that forces Mot's capitulation and gives Baal the throne.*]

> [Mot] returned to Baal on the summit of Sapan.[3]
>   He raised his voice and called out:
> "You gave my brothers as my food, O Baal,
>   My mother's sons for me to eat!"[4]
>
> They eyed each other like warriors;
>   Mot was strong, Baal was strong.
> They gored each other like buffalo;
>   Mot was strong, Baal was strong.
> They bit each other like serpents;
>   Mot was strong, Baal was strong.
> They dragged each other like thoroughbreds.
>   Mot fell, Baal fell.
>
> On high, Shapshu called out to Mot:
>   "Hear now, Mot, son of El:
> How can you trade blows with Mighty Baal?
>   Will Bull El, your father, listen to you then?
> Surely he will remove the support of your seat,
>   Surely he will overturn the throne of your kingship,
>   Surely he will break the scepter of your rule."

2. For a translation of the whole myth, see Mark S. Smith's in Simon B. Parker, ed., *Ugaritic Narrative Poetry* (SBLWAW 9; Atlanta: Scholars Press, 1997), 81–176.

3. Modern name Jebel al-Aqraʿ, a relatively tall (5,600-foot) mountain a few miles north of Ugarit; the biblical Mount Zaphon (e.g., Isa. 14:13).

4. A scene in which Baal gave Mot his own brothers to eat has not survived, although both are described as "sons of El" (*bn ilm*), and Mot did swallow Baal himself earlier in the myth.

Mot, the son of El, was afraid,
    The Beloved of El, the Warrior, was frightened.
Mot trembled at her voice,
    He [. . .]
"Let Baal be enthroned on [his] royal [throne,]
    On [the resting place, the throne] of his dominion."

KARATEPE GATE INSCRIPTION OF AZATIWADA

What: Linear alphabetic inscription in stone on entrance to citadel
When: ca. 730–710 BCE
Where: Karatepe
Language: Phoenician (versions also exist in Hieroglyphic Luwian)
Translation: By the author[5]

§1   I am Azatiwada, whom Baal blesses, the servant of Baal, whom Awariku,
      king of the Danunians, exalted. Baal made me father and mother to the
      Danunians.

§2   I restored[6] the Danunians; I extended the land of the Plain of Adana,[7] from
      the rising of the sun to its setting, and in my days the Danunians had every
      blessing, and abundance and luxury, and I filled the storehouses of Pahar,
      and I set horse against horse, and shield against shield, and army against
      army, for the sake of Baal and for the sake of the gods. I shattered the wicked
      ones,[8] and I drove out all the evil in the land. I set up the house of Adana in
      luxury, and I created luxury for the lineage of Adana.

§3   Now, I sat on the throne of my father, and I established peace with every
      king; indeed, every king has accepted me as a father[9] because of my justice,
      and because of my wisdom, and because of the goodness of my heart.

§4   And I built fortresses at all the frontier borders, in the places which there
      were evil people, chiefs of robber bands, none of whom had formerly sub-
      mitted to the House of Mopsos. But I, Azatiwada, put them beneath my feet.
      I built fortresses in those places, so that the Danunians could live in secu-
      rity. I humbled mighty lands in the west which none of the kings before me
      had humbled—but I, Azatiwada, humbled them and brought them down! I
      deported them to the edges of my borders in the east, and I settled Danu-
      nians in their place. Therefore, in my days at all the borders of the Plain
      of Adana, from the rising of the sun to its setting, in the places which were
      formerly dreaded, where (even) a man would fear to walk along the road, in

5. Based on the Phoenician text presented in Halet Çambel, *Corpus of Hieroglyphic Luwian Inscriptions*, vol. 2, *Karatepe-Aslantas* (Berlin: Walter de Gruyter, 1999), 48–58. The numbered paragraphs
presented here are for reference only and do not correspond to divisions in the original text.
    6. Lit., "caused to live."
    7. Adana is a region in southeastern Asia Minor.
    8. Or "scoffers" (Phoenician: *mlṣm*). Cf. Ps. 1:1; Prov. 1:22, etc.
    9. Such familial terminology was commonly used in the ANE to reflect power relationships.

my days women could stroll[10]—by the grace of Baal and the gods. And so in all my days there was abundance and luxury and good living and security for the Danunians and for the whole Plain of Adana.

§5   Now, I built this city, and I gave it the name Azatiwaddiya.[11] Since Baal and Resheph Ṣprm[12] sent me to build it, I built it for the sake of Baal and for the sake of Resheph Ṣprm—with abundance and luxury and good living and security, in order to protect the Plain of Adana and the House of Mopsos. For in my days, the land of the Plain of Adana had abundance and luxury, and there were no plagues for the Danunians in my days. So I built this city and I have made its name Azatiwaddiya, and I enthroned Baal Krntryš.[13]

§6   A sacrifice shall be brought for every occasion—an annual sacrifice of one ox, and in the plowing season one sheep, and in the harvest season one sheep. May Baal Krntryš bless Azatiwada with life and with peace and with mighty strength over every king, so that Baal Krntryš gives to Azatiwada length of days, and a multitude of years, and pleasant principality, and mighty strength over every king.

§7   Let this city possess grain and wine; let this people that dwells in it possess cattle and sheep and grain and wine; let them multiply greatly and become exceedingly mighty; and let them serve Azatiwada and the House of Mopsos exceedingly well, for the sake of Baal and for the sake of the gods.

§8   Now, if a king among kings, or a prince among princes, or a man of note erases the name of Azatiwada from this gateway, and puts (his) name (there); indeed, if he covets this city, and tears out this gate which Azatiwada has made, and makes another gate, and puts (his) name on it; if in greediness he tears it out, if in hatred and in evil he tears out this gate, then may Baal of Heaven and El, the creator of the earth, and Shamash[14] and all the divine assembly wipe out that kingdom and that king and that man of note. Let the name Azatiwaddiya be forever like the names of Shamash and Yarach![15]

DISCUSSION

Baal was one of the most widely worshiped gods in the ancient Near East. He probably originated as a Syro-Palestinian deity, and his name appears in lists of gods as early as the third millennium BCE. His cult spread to Egypt by the early second millennium and was later spread throughout the Mediterranean region by the seafaring Phoenicians. Baal's

10. Translation uncertain.
11. I.e., Azatiwada has named the city after himself.
12. If Ṣprm is not a place name, then it probably means "Resheph of the goats" or "Resheph of the birds."
13. Krntryš may refer to Cilicia (a region on the southeast coast of Asia Minor), or it may mean "mace-bearing."
14. The sun-god.
15. The moon-god.

worship was pervasive in Syria-Palestine in the Bronze Age, and the situation was not much different during the Iron Age.

One must ask whether it makes sense to treat all of the many, widespread references to Baal as referring to a single deity, or whether each site ought to be understood as worshiping its own version of Baal. To take one example, Ugaritic god lists include sacrifices to multiple Baals, such as "Baal of Ugarit," "Baal of Aleppo," and "Baal (of) Zaphon." Another god list includes six entries that simply read "Baals."[16] A similar question can be asked about Yhwh, since there are references in extrabiblical inscriptions to "Yhwh of Samaria" and "Yhwh of Teman."

In the case of Baal, the matter is complicated further by the fact that the word ba'al in Hebrew is a common noun meaning "lord, master" (as do similar terms in other Semitic languages). Therefore it can be applied to gods who go by other names. For example, Baal is very similar to Hadad/Adad, a Syrian and Mesopotamian storm-god, and it has been suggested that "Baal" originated as a title of Hadad, much as Israelites called Yhwh "Lord" (Hebrew ʾadonay).

There is no doubt that Baal would have been understood somewhat differently in different places, but it is difficult to reconstruct the particularities of his various manifestations, because there is less information about Baal's mythology than one might hope; the data from most locations consists only of fragmentary hints such as theophoric names.[17] The two primary corpora that shed light on Baal's mythology are the Ugaritic texts and the Bible. The Karatepe Gate Inscription (above) is one of the few additional texts from the Iron Age that tell us anything about Baal.

Not surprisingly, the picture of Baal that emerges from texts written by Baal worshipers is very different from that of the Bible. The most extensive myths about Baal (native or otherwise) come from Ugarit, a Bronze Age Phoenician city. In addition to the primary mythological poems, he is referred to in numerous other Ugaritic texts, such as incantations and god lists. As in Azatiwada's inscription, Baal emerges at Ugarit as a national deity, a patron of the city-state's royal line, and he also has a warrior aspect. At Ugarit, Baal is further described as a judge and a healer, in which function he may even have been thought to have the power to raise the dead. A final major aspect of Baal was as a god of fertility—both human fertility (esp. in the sense of supporting royal succession) and the fertility of the land. In this role as a grain deity, he could be called "Son of Dagan," another god associated with grain. Progeny and agricultural produce were of crucial importance in the life of ancient people, so it is not hard to see why Baal was such a significant deity.

In the Karatepe inscription, Baal is portrayed as a royal patron deity who brought Azatiwada to the throne, supported him in battle, and even gave him long life. Azatiwada, in turn, established Baal's worship in his land. In the inscription, Baal is given two different epithets (*Krntryš* and "of Heaven"), which probably does not indicate two different deities, but rather two different epithets of the same god. The Karatepe inscription also refers to El and Shamash, versions of whom appear in the Ugaritic Baal myth as well. Karatepe

---

16. Dennis Pardee, *Ritual and Cult at Ugarit* (SBLWAW 10; Atlanta: SBL, 2002), 15.

17. Theophoric (lit., "god-bearing") names are those that include a divine element. Biblical names that end in "-iah" or "-jah" (Isaiah, Hezekiah, Elijah, etc.) include the element "Yah(u)," for Yhwh. Names such as Jerubaal and Ishbaal include the theophoric element for Baal.

was not far from Ugarit, so even though the text came hundreds of years later than the Ugaritic myths, it is not surprising that its theological emphases have a basic similarity.

The Bible frequently refers to plural "Baals" (Judg. 2:11; 1 Kgs. 18:18, etc.), and there are scattered references to specific manifestations of Baal, such as "Baal of Peor" (Num. 25:3, etc.) and "Baal-zebub" (2 Kgs. 1:2, etc.). Just as significant, numerous names of people and places in the Old Testament include the element "Baal": Jerubbaal ("Let Baal contend") is another name for the judge Gideon; Ishbaal ("Man of Baal") and Meribaal ("Baal is lord" or "Beloved of Baal") were a son and grandson of Saul, respectively. Among the many Baalistic place names are Baal-gad, Bamoth-baal, Baale-judah.[18] Many of these sites appear to have been named only after the Israelites settled in Palestine, so they cannot be dismissed as mere survivals of Canaanite names.

Were the ancient Israelites and Judeans indeed enthusiastic Baal worshipers, perhaps in addition to worshiping Yhwh? The data are mixed. On the one hand, Jeffrey Tigay has shown that personal names incorporating Baal are a minority of occurrences both in the Bible and in inscriptions that have been recovered archaeologically; Yahwistic names make up the great majority of such names, and Tigay takes this to reflect a strong national religious preference for Yhwh. On the other hand, the numerous Baalistic personal names, the place names (which Tigay did not include in his analysis), and biblical stories suggest that Israelites and Judeans were inclined toward the worship of Baal in his various forms. In 1 Kings 18 (above), Elijah describes himself as the only surviving prophet of Yhwh in comparison to hundreds of Baalistic prophets. One can add the description of the cycle of apostasy in Judges 2, in which it is said that the Israelites repeatedly "did what was evil in the sight of Yhwh and worshiped the Baals; and they abandoned Yhwh" (2:11–12). This pattern of vacillation was viewed by later Judean historians as typical of the people's religious practices. One need not treat such stories as journalistic, firsthand accounts to think they were concerned with addressing a perceived problem with the people's adherence to Yhwh throughout the nation's history.

Although readers of the Bible may already have encountered stories of the Israelites' attraction to Baal, many may find it surprising that numerous aspects of the Ugaritic gods are also present in the biblical portrayal of Yhwh as the God of Israel. This is true of the Ugaritic El (who is called a father and sits at the head of a divine council; cf. Ps. 82) and Anat (whose warrior aspect finds echoes in numerous biblical descriptions of the Divine Warrior; cf. Isa. 34). Yet it is Baal who perhaps has the greatest degree of commonality with the biblical portrayal of Yhwh. Baal is presented as a ruler on a throne (cf. Isa. 6:1) and as a rider of clouds (cf. Ps. 68:4); he lives on a mountain (cf. Mount Sinai, "Mount Zion"); he brings rain (cf. Deut. 28:12; Jer. 5:24) and his voice shakes the earth like thunder (cf. Ps. 29:3–4); he slays the serpentine monsters of river and sea (Isa. 27:1; Job 26:12–13).

Yhwh and Baal were probably described with some of these same characteristics from their (somewhat obscure) literary beginnings, but it is clear that the striking similarities are also partly a result of purposeful adoption of Baalistic characteristics into the portrait of

---

18. One of the most striking examples is "Baal-zephon," which is supposed to be a location south of Israel on the people's route out of Egypt, but which clearly preserves the ancient tradition of Baal's enthronement on the heights of northern Mount Zaphon.

Yhwh by the authors of the Bible. In Hosea 2:8, one can see the rhetorical effort of a prophet of Yhwh to assert that it was Yhwh who was to be credited with blessings that ancient inhabitants of the Levant might otherwise have attributed to Baal—"it was I who gave [Israel] the grain, the wine, and the oil." The text as a whole presents Yhwh as a righteous husband who has provided for his wife (the people), but has been spurned by her anyway; Yhwh is justifiably angry about the abandonment, yet still longs to be reunited (2:15–17).

Both in prophetic disputations that indicate "confusion" of Yhwh and Baal, and in the images of the two gods as historical benefactors of their respective nations, it is apparent that they were perceived in similar ways; yet at the same time, Yahwistic theologians began to protest more forcefully against any confusion between the two deities and to exclude the worship of Baal. Purges of Baalistic worship were carried out in both the northern kingdom (by Jehu; 2 Kgs. 10:18–28) and the southern (by Jehoshaphat [2 Kgs. 3:2] and Josiah [23:4–5]).

Mark Smith has conceptualized the processes by which Israelites assigned to Yhwh the attributes of other gods as *convergence*, and the process by which they eventually rejected the other gods as *differentiation*. This model of convergence-and-differentiation draws on work by earlier scholars (e.g., Frank Moore Cross) on the continuities between Ugaritic and Israelite mythology, but Smith particularly emphasizes that Yhwh's adoption of the roles, characteristics, and even epithets of other gods is best understood as a form of *rhetorical* competition between the worshipers of different gods.

The portrayal of Yhwh in the Bible is also marked by significant differences from Baal, of course. For example, there are indications in the Ugaritic texts that the gods of that pantheon had active sex lives, whereas Yhwh is never portrayed in that way. Furthermore, Yhwh has no serious divine rivals in the Bible; his aforementioned victories over the powers of watery chaos are presented as *faits accomplis*, rather than being narrated with any sense of suspense. Baal is much more consistently presented as having rivals and weaknesses. For example, in the Ugaritic myth Baal is swallowed up by Mot, descends to the underworld, and only returns through the help of Anat. Yhwh is never defeated, and although he has contact with the underworld in the Hebrew Bible, he does not die. The polytheistic context of the Baal myth allows Baal to "die"; even without him, divine actors such has El and Anat are still on stage to move the story forward.

The worship of Yhwh and Baal were probably in conflict to some degree throughout the histories of Israel and Judah; early inscriptions such as the Mesha Stela (chap. 10) amply demonstrate that the deities of different Levantine nations were long thought to be opposed to each other—at least indirectly, through their human representatives. Furthermore, Yhwh's jealousy was probably an attribute of great antiquity (Exod. 20:5). However, within the corpus of biblical writings, it is primarily in the later preexilic and the postexilic periods that one sees a new emphasis on the exclusion of foreign gods and practices.

REFLECTION QUESTIONS

1. What are some similarities between the portrayals of Baal in the biblical and extrabiblical texts in this chapter? What are some differences?

2. How does the relationship between god and king affect the way deities are portrayed in the above texts?

3. Although the biblical texts above make it clear that the authors condemned the worship of Baal, they do not say why. It is not self-evident why, in a wholly polytheistic ancient Near Eastern world, ancient Israelites and Judeans should have sought to exclude the worship of other gods. Why do you think they did so?

4. Which do you think is more complicated: a pantheon full of deities who have various functions, attributes, and personae, or one deity in whom all of the functions and aspects of deity are contained?

5. Who gets to define the nature and character of a deity? What is the proper basis for such a definition?

FURTHER READING

Cross, Frank Moore. *Canaanite Myth and Hebrew Epic: Essays in the History of the Religion of Israel.* Cambridge, MA: Harvard University Press, 1973.

Herrmann, Wolfgang. "Baal." Pages 132–39 in *Dictionary of Deities and Demons in the Bible.* 2nd rev. ed. Edited by Karel Van Der Toorn, Bob Becking, and Pieter W. Van Der Horst. Leiden: Brill, 1999.

Na'aman, Nadav. "Baal Toponyms." Pages 140–41 in *Dictionary of Deities and Demons in the Bible.* 2nd rev. ed. Edited by Karel Van Der Toorn, Bob Becking, and Pieter W. Van Der Horst. Leiden: Brill, 1999.

Pardee, Dennis. *Ritual and Cult at Ugarit.* SBLWAW 10. Atlanta: Society of Biblical Literature, 2002.

Smith, Mark S. *The Early History of God: Yahweh and the Other Deities in Ancient Israel.* 2nd ed. Biblical Resource Series. Grand Rapids: Eerdmans, 2002.

———. *The Origins of Biblical Monotheism: Israel's Polytheistic Background and the Ugaritic Texts.* Oxford: Oxford University Press, 2001.

Tigay, Jeffrey H. *You Shall Have No Other Gods: Israelite Religion in the Light of Hebrew Inscriptions.* Harvard Semitic Studies 31. Atlanta: Scholars Press, 1986.

PART V

Writings

Proverbs and Wisdom Instructions

Instruction of Amenemope and Proverbs 22:17–24:22

INSTRUCTION OF AMENEMOPE

What: Hieratic text on papyrus scroll, 3.7 m × 24 cm
When: Sixth century BCE; fragmentary copies as early as Twenty-first Dynasty (1069–945). Composed either then or near the end of the immediately preceding New Kingdom.
Where: Most complete copy is from Akhmim, (north of Abydos); other partial copies exist.
Language: Egyptian
Translation: W. K. Simpson[1]

The beginning of the instruction about life,
    The guide for well-being,
All the principles of official procedure,
    The duties of the courtiers;
To know how to refute the accusation of one who made it,
    And to send back a reply to the one who sent him;
To set one straight on the paths of life,
    And make him prosper on earth;
To let his heart settle down in its chapel,[2]
    As one who steers him clear of evil;
To save him from the talk of others,
    As one who is respected in the speech of men.

Written by the superintendent of the land, experienced in his office,
    The offspring of a scribe of the Beloved Land,

---

1. W. K. Simpson, ed., *The Literature of Ancient Egypt: An Anthology of Stories, Instructions, and Poetry* (3rd ed.; New Haven, CT: Yale University Press, 2003), 223–43.
2. In the amulets of the New Kingdom, the heart is portrayed in a kind of shrine or chapel; the image here probably symbolizes composure. The heart was also the organ from which the Egyptians believed that thought originated (see also the role of Ptah's heart in the Memphite Theology in chap. 3).

The superintendent of produce, who fixes the grain measure,
  Who sets the grain tax amount for his lord,
Who registers the islands which appear as new land over the cartouche of His Majesty,[3]
  And sets up the land mark at the boundary of the arable land,
Who protects the king by his tax rolls,
  And makes the Register of the Black Land.[4]
The scribe who places the divine offerings for all the gods,
  The donor of land grants to the people,
The superintendent of grain who administers the food offerings,
  Who supplies the storerooms with grain.
A truly silent man in Tjeni in the Ta-wer nome,[5]
  One whose verdict is "acquitted" in Ipu,
The owner of a pyramid tomb on the west of Senut,
  As well as the owner of a memorial chapel in Abydos,
Amenemope, the son of Kanakht,
  Whose verdict is "acquitted" in the Ta-wer nome.
For his son, the youngest of his children,
  The least of his family,
Initiate of the mysteries of Min-Kamutef,[6]
  Libation pourer of Wennofre;[7]
Who inducts Horus upon the throne of his father,
  His stolist in his august chapel,
[. . .] secret [. . .]
  The seer of the Mother of God,
The inspector of the black cattle of the terrace of Min,
  Who protects Min in his chapel,
Horemmaakheru is his true name,
  A child of an official of Ipu,
The son of the sistrum player of Shu and Tefnut,[8]
  The chief singer of Horus, the lady Tawosret.[9]
He says:

Chapter 1

Give your ears and hear what is said,
  Give your mind over to their interpretation:
It is profitable to put them in your heart,
  But woe to him that neglects them!
Let them rest in the shrine of your belly
  That they may act as a lock in your heart;

3. When the annual Nile floods subsided, newly formed islands in the river were immediately designated as royal property.

4. A common term for Egypt.

5. A nome was an administrative division in Egypt. Tjeni in the Ta-wer nome (Abydos) was the great temple and cult site of the god Osiris, where many royal and private memorial buildings were dedicated. Ipu and Senut were in the Panopolite nome to the north of Abydos, the area of modern Akhmim.

6. The patron god of Akhmim.

7. Wennofre is an epithet of Osiris, the Egyptian god of the underworld and the dead.

8. Shu, Tefnut, and Horus are all Egyptian deities.

9. The final pharaoh of the Nineteenth Dynasty.

Now when there comes a storm of words,
    They will be a mooring post on your tongue.
If you spend a lifetime with these things in your heart,
    You will find it good fortune;
You will discover my words to be a treasure house of life,
    And your body will flourish upon earth.

Chapter 2

Beware of stealing from a miserable man
    And of raging against the cripple.
Do not stretch out your hand to strike an old man,
    Nor snip at the words of an elder.
Don't let yourself be sent on a fraudulent business,
    Nor desire the carrying out of it;
Do not get tired because of being interfered with,
    Nor return an answer on your own.
The evildoer, throw him (in) the canal,
    And he will bring back its slime.
The north wind comes down and ends his appointed hour,
    It is joined to the tempest;
The clouds are high, the crocodiles are nasty,
    O hot-headed man, what are you like?
He cries out, and his voice (reaches) heaven.
    O Moon, make his crime manifest!
Row that we may ferry evil away,
    For we will not act according to his (evil) nature;
Lift him up, give him your hand,
    And leave him (in) the hands of God;
Fill his gut with your own food
    That he may be sated and ashamed.
Something else of value in the heart of God
    Is to stop and think before speaking.

Chapter 3

Do not get into a quarrel with the argumentative man
    Nor incite him with words;
Proceed cautiously before an opponent,
    And give way to an adversary;
Sleep on it before speaking,
    For a storm come forth like fire in hay is
The hot-headed man in his appointed time.
    May you be restrained before him;
Leave him to himself,
    And God will know how to answer him.
If you spend your life with these things in your heart,
    Your children shall observe them.

Chapter 4

The hot-headed man in the temple
    Is like a tree grown in an enclosed space;

In a moment is its loss of foliage.
    It reaches its end in the carpentry shop;
It is floated away far from its place,
    Or fire is its funeral pyre.
The truly temperate man sets himself apart,
    He is like a tree grown in a sunlit field,
But it becomes verdant, it doubles its yield,
    It stands before its owner;
Its fruit is something sweet, its shade is pleasant,
    And it reaches its end in a grove.

Chapter 5

Do not take by violence the shares of the temple,
    Do not be grasping, and you will find abundance;
Do not take away a temple servant
    In order to do something profitable for another man.
Do not say today is the same as tomorrow,
    Or how will matters come to pass?
When tomorrow comes, today is past;
    The deep waters become a sand-bank.
Crocodiles are uncovered, the hippopotamuses are on dry land,
    And the fishes gasping for air;
The wolves are fat, the wild fowl in festival,
    And the nets are drained,
Every temperate man in the temple says,
    "Great is the benevolence of Re."[10]
Adhere to the silent man, you will find life,
    And your body shall flourish upon earth.

Chapter 6

Do not displace the surveyor's marker on the boundaries of the arable land,
    Nor alter the position of the measuring line;
Do not be covetous for a single cubit of land,
    Nor encroach upon the boundaries of a widow.
One who transgresses the furrow shortens a lifetime,
    One who seizes it for fields
And acquires by deceptive attestations,
    Will be lassoed by the might of the Moon.
To one who has done this on earth, pay attention,
    For he is an oppressor of the feeble;
He is an enemy worthy of your overthrowing;
    Life is taken from his eye;
His household is hostile to the community,
    His storerooms are broken into,
His property is taken away from his children,
    And his possessions are given to someone else.
Take care not to topple over the boundary marks of the fields,

10. The sun-god.

Not fearing that you will be brought to court;
Man propitiates God by the might of the Lord[11]
    When he sets straight the boundaries of the arable land.
Desire, then, to make yourself prosper,
    And take care for the Lord of All;[12]
Do not trample on the furrow of someone else,
    Their good order will be profitable for you.
So plough the fields, and you will find whatever you need,
    And receive the bread from your own threshing floor:
Better is a bushel which God gives you
    Than five thousand deceitfully gotten;
They do not spend a day in the storehouse or warehouse,
    They are no use for dough for beer;
Their stay in the granary is short-lived,
    When morning comes they will have vanished.
Better, then, is poverty in the hand of God
    Than riches in the storehouse;
Better is bread when the mind is at ease
    Than riches with anxiety.

Chapter 7

Do not set your heart upon seeking riches,
    For there is no one who can ignore Destiny and Fortune.[13]
Do not set your thoughts on superficial matters:
    For every man there is his appointed time.
Do not exert yourself to seek out excess
    And your allotment will prosper for you;
If riches come to you by thievery
    They will not spend the night with you;
As soon as day breaks they will not be in your household;
    Although their places can be seen, they are not there.
When the earth opens up its mouth, it levels him and swallows him up,
    They will plunge in the deep;
They will make for themselves a great hole which suits them.
    And they will sink themselves in the underworld.
Or they will make themselves wings like geese,
    And fly up to the sky.
Do not be pleased with yourself (because of) riches acquired through robbery,
    Neither be sorry about poverty.
As for an officer who commands one who goes in front of him,
    His company leaves him;
The boat of the covetous is abandoned (in) the mud,

11. See following note on "Lord of All."
12. The phrase "Lord of All" appears also in earlier wisdom instructions, such as that of King Amenemhet, which dates to the Old Kingdom. Although its significance here is contested—it could refer to either the pharaoh or a high god such as Osiris—it should not be confused by readers with the use of "Lord" in the Bible to denote Yhwh. On the other hand, it is conceivable that the nonspecificity of the term could have made the text more appealing for an Israelite scribe to adapt.
13. The reference is to Shay and Emutet, deities of destiny and fortune.

While the skiff of the truly temperate man sails on.
When he rises you shall offer to the Aten,[14]
    Saying, "Grant me prosperity and health."
And he will give you your necessities for life,
    And you will be safe from fear.

Chapter 8

Set your deeds throughout the world
    That everyone may greet you;
They make rejoicing for the Uraeus,[15]
    And spit against the Apophis.[16]
Keep your tongue safe from words of detraction,
    And you will be the loved one of the people,
Then you will find your (proper) place within the temple
    And your offerings among the bread deliveries of your lord;
You will be revered, when you are concealed (in) your grave,
    And be safe from the might of God.
Do not accuse a man,
    When the circumstance of (his) escape is unknown.
Whether you hear something good or bad,
    Put it outside, until he has been heard;
Set a good report on your tongue,
    While the bad thing is concealed inside you.

Chapter 9

Do not fraternize with the hot-tempered man,
    Nor approach him to converse.
Safeguard your tongue from talking back to your superior,
    And take care not to offend him.
Do not allow him to cast words only to entrap you,
    And be not too free in your replies;
With a man of your own station discuss the reply;
    And take care of speaking thoughtlessly;
When a man's heart is upset, words travel faster
    Than wind over water.
He is ruined and created by his tongue,
    When he speaks slander;
He makes an answer deserving of a beating,
    For his freight is damaged.
He sails among all the world,
    But his cargo is false words;
He acts the ferryman in twisting words:
    He goes forth and comes back arguing.
But whether he eats or whether he drinks inside,

14. The divine sun disk.
15. The uraeus is the serpent on the pharaoh's headdress, which in mythology is his protector from his enemies.
16. Apophis is the great, swallowing serpent of the Egyptian underworld.

His accusation (waits for him) outside.
The day when his evil deed is brought to court
    Is a disaster for his children.
Even Khnum[17] will straightway come against him, even Khnum will
    straightway come against him,
The potter of the ill-tempered man,
[. . .]
It is to knead and bake the hearts that he molds
    He is like a wolf cub in the farmyard,
And he turns one eye to the other (squinting),
    For he sets families to argue.
He goes before all the winds like clouds,
    He changes his hue in the sun;
He crocks his tail like a baby crocodile,
    He curls himself up to inflict harm,
His lips are sweet, but his tongue is bitter,
    And fire burns inside him.
Do not fly up to join that man
    Not fearing you will be brought to account.

Chapter 10

Do not address an intemperate man in your (unrighteousness)
    Nor destroy your own mind;
Do not say to him, "May you be praised," not meaning it
    When there is fear within you.
Do not converse falsely with a man,
    For it is the abomination of God.
Do not separate your mind from your tongue,
    All your plans will succeed.
You will be important before others,
    While you will be secure in the hand of God.
God hates one who falsifies words,
    His great abomination is duplicity.

Chapter 11

Do not covet the property of the dependent
    Nor hunger for his bread;
The property of a dependent is an obstruction to the throat,
    It makes the gullet throw it back.
It is by false oaths that he has brought himself up,
    While his heart slips back inside him.
It is through the "disaffected" that "effectiveness" is "weakened,"[18]
    And then evil will topple good.
If you are at a loss before your superior,
    And are confused in your speeches,

17. A major Egyptian deity associated with building and creation; thus the potter who molds living things.
18. Simpson alternatively suggests: "Do not let disaffection wear away success."

Your flatterings are turned back with curses,
    And your prostrations by beatings.
Whoever fills the mouth with too much bread swallows it and spits up,
    So you emptied of your good.
To the examination of a dependent pay attention
    While the staves touch him,
And while all his people are fettered with manacles:
    Who is to have the execution?
When you are too free before your superior,
    Then you are in bad favor with your subordinates.
So steer away from a dependent on the road,
    That you may see him but keep clear of his property.

Chapter 12

Do not covet the property of an official,
    And do not fill (your) mouth with too much food arrogantly;
If he sets you to manage his property,
    Respect his, and yours will prosper.
Do not deal with the intemperate man,
    Nor associate yourself to a disloyal party.
If you are sent to transport straw,
    Abstain from profiting thereby,
If a man is detected in a dishonest transaction,
    Never again will he be employed.

Chapter 13

Do not lead a man astray (with) reed pen on papyrus:
    It is the abomination of God.
Do not witness a false statement,
    Nor remove a man (from the list) by your order;
Do not reckon with someone who has nothing,
    Nor make your pen be false.
If you find a large debt against a poor man,
    Make it into three parts;
Release two of them and let one remain:
    You will find it a path of life;
You will pass the night in sound sleep; in the morning
    You will find it like good news.
Better it is to be praised as one loved by men
    Than wealth in the storehouse;
Better is bread when the mind is at ease
    Than riches with troubles.

Chapter 14

Do not ingratiate yourself with a person,
    Nor exert yourself to seek out his hand,
If he says to you, "take a bribe,"

There is no need to respect him.
Do not be afraid of him, nor bend down your head,
    Nor turn aside your gaze.
Address him with your words and say to him greetings;
    When he stops, your chance will come;
Do not repel him at his first approach,
    Another time he will be apprehended.

Chapter 15

Do well, and you will attain influence.
    Do not dip your reed against a transgressor.
The beak of the Ibis is the finger of the scribe,[19]
    Take care not to disturb it;
The Ape (Thot) dwells (in) the temple of Khmun,[20]
    While his eye travels around the Two Lands;[21]
If he sees one who cheats with his finger (that is, a false scribe),
    He takes away his provisions by the flood.
As for a scribe who cheats with his finger,
    His son shall not be enrolled.
If you spend your life with these things in your heart,
    Your children shall observe them.

Chapter 16

Do not tilt the scale nor falsify the weights,
    Nor diminish the fractions of the grain measures;
Do not wish for the grain measures of the fields
    To cast aside those of the treasury.
The Ape sits by the balance,
    While his heart is the plummet.
Who is a god as great as Thot,
    The one who discovered these things,[22] in order to create them?
Do not get for yourself short weights;
    They are plentiful, yea, an army by the might of God.
If you see someone cheating,
    At a distance you must pass him by.
Do not be avaricious for copper,
    And abjure fine clothes;
What good is one cloaked in fine linen,
    When he cheats before God.
When jewels are heaped upon gold,
    At daybreak they turn to lead.

19. The Ibis here is Thoth, patron god of the scribe.
20. The Egyptian name for Hermopolis, the town of Thoth.
21. Upper and Lower Egypt.
22. Possibly a reference to the invention of hieroglyphic writing.

Chapter 17

Beware of tampering with the grain measure
     To falsify its fractions;
Do not act wrongfully through force,
     Cause it not to be empty inside,
May you have it measured exactly as it arrived,
     Your hand stretching out with precision.
Make not for yourself a measure of two capacities,
     For then it is toward the depths that you will go.
The measure is the eye of Re,
     Its abomination is the thief.
As for a grain measurer who multiplies and subtracts,
     His eye will seal up against him.
Do not receive the harvest tax of a cultivator,
     Nor set a papyrus against him to harm him.
Do not enter into collusion with the grain measurer,
     Nor defraud the share of the Residence,
More important is the threshing floor for barley
     Than swearing by the Great Throne.

Chapter 18

Do not go to bed fearing tomorrow,
     For when day breaks how will tomorrow be?
     Man knows not what tomorrow will be!
God is success,
     While man is failure.
The words which men say pass on one side,
     The things which God does pass on another side.
Do not say, "I am without fault,"
     Nor try to seek out trouble.
Fault is the business of God,
     It is sealed with his finger.
There is no success in the hand of God,
     Nor is there failure before Him;
If one turns himself about to seek out success,
     In a moment He destroys him.
Be strong in your heart, make your mind firm,
     Do not steer with your tongue;
The tongue of a man is the steering oar of a boat,
     But the Lord of All is its pilot.

Chapter 19

Do not enter the council chamber in the presence of a magistrate
     And then falsify your speech.
Do not go up and down with your accusation
     When your witnesses stand readied.
Do not overstate (through) oaths in the name of your lord,
     (Through) pleas (in) the place of interrogation.

Tell the truth before the magistrate,
    Lest he gain power over your body;
If you petition before him the next day,
    He will concur with all you say;
He will present your case (in) court before the Council of the Thirty,
    And it will be decided another time as well.

Chapter 20

Do not defraud a person in the law court
    Nor put aside the just man.
Do not pay attention to garments of white.
    Nor scorn one in rags.
Take not the bribe of the strong man,
    Nor repress the weak for him.
Maat[23] is a great gift of God;
    he gives it to whom he wishes.
The strength of one like him
    Saves a poor wretch from his beatings.
Do not make for yourself false enrollment lists:
    For they are punishable offenses (deserving) death;
They are serious oaths which promote respect;
    And they are to be investigated by a reporter.
Do not falsify the oracles on a papyrus
    And (thereby) alter the designs of God.
Do not arrogate to yourself the might of God
    As if Destiny and Fortune did not exist.
Hand property over to its (rightful) owners,
    And seek out life for yourself;
Let not your heart build in their house,
    For then your neck will be on the execution block.

Chapter 21

Do not say, find for me a strong patron,
    For a man in your town has afflicted me.
Do not say, find for me an active intercessor,
    For one who hates (me) has afflicted me.
Indeed, you cannot know the plans of God;
    You cannot perceive tomorrow.
Sit yourself at the hands of God:
    Your tranquility will overthrow (the adversaries).
As for a crocodile deprived of his tongue,
    His significance is negligible.
Empty not your soul to everybody
    And do not diminish thereby your importance;
Do not pour out your words to others,
    Nor fraternize with one who is too rash.

---

23. The Egyptian term for justice and righteousness. This translation departs from Simpson's in favor of Lichtheim's (*AEL* II.158).

Better is a man whose report is inside him
    Than one who tells it to disadvantage.
One cannot run to attain perfection;
    One cannot create (only) to destroy it.

Chapter 22

Do not provoke your adversary,
    And do not (let) him say his innermost thoughts;
Do not fly up to greet him
    When you cannot see how he acts.
May you first comprehend his accusation
    Be calm and your chance will come.
Leave it to him and he will empty his soul;
    Sleep knows how to find him out;
Touch his feet, do not disrespect him;
    Fear him, do not underestimate him.
Indeed, you cannot know the plans of God,
    You cannot perceive tomorrow.
Sit yourself at the hands of God;
    Your tranquility will overthrow them.

Chapter 23

Do not eat a meal in the presence of a magistrate,
    Nor set to speaking first.
If you are sated, pretend to chew,
    Enjoy yourself with your saliva.
Look at the cup in front of you,
    And let it suffice your need.
Even as a noble is important in his office,
    So he is like the abundance of a flooded well.
Do not listen to the proposition of an official indoors,
    And then repeat it to another outside.
Do not allow your discussions to be brought outside
    Lest your heart be grieved.
The heart of a man is the beak of God,
    So take care not to slight it;
A man who stands (at) the side of an official
    Should not have his name known (in the street).

Chapter 25

Do not laugh at a blind man nor taunt a dwarf,
    Neither interfere with the condition of a cripple;
Do not taunt a man who is in the hand of God,
    Nor scowl at him if he errs.
Man is clay and straw,
    And God is his potter;
He overthrows and He builds daily,
    He impoverishes a thousand if He wishes.
But He makes a thousand into officials

When He is in His hour of life.
How fortunate is he who reaches the West,
    When he is safe in the hand of God.

Chapter 26

Do not sit in the beer hall
    Nor join someone greater than you,
Whether he be low or high in his station,
    An old man or a youth;
But take as a friend for yourself someone compatible:
    Re is helpful though he is far away.
When you see someone greater than you outside,
    Follow him, respect (him).
And give a hand to an old man filled with beer:
    Respect him as his children would.
The strong arm is not weakened when it is uncovered,
    The back is not broken when one bends it;
A man is not denigrated when he speaks sweet words,
    More so than a rich man whose words are straw.
A pilot who sees into the distance
    Will not let his ship capsize.

Chapter 27

Do not reproach someone greater than you,
    For he has seen the Sun before you;
Do not let yourself be reported to the Aten when he rises,
    With the words, "Again a young man has reproached an elder."
Very painful in the sight of Re
    Is a young man who reproaches an elder.
Let him beat you with your hands folded,
    Let him reproach you while you keep quiet.
Then when you come before him in the morning
    He will give you bread freely.
As for bread, the dog of his master
    Barks to the one who gives it.

Chapter 28

Do not identify a widow if you have caught her in the fields,
    Nor fail to give way if she is accused.
Do not turn a stranger away (from) your oil jar
    Double it (more than) for your (own) family.
God loves him who cares for the poor,
    More than him who respects the wealthy.

Chapter 29

Do not turn people away from crossing the river
    When you have room in (your) ferryboat;

If an oar is given you in the midst of the deep waters,
    So bend back your hands (to) take it up.
It is not an abomination in the hand of God
    If the crew does not agree.
Do not acquire a ferryboat on the river,
    And then attempt to seek out its fares;
Take the fare from the man of means,
    But (also) accept the destitute (without charge).

Chapter 30

Mark for yourself these thirty chapters:
    They please, they instruct,
They are the foremost of all books;
    They teach the ignorant.
If they are read before an ignorant man,
    He will be purified (of his ignorance) through them.
Fill yourself with them; put them in your mind
    And get men to interpret them.
As for a scribe who is experienced in his position,
    He will find himself worthy of being a courtier.
It is finished.
By the writing of Senu, son of the god's father Pamiu.

PROVERBS 1:1–7; 22:17–24:22

When: Unknown
Where: Jerusalem
Language: Hebrew
Translation: NRSV[24]

1:1The proverbs of Solomon son of David, king of Israel:

    2For learning about wisdom and instruction,
        for understanding words of insight,
    3for gaining instruction in wise dealing,
        righteousness, justice, and equity;
    4to teach shrewdness to the simple,
        knowledge and prudence to the young—
    5Let the wise also hear and gain in learning,
        and the discerning acquire skill,
    6to understand a proverb and a figure,
        the words of the wise and their riddles.
    7The fear of Yhwh is the beginning of knowledge;
        fools despise wisdom and instruction.
    . . . .
    22:17The words of the wise:

24. The NRSV text is slightly altered. In addition to the added numbering (see note below), line spaces have been rearranged and God is called "Yhwh" instead of "the LORD."

Incline your ear and hear my words,
    and apply your mind to my teaching;
[18]for it will be pleasant if you keep them in your belly,
    if all of them are ready on your lips.
[19]So that your trust may be in Yhwh,
    I have made them known to you today   yes, to you
[20]Have I not written for you thirty sayings[25]
    of admonition and knowledge,
[21]to show you what is right and true,
    so that you may give a true answer to those who sent you?

(1)[26] [22]Do not rob the poor because they are poor,
    or crush the afflicted at the gate;
[23]for Yhwh pleads their cause
    and despoils of life those who despoil them.

(2) [24]Make no friends with those given to anger,
    and do not associate with hotheads,
[25]or you may learn their ways
    and entangle yourself in a snare.

(3) [26]Do not be one of those who give pledges,
    who become surety for debts.
[27]If you have nothing with which to pay,
    why should your bed be taken from under you?

(4) [28]Do not remove the ancient landmark
    that your ancestors set up.

(5) [29]Do you see those who are skillful in their work?
    they will serve kings;
    they will not serve common people.

(6) [23:1]When you sit down to eat with a ruler,
    observe carefully what is before you,
    [2]and put a knife to your throat
        if you have a big appetite.
[3]Do not desire the ruler's delicacies,
    for they are deceptive food.

(7) [4]Do not wear yourself out to get rich;
    be wise enough to desist.

---

25. The Hebrew text here contains a small copying error, a single vowel which must be corrected in order to render the text comprehensible. The number 30 has significance in Egyptian culture; it corresponds to the number of judges in both the human court referred to in Amenemope 19.11, and (in some mythological texts) the number of judges who judge the dead. That may explain why thirty chapters were composed for the instruction. The error in the copying of the biblical text was probably due to later Hebrew scribes' not being aware of the number's significance (Michael V. Fox, *Proverbs 10–31* [AB 18B; New Haven, CT: Yale University Press, 2009], 710–11).

26. The sayings are numbered 1–30 here, a division not indicated in the original text, to help the reader recognize the "thirty sayings."

⁵When your eyes light upon it, it is gone;
   for suddenly it takes wings to itself,
   flying like an eagle toward heaven.

(8) ⁶Do not eat the bread of the stingy;
   do not desire their delicacies;
   ⁷for like a hair in the throat, so are they.
"Eat and drink!" they say to you;
   but they do not mean it.
⁸You will vomit up the little you have eaten,
   and you will waste your pleasant words.

(9) ⁹ Do not speak in the hearing of a fool,
who will only despise the wisdom of your words.

(10) ¹⁰Do not remove an ancient landmark
   or encroach on the fields of orphans,
¹¹for their redeemer is strong;
   he will plead their cause against you.

(11) ¹²Apply your mind to instruction
   and your ear to words of knowledge.

(12) ¹³Do not withhold discipline from your children;
   if you beat them with a rod, they will not die.
   ¹⁴If you beat them with the rod, you will save their lives from Sheol.

(13) ¹⁵My child, if your heart is wise, my heart too will be glad.
¹⁶My soul will rejoice when your lips speak what is right.

(14) ¹⁷Do not let your heart envy sinners,
   but always continue in the fear of Yhwh.
¹⁸Surely there is a future,
   and your hope will not be cut off.

(15) ¹⁹Hear, my child, and be wise,
   and direct your mind in the way.
²⁰Do not be among winebibbers,
   or among gluttonous eaters of meat;
²¹for the drunkard and the glutton will come to poverty,
   and drowsiness will clothe them with rags.

(16) ²²Listen to your father who begot you,
   and do not despise your mother when she is old.
²³Buy truth, and do not sell it;
   buy wisdom, instruction, and understanding.

(17) ²⁴The father of the righteous will greatly rejoice;
   he who begets a wise son will be glad in him.
²⁵Let your father and mother be glad;
   let her who bore you rejoice.

(18) ²⁶My child, give me your heart,
  and let your eyes observe my ways.
²⁷For a prostitute is a deep pit;
  an adulteress is a narrow well.
²⁸She lies in wait like a robber
  and increases the number of the faithless.

(19) ²⁹Who has woe? Who has sorrow?
  Who has strife? Who has complaining?
Who has wounds without cause?
  Who has redness of eyes?
³⁰Those who linger late over wine,
  those who keep trying mixed wines.

(20) ³¹Do not look at wine when it is red,
  when it sparkles in the cup
  and goes down smoothly.
³²At the last it bites like a serpent,
  and stings like an adder.
³³Your eyes will see strange things,
  and your mind utter perverse things.
³⁴You will be like one who lies down in the midst of the sea,
  like one who lies on the top of a mast.
³⁵"They struck me," you will say, "but I was not hurt;
  they beat me, but I did not feel it.
  When shall I awake? I will seek another drink."

(21) ^{24:1}Do not envy the wicked,
  nor desire to be with them;
²for their minds devise violence,
  and their lips talk of mischief.

(22) ³By wisdom a house is built,
  and by understanding it is established;
⁴by knowledge the rooms are filled
  with all precious and pleasant riches.

(23) ⁵Wise warriors are mightier than strong ones,
  and those who have knowledge than those who have strength;
⁶for by wise guidance you can wage your war,
  and in abundance of counselors there is victory.

(24) ⁷Wisdom is too high for fools;
  in the gate they do not open their mouths.
⁸Whoever plans to do evil will be called a mischief-maker.
⁹The devising of folly is sin,
  and the scoffer is an abomination to all.

(25) ¹⁰If you faint in the day of adversity, your strength being small;
¹¹if you hold back from rescuing those taken away to death,
  those who go staggering to the slaughter;
¹²if you say, "Look, we did not know this"—

does not he who weighs the heart perceive it?
   Does not he who keeps watch over your soul know it?
   And will he not repay all according to their deeds?

(26) [13]My child, eat honey, for it is good,
   and the drippings of the honeycomb are sweet to your taste.
[14]Know that wisdom is such to your soul;
   if you find it, you will find a future,
   and your hope will not be cut off.

(27) [15]Do not lie in wait like an outlaw against the home of the righteous;
   do no violence to the place where the righteous live;
[16]for though they fall seven times, they will rise again;
   but the wicked are overthrown by calamity.

(28) [17]Do not rejoice when your enemies fall,
   and do not let your heart be glad when they stumble,
[18]or else Yhwh will see it and be displeased,
   and turn away his anger from them.

(29) [19]Do not fret because of evildoers.
   Do not envy the wicked;
[20]for the evil have no future;
   the lamp of the wicked will go out.

(30) [21]My child, fear Yhwh and the king,
   and do not disobey either of them;
[22]for disaster comes from them suddenly,
   and who knows the ruin that both can bring?

SUGGESTIONS FOR COMPARISON

Proverbs	Amenemope[27]
22:17	1.1–2
22:18–19	1.3–8
22:20	30.1
22:21	Prologue: 5–6
22:22–23	2.1–2
22:24–25	9.1–2
22:26–27	——
22:28; 23:10	6.1–4
22:29	30.9–10
23:1–3	23.1–6

27. A simplified numbering system is adopted here for Amenemope. The text is often cited according to its column and line number, a system that can be accessed in Simpson's own volume or other scholarly publications.

23:4–5	7.1–16
23:6–7	11.1–4
23:8	11.13–14
23:9	21.11–14
23:10–11	6.1–4

DISCUSSION

Two different literary forms are combined in the texts presented in this chapter: proverbs and wisdom instructions. A proverb is "a short pithy saying in common and recognized use; a concise sentence, often metaphorical or alliterative in form, which is held to express some truth ascertained by experience or observation and familiar to all." This definition from the *Oxford English Dictionary* captures a number of key aspects: brevity, wit, orality, cultural familiarity, and reference to the social environment. A wisdom instruction usually contains proverbial sayings but is framed as a speech from a figure of higher stature to a student; often they present themselves as the words of a father (especially a king) to a son.

The tradition of wisdom instruction was both ancient and enduring in Egypt. The earliest exemplars, such as the instructions of Hardedef and Ptahhotep, likely date to the Old Kingdom (late 3rd millennium BCE). The Instruction of Amenemope is relatively late compared to those classical exemplars, but the tradition continued into the second half of the first millennium. Texts such as the Instruction of Ankhsheshonq and Papyrus Insinger attest the genre as late as the Ptolemaic period (332–30 BCE) and are written in demotic, a later form of the Egyptian language.

A common narrative technique in Egyptian wisdom literature is to provide a framing story in which a father imparts wisdom to his son. The social location of each instruction may vary; for example, Ptahhotep was a famed adviser to pharaohs, whereas Amenemope's status appears to have been lower. Although the extant Egyptian instruction texts are written in the name of various figures, in general it is possible to perceive a democratization over time—initially instructions were ascribed to pharaohs and other lofty figures, whereas the later demotic instructions contain wisdom for more common people. Amenemope is generally seen as occupying a middle position in this process.

Another shift over time is the "religionization" of Egyptian wisdom. This took a couple of different forms, including (1) a focus on discerning divine will in contrast to observation of natural phenomena and (2) heightened expressions of piety rather than emphasis on personal flourishing. An example of this is the couplet in Amenemope 2.19–20: "Lift him up, give him your hand, / And leave him (in) the hands of God." The divine nature of Egyptian wisdom manifests itself in various ways, including in references to deities. Interestingly, Maat, the divinized personification of wisdom in Egyptian thought, does not figure prominently in the Instruction of Amenemope. Instead, the common noun *maat*, "wisdom," is mentioned as a "gift of God" in 20.7. Another way to consider the religionization of wisdom is to note certain similarities between the wisdom sayings and the denials of guilt in the "negative confession" of Book of the Dead, Spell 125 (in chap. 22

of this volume)—the good advice for this life was also a key to surviving and succeeding in the afterlife. In each of these cases one can see that "Egyptian ethics were 'practical ethics'—that is, moral values linked to practical matters and expressed in the form of personal, down-to-earth observations and admonitions."[28]

There is no canonical Egyptian list of morals or ethical values, but in the "sheer repetition" of examples, Miriam Lichtheim thought it was possible to identify the principal virtues and vices. She wrote, "The leading virtues were: honesty and truthfulness; justice, kindness, and generosity; temperance and patience; thoughtfulness, diligence, and competence; loyalty and reliability. Vices and crimes were headed by Greed and its breed of Rapacity, Theft, Lying and Deceit. Among the deeds of aggression, Anger, Quarreling, and Calumny stood out. Disobedience, Sloth, and Neglect formed the rear."[29] Most of these virtues and vices are referred to in Amenemope.

Another theological aspect of Amenemope on which a student of the Bible is likely to remark is the repeated references to "god" (in Egyptian, *netjer*), which are left unspecified. This is characteristic of Egyptian wisdom instructions, to the point that some prominent Egyptologists have described such texts as monolatrous or henotheistic.[30] Amenemope is certainly not monotheistic, however. One can see in the same texts numerous references to named divinities; there was certainly no effort to exclude the multiplicity of gods. (As in other instructions, one sees in Amenemope a number of references to solar deities such as Re and the Aten, and here specifically one sees particular emphasis on Thoth.) Furthermore, one notes the controversy that was caused in ancient Egypt by the one real push for monotheism, that of Akhenaten (see chap. 23). Instead, what one sees in these instructions is the effort to make the text relevant to many contexts and people in a polytheistic society. The readers of a wisdom instruction might function in contexts that affirmed the power of many different gods; thus, *netjer* is "a neutral term that will cover any individual deity and hence any particular situation that the pupil, and later the official, might encounter."[31] Nevertheless, since Amenemope has been adopted more directly than most other ancient Near Eastern texts that influenced the authors of the Bible, it behooves the reader to consider whether the nonspecific nature of its terminology for god made it seem more acceptable to the biblical authors.

Proverbs and instruction texts similar to Amenemope are found outside Egypt and Israel, but they are not numerous. Collections of Sumerian proverbs from as early as the

---

28. Nikolaos Lazaridis, "Ethics," in *UCLA Encyclopedia of Egyptology* (ed. Elizabeth Frood and Willeke Wendrich; Los Angeles, 2008), 1. Accessed at http://digital2.library.ucla.edu/viewItem .do?ark=21198/zz000s3mhn.

29. Miriam Lichtheim, "Didactic Literature," in *Ancient Egyptian Literature: History and Forms* (ed. Antonio Loprieno; New York: Brill, 1996), 261–62.

30. For more complete discussion of henotheism (the temporary worship of one god alone) and monolatry (permanent adherence to one god while still acknowledging the existence of others), see chap. 23. For discussion from an Egtypological standpoint, see Erik Hornung, *Conceptions of God in Ancient Egypt: The One and the Many* (trans. J. Baines; Ithaca, NY: Cornell University Press, 1982), 230–50. Similar ideas have been advanced about unspecified references to "god" in Mesopotamian wisdom compositions. For a recent example, see Takoyoshi Oshima, *The Babylonian Theodicy* (SAACT 9; Winona Lake, IN: Eisenbrauns, 2013), xlviii.

31. Hornung, *Conceptions of God*, 57.

mid-third millennium continued to be copied and quoted in Mesopotamia into the first millennium.[32] Like much of Mesopotamian literature, they have been found in the library of Ashurbanipal. Some of these may sound familiar to a reader of Proverbs ("Wealth is far away; poverty is near" [cf. Prov. 14:23]; "To have, and insist on more, is abominable" [cf. Prov. 1:19]), some are inscrutable ("A palace is an ox; let its tail be caught!"), while in other cases it is not clear that the collected sayings are proverbs at all ("My youthful vigor left my loins like a runaway donkey"). Mesopotamian proverbs are more often humorous than those from other cultures and are sometimes phrased as riddles.

The wisdom-instruction genre is not very well attested in Mesopotamia; it appears that other wisdom genres, such as dialogues, disputations, and hymns, predominated. However, a few fragmentary examples have survived; in particular, the opening of the fragmentary "Instructions of Shuruppak" is very similar ("O my son, I offer you instruction, take my instruction," etc.) and shows that the primarily Egyptian genre was not completely unknown in the East. The somewhat longer "Counsels of Wisdom" are also addressed to a son.[33] There is also a fragmentary wisdom instruction found at both Ugarit and Emar, reflecting a knowledge of the genre in the West during the Bronze Age. The tradition is found later in the "Words of Aḥiqar," attested earliest in Aramaic around 500 BCE (the narrative framework of the instructions is discussed as a court tale in chap. 5).

The similarities between Proverbs 22:17–23:11 and Amenemope have attracted special attention; probably no other pair of biblical and ancient Near Eastern texts have as much in common. A number of parallels between Amenemope and Proverbs 22:17–23:11 are listed in the chart above, and parallels can be identified elsewhere in Proverbs. Some further similarities between the two texts are obscured by translations or are perceptible only to those who know the languages. For example, the phrase "keep them in your belly" in Proverbs 22:18 is not idiomatic in Hebrew and appears instead to be a direct adoption of a common Egyptian phrase (see Amenemope 1.5). Similarly, the "hothead" of Proverbs 22:24–25 is an unusual Hebrew phrase, but seems to be an adoption of a common Egyptian one used in the Amenemope parallel (9.1–2).

The fullest text of Amenemope was rediscovered in 1888 but not published until the editions of E. A. Wallis Budge in the 1920s. Since the complete text presented above is from a sixth-century copy, some scholars initially argued that the Egyptian text had been influenced by the biblical proverbs (they were emboldened by the biblical story in 1 Kgs. 10 that Solomon's wisdom attracted dignitaries from the south).[34] However, now that additional early copies of Amenemope have appeared, there is no longer any doubt about its historical priority to Proverbs. The antiquity of the wisdom-instruction tradition

---

32. Bendt Alster, *Proverbs of Ancient Sumer: The World's Earliest Proverb Collections* (Bethesda, MD: CDL Press, 1997); W. G. Lambert, *Babylonian Wisdom Literature* (Oxford: Clarendon, 1960), 222–82.

33. Lambert, *Babylonian Wisdom Literature*, 92–117.

34. For a summary of some of the positions that have been advanced (for example, biblical priority or a Semitic original preceding both texts), see William McKane, *Proverbs: A New Approach* (Philadelphia: Westminster, 1970), 371; or, more recently, Tremper Longman III, *Proverbs* (Grand Rapids: Baker Academic, 2006), 52–54.

within Egyptian culture, which begins more than a thousand years before Proverbs, should have made this the default assumption.

The next question that arises is how the influence functioned. In particular, should one assume that the author of the later text worked from a copy of the earlier text ("direct literary influence")? Or did the later author simply partake of a shared body of "traditions," perhaps transmitted orally in the case of wisdom? To many scholars, it has seemed clear that the level of similarity requires that the author was working with a copy or a translation of Amenemope. The Egyptologist Miriam Lichtheim wrote, "It can hardly be doubted that the author of Proverbs was acquainted with the Egyptian work and borrowed from it" (*COS* 1.115). The fact that Amenemope continued to be copied at least into the middle of the first millennium means that it continued to be a part of the scribal culture throughout the period in which Hebrew proverbs were being compiled.

Other scholars (R. N. Whybray, for example) have been less convinced of a direct literary relationship between the two texts. Notably, Proverbs used only pieces of Amenemope, often the opening lines of a given chapter. Furthermore, it presents the chapters in a different sequence compared to the Egyptian text. This could be attributed to intentional reshaping by a scribe who had a copy of Amenemope, but it also opens the door to other theories. It is possible that the author of Proverbs was transmitting an oral tradition. Or perhaps the author of Proverbs was working from a text that was not exactly like Amenemope; in that case, both might have been based on an original compilation of sayings that both authors adapted in their own ways. (This last theory would be similar to the popular idea of a common source for the New Testament Gospels.)

The opening verses of the book of Proverbs ascribe them to Solomon. Interestingly, in light of the historical priority of the Egyptian texts, 1 Kings 4:30 compares Solomon's wisdom favorably to that of neighboring empires, saying that it "surpassed the wisdom of all the people of the east, and all the wisdom of Egypt." Lichtheim assumed that literary influence from Egyptian wisdom came during the Ramesside period, but it is nearly impossible that such influence could have taken place prior to the Israelite united monarchy and the development of a specifically Israelite scribal culture (see introduction).

Indeed, the question of the provenance of the book of Proverbs is more complicated than it might appear at first glance. In Proverbs 25:1, one reads, "*These, too,* are proverbs of Solomon that the officials of King Hezekiah of Judah copied." This calls attention to the likelihood that Judean scribes were working with Egyptian wisdom traditions in the Neo-Assyrian period.[35] As noted in the introduction, extrabiblical data for the period of the united monarchy are scarce, but there is reason to believe that contacts between Egypt and Israel/Judah grew closer in the eighth century, when pressure from the Neo-Assyrian Empire caused Levantine nations to look southward for military support. Thus, whatever the role of Solomon's court in compiling and producing wisdom texts, there was a later round of such literary production under Hezekiah. Where the biblical data is equivocal, the extrabiblical data thus far suggests focusing on the later period, namely, the late eighth century.

---

35. R. N. Whybray, "The Sage in the Israelite Royal Court," in John G. Gammie and Leo G. Perdue, eds., *The Sage in Israel and the Ancient Near East* (Winona Lake, IN: Eisenbrauns, 1990), 138.

If Proverbs was compiled after Solomon's time, this process would be similar to the collecting of teachings from elsewhere in the ancient world, such as Plato's stories about Socrates or the aforementioned Instruction of Ptahhotep, for which the earliest date usually suggested (6th Dynasty) is long after Ptahhotep's death. Because oral literature was much more developed in the ancient world than most moderns can imagine, to say that these words were written down much later does not necessarily rule out the original figures as sources of at least some of the proverbs. Indeed, it raises the question of what authorship was in the ancient world. In a time when scribes were primarily technicians, and in cultures in which extreme wisdom was often ascribed to kings who did not write down their words, what does it mean to say that these are the "proverbs of Solomon"?

REFLECTION QUESTIONS

1. Choose one or more of the suggested pairs of texts for comparison (above) and describe how the two are similar and different.

2. Do you think that the similarities between the two texts are best ascribed to direct literary influence, a common oral tradition, or something else?

3. Markers in each text reveal what culture it comes from. What are some examples? Assuming the biblical text is later, where can you see the biblical author adapting Egyptian source material?

4. Some scholars (e.g., R. N. Whybray) have argued against dependence of Proverbs on Amenemope based on the fact that the close parallels between the two texts end at Proverbs 23:11, whereas the biblical "thirty sayings" continue until 24:22. Do you accept this argument? If not, what significance would you ascribe to this partial independence of the biblical text?

5. In addition to the example cited (2.19–20), where do you see "religionization" of wisdom in Amenemope? Where do you see a parallel phenomenon in the Proverbs passage? Does one strike you as more "religionized" than the other?

6. What are practical or ethical benefits and risks of the religionization of wisdom?

7. How does the idea of *maat* (or wisdom) as a "gift of God" in Amenemope 20.7 compare with the biblical text's ideas about the origins of wisdom?

8. To whom would the Instruction of Amenemope have been most useful? Where in society do you imagine its author and recipient were located?

9. To whom would the "words of the wise" (Prov. 22:17–24:22) have been most useful? Where in society do you imagine its author and recipient were located?

10. Are the main emphases of each text distinctive from each other? If so, how? Did being wise mean something different in one culture than in the other?

11. The book of Proverbs and Amenemope both make reference to settings in the royal court, but both also endured in circulation after the end of their respective dynasties. What do you think allowed these texts to retain their value and authority?

12. How does it affect your understanding of biblical wisdom to know that these are, in part, "foreign" texts incorporated into the Jewish and Christian canons?

FURTHER READING

Alster, Bendt. *Proverbs of Ancient Sumer: The World's Earliest Proverb Collections.* Bethesda, MD: CDL Press, 1997.

Crenshaw, James L. *Old Testament Wisdom: An Introduction.* Louisville, KY: John Knox Press, 1981. (Esp. "Egyptian and Mesopotamian Wisdom Literature," 212–35.)

Emerton, J. A. "The Teaching of Amenemope and Proverbs XXII 17–XXIV 22: Further Reflections on a Long-standing Problem." *VT* 51 (2001): 431–65.

Fox, Michael V. *Proverbs 10–31.* AB 18B. New Haven, CT: Yale University Press, 2009.

Gammie, John G., and Leo G. Perdue, eds. *The Sage in Israel and the Ancient Near East.* Winona Lake, IN: Eisenbrauns, 1990.

Hornung, Erik. *Conceptions of God in Ancient Egypt: The One and the Many.* Ithaca, NY: Cornell University Press, 1982. (Esp. 33–65.)

Lambert, W. G. *Babylonian Wisdom Literature.* Oxford: Clarendon, 1960.

Perdue, Leo G. *The Sword and the Stylus: An Introduction to Wisdom in the Age of Empires.* Grand Rapids: W. B. Eerdmans Pub. Co., 2008.

Römheld, Diethard. *Wege der Weisheit: Die Lehren Amenemopes und Proverbien 22:17–24:22.* Beihefte zur Zeitschrift für die alttestamentliche Wissenschaft 184. Berlin: Walter de Gruyter, 1989.

Shupak, Nili. "The Instruction of Amenemope and Proverbs 22:17–24:22 from the Perspective of Contemporary Research." Pages 203–20 in *Seeking Out the Wisdom of the Ancients: Essays Offered to Honor Michael V. Fox on the Occasion of His Sixty-Fifth Birthday.* Edited by Ronald L. Troxel, Kelvin G. Friebel, and Dennis R. Magary. Winona Lake, IN: Eisenbrauns, 2005.

Whybray, R. N. *The Book of Proverbs: A Survey of Modern Study.* Leiden: Brill, 1995. (Esp. 78–85.)

21

Responses to Human Suffering

Ludlul bēl nēmeqi *and Job*

JOB 1–2; 16:6–17:16; 38; 40:1–14; 42:1–17

When: Unknown
Where: Jerusalem
Language: Hebrew

LUDLUL BĒL NĒMEQI ("LET ME PRAISE THE LORD OF WISDOM . . .")

What: Cuneiform text reconstructed from more than fifty fragmentary clay tablets
When: Probably late Kassite period (1300–1155 BCE) or Second Dynasty of Isin (1157–1026 BCE)
Where: Likely composed in Babylon. Copies recovered from Babylonia (Babylon, Kish, Sippar) and Assyria (Ashur, Nimrud, Nineveh, Sultantepe)
Language: Akkadian
Translation: Amar Annus and Alan Lenzi[1]

Tablet I

I will praise the lord of wisdom, the cir[cumspect] god,
Angry at night (but) relenting at daybreak.
Marduk, the lord of wisdom, the circumspect god,
Angry at night (but) relenting at daybreak.
5 Whose fury, like a violent storm, is a wasteland,
But whose blowing, like a breeze of the morning hours, is pleasant.
(Who) in his anger is irresistible, his fury a flood,

1. Adapted from Amar Annus and Alan Lenzi, *"Ludlul Bēl Nēmeqi": The Standard Babylonian Poem of the Righteous Sufferer* (SAACT 7; Helsinki: The Neo-Assyrian Text Corpus Project, 2010), 31–44.

(But) his mind turns back, his mood relents.

The brunt of whose hand the heavens cannot bear,

10   (But) whose palm is (so) gentle it rescues the dying.

Marduk, the brunt of whose hand the heavens cannot bear,

(But) whose palm is (so) gentle it rescues the dying.

On account of whose wrath, graves are opened,

(But) then he raises up the fallen from disaster.

15   (When) he frowns, the divine guardian and protective spirit withdraw.

(But when) he takes notice, his god turns back to him whom he had rejected.

His grievous punishment is immediately overbearing,

(But) he (also) shows pity and instantly becomes motherly.

He hastens to treat his beloved (?) kindly,

20   And like a cow with a calf, he is ever attentive.[2]

His beatings are barbed, they pierce the body,

(But) his bandages mo[lli]fy, they revive (the one afflicted by) the
      Namtar-demon.

He speaks and imputes guilt,[3]

(But) on the day of his justice liability and guilt are absolved.

25   He is the one (who) makes (one) acquire the [sh]ivering-demon,

(But) with his incantation he e[xp]els chills and cold tremors.

Who makes slight (?) the [devasta]tion (?) of Adad, the blow of Erra,[4]

(But) who reconciles (one's) enraged god and goddess.

The lord, he sees [eve]rything in the heart of the gods,

30   (But) no on[e among the god]s knows his way.

Marduk, he sees [eve]rything in the heart of the gods,

(But) no god can learn his counsel.

As heavy as is his hand, his heart is merciful.

As murderous as are his weapons, his intention is life-sustaining.

35   Without his consent, who could assuage his striking?

Apart from his intention, who could stay his hand?

I, who ate mud like a fish, will extol his anger.

He quickly bestowed favor, just as he revived the dead.

I will teach the people their plea for favor is near.

40   May his favora[ble] concern carry off their sin.

Fr[om] the day Bel[5] punished me,

And the hero Marduk was angry [wi]th me,

My god rejected me, he disappeared,

My goddess left, she departed from (my) side.

---

2. Lit., "he keeps turning around behind him." Marduk keeps looking behind him at his protégé, who is following, as a cow might look back to check on its calf.

3. Lit., "makes one acquire guilt."

4. Adad is a Mesopotamian storm-god. Erra was associated with the underworld but was also thought of as a destroyer of human civilization by means of disease, war, and fire.

5. "Bel" (meaning "Lord") is another name for Marduk.

45 [The protec]tive spirit of good fortune who (was) at my side [spl]it off,
    My divine guardian became terrified and was seeking out another.
    My dignity was taken, my masculine features obscured,
    My characteristic manner was cut off, it jumped for cover.
    Portents of terror were established for me,
50 I was expelled from my house, (and) I wandered about outside.
    My omens were confused, equivocal every day,
    My oracle was not decided by diviner and dream interpreter.
    What I overheard in the street (portended) evil for me,
    (When) I lay down at night, my dream was terrifying.
55 The king, the flesh of the gods, the sun of his people,
    His heart was angry (with me) and made forgiving me difficult.
    Courtiers were plotting malicious speech against me,
    They gathered themselves, they were inciting calumny.
    If the first (says), "I will make him pour out his life,"
60 The second says, "I will make (him) vacate his post,"
    Likewise the third: "I will seize his office,"
    The fourth says, "I will take over his household,"
    (And) the fifth overturned the opinion of the fifty,
    The sixth and the seventh followed as close as his protective spirit.
65 The band of seven gathered their pack,[6]
    Relentless as a [devil], they were like a demon.
    Their flesh was one, but each had a mouth,
    They [un]leashed (their) rage against me, they were set ablaze like fire.
    They set slander and obstruction in alliance against me,
70 My eloquent speech they hindered as with reins.
    My lips, which prattled constantly: I became as a deaf-mute,
    My resounding cries trailed off into silence.
    My proud head bowed to the ground,
    Terror weakened my stout heart.
75 A lad turned back my burly chest,
    My ever-active arms were continually covered, they clutched each other.
    I, who walked about as a lord, learned to slink,
    I was (once) dignified but became a slave.
    From (my) extensive family I became alienated.
80 (When) I walked through the street, fingers were pointed (at me),
    (When) I entered the palace, eyes would squint (at me).
    My city looked angrily at me as an enemy,
    My country (was) hostile, as if a foreign land.
    My brother became a stranger,
85 My friend became an enemy and a demon.
    In a rage (my) comrade would denounce me,

6. "The seven" is a common grouping of demons in Mesopotamian mythology.

My colleague would defile (his) weapon for spilling blood.
(My) best friend would slander me,
My slave openly cursed me in the assembly,
90 (My) slave girl defamed (me) before the crowd.
(When) an acquaintance saw me, he hid,
My family treated me as a stranger.
A grave lay open for one speaking well of me,
The one uttering slander against me was promoted.
95 (As for) the one speaking calumny against me, a god (was) his helper.
Death hastened for the one who said "mercy!"
The one who did not help: life became his protective spirit.
I did not have one who walks at my side, I did not see one who shows mercy.
They distributed my things to the commoners,
100 The opening of my canals they ruined with silt.
They drove out the work song from my fields,
My city fell silent like a foreign city.
They caused another to take my cultic offices,
And they installed an outsider in my cultic obligations.
105 The day (was) sighing, the night lamentation,
(every) month a daze, the year misery.
Like a dove I would moan all day,
Like a singer I would wail my lamentation.
With perpetual weeping my eyes [. . .]
110 My cheeks burned with tears for a fifth time.
My face was darkened by the apprehension of my heart,
Terror and panic turned my flesh pale.
My guts trembled in perpetual fear,
I [. . .] like a burning fire.
115 (My) prayer became like an ever-burning flame,
My prayer (was) a brawl, like a quarrel.
I sweetened my lips, (but) they were obscure like darkness,
I would speak sharply, (but) my conversation (was) a stumbling block.
Perhaps good fortune will come to me at daybreak,
120 (When) the new moon appears, (perhaps) my sun will shine on me.

Tablet II

One year to the next, the allotted time passed.
I turned about and evil (was everywhere),
My bad luck was increasing, I could not find prosperity.
I called to (my) god, (but) he did not pay attention to me,
5 I implored my goddess, (but) she did not lift her head to me.
The diviner could not determine the situation with divination,

The dream interpreter could not clarify my case with libanomancy.[7]
I prayed to the dream god, but he did not reveal anything to me,
The exorcist with (his) rituals did not release the divine anger (against me).
10   What strange conditions everywhere!
I looked behind (me), harassment (and) trouble!
Like one who had not made libations for (his) god,
And did not invoke (his) goddess with a food offering,
(Who) did not engage in prostration, was not seen bowing down,
15   From (whose) mouth prayers (and) supplications have ceased,
(Who) abandoned the day of (his) god, disregarded the festival,
Became negligent and despised their rites,
(Who) did not teach his people to fear and to pay heed to (the gods),
(Who) did not invoke his god (when) he ate his food,
20   (Who) abandoned his goddess, did not bring a flour-offering,
(Like) the one who raves (?), (and) forgot his lord,
(Who) invoked the solemn oath of his god in vain, (that was who) I was like.
In fact, I was attentive to prayers and supplications,
Prayer was common sense, sacrifice my rule.
25   The day to fear the gods (was) a delight to my heart,
The day of the goddess's procession (was) wealth (and) weal.
The king's prayer: it (was) a pleasure,
And his fanfare (was) truly a delight.
I taught my land to observe the rites of the god,
30   I instructed my people to revere the name of the goddess.
I made (my) praises of the king like a god's,
And taught the masses fear for the palace.
Would that I knew these things were acceptable to the god!
That which is good to oneself (may be) a sacrilege to the god,
35   That which is wretched to one's heart may be good to one's god.
Who (can) learn the plan of the gods in the heavens?
Who understands the counsel of the deep?
Where did humanity learn the divine decree of the gods?
The one who lived by might died in distress.
40   In one moment a person is worried, (then) suddenly becomes exuberant.
In one instant he sings with jubilation,
The next he groans like a mourner.
Their (i.e., human beings') destiny changes in a blink of the eye.
(When) they are hungry, they become as corpses,
45   (When) they are sated, they rival their god.
In the good times they speak of ascending to the heavens,

---

7. Lit., "with incense." Libanomancy is divination via the observation of smoke from burning incense.

(When) they become distressed, they talk of descending to the netherworld.
I have reje[ct]ed these things, I have not learn[ed] their meaning.
[As for] me, the wear[ied one], a storm was dr[iv]ing (me).

50 Debilitating sickness advanced against me,
Evil wind [from] the horizon blew against me.
Headache cropped up from the surface of the netherworld,
A wicked demon/cough came forth from its Apsu.[8]
An un[relen]ting ghost came forth from Ekur,[9]

55 Lamashtu[10] c[ame d]own from the midst of the mountain.
Chills gave way (?) with the inundation,
Debility broke through (?) with the crops.
They (all) joined their forces [and] together approached me,
They surroun[ded (my) hea]d, they covered my skull.

60 [My countena]nce was gloomy, my eyes welled-up (with tears),
They strained my neck muscles, they made (my) neck limp,
They struck my chest, they have beaten (my) breast,
They took hold of my back, they inflicted convulsions (on me),
In my chest they kindled a fire,

65 They roiled my innards, they twisted my guts,
They infected [my lun]gs with coughing (and) phlegm,
They afflicted my limbs with disease,[11] they made my belly feel queasy.
My tall stature they demolished like a wall,
My broad build they leveled like rushes.

70 I was thrown down like a dried fig, I was cast down on (my) face.
A malevolent demon clothed my body (as) a garment,
Sleep covered me like a net.
They were staring, but my eyes could did not see,
They were open, but my ears could not hear.

75 Numbness had seized my entire body,
Paralysis had fallen upon my flesh.
Stiffness had seized my arms;
Impotence had fallen upon my loins;
My feet forgot mobility.

80 [A bl]ow overtook (me); I was choking like one fallen;
The edict of death had covered my face.
(If) my inquirer [took n]otice of me, I would not answer,

---

8. The Apsu was the primordial deep in Mesopotamian mythology, a freshwater ocean that was thought to lay beneath the land and was home to various supernatural powers.

9. "Ekur," which literally means "mountain house," refers to the home of demons in the distant netherworld.

10. Lamashtu was a kind of superdemon, even a demigoddess, who was believed to attack pregnant women and infants.

11. The nature of the disease (Akkadian *li'bu*) is not clear; the term is alternately associated with fevers and skin rashes.

"[Wo]e!" they would cry; I did not possess myself.
A trap was laid on my mouth,
85   And a bolt barred my lips.
My [ga]te was bolted, my watering place sealed up.
(My) hunger was [pro]longed, my thr[oa]t closed up.
If (it was) grain, I would swallow it like stinkweed;
Beer, the sustenance of people, had become displeasing to me.
90   Indeed, (my) sickness had been too long.
Through lack of food, my countenance had chan[ged],
(My) flesh had wasted away, my blood drai[ned].
(My) bones became visible, covering [my sk]in,
(My) tissues were inflamed, affli[cted] with jaundice (?).
95   I took to a sickbed of confinement, going out (was) a hards[hip],
(My) house became my prison.
A fetter for my flesh, my arms were useless,
A shackle to my person, my feet were done for.
My afflictions were severe, the wound gra[ve].
100   The whip that beat me was full of thorns,
A goad covered with thorns pricked me.
All day long a persecutor would pursue [me],
Nor at night did he let me breathe freely for a moment.
Through constant turning my sinews/joints were loosened/parted,
105   My limbs were splayed, (just) hanging apart.
I spent the night in my own filth like an ox,
I wallowed in my own excrement like a sheep.
The exorcist was scared (?) by my symptoms,[12]
And the diviner became confused by my omens.
110   The exorcist did not clarify the nature of my illness,
And the diviner did not give the duration for my sickness.
(My) god did not rush in to help, he did not take my hand,
(My) goddess did not have mercy on me, she did not come to my side.
(My) grave lay open, my funerary goods prepared,
115   Before my death, mourning for me was completed.
My entire land said about me, "How wronged he is!"
(When) my ill-wisher heard, his face lit up,
(When) they informed my nemesis, her mood brightened.
The day grew dark for my entire family,
120   For those among (my) friends their sun darkened.

---

12. Alternatively, "My symptoms removed [lit., stripped away] the exorcist." The verb is sometimes used to describe the removal of an evil or sickness from a person's body. According to the alternative rendering, this line attests an ironic, metaphorical usage of the verb: the sickness removed the one who normally removed sickness.

Tablet III

His hand was (so) heavy I could not bear it.
(My) dread of him was [ove]rwhelming, I [. . .]
His furious [pun]ishment (was) a [. . .] flood,
Whose advance was [aggres]sive (?), it [. . .]
5 [Sev]ere, serious illness does not [. . . my p]erson,
I forgot alertness, [. . .] made me delirious.
[D]ay and night alike I would m[oan],
Dreaming (and) waking moments both aff[licted me].
(There was) a singular man, extraordinary in fo[rm],
10 Magnificent in physique, clothed in new gar[ment]s.
Because (I was just) waking up, his outline la[cke]d form,
He was clad in radiance, clothed in a[w]e.
[He en]tered and stood [over m]e.
(When) [I saw] him, [my] flesh was paralyzed.
15 [He said], "[You]r lord sent [me]."

[*The intervening lines, partly broken, describe how three more figures appeared to Shubshi in his dreams, in order to heal him. He refers in a broken passage to the removal of his "acts of negligence," and to his "sin" and his "iniquity," so it appears that he ends up taking responsibility for his own suffering.*]

[He a]pplied his spell, which drives away ev[il],
[He dr]ove the evil wind back to the horizon.
70 He drove the headache back to the surface of the netherworld,
[He se]nt the wicked demon/cough (back) down to the Apsu.
He returned the unrelenting ghost to Ekur,
He overthrew Lamashtu, he made (her) disap[pear].
He made the current, the waters receive (my) chills,
75 He tore out the root of debility like a plan[t].
Unpleasant sleep, pouring out of slumber,
Like smoke with which the heavens are filled, he sent away.
(My) turning to people with "woe" and "alas,"
He removed like fog, he . . . the netherworld.
80 Constant headache, which was as hea[vy] as a [grind]ing stone,
He withdrew like the dew of ni[gh]t, he dr[ove] (it) away from me.
My blurred eyes were cov[er]ed with the pall of de[ath],
He removed (it) far, far away, he brightened (my) vis[ion].
My ears, which were clogged, stopped up like a deaf man's,
85 He removed their wax, he opened (my) hearing.
My nose, [whose br]eathing was blocked with the onset of fever,
He relieved its illness so that I could breathe [(freely)].
My lips, which were raging (and) took [. . .]
He wiped away their fear, he rel[eased] their bond.
90 My mouth, which was closed up so that speaking (was) diff[icult],

He polished like copper, its dirt [. . .]
My [tee]th, which were clenched, bo[und] together,
He opened their binding and [. . .] their base/jaw (?).
(My) tongue, which was bound (so that) it was [no]t a[ble] to move about,
95   He wiped away its thickness so that [my] speech became clear (?).
(My) throat, which was constricted, blocked as with a lump,
He made well and c[aus]ed it to sound its songs like a reed flute.
My gullet, which was swollen, would not [acc]ept [food],
Its swelling went down, and he opened its stoppage.
. . .

Tablet IV

My [lo]rd [soo]thed me,
My [lo]rd bandaged me.
My [lo]rd removed affliction from me,
My [lo]rd revived me.
5   [From the pi]t he rescued me,
[. . . he g]athered me up.
[From disas]ter he raised me up,
[. . .] out of the Hubur River he pulled me,
[. . .] he clasped my hand.
10   [He who] struck me,
Marduk, restored me.[13]
He struck the hand of my striker,
Marduk made him throw down his weapon.
On the mouth of the lion e[at]ing me,
15   Marduk put a muzzle.

[intervening lines damaged]

Who might it have been but (?) the Lord (who) released me,
That life might be shown to me just in time?
He would not let me go down to the netherworld,
30   (Though) I walked about (?) in the state of a ghost.
Who might it have been but (?) Marduk (who) abandoned me,
So that I became prey for demons,
(And) walked about on high (??) as a corpse (?) be[fore him (?)]?[14]
With the washing of (my) matted hair [. . .]
35   My ablution of renewal, and [. . .]
The affliction which he heard in (my) prayer [. . .]

13. Lit., "raised up my head."
14. These two lines are very difficult to understand; this translation differs from that of Annus and Lenzi.

For prostration and supplication to Esagi[l][15] [. . .]

I, who went down to the grave, entered the Gate of the R[ising Sun] again.

In the Gate of Abundance, abundance [. . .]

40   In the Gate of [. . .] the Divine Guardian my divine guardian appro[ached me].

In the Gate of Well-Being I encou[ntered] well-being.

In the Gate of Life I was granted life.

In the Gate of the Rising Sun I was counted among the living.

In the Gate of Brilliant Astonishment my signs became clear.

45   In the Gate of the Release from Guilt my bond was released.

In the Gate of Praise my mouth inquired.

In the Gate of Release from Sighing my sighing was released.

In the Gate of Pure Water I was sprinkled with water of purification.

In the Gate of Well-being I was seen with Marduk.

50   In the Gate Sprinkled with Luxury I kissed the feet of Zarpanitu.[16]

With prayer and intense supplication I continually entreated before them,

I offered sweet incense before them.

I presented an offering, a gift, heaped up donations,

I sacrificed fattened bulls, slaughtered prime sheep (?),

55   I continually poured out sweet, fine beer (and) [p]ure wine.

[*intervening lines damaged*]

The citizens of Babylon saw how [Marduk] revived (me),

70   The mouths of all of them extolled [his] greatness.

"Who would have said he would see (the light of) his sun (again)?

Who could have imagined he would stroll along his street (again)?

Without Marduk, who would have revived (him) from his deathly condition?

If not for Zarpanitu, which goddess would have given (him) his life?

75   Marduk is able to restore from the grave,

Zarpanitu is experienced at sparing from disaster.

Wherever the earth is established, the heavens stretched out,

(Wherever) the sun shines (and) fire blazes,

(Wherever) water flows (and) wind blows,

80   Those whose lump of clay Aruru pinched off,[17]

[Li]ving beings, (who) walk along,

As many [peo]ple as there are, praise Marduk!"

[*Last 38 lines fragmentary*]

15. The temple of Marduk in Babylon, literally "the lofty house."

16. Zarpanitu was a goddess of childbirth and the wife of Marduk. As the following lines empha-size, restoration of the sufferer to good health is imagined as rebirth or rising from the grave.

17. Aruru was another mother-goddess associated with childbirth. In Mesopotamia the creation of humankind was often envisioned as introducing life into clay by a goddess (cf. Gen. 2:7).

DISCUSSION

For nearly as long as there are records of religion in the ancient Near East, there are accounts of human complaints to the gods about suffering and also dialogues that debate the causes of human suffering. Later chapters discuss prayers of lament by individuals (chap. 24) and on behalf of cities (chap. 25); while the texts in this chapter certainly contain some similar language, they are distinguished from laments by their approach to the topic—a multifaceted and universalizing viewpoint that is closer to wisdom literature than to prayer. They have been recognized as viewing human suffering from a wider perspective.

The earliest of these reflections on human suffering are relatively fragmentary, such as the Old Babylonian "Dialogue between a Man and His God," in which "a young man" implores his god with prayer and groaning, saying that he has "debated with" himself, wondering whether he has done something wrong, but denying it in the next breath. He suffers from both physical ills and social ostracism. In the end, the god heals him, saying, "Let not your heart be despondent." He sends the man on his way with an exhortation to "Feed the hungry (and) water the thirsty," reassuring him that "the gate of life and well-being is open to you" (COS 1.151). A similar Akkadian text (RS 25.460), which names Marduk as the oppressing/saving deity and is thus akin to a compact version of *Ludlul bēl nēmeqi*, was discovered at Late Bronze Age Ugarit.

Still another Akkadian text, usually called the Babylonian Theodicy,[18] supplies a close analogue for the dialogue between Job and his friends. In the Babylonian Theodicy, however, there is only one friend, and no narrative introduction has survived, although the friend's opening comments suggest that more narrative may have been present in the text's original (unbroken) form. A couple of exchanges give the flavor of this composition, which likely dates to the eleventh century BCE and has survived in nine copies from the first millennium:

Sufferer: I am without recourse, heartache has come upon me.
I was the youngest child when fate claimed (my) father,
My mother who bore me departed to the land of no return,
My father and mother left me, and with no one my guardian!

Friend: Considerate friend, what you tell is a sorrowful tale,
My dear friend, you have let your mind harbor ill.
You make your estimable discretion feeble-minded,
You alter your bright expression to a scowl.
Of course our fathers pay passage to go death's way,
I too will cross the river of the dead,
as is commanded from of old.

. . . .

Sufferer: Those who seek not after a god can go the road of favor,
Those who pray to a goddess have grown poor and destitute.
Indeed, in my youth I tried to find out the will of (my) god,
With prayer and supplication I besought my goddess.

18. See below for a definition and discussion of the term "theodicy."

> I bore a yoke of profitless servitude:
> (My) god decreed (for me) poverty instead of wealth.
> A cripple rises above me, a fool is ahead of me,
> Rogues are in the ascendant, I am demoted.

Friend: O just, knowledgeable one, your logic is perverse,
> You have cast off justice, you have scorned divine design.
> In your emotional state you have an urge to disregard
>   divine ordinances,
> . . . .
> The strategy of a god is [as remote as] innermost heaven,
> The command of a goddess cannot be dr[awn out].[19]

The main topic of the dialogue has been summarized as "the importance of worshiping the gods despite occasional sentiments of injustice."[20] The friend's efforts to shame the sufferer with charges of heresy and blasphemy are most reminiscent of Job (they are otherwise unusual among ANE wisdom compositions). Just like Job's friends, he presents himself as one who speaks for orthodoxy. For example, in Job 15:2–6, Eliphaz says,

> Should the wise answer with windy knowledge, and fill themselves with the east wind?
> Should they argue in unprofitable talk, or in words with which they can do no good?
> But you are doing away with the fear of God, and hindering meditation before God.
> For your iniquity teaches your mouth, and you choose the tongue of the crafty.
> Your own mouth condemns you, and not I; your own lips testify against you.

Despite these similarities, the Babylonian Theodicy is quite different from Job in that it has no particular narrative shape or progression. Furthermore, it makes no effort, not even a superficial one, to settle the issues that it raises, and the speaker closes the composition still in distress and misfortune.

Instead, it is the composition titled *Ludlul bēl nēmeqi* that arguably offers the most striking comparison with the biblical book of Job; it has been termed "The Babylonian Job" or a "Poem of the Righteous Sufferer." The reasons that *Ludlul* and Job are so often compared are not difficult to identify: in both texts, a man of high social standing is suddenly afflicted. Their misfortunes are diverse: physical ailments, economic losses, and a collapse of their social standing. Such a combination of seemingly unrelated types of suffering can also be seen in prayers of lament (chap. 24). In each case, the suffering is compounded by the silence of the god (*Ludlul* II.4–9; Job 30:20), a theme that also finds expression in the Bible in, e.g., 1 Samuel 28:6 and Isaiah 8:17. Even the rhetoric that the sufferers use is similar: to take only one example, both liken their suffering to the onset of death (*Ludlul* II.114–15; Job 17:1, 13–16). Eventually, however, each man is restored.

The historical context and authorship of these two texts sheds little light on them. The speaker in *Ludlul* is identified as Shubshi-meshre-shakkan, a relatively uncommon name, but one that is attested for a high-ranking official during the reign of the Kassite

---

19. Translation by Benjamin R. Foster, *COS* 1.154.

20. Takoyoshi Oshima, *The Babylonian Theodicy* (SAACT 9; Winona Lake, IN: Eisenbrauns, 2013), xvii.

Babylonian king Nazimurutash (r. ca. 1307–1282).[21] This is only to say that the poem may have become attached to a real figure, not that he is necessarily its author. The perfect storm of comprehensive suffering that overwhelms Shubshi is certainly best identified as a literary archetype rather than the experience of any historical individual. Still, *Ludlul* can be plausibly connected to at least a general historical horizon.

The book of Job's relationship to historical context is even more mysterious. It makes no reference to historical events and comprises some of the most difficult Hebrew in the Bible; even the identity of Job's "land of Uz" is uncertain. The book seems determined to remove itself from the familiar guideposts of time and space, as if to focus the reader on the theological and philosophical issues that it raises. Furthermore, its shifts in literary form and genre (notably from prose to poetry and then back) may well indicate that it is a composite work, in which some sections predated others. In short, it bristles with complexities that make it one of the most difficult books to place in a historical context. Although Job treats enduring theological themes and at least nods to certain archaic linguistic forms, most interpreters place the finished composition in the exilic or postexilic period. The problems of suffering and the justice of God were sharpened for Hebrew authors in a new way in the wake of Jerusalem's fall to the Babylonians in 586, as is so evident elsewhere in the Bible. Although the book of Job focuses on individual rather than corporate suffering, it is not hard to imagine its significance for an exilic community.

Because of the similarities between Job and *Ludlul*, it was initially assumed that one had directly influenced the other. If that were the case, the influence could only have derived from the Akkadian text, since it was composed when the Hebrew language did not yet exist. In 1906, the eminent Semitist Morris Jastrow made this quite explicit:

> It is difficult to resist the impression that [*Ludlul*] may have suggested to the Hebrew philosopher to take up the old story of the pious sufferer, as it had developed among the Hebrews in post-exilic days, and to furnish, in contrast to the Babylonian treatment, a Jewish discussion of the eternal problem of human suffering—precisely as in the creation and deluge myths we have the Jewish treatment of themes the material for which was furnished by Babylonian tradition.[22]

Jastrow's article generated immediate disagreement, on the basis that the two texts had too many differences to be related even indirectly.[23] And indeed, as more similar texts have come to light—not only from Mesopotamia but from Egypt as well—it has become increasingly clear that such theological ideas and literary forms were in fact widely dispersed throughout the ancient world.[24]

---

21. Two of the other names in the poem, Laluralimma and Ur-Nintinugga, are also of Kassite origin. For further discussion, see Annus and Lenzi, *"Ludlul Bēl Nēmeqi,"* xvi–xix, and Karel van der Toorn, "Theodicy in Akkadian Literature," in *Theodicy in the World of the Bible* (ed. Antti Laato and J. C. De Moor; Leiden: Brill, 2003), 76–77.

22. Morris Jastrow, "A Babylonian Parallel to the Story of Job," *JBL* 25 (1906): 190.

23. E.g., Simon Landersdorfer, *Eine babylonische Quelle für das Buch Job? Eine literar-geschichtliche Studie* (St. Louis: Herder, 1911).

24. The sort of wisdom texts cast as dialogue are by no means limited to Mesopotamia and Israel; one could also fruitfully compare Egyptian dialogues such as the "Dispute of a Man with His Ba." Indeed, the tone of certain "pessimistic" Egyptian wisdom texts (which despair of the justice and

More recently, the matter has been reframed so scholars speak of the book of Job's participation in a set of cultural forms and traditions, rather than positing literary dependence of one text on another. There has been a salutary tendency to consider Job as taking part in the wider world of ancient Near Eastern wisdom. A particularly strong statement comes from Leo G. Perdue: "The extraordinary parallels between the themes, language, and forms of Babylonian wisdom and those of the Joban poetry . . . would derive only from a direct knowledge of Babylonian wisdom resources and perhaps even an acquaintance with their sages and teachers."[25] The crucial difference between this formulation of the matter and Jastrow's is that Perdue makes no claim that the author of Job ever read *Ludlul* itself, nor that he was directly influenced by *Ludlul*, only that the kinds of questions and forms that are found in Mesopotamian wisdom would have shaped the Joban author's thinking.

There is no doubting the utility of comparing the two texts, but a close reading can end up raising the question of whether the two texts are really *about* the same thing *at all*, despite their similar narrative arcs. In the first place, Job is described at the very outset of his story as "blameless and upright," whereas the status of *Ludlul's* Shubshi-meshre-shakkan before Marduk is far less clear. The key lines are I.23–24: "He speaks and imputes guilt;[26] but on the day of his justice, liability and guilt are absolved." He acknowledges that he has been found guilty, but in these lines he suggests that it is Marduk's own decision to make him guilty. Shubshi refers to suffering defamation and "calumny" (I.90, 95), which suggest an innocent man who has been wronged, but the reader has only his own word for it, not that of an apparently omniscient narrator. Later, he asserts that he has been "attentive to prayers and supplications," offering the right sacrifices and even teaching the masses. In the end, however, he has to admit that he has no idea if he has done right in the eyes of the gods: "Would that I knew these things were acceptable to the god!" (II.23, 33, cf. 24–32). Job is also described as religiously fastidious (1.5, 8), but he is much more certain of his own righteousness than Shubshi; instead, it is Bildad (8:9), Elihu (36:26), and God who call him ignorant; only belatedly does Job seem to acquiesce (42:1–3).

The two stories also differ structurally in that *Ludlul* has no narrative frame to give a perspective outside that of the speaker, nor are there any friends to lend their opinions.[27]

---

goodness of human life) is very similar to Job; other Egyptian texts, including most famously "The Eloquent Peasant," have verse accounts framed in narrative prose, just as Job does. In the final accounting, no single Egyptian text offers as close a comparison as *Ludlul*, but they do make us aware that many of the literary features of Job were widespread, so that we should not assume too direct a relationship between any two specific texts.

25. Leo G. Perdue, "Exilic Wisdom and the Babylonian Sapiential Tradition: The Book of Job," in *Wisdom Literature: A Theological History* (Louisville, KY: Westminster John Knox Press, 2007), 84; cf. 88.

26. More literally, "causes one to acquire guilt."

27. Although the claims here are modest, it is somewhat risky to draw conclusions about the structure of *Ludlul* because of its fragmentary nature. Quite recently, T. Oshima has argued that the poem included five tablets and many more lines than most scholars have assumed ("How Many Tablets Did Ludlul Bēl Nēmeqi Consist Of?" *Nouvelles assyriologiques breves et utilitaires* [2012]: 28–30).

In sum, *Ludlul* is monovocal, whereas Job is polyphonic.[28] Another voice present in Job that is absent from *Ludlul* is that of the god who is addressed: Yhwh speaks for himself, whereas Marduk does not. (Although the ending is broken, there is nothing to suggest that Marduk had a speaking part in *Ludlul*.) Furthermore, Yhwh's spoken response is strikingly different from Marduk's unspoken response, such that one could draw conclusions about the personalities of the deities and the way they were seen to relate to their worshipers.

These differences are among the hints that these texts are more difficult to classify than has sometimes been acknowledged. They are often considered under the category of theodicy. The *Oxford English Dictionary* defines theodicy as "a vindication of the divine attributes, esp. justice and holiness, in respect to the existence of evil." Theodicy intends, as Milton said of his *Paradise Lost*, to "justify the ways of God to men."

Is that what these texts do? *Ludlul* certainly extols Marduk as a god who saves even from death. It has commonly been identified as part of a larger effort in the Kassite period to exalt Marduk, much like *Enuma Elish*, and some scholars rightly point out its affinities with the individual thanksgiving psalms in the Bible. But even in praising Marduk, it casts him in a somewhat equivocal light. As we have seen, the same text also identifies Marduk as the one who put Shubshi in his position in the first place, and there is no reason given for the deity's initial wrath; there is something arbitrary about it all. If this were a justification of Shubshi's suffering or Marduk's wrath, it would not be a very effective or helpful one.

In addition to *Ludlul*'s "doxological purpose," there are still other ways to look at its purpose and function. The account of Shubshi's restoration in Tablet III is an almost perfect mirror image of his physical affliction in Tablet II, down to some of the same phrases. Thus the catalog of ailments and their treatments could have allowed it to function as a kind of magico-medical text, a reference work to be used by religious experts who tended to ailing people who could afford their services. These same passages are clearly similar to, and in some cases drawn directly from, Mesopotamian prayers and incantations. Like those texts, it vacillates between confessions of guilt and protests of innocence.

Similarly, it is not clear to everyone that the book of Job vindicates Yhwh. It suggests that God allows Job to suffer due to a combination of pride and caprice: Satan claims that Job is righteous only because he has never suffered, and God takes the bet. This hardly seems like a justification of God. Indeed, it is Job's friends who are most interested in defending and justifying God, and in the end God dismisses them: "My wrath is kindled against you . . . for you have not spoken of me what is right" (Job 42:7). Nor is God any more willing to give an account of himself, responding instead with a withering barrage of questions ("Where were you when I laid the foundation of the earth?" [Job 38:4] etc.) intended to establish that Job has no right question God. This brief summary risks taking lightly the long and rich history of attempts to determine the book's meaning,[29] but it may

---

28. Carol A. Newsom, *The Book of Job: A Contest of Moral Imaginations* (Oxford: Oxford University Press, 2003), 3–31.

29. In particular, we may note that we have not addressed the speeches of Elihu or the claim of some interpreters that Yhwh's speeches function "to declare his mastery in and over creation, and so to renew his ancient pledge and in this way reawaken faith" (E. W. Nicholson, "The Limits

simply not offer the answers that many readers seek. In sum, if either Marduk or Yhwh is vindicated, it is not by some intellectual breakthrough, but by the practical restoration that each offers in the end.

F. Rachel Magdalene, noting the clear similarities between Job and the aforementioned Mesopotamian incantations, goes a step further by connecting Job to Babylonian trial law, suggesting that Job and Yhwh end up both having to answer charges brought by Satan.[30] While clearly the book in its complete form far exceeds any ancient legal form, this perspective has the potentially fruitful effect of presenting the speeches in the book as *testimonies* to be assessed by the reader, who is put in the position of a juror. This is a reflection of the way the book does indeed function: readers of Job are left, at the end of the book, to decide what it all means. The variety of possible conclusions is demonstrated by the book's history of interpretation.

Viewed in historical perspective, the tensions that persist beyond the end of the book of Job are probably anything but accidental. Who in the ancient Near East was any more qualified to cry out to their God than the desolated Judeans in Babylon, whose city was in ruins and whose whole culture was on the brink of annihilation? Job's theological depth and complexity are likely a direct result of the exilic experience—not only in that suffering led to more impassioned questioning and a refusal to embrace easy answers, but also in that the exposure to Babylonian culture brought the Judean thinkers into more direct conversation with a whole range of other people's ideas about the gods and their ways.

REFLECTION QUESTIONS

1. What information does the reader get from the framing narrative in Job that is missing from *Ludlul*? What effect does the addition of this information have on the way Job's story comes across?

2. What is the effect of adding conversation partners to answer Job's speeches, as compared with *Ludlul*, where Shubshi-meshre-shakkan is the only major speaker?

3. How is Shubshi-meshre-shakkan restored? How is Job restored? What does the contrast between these two restorations lead you to conclude about the purpose of each text?

4. Do you consider God's speeches at the end of the book of Job to be an adequate resolution to the issues the book raises? What about God's "restoration" of Job's family and property? Why or why not?

5. Jastrow wrote that "Job is of an infinitely higher order" than *Ludlul* in both intellectual and literary terms. Do you agree or disagree, and why?

6. How do the endings of *Ludlul* and Job compare in mood and message?

---

of Theodicy as a Theme of the Book of Job," in *Wisdom in Ancient Israel: Essays in Honour of J. A. Emerton* [ed. John Day, Robert P. Gordon, and H. G. M. Williamson; Cambridge: Cambridge University Press, 1995], 82). For an analysis of the Elihu and Yhwh speeches and an argument that they do not offer any final word, see Newsom, *Book of Job*, 200–258.

30. F. Rachel Magdalene, *On the Scales of Righteousness: Neo-Babylonian Trial Law and the Book of Job* (Providence, RI: Brown Judaic Studies, 2007).

7. To what text(s) in the Bible could you compare the closing (extant) lines of *Ludlul*?

8. Based on these two texts, how would you compare the responses of Marduk and Yhwh to suffering? How are their personalities described? How do they relate to human beings?

FURTHER READING

Annus, Amar, and Alan Lenzi. *Ludlul bēl nēmeqi: The Standard Babylonian Poem of the Righteous Sufferer*. Helsinki: Neo-Assyrian Text Corpus Project, 2010.

Jastrow, Morris. "A Babylonian Parallel to the Story of Job." *JBL* 25 (1906): 135–91.

Lambert, W. G. *Babylonian Wisdom Literature*. Oxford: Clarendon, 1960.

Landersdorfer, Simon. *Eine babylonische Quelle für das Buch Job? Eine literar-geschichtliche Studie*. St. Louis: Herder, 1911.

Lenzi, Alan. "The Curious Case of Failed Revelation in *Ludlul Bēl Nēmeqi*: A New Suggestion for the Poem's Scholarly Purpose." In *Mediating between Heaven and Earth: Communication with the Divine in the Ancient Near East*. Edited by C. L. Crouch, J. Stökl, and A. Zernecke. Library of the Hebrew Bible/Old Testament Studies. London: T & T Clark, 2012.

Magdalene, F. Rachel. *On the Scales of Righteousness: Neo-Babylonian Trial Law and the Book of Job*. Providence, RI: Brown Judaic Studies, 2007.

Moran, William L. "The Babylonian Job." Pages 182–200 in *The Most Magic Word: Essays on Babylonian and Biblical Literature*. Edited by Ronald S. Hendel. Washington, DC: Catholic Biblical Association of America, 2002.

Newsom, Carol A. *The Book of Job: A Contest of Moral Imaginations*. Oxford: Oxford University Press, 2003.

Nicholson, E. W. "The Limits of Theodicy as a Theme of the Book of Job." Pages 71–82 in *Wisdom in Ancient Israel: Essays in Honour of J. A. Emerton*. Edited by John Day, Robert P. Gordon, and H. G. M. Williamson. Cambridge: Cambridge University Press, 1995.

Oshima, Takayoshi. *Babylonian Poems of Pious Sufferers: Ludlul Bel Nemeqi and the Babylonian Theodicy*. Orientalische Religionen in der Antike. Tübingen: Mohr Siebeck, 2014.

Perdue, Leo G. "Exilic Wisdom and the Babylonian Sapiential Tradition: The Book of Job." Pages 77–135 in *Wisdom Literature: A Theological History*. Louisville, KY: Westminster John Knox Press, 2007.

Toorn, Karel van der. "Theodicy in Akkadian Literature." Pages 57–89 in *Theodicy in the World of the Bible*. Edited by Antti Laato and J. C. De Moor. Leiden: Brill, 2003.

22

Prayers Regarding Wrongdoing

Prayers from Mesopotamia, Egypt, and the Psalms

Prayers Confessing Wrongdoing

PSALM 51

When: Unknown
Where: Jerusalem
Language: Hebrew

PRAYERS "FOR APPEASING THE HEART OF AN ANGRY GOD" (DINGIR.ŠÀ.DIB.BA INCANTATIONS)

What: Cuneiform text reconstructed from multiple clay tablets
When: Seventh–sixth centuries BCE
Where: Nineveh, Ashur, Susa, and Babylon
Language: Akkadian
Translation: Adapted from W. G. Lambert[1]

> Ea, Shamash, and Marduk,[2] what are my iniquities?
> A bane has confronted me, evil has taken control of me.
> My father begat me, my mother bore me.
> They strove and like a snake I [. . .]
> 5   I came forth from the darkness and saw you, O Shamash.

---

1. W. G. Lambert, "DINGIR.ŠÀ.DIB.BA Incantations," *JNES* 33 (1974): 267–322. A new translation of part of this text, with commentary, can be found in *Akkadian Prayers and Hymns: A Reader* (ed. Alan Lenzi; Society of Biblical Literature Ancient Near East Monographs 3; Atlanta: SBL, 2011).

2. Ea was god of the subterranean freshwater ocean, Apsu, and was also a determiner of destinies. Shamash was a sun deity and oversaw justice. Marduk was the city deity of Babylon and (in the Babylonians' view) head of the Mesopotamian pantheon.

An evil wind has overturned my [. . .]s,
A mighty storm has bowed my head,
Like a bird my pinions have been cut off,
I have shed my wings and am unable to fly.
10   Palsy has seized my arms,
Impotence has fallen on my knees.
I moan like a dove night and day,
I am inflamed, weeping bitterly,
Tears flow from my eyes.
15   Shamash, there is peace in your presence:
Release and remove the iniquities of my father and mother.
Get out, curse! Drive it out, O Ea, king of the Apsu,[3]
[And] Asalluhi, lord of exorcism.[4]
May my guilt be distant, 3,600 leagues away,
20   May the river receive it from me and take it down to its depths.
Ea, Shamash, and Marduk, help me,
That I may be clean in your presence, pure before you.

My god, I did not know how severe your punishment is.
I frivolously took a solemn oath in your name,[5]
25   I profaned your decrees, I went too far,
I [. . .] your mission in trouble,
I transgressed your way much,
I did not know, much [. . .]
My iniquities are many: I know not what I did.
30   My god, expunge, release, suppress the anger of your heart,
Disregard my transgressions, receive my prayers,
Turn my sins into virtues.
Your hand is terrible, I have experienced your punishment.
Let him who reverences his god and goddess learn from my example.
35   My god, be reconciled; my goddess, relent.
Turn your faces to the petition manifest in my raised hands.
May your fierce hearts rest,
May your reins be appeased, grant me reconciliation
That I may sing your praises without forgetting to the widespread people.

---

40   My god, my lord, who created my "name,"[6]
Who guards my life, who brings my progeny into existence,
My fierce god, may your heart rest,

---

3. See previous note.
4. A god of magical knowledge associated with Ea. In Standard Babylonian texts like this one, this name can be used for Marduk as well; Marduk effectively absorbed Asalluhi's persona.
5. See Exod. 20:7; Lev. 19:12; and the Votive Stela of Neferabu with Hymn to Ptah, line 21 (below).
6. Probably in the sense of "reputation."

My angry goddess, be reconciled to me.

Who knows, my god, your abode?
45   I never saw your holy station, your chamber.
I am constantly in grief; my god, where are you?
Avert the anger you have had for me,
Turn your face to the holy divine meal of fat and oil
That your lips may receive good things. Command that I may prosper,
50   Command my health with your holy mouth.
Remove me from evil that I may be saved with you.
Decree for me a destiny of health,
Lengthen my days, grant me health.

It is an incantation for appeasing the wrath of a god.

55   My god, holy one, creator of all peoples are you.
I am feeble, my fear is much.
May the earth, which received (it), draw my fear to the Apsu,
May turbulent (waters) receive my fears,
May [smooth] (waters) receive (them) from me,
60   May [well ordered] (waters) permanently change places with me.
[May it draw] the iniquity of the irreverent [(and take it)] before you.
[I] have bowed beneath [you] for your reconciliation,
[May I succeed] and prosper [that I may sing] your praises.

It is an incantation for appeasing the wrath of a god.

[65–70: Ritual section]

. . .
My god, great one, who grants life,
110   Who gives judgments, whose command is not altered,
[. . .] you, my god, I have stood before you, I have sought you, my god, [I have
bowed] beneath you.
Accept my prayers, release my bond.
Release my curses, tear out the [. . .] of my evil, drive away my trouble.
Drive out from my body illness from known and unknown iniquity,
115   The iniquity of my father, my grandfather, my mother, [my] grandmother,
The iniquity of my elder brother and elder sister,
The iniquity of clan, kith and kin,
Which has come upon me because of the raging of the wrath of my god and
goddess.
Now I burn their images before your great divinity.
120   Release my bond, grant me reconciliation.

In respect of offence, iniquity, transgression and sin
I have offended against my god, sinned against my goddess, have committed
[All] my iniquities, all my sins, all my transgressions.

I promised and then reneged; I gave my word but then did not pay.
125   I did wrong, I spoke improper things,
      I repeated [what should not be uttered], improper things were on my lips.
      In innocence I went too far.
      [. . .] my god, forgive.
      May [my transgressions] be released, [turn] my sins into virtues.
130   [. . .] you determine.
      [. . .] who sinned, save completely.
      Who is there who has not sinned against his god?
      Who (is there) that has kept the commandment forever?
      All of mankind who exist are sinful.
135   I, your slave, have committed every sin.
      I stood at your service, but [. . .] falsehood,
          I spoke lies, I pardoned my own sins,
      I spoke improper things, you know them all.
      I committed offence against the god who created me,
140   I did an abomination, ever doing evil.
      I coveted your abundant property,
      I desired your precious silver.
      I raised my hand and desecrated what should not be so treated.
      In a state of impurity I entered the temple.
145   Constantly I committed a terrible abomination against you,
      I transgressed your rules in what was displeasing to you.
      In the fury of my heart I cursed your divinity,
      I have continually committed iniquities, known and unknown.
      I went the full length of my wishes, I committed sacrilege.
150   Enough, my god! Let your heart rest.
      May the goddess who was angry fully subside.
      Release the pent-up wrath of your heart,
      May your inner being[7] by which I swore be reconciled with me.
      Though my iniquities be many, release my bond,
155   Though my transgressions be seven, let your heart rest,
      Though my sins be many, show great kindness and cleanse [me].
      [My god], I am exhausted, take my hand,
      [. . . on] the ground, support [my] head.
      [. . .] my lord, save with my life,
160   [Drive from] my body grief and distress . . .
161–171 [missing or fragmentary]
      [. . .] which I enter, let me bear life.
      [. . .] That the day may rejoice [for] the shepherd of the peoples,
      [That I may] sing of you and praise your divinity,
175   That I may sing your praises [to] the numerous [peoples].

---

7. Akkadian *qiribki*.

VOTIVE STELA OF NEFERABU WITH HYMN TO MERTSEGER

What: Hieroglyphic inscription on rectangular limestone slab, 20 cm x 54 cm
When: Nineteenth Dynasty (ca. 1295–1186 BCE)
Where: Deir el-Medina
Language: Egyptian
Translation: Miriam Lichtheim, *AEL*, II.107–9

Giving praise to the Peak of the West,[8]
Kissing the ground to her *ka*.[9]
I give praise, hear (my) call,
I was a truthful man on earth!
5[10] Made by the servant in the Place of Truth,[11] Neferabu, justified.

(I was) an ignorant man and foolish,
Who knew not good from evil;
I did the transgression against the Peak,
And she taught a lesson to me.
10 I was in her hand by night as by day,
I sat on bricks like the woman in labor,
I called to the wind, it came not to me,
I libated to the Peak of the West, great of strength,
And to every god and goddess.

15 Behold, I will say to the great and small,
Who are in the troop:
Beware of the Peak!
For there is a lion within her!
The Peak strikes with the stroke of a savage lion;[12]
20 She is after him who offends her!

I called upon my Mistress,
I found her coming to me as sweet breeze;
She was merciful to me,
Having made me see her hand.
25 She returned to me appeased,
She made my malady forgotten;
For the Peak of the West is appeased,
If one calls upon her.

8. That is, Mertseger, a guardian goddess of the Theban necropolis who was viewed as dwelling in, or being identical with, a mountain peak of the western desert.
9. The *ka* is an aspect of the Egyptian soul.
10. Line numbers are for reference purposes only and do not correspond to the original text.
11. In the Theban necropolis.
12. Note that the God of Israel is often portrayed as a lion, esp. in the biblical prophetic books, e.g., Isa. 31:4; 38:13.

So says Neferabu, justified.

30 He says:
Behold, let hear every ear,
That lives upon earth:
Beware the Peak of the West!

VOTIVE STELA OF NEFERABU WITH HYMN TO PTAH

What: Hieroglyphic inscription on a round-topped limestone stela, 39 cm × 28 cm
When: Nineteenth Dynasty (ca. 1295–1186 BCE)
Where: Deir el-Medina
Language: Egyptian
Translation: Miriam Lichtheim, *AEL*, II.109–10

(Ptah is depicted seated, next to the text: "Ptah, Lord of maat, *King of the Two Lands, the fair-faced on his sacred seat." Beneath him is the kneeling figure of Neferabu.)*

Praisegiving to Ptah,[13] Lord of *maat*,[14]
King of the Two Lands,[15]
Fair of face on his great seat,
The One God among the Ennead,[16]
5[17] Beloved as King of the Two Lands.
May he give life, prosperity, health,
Alertness, favors, and affection,
And that my eyes may see Amun[18] every day,
As is done for a righteous man,
10 Who has set Amun in his heart!
So says the servant in the Place-of-Truth, Neferabu, justified.

(Reverse)

Beginning of the recital of the might of Ptah, South-of-his-Wall,[19]
by the servant in the Place of Truth[20] on the West of Thebes, Neferabu,
    justified.
He says:

13. Ptah is a complex deity, associated with craftsmanship, and therefore also with creation. He is portrayed anthropomorphically.

14. *Maat* is an Egyptian term for justice. It is sometimes personified as a goddess.

15. Upper and Lower Egypt.

16. The Ennead (from the Greek *ennea*, "nine") was a group of nine primary Egyptian deities. To call a deity "One God" was a term of honor, suggesting henotheistic worship of that god as primary.

17. Line numbers are for reference purposes only and do not correspond to the original text.

18. Amun was a high god and a creator god in Egypt; interestingly, in light of this phrase, he was characterized by hiddenness.

19. This epithet seems to have referred to the position of a shrine within Ptah's temple at Memphis.

20. In the Theban necropolis.

15   I am a man who swore falsely by Ptah, Lord of *maat*,
      And he made me see darkness by day.
      I will declare his might to the fool and the wise,
      To the small and great:
      Beware of Ptah, Lord of *maat*!
20   Behold, he does not overlook anyone's deed!
      Refrain from uttering Ptah's name falsely,
      Lo, he who utters it falsely, he falls!
      He caused me to be as the dogs of the street,
      Since I am in his hand;
25   He made men and gods observe me,
      Since I am a man who has sinned against his Lord.
      Righteous was Ptah, Lord of *maat*, toward me,
      When he taught a lesson to me!
      Be merciful to me, look on me in mercy!
30   So says the servant in the Place-of-Truth on the West of Thebes,
      Neferabu, justified before the great god.

SUGGESTIONS FOR COMPARISON

Psalm 51	*DINGIR.ŠÀ.DIB.BA*	*Hymn to Mertseger*	*Hymn to Ptah*
vv. 1–2	lines 30–32	line 23	line 29
vv. 3–4	lines 23–29	lines 6–8	lines 26–28
v. 5	lines 4–6		
vv. 9–10	lines 16, 31–32, 114–17	lines 24–26	
vv. 13–15	lines 39, 172–75	lines 30–33	lines 17–18

DISCUSSION

Patrick Miller observed that "when Israel began to pray to the Lord, it did so in the midst of peoples whose arms had long been raised and whose heads has been bowed to the gods that directed their lives and delivered them from danger."[21] Many aspects of the prayer traditions found in the Psalms had already taken shape in the ancient Near East centuries before Israel existed.

When it comes to individual prayers of supplication, Mesopotamia provides a particularly extensive body of texts for comparison. Prayers in forms similar to those presented here go back to the third millennium BCE. Some of the earliest Mesopotamian prayer tablets were so-called letter-prayers; these were composed as letters to a god and then placed in the god's sanctuary as if they were being delivered to a divine recipient. Other

---

21. Patrick D. Miller, *They Cried to the Lord: The Form and Theology of Biblical Prayer* (Minneapolis: Fortress Press, 1994), 3.

early prayers for wealthy supplicants were inscribed on the bases of statues of the patron in a posture of prayer, which were also placed in the temple to represent the person as continually praying to the god.

As the tradition developed, the "prayers for appeasing the heart of an angry god" (often called by an abbreviated Sumerian title, DINGIR.ŠÀ.DIB.BA[22]) were only one among a number of types of Mesopotamian incantation series: Some are very similar to these, while others have more formal addresses including lengthy praises to the gods. Still others include more elaborate ritual actions (such as burning items to dispel the evil that was thought to be causing the supplicant's suffering) or are aimed at specific problems, such as headaches or male impotence.

The "prayers for appeasing the heart of an angry god" presented above are versions from relatively late collections. Much as the psalms were composed for specific occasions and only later collected into the Psalter as we know it, the DINGIR.ŠÀ.DIB.BA prayers also had a long history of production and recompilation, and they are preserved both individually and as part of larger ritual complexes, which may include instructions for ritual actions. Some of these were specifically used in kingly rituals in Mesopotamia, as the royal psalms may have been in Israel. The text presented here is a composite of sixteen tablets from the Neo-Assyrian and Late Babylonian period; although no one ancient source had exactly this arrangement of texts, it gives a sense of how a compilation of such prayers might have looked.

Both the psalms and the Mesopotamian prayers in this chapter address the gods less formally than did many ancient Near Eastern texts. Based on the idea that "the level of formality in ritual is often directly related to the social distance or proximity between the parties involved," Alan Lenzi has argued that the brief opening addresses suggest a "familiar connection between the supplicant and the deity." On that basis, he finds support for "a personal aspect to the god presented in the Psalter's laments of the individual."[23]

The type of Mesopotamian prayers presented here are typically addressed to *unnamed* personal gods and goddess. It is not likely that these gods were actually considered nameless, but rather that the prayers in their written form were composed so as to be useful in addressing *any* deity. The idea of a personal god may have originated with rulers in early periods of Mesopotamian history, but by the time of these texts it is likely that nonroyal individuals could also think of themselves as having a god or goddess who was specifically concerned with them. Sometimes such personal gods were cited as protecting, comforting presences; for example, there are references to the personal god as the speaker's creator and the guarantor of his or her progeny. However, the prayers here assumed that the gods had been provoked to anger, leading to the misfortune or suffering of the speaker.

It is generally agreed that "in [Mesopotamian prayers from] later periods there is a stronger emphasis on . . . sin/divine anger/suffering."[24] A "medical" text demonstrates the large number of problems that could be attributed to the wrath of a personal god:

22. Sumerian words are usually transcribed in small capital letters.

23. Alan Lenzi, "Invoking the God: Interpreting Invocations in Mesopotamian Prayers and Biblical Laments of the Individual," *JBL* 129 (2010): 304.

24. Tzvi Abusch, "Witchcraft and the Anger of the Personal God," in *Mesopotamian Magic: Textual, Historical, and Interpretative Perspectives* (ed. Tzvi Abusch and Karel van der Toorn; Groningen: Styx Publications, 1999), 91.

If a man has experienced something untoward and he does not know how it happened to him; he has continually suffered losses: losses of barley and silver, losses of male and female slaves, cattle, horses, and sheep; dogs, pigs, and servants dying off altogether; he has heart-break time and again; he constantly gives orders but no (one) complies, calls but no (one) answers; the curse of numerous people; when lying (in his bed) he is repeatedly apprehensive, he contracts paresis,[25] he is filled with anger against god and king . . . his limbs are hanging down, from time to time he is apprehensive, he does not sleep day or night, he often sees terrifying dreams, he often gets paresis, his appetite for bread and beer is diminished, he forgets the word he spoke: *that man has the wrath of the god and/or the goddess on him; his god and his goddess are angry with him.*[26]

In keeping with this wide variety of possibilities, catalogs of diverse forms of suffering can be seen in both the Mesopotamian prayers presented above and in the psalms. In much the same way that the Mesopotamian prayers hunt for a cause of the suffering and cover more ground than any individual sufferer was likely to experience at one moment, so too the psalms often combine a dizzying array of physical, social, and even military problems (e.g., Ps. 22; see also Job). For this reason, many psalms are thought to have served a "medical" purpose in the religious worlds of ancient Israel and Judah: that is, like the Mesopotamian texts presented here, psalms may have been read and accompanied by ritual practices, such as sacrifices, that are now lost in most cases.[27]

Sometimes scholars have sought to distinguish psalms from Mesopotamian texts such as these by arguing that the psalms are *prayers*, while the Mesopotamian texts are *magical incantations*. The essential distinction they have tried to make is that the psalms assume that God acts freely toward the supplicant, while in other ancient Near Eastern texts, the authors assume that the right sequence of words and actions will *assure* the gods' favor.

This distinction between prayer and magic is necessarily based on the form of these texts as we read them today—Mesopotamian prayer texts have been preserved with rubrics, that is, ritual instructions. Those that would have accompanied the Mesopotamian prayers above have been lost, but those on similar tablets read, for example, "You recite this [incantation] three times and it will be released," or "He shall stand facing the ritual paraphernalia of a man's god and goddess and he shall recite [the prayer]." Psalms, on the other hand, typically omit such instructions. However, it is possible that the ritual instructions for the psalms were lost in the process of their transmission. A significant number of the psalms were probably originally composed in the preexilic period, but the form of the Psalter as it comes to us is a product of the postexilic period. The way these psalms were incorporated into worship surely changed over the hundreds of years of the Bible's formation and has continued to change ever since. Therefore, distinctions between biblical psalms and Mesopotamian prayers are best made only in a qualified manner.

25. A nerve disease that is often an aftereffect of syphilis.

26. This text, along with discussion and citations, may be found at Abusch, "Witchcraft," 85. Emphasis added.

27. Sigmund Mowinckel, *The Psalms in Israel's Worship* (2 vols. in 1; Grand Rapids: Eerdmans, 2004), 2:1–25.

Two prayers from the tombs of "middle-class" workmen in Deir el-Medina are also presented above. They supply relatively close cognates to the psalms and Mesopotamian prayers, confessing the speaker's wrongdoing and the righteousness of the gods, while simultaneously subtly imploring the gods for mercy. Fragmentary antecedents for these hymns are found on hieratic ostraca from the tomb of Amenhotep II (18th Dynasty, end of the 15th c. BCE),[28] but such a sparse collection of data hardly establishes penitence as a major theme of ancient Egyptian religion. Prior to the New Kingdom there are no known examples of this kind of religious text in Egypt. Some scholars think that the emphasis on the king as the focus of Egyptian religion during the Amarna period led to a backlash in subsequent periods, which included an emphasis on all worshipers' personal closeness to God.

Certain aspects of the Egyptian texts are reminiscent of the others, including the vagueness of the "transgression" in the Mertseger hymn. (The Ptah hymn is clearer, identifying taking the god's name in vain as the wrongdoing.) The texts also reflect the variety of outcomes found elsewhere: The supplication to Ptah appears unfulfilled at the time of its writing ("Be merciful to me!"), whereas the Mertseger prayer already attests satisfaction ("She was merciful to me, having made me see her hand"). The Egyptian texts differ, however, in that they do not address the gods directly; this creates the impression of a more impersonal relationship between god and worshiper.

In chapter 20, the divine figure of Maat was introduced. The goddess Maat was the personification of an abstract concept by the same name. The term *maat* meant "justice" and "cosmic order," but also "truth" and "balance." The opposite of *maat* was *isfet*, meaning "wrongdoing, chaos." In Egyptian theological rhetoric, then, to do wrong was to upset the balance of the world—further incentive to proclaim one's innocence rather than admit guilt. This helps to explain why, in general, Egyptian religion has been considered less open to admissions of guilt[29] in spite of the fact that wrongdoing and feelings of guilt were surely well attested in Egyptian society. An impenitent tone predominates in the surviving texts—for example, the well-known "negative confession" of the Book of the Dead, Spell 125 (below).

The Mesopotamian and biblical confessions sit side by side in their collections with denials of wrongdoing—in the same compilation in the case of the Mesopotamian texts, while Psalm 26 is an example from the Psalter. Some of these claims of innocence are presented in the second half of this chapter. The juxtaposition of the embrace and denial of personal guilt may strike present-day readers as odd or contradictory, but it appears that ancient worshipers felt a need for both approaches.

28. Edward F. Wente Jr., "Penitential Hymns," in *The Literature of Ancient Egypt: An Anthology of Stories, Instructions, and Poetry* (ed. W. K. Simpson; 3rd ed.; New Haven, CT: Yale University Press, 2003), 284.

29. Edward R. Dalglish, *Psalm Fifty-One: In the Light of Ancient Near Eastern Patternism* (Leiden: Brill, 1962), 8.

Prayers Denying Wrongdoing

PSALM 26

When: Unknown
Where: Jerusalem
Language: Hebrew

BOOK OF GOING FORTH BY DAY
(BOOK OF THE DEAD), SPELL 125

What: One of nearly 200 spells that could be included in a funerary text; recorded on various media, but often on a papyrus scroll
When: Existing copies date to the Eighteenth Dynasty (1550–1295 BCE); perhaps composed earlier
Where: Thebes; copies have also been discovered in other locations
Language: Egyptian
Translation: R. O. Faulkner, *The Ancient Egyptian Book of the Dead* (1972)[30]

§1 [*Rubric:*] [31]
What should be said when arriving at this Hall of Justice, purging [the deceased][32] of all the evil which he has done, and beholding the faces of the gods
§2 [*Opening address to Osiris:*]
Hail to you, great god, Lord of Justice![33] I have come to you, my lord, that you may bring me so that I may see your beauty, for I know you and I know your name, and I know the names of the forty-two gods of those who are with you in this Hall of Justice, who live on those who cherish evil and who gulp down their blood on that day of the reckoning of characters in the presence of Wennefer.[34] Behold the double son of the Songstresses; Lord of Truth is your name.
§3 [*Negative confession*]
　　Behold, I have come to you, I have brought you truth, I have repelled falsehood for you.
　　I have not done falsehood against men,
　　I have not impoverished my associates,

---

30. R. O. Faulkner, trans., *The Ancient Egyptian Book of the Dead* (New York: Limited Editions Club, 1972); reprinted with the permission of MBI, inc. See also Raymond O. Faulkner, Ogden Goelet, Eva Von Dassow, and James Wasserman, *The Egyptian Book of the Dead: The Book of Going Forth by Day* (San Francisco: Chronicle Books, 1998).
31. Subheadings and line numbers are provided only for convenient reference. They do not correspond to the original text.
32. The name of the person for whom the text was prepared would be inserted here.
33. Refers to Osiris, who oversees the judgment of the dead.
34. Also a reference to Osiris. The epithet *wn-nfr* meant, roughly, "He who is permanently benign and youthful."

I have done no wrong in the Place of Truth,[35]
5   I have not learned that which is not,
I have done no evil,
I have not daily made labor in excess of what was due to be done for me,
My name has not reached the offices of those who control slaves,
I have not deprived the orphan of his property,
10   I have not done what the gods detest,
I have not slandered a servant to his master,
I have not caused pain,
I have not made hungry,
I have not made to weep,
15   I have not killed,
I have not commanded to kill,
I have not made suffering for anyone,
I have not lessened the food-offering in the temples,[36]
I have not destroyed the loaves of the gods,
20   I have not taken away the food of the spirits,
I have not copulated,[37]
I have not misbehaved,
I have not lessened food-supplies,
I have not diminished the aroura,[38]
25   I have not encroached upon fields,
I have not laid anything upon the weights of the hand-balance,
I have not taken anything from the plummet of the standing scales,
I have not taken the milk from the mouths of children,
I have not deprived the herds of their pastures,
30   I have not trapped the birds from the preserves of the gods,
I have not caught the fish of their marshlands,
I have not diverted water at its season,
I have not built a dam on flowing water,
I have not quenched the fire when it is burning,
35   I have not neglected the dates for offering choice meats,
I have not withheld cattle from the god's-offerings,
I have not opposed a god in his procession.[39]
I am pure, pure, pure, pure!
§4 [*Statement of innocence:*]

35. A reference to the Theban necropolis.

36. This introduces a section concerned with the maintenance of the gods' cults. The combination of religious and moral concerns might be compared to the biblical Ten Commandments.

37. Some version add, "with a male."

38. A measure of land area, about 2,756 square meters.

39. Processions of divine statues sometimes had divinatory purposes in ancient Egypt, so interfering with such a procession could be tantamount to interfering with the will of the god.

My purity is the purity of that great *Bennu*-bird[40] which is in Heracleopolis, because I am indeed the nose of the Lord of Wind who made all men live on that day of completing the Sacred Eye in Heliopolis in the second month of winter last day, in the presence of the lord of this land. I am he who saw the completion of the Sacred Eye[41] in Heliopolis, and nothing evil shall come into being against me in this land in this Hall of Justice, because I know the names of these gods who are in it.

§5 [*Address to the God of the Hall of Justice:*]

Thus says [the deceased]: Hail to you, you gods who are in this Hall of Justice! I know you and I know your names, I will not fall to your knives; you shall not bring the evil in me to this god in whose suite you are, no fault of mine concerning you shall come out, you shall tell the truth about me in the presence of the Lord of All, because I have done what was right in Egypt, I have not reviled God, and no fault of mine has come out regarding the reigning king.

Hail to you, O you who are in the Hall of Justice, who have no lies in your bodies, who live on truth and gulp down truth in the presence of Horus who is in his disk. Save me from Babai, who lives on the entrails of the old ones on that day of the great reckoning.

Behold, I have come to you without falsehood of mine, without crime of mine, without evil of mine, and there is no one who testifies against me, for I have done nothing against him.

§6 [*Positive statement of rectitude*]

> I live on truth, I gulp down truth,
> I have done what men say and with which the gods are pleased.
> I have propitiated God with what he desires;
> I have given bread to the hungry,
> water to the thirsty, clothes to the naked,
> and a boat to him who was boatless,
> I have given god's offerings to the gods
> and invocation-offerings to the spirits.

§7 [*Summary prayer*]

> Save me, protect me,
> without your making report against me in the Presence,
> for I am pure of mouth and pure of hands,
> one to whom is said 'Twice welcome!' by those who see him. . . .[42]

PRAYERS "FOR APPEASING THE HEART OF AN ANGRY GOD" (DINGIR.ŠÀ.DIB.BA INCANTATION SERIES)

What: Cuneiform text reconstructed from multiple clay tablets
When: Seventh–sixth centuries BCE
Where: Nineveh, Ashur, Susa, and Babylon
Language: Akkadian
Translation: Adapted from W. G. Lambert, *JNES* 33 (1974): 274–91.

---

40. Many birds were associated with the afterlife in Egyptian myth. The *Bennu* appears to derive its name from the Egyptian verb "to rise," and thus symbolizes the power of resurrection for the deceased.

41. The eye of Horus, a symbol of protection against evil.

42. The prayer continues in the same vein, employing mythological concepts that would require more explanation than is desirable for the purpose of this comparison.

[As the line numbers indicate, this is a section of the same compilation presented above.]

[As for me], my god, what have I done? My god, [my] lord, [what have I done?]
[My goddess], my [lady], what have I done?
My god who begat me, what have I done?
[My goddess who bore me. what have I done?]
75   My [. . .], what have I done?
Merchant [, what have I done?]
[. . .] who holds the balances. [. . .]
O one whose house-born slave am I, what have I done?
O one whose slave am I, what have I done?
80   I have not held back from him the ox in the stall,
I have not held back from him the sheep in the pen,
I have not held back from him the valuables which I owned.
The food I found I did not eat to myself,
The water I found I did not drink to myself.
85   Like the one who ate to himself the food he found, where did you send me?
Like one who drank to himself the water he found, where did you send me?
Like the one who frivolously uttered an oath by his god, where did you send me?
My god, you have carried off my wife, you have carried off my son.
My god, receive my hands uplifted in sighing.
90   Like river water I do not know where I am going,
Like a boat I do not know at which quay I put in.
I have fallen, raise me up. I have slipped, take my hand.
My god, I have fallen, raise me up. I have slipped, [take] my hand.
In still waters be my oar,
95   In deep waters be my steering paddle.
Do not hand me over to an evil day.
Do not turn me over to a day of storm.
The food I found I ate with sighing,
The water I found I drank with sighing.
100   Like one who goes down in the marshes, I have fallen in the mud.
You look with favor, look with steadfast favor on me.
Like a marsh, you have filled me with weeping; comfort me.
You look with favor, look with steadfast favor on me.
The man on whom you look with favor lives.
105   You look with favor, look with steadfast favor on me.
At the glance of your eyes that man lives.
You look with favor, look with steadfast favor on me.
For me may the heart of my god become as it was.

SUGGESTIONS FOR COMPARISON

Psalm 26		DINGIR.ŠÀ.DIB.BA	Book of the Dead 125
Assertion of innocence	v. 1	lines 71–74	§3–4
Denial of wrongdoing	vv. 4–6	lines 80–84	§3.2–38
Prayer against harm	v. 9	lines 96–97	§5
Prayer for favor	v. 11	lines 101–8	§5, 7
Promise of praise	vv. 7, 12	lines 39, 172–75	—[43]

DISCUSSION

The Egyptian Book of Going Forth by Day, commonly called the Book of the Dead, was popular throughout the later parts of Egyptian history, from the Eighteenth Dynasty into the Roman period. More than three thousand copies have survived, and it eventually attained a canonical form, in which it had 162 or 165 spells; other forms, both shorter and longer, have also survived.

As the title suggests, the Book of Going Forth by Day is a book of spells intended to give the deceased person the supernatural power to overcome death and become divinized—not only to attain the happy afterlife, but to go forth from the darkness of the tomb and receive offering in the land of the living. This had been a religious ambition throughout Egyptian history, probably for a wide spectrum of people. However, the number of people with the capacity to record their hopes in writing increased over time. In the Old Kingdom (2686–2160 BCE) it was primarily pharaohs (along with a few queens) who were known to have aspired to become a god in the afterlife (in the Pyramid Texts); in the Middle Kingdom (2055–1650), royal courtiers also recorded such hopes in the Coffin Texts; and by the New Kingdom (1550–1069) and later, such afterlife texts were even more widely available to anyone who could pay for their production. Many of the spells in the New Kingdom versions of the Book of Going Forth by Day are related, in theme and content, to the spells of the earlier books. Depending on the period, these texts might be written in a papyrus scroll buried with the body, or painted on the sarcophagus or tomb walls.

One of the centerpieces of the Book of Going Forth by Day is the judgment of the dead. The ordeal is described in various ways, but in the main scene the deceased appears in a tribunal where Osiris presides along with forty-two divine judges. Iconographic portrayals of this scene vary, but commonly Thoth records the verdict and Anubis acts as "lord of the balances." The deceased's heart is weighed against a feather, symbolizing *maat* ("justice"). If the deceased is found to be unburdened by guilt, the deceased goes on to join Osiris as an *akh*, or "powerful spirit." If not, the monster Ammut awaits to devour the heart, and the person experiences the second and final death. Other Egyptian texts and art portray the torture and destruction of damned souls in ways that anticipate later Western images of hell.

---

43. Although the promise of praise is generally not used as a motivating factor in the address to the deity in this text, there is hymnic praise language, e.g.: "Hail to you, O you who are in the Hall of Justice, who have no lies in your bodies, who live on truth and gulp down truth."

The fundamental tension in these texts is between justice (*maat*) and wrongdoing (*isfet*). Because of the importance of innocence in this process, Spell 125 of the Book of the Dead is a thoroughgoing denial of wrongdoing—surely the most extensive such denial in the ancient world. It comprises a "negative confession," in which the deceased person comes before the tribunal of gods in the Hall of Justice and disavows wrongdoing.

Even in the Egyptian Book of the Dead, whose protests of innocence we have just noted, the same juxtaposition of approaches to guilt can be seen. It is less often noted that in Spell 126, which follows directly after the "negative confession," the speaker prays to another set of judges ("the baboons who sit in the bow of the bark of Re") to "expel my evil, grip hold of my falsehood"! So immediately after Spell 125's protestation of purity, the deceased acknowledges that he needs evil and falsehood expunged from him. As with other aspects of ancient Near Eastern religions, it seems that the compilers (and those who prayed the prayers) were untroubled by the contrast. They were less concerned about establishing logical, systematic statements of doctrine, and more concerned about supplying proper rhetoric for a wide range of situations. In the cases presented here, a concern for rhetorical comprehensiveness seems apparent—a prayer for the one who feels guilty, a prayer for the one who does not. The ritual (some would call it "magical") aspect of the spell means that it was not understood as a statement of fact, but as a way to conjure a state of being for the deceased. Such spells have sometimes been likened to priestly initiation rites or other rites of passage that invoke a new identity.

The Mesopotamian text above is taken from the middle of the same DINGIR.ŠÀ.DIB.BA compilation that is presented earlier in this chapter, but it takes a different approach to appeasing the angry god. Like the Book of the Dead text, it includes some denials or specific transgressions. But it also includes a third possibility: agnosticism about the wrongdoing. The speaker asks over and over: *What have I done?* It is possible that these various strategies (confession, denial, agnosticism) were all used by the same supplicant, to "cover all the bases." (Yet another distinct strategy is employed in lines 132–34: the assertion that everyone is sinful; cf. Rom. 3:23.) However, it is also possible that the compilations of texts were like templates or prayer books, from which a supplicant (or more likely a religious professional who could read the texts) might draw pieces according to need.

Psalm 26 is an unusual exemplar, and commentators have remarked on its impenitent tone. It is also distinguished from the other texts in this section by its strongly communal focus. The psalmist seeks to distance himself from the "company of evildoers" (the worthless, the hypocrites, the wicked, the bloodthirsty, the sinners) in order to stand in "the great congregation," worshiping Yhwh. The speaker's personal fate is still very much in view, but both good and evil are imagined in terms of community, in a way that is not apparent in the other two texts. Many of the contrasting terms for the righteous and the wicked are found in wisdom psalms such as Psalm 1, but from a less personal perspective.

It is not clear what prompted the prayer of Psalm 26. Does the injunction—"Do not sweep me away with sinners, nor my life with the bloodthirsty"—mean that the psalmist is in danger? Or is that request merely prophylactic? In any case, it is striking that the author inserts it despite his apparent confidence in his own righteousness. Either, like the speaker in Book of the Dead, Spell 126, he senses the need for additional grace and expiation despite his innocence, or he is not completely confident in the machinery of divine justice.

In closing, these examples of personal piety from across the ancient Near East invite one to reflect on how individuals conceived of their relationship to the divine in general. The Egyptologist Barry J. Kemp has expressed skepticism about the magnitude of the role religion played in the lives of ancient Egyptians, and the extent to which their ethics were based on religious ideas:

> The Egyptians possessed a developed theology which centered on knowledge of a hidden cosmos, but this is likely to have been seriously pursued only by a very few as a specialized academic study. It was possible for people (including the inhabitants of Deir el-Medina village) to buy some of this knowledge in written form (Coffin Texts, Book of the Dead) as an aid to survival after death, but it did not serve as a guide to living and so there was not, as far as we can see, a distinctively religious way of conducting one's life.[44]

This portrait is certainly a recognizable one: in looking around at our contemporaries, most readers will know many for whom religion is an afterthought unless there is a funeral or wedding to attend. The data from which we construct a picture of ancient peoples is far from complete; indeed, for the most part it is scant. Should one imagine them as walking around with a constant awareness of the divine, and perhaps living in dread of having given offense? Or were they driven to seek expert guidance in supplicating the gods only in extreme distress, as a person today might seek a medical specialist only as a last resort?

REFLECTION QUESTIONS

1. What reasons does each text in the first section give (or suggest) for the god's anger and the speaker's suffering?

2. What can you infer from each text about the supplicant's view of God or the gods? Are the gods being addressed trustworthy? Are they omniscient? Are their standards and purposes clear?

3. What common features do you find in the penitential texts? In the texts that protest innocence? Are there aspects of each that you find distinctive?

4. Do you see indications in the psalms that they might have been used in ritual (e.g., sacrificial) settings? How might such settings have compared with the use of the other texts in their respective cultures?

5. Would you characterize the Mesopotamian texts as prayers or magical incantations? Why?

6. What do the similarities and differences between these texts suggest about ancient Israel and Judah's practices of prayer and views about God?

7. Do you see indications in each of the texts of a "familiar connection" between the speaker and the deity? Do you sense any distinction in tone between the texts where a deity is named and those where one is not? Is there a tension between intimacy with the god(s) and claims about their power?

---

44. Barry J. Kemp, "How Religious Were the Ancient Egyptians?" *Cambridge Archaeological Journal* 5 (1995): 25–54.

8. It has been suggested that the difference between monotheistic and polytheistic religious systems accounts for some of the differences between these texts. Do you agree or disagree?

FURTHER READING

Abusch, Tzvi. "Witchcraft and the Anger of the Personal God." Pages 83–121 in *Mesopotamian Magic: Textual, Historical, and Interpretative Perspectives*. Edited by Tzvi Abusch and Karel van der Toorn. Groningen: Styx Publications, 1999.

Dalglish, Edward R. *Psalm Fifty-One: In the Light of Ancient Near Eastern Patternism*. Leiden: Brill, 1962.

Hallo, William W. "Lamentations and Prayers in Sumer and Akkad." In *Civilizations of the Ancient Near East*. Edited by Jack M. Sasson. New York: Scribner, 1995.

Lambert, W. G. "DINGIR.ŠÀ.DIB.BA Incantations." *JNES* 33 (1974): 267–322.

Lenzi, Alan. "Invoking the God: Interpreting Invocations in Mesopotamian Prayers and Biblical Laments of the Individual." *JBL* 129 (2010): 303–15.

Miller, Patrick D. *They Cried to the Lord: The Form and Theology of Biblical Prayer*. Minneapolis: Fortress Press, 1994. (Esp. 3–31, "Israel's Neighbors at Prayer.")

Mowinckel, Sigmund. *The Psalms in Israel's Worship*. 2 vols. in 1. Grand Rapids: Eerdmans, 2004.

23

Hymns of Praise with Solar Imagery

The Great Hymn to the Aten and Psalm 104

PSALM 104

When: Unknown
Where: Jerusalem
Language: Hebrew

THE GREAT HYMN TO THE ATEN

What: Hieroglyphic text inscribed on the wall of the Tomb of Ay
When: 1352–1336 BCE (18th Dynasty)
Where: Ahketaten, Egypt (present-day El Amarna)
Language: Egyptian
Translation: Miriam Lichtheim, *AEL* II.96–99

(*Prologue:*)

Adoration of *Re-Harakhti-who-rejoices-in-lightland In-his-name-Shu-who-is-Aten*, living forever; the great living Aten who is in jubilee, the lord of all that the Disk encircles, lord of sky, lord of earth, lord of the house-of-Aten in Akhet-Aten; (and of) the King of Upper and Lower Egypt, who lives by Maat, the Lord of the Two Lands, *Neferkheprure, Sole-one-of-Re*; the Son of Re who lives by Maat, the Lord of Crowns, Akhenaten, great in his lifetime; (and) his beloved great Queen, the Lady of the Two Lands, *Nefer-nefru-Aten Nefertiti*, who lives in health and youth forever. The Vizier, the Fanbearer on the right of the King,

Ay—He says:[1]

---

1. The hymn is thought to have been composed originally for the king, Akhenaten (see prologue and lines 123–25), and secondarily adapted to use in the tomb of the courtier Ay, which is why Ay is the speaker here.

357

1[2]   Splendid you rise in heaven's lightland,[3]
      O living Aten, creator of life!
   When you have dawned in eastern lightland,
      You fill every land with your beauty.
5   You are beauteous, great, radiant,
      High over every land;
   Your rays embrace the lands,
      To the limit of all that you made.
   Being Re, you reach their limits,[4]
10   You bend them (for) the son whom you love;
   Though you are far, your rays are on earth,
      Though one sees you, your strides are unseen.
   When you set in western lightland,
      Earth is in darkness as if in death;
15   One sleeps in chambers, heads covered,
      One eye does not see another.
   Were they robbed of their goods
      That are under their heads,
      People would not remark it.
20   Every lion comes from its den,
      All the serpents bite;
   Darkness hovers, earth is silent,
      As their maker rests in lightland.
   Earth brightens when you dawn in lightland,
25   When you shine as Aten of daytime;
   As you dispel the dark,
      As you cast your rays,
   The Two Lands[5] are in festivity.
      Awake they stand on their feet,
30   You have roused them;
      Bodies cleansed, clothed,
      Their arms adore your appearance.
   The entire land sets out to work,
      All beasts browse on their herbs;
35   Trees, herbs are sprouting,
      Birds fly from their nests,

---

2. The line numbers here are only for readers' reference; they do not correspond to any original text.

3. I.e., the horizon.

4. This line contains an untranslatable play on words between *Ra‘* the sun(-god) and the common noun *ra‘* meaning "end, limit."

5. Upper and Lower Egypt.

Their wings greeting your *ka*.[6]
    All flocks frisk on their feet,
All that fly up and alight,
40   They live when you dawn for them.
Ships fare north, fare south as well,
    Roads lie open when you rise;
The fish in the river dart before you,
    Your rays are in the midst of the sea.
45 Who makes seed grow in women,
    Who creates people from sperm;
Who feeds the son in his mother's womb,
    Who soothes him to still his tears.
Nurse in the womb,
50   Giver of breath,
To nourish all that he made.
    When he comes from the womb to breathe,
On the day of his birth,
    You open wide his mouth,
55 You supply his needs.
    When the chick in the egg speaks in the shell,
You give him breath within to sustain him;
    When you have made him complete,
To break out from the egg,
60   He comes out from the egg,
To announce his completion,
    Walking on his legs he comes from it.
How many are your deeds,
    Though hidden from sight,
65 O Sole God beside whom there is none!
    You made the earth as you wished, you alone,
All peoples, herds, and flocks;
    All upon earth that walk on legs,
    All on high that fly on wings,
70 The lands of Khor and Kush,
    The land of Egypt.
You set every man in his place,
    You supply their needs;
Everyone has his food,
75   His lifetime is counted.
Their tongues differ in speech,
    Their characters likewise;

6. The *ka* is a complex concept in Egyptian mythology, but can be understood as "life force."

Their skins are distinct,
    For you distinguished the peoples.

80   You made Hapy in *duat*,[7]
      You bring him when you will,
To nourish the people,
    For you made them for yourself.
Lord of all, who toils for them,
85   Lord of all lands, who shines for them,
Aten of daytime, great in glory!
    All distant lands, you make them live,
You made a heavenly Hapy descend for them;
    He makes waves on the mountains like the sea,
90   To drench their fields and their towns.
How excellent are your ways, O Lord of eternity!
    A Hapy from heaven for foreign peoples,
And all lands' creatures that walk on legs,
    For Egypt the Hapy who comes from *duat*.

95   Your rays nurse all fields,
    When you shine they live, they grow for you;
You made the seasons to foster all that you made,
    Winter to cool them, heat that they taste you.
You made the far sky to shine therein,
100   To behold all that you made;
You alone, shining in your form of living Aten,
    Risen, radiant, distant, near.
You made millions of forms from yourself alone,
    Towns, villages, fields, the river's course;
105   All eyes observe you upon them,
    For you are the Aten of daytime on high.
    . . .

You are in my heart,
    There is no other who knows you,
Only your son, Neferkheprure, Sole-one-of-Re,
110   Whom you have taught your ways and your might.
(Those on) earth come from your hand as you made them,
    When you have dawned they live,
When you set they die;
    You yourself are lifetime, one lives by you.

---

7. Hapy is the divinized personification of the Nile flood that brought fertility to the land. The *duat* is the underworld. Thus the claim is that Aten brings forth the flood from beneath the ground.

115   All eyes are on (your) beauty until you set,
        All labor ceases when you rest in the west;
     When you rise you stir [everyone] for the King,
        Every leg is on the move since you founded the earth.
     You rouse them for your son who came from your body,
120   The King who lives by Ma'at, the Lord of the Two Lands,
     Neferkheprure, Sole-one-of-Re,
        The Son of Re who lives by Ma'at, the Lord of crowns,
     Akhenaten, great in his lifetime;
        (And) the great Queen whom he loves, the Lady of the Two Lands:
125 Nefer-nefru-Aten Nefertiti, living forever.

SUGGESTIONS FOR COMPARISON

Hymn to the Aten	Psalm 104
lines 3–8	vv. 1b–2a
lines 35–38	vv. 16–17
lines 80–94	vv. 10–13
lines 20–44	vv. 20–26
lines 111–14	vv. 28–30

DISCUSSION

The Great Hymn to the Aten is the most impressive literary text that survives from the Amarna period, and it serves as a witness to the most unusual religious movement of ancient Egyptian history.

There was a long history of solar religion in ancient Egypt—it was the focal point of the cult at Heliopolis—and so there were also hymns of praise to sun-gods. To some degree, the hymn presented here shares in that literary tradition. However, the reign of Amenhotep IV (1372–1355 BCE) saw a great religious upheaval when the king underwent a conversion experience and mandated that his kingdom should follow him in worshiping the Aten, the deified sun disk, as the one true god. This came at the expense of the whole pantheon of Egyptian deities, their temples, and their personnel, but Aten particularly displaced Amun-Re from his role as high god. Akhenaten sought to efface references to Amun throughout the land, even as far away as Nubia.

To make a clean break, the king chose a new capital city on virgin ground and named it Akhetaten ("Horizon of the Sun Disc"). The site's modern Arabic name is El Amarna, thus the period is often called the Amarna period. Amenhotep even changed his own name to Akhenaten ("Agreeable to Aten"); he also changed other throne names that had linked the kingship to Thebes.

Akhenaten has inspired a vast amount of scholarship because he is such a striking figure. He has been called "the heretic king" (by Redford) and "the first individual in human history" (by the Egyptologist J. H. Breasted).[8] Some have theorized that Akhenaten was threatened by the power of the priests of Amun, or that he had a particular dislike for the underworld cult of Osiris. In any case, it required innovation and fortitude to make the kind of major shift that Akhenaten undertook, and indeed the Amarna period was marked by innovation in many areas beyond theology, from sculpture to literature. For example, the sole worship of one god meant that Aten had to embody both male and female (e.g., the epithet "nurse in the womb" in line 49), and so in Amarna period sculpture men and women are portrayed similarly, as a form of *imitatio Dei*. The men are androgynous, with large hips, slender upper bodies, and pregnant-looking bellies, a startling break with many centuries of artistic tradition.

Some historians have argued that Amarna religion did not strictly exclude other gods, nor was it a complete break with the past, since Akhenaten's father, Amenhotep III, had promoted the Heliopolis sun cult (albeit in a less extreme way). However, Amarna religion did focus exclusively on the worship of the Aten/sun disk, and couplets such as this one (lines 65–66) leave little room for other deities:

> O Sole God beside whom there is none!
> You made the earth as you wished, you alone.

Indeed, such claims sound very much like the widely recognized monotheistic statements of Second Isaiah (e.g., Isa. 45:5–6: "I am the LORD, and there is no other; besides me there is no god. I arm you, though you do not know me, so that they may know, from the rising of the sun and from the west, that there is no one besides me; I am the LORD, and there is no other"). It should be noted, however, that as with any religious dogma, Amarna religion did not gain universal acceptance even in its own time: excavations from the site have turned up amulets of gods other than Aten. Despite the attempt to remove all worship of other gods, individuals still retained some relation to them.

When discussing the theologies of these texts, it will be useful for the reader to be aware of some more precise terminology:

- *Monotheism*, properly speaking, has come to be defined as not only the worship of a single god, but also the straightforward denial of the existence of other gods. (E.g., Isa. 45:21: "There is no other god besides me.")
- Short of strict monotheism, one may speak of *monolatry*, in which a group acknowledges the existence of other gods but forbids worshiping them. (E.g., Deut. 6:13–14: "Yhwh your God you shall fear; him you shall serve, and by his name alone you shall swear. Do not follow other gods, any of the gods of the peoples who are all around you.")
- *Henotheism* has been described as a more temporary form of monolatry, for example, a period of strict adherence to the worship of one god in an effort to avert a crisis (e.g., Josh. 2:10–19).
- *Summodeism* allows worshipers to call on the names of various gods, but "the deities are regarded as aspects or functions of a chief god, with political power often key to its

---

8. Donald B. Redford, *Akhenaten, the Heretic King* (Princeton, NJ: Princeton University Press, 1984); James Henry Breasted, *A History of Egypt* (2nd ed.; New York: Charles Scribner's Sons, 1909), 356.

expression."[9] The Babylonian god Marduk was famously given "fifty names" when he conquered Tiamat and assumed reign over the gods in the myth *Enuma Elish* (see chap. 3).

- Closely related to summodeism is the idea of *diffused monotheism*, in which one God is supreme and all-powerful, but "delegates certain portions of his authority to particular divine functionaries who work as they are commissioned by him."[10]

Because a single hymn such as the one presented here may reflect only a single episode of worshipful rhetoric, it would be difficult to conclude from it alone which phenomenon one is dealing with. One does have other significant data, however. As part of his reform, Akhenaten closed many temples of other gods around the country. In addition to its religious impact, this decision had an economically centralizing effect. In Egypt as elsewhere in the Near East, religion, politics, and economics were intertwined, so closing temples had the effect of disrupting distribution of goods across the country, with no other system to take its place. These pragmatic issues probably contributed to the backlash against Amarna religion after Akhenaten's death.

From a theological standpoint, Amarna religion promised the availability of the divine—in both iconography and literature from the period, one sees a focus on the sun disk's rays, which shed light on all. This was a contrast to Amun, who was known as a hidden god, at least theoretically. Although it is difficult to assess whether this had much impact in practical terms, this emphasis on the sun's accessibility expressed itself in broad-minded, universalistic rhetoric that emphasized the Aten's blessings for all creation. Aten was also accessible in that he was supposed to be *within* his worshipers—for example, "You are in my heart" (line 107)—although again here one is dealing with elite compositions, so it is not clear to what extent Aten was considered accessible to common people. Even Ay's hymn seems to have been originally a royal composition, and the king played a large role in Atenism as the contact with the divine.

Another major religious impact of Amarna religion was the deemphasizing of mortuary religion, which was near the heart of Egyptian religion before and after. Ancient Egyptians' preparations for death are most famously represented by the practice of mummification, but along with the treatment of the body came a vast array of mythology, from the roles of various deities in the deceased's afterlife journey to magical spells intended to help the deceased reach the happy afterlife. All this was banished from Amarna religion because the underworld was viewed as inaccessible to the sun—a stunning disjunction from earlier Egyptian religion.[11]

For all these reasons, the Atenism of the Amarna period was short-lived. Only a few years after Akhenaten's death, his heir Tutankhaten moved the royal court back to

---

9. Mark S. Smith, *God in Translation: Deities in Cross-Cultural Discourse in the Biblical World* (FAT 57; Tübingen: Mohr Siebeck, 2008), 169.

10. Nili Fox, "Concepts of God in Israel and the Question of Monotheism," in *Text, Artifact and Image: Revealing Ancient Israelite Religion* (ed. Gary Beckman and Theodore J. Lewis; Providence, RI: Brown Judaic Studies, 2006), 329–31.

11. The tomb of Akhenaten was not placed in the west, as was traditional, but rather on the east, the place of the rising sun. As lines 13–23 of the hymn indicate, Amarna religion considered the setting of the sun to allow chaos and dangerous creatures to emerge. Rebirth only occurred with the new rising sun, and so the king wanted to be associated with the latter.

Memphis and changed his name to Tutankhamun (this was the famous "King Tut"). The new king, seemingly influenced by one of his tutors, who was a religious traditionalist, returned Amun to primacy among the gods and essentially restored the nation's religious practices to their pre-Amarna state. Tutankhamun even embarked on a massive mission to deface the name of Akhenaten on statues and monuments, erasing the latter's memory and thereby consigning him to the dreaded "second death." Akhenaten's "monotheistic heresy" was ended and blotted out. Within thirty years of its founding, Akhetaten was abandoned. So great was later generations' disdain for Akhenaten's innovation that little there was deemed worth taking—which is why we have such famous texts and artifacts as the Amarna letters and the bust of Nefertiti, both of which were abandoned there.

Psalm 104 comes from centuries later than the Hymn to the Aten. Unlike many of the biblical texts discussed in this book, it is very difficult to ascertain when it may have been written, since psalmic poetry changed relatively little over time; Israel and Judah were also in contact with Egypt over a long period of time.

The hymn form in the Bible has also been called a "psalm of descriptive praise" by Claus Westermann. The form is simple—in its most basic form consisting only of a call to praise and a description of the reasons. In Psalm 104, one sees (self-)exhortation to praise at both the beginning and the end. (Arguably the same can be said of the Hymn to the Aten, in that it opens with "adoration," and concludes with the assertion that the Aten "rouses" everyone.) Other biblical hymns of praise focused on creation include Psalms 8; 33; and 145.[12]

Psalm 104 is by no means the only place in the Bible where one finds solar imagery for Yhwh. Psalm 84:11 says, "Yhwh is a sun and a shield." One might also mention Psalm 19: "The heavens are telling the glory of God; and the firmament proclaims his handiwork. . . . In the heavens he has set a tent for the sun, which comes out like a bridegroom from his wedding canopy, and like a strong man runs its course with joy. Its rising is from the end of the heavens, and its circuit to the end of them; and nothing is hid from its heat" (vv. 1, 4–6). There, of course, the sun is not directly equated with Yhwh, but that may be said for Psalm 104 as well.

Historically speaking, there seems to have been a solar aspect to Judean religion, at least in the preexilic period. That is to say, one way that people worshiped Yhwh was *as the sun*. There are various indications of this; Ezekiel 8:16 tells of people in Yhwh's temple "prostrating themselves to the sun." And 2 Kings 23:11 reports that Josiah "removed the horses that the kings of Judah had dedicated to the sun, at the entrance to the house of Yhwh, by the chamber of the eunuch Nathan-melech, which was in the precincts; then he burned the chariots of the sun with fire."[13] Although there is a repeated Deuteronomistic polemic against "the host of heaven," the particular description in 2 Kings 23:11 does not have the character of a stylized polemic, and so probably preserves historical facts.

---

12. One can also see creation themes in Pss. 19:1–6; 29; 66:1–12; 103; 113; 139; and 148.

13. One can also note the survival of solar imagery for God in the New Testament, e.g., Rev. 21:23: "The city has no need of sun or moon to shine on it, for the glory of God is its light, and its lamp is the Lamb."

Equally telling is a tenth-century cult stand from the town of Ta'anach, in Judah, the top register of which shows a sun disk supported by a horse; this is framed by what appear to be the arms of a throne, and the sides of the same register portray cherubim, just as the divine throne in Jerusalem had. (The empty space in the third register from the top is thought to be an aniconic "representation" of Yhwh, while the second and fourth registers, depicting a sacred tree and a naked goddess with lions, respectively, are usually thought to be representations of Asherah.) The Ta'anach cult stand is perhaps the strongest single piece of extrabiblical evidence that Judeans associated Yhwh with the sun, though one can also point to Iron Age horse figurines with a sun disk above their heads that have been excavated at Lachish, Hazor, and Jerusalem, plus two seals depicting bulls with solar disks between their horns from Ramat Rachel.

Similarities between biblical religious imagery and that of neighboring cultures are not unusual. The question is how such imagery is uniquely adapted to each culture and religion. In the case of Psalm 104's solar imagery that is reminiscent of the Great Hymn to the Aten, it has been suggested that there is a pattern of correspondence between the psalm and the creation narrative of Genesis 1:[14]

Psalm 104	Genesis 1
vv. 1–4	vv. 6–8
vv. 5–9	vv. 9–10
vv. 10–13	vv. 6–10
vv. 14–18	vv. 11–12
vv. 19–23	vv. 14–18
vv. 24–26	vv. 20–22
vv. 27–30	vv. 24–30

If one accepts this set of correspondences as more than random, then it shows a Judean scribe adapting preexisting imagery to the purpose of the worship of Yhwh in light of existing ideas about Yhwh's creative powers. Given the uncertainty about the date of Psalm 104, the direction of influence is not certain, nor can one rule out the existence of some third unknown source for both existing texts.

A final aspect of the relationship between the two texts that must be mentioned briefly is the theory that Israel's monotheism was brought from Egypt to the Levant by Moses at the time of the exodus. Because there is no evidence for the exodus or Moses outside the Bible, they are largely inaccessible to historical methods. We can say that there was generally contact between Egypt and the Levant in the time of Akhenaten, but this is also true of later periods. Thus it would be difficult to argue in any specific way for transmission of the idea of monotheism from New Kingdom Egypt to Israel.

Admittedly, it is striking that Israel claimed one of its theological taproots—the exodus and the delivery of the law to Moses—so close in time and space to another (attempted) monotheistic revolution. But that observation can only be a topic for musing, given the

---

14. Bernhard H. Anderson, *Creation Versus Chaos: The Reinterpretation of Mythical Symbolism in the Bible* (Philadelphia: Fortress Press, 1987), 91–93.

current state of our knowledge. The more promising avenue of historical study is to note the strong connections between Egypt and Israel throughout the first millennium BCE. In addition to the many examples cited in the introduction to this volume, the mysterious statement of Isaiah 19:18 is particularly provocative in connection with solar worship: "On that day there will be five cities in the land of Egypt that speak the language of Canaan and swear allegiance to the LORD of hosts. One of these will be called the City of the Sun." Among the many results of the contact between Egypt and the Levant, some transmission of solar divine imagery seems highly likely.

REFLECTION QUESTIONS

1. What characteristics, powers, and effects are common to Aten in the Egyptian hymn and to Yhwh in the psalm?

2. What is the relation of the deity in each hymn to the sun?

3. What happens at night in the Egyptian hymn, and how is night described? In the psalm?

4. How does the presence of the king affect the theology of the Aten hymn? Does its royal character differentiate it from the psalm?

5. Given that the Egyptian hymn predates the psalm, do you think that Israelites who recited or heard such a psalm would have been aware of its resonance with Egyptian hymns? How do you think they would have made sense of the similarities if they had been pointed out?

6. What are some key differences between the Aten hymn and the psalm?

7. Do you think that solar religion was viewed as part of Yahwistic worship by its practitioners? If so, why did Yahwistic reformers such as Ezekiel and Josiah view it negatively?

8. These texts show that the same imagery can be applied to multiple deities. What impact might that recognition have on our understanding (or use) of religious imagery in our own times?

FURTHER READING

Anderson, Bernhard H. *Creation Versus Chaos: The Reinterpretation of Mythical Symbolism in the Bible.* Philadelphia: Fortress Press, 1987.

Foster, John L. "The Hymn to Aten: Akhenaten Worships the Sole God." Pages 1751–61 in *Civilizations of the Ancient Near East*, vol. 3. New York: Charles Scribner's Sons, 1995.

Fox, Nili. "Concepts of God in Israel and the Question of Monotheism." In *Text, Artifact and Image: Revealing Ancient Israelite Religion*. Edited by Gary Beckman and Theodore J. Lewis. Providence, RI: Brown Judaic Studies, 2006.

LeMon, Joel M. *Yahweh's Winged Form in the Psalms: Exploring Congruent Iconography and Texts.* Orbis biblicus et orientalis 242. Fribourg: Academic Press, 2010.

Redford, Donald B. *Akhenaten, the Heretic King.* Princeton, NJ: Princeton University Press, 1984.

Smith, Mark S. "The Near Eastern Background of Solar Language for Yahweh." *JBL* 109 (1990): 29–39.

Taylor, Glen. *Yahweh and the Sun.* JSOTSup 111. Sheffield: JSOT Press, 1993.

Vernus, Pascal. *Sagesses de l'Égypte pharaonique.* Paris: Imprimerie nationale, 2001. (Esp. 299–346.)

Westermann, Claus. *The Psalms: Structure, Content and Message.* Minneapolis: Augsburg, 1980. (Esp. 81–96.)

24

Prayers of Lament

Hittite Plague Prayers and Psalms 88–89

PSALM 88

When: Unknown
Where: Jerusalem
Language: Hebrew

PSALM 89

When: Unknown (mid-sixth century BCE?)
Where: Jerusalem
Language: Hebrew

[*Note that Ps. 89:52 in English translations—"Blessed be Yhwh forever. Amen and Amen"—is actually a liturgical closing to the third book of the Psalter. It is not part of the literary structure of Ps. 89.*]

MURSILI'S "FIRST" PLAGUE PRAYER TO THE ASSEMBLY OF GODS AND GODDESSES (CTH 378.1)

What: Cuneiform text on clay tablet
When: ca. 1310 BCE
Where: Hattusas (near modern Boğazkale, Turkey)
Language: Hittite
Translation: Itamar Singer[1]

---

1. Itamar Singer, *Hittite Prayers* (SBLWAW 11; Atlanta: Society of Biblical Literature, 2002), 61–64.

367

§1 (obv. 1–7) [All] you male [gods], all female gods [of heaven (?)], all male gods [of the oath], all female gods of the oath, [all] male primeval [gods], all female (primeval) gods, you gods who have been summoned to assembly for bearing witness to the oath on this [matter], mountains, rivers, springs, and underground watercourses. I, Mursili, [great king (?)], your priest, your servant, herewith plead with you. [Listen] to me O gods, my lords, in the matter in which I am making a plea to you!

§2 (obv. 8–15) O gods, [my] lords! A plague broke out in Hatti, and Hatti has been severely damaged by the plague. And since for twenty years now in Hatti people have been dying, the affair of Tudhaliya the Younger, son of Tudhaliya, started to weigh on [me]. I inquired about it to the god through an oracle, and the affair of Tudhaliya was confirmed by the deity. Since Tudhaliya the Younger was their lord in Hatti, the princes, the noblemen, the commanders of the thousands, the officers, [the corporals (?)] of Hatti and all [the infantry] and chariotry of Hatti swore an oath to him. My father also swore an oath to him.

§3 (obv. 16–22) [But when my father] wronged Tudhaliya, all [the princes, the noblemen], the commanders of the thousands, and the officers of Hatti [went over] to my father. The deities by whom the oath was sworn [seized] Tudhaliya and they killed [Tudhaliya]. Furthermore, they killed those of his brothers [who stood by] him . [. . .] they sent to Alashiya (Cyprus) and [. . .]. And [since Tudhaliya the Younger] was their [lord], they [. . .] to him [. . .]. [. . .] and the lords transgressed the oath [. . .].

§4 (obv. 23–40) [But, you, O gods], my [lords], protected my father. [. . .]. And because Hatti [was attacked (?)] by the [enemy, and the enemy] had taken [borderlands] of Hatti, [my father kept attacking the enemy lands] and kept defeating them. He took back the borderlands of Hatti, which [the enemy had taken] and [resettled] them. Furthermore, [he conquered] still other foreign lands [during his] kingship. He sustained Hatti and [secured] its borders on each side.

During his reign the entire land of Hatti did well. [Men (?)], cattle and sheep became numerous in his days, and the civilian prisoners who [were brought] from the land of the enemy survived as well. Nothing perished.

But now you, O gods, [my lords], have eventually taken vengeance on my father for this affair of Tudhaliya the Younger. My father [died (?)] because of the blood of Tudhaliya, and the princes, the noblemen, the commanders of the thousands, and the officers who went over [to my father], they also died because of [that] affair. This same affair also came upon the land of Hatti, and the population of the land of [Hatti] began to perish because of [this] affair. Until now Hatti [. . .], but now the plague [has become] even [worse]. Hatti has been [severely] damaged by the plague, and it has been decimated. I, Mursili, [your servant], cannot [overcome] the worry [of my heart], I can no longer [overcome] the anguish of my soul.

§5 (obv. 41–47) [*Very fragmentary passage in which Mursili apparently continues to plead with the oath-deities concerning their vengeance of Tudhaliya's blood*]

§6 (rev. 8′–12′) [Now,] I have confessed [it to you, O gods (?). Because] my father [killed (?)] Tudhaliya [and . . .], my father therefore [performed] a ritual (for the expiation) of blood. But [the land of] Hatti did not [perform] anything for itself. I performed [the ritual of the blood], but the land did not perform anything. They did nothing on behalf [of] the land.

§7 (rev. 13'–20') Now, because Hatti has been severely oppressed by the plague, and the population of Hatti continues to die, the affair of Tudhaliya has troubled the land. It has been confirmed for me by [the god], and I have further investigated [it] by oracle. They are performing before you, [O gods], my lords, the ritual of the oath which was confirmed for you, [O gods], my lords, and for your temples, with regard to the plague of the land and they are clearing [it (i.e., the oath obligation) before] you. And I am making restitution to you, O gods, my lords, with reparation and a propitiatory gift on behalf of the land.

§8 (rev. 21'–40') Because you, O gods, my lords, [have] taken vengeance for the blood of Tudhaliya, those who killed Tudhaliya [have made] restitution for the blood. But this bloodshed is finished in Hatti again: Hatti too has already made restitution for it. Since it has now come upon me as well, I will also make restitution for it from my household, with restitution and a propitiatory gift. So may the soul of the gods, my lords, again be appeased. May the gods, my lords, again be well disposed toward me, and let me elicit your pity. May you listen to me, to what I plead before you.

I have [not] done any evil. Of those who sinned and did the evil, no one of that day is still here. They have already died off. But because the affair of my father has come upon me, I am giving you, O gods, my lords, a propitiatory gift on account of the plague of the land, and I am making restitution. I am making restitution to you with a propitiatory gift and reparation. May you gods, my lords, again [have] mercy on me, and let me elicit your pity.

Because Hatti has been oppressed by the plague, it has been reduced in size. [And those makers of offering bread and libation pourers who used to prepare] the offering bread and the libation for the gods, my lords, [since Hatti] has been severely oppressed by [the plague], [they have died] from the plague. [If the plague] does not subside at all, and they continue to die, [even those] few [makers of offering bread] and libation pourers [who still remain will die, and nobody will prepare] for you offering bread and libation any longer.

§9 (rev. 41'–51') May [you gods, my lords], have mercy on [me again] because of the offering bread and the libation which [they prepare for you], and let me elicit your pity. Send the plague [away from Hatti]. Let those few makers of offering bread [and pourers of libation] who [still remain] with you not be harmed, and let them not go on dying. Let them prepare [the offering bread] and the libation for you. O gods, my lords, turn the plague [away, and send] whatever is evil to the enemy land. Whatever has happened in Hatti because of Tudhaliya, send it [away] O gods, [my lords]. Send [it] to the enemy land. May you again have mercy on Hatti, and let [the plague] subside. Furthermore, [because] I, your priest, your servant, elicit your pity, may you have mercy on me. Send away the worry from my heart, take away the anguish from my soul!

Colophon

(rev. 52'–53') [One tablet], complete. When Mursili made a plea [because of the plague . . .].

DISCUSSION

One of the most basic human religious instincts is to cry out for divine relief from suffering. Prayers of lament arose out of a background similar to other ancient Near Eastern prayers (see chap. 22), but the prayers in this chapter are distinguished by their remaining "in darkness," in lament, to their very end. Most psalmic prayers portray the reversal of the supplicant's suffering and thus shift to praise that affirms divine grace toward the end, but these prayers leave their speakers still waiting for divine intervention.

The prayer by Mursili II presented in this chapter is full of pathos. In the fourteenth century BCE, the Hittites dominated Asia Minor and beyond, peaking with the long and successful reign of Suppiluliuma I. However, the Hittite military apparently brought back a deadly disease from one of its more distant campaigns, resulting in a lengthy plague that killed a large number of people. Six years later, Suppiluliuma himself seems to have succumbed, and his first heir died just over a year later.[2] This brought Mursili to the throne at a very young age. The present text is from a few years later; with the plague having ravaged the land for some two decades, the king cries out for relief. Although it could be considered a communal lament (like a city lament; see chap. 25), the king speaks individually on behalf of the people, and his distress at being unable to alleviate his nation's suffering is apparent. There are about a half-dozen other major exemplars of the "plague prayers," all by Mursili.

The Hittites, in contrast to the psalmists, did not compose prayers of thanksgiving, although they did write hymns of praise.[3] Most Hittite prayers contain both hymnic material and requests for help; the so-called plague prayers are unique in having almost no hymnic content.

Mursili attributes his people's suffering to a vow broken by his father. (It is perhaps not accidental that the latter is not named, if he is supposed to be out of favor with the gods.) Suppiluliuma apparently attained the throne by killing the legitimate heir, Tudhaliya the Younger. This presents Mursili with a difficult rhetorical situation: he must acknowledge that "the gods protected [his] father" (§4), while still attributing the present suffering to a past transgression. He does this by averring that his father performed a ritual to expunge his own blood-guilt, but that he neglected to do so on behalf of the whole nation, which was also held guilty by the gods.

This theme of delayed punishment is hardly unique in the ancient Near East; it is also present in the Bible. The books of Kings attribute the fall of the northern kingdom to the sin of Jeroboam that had been committed two centuries earlier (1 Kgs. 13:34; 2 Kgs. 17:21–22), and the fall of the southern kingdom to the sin of Manasseh, even though it took place half a century after the end of his reign (2 Kgs. 21:9–17; 23:26; 24:3). A similarly dire fate is proclaimed by Isaiah to Hezekiah concerning the time of his sons (Isa. 39:5–8). In all these cases, the interpretation of history reflects a belief that the sins of

---

2. Billie Jean Collins, *The Hittites and Their World* (SBLABS 7; Atlanta: SBL, 2007), 49.

3. Singer states that the Hittites "expressed their gratitude to their gods through pious deeds, such as the erection and embellishment of temples, or the dedication of cult objects" (*Hittite Prayers*, 5).

the present do not merit the suffering that has come; therefore the guilt that brought the punishment must lie in the past.

Mursili's effort to project the reason for the plagues onto the past also allows him to indulge in a simultaneous rhetoric of guilt and innocence: He acknowledges that an error or oversight has taken place, but adds, "I have [not] done any evil" (§8). If that is not enough, he adds, "of those who sinned and did the evil, no one of that day is still here"! That is, he alerts the gods to the fact that there is no one left from the sinful generation to punish. The idea that an entire generation could be pervasively guilty is present also in the biblical account of the flood (Gen. 6:5; 7:1: "Yhwh said to Noah, 'Go into the ark, you and all your household, for I have seen that you alone are righteous before me in this generation'"), and when Deuteronomy explicitly engages the generations to come in the covenant with Yhwh (Deut. 6:20–25; 29:14–15), it may be to rule out the kind of rhetoric that excuses a later generation.

Numerous versions of Mursili's plague prayers have survived, and other prayers give other reasons for the plague, such as a failure to sacrifice to god Mala of the river Euphrates, or Suppiluliuma's violation of a treaty with Egypt.[4] There are also prayers directed toward different deities: toward Arinna, toward the storm-god, and even toward a deified deceased king, Telepinu. A tragic picture emerges of Mursili pursuing various explanations as the plague wore on, probably in consultation with his advisers and religious professionals.

The historical situation of Psalm 89 is quite likely the aftermath of the fall of Jerusalem. The Hebrew verb used for "plunder" in verse 41 ("All who pass by plunder him; he has become the scorn of his neighbors") is used for the Babylonian destruction in other contexts. The devastation that befell Jerusalem and its temple in 586 was nearly complete (see chap. 25). Many nations that suffered similar destructions were lost to history, as were the gods they worshiped; it is thus something of a wonder that the worshipers of Yhwh continued to recount the promises made to earlier generations after they seemed to be irrevocably broken, and to seek God's favor when it seemed to have been taken away once and for all.

Psalm 88 has a more private character, with its allusions to personal suffering and death. This sort of mixed imagery of suffering is fairly common in psalms and may reflect their lengthy process toward canonization (as opposed to the Hittite prayers, which have been recovered in the form of their first composition).[5] It is not hard to imagine Psalm 88 speaking to the same historical context as Psalm 89, but it is just as likely that it was composed for some other situation and placed here secondarily for its resonance with the events mentioned in Psalm 89. It is commonly theorized that these two psalms, with their uncommonly somber endings, were placed at the end of the third book of the Psalter as a liturgical reflection on the end of the kingdom of Judah.

There are numerous similarities between the psalms presented here and the Hittite prayers. Psalm 89 recalls past protection and salvation by Yhwh (89:1–37), and in light

---

4. Trevor Bryce, *The Kingdom of the Hittites* (Oxford: Clarendon Press, 1998), 224.

5. It is also notable that the psalms are in poetic form. The nature of Hittite poetic form is still being debated, but the text presented here certainly appears to be prose.

of that, it struggles to understand the rejection the nation is experiencing (89:38–51). There is a jarring shift of tone between the hymnic praises of the former section and the mournful lament of the latter. This combination of disparate elements is surely intentional on the part of the psalmist, even if the hymnic material reflects long-standing literary traditions.

Like the Hittite prayer, Psalm 89 has a strongly royal character. As in the case of Mursili, the Davidic heir speaks on behalf of the nation. But whereas the Hittite prayer sought to drive a wedge between the generations in order to absolve the present one, the psalm strongly asserts the connection to past generations by invoking the later king's expectation to inherit the promises made to his ancestor David (e.g., 89:3–4). Another significant difference is in the role of kingship in the two nations; the pressure on Mursili was even greater because the Hittite king was also the chief priest (§§1, 9). Although the Davidic ruler was anointed like a priest (vv. 20, 38, 51), there is no suggestion in Psalm 89 that he functioned as one.

Hittite prayers were quite literally arguments before the gods: the Hittite term for a prayer, *arkuwar*, is etymologically related to the English word "argument."[6] The supplicant was in effect arguing a case before divine judges. (One of the Hebrew words for prayer, *tefillah*, has similar judicial associations.) Although the preceding discussion of perceived causes of suffering in the Hittite prayers makes clear that the authors were concerned with issues of justice and wrongdoing, both they and the psalmists also appeal to divine self-interest in an attempt to motivate. Mursili notes that the plague has killed off many of those who prepare and give the offerings to the gods. If the plague continues, he boldly asserts, "[nobody will prepare] for you offering bread and libation any longer" (§8). The exact significance of the loss of sacrifice is not made clear in this text, but other Hittite texts state that the sacrifices are the food of the gods,[7] so perhaps the implication is that their very survival is at stake. Only rarely do psalmic appeals suggest that Yhwh is motivated by sacrifices (e.g., Pss. 20:3; 51:18–19; 54:6); more often, Yhwh's desire for sacrifice is diminished (Pss. 50:12–13; 69:30–31). The motivation that is expressed more often, including in these psalms, is Yhwh's desire for praise. With pointed rhetorical questions, Psalm 88:10–11 calls attention to the potential silencing: "Do the shades rise up to praise you? Is your steadfast love declared in the grave, or your faithfulness in Abaddon?" Although the requests of the psalmists are less explicitly named than those in the Hittite prayers, they are certainly implied: the laments about a lack of help invoke divine help; and the remembrances of past deliverance express a longing for future deliverance.

One notable distinction between the Hittite prayer and the psalms presented here is that the psalms make no effort to identify a reason for the divine wrath. Other psalms confess wrongdoing (e.g., Ps. 51:3–5), but that is not the case here. These psalms are focused on alerting God to the suffering of the speakers. In fact, they come close to laying the responsibility at the feet of God, as if God had been negligent and even broken promises (e.g., 89:49: "O Yhwh, where is your steadfast love of old, which by your faithfulness

---

6. Singer, *Hittite Prayers*, 5.

7. Paul Sanders, "*Argumenta ad Deum* in the Plague Prayers of Mursili II and in the Book of Psalms," in *Psalms and Prayers* (ed. Bob Becking and Eric Peels; OtSt 55; Leiden: Brill, 2007), 186.

you swore to David?"), but they stop short of explicit accusations or protests of innocence. One way to interpret this reticence to identify causes is that the suffering is so great that its reasons recede from importance in the mind of the speaker. The cry is loud and clear: Make it stop.

REFLECTION QUESTIONS

1. To what does Mursili attribute the plagues?
2. To what do the psalmists attribute their suffering, and what is the nature of that suffering in each case?
3. Mursili is the named speaker of the Hittite text, whereas the speaker is not specified in the psalms. How would you compare the speaking voices in each text? Whom do you imagine originally speaking the psalms?
4. How does the nation's history with the gods in question figure in each text?
5. What does Mursili assume will motivate the gods and goddesses to relent? Can you find examples in the Bible where the same assumption is operable?
6. What do the psalmists hope will motivate Yhwh to relent?
7. Which of the arguments in these texts strikes you as the most potentially effective, and why?
8. How would you compare the tone of the Hittite prayer and the psalms (to the best of your ability, although translation obscures some of the nuances of the originals)?

FURTHER READING

Bryce, Trevor. *The Kingdom of the Hittites*. Oxford: Clarendon Press, 1998. (Esp. 223–25.)
Greenberg, Moshe. "Hittite Royal Prayers and Biblical Petitionary Psalms." Pages 15–27 in *Neue Wege der Psalmenforschung*. Edited by Klaus Seybold and Erich Zenger. Freiburg: Herder, 1994.
Sanders, Paul. "*Argumenta ad Deum* in the Plague Prayers of Mursili II and in the Book of Psalms." Pages 181–217 in *Psalms and Prayers: Papers Read at the Joint Meeting of the Society of Old Testament Study and Het Oudtestamentisch Werkgezelschap in Nederland en België, Apeldoorn, August 2006*. Edited by Bob Becking and Eric Peels. OtSt 55. Leiden: Brill, 2007.
Singer, Itamar. *Hittite Prayers*. SBLWAW 11. Atlanta: Society of Biblical Literature, 2002.

25

City Laments

Lamentations over the Destructions of Sumer, Ur, and Jerusalem

LAMENTATIONS

When: After 586 BCE
Where: Jerusalem
Language: Hebrew

LAMENTATION OVER THE DESTRUCTION OF SUMER AND UR

What: Cuneiform text reconstructed from forty-seven fragmentary tablets
When: ca. 1740 BCE
Where: Copies from Nippur, Ur, and Larsa
Language: Sumerian
Translation: Piotr Michalowski[1]

> To overturn the (appointed) time, to forsake the (preordained) plans,
> The storms gather to strike like a flood.
> To overturn the (divine) decrees of Sumer,
> To lock the favorable reign in its abode,
> 5   To destroy the city, to destroy the temple,
> To destroy the cattle pen, to level the sheep fold,
> That the cattle not stand in the pen,
> That the sheep not multiply in the fold,
> That its watercourses carry brackish water,
> 10   That weeds grow in the fertile fields
> That "mourning" plants grow in the steppe,

1. Piotr Michalowski, *The Lamentation over the Destruction of Sumer and Ur* (Winona Lake, IN: Eisenbrauns, 1989).

That the mother does not seek out her child,
That the father not say, "Oh, my (dear) wife!"
That the junior wife not take joy in (his) embrace,
15   That the young child not grow vigorous on (her) knee,
That the wet-nurse not sing lullabies,
To change the location of kingship,
To defile the rights and decrees,
To take away kingship from the land,
20   To cast the eye (of the storm) on all the land,
To forsake the divine decrees by the order of An and Enlil,[2]
After An had frowned upon all the lands,
After Enlil had looked favorably on an enemy land,
After Nintu had scattered the creatures that she had created,
25   After Enki had altered (the course of) the Tigris and Euphrates,
After Utu had cast his curse on the roads and highways,
In order to forsake the divine decrees of Sumer, to change its (preordained)
        plans,
To alienate the (divine) decrees of the reign of kingship of Ur,
To defile the Princely Son in his (temple) Ekishnugal,[3]
30   To break up the unity of the people of Nanna,[4] numerous as ewes,
To change the food offerings of Ur, the shrine of magnificent food offerings,
That its people no longer dwell in their quarters, that they be given over (to
        live) in an inimical place,
That (the soldiers of) Shimashki and Elam,[5] the enemy, dwell in their place,
That its shepherd be captured by the enemy, all alone,
35   That Ibbi-Sîn[6] be taken to the land of Elam in fetters,
That from the mountain Zabu, which is on the edge of the Sealand, to the bor-
        ders of Anshan,[7]
Like a bird that has flown its nest, he not return to his city,
That on the two banks of the Tigris and Euphrates "bad weeds" grow,
That no one set out for the road, that no one seek out the highway,
40   That the city and its settled surroundings be razed to ruins,

---

2. The deities listed in lines 21–26 are all prominent in the Sumerian pantheon. They have different associations—An with the heavens, Enlil with storms, Enki with underground sources of water, Nintu with procreation, Utu with the sun—and they are portrayed as carrying out harm in each of those spheres.

3. The temple of Nanna at Ur.

4. Nanna was the city god of Ur. He was a moon-god and the son of Enlil. He is called "the Princely Son" in the previous line, and Su'en elsewhere in this text. Su'en later contracted to Sîn, a name used for the Mesopotamian moon-god in other texts in this volume.

5. Shimashki and Elam were both to the east of Sumer, in present-day Iran.

6. Ibbi-Sîn was the last king in the Ur III dynasty. He failed to control the region and was deported to Susa in 2004 BCE.

7. Much as the biblical stock phrase "from Dan to Beer-sheba" was meant to indicate the whole land of Israel, this seems to indicate the whole land of Sumer.

To slaughter its numerous black-headed people,

That the hoe not attack the fertile fields, that seed not be planted in the ground,

That the sound of the song of the one tending the oxen not resound on the plain,

That butter and cheese not be made in the cattle pen, that dung not be laid on the ground,

45 That the shepherd not enclose the sacred sheep fold with a fence,

That the song of churning not resound in the cattle pen,

To decimate the animals of the steppe, to finish off (all) living things,

That the four-legged creatures of Shakan[8] not lay dung on the ground,

That the marshes (be so dry as to) be full of cracks, that it not have any (new) seed,

50 That *saghul*-reeds grow in the canebrake, that they be covered by a stinking morass,

That there be no new growth in the orchards, that it all collapse by itself—

The city of Ur is a great charging aurochs, confident in its own strength,

It is the primeval city of Lordship and Kingship, built on sacred ground—

To quickly subdue it like a yoked ox, to bow its neck to the ground,

55 (the gods) An, Enlil, Enki, and Ninmach[9] decided its fate.

Its fate, which cannot be changed, who can overturn it—

Who can oppose the commands of An and Enlil?

An frightened the (very) dwelling of Sumer, the people were afraid,

Enlil blew an evil storm, silence lay upon the city,

60 Nintu bolted the door of the storehouses of the land,

Enki blocked the water in the Tigris and Euphrates,

Utu took away the pronouncement of equity and justice,

Inanna[10] handed over (victory in) strife and battle to a rebellious land,

Ningirsu[11] wasted Sumer like milk poured to the dogs.

65 Revolt descended upon the land, something that no one had ever known,

Something unseen, which had no name, something that could not be fathomed.

The lands were confused in their fear,

The god of that city turned away, its shepherd vanished.

The people, in fear, breathed only with difficulty,

70 The storm immobilizes them, the storm does not let them return,

There is no return for them, the time of captivity does not pass.

This is what Enlil, the shepherd of the black-headed people, did:

Enlil, to destroy the loyal household, to decimate the loyal man,

To put the evil eye on the son of the loyal one, on the first-born,

---

8. A god of goats and other hooved animals.

9. A mother-goddess associated with the creation of humankind.

10. An important female deity with complex mythology, Inanna (later Ishtar) was associated with warfare, among other things.

11. Ningirsu was a local manifestation of the warlike Ninurta, and also the city deity of Lagash.

75   Enlil then sent down Gutium[12] from the mountains.
     Their advance was as the flood of Enlil that cannot be withstood,
     The great storm of the plain filled the plain, it advanced before them,
     The teeming plain was destroyed, no one moved about there.
     The dark time was roasted by hailstones and flames,
80   The bright time was wiped out by a shadow.
     [[On that bloody day, mouths were crushed, heads were crashed,
     The storm was a harrow coming from above, the city was struck (as) by a hoe.]][13]
     On that day, heaven rumbled, the earth trembled, the storm worked without
           respite,
     The heavens were darkened, they were covered by a shadow, the mountains roared,
     The sun lay down at the horizon, dust passed over the mountains,
     The moon lay at the zenith, the people were afraid.
     [. . .]
     There were corpses (floating) in the Euphrates, brigands roamed [the roads].
95   [The father turned away from his wife], he says not, "Oh, my wife!"
     [The mother turned away from her child], she says not, "Oh, my child!"
     (The one) who had a productive estate [says not], "Oh, my estate!"
     The rich left his possessions and took an unfamiliar path.
     In those days the kingship of the land was defiled,
100 The crown that had been on the head (of the king) [. . .] by itself.
     The lands that had taken the same road (in obedience to Ur), were split into
           factions,
     The food offerings of Ur, the shrine (that received) magnificent food offerings,
           were changed (for the worse).
     Nanna traded away his people numerous as ewes.
     Its king sat immobilized in the palace, all alone.
105 Ibbi-Sîn was sitting in anguish in the palace, all alone.
     In the Enamtila,[14] the palace of his delight, he was crying bitterly.
     The devastating flood was leveling (everything),
     Like a great storm it roared over the earth, who could escape it?
     To destroy the city, to destroy the temple,
110 That traitors would lay on top of loyal men, and
     The blood of traitors flow upon loyal men.
     The first *kirugu*.[15]

12. The Gutians were a group of people, apparently centered in the Zagros Mountains, who troubled the Mesopotamians with raids for centuries near the end of the third millennium BCE, and even ruled for a while in more northern areas.

13. These two lines, numbered 80α and 80β, are not present in all copies of the text. In general, readers who would like to cite the text for scholarly purposes are encouraged to consult the original edition by Michalowski.

14. In Sumerian, Enamtila means "house of life," and it usually refers to the temple of Enlil. Here it seems to refer to the palace of Ibbi-Sîn. The significance of this is not clear.

15. *Kirugu* is the Sumerian word for "song."

The storms gather to strike like a flood.
—the antiphon[16] of the *kirugu*.

115   The temple of Kish, Hursagkalama, was destroyed,
       Zababa[17] took an unfamiliar path away from his beloved dwelling,
       Mother Ba'u was lamenting bitterly in her Urukug,
       "Alas, the destroyed city, my destroyed temple!" bitterly she cries.
       [*broken lines*]
       Kazallu, the city of teeming multitudes, was wrought with confusion,
       Numushda took an unfamiliar path away from the city, his beloved dwelling,
125   His wife Namrat, the beautiful lady, was lamenting bitterly,
       "Alas, the destroyed city, my destroyed temple!" bitterly she cries.
       Its river bed was empty, no water flowed,
       Like a river cursed by Enki, its opening channel was dammed up,
       On the fields fine grains grew not, people had nothing to eat,
130   The orchards were scorched like an oven, its (surrounding) steppe was
           scattered,
       The wild animals, the four-legged creatures did not run about,
       The four-legged creatures of Shakan could find no rest.
       Lugalmarada stepped outside his city,
       Ninzuana took an unfamiliar path away from her beloved dwelling,
135   "Alas, the destroyed city, my destroyed temple!" bitterly she cries.
       Isin, the shrine that was not a quay, was split by (onrushing) waters,
       Ninisina, the mother of the land, wept bitter tears,
       "Alas, the destroyed city, my destroyed temple!" bitterly she cries.
       Enlil smote Duranki with a mace,
140   Enlil established lamenting in his city, the shrine of Nippur,
       Mother Ninlil, the lady of the Kiur, wept bitter tears,
       "Alas, the destroyed city, my destroyed temple!" bitterly she cries.
       Kesh, built all alone on the high steppe, was haunted,
       Adab, which stretches out along the river, was deprived of water.
145   The snake of the mountain made his lair there, it became a rebellious land;
       The Gutians bred there, issued their seed.
       Nintu wept bitter tears over her creatures that she had created,
       "Alas, the destroyed city, my destroyed temple!" bitterly she cries.
       In Zabala the sacred Giguna was haunted,
150   Inanna abandoned Uruk, went off to enemy territory.
       In the Eanna the enemy laid his eyes upon the sacred Gipar shrine.

16. The antiphon typically summarizes the *kirugu* or song that it follows. The English term is taken from choral singing, though it not clear how these compositions were performed.

17. Essentially the entire second *kirugu* (song) is a listing of goddesses (and one god, Lugal-banda) who are forced to flee and then cry out for their cities. It would be unwieldy to attempt to identify each place and deity.

The sacred Gipar[18] of the *en*-ship[19] was defiled,
Its *En* priest[20] was snatched from the Gipar (and) carried off to enemy territory.
"Alas, the destroyed city, my destroyed temple!" bitterly she cries.
155   A violent storm blew over Umma, the brickwork in the midst of the "highland,"
Shara took an unfamiliar path away from the Emach, his beloved dwelling,
Ninmul cried bitter tears over her destroyed city,
"O my city, whose charms can no longer satisfy me!" bitterly she was crying.
Girsu, the city of heroes, was afflicted with a lightning storm,
160   Ningirsu took an unfamiliar path away from the Eninnu,
Mother Ba'u wept bitter tears in her Urukug,
"Alas, the destroyed city, my destroyed temple!" bitterly she cries.
On that day the word (of Enlil) was an attacking storm—who could fathom it?
The word of Enlil is destruction on the right, is . . . on the left,
165   This is what Enlil did in order to decide the fate of mankind:
Enlil brought down the Elamites, the enemy, from the highlands.
Nanshe, the Noble Son, was settled outside the city.
Fire approached Ninmar in the shrine Guabba,
Large boats were carrying off its precious metals and stones.
170   The lady—sacred Ninmar—was despondent because of her perished goods.
Then the day, burning like [. . .],
The province of Lagash was handed over to Elam.
And then the Queen also reached the end of her time,
Ba'u, as if she were human, also reached the end of her time:
175   "Woe is me, he (Enlil) has handed over (the city to the) storm,
He has handed (it) over to the storm that destroys cities,
He has handed (it) over to the storm that destroys temples!"
Dumuziabzu was full of fear in the temple of Kinunirsha,
Kinunirsha, the city of her noble youth, was ordered to be plundered.
180   The city of Nanshe [. . .] was delivered to the foreigners,
Sirara, her beloved dwelling, was handed over to the evil ones,
"Alas, the destroyed city, my destroyed temple!" bitterly she cries.
Its sacred Gipar of *en*-ship was defiled,
Its *En* priest was snatched from the Gipar (and) carried off to enemy territory.
185   A mighty arm was set over the bank(s) of the Idnuna-Nanna canal,
The settlements of Edana-Nanna were destroyed like a mighty cattle pen.
Its refugees, like stampeding goats, were chased by dogs.

---

18. In Sumerian, *gipar* means "storehouse," but it is used here as a designation for part of the sacred precinct of a goddess.

19. The Sumerian word *en* is used frequently from this point on. It means "lord, ruler," so that "*en*-ship" means "lordship."

20. See note above. As in English, "lordship" has both political and religious connotations. An "*En*-priest" is therefore a high priest who probably also had power in spheres of life that one would consider political today.

They destroy Gaesh like milk poured out to dogs,

Its finely fashioned statues they shatter,

190 "Alas, the destroyed city, my destroyed temple!" bitterly she cries.

Its sacred Gipar of *en*-ship was defiled,

Its *En* priest was snatched from the Gipar (and) carried off to enemy territory.

A lament was raised at the dais that stretches out toward heaven,

Its heavenly throne was not set up, it was not fit to be crowned,

195 Was cut down as if it were a date palm and tied together.

Ashu, the estate that stretches out along the river, was deprived of water,

At the place of Nanna where evil had never walked, the enemy walked,

Thus the temple was treated.

The Epuchruma was emptied,

200 Kiabrig, which used to be filled with numerous cows and numerous calves, was
destroyed like a mighty cattle pen,

Ningublaga took an unfamiliar path away from the Gabur,

Niniagara wept bitter tears all alone,

"Alas, the destroyed city, my destroyed temple!" bitterly she cries.

Its sacred Gipar of *en*-ship was defiled,

205 Its *En* priest was snatched from the Gipar (and) carried off to enemy territory.

Ninazu deposited (his) weapon in a corner in the Egida.

An evil storm swept over Ninhursag at the Enutura,

Like a dove she flew from the window, she stood away on the plain.

"Alas, the destroyed city, my destroyed temple!" bitterly she cries.

210 In the Gishbanda, the temple that was filled with lamentation, "lamentation"
reeds grew,

Ningizzida took an unfamiliar path away from the Gisbanda,

Ninazimua, the queen of the city, wept bitter tears,

"Alas, the destroyed city, my destroyed temple!" bitterly she cries.

On that day, the storm forced people to live in darkness,

215 In order to destroy Ku'ara, it forced people to live in darkness.

Ninechama in fear wept bitter tears,

"Alas, the destroyed city, my destroyed temple!" bitterly she cries.

Asarluhi put his robes on with haste [. . .],

Lugalbanda took an unfamiliar path away from his beloved dwelling,
Ninsun [. . .]

220 "Alas, the destroyed city, my destroyed temple!" bitterly she cries.

Eridu, floating on great waters, was deprived of drinking water,

[*broken lines*]

Enki took an unfamiliar path away from Eridu,

Damgalnuna, the mother of the Emah, wept bitter tears,

"Alas, the destroyed city, my destroyed temple!" bitterly she cries.

Its sacred Gipar was defiled,

250 Its *En* priest was snatched from the Gipar (and) carried off to enemy territory.

In Ur no one went to fetch food, no one went to fetch drink,
(But) the one who went to fetch food went away from the food, and so will not
    return,
The one who went to fetch drink went away from the drink, and so will not
    return.
To the south, the Elamites stepped in, slaughtering [. . .],
255   To the north, the vandals, the enemy [. . .],
The Tidnumites[21] daily strapped the mace to their loins,
To the south, the Elamites, like an onrushing wave, were [. . .],
To the north, like chaff blowing in the wind, [they . . .] over the steppe,
Ur, like a great charging aurochs, bowed its neck to the ground.
260   This is what Enlil, the one who decides the fates, then did:
For the second time he sent down the Elamites, the enemy, from the
    mountains.
The foremost temple, firmly founded [. . .],
In order to destroy Kisiga, ten, [nay five me]n [. . .]
Three days and three nights did not pass [. . .] the city was raked (as by) a hoe,
265   Dumuzi went out of Kisiga like a prisoner of war, his hands were fettered.

[*broken lines*]

She rode away from her possessions, she went to the mountains,
    She loudly sang out a lament over those brightly lit mountains:
"I am a Lady, (but) I had to ride away from my possessions, and now I am a
    slave in these parts,
I had to ride away from my precious metals and stones, and now I am a slave in
    these parts,
275   There, slavery, [. . .] people, who can [. . .] it?
There, slavery, Elam [. . .], who can [. . .] it?"
"Alas, the destroyed city, my destroyed temple!" bitterly she cries.
Her Majesty, though not the enemy, went to enemy land.

[*broken lines*]

[The second] k[irugu.]
Enlil threw open the door of the grand gate to the wind.
In Ur no one went to fetch food, no one went to fetch drink,
Its people rush around like water churning in a well,
295   Their strength has ebbed away, they cannot (even) go on their way.
Enlil afflicted the city with an inimical famine.
He afflicted the city with something that destroys cities, that destroys temples,
He afflicted the city with something that cannot be withstood with weapons,
He afflicted the city with dissatisfaction and treachery.
300   In Ur, which was like a solitary reed, there was not (even) fear,
Its people, like fish being grabbed (in a pond) sought shelter,

---

21. The Tidnumites were a group of Amorite tribespeople.

Everyone lay spread about, no one could rise.

At the royal station that was on top of the platform there was no food,

The king who was used to eating marvelous food grabbed at a (mere) ration,

305 (As) the day grew dark, the eye (of the sun) was eclipsing, (the people) experienced hunger,

There was no beer in his (the king's) beer-hall, there was no more malt (for making) it,

There was no food for him in the palace, it was made unsuitable to live in,

Grain filled not his lofty storehouse, he could not (send there for supplies) to save his life.

The grain stacks and grain depots of Nanna held no grain,

310 The evening meal in the great dining hall of the gods was defiled,

Beer, wine, and honey ceased (to flow) in the great dining hall,

The butcher knife that used to slay sheep and oxen lay hungry in the grass,

Its mighty oven no longer processed sheep and oxen, it no longer emitted the aroma (of roasting meat).

The sounds of the Bursag of Nanna were stilled,

315 The temple, which used to bellow like a bull, was silenced,

Its holy deliveries were no longer fulfilled, its [. . .] were alienated,

The mortar, pestle, and grinding stone lay idle, no one bends down (to use them).

The Shining Quay of Nanna was silted up.

The sound (of water lapping against) the prow of the boat ceased, there was no rejoicing,

320 The Unuribanda of Nanna was heaped with dust.

The rushes grew, the rushes grew, the "mourning reeds" grew (and as a result),

Boats and ships ceased docking at the Shining Quay.

Nothing moved on the watercourse that was fit for large ships.

The rites of the festivals at the place of the "plans" were altered,

325 The boat with first fruit-offerings no longer brings the first fruit offerings to the father who begat him (Nanna),

Its food offerings could not be taken to Enlil in Nippur.

Its watercourse was empty, (and so) ships could not travel,

There were no paths on both of its banks (for) long grasses grew (there).

The reed fence of the fecund cattle pen of Nanna was torn out,

330 The garden huts were overrun, (their) walls were breached,

The cow and her young were captured (and) carried off to enemy territory.

The *munzer*-fed cows[22] took an unfamiliar path, in a steppe that they did not know,

Gaiau,[23] who loves cows, dropped his weapon in the dung,

---

22. Sumerian *munzer* may refer to the licorice plant.
23. A minor deity known as "the shepherd of Sîn."

Shunidu,[24] who stores the butter and cheese, did not store the butter and cheese.

335   Those who are unfamiliar with butter were churning the butter,
Those who are unfamiliar with milk were [. . .]ing the cream.
The sound of the churning vat did not resound in the cattle pen,
Like mighty fire that used to burn (but now) its smoke is extinguished,
[. . .] the great dining hall of Nanna [. . .],

340   Su'en[25] wept to his father Enlil:
"O father who begot me, why have you turned away from Ur the city that was
      built for you?
O Enlil, why have you turned away from Ur, the city that was built for you?"
The boat with first fruit-offerings no longer brings the first fruit-offerings to
      the father who begot him,
Its food offerings could no longer be brought to Enlil in Nippur.

345   The En-priests of the city and of the countryside were carried off by phantoms,
Ur, like a city that has been wrought by the hoe, became a ruined mound,
The Kiur, the place of Enlil's flour offerings, became a haunted shrine.
O Enlil, your city [. . .] an empty wasteland,
Nippur; your city [. . .] an empty wasteland.

350   The dogs of Ur no longer sniff at the base of the city wall.
The one who (used to) drill large wells, (now just) scratches the ground in the
      market place.
"My father who bore me, my city, which is all alone, return to your embrace,
Enlil, my (city of) Ur, which is all alone, return to your embrace,
My Ekishnugal, which is all alone, return to your embrace!

355   May you bring forth offspring in Ur, may you multiply (its) people,
May you restore the (divine) decrees of Sumer that have been forgotten!"
The third *kirugu*.

Oh, the righteous temple, the righteous temple! Oh, its people, its people!
—the antiphon of the *kirugu*.

360   Enlil then answers his son Su'en:
"There is lamentation in the haunted city, 'mourning' reeds grow there,
In its midst there is lamentation, 'mourning' reeds grow there,
In it (the population) pass their days in sighing.
My son, the Noble Son [. . .], why do you concern yourself with crying?
O Nanna, the Noble Son [. . .], why do you concern yourself with crying?
The judgment of the assembly cannot be turned back,

365   The word of An and Enlil knows no overturning,
Ur was indeed given kingship (but) it was not given an eternal reign.

24. A minor deity who was called the son of Gaiau and a "herdsman of Sîn."
25. Another name for Nanna; see note to line 30.

From time immemorial, since the land was founded, until the population multiplied,
Who has ever seen a reign of kingship that would take precedence (forever)?
The reign of its kingship had been long indeed but had to exhaust itself.
370 O my Nanna, do not exert yourself (in vain), leave your city!"
Then, (upon hearing this), His Majesty, the Noble Son, became distraught,
Lord Asimbabbar, the Noble Son, grieved,
Nanna, who loves his city, left his city,
Su'en took an unfamiliar path away from his beloved Ur.
375 Ningal [. . .] in order to go to an alien place,
Quickly clothed herself (and) left the city.
(All) the Anunna stepped outside of Ur,
Ur [. . .] approached,
The trees of Ur were sick, the reeds of Ur were sick,
The trees of Ur were sick, the reeds of Ur were sick,
380 Laments sounded all along its city wall.
Daily there was slaughter before it.
Large axes were sharpened in front of Ur,
The spears, the arms of battle, were being launched,
The large bows, javelin, and siege-shield gather together to strike,
385 The barbed arrows covered its outer side like a raining cloud,
Large stones, one after another, fell with great thuds.
Daily the evil wind returns to (attack) the city.
Ur, which had been confident in its own strength, stood ready for slaughter,
Its people, oppressed by the enemy, could not withstand (their) weapons.
(Those) in the city who had not been felled by weapons, died of hunger,
390 Hunger filled the city like water, it would not cease,
(This) hunger contorts (people's) faces, it twists their muscles.
Its people are (as if) surrounded by water, they gasp for breath,
Its king breathed heavily in his palace, all alone,
Its people dropped (their) weapons, (their) weapons hit the ground,
395 They struck their necks with their hands and cried.
They sought counsel with each other, they searched for clarification,
"Alas, what can we say about it, what more can we add to it?
How long until we are finished off by (this) catastrophe?
Ur—inside it there is death, outside it there is death,
400 Inside it we are being finished off by famine,
Outside it we are being finished off by Elamite weapons.
In Ur the enemy has oppressed us, oh, we are finished!"
They take refuge behind it (the city walls), they were united (in their fear).
The palace that was destroyed by (onrushing) waters has been defiled, its bolt was torn out,
405 Elam, like a swelling flood wave, left only the spirits of the dead.
In Ur (people) were smashed as if they were clay pots,

Its refugees were (unable) to flee, they were trapped inside the walls,
Like fish living in a pond, they seek shelter.
The enemy seized the Ekishnugal of Nanna.
The statues that were in the treasury were cut down,
The great stewardess Niniagara cut herself off from the storehouse,
410   Its throne was cast down before it, she threw herself down into the dust.
Its mighty cows with shining horns were captured, their horns were cut off,
Its unblemished oxen and grass-fed cows were slaughtered, they were cut down
    as if they were date palms, and their (carcasses) were tied together.
The palm tree, (strong) as mighty copper, the heroic weapon,
Was torn out like (mere) rushes, was plucked like (mere) rushes, its trunk was
    turned sideways,
415   Its top lay in the dust, there was no one to raise it,
The midriffs of its palm fronds were cut off and their tops were burnt off,
Its date clusters that used to fall on the well were torn out.
The fertile reeds, which grew in the sacred [. . .], were defiled,
The great tribute that they had collected was hauled off to the mountains.
420   The great door ornament of the temple was felled, its parapet was destroyed,
The wild animals that were intertwined on its left and right
Lay before it like heroes smitten by heroes,
Its open-mouthed dragons (and) its awe-inspiring lions
Were pulled down with ropes like captured wild bulls and carried off to enemy
    territory.
425   The fragrant aroma of the sacred seat of Nanna was destroyed like that of a
    cedar grove,

[*broken lines*]

Verdicts were not given at the Dublamach,[26] the place where oaths used to be
    taken,
The throne was not set up at its place of judgment, justice was not
    administered.
440   Alamus[27] threw down his scepter, his hands trembled.
(Musicians) no longer played the *balag* instrument[28] in the sacred bedchamber
    of Nanna,
The sacred box that no one had set eyes upon was seen by the enemy,
The divine bed was not set up, it was not spread with clean hay,
The statues that were in the treasury were cut down,
445   The temple cook, the dream interpreter, and the "seal keeper" did not prepare
    the ceremony,
They stood in submission and were carried off by the foreigners.

---

26. The Dublamach is called "the place where justice is rendered" in royal inscriptions. It is not clear what or where it was.
27. Alamus was called the vizier of Nanna.
28. Probably a type of drum, although its identity is not certain.

The holy *azga*-priests of the sacred lustrations, the linen clad priests,
Forsake the sacred rites and decrees, they go off to a foreign city.
In his grief Su'en approached his father,
450 He went down on his knee in front of Enlil, the father who begot him.
"O father who begot me, how long will the enemy eye be cast upon my
   account, how long?
The *en*-ship and the kingship that you bestowed [. . .],
Father Enlil, the one who advises with just words,
The wise words of the land [. . .],
455 Your inimical judgment [. . .],
Look into your darkened heart, terrifying like waves!
O father Enlil, the fate that you have decreed cannot be explained!
[. . .] of *en*-ship, my ornament."
[. . .] he put on a mourning garment.
460 Enlil then provides a favorable response to his son:
"My son, the city that was built for you in joy and prosperity, it was given to
   you as your reign,
The destroyed city, the great wall, the walls with broken battlements: all this is
   part of the (appointed) reign,
[. . .]
[. . .] your dwelling—the Etemenniguru—that was properly built.
465 Ur shall be rebuilt in splendor, may the people bow down (to you),
There is to be bounty at its base, there is to be grain,
There is to be splendor at its top, the Sun will rejoice there!
Let an abundance of grain embrace its table,
May Ur, the city whose fate was pronounced by An, be restored for you!"
470 Having pronounced his blessing, Enlil raised his head toward the heavens
   (saying):
"May the land, north and south, be organized for Nanna,
May the road(s) of the land be set in order for Su'en!
Like a cloud hugging the earth, they shall submit to him,
By order of An and Enlil (abundance) shall be bestowed!"
475 Father Nanna stood in his city of Ur with head raised high (once again),
The hero Su'en entered into the Ekishnugal.
Ningal refreshed herself in her sacred living quarters,
In Ur she entered into her Ekishnugal.
The fourth *kirugu*.

There is lamentation in the haunted city, "mourning" reeds grew there,
480 In its midst there is lamentation, "mourning" reeds grew there.
Its people spend their days in moaning.
—the antiphon of the *kirugu*.

O bitter storm, retreat; O storm, storm return to your home!
O storm that destroys cities, retreat; O storm, storm return to your home!

485   O storm that destroys temples, retreat; O storm, storm return to your home!
Indeed, the storm that blew on Sumer, blew on the foreign lands,
Indeed, the storm that blew on the land, blew on the foreign lands,
It has blown on Tidnum, it has blown on the foreign lands,
It has blown on Gutium, it has blown on the foreign lands,
490   It has blown on Anshan, it has blown on the foreign lands,
(And) it leveled Anshan like a blowing evil storm.
Famine has overwhelmed the evil doer—may (that) people submit!
May An not change the decrees of heaven, the plans to treat the people with
    justice,
May An not change the decisions and judgments to lead the people properly,
495   Travel on the roads of the land—may An not change it,
May An and Enlil not change it—may An not change it,
May Enki and Ninmach not change it—may An not change it,
That the Tigris and Euphrates (again) carry water—may An not change it,
That there (again) be rain in the skies and good crops on the ground—may An
    not change it,
500   That there be water courses with water and fields with grain—may An not
    change it,
That the marshes support fish and fowl—may An not change it,
That fresh reeds and new shoots grow in the canebrake—may An not change it,
May An and Enlil not change it,
May Enki and Ninmach not change it,
505   That the orchards bear honey-plants and grapevines—may An not change it,
That the high plain bear the *mashgurum* plant[29]—may An not change it,
That there be long life in the palace—may An not change it,
That the Sealand bring forth abundance—may An not change it,
That the land be populated from north to south—may An not change it,
510   May An and Enlil not change it—may An not change it,
May Enki and Ninmach not change it—may An not change it,
That cities be rebuilt, that the people be numerous—may An not change it,
That in the whole universe the people be cared for—may An not change it!
O Nanna, your kingship is sweet, return to your place!
515   May a good abundant reign be long lasting in Ur!
Let its people lie down in safe pastures, let them copulate!
O mankind [. . .]
O Nanna—oh, your city! Oh, your temple! Oh, your people!
The fifth *kirugu*.

29. Identity unknown, but apparently a mark of a flourishing land.

DISCUSSION

One of the most remarkable effects of studying the long history of the ancient Near East is that it allows us to recognize that the political structures that can seem so permanent and meaningful are instead relatively ephemeral. Cities, nations, and civilizations come and go, rise and fall. Modern readers may be more familiar with the individual laments of the psalms (see chap. 24), but a separate genre mourned the fall of cities and reflected on the reasons and significance of such events.

Lamentation over the Destruction of Sumer and Ur

There are five surviving Mesopotamian city laments. They are all written in Sumerian, and although they draw on even older traditions, they responded specifically to the destruction of Sumerian cities at the end of the Ur III period (end of the 21st c. BCE) and the early Isin period (20th c. BCE). They include laments over Ur, Nippur, Eridu, and Uruk, and over Sumer and Ur together.

The Third Dynasty of Ur, the fall of which is lamented in the text above, had been one of the grandest in ancient Near Eastern history up to that point. Though regional in its power, it developed an extraordinarily organized, centralized system of production for goods such as textiles and metals, and tens of thousands of Sumerian documents have been discovered in its archives. Their king Ur-Namma recorded one of the earliest known Mesopotamian law codes (see chap. 7), and the kings of Ur also built some of the earliest ziggurats, for which Mesopotamia is famous. It is not hard to understand why poets might have mourned the fall of this civilization after it was overrun at the end of the twenty-first century BCE.

The five extant city laments are diverse in content and form, but they share certain themes. They all portray the total destruction of the city and its people, the role of the gods in deciding to destroy it, and the abandonment of the city by its patron deities (though its goddess often pleads for its deliverance). They also describe or presume the restoration of the city and/or temple and the return of the patron deity. Finally, they close with a prayer to the deity "involving either praise, plea, imprecation against the enemy, self-abasement, or a combination of these elements."[30]

The destruction of the city in each of the Sumerian city laments is described as being carried out by the onslaught of a massive storm. Many discussions of the texts treat this "storm" as a metaphor for a military attack by foreigners. In the case of Ur, the city-state was indeed threatened by Amorite tribes in the West, and eventually overrun by Elamites from the East (LSUr 401–5). However, the texts themselves at certain points indicate an even more comprehensive coincidence of factors, including drought, famine, and plague. It is difficult to separate these factors from military attack, since a besieged city often

---

30. W. C. Gwaltney, "The Biblical Book of Lamentations in the Context of Near Eastern Literature," in *Scripture in Context II: More Essays on the Comparative Method* (ed. W. W. Hallo, J. C. Moyer, and L. G. Perdue; Winona Lake, IN: Eisenbrauns, 1983), 202–3.

suffers drought and plague, but it seems plausible that such a major historical collapse of a well-organized state required an exceptional set of conditions.[31]

There is not much data to shed light on how (or whether) the city laments were used in ritual and worship. It is often thought that they were used when the Mesopotamians tore down and restored a temple, which would fit with images of restoration at the end of the text, but not so well with the picture of widespread suffering. Later lament forms (called *balag*s and *ershemma*s) that derived from the city laments were used when a sanctuary was to be razed and restored (the restoration and remodeling of temples was a major pastime of ancient Near Eastern rulers), but also during the *akitu* festivals (see chap. 8), to avert portended evil, and simply on certain fixed days in the religious calendar.

The later laments known as *balag*s and *ershemma*s began to appear around the same time that the city laments disappeared (in the Old Babylonian period, ca. 2000–1500), and they continued to be copied into the late first millennium. They preserve much of the material in the city laments, and so are demonstrably derived from the earlier compositions. However, they are "generalized [so as to be] easily adaptable to different cities, occasions, and times," and most scholarly interpreters find them comparatively "mechanical, often boring, repetitive, and unimaginative."[32] Although "their longevity and broad range of use suggest . . . that the ancients found great merit in them,"[33] they lack the poetic freshness and emotional force that make the older city laments more comparable to Lamentations.

One possible interpretation of the data is that the city laments were indeed composed to recount the fall of cities when the events were fresh, and that they were later adapted to regular cultic use in a bowdlerized form that was supposed to achieve the same cultic effect with less drama.

Lamentations

The book of Lamentations is made up of five poems, one per chapter. While the five are not uniform in all ways and can be analyzed separately, attempts to argue that different chapters were composed by different authors at different times have not been widely convincing. That is not to say they are certainly all by the same author, only that the data is at best equivocal. Since the poems show practically none of the hopes that were characteristic of the period after the return from the Babylonian exile, it is usually assumed that they were composed during the exile. Although the text is not a journalistic report of the destruction of Jerusalem, the visceral violence and terror of certain passages has indicated to many that its composition took place close to the destruction of the city in 586.

The Babylonian Chronicle confirms that Nebuchadnezzar had campaigned to Jerusalem in 597 and installed "a king of his own choosing" (Zedekiah) on the throne after the Judeans failed to pay the tribute at that time (see chap. 12). But that chronicle breaks off after 594. Second Kings 24:20–25:2 reports that Zedekiah, Nebuchadnezzar's hand-picked

31. H. L. J. Vantisphout, "The Death of an Era: The Great Mortality in the Sumerian City Laments," in *Death in Mesopotamia* (ed. B. Alster; Copenhagen: Akademisk Forlag, 1980), 85–86.

32. F. W. Dobbs-Allsopp, *Weep, O Daughter of Zion: A Study of the City-Lament Genre in the Hebrew Bible* (Biblica et orientalia 44; Rome: Pontificio Istituto Biblico, 1993), 13.

33. Gwaltney, "Biblical Book of Lamentations," 205.

puppet ruler, rebelled against him,[34] so that he besieged Jerusalem for nearly two years. At that point, Nebuchadnezzar was through trying to work with this distant kingdom; although the Assyrians were famous for their savagery in warfare and their deportations, the Babylonians were actually even less interested in managing their provinces. Nebu-chadnezzar destroyed Jerusalem, apparently with extreme vengeance, razing the city and not rebuilding it. The Babylonians went on to exploit the surrounding farmland from a small administrative center in Mizpah, but they never rebuilt Jerusalem at all.

As for the events that took place in the city when it was destroyed, Lamentations itself is one of the only sources. The picture is grim:

> Look, O Yhwh, and consider! To whom have you done this?
> Should women eat their offspring, the children they have borne?
> Should priest and prophet be killed in the sanctuary of Yhwh?
> The young and the old are lying on the ground in the streets;
> my young women and my young men have fallen by the sword;
> in the day of your anger you have killed them,
> slaughtering without mercy.
>
> (Lam. 2:20–21)

Jerusalem was a strongly fortified city, but it was not prepared to hold out for years. The images of the suffering of those within are if anything more horrifying than the images of the slaughter itself:

> Happier were those pierced by the sword than those pierced by hunger,
> whose life drains away, deprived of the produce of the field.
> The hands of compassionate women have boiled their own children;
> they became their food in the destruction of my people.
>
> (Lam. 4:9–10)

The language is poetic and sometimes metaphorical, but actually more consistently naturalistic in its portrayal of the city's destruction than the Sumerian laments. The destruction is repeatedly attributed to Yhwh, the national god (Lam. 1:5), but it is com-paratively clear that the suffering inflicted is related to a military siege and defeat. Super-natural storms and floods are not in view, as they are in the Sumerian text.

As with the Mesopotamian laments, the book of Lamentations may have had a liturgi-cal function in mourning the destruction of the city and temple. The fall of Jerusalem is said to have taken place in the fifth month (2 Kgs. 25:8), and Jeremiah 41:5 may testify to an early effort to commemorate the event when "eighty men arrived from Shechem and Shiloh and Samaria, with their beards shaved and their clothes torn, and their bodies gashed, bringing grain offerings and incense to present at the temple of Yhwh." In the postexilic period, Zechariah 7:3–5 and 8:19 testify to fasting, mourning, and lamenting at various times, including in the fifth month. Even more strikingly, the book of Ezra

---

34. Rebellion most often means a refusal to pay the tribute in cases such as this. Ezek. 17:15 reports that Zedekiah rebelled "by sending ambassadors to Egypt, in order that they might give him horses and a large army." Sending ambassadors to Egypt likely entailed sending the tribute to them instead of Babylon.

recounts that when sacrifice and worship were reestablished on the site of the temple, it was not an occasion of unalloyed joy, but of rejoicing and weeping together:

> Many of the priests and Levites and heads of families, old people who had seen the first house on its foundations, wept with a loud voice when they saw this house, though many shouted aloud for joy, so that the people could not distinguish the sound of the joyful shout from the sound of the people's weeping, for the people shouted so loudly that the sound was heard far away. (Ezra 3:12–13)

This incorporation of weeping into the rituals of rebuilding a temple is reminiscent of one of the uses of the Mesopotamian laments (see above). It is possible that Lamentations was recited at that time and regularly at the annual fasts.

Certain major differences also emerge in the comparison. For example, in the Lamentation over the Destruction of Sumer and Ur, no reason is given for the city's destruction. Since no explanation is given, the gods seem to act capriciously—"An, Enlil, Enki, and Ninmach decided its fate" (LSUr 55). By contrast, Lamentations lays the fault for the cataclysm squarely at the feet of the people: "Jerusalem sinned grievously, so she has become an object of scorn" (Lam. 1:8, cf. 3:39; 5:7, 16).

The Question of Influence

There is a vast historical gap, approximately a millennium, between the Sumerian and biblical texts presented here. There are no copies of the Sumerian city laments later than the Old Babylonian period (ca. 1500 BCE), while Lamentations probably dates to the sixth century BCE. In light of that gap, one of the first critical issues that any comparison of these texts must address is how there could be any relationship at all. Along with the historical distance, the lack of closely parallel phraseology has caused some scholars to renounce any literary relationship between the texts. As McDaniel wrote, "It seems best to abandon any claim of literary dependence or influence of the Sumerian lamentations on the biblical Lamentations. At most the indebtedness would be the *idea* of a lamentation over a beloved city. But since there is such a natural corollary to individual and collective lamentations or funeral laments, indebtedness may properly be discarded."[35]

This judgment, made more than forty years ago, now appears too dismissive. One link between the two periods is formed by the later Mesopotamian liturgical laments (*balag*s and *ershemma*s) discussed above. Since these were still being copied in the late first millennium, they were still in use when the Judeans went into exile in Babylon. The idea that Hebrew authors were influenced by Babylonian compositions has been one of the assumptions of many who see similarities between Lamentations and the city laments. As C. J. Gadd wrote, referring to Psalm 137, "Certainly not all of the harps were left hanging by the waters of Babylon, and some were attuned to sing at home the songs of a strange land."[36]

---

35. Thomas McDaniel, "The Alleged Sumerian Influence upon Lamentations," *VT* 18 (1968): 209.
36. C. J. Gadd, "The Second Lamentation for Ur," in *Hebrew and Semitic Studies* (Festschrift for G. R. Driver; ed. D. W. Thomas and W. D. McHardy; Oxford: Clarendon Press, 1963), 61 n. 2.

Another piece of data that helps to close the gap between the Sumerian and Judean texts is the existence of suggestive pieces of the city-lament form within the earlier Hebrew prophets, for example, the eighth-century prophet Amos's description of Israel's decimation:

> Fallen, no more to rise, is maiden Israel;
> > forsaken on her land, with no one to raise her up.
> For thus says Yhwh GOD:
> The city that marched out a thousand shall have a hundred left,
> > and that which marched out a hundred shall have ten left.
> > > > (Amos 5:2–3)

Jeremiah 31:15 also shows possible influence of the city-lament genre in its portrait of the weeping of Rachel; as the wife of the patriarch Jacob, the personification of Israel, she is a natural analogue for the weeping national goddess in the city laments:

> A voice is heard in Ramah,
> > lamentation and bitter weeping.
> > Rachel is weeping for her children;
> > she refuses to be comforted for her children,
> > because they are no more.

One can compare the personification of Zion in Lamentations 1:17.

On the basis of these and numerous other passages in the prophets (particularly in the oracles against the nations; cf. chap. 16), Hillers and Dobbs-Allsopp have argued that Israel and Judah had their own *native* city-lament genre. While all these biblical texts must in some way hark back to earlier prototypes, the genre does seem fully absorbed into its West Semitic context. It does not have such Mesopotamian features as polytheism and lengthy lists (LSUr 115–275, etc.).[37] Even a feature that appears similar at first, such as the five *kirugu* (songs) of the Mesopotamian lament and the five chapters of Lamentations, turns out not to be significant for comparison, since other city laments had different numbers of *kirugu* and there is no correlation between the content of the corresponding sections.

The idea of a native city-lament genre also accounts for the lack of numerous close parallels in the wordings of the two texts better than the notion of direct literary influence. There are a few—for example, Lam. 4:5 ("Those who feasted on delicacies perish in the streets") can be compared with LSUr 304 ("The king who was used to eating marvelous food grabbed at a [mere] ration"; cf. LSUr 312–13).[38] But even that image is part of a more widespread ancient Near Eastern literary motif of the "world upside down"—the

---

37. Dobbs-Allsopp, *Weep, O Daughter*, 158.

38. There are other parallels between Lamentations and the later lament forms; for example, compare Lam. 1:10 ("She saw the heathen enter her sanctuary") with the Mesopotamian lament, "That enemy has caused men wearing shoes to enter (my) cella. That enemy has brought the unwashed into the chamber. He has laid his hands on it and I am afraid" (Delbert R. Hillers, *Lamentations* [2nd ed.; AB 7A; New York: Doubleday, 1992], 32–33).

social order is portrayed as inverted in bad times—so that it is not necessarily a case of direct influence.

Instead, it is the accumulation of thematic similarities that makes the most compelling case for a relationship between these texts. Dobbs-Allsopp[39] identified nine characteristics of the city-lament genre, of which eight are at least partially relevant to its biblical manifestations (since both compositions are lengthy, the examples given here are not intended to be exhaustive):

1. *Subject and mood:* Each text concerns the destruction of a city and is "mournful and somber" in mood.

2. *Structure and poetic technique:* City-lament texts include speech from various points of view, and employ techniques such as portraying the reversal of the city's formerly happy order (e.g., LSUr 300–32; Lam. 1:1; 2:1; 4:1–10). Parallelism is also used in both, as is the alternation of first-, second-, and third-person speech (which creates an impression of comprehensiveness in the lament).

3. *Divine abandonment:* The gods of the city to be destroyed leave it before the destruction happens (e.g., LSUr 115–278; Lam. 2:7; 5:20).[40]

4. *Assignment of responsibility:* Although the reasons vary between the Sumerian and biblical compositions, each of them gives some reason for the city's destruction. (e.g., LSUr 22–26, 55–57; Lam. 1:5, 8–9; 4:13; 5:16, etc.)

5. *The divine agent:* In each of these texts the gods are portrayed as playing a role in the city's destruction. In each case, the gods employ foreign nations (e.g., LSUr 72–84, 163–69; Lam. 1:10) and natural forces (e.g., LSUr 59, etc.; Lam. 1:13) in the destruction. In Lamentations, Yhwh takes a particularly active role in the destruction as the Divine Warrior (2:1–9).

6. *Destruction:* Each text portrays the destruction of the city, its sanctuaries, its people—its entire society and culture.

7. *The weeping goddess:* This characteristic is less prominent in Lamentation over the Destruction of Sumer and Ur (cf. lines 115–18), but is a major feature of the similar Lament for Ur, where Ningal weeps after her petition for her city is denied. In the Bible, the monotheistic tendencies of the Judean authors made goddess imagery unsuitable, and so it is the personified Daughter Zion who weeps (e.g., Lam. 1:2).

8. *Lamentation:* This mourning over the fate of each city is what gave the genre its name (e.g., LSUr 361–62, 380; Lam. 1:4, 16; 2:5, 11; 5:15)

9. *Restoration of the city and the return of the gods:* It has been theorized that the Sumerian compositions were used as ritual texts for ceremonies celebrating a city's (or a temple's) restoration, since each one concludes with reports of and/or prayers for the well-being of the destroyed city (LSUr 483–516). Lamentations does not reach this last point; it is only hoped for (5:21).

In the end, the objections raised by McDaniel do not quite convince; it is quite true that any of the individual motifs that he notes could be random, but the constellation of them in both places makes the two compositions seem similar.

Perhaps the most important modification of earlier assumptions that needs to be made is the admission that certainty about the path of the influence is impossible, and that

---

39. Dobbs-Allsopp, *Weep, O Daughter,* 30–96.

40. The image of Zion as a widow may also reflect abandonment by her divine spouse, Yhwh (cf. Hos. 1–3; Isa. 5:1–7). See also chap. 18 of this volume.

indeed it may have come indirectly through multiple channels. This recognition would actually be a return to an older position held by a leading Sumerologist such as S. N. Kramer, who wrote that "Sumerian influence penetrated the Bible through Canaanite, Hurrian, Hittite, and Akkadian literature."[41] Dobbs-Allsopp points out that current literary theory has come to a more complex understanding of influence:

> Even assuming the fact of some type of literary influence, the idea that text A must be the direct source of text B is somewhat simplistic. Often the 'emitter' and 'receiver' of literary influence are not directly linked, but are connected by 'intermediaries.' . . . Moreover, given the geographical proximity of cultural areas within the ancient Near East, one cannot discount the possibility that these Mesopotamian traditions entered the Hebrew Bible orally.[42]

This freer approach to the relationship between the texts helps one to compare aspects of the compositions that do not seem similar at first. For example, it is noted above that Lamentations does not partake in the Mesopotamian habit of making lengthy lists. However, chapters 1–4 are each in the form of an acrostic—that is, each line (or group of lines) begins with a letter of the alphabet, in alphabetic order. (This feature cannot be conveyed in translation.) It seems that both of these literary techniques—lists and acrostics—were likely intended to convey a *comprehensive* account of suffering by covering all the bases.

This brings up a final point: there is a purpose to the literary forms of lament in the ancient Near East; their formalism provides a way to structure grief so as to control it. Like a funeral liturgy in a prayer book, they provide words for those who may be too overwhelmed by grief to produce their own: *Ashes to ashes, dust to dust.* Like any literature, there is the potential for liturgies to become ossified and lose their power (as happened with the *balag*s and *ershemma*s), but the texts in this chapter still straddle the gap between the raw suffering of the event and its muted commemoration in later liturgy.

REFLECTION QUESTIONS

1. How would you compare and/or contrast the tone and imagery of the two laments?
2. How conscious do you think the author or authors of Lamentations were that their composition had affinities with other laments for fallen cities?
3. What effect does the shift from (Mesopotamian) polytheism to (Judean) monotheism have on the way that these texts "think" theologically? Where is blame assigned in each case for the suffering inflicted on the cities?
4. Related to the last question, what is known and unknown in each text about God or the gods?
5. What does the ending of each text do to the meaning of the whole? What do you think is the relationship of each ending to the historical circumstances in which it was composed or read?

41. Samuel Noah Kramer, *The Sumerians: Their History, Culture, and Character* (Chicago: University of Chicago Press, 1963), 291.
42. Dobbs-Allsopp, *Weep, O Daughter*, 5–6.

6. What effect would it have to recite texts such as these in a community to commemorate the fall of a city? What lessons does each text seem to want to convey about these past events?

7. If your city were destroyed, or your nation were conquered, and you had to write something to commemorate that event, would you write something like these texts? Why or why not?

FURTHER READING

Dobbs-Allsopp, F. W. *Weep, O Daughter of Zion: A Study of the City-Lament Genre in the Hebrew Bible*. Biblica et orientalia 44. Rome: Pontificio Istituto Biblico, 1993.

Gwaltney, W. C. "The Biblical Book of Lamentations in the Context of Near Eastern Literature." Pages 191–211 in *Scripture in Context II: More Essays on the Comparative Method*. Edited by W. W. Hallo, J. C. Moyer, and L. G. Perdue. Winona Lake, IN: Eisenbrauns, 1983.

Hillers, Delbert R. *Lamentations*. 2nd ed. AB 7A. New York: Doubleday, 1992.

Kramer, Samuel Noah. "Sumerian Literature: A General Survey." Pages 327–52 in *The Bible and the Ancient Near East: Essays in Honor of William Foxwell Albright*. Edited by G. E. Wright. Garden City, NY: Doubleday, 1961.

———. "Sumerian Literature and the Bible." *Analecta Orientalia* 12 (*Studia Biblica et Orientalia* 3) (1959): 185–204.

McDaniel, Thomas. "The Alleged Sumerian Influence upon Lamentations." *VT* 18 (1968): 198–209.

Michalowski, Piotr. *The Lamentation over the Destruction of Sumer and Ur*. Winona Lake, IN: Eisenbrauns, 1989.

Vanstiphout, H. L. J. "The Death of an Era: The Great Mortality in the Sumerian City Laments." Pages 83–89 in *Death in Mesopotamia*. Edited by B. Alster. Copenhagen: Akademisk Forlag, 1980.

26

Persian Edicts

Letter to Gadatas and Ezra 6:1–12

EZRA 6:1–12

When: Ca. 520 BCE (see below)
Where: Jerusalem
Language: Aramaic

LETTER TO GADATAS

What: Greek text on marble stela recording letter from Darius
When: 521–486 BCE (existing stela is a Roman-period copy)
Where: Near Magnesia of Maeander (Asia Minor)
Language: Greek
Translation: By the author

Thus says the King of Kings, Darius, son of Hystapes, to Gadatas, his servant: I have learned that you do not obey my orders in all things. For on the one hand, you work my land, planting the produce from Beyond (the) Euphrates as far as the coast of the region of Asia. I commend your intent, and on account of all these things there will be established for you great gratitude in the King's house.

On the other hand, because you lose sight of my wishes regarding the gods, I will cause you to experience my offended anger if you do not change. Indeed, you have exacted tribute from the gardener-priests of Apollo, and you assigned [them] profane land to dig, not recognizing my ancestors' purpose on behalf of the god who spoke to the Persians only truth, and to the . . .

[*Text breaks off*]

DISCUSSION

In the first half of the first millennium BCE, imperial rule increasingly became the norm in the Near East. The Assyrians, Babylonians, and Persians controlled successively larger empires. Under such conditions, officials in far-flung locales sometimes depended on a judgment from the distant imperial court. Unfortunately, little is known about the way the Persians ran their empire, and many of the records that have survived are from foreign nations (see also chap. 27). Despite the empire's relatively long endurance and vast extent, there are few records of its concrete management of such matters.

The Letter to Gadatas is thus an important and rare witness to Persian imperial policy toward the temples and religious personnel in the outlying provinces. The authenticity of the letter has sometimes been questioned, partly because it is in Greek rather than Persian or Aramaic (the administrative language thought to have been used in the Western provinces), and partly because it exists only in a copy that can be assigned to the Roman period based on the style of the carving.[1] However, it is now widely accepted to be a late copy of a Greek translation of an authentic Persian decree.

The Persian Empire was divided into provinces administered by governors known as satraps. There was a residence near Magnesia for the satrap of Sardis, and it has been reasoned that Gadatas held that office; it was also normal for a governor's duties to include the maximization of a region's horticultural output. Gadatas is praised for cultivating exotic plants in new areas, but it appears he has been a bit too zealous in exploiting the labor of the local priests, who had their own temple precincts to tend and had been exempted from paying tribute and performing forced labor. A comparable decree is found in Ezra 7:24, part of a decree by the Persian emperor Artaxerxes (r. 464–424): "We also notify you that it shall not be lawful to impose tribute, custom, or toll on any of the priests, the Levites, the singers, the doorkeepers, the temple servants, or other servants of this house of God."

There are other indications outside the Bible that Darius (r. 521–486) took an interest in the religions of the subject peoples. For example, the Greek historian Diodorus Siculus (1st c. BCE) wrote,

> Darius the father of Xerxes . . . was incensed at the lawlessness which his predecessor, Cambyses, had shown in the treatment of the sanctuaries of Egypt, and aspired to live a life of virtue and of piety towards the gods. Indeed he associated with the priests of Egypt themselves, and took part with them in the study of theology and of the events recorded in their sacred books; and when he learned from these books about the greatness of soul of the ancient kings and about their goodwill towards their subjects he imitated their manner of life. For this reason he was the object of such great honor that he alone of all the kings was addressed as a god by the Egyptians in his lifetime, while at his death he was accorded equal honors with the ancient kings of Egypt who had ruled in strictest accord with the laws. (1.95.4–5)

Of course, this story was written long after the events it narrates, but it seems reasonable to give some credence to the way a person was remembered.

---

1. Pierre Briant, *From Cyrus to Alexander: A History of the Persian Empire* (trans. Peter T. Daniels; Winona Lake, IN: Eisenbrauns, 2002), 491.

It may seem odd that a text such as the Letter to Gadatas would have been copied hundreds of years after it was issued, especially at a time when the imperial power that issued it had been superseded. Then again, the perceived antiquity of the decree may have been part of its appeal. Although Darius's words no longer had the force of law, it was surely worth something to be able to assert that one's sacred rites had been established long ago. The claim that "it has always been this way" still carries weight in many instances.

To say that the Persian decrees in Ezra 1:2–4 and 6:1–12 are also based on authentic documents risks oversimplifying the process of copying and editing, and ignoring the likely modifications that such a process would have introduced; nevertheless, that is the basic direction in which the data point. H. G. M. Williamson (1983; 2008) has argued for that conclusion on the basis of formal and linguistic aspects of the text.[2] Furthermore, the governor Tattenai named in Ezra 6:6, 13 is also attested in the same capacity in a letter from the same time period unearthed in Babylon.[3]

If the documents are based on authentic originals, and if work on the Second Temple resumed in the second year of Darius's reign, as Ezra 4:24 reports, then the original decree is to be dated to 520. Like the Letter to Gadatas, the decrees in the Bible as we have them underwent a lengthy process of transmission, since they have been incorporated into the book of Ezra, which was not completed until at least the late fifth century.[4] Arguably the local authorities in both cases made it a point to transcribe and preserve the statement of imperial favor; in a world without hard drives and Google searches, the transmission of such documents was a way to guarantee that their special rights and status were not forgotten.

While the decrees regarding the Jerusalem temple were epoch-making for the Judeans, they were apparently not extraordinary for the Persian political establishment. Cyrus had similarly ensured himself a warmer reception in Babylon by protecting and supporting its temples, as he reported in his well-known cylinder inscription. Some historians have asserted that support for local religions was a policy of the Achaemenid empire. However, most ancient Near Eastern empires did not adhere to strict policies in their treatment of conquered peoples. Indeed, it is not clear that Persian treatment of foreign temples was uniform. Greek historians such as Herodotus (*Hist.* 3) and Strabo (*Geogr.* 17.1.27, 46) reported that the Persian Cambyses (r. 529–522) desecrated and destroyed Egyptian temples. However, the native Egyptian records tell a different story—although there were some depredations and loss of revenue, in general the temples were treated with respect.

Thanks to the Persians' own rhetoric and their rapturous reception in the Bible, they are sometimes portrayed as the world's first champions of human rights and religious

---

2. H. G. M. Williamson, "The Aramaic Documents in Ezra Revisited," *JTS* 59 (2008): 41–62; and Williamson, "The Composition of Ezra i–vi," *JTS* 34 (1983): 1–30.

3. Diana Edelman, *The Origins of the 'Second' Temple: Persian Imperial Policy and the Rebuilding of Jerusalem* (London: Equinox, 2005).

4. "The scribe Ezra" appears also in Neh. 8, and the mission of Nehemiah was likely not until the middle of the fifth century (see chap. 27). The appearance side-by-side of figures who are generally thought to have lived about a half century apart raises historical problems, of course. But from a literary standpoint, the two books show signs of common shaping, so they are often considered as a literary unity.

tolerance. It is important to note that, whatever noble impulses they may have had, they were driven also by pragmatic concerns when they authorized support for outlying areas such as Judah. As with the treatment of Babylon reported in the Cyrus Cylinder, it is probable that Cyrus's decrees regarding the Jerusalem temple and the return of the Jews had political objectives in mind.

Numerous theories have been propounded about Cyrus's reasons.[5] He was probably already anticipating an expedition against Egypt, which was on the other side of Judea. There were also a number of uprisings in the western part of the empire in the fifth century, so it was a natural time for the Persians to seek to create nodes of passionate loyalists in the imperial grid. By granting the Judeans this favor, he ensured their allegiance and at least their pacifism, if not perhaps their outright participation (the Persian army was made up of diverse troops from all over the empire). The Persians had a massive empire and could not have ruled it entirely by force.

From this perspective, inspired acts of graciousness and generosity (such as helping to rebuild the Jerusalem temple) can also be seen as pragmatic attempts to reconcile local subjects to centralized power. The maintenance and reinforcement of the empire remained the Persians' fundamental objective.

REFLECTION QUESTIONS

1. What literary, ideological, or rhetorical aspects of each inscription strike you as authentic? That is, what aspects of each text strike you as something a Persian ruler would actually have decreed?

2. What aspects of each text strike you as strange for a Persian emperor to decree?

3. If there are sections of either text that appear not to directly reflect an imperial document, what might have been the impetus for scribal copyists to alter or augment the text?

4. What would the effect of each decree have been among the temple officials in Magnesia and Jerusalem, respectively? Among the broader populations in each area?

5. What could have been some reasons for the Persians' apparent indulgence of foreign religions, other than a philosophical respect for religious pluralism?

6. Can you think of public actions in your own world that could be interpreted as either inspired or pragmatic, or both?

FURTHER READING

Briant, Pierre. *From Cyrus to Alexander: A History of the Persian Empire*. Translated by Peter T. Daniels. Winona Lake, IN: Eisenbrauns, 2002.

Edelman, Diana. *The Origins of the 'Second' Temple: Persian Imperial Policy and the Rebuilding of Jerusalem*. London: Equinox, 2005.

---

5. For a more complete accounting of the theories, see Edelman, *Origins of the 'Second' Temple*, 3–9, 332–51.

Grabbe, Lester L. "The 'Persian Documents' in the Book of Ezra: Are They Authentic?" Pages 531–70 in *Judah and the Judeans in the Persian Period*. Edited by O. Lipschits and M. Oeming. Winona Lake, IN: Eisenbrauns, 2006.

Williamson, H. G. M. "The Aramaic Documents in Ezra Revisited." *JTS* 59 (2008): 41–62.

———. "The Composition of Ezra i–vi." *JTS* 34 (1983): 1–30.

27

Autobiographies

Udjahorresne and Nehemiah

NEHEMIAH 1:1–2:8; 5:16–19; 13:6–31

When: Fifth century
Where: Jerusalem
Language: Hebrew

INSCRIPTION OF UDJAHORRESNE

What: Hieroglyphic inscription on green basalt statue of standing figure holding a *naos*
   (or shrine), Vatican Museum, 0.7 meter tall
When: ca. 520 BCE
Where: Sais
Language: Egyptian
Translation: Miriam Lichtheim, *AEL*, III.37–40

[Text on the front and roof of the naos:]

(1) An offering that the King gives (to) Osiris-Hemag:[1] A thousand of bread, beer, oxen, and fowl, everything good and pure, for the *ka*[2] of the one honored by the gods of Sais, the chief physician, Udjahorresne.

An offering that the King gives (to) Osiris who presides over the Palace: A thousand of bread, beer, oxen, and fowl, clothing, myrrh, and unguent, and every good thing, for the *ka* of the one honored by all the gods, the chief physician, Udjahorresne.

---

1. The manifestation of Osiris (god of the underworld) that was characteristic of Sais. The name is not entirely clear, but seems to mean something like "Osiris made of carnelian." Carnelian is a semiprecious stone, varying in color from orange to brownish-red.
2. In Egyptian mythology, one of the elements of the soul.

(3) O Osiris, lord of eternity! The chief physician, Udjahorresne, has placed his arms about you as protection.[3] May your *ka* command that all blessings be done for him, according as he protects your chapel forever.

[*Text under the right arm:*]

(7) The one honored by Neith-the-Great,[4] the mother of god, and by the gods of Sais, the prince, count, royal seal-bearer, sole companion, true beloved King's friend, the scribe, inspector of council scribes, chief scribe of the great outer hall, administrator of the palace, (9) commander of the royal navy under the King of Upper and Lower Egypt, Khenemibre,[5] commander of the royal navy under the King of Upper and Lower Egypt, Ankhkare,[6] Udjahorresne; engendered by the administrator of the castles (of the red crown), chief-of-Pe priest, *rnp*-priest, priest of the Horus Eye, prophet of Neith who presides over the nome of Sais, Peftuaneith; (11) he says:

The Great Chief of all foreign lands, Cambyses[7] came to Egypt, and the foreign peoples of every foreign land were with him.[8] When he had conquered this land in its entirety, they established themselves in it, and he was Great Ruler of Egypt and Great Chief of all foreign lands.

His majesty assigned to me the office of chief physician. (13) He made me live at his side as companion and administrator of the palace. I composed his titulary, to wit his name of King of Upper and Lower Egypt, Mesutire.[9]

I let his majesty know the greatness of Sais, that it is the seat of Neith-the-Great, the mother who bore Re[10] and inaugurated birth when birth had not yet been; and the nature of the greatness of the temple of Neith, that it is heaven in its every aspect; and the nature of the greatness of the castles of Neith, (15) and of all the gods and goddesses who are there; and the nature of the greatness of the Palace, that it is the seat of the Sovereign, the Lord of Heaven;[11] and the nature of the greatness of the Resenet and Mehenet sanctuaries; and of the House of Re and the House of Atum,[12] the mystery of all the gods.

[*Text under the left arm:*]

(16) The one honored by his city-god and all the gods, the prince, count, royal seal-bearer, sole companion, true beloved King's friend, the chief physician, Udjahorresne, born of Atemirdis, he says:

I made a petition (18) to the majesty of the King of Upper and Lower Egypt, Cambyses, about all the foreigners who dwelled in the temple of Neith, in order to have them expelled from it, so as to let the temple of Neith be in all its splendor, as it had been before. His majesty commanded to expel all the foreigners (20) [who] dwelled in the

3. Note that the statue is holding a shrine to Osiris.
4. Neith was the patron goddess of Sais.
5. Throne name of King Amasis.
6. Throne name of King Psamtik III.
7. Cambyses ruled the Persian Empire 529–522.
8. The Persian army was famous for incorporating fighting units from all over the empire.
9. The throne name of Cambyses, which means "Offspring of Re."
10. An Egyptian solar deity.
11. Osiris.
12. All temples in Sais.

temple of Neith, to demolish all their houses and all their unclean things that were in this temple.

When they had carried [all their] personal [belongings] outside the wall of the temple, his majesty commanded to cleanse the temple of Neith and to return all its personnel to it, (22) the [. . .] and the hour priests of the temple. His majesty commanded to give divine offerings to Neith-the-Great, the mother of god, and to the great gods of Sais, as it had been before. His majesty commanded [to perform] all their festivals and all their processions, as had been done before. His majesty did this because I had let his majesty know the greatness of Sais, that it is the city of all the gods, who dwell there on their seats forever.

[*Text on the left side of the naos base:*]

(24) The one honored by the gods of Sais, the chief physician, Udjahorresne, he says:

The King of Upper and Lower Egypt, Cambyses, came to Sais. His majesty went in person to the temple of Neith. He made a great prostration before her majesty, as every king has done. He made a great offering (26) of every good thing to Neith-the-Great, the mother of god, and to the great gods who are in Sais, as every beneficent king has done. His majesty did this because I had let his majesty know the greatness of her majesty Neith, that she is the mother of Re himself.

[*Text on the right side of the naos base:*]

(28) The one honored by Osiris-Hemag, the chief physician, Udjahorresne, he says:

His majesty did every beneficence in the temple of Neith. He established the presentation of libations to the Lord of Eternity[13] in the temple of Neith, as every king had done before. (30) His majesty did this because I had let his majesty know how every beneficence had been done in this temple by every king, because of the greatness of this temple, which is the seat of all the gods everlasting.

[*Text on the left wall of the naos and on the statue's garment:*]

(31) The one honored by the gods of the Saite nome,[14] the chief physician, Udjahorresne, he says:

I have established the divine offering of Neith-the-Great, the mother of god, according to his majesty's command for all eternity. I made a (pious) foundation for Neith, mistress of Sais, of every good thing, as does a servant (33) who is useful to his lord.

I am a man who is good in his town. I rescued its inhabitants from the very great turmoil when it happened in the whole land,[15] the like of which had not happened in this land. I defended the weak (35) against the strong. I rescued the timid man when misfortune came to him. I did for them every beneficence when it was time to act for them.

[*Text on the right wall of the naos and on the statue's garment:*]

The one honored by his city-god, the chief physician, Udjahorresne, he says:

I am one honored by his father, praised by his mother, the intimate of his brothers. I established them in the office of prophet. I gave them a productive field by his majesty's

---

13. Osiris.
14. A nome was a regional administrative division within Egypt.
15. A reference to the Persian conquest; see also lines 40–41.

command for (39) all eternity. I made a fine tomb for him who lacked one. I supported all their children. I established all their households. I did for them every beneficence as a father does for his son, when the turmoil happened in (41) this nome, in the midst of the very great turmoil that happened in the whole land.

[Text on the back plinth:]

(43) The prince, count, royal seal-bearer, sole companion, prophet of those by whom one lives,[16] the chief physician, Udjahorresne, born of Atemirdis, he says:

The majesty of the King of Upper and Lower Egypt, Darius, ever-living, commanded me to return to Egypt—when his majesty was in Elam and was Great Chief of all foreign lands and Great Ruler of Egypt—in order to restore the establishment of the House of Life [in all its parts],[17] after it had decayed. The foreigners carried me from country to country. They delivered me to Egypt as commanded by the Lord of the Two Lands.

I did as his majesty had commanded me. I furnished them with all their staffs consisting of the wellborn, no lowborn among them. I placed them in the charge of every learned man (45) [in order to teach them] all their crafts. His majesty had commanded to give them every good thing, in order that they might carry out all their crafts. I supplied them with everything useful to them, with all their equipment that was on record, as they had been before.

His majesty did this because he knew the worth of this guild in making live all that are sick, in making endure forever the names of all the gods, their temples, their offerings, and the conduct of their festivals.

[Text on the right side of the statue base:]

(46) The chief physician, Udjahorresne, he says:

I was one who was honored by all his masters, my being. They gave me ornaments of gold and did for me every beneficence.

[Text on the left side of the statue base:]

(47) One honored by Neith is he who shall say:

"O great gods who are in Sais! Remember all the benefactions done by the chief physician, Udjahorresne. And may you do for him all benefactions! May you make his good name endure in this land forever!"

DISCUSSION

The Persian conquest of the Near East progressed rapidly. Cyrus II took the throne in 550, and by 539 he had conquered Babylon, which had previously controlled most of the Near East. By 525, Cyrus's successor, Cambyses II, had campaigned to Egypt, and thus controlled the largest empire that the world had known. One reason for the rapidity of the Persian conquest was that most of the Near East had already been pacified by the Assyrians and the Babylonians. Although Egypt and the Levant had tasted some brief

---

16. I.e., prophet of the gods.
17. There is a break in the text at this point. This is the restoration suggested by Lichtheim.

independence when Mesopotamian power waned in certain periods, but they had been under foreign domination for much of the previous two centuries.

The power structures of the region could change rapidly, the Inscription of Udjahorresne suggests that some Egyptians flourished under Persian rule. Although later Greek historians recorded that the Persians pillaged certain Egyptian temples in retaliation for revolts,[18] and indeed Udjahorresne speaks of having to rescue people in his village (lines 33–34), there is no reason to believe that their general policy was any different in Egypt than elsewhere. (The Greek historians' portrayals of the Persians were surely influenced by the fact that the two nations were enemies.) It is clear that Cambyses adopted Egyptian royal self-portrayals that were associated with native pharaohs in order to ingratiate himself to the local people.

Despite the efforts of the Persians to endear themselves, the position of local elites under imperial rule would have been fraught with tensions between new rulers and old customs. They must have felt some allegiance to preexisting power structures and to indigenous cultural traditions. (This was probably even more true in Egypt, where the indigenous traditions were more ancient and had not been interrupted by a long exile, as in Judah.) The two texts in this chapter are the stories of officials who collaborated with the Persians, and they reflect, in subtle ways, the political and cultural tensions of their times.

The Inscription of Udjahorresne comes from Sais, which was the capital of the Twenty-sixth Dynasty that immediately preceded Persian rule. Naturally, pharaohs composed royal inscriptions describing their achievements, just as kings did elsewhere in the ancient Near East. But in Egypt, autobiographical texts are also common in the tombs of courtiers; they are some of the most important sources for Egyptian history. Such autobiographies served not only to identify the tomb owner, but also to describe the tomb owner's worthy life and assert his or her righteousness in the judgment of the dead.

Udjahorresne seems to have experienced a midlife career change, in that he was named "chief physician" by Cambyses. Of course, in this ancient context, "physician" meant a different set of responsibilities from those that physicians have in our times. Among other duties, Udjahorresne seems to have been responsible for a cult of healing based in the temples of Sais (line 45). It is not made clear how a former "commander of the royal navy" ingratiated himself to the Persians enough to be awarded a high rank under the new regime, but he finds himself in a dual position of feeling responsibility both to the Persian king and to his own people and religion.

In the case of Judah, Cyrus's conquest was more than acceptable; it was actively welcomed by a significant portion of the population, who deemed it far preferable to the rule of the Babylonians. Whereas the Babylonians destroyed Jerusalem and seem to have had a policy that it could not be rebuilt, Cyrus issued an edict in 536 to return the exiled Judeans from Babylon back to Judah. According to the book of Ezra, Persian rulers even funded the rebuilding of the Judean temple (see chap. 26). It is not hard to see why a biblical prophet might deem Cyrus a messiah (Isa. 45:1). The Persians' relative beneficence toward Judah was part of a general policy of indulgence and religious tolerance toward

18. Cf. Herodotus *Hist.* 3; Plutarch *Is. Os.* 2.6; Aelian *Var. hist.* 6.8.

conquered nations that was intended to pacify and manage the large empire without the costs of constant warfare that had helped to fell the Mesopotamian powers.

Despite the warm reception that Cyrus received in the Bible, he did not restore Judah to its preexilic state. It remained under Persian rule, part of a larger province known as "Beyond the River" (Heb. *Eber-hannahar*). Within the larger province, it is possible to speak of a smaller political entity, Yehud. Although in Hebrew it is named identically to the preexilic kingdom of Judah, scholars often distinguish it by calling it Yehud, which is the Aramaic form found both in the Bible (Dan. 2:25; 5:13; 6:13; Ezra 5:1, 8; 7:14) and on coins from the period.

When looking at the Persian period, one can for the first time use the terms "Jew" and "Jewish" to describe an ethnic or religious identity. There were diaspora communities at this time in Babylonia, Persia, and Egypt, and Aramaic was becoming their primary language in many cases. Because the people who had coalesced in Israel and Judah during the Iron Age came to be no longer defined primarily by their land or language, one can speak of scattered communities of "Jews" rather than "Judeans."

Nehemiah is one of the few books of the Bible that describes life in the Persian period. The date of Nehemiah's mission to Jerusalem is generally agreed upon: Nehemiah 2:1 indicates that it was in the twentieth year of Artaxerxes—presumably Artaxerxes I,[19] which would mean 445 BCE, and 5:14 reports that he governed the city until Artaxerxes' thirty-second year (433). This means that he came to the city seventy years after the dedication of the Second Temple and found it still struggling. The postexilic period was not a time of prosperity in Judah (as reflected in Neh. 5:1–5), and Jerusalem in particular was not an attractive place to live because it was still in ruins.[20]

There are few extrabiblical historical sources with which one can compare Nehemiah's (and Ezra's) accounts except for scattered reports such as the Letter to Gadatas (chap. 26) and a collection of administrative tablets unearthed at Persepolis.[21] Each of these sources pertains to Persian governance elsewhere in the empire; there are practically no Persian sources regarding imperial governance of Palestine. Comparison of these very limited sources shows that, however much the books of Ezra and Nehemiah have been shaped in the process of their compilation, they bear the distinct imprint of Persian rule; this is true both in narrow ways (such as their use of language) and in broad ways (such as the attitude that they portray the empire taking toward foreign religions).

---

19. Artaxerxes II and Artaxerxes III ruled primarily in the fourth century BCE, probably too late for Nehemiah's mission. There is a letter among the Elephantine Papyri from about 408 that refers to "the sons of Sanballat the governor of Samaria." This would fit well if the Sanballat who figures prominently in Nehemiah lived in the third quarter of the fifth century, as the dating of Nehemiah's mission to 445 would suggest.

20. Neh. 7:4: "The city was wide and large, but the people within it were few and no houses had been built." Neh. 11:1–2: "Now the leaders of the people lived in Jerusalem; and the rest of the people cast lots to bring one out of ten to live in the holy city Jerusalem, while nine-tenths remained in the other towns. And the people blessed all those who willingly offered to live in Jerusalem."

21. H. G. M. Williamson, *Studies in Persian Period History and Historiography* (FAT 38; Tübingen: Mohr Siebeck, 2004), 212–31.

Nehemiah's governorship (5:14) and his limited authority within Judah is also consistent with what is known about Persian imperial rule. Although native Persians were installed like colonists on sizable plots of land in the provinces, local authorities continued to enjoy a certain degree of autonomy. Unlike the situation when Judah first lost its autonomy when Jerusalem fell to the Babylonians, it is difficult to perceive indications of anti-Persian political reaction in the postexilic biblical books. However, there are certainly indications of an effort by some in Yehud to preserve their ethnic and religious identity. Indeed, some historians would say they were trying to *create* such an identity, or at least re-create one.

The negotiation of political and religious identity under imperial rule is a major theme of many of the postexilic biblical books, including not only those already discussed but also Daniel and Esther (and perhaps even the Joseph narratives). Readers should consider that cultural influence will function differently under different power relationships, although that factor is not often mentioned explicitly in comparative scholarship. For example, the adoption of foreign ideas may be much less problematic when the adopting culture is securely in power than when it is in an imperialized position and trying to defend and preserve its own traditions.

One striking similarity between the two texts is that both Udjahorresne and Nehemiah undertake to purify their respective temples and worship, and in each case there is an element of ethnic cleansing (Udj. 18–22, 44–45; Neh. 13). Although Udjahorresne predates Nehemiah by the better part of a century, comparison does not suggest that there was any literary influence between the two texts. The Egyptian autobiography form may well have been known in Yehud, but the similarities are primarily based on similar social forces surrounding their composition.

REFLECTION QUESTIONS

1. What indications do Udjahorresne and Nehemiah give of their deference to Persian power? Are there indications of Persian influence on these texts?

2. What signs of deference do these texts each record on the part of Persian rulers toward provincial interests?

3. How do Udjahorresne and Nehemiah maintain their own national-cultural identities in the face of Persian power?

4. Can you think of examples from the modern world of the encounter between imperial and indigenous powers? How does cultural influence work in such cases?

5. How is religion linked to politics (and specifically to political power) in these texts, and in our own times?

6. For what does Udjahorresne hope to be remembered? For what does Nehemiah hope to be remembered?

7. What seem to be the main goals of each text? That is, what were the authors trying to achieve by writing them?

8. How do the goals of Nehemiah's memoir compare with, say, Genesis or Exodus? With Samuel–Kings? How does Nehemiah's account fit into the larger story of writing and historiography in Israel and the ancient Near East?

9. There is a debate over whether Nehemiah's "memoirs" are real sources—that is, whether they were composed by a real governor of Jerusalem or were later literary inventions. How might comparison with the Udjahorresne inscription shed light on that question?

10. Both Udjahorresne and Nehemiah undertake significant changes in their spheres of authority. How do they each justify those changes?

11. Why do you think Nehemiah's memoirs were included in the biblical canon?

FURTHER READING

Baines, John. "On the Composition and Inscriptions of the Vatican Statue of Udjahorresne." Pages 83–92 in *Studies in Honor of William Kelly Simpson*, vol. 1. Edited by Peter Der Manuelian. Boston: Museum of Fine Arts, 1996.

Blenkinsopp, Joseph. *Ezra-Nehemiah: A Commentary*. OTL. Philadelphia: Westminster Press, 1988.

———. "The Mission of Udjahorresnet and Those of Ezra and Nehemiah." *JBL* 106 (1987): 409–21.

Lloyd, Alan B. "The Inscription of Udjahorresnet: A Collaborator's Testament." *Journal of Egyptian Archaeology* 68 (1982): 166–80.

Williamson, H. G. M. *Ezra, Nehemiah*. Word Biblical Commentary 16. Waco, TX: Word Books, 1985.

———. *Studies in Persian Period History and Historiography*. FAT 38. Tübingen: Mohr Siebeck, 2004.

Index of Scripture and Other Ancient Sources

This volume and its index order the canon according to Torah-Prophets-Writings.

Index of Subjects

(*excluding references in primary texts*)

421

CPSIA information can be obtained at www.ICGtesting.com
Printed in the USA
BVOW04s1233110515

399581BV00005B/10/P